P9-CAR-259

The Social Basis of Health and Healing in Africa

COMPARATIVE STUDIES OF HEALTH SYSTEMS AND MEDICAL CARE

General Editor

John M. Janzen

□

Founding Editor

Charles Leslie

□

Editorial Board

Don Bates, M.D.,
McGill University

Frederick L. Dunn, M.D.,
University of California, San Francisco

Kris Heggenhougen,
Harvard University

Brigitte Jordan,
Michigan State University

Shirley Lindenbaum,
The Graduate School and
University Center of the City of New York

Patricia L. Rosenfield,
The Carnegie Corporation of New York

Paul U. Unschuld,
University of Munich

Francis Zimmermann,
Centre National de la Recherche Scientifique, Paris

□

For a complete list of titles in this series, please contact the
Sales Department
University of California Press
2120 Berkeley Way
Berkeley, CA 94720

The Social Basis of Health and Healing in Africa

EDITED BY

Steven Feierman and John M. Janzen

Sponsored by the
Joint Committee on African Studies
of the
American Council of Learned Societies
and the
Social Science Research Council

UNIVERSITY OF CALIFORNIA PRESS
Berkeley Los Angeles Oxford

RA
418.3
.A35
S63
1992

University of California Press
Berkeley and Los Angeles, California

University of California Press
Oxford, England

Copyright © 1992 by The Regents of the University of California

Library of Congress Cataloging-in-Publication Data

The Social basis of health and healing in Africa / edited by Steven Feierman and John M. Janzen; sponsored by the Joint Committee on African Studies of the American Council of Learned Societies and the Social Science Research Council.
p. cm.—(Comparative studies of health systems and medical care)
Includes bibliographical references and index.
ISBN 0-520-06680-4 (alk. paper).—ISBN 0-520-06681-2 (pbk. : alk. paper)
1. Social medicine—Africa. 2. Healing—Africa. 3. Medical anthropology—Africa. I. Feierman, Steven, 1940– . II. Janzen, John M. III. Joint Committee on African Studies. IV. Series.
RA418.3.A35S63 1992
362.1′096—dc20 90-44243
CIP

Printed in the United States of America

1 2 3 4 5 6 7 8 9

The paper used in this publication meets the minimum requirements of American National Standard for Information Sciences—Permanence of Paper of Printed Library Materials, ANSI Z39. 48-1984 ∞

22184509

CONTENTS

POSTCOLONIAL MEDICINE

MAPS

FIGURES

TABLES

PREFACE

The purpose of the present volume is to offer, in a reasonably compact single work, studies of social conditions shaping health in Africa and an overview of the therapeutic traditions that have been marshaled to confront disease.

This book is a distillation of the "Medicine and Society in Africa" project sponsored by the Joint Committee on African Studies of the Social Science Research Council and the American Council of Learned Societies during the 1980s. It included a series of research planning workshops, special sessions at annual meetings of the African Studies Association, an international conference, and several publications. A bibliography in *Health and Society in Africa* (1979) by Steven Feierman identified a body of literature relevant to the project's inquiry; a volume titled *The Social History of Disease and Medicine in Africa* (1979), edited by John M. Janzen and Steven Feierman, presented papers on specific diseases and therapeutic traditions; another volume, titled *Causality and Classification in African Health and Medicine* (1981), edited by J. M. Janzen and Gwyn Prins, brought together papers of a conference on therapeutic traditions as conceptual systems and as embedded in broad historical change; and a review paper by Steven Feierman, "Struggles for Control: The Social Roots of Health and Healing in Modern Africa" (1985), took stock of the growing body of literature on the social organization of therapy, the social context of ill health, and the impact of healers or physicians on socially produced health conditions. Other papers on the political economy of health are incorporated here, or have appeared in a special journal issue edited by Randall Packard, Ben Wisner, and Thomas Bossert (1989).

Despite this backdrop of publications and conferences, the present work is still far from being a definitive statement on the social analysis of health and healing in Africa. Thousands of articles appear annually on particular health issues of pressing practical importance. The conditions of health themselves change from year to year. We are painfully aware that in the near-decade that this project has run its course, serious new health challenges have emerged. Chloroquine-resistant malaria has become a major threat on the eastern side of the continent. A new epidemic without known cure, acquired immune deficiency syndrome (AIDS), has become especially serious in Central Africa, although it has global dimensions as well. In the same decade health authorities in a number of countries have taken important initiatives to make inoculations more widely available to infants and young children.

The place of social analysis in dealing with these issues may not be immediately apparent. However, it is difficult to imagine improvement without sharper analysis, which may lead to critiques of policies and programs by governments, by nongovernmental agencies, and by those people outside official spheres who are working for constructive social change.

Four areas of discovery in the project, reflected in the papers and introductions of this volume, may be summarized. First is the reaffirmation of the importance of placing disease and health within a social, political, economic, and cultural context. Such a perspective has often been stressed in the abstract; it has become a truism. Yet all too frequently we see descriptions of, or efforts to deal with, particular diseases narrowly in terms of the biological or technical levels of understanding, rather than in terms of the wider social and economic conditions that promote those diseases. One of the most blatant examples of this is tuberculosis in southern Africa. An endemic disease whose causes, conditions, and cures are almost common knowledge still rages widely in association with poverty and poor working conditions. Similarly we see, all too frequently, efforts to describe, or to recommend the use of, therapeutic interventions and health measures that would be impossible to implement, given infrastructural and institutional capabilities, and are thus fated to fail.

Related to this is a second point: the importance of seeing change in society as affecting health levels, rather than seeing disease outside of social context. This has led to a growing conviction that only historical studies stressing change can do justice to the analysis of why specific diseases emerge, why they persist, and what are their consequences in the life of society.

A third point is the importance of seeing therapeutic practices not as tight "systems" or isolated institutions, but as loosely linked sets of practices. We utilize the concept of therapeutic traditions in this work to describe historically continuous streams of interrelated theory and practice. Within each stream are sets of concepts concerning illness causation, anatomy, society, or self, as they relate to bodies of therapeutic practice, and also to the inherited occupational roles within which healers work. We have little use, however, for the description of medicine as "traditional," euphemistic for static, irrational, unconscious, collective, and ineffectual; the opposite of "modern," euphemistic for dynamic, rational, conscious, individualistic, and effectual.

Nor do we find it helpful to speak of "ethnomedicine," whether this be a rewording of tribally bounded medical customs, or even of all medical practices in a society. As already mentioned, therapies may best be accounted for in the context of larger cultural, social, political, and economic sets. Just as disease is not an independent variable in social analysis, so therapeutics is also embedded in and reflecting the concepts, values, institutions, and power relations around it.

A final insight of the "Medicine and Society" project lies in the view that the maintenance of health is a process that, whether at the household, lineage, community, or professional and national level, requires effective organization to succeed. In other words, health, however defined, is not something that "just happens": it is maintained by a cushion of adequate nutrition, social support, water supply, housing, sanitation, and continued collective defense against contagious and degenerative disease. Such a view is necessary if we are to understand those contexts in today's Africa where health levels deteriorate, and where they improve. It is also a useful perspective from which to understand why, in settings where state services do not exist, or have collapsed, household, family, or wider network-type supports may to a degree "maintain health."

The "Medicine and Society" project was fortunate to have the participation of many active and productive scholars. A number of project participants published their own collections on portions of the broader field of knowledge. Among these, Dennis Cordell and Joel Gregory published *African Population and Capitalism* (1987) on the social conditons of population growth and decline. Murray Last (together with Gordon Chavunduka) edited a collection on the process by which local African healers have pressed toward professionalization (Last and Chavunduka 1986). Ismail Abdalla (together with B. DuToit) published a volume on the role of Islam, Christianity, and science in local African healing (DuToit and Abdalla 1985). P. Stanley Yoder (1982) edited a collection of essays on local medical systems.

It proved impossible for the project to produce authoritative work on AIDS in Africa. New data were pouring in as the volume neared completion; the social interpretations of AIDS in Africa advanced by the scientific community were often weak and sometimes biased (see Sabatier 1988). The basic epidemiology of heterosexually transmitted AIDS in Africa is still only partially understood. The answers, when they come, will depend on a careful and subtly defined sense of the historical context in which the disease has emerged.

We hope that this volume has, nevertheless, contributed to an understanding of the picture of health problems on the African continent, of the measures that must be taken to improve that picture, and to an understanding of the means people in fact use to maintain their health. Too many currently available scholarly projects on the subject of African health fail to document the full range of therapies and health-maintaining strategies that people use. Too many also fail to place declining health in a context of the political economy. We hope this work will contribute to the dissipation of intellectual mythologies that cloud understanding of the fabric of health.

Finally, we wish to acknowledge the many scholars and practitioners who have participated in the "Medicine and Society in Africa" project with their research, writing, lectures, and practical interventions. In a special way we recognize Martha Gephart of the Social Science Research Council and the members of the Joint Committee on African Studies for their support.

John M. Janzen Steven Feierman

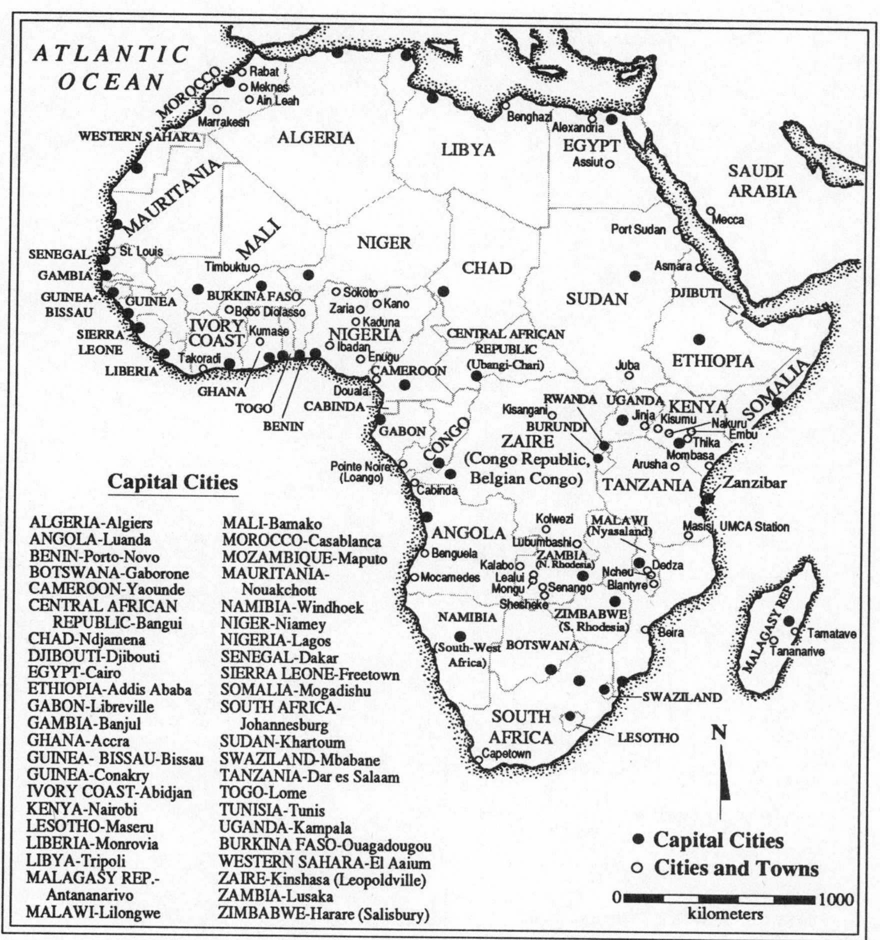

Map 1. Contemporary Nations of Africa

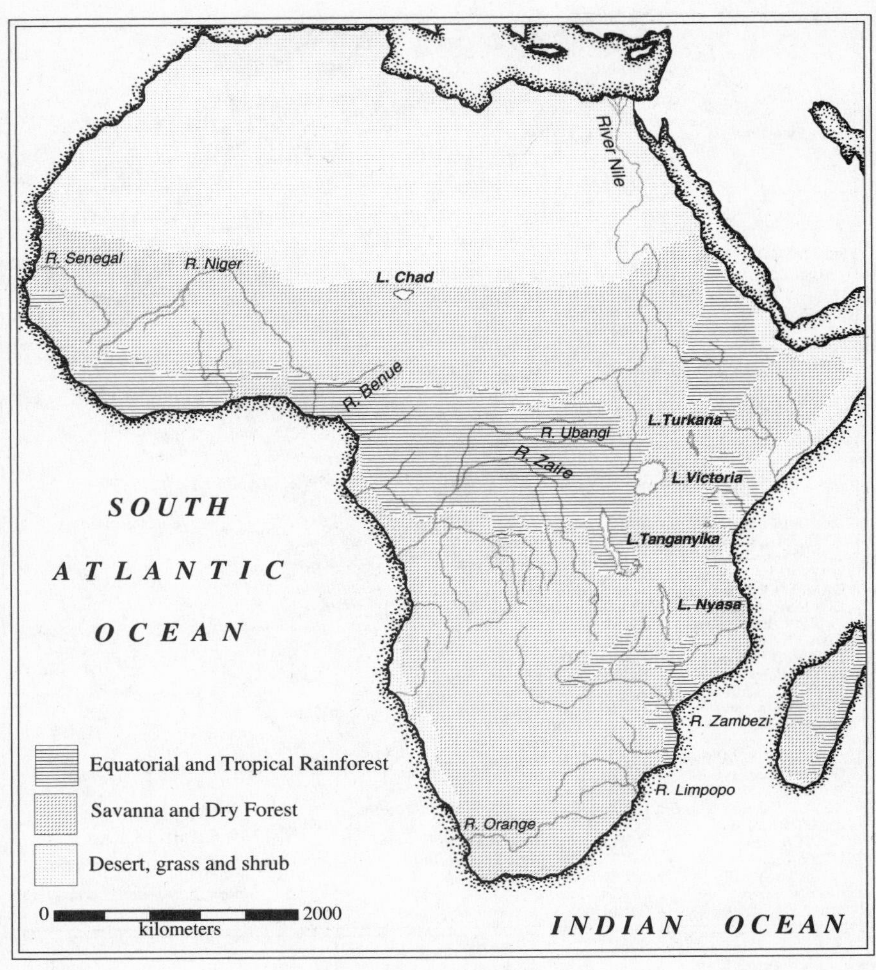

Map 2. African Vegetation and Mineral Resources

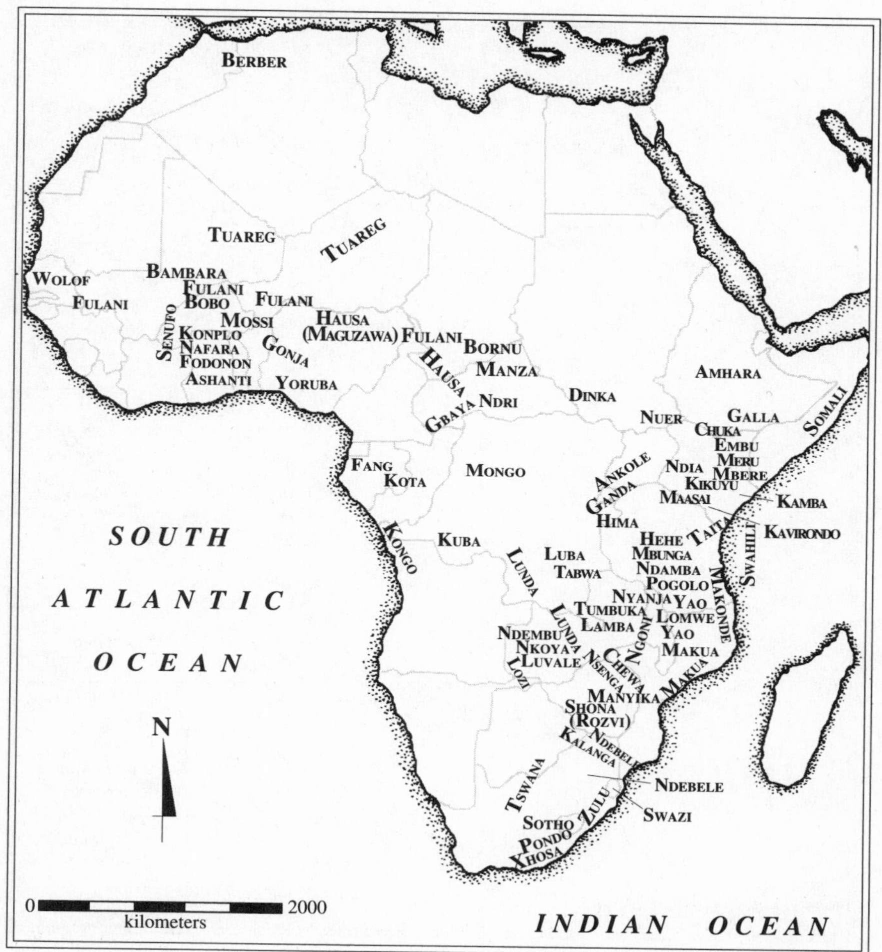

Map 3. Ethnic Distributions

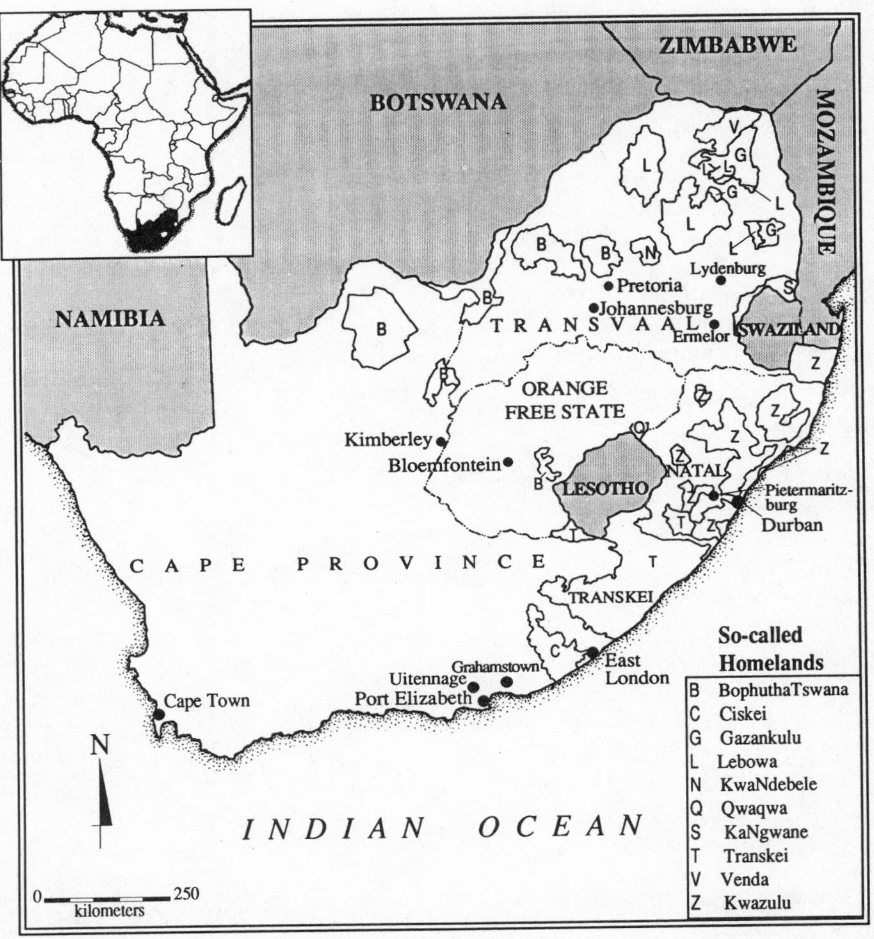

Map 4. South African Political Regions, Boundaries, and Cities

PART ONE

Introduction

This book explores health and healing within the larger picture of changing African societies and cultures. The path of change in health and disease (like that of healing) cannot be understood apart from change in farming, household organization, politics, and migration, among many other elements. When farmers clear the forest, malaria often spreads. When governments build irrigation works, the threat of schistosomiasis usually deepens. If mothers take work time to farm in place of cooking, child malnutrition ordinarily becomes more of a problem. Anyone who wishes to understand the causes of health and illness must therefore inquire into the ecology of forests, the particular way governments build irrigation works, and the complex causes of change in how women organize their workdays. Changing patterns of disease, in Africa as elsewhere in the world, are an integral part of changing society.

Healing, like health, is obviously rooted in the social and cultural order. If we ask about the cultural definition of a living person, then we are addressing profound general questions about morality, about life and death. What separates the living from the dead? How do ancestors come to act in the lives of their descendants? Why are some kinds of social acts (incest, perhaps) seen as dangerous to the health of the perpetrator's relatives? The cultural definition of the individual's place in society, and of the human body and its parts, is inseparable from healing practices. To define dangerous behavior, and to define evil, is to define some causes of illness. As the definition of evil changes, so does the interpretation of illness. To understand change in healing, we must understand what it is that leads people to alter the definition of dangerous social behavior.

It can easily be accepted that health and healing in Africa are shaped by broad social forces. The question is how they are shaped and what is the process. In answering this question the authors of this book's essays focus on a few main themes.

OPEN QUESTIONS ON THE STUDY OF AFRICAN HEALING

On the subject of healing the late 1970s saw an old paradigm disintegrate under the weight of anomalous information. The old paradigm pictured an African map divided among hundreds of ethnic groups, each with clear boundaries. Each ethnic group was described as having its own set of traditional medical ideas and practices. An ethnic group's healing practices, according to this paradigm, were ordered according to a coherent set of principles defining the different types of forces that cause illness or other misfortune (Horton 1967). These forces might include ancestors, nature spirits, and witches. Healers and diviners did the job of matching the patient's illness with the appropriate niche in the ordered cosmology, thus making a ritual diagnosis.

There were problems with this picture. Ethnographers discovered that in many cases patients did not interpret their own illnesses as caused by supernatural or moral forces, even when the patients recognized a hierarchy of such forces. The nonconforming illnesses had natural causes. Ancestors were not responsible, nor were nature spirits, witches, or sorcerers. The people who suffered these illnesses, or who treated them, said that they "just happened" (Gillies 1976).

The new category of illnesses that "just happened" came into scholarly view as part of a body of new ethnographic information (Chavunduka 1978; Janzen 1978*b*). This reported the world as seen through the eyes of patients. Most previous ethnographies had reported the practices of individual healers, or of categories of healers. Each type of healing had its theory of what causes illness. All practitioner-informants had their own personal interpretive frameworks. The ethnographic study of healing with one healer-informant, or with one category of healers, was likely to lead to a well-ordered description of a hierarchy of illness-causing forces as seen from that particular point of view. What patients see, in Africa as in many other parts of the world, is a diverse, heterogeneous set of options for treatment—options that vary from place to place. In one place a patient, in the course of a single illness, might consult dispensary attendants, Christian or Muslim religious practitioners, medical doctors, specialists in sorcery cures, spirit-possession healers, herbalists, and others. An ethnographer who studies the world from the point of view of patients or their lay attendants is likely to see a much more varied, perhaps chaotic, picture of therapeutic ideas and practices.

As scholarly knowledge of therapies in any one place became more diverse, the map of neat ethnic territories became confused. Each therapy, each type of practitioner and set of ideas, has its own map. It is rare for the boundaries of a type of therapy to coincide neatly with the boundaries of an ethnic group, or with those of other therapies in the same general area. Very few of the therapy-distribution maps overlap. In East Africa, for example, Muslims (and Muslim practitioners) are scattered all across the map of the region. The map of Muslims does not match any ethnic map. Nor do maps of spirit-possession practices overlap with ethnic ones. The therapeutic map is no longer divided among bounded ethnic groups. There are actually many maps of therapies within each local region; no two therapy-distribution maps have the same shape.

Anthropologists and historians, when they began to understand that therapies were diverse and not necessarily ethnically based, turned to new sets of questions. There was, for example, a question about the nature of coherence in the midst of therapeutic diversity. It was easy enough to picture the patient's helping relatives choosing among a wide range of alternatives, as though walking through a well-stocked supermarket, taking one therapy or another off the shelf from among an endless array. The problem with this image, however, is that therapies are not neatly laid out on ordered shelves, nor are they contained in cans, or tins, or jars. The interpretation of illness raises questions about the meaning of life and death, and about the causes of misfortune. Naming the condition is central to the therapeutic process, and each name carries profound implications. For a patient to learn in hospital that she has infectious hepatitis can mean that she and her physician share a picture of the nature of infection. More importantly, it can mean that she and the physician see the body as "knowable and treatable in isolation from the human mind and human relations" (Hahn 1982). But then what if the same patient, for the same illness, is also treated for sorcery and then later for Christian spirit possession? Does this mean that the patient and the patient's relatives are buying and then discarding entire theories of the nature of the person—one biomedical, a second focusing on moral relations within the community, and a third based on a Christian view of the supernatural? Or is it true that the patient's relatives hold a single coherent view of the nature of illness, a view related in only limited ways to the views of the various practitioners? Is the lay image of the person's place in the universe of misfortune a coherent and orderly one, or is it diverse, incoherent, and lacking in order?

Scholars of the most recent generation have answered questions like these in very different ways. Gwyn Prins writes in this volume (chap. 13) about persistent "core concepts," a kind of center of gravity for a shared picture of reality. Murray Last, also in this volume (chap. 16), takes the opposite view. He writes that "medicine is being seen not so much as a medical system but as part of the necessary cultural camouflage . . . that enables one to survive, preferably unnoticed, in a diverse society." In his view the laypeople of the area he describes neither know nor want to know about the parts of their medical culture. We cannot describe Last's answer (or Prins's) as the authoritative one, for the issues will continue to provoke debate. But it is important to see that the patient's eye view of therapeutic diversity raises important questions about the coherence of healing knowledge.

Since the therapeutic map began to lose its clear lines—when ethnomedical boundaries were opened—the course of historical change has needed a new interpretation. It is now impossible to study the history of isolated ethnomedical systems. The history of each set of practitioners and practices, distributed across language or ethnic lines, has its own internal logic. To understand the history of Islamic healing in any one small place the historian or anthropologist needs to understand the broader history of Islam and of healing within it, as Ismail Abdalla (chap. 6, this volume) has shown. Restricting knowledge of Islamic therapies to any one locality will not reveal the most important lines of development. Similarly, one cannot understand the medicine of Christian mission hospitals as strictly local, separate from the wider history of missions and of hospitals. The same point holds for therapies that are not tied to Islam, or to Christianity, or to any world religion. African healers, practicing therapies that originate on the African continent, carry their knowledge from place to place without necessarily halting at ethnic or language boundaries. Many cults of affliction in Zambia, for example, have spread from one part of the country to another. The most popular cults acquire patients and practitioners in a number of districts (Van Binsbergen 1981). Other cults have spread across international borders, originating in Angola and then spreading to Zambia.

The history of healing in Africa has come to resemble the history of religion in a place that experiences broad religious diversity. The history of religion can be written as a story of competing traditions, each with its own ideas and institutions, material interests, and authority structures: the history, for example, of institutionalized Islam or Christianity. Or it can be written as the story of choice within a community. Do men choose one religion and women, another? Do religious divisions emerge between merchants and workers, or between literate people and illiterate ones? For a full account of religion in Dar es Salaam, for example, we would need histories of Islamic brotherhoods (with roots elsewhere in the Islamic world), histories of Catholicism, of evangelical Lutheran Protestantism, and of charismatic versions of Christianity. Each religious tradition must be treated fully on its own, with Dar es Salaam as a mere stopping place. But then we would need to understand local choice—which people in Dar es Salaam have chosen Catholicism, or Islam, and why they have made their own choices.

As in the case of religion, the history of therapy is a history of multiple streams of healing traditions, but with a difference. It is rare to find an individual who will take communion in a Catholic church on one day, begin to fast for Ramadan on the next, and sacrifice to the ancestors on the third. The world religions in particular tend to be exclusive. It is quite usual, by contrast, for a patient to be treated for sorcery on one day, at a hospital on the second, and for spirit possession on the third. The patterns of choice work themselves out in complex ways within individual illness episodes. Nevertheless, the history of healing is a history of multiple traditions, each one with its own distribution in time and space. The contributions to this volume trace several traditions—the history of Lemba (an Equatorial African cult of affliction), the history of Islamic medicine in Hausaland in northern Nigeria, and the history of Godly Medicine among Anglican missionaries in Tanganyika.

The healing traditions have been forced to provide interpretations of a rapidly changing reality. Conditions of health and disease have changed fundamentally in most parts of Africa over the past century. Each healing tradition (the tradition of cults of affliction, the biomedical one, the Islamic one, and each of the others) has had to find answers to very new questions. When tuberculosis spread to the far-flung rural homes of southern African mine workers, the healing traditions, or rather their practitioners, were forced to respond. Healing conceptions and rituals often seem to be addressing the eternal problems of the human condition—what is the nature of evil, of pollution, of danger, of the relationship between the living and the dead, or between people and spirit. But therapeutic practices are used, in most cases, to treat illness. If illness changes rapidly, then so, too, must healing. In fact, the causal chain forms a double loop here. Healing is rooted in society; as society changes, healing changes with it. Health and disease are rooted in society; as society changes, these also change. Yet changes in healing must respond to changes in health. Neither of the loops can be understood in isolation.

OPEN QUESTIONS ON THE STUDY OF HEALTH AND DISEASE

The varied record of health in Africa over the past century is inseparable from the history of change in control over political institutions and change in the organization of economic production. The continent has seen drastic changes in its basic political and economic framework. In the early years of colonial rule some governments relied on forced labor; in parts of colonial Africa, especially in the eastern and southern parts of the continent, male workers migrated from rural homes, leaving their families behind; in the postcolonial years class differentiation has become more pronounced, with some workers permanently separated from their roots in the countryside. Each different pattern of production and of political control is associated with a particular distribution of health problems. The outcomes are not predictable in any simple way, for they are shaped by changes in the natural environment and by the struggles of workers against their employers and against government, and by farmers against the onerous demands of the state. Nevertheless, important regularities emerge.

Cordell, Gregory, and Piché (chap. 1, this volume) show just how strong the associations are between health and political or economic control. In Ubangi-Shari (later Central African Republic), the years of French rule before World War I were a brutal time. The territory was governed by concessionary companies that forced Africans to collect rubber and other wild products. Many people fled from their homes and farms, leading to a decline in food production. During this period the population dropped, death rates rose, and fertility diminished. The declining likelihood of survival grew directly out of political and economic exploitation. Ubangi-Shari was similar in these respects to King Leopold's Congo (later the Belgian Congo, and now Zaire), in the same period.

As colonial control changed, so, too, did health problems. The 1920s saw a shift to an economy based on cultivation rather than the collection of wild products. The government now compelled farmers to grow cotton, which required intense labor at the same time as the major grain crops—sorghum and millet. The authors hypothesize that hungry-season malnutrition first became a problem in that period. In a general way, the significant point is this. States of health emerge from the basic organization of daily life, as shaped by the entire framework of political and economic control.

One additional example will illustrate the point more fully. It is the story of change in farming after World War II in a single village in the Gambia—Genieri, which became the subject of a detailed series of studies over nearly twenty years (Haswell 1953, 1963, 1975). In this place one of the central agricultural problems, with profound importance for health, was a shortage of food during the most difficult time of the year. This was a time when the new year's rice crop was maturing, making heavy labor demands on women, who did the weeding. It was also a time when the previous year's rice had been exhausted, leaving people hungry, and when some infectious diseases took their greatest toll among infants and young children.

One of the most important ways women, who were the major rice farmers, found hungry-season food was from men's millet farming. Within the large kinship-based compounds, each taking in a number of households, men would join together in cooperative work parties to raise millet. This provided a small proportion of the year's calories, but a proportion available at a desperately important time.

In the postwar period, the men of Genieri began to rapidly expand the amount of time they gave to farming peanuts—a crop that belonged to each man as his personal property and not as the wealth of the compound. A household could live well through the hungry season, without a compound's millet, if it had peanut money for buying food. In some cases, young and vigorous men withdrew from the compounds, leaving millet farming behind, confident that they could live comfortably through the hungry season using cash from their peanut crops. The government tried to help keep up food production, despite the withdrawal of some men's labor, by building causeways to open up new lands for wet rice. The earlier relatively uniform system of large compounds was replaced by a more diverse pattern: some people still lived in large compounds; others, in relatively unattached households.

This set of changes created a much more diverse social picture than had existed before, with its own profound implications for health. When compounds broke up, there were poor households, some of them woman-centered, which in an earlier period would have been parts of compounds, and which now lost some of their hungry-season food and some health care support. At times the poorer people worked for others to get money for their hungry-season food requirements. Male peanut farmers were affected by fluctuations in the price of peanuts on commodity markets. If they borrowed money for food or farming costs from village moneylenders, their ability to repay depended on unpredictable prices. Some of the most influential men had access to rice at government-controlled prices, or to cooperative credit at rates below those charged by the moneylender. In the early 1970s there were still some large compounds, and these were especially prosperous if they included a successful moneylender, or a man with solid political connections, or in some cases a Koranic scholar with a large following. Some households were very poor, and isolated woman-centered households most probably fared the worst.

This example illustrates the complexity of the relationship between political and economic change and changing health conditions. Initially, the system of farming changed because of decisions by some farming men to grow peanuts. This ended an entire system of growing hungry-season food, and it left some women (and their children) without the nutritional support of compounds. Then the entire system of credit, moneylending, and government control over commercial rice supplies came into play. The precise consequences for health depended on where, in this entire system, the individual was located: in a woman-centered household, or in a large compound that included a moneylender, or in the household of a government official. No one decision or level of control dictated the precise shape of the new system: it emerged from governmental decisions about rice farming, from the way in which the official marketing apparatus passed on to farmers the fluctuations in peanut prices, from the kinship strategies of local men as peanut farmers, from the social organization of Koranic scholars' compounds, from the precise form of governmental control over food supplies, and from the methods local people developed for dealing with the insecurities of world commodity markets.

In spite of the complexity and particularity of these processes, and of others like them around the continent, it is possible to point to a few broad regularities in the way political and economic change has affected states of health in the twentieth century. These include simplification of the food crop regime, a weakening of kinship-based support mechanisms, and the emergence of profound health consequences growing out of inequalities in the payment of social costs for competing groups of workers.

During the twentieth century the regime of food crops has become consistently simpler. This has come about because of changes in the organization of labor and of marketing. Peasant households use more of their labor for commercial crops or wage labor, reducing the work time for food crop cultivation. The sexual division of labor changes. Some old food crops are abandoned, some preserved, and some new ones chosen. The preferred food crops often make lower demands on soil or labor. This was so in the case of cassava, which was adopted as a replacement for millet and sorghum in Ubangi-Shari (chap. 1, this volume), and which spread widely around the continent. Cassava was not as rich nutritionally as the crops it replaced. In some cases peasants adopt new food crops because they are suitable for marketing, leaving cultivators free to decide after harvest on the proportion of the annual crop to be eaten and the proportion to be sold.

The overall pattern of change in rural society and in its crop regimes leads to an intensification of hungry-season malnutrition (Chambers et al. 1981). It leads also to inequalities in how malnutrition is distributed (Haswell 1975). Rural networks of social support change, leaving some community members unprotected during the hungry season of each year and during famine times. Amartya Sen, in his discussion of entitlements (1981), shows that hunger only rarely emerges from scarcity in the total amount of food a society produces. The people who suffer hunger are those who are not *entitled* to food. These may be whole segments of a national population who (because they are powerless or in political disfavor) are deprived in periods of famine, or they may be vulnerable categories of individuals hidden within local communities.

Another widespread set of regularities in the twentieth century has been in patterns of inequality in the health consequences of the particular form of social organization of economic production. The inequality can be racial, as in the much higher likelihood that black mine workers in South Africa will suffer disabling accidents than will white mine workers. It can be based on class, as in the greater likelihood, in some observations, that children of bureaucrats will receive hospital care than will children of the urban poor. Or the inequalities can emerge within a class, as in the greater likelihood that peasant women without husbands will raise malnourished children than will married peasant women with resident husbands. The evolution of inequalities is the result of the entire process of bargaining and political mobilization involving the state, capital, workers' organizations, and popular political movements. Indeed, it is the result of the contest among all the major players in national (or colonial) political and economic competition.

For example, in South Africa in the late 1970s the children of white workers suffered almost no cases of kwashiorkor, the nutritional disease that was very common among the children of black workers. The two most common blanket explanations are that this state of affairs was the consequence of racism or of capitalism, both of which are in fact defining elements in the political and economic life to South Africa. But then how are we to explain that kwashiorkor existed among white children in the 1930s? Racism and capitalism defined the general social context in both periods; the differences were in the specific nature of the class and ethnic alliances on which the state's power rested. The full story has to do with Afrikaner nationalism, as supported in the 1940s by white workers, white farmers, and other parts of the white electorate. A government came to power in 1948 that (because of the particular pattern of alliances) was devoted to improving the health of poor white children but not of black children (Feierman 1985; Marks and Andersson, chap. 5, this volume; O'Meara 1983).

Similarly, the fact that African children in the city are much more likely to survive to the age of five than are African children in the countryside is the consequence of an extended series of struggles by urban African political movements and trade union organizations. Rent strikes, bus boycotts, and labor actions in the years since World War II have all played a role (Lodge 1983). Manufacturing employers, who invest in workers' skills, have also been more anxious than white farmers or mine managers to see public investment in urban health.

Despite the complexity of the forces in each particular case, there are strong regularities in the distribution of health care and of ill health in twentieth-century Africa. Most colonial health care systems provided care and public health services to white people in the early days, and next to African men at the workplace. In the Ivory Coast in 1952, for example, all eleven major hospitals were found in the rich southern part of the territory, where European enterprise was concentrated (Lasker 1977, 288). Government health services came quite late (after World War II) to African women and children, and to the rural population. Not before this late period, in most colonies, were maternity services introduced (Feierman 1985, 122ff.). Because of the urban bias of colonial medicine, and of the greater political bargaining power of city-dwellers up to the present, urban life expectancy is longer than rural, and urban infant mortality is lower, almost everywhere on the continent. The introduction to part II reviews some of the evidence for this.

The present interpretation, that health can be understood only within the context of political and economic control, leaves us with important open questions. These are questions on which social scientists have not reached clear consensus. The first of these is on the triangular relationships among the politics of class, policies governing the fundamental direction of the economy, and policies governing social issues including health. In the central political battles that change a nation's entire direction, health issues are usually secondary. The central issues (if they are about more than the access of competing groups to political power) usually concern the shape of the productive economy. Are there to be large farms or small farms? Are factories to get more support than plantations? Will factory owners be national citizens or outsiders? Each decision concerning one of these issues carries implications about a series of other decisions affecting health. The degree of freedom accorded to factory owners usually shapes the quality of regulations on occupational health and on pollution. The question here is, can reformist health policies be successful if they are not part of a broader class politics?

Marks and Andersson's essay in this volume raises that issue. It discusses a failed attempt in 1944 at health reform in South Africa. This was a plan formulated by influential health officials to create a national network of institutions combining health care, health education, public health, and health maintenance. If the attempt had been successful, it would have reduced the striking inequalities still present between the health of whites and blacks, and between the health of Africans in the city and in the countryside.

The initiative failed, but not for lack of intelligence or imagination among planners. The failure grew out of the politics of race, class, and nationality in South Africa. The issue is sometimes interpreted as one of resources; could the South African government at that moment afford to build expensive health institutions? But the turning in the road was really a very different one, involving the entire array of political and economic forces. How could the government at that time respond to both the pressure for city services by urban African squatters and the countervailing pressure by white farmers to keep Africans out of the city and to keep farm wages low? If the government had permitted black people to move freely into the city, and if it had provided a minimum of social and health services there, then many blacks would have left the white-owned farms, where health conditions and wages were appalling. The white farmers demanded that blacks be prohibited from migrating to the cities, and that health and social services in the cities not be so high as to help lure away their labor. Struggles for health are tied to a society's central struggles (Sanders 1985). Marks and Andersson let us see the place of health issues, as interpreted by health professionals, in defining the nation's central conflicts.

A final set of open issues, alongside the relationship between class politics and health policies, is the question of production and reproduction. In the sphere of economic production people work to make goods and to provide economically valued services. The sphere of reproduction encompasses procreation along with the maintenance and preservation of life. Childbirth is included here, along with the intimate care that close relatives give to the sick and to those too old or too weak to work. The assumptions hidden by the definition of these spheres have been challenged by a generation of feminist scholarship. This academic tradition shows that the organization of production shapes (and is shaped by) the intimate organization of gender at the domestic level.

Feminist definitions of reproduction are usually broad ones, beyond the reproduction of children through pregnancy and childbirth. Domestic labor, these works argue, is undervalued in capitalist societies because it is not sold. It is tied to a women's sphere, which, even though defined in the first instance by biological reproduction, also takes in the other unpaid work that women do. In the paid labor force women are overrepresented in nurturing and service jobs. Pay for these jobs is low because the work resembles women's unpaid domestic labor (Strobel 1983, 111–112).

The relationship between the two spheres in Africa is important for health. The rural organization of production shapes health by determining the quality of the food supply and the use of the natural environment (and through the environment, the distribution of disease). The organization of reproduction is explicitly devoted to health issues: to childbirth and care of the sick. The interplay between the two, between production and care-giving, is at the heart of health organization. The relationships are so entangled, however, that scholars continue to work on the issues, with no one approach sweeping the field. No orthodoxy has emerged. One problem with the terms is that they make two parallel sets of distinctions, not always found together in reality. "Reproduction" is assumed to have something to do with procreation, or maintenance, or care-giving. It is also seen as related to social ties at an intimate or private level. The definitions leave open the question of how to define women's farm production for private use, or how to define care-giving on a public scale.

Despite difficulties with terminology, production and reproduction point to a cluster of concrete questions on African health. Each question has rich implications; none is to be resolved in any clear way. First, what is the relationship between a society's overall needs for labor, as defined by the holders of power, and the intimate control over pregnancy and childbirth? Colonial authorities in most parts of the continent wanted to increase labor supplies. At the same time, women in some societies were shortening the periods of sexual abstinence after childbirth. They were shortening the space between children, increasing the labor supply (Schoenmaeckers et al. 1981). Were they responding to the demands of authority? What was the mechanism by which public authorities influenced intimate decisions on sexual practice? Was this an accidental relationship between presumed cause and presumed effect? The answers are unknown.

The second set of questions is more widely discussed. When colonial economies use cheap labor or migrant labor, the cost of labor's reproduction is usually paid within the domestic group and the local kinship network (Meillassoux 1975). Neither the state nor employers pay the cost of healthy childbirth, of health care for the young, or of pensions for those who have left the work force. This is well known and well documented. We do not know very much, however, about the child-rearing and childbirth strategies of different types of households, or about their health effects. In a migrant economy, survival chances differ among children whose mothers are widowed, or divorced, or living far from their natal families, or dead. We do not know exactly how. Nor do we know much about the relationship between women's career patterns and their states of health. With rare exceptions, these questions are in the earliest stages of exploration.

Third, women's relative power at the intimate domestic level is related in unspecified ways to women's participation in public affairs. It is probable that participation in national politics wins for women improvement in private reproductive health. Once again, the core of what we need to understand has to do with the relationship between the most intimate sphere of people's everyday lives and overarching political and economic power.

HEALTH AND MEDICINE IN THE ACTIVE VOICE

Change in disease and in the basic organization of everyday life necessarily leads to change in the measures people take to preserve health, and in healing practices. It is important to recognize that change in the way Africans cope with disease does not merely occur as an automatic reflex, devoid of conscious reflection or creativity. The reality of African healing, when examined closely, is very far from the tired image of an inert, static, un-self-conscious tradition.

Much of what is important about African healing becomes clear only when healers and patients and their relatives are pictured actively creating the particular healing gesture, reshaping healing institutions, and finding the meaning of misfortune. Individuals of course use received language and knowledge, and they act within received institutions, but the language, the knowledge, and the institutions change over time in ways that can be apprehended only if we picture African peasants and city-dwellers as active creators. We need to describe African medicine in the active voice.

The patient's relatives, who try to understand and come to terms with illness, explore the world of misfortune and of therapeutic possibilities as they find it at that moment. In her essay in this volume (chap. 15), Christopher Davis-Roberts reports the illness of a three-year old girl, Malaika ("the Angel," "the Messenger"), who suffered a puzzling series of symptoms—swellings emitting pus, fevers, hives, and other symptoms. Malaika's father, together with the observing anthropologist and others who cared for the child, watched the symptoms unfold through time and tried to understand them despite their ambiguity. The anthropologist contributed tetracycline and penicillin; Malaika's father hunted for a trader who might sell niridazole (used for treatment of schistosomiasis) and (at another time) tried to understand those relationships among his wife's relatives which might have led Malaika to suffer. The process of creation was a subtle one. It is impossible to say whether any particular therapeutic idea changed as Malaika's treatment unfolded through time. But it is certain also that there was nothing automatic, culturally programmed, or self-evident about the illness, its definition, or the therapy. Those who cared for Malaika acted and by doing so defined themselves in relation to one another, defined the illness, and defined the ultimate causes of misfortune in life as they understood it.

The act of creation in healing is often much more direct and obvious than this, and less subtle, a response to new challenges and opportunities, as when Nigerian healers built businesses for the mass production and transport of herbal remedies. In colonial Northern Rhodesia, as described by Prins, Lozi carefully evaluated the skills of the first European physicians and brought patients who, having been screened by their fellow Lozi, were found to have appropriate conditions. African healers went into business on a large scale selling charms to protect migrant workers from the attack medicines of the many strangers and chance acquaintances they met. The workers, we know, also took measures to protect themselves against the worst dangers of employment. Migrants created communication networks for reporting health conditions—networks that were invisible to the colonial rulers, but which enabled laborers at the mines to avoid employers with the worst records for preserving health.

Also invisible to the authorities were the formal meetings that Zulu diviners began to hold in the city to enforce orthodox practice and to ensure that new generations of diviners would remain true to the core principles of Zulu cosmology (Ngubane 1977). This institution for enforcing the correct practice of tradition was nevertheless active and creative, for it imposed new forms of organization and unity on diviners who were otherwise expected to regulate their occupation along lines laid down by government authorities.

Zulu Christians in separatist churches created entirely new bodies of healing practice and theory. Prophets like Isaiah Shembe found inspiration in their dreams to introduce a new order of religious practice in Zionist churches (Sundkler 1961), using the profoundly evocative symbols of precolonial Zulu religion to carry a Christian message. The congregations are communities of suffering and healing. Most new members join because they are ill and hope to find relief from their afflictions (West 1975).

To see African healers and patients as active and creative, altering received knowledge and practice, on a quest for original understanding, is to take a position that is at odds with much of current thinking on social history and the history of ideas. *Annales* historians see continuities over the long term as profoundly important. The seemingly creative acts of individuals are but variations on a continuing theme. Poststructuralists see us all as imprisoned by our language, impotent because we do not understand that our most important statements are the ones our discourse leaves unsaid and therefore hidden from our own view. Yet the present work insists that African patients and healers think creatively and act with purpose. Their consciousness counts in ways that have always been recognized by scholarship on the creation of European culture, but rarely by scholarship on African culture.

The scattered evidence on the precolonial period reveals a picture of active creation. Janzen's account of consecrated healing knowledge in Equatorial Africa demonstrates that different medicines and different forms of organization dominated in each historical era. Lemba, for example, served in the seventeenth century as a form of sacred knowledge to preserve the health of the king, but then changed in successive generations. Later the kingdoms fragmented; a network of traders tied the region together, using their joint influence in place of royal authority; the merchants served as the senior Lemba priests, using the sacred knowledge as the medicine of government. In the nineteenth century, when venereal diseases threatened fertility, Lemba carried weight as "the government of multiplication and reproduction." The full story, if it were known, would tell of individuals in each generation working to change Lemba's emphasis, applying the sacred knowledge to new domains of experience, and creating new forms of knowledge. The historical records reveals more about the knowledge created than about the creators.

Lemba did not belong to a single ethnic group or linguistic unit. Its senior practitioners stretched across a whole region. They were merchants and judges drawn from a number of places; they formed a web of influential leaders who shared in the sacred medicine of government. It was occupation, not ethnicity, which defined the Lemba priesthood; social variation, not homogeneous "tribal" practice, which determined access to healing knowledge.

THERAPEUTICS IN TOTAL SOCIAL HISTORY

Healing ideas and practices are not a separate domain. They are an integral part of politics, kinship relations, religion, trade, farming, and sexual life. As these evolve, so does healing. It must therefore be understood within the totality of society's social and cultural history. When Africans converted to Christianity, as Ranger shows, missionaries expected that their change of religion would lead them to change their healing practices. The discussion of whether to consult an *mganga* or a physician was not narrowly medical; it revolved around questions of good and evil. Missionaries saw physicians as successors to Christ the Healer. Missionaries treated African choices of therapy as choices of theology. Ranger writes about a missionary (not atypical) who withheld medicine for a child's sores until the mother agreed to cut off all charms. "I told her . . . [the missionary wrote] that I could do nothing till she gave up the medicine of the devil" (1978*b*, 262). This sort of intolerance was not uncommon. Church authorities, faced with cases of madness that had been attributed to witchcraft, sometimes saw the choice between therapies as one between good and evil. Medicine in this case is not separate from theology. To understand the evolving therapy, one needs to understand the evolution of religious thought.

Medical thought takes on the characteristic ideas of society as a whole. In West Africa in the early colonial years, Curtin shows, public health practice was inextricably linked to the pattern of race relations. The Europeans who planned West Africa's cities assumed that segregation was healthy for whites, that the health of colonialists would be preserved only if they were kept separate from the conquered Africans. The medical justifications for segregation changed with time and place. At times it was plague that seemed to required urban segregation. In some places no Africans were allowed near European quarters, for they were presumed to have malaria parasites in their blood. In other places African servants were allowed, but not other Africans. The medical justifications of the precise health rules were often obscure. In Dakar racial segregation evolved as a plague measure, but continued after the plague threat ended. Africans wealthy enough to live in the European manner built houses alongside the French. Race, culture, and disease merged in a strange complex. Its precise form varied locally. W. J. Simpson of the London School of Hygiene and Tropical Medicine wrote (1914, 9–10,109):

> It has to be recognized that the standards and mode of life of the Asiatic do not ordinarily consort with the European, whilst the customs of the Europeans are at times not acceptable to the Asiatics, and that those of the African unfamiliar with and not adapted to the new conditions of town life will not blend with either. Also that the diseases to which these different races are respectively liable are readily transferable to the European and vice versa, a result especially liable to occur when their dwellings are near each other.

The solution, therefore, Simpson wrote, was to plan separate quarters for Europeans, Asians, and Africans. The racial ideas of the conquerors shaped their understanding of medical problems. Their medical ideas shaped the landscape, and with it the pattern of urban disease. In the case of urban planning as in mission medicine, health practice was incorporated into broader patterns of social and cultural change.

A similar integration is visible in kinship-based therapies. The case of Malaika, described by Davis-Roberts, revolved around the dilemma created when a dead man's relatives blamed his wife for his death. The relatives refused to follow the normal practice of widow inheritance. The disinherited widow then went mad. It was, then, the widow's granddaughter Malaika who suffered illness because of the disturbed relationships. The appropriate therapy for Malaika was one that would treat the complex of relationships.

Widow inheritance, which was at the heart of the family relations affecting

Malaika, is a continuation, after a husband's death, of the relationship between two social groups linked in marriage. If the changing economy should render widow inheritance an unattractive option, the custom would disappear. If this were to happen, the set of therapeutic practices of the kind used to cure Malaika would change also. The history of therapies can be understood only as part of a total history of kinship and the economy.

As kinship patterns change, so, too, do the networks of relatives who manage therapy. Once again, the evolution of therapy is inseparable from the history of local social organization, and of the larger society. We see this in Lower Zaire, in the case of a woman named Lwezi Louise (Janzen 1978*b*). Lwezi fell ill with periodic fever and chills, radiating back pack, pain in her joints, loss of appetite, and general malaise. Her relatives took her through a long series of therapies. They shuttled from one to another, in a characteristic way. Lwezi's relatives tried a dispensary, a *nganga*, a Christian prophet, and a second dispensary. The relatives wanted also to make a therapeutic adjustment to Lwezi's kinship relations. Lwezi had married a man in the city who had not made the customary payment to her father. Lwezi's father, upset at this improper marriage, withheld his paternal blessing. Lwezi Louise's brothers offered to pay the gift to their father in the husband's place. But the father felt that if he accepted the gift he would relinquish authority over his daughter. Lwezi's husband, having failed to pay, would not take up that authority. The father therefore refused to accept the payment from his sons, Lwezi's brothers. His judgment was supported by the local Christian pastors. "The pastors on both sides rejected this, noting that it would set Lwezi free, with a blessing, to become a public woman" (Janzen 1978*b*, 107).

This decision demonstrates that Lwezi Louise could not be cured if the therapy itself undermined patterns of authority. Kinship was central, therapeutic action peripheral. Because of this, any understanding of therapy management must be based on a clear analysis of kinship authority. We return once again to an earlier conclusion: that change in therapy is part of a total picture of change in culture and community organization.

CONTROL OVER THERAPY

The story of healing is one of public power and private choice. The public and the private interact in unexpected ways. In virtually every African country, governments encourage people to choose biomedicine—the medicine of hospitals, dispensaries, and clinics. Yet in most countries hospital medicine is available to only a part of the population. In most countries popular medicine, as practiced by local so-called traditional healers is illegal or extralegal. Yet patients make the majority of their visits for treatment to local healers. Actual patterns of health care emerge from the midst of these paradoxes.

Even at a time when many African governments publicly acknowledge the value of local healing traditions, most of the colonial laws that rendered popular healing illegal remain on the books. The result is a peculiar situation in which the herbal knowledge of popular practitioners is seen by governments as a national treasure, and yet many healing acts are illegal, although they are rarely subject to prosecution. French law, which is still in force in most of Francophone Africa, makes it illegal for anyone but a licensed physician to perform "medical acts." British law, which remains on the books in many Anglophone countries, makes alternative medical practice legal so long as the practitioner does not take measures "implying that he is registered," but so-called antiwitchcraft laws, which survive in many of the countries that had been British colonies, were so broad as to prohibit almost any kind of popular medical practice (Stepan, 1983, 297, 311).

Even when popular healing practice is recognized as legal, it can place the practitioner in an ambiguous legal position. Because healers are not recognized as medical practitioners, a healer can be charged with unauthorized practice, or even with murder, in the case of a patient's death. Today, healers' associations are working to improve the legal status of their members (Last and Chavunduka 1986). These efforts have enjoyed little success so far. Most governments issue statements on the positive value of traditional healing, but do little to incorporate local healing, or even to remove the penalties against it. Only local midwives have been included in government health establishments in any useful way (Pillsbury 1982).

The actual legal situation in most places and at most times is at a stalemate. The authorities usually leave healers alone, neither licensing nor persecuting them. Healers protect themselves, often by becoming invisible. On rare occasions individual healers win favor with powerful politicians. Others protect themselves by forming public pressure groups. These latter strategies can be dangerous. Politicians fall from power, leaving their friends vulnerable. Popular movements sometimes seem threatening to power-holders; seen from the government's point of view their leaders look suspiciously like rebels. But the most common response by healers is neither to seek patronage nor to build a following. It is to become invisible. The most common response by governments is to accept this and ignore the issue.

Licensing of healers is problematic since governments, in awarding licenses, would be forced to accept the conceptual framework underlying popular healing. A responsible government would prohibit malignant medical practices while permitting legitimate healers to carry on. But how is a government to demonstrate in a court of law that this healer is practicing witchcraft while that one is benevolent? It is impossible, and so governments back off.

The other alternative would be to close down all popular healers, making no distinctions. This is unfeasible because popular healers provide so much of actual health care. If a government arrested or closed down all popular healers, and if the patients all went to government facilities instead, the government would be overwhelmed. Clinics and dispensaries would be flooded with patients, unable to carry on. Many patients would, in any event, resist. There are some treatments for which dispensary medicine is no substitute.

Despite the complex legal situation, it is important to search for patterns of authority and control in African healing. Whoever controls the diagnosis of illness (most often someone drawn from the lay population) shapes cultural ideas on misfortune and evil. The power to name an illness is the power to say which elements in life lead to suffering. To define illness is also to decide when a person can legitimately be excused from work or other obligations. The explanation of illness is often tied up with conflicts in the life of a household or community. Here again, control over healing carries weight in larger affairs. These matters are too important to float freely, uncontrolled by any authority. Yet the organization of medical practice and medical knowledge conspire against the emergence of definitive professional authority. Medical ideas are not codified in one coherent system. Traditions of healing (spirit possession, sorcery, biomedicine) evolve separately, each with its own logic and boundaries. Even though physicians control government definitions of legality, they are unsuited to serve as gate-keepers. They cannot direct patients to the various healers because they do not share the values of the patients or of the healers. Some popular healers are well suited to serve as gate-keepers but have no legal standing. Indeed, they are themselves legally vulnerable.

Therapy managers, drawn from among the patient's relatives, neighbors, and friends, are at the heart of African healing. This has become clear since the late 1970s (Janzen 1978*b*). Therapy managers are defined solely through their relationship to the patient and the patient's particular illness. The therapy managers help to choose among healers. In some cases they pay for care. Some African hospitals do not provide food; they leave this to the therapy managers. These helpers also serve, quite often, as the patient's nurses in hospital.

Therapy management fulfills two quite separate functions, organized in different ways. The first is authoritative diagnosis and control over treatment. These are in the hands of the one person (or limited group) who has juridical authority over the patient. The holder of authority is sometimes the patient's father, sometimes the lineage head, and sometimes the husband. Adult men and independent women at times make therapy management decisions for themselves. The second function is supportive care. Whereas juridical authority is limited to a few hands, supportive care is distributed widely. Neighbors, old friends, passers-by, and distant relatives all offer, on occasion, to help out. They all suggest possible diagnoses and treatments. But they can share in the final decisions only if they are invited by authority-holders.

Therapy managers of both kinds are defined through their helping relationship to the patient. In the nature of things, most are not healers. If a patient's relative happens to be a healer, that person can also be a therapy manager. The person who combines the two roles of healer and therapy manager is especially influential. Most of the people who know the patient's personal circumstances do not have technical medical competence. Most of the people with technical competence do not know the patient. The healer-relative holds technical as well as personal knowledge and therefore plays an especially important role. Therapy management does not have a distinctive institutional hierarchy; it is fully embedded within general patterns of control over domestic and community affairs. The person with juridical authority over the patient in the sphere of health care (typically in many places the patient's father, husband, or elder brother) holds other kinds of authority at the same time. When making a health decision, he (it is rarely a woman) considers other issues at the same time. He considers his own interests and all conflicting interests within the community. The cases of Malaika and of Lwezi Louise illustrate the inseparability of therapy management and local social organization. Close relatives do not form separate sets of institutions for health care and for economic production. They plan together as relatives and deal with whatever problems arise—whether a daughter's illness or falling crop prices.

At this intimate level local politics, economic production, and therapy are integrated, often in complex ways. The daily activities that shape health and disease move ahead alongside health care. This is the fundamental level at which health and health care are integrated.

THE DESIGN OF THE BOOK

The essays that follow are divided into two groups: the first (part II), on the decline and rise of population in the regions of Africa, with an emphasis on the history of patterns of ill health; and the second (part III), on the history of the diverse traditions of therapeutics in Africa. The two groups are interdependent. The accounts of the health consequences of migratory labor in South Africa by Packard (chap. 4) and by Marks and Andersson (chap. 5) in part II also discuss, of necessity, crucial events and forces that shaped the South African health care system. Prins (chap. 13), writing in part III, on therapeutics, returns to the epidemiology of tuberculosis in order to set out the challenging disease environment within which Lozi healers shaped changing therapies.

The essays in both of the remaining sections of the book locate their subject matter within a broader social and cultural context. Neither disease nor therapeutic practices are treated as isolated medical subjects, cut off from the wider history of Africa.

Cordell, Gregory, and Piché (chap. 1) explore the significance of what they call the "demographic regime," the dynamic relationship of mortality, fertility, and migration within the context of changes in state policies and class structure, as mediated by the health environment. They explore the significance of their model through a discussion of the political, economic, and disease history of the Central African Republic and Burkina Faso.

Marc Dawson, in his essay (chap. 3) on smallpox in precolonial and early colonial Kenya, describes the dynamic interplay between the evolution of strains of the virus and the patterns of human activity in which epidemics emerged. The upheavals of the early colonial period brought famine, which led people to trade, to raid one another, and to gather in the few locations where food was available. The movement of people and the concentration of nonimmune people searching for food led to the most devastating smallpox epidemic of the past century.

Megan Vaughan (chap. 2) writes about the social context of hunger, which, in her view, is unequally distributed on the basis of fundamental divisions within the community. She asks about individuals who had greater or smaller entitlements to food during Malawi's famine of 1949, and finds that individuals located at different points within the organization of power and production (with the distinctions based partly on gender) enjoyed very different entitlements to food during the famine.

The same relationship between ill health and social inequality (this time on the basis of race and class) is at the heart of the two essays on South Africa, by Packard (chap. 4) and by Marks and Andersson (chap. 5). The history of tuberculosis, of malnutrition, and of nutritionally related infectious disease is bound up with the entire pattern of South African mine labor, migrations, and racial domination.

The essays on therapeutics in part III are grouped into four sections, on precolonial, colonial, and postcolonial medicine and on twentieth-century African medicine.

With the transition from the precolonial to the colonial period, authority over public efforts to bring health to the populace shifted from African to European hands. Janzen (chap. 7) and Waite (chap. 8), writing in the precolonial section about parts of the region in which Bantu languages are spoken, show that in precolonial African polities public healing was a core concern. Chiefs took part in healing and the leaders of healing cults participated in public politics. Waite describes how chiefs and priests administered a system of public health over much of the region. Janzen tells us that when chiefship declined in western Equatorial Africa, cult authorities assumed governmental functions. He explains that when we see the therapeutic institutions of that region from within, "artificial dichotomies between religion and government, or medicine and politics are put aside." Lemba, the therapeutic cult, was at the same time a central governmental institution of the nineteenth century and an association of wealthy traders which regulated commerce.

In early colonial West Africa (as in precolonial Lemba) as described by Philip Curtin (chap. 9), the holders of wealth and of power had a disproportionate say when it came to interpreting specialized knowledge about the public conditions needed for good health. Curtin describes the great advances in scientific knowledge about malaria that came at the end of the nineteenth century. He then shows how colonial authorities used the new knowledge to legitimate racial segregation in West Africa's towns even though segregation was ineffective in controlling malaria. Public health measures, in colonial as in precolonial Africa, were the outcome of negotiation among power groups. The African middle class in colonial turn-of-the-century Accra, in Ghana, fought against malaria-control segregation and defeated it.

Abdalla's essay on Islamic medicine in West Africa (chap. 6) shows the important role played early in the precolonial period by cosmopolitan religion and cosmopolitan healing practices. Islamic medicine encompassed a diverse body of conceptions and practices, including humoral medicine (resembling that of the Mediterranean world) and the more strictly religious medicine of the Prophet. Abdalla defines Islamic medicine as the medicine of Islamdom, thus encompassing all the diverse conceptions and practices of the Islamic world, regardless of whether the particular practices had Islamic theological roots.

Parallels emerge in some limited respects between Abdalla's (chap. 6) description of Islamic healing and Ranger's (chap. 10) of Anglican healing in colonial Tanzania. Ranger shows that scientific hospital medicine was treated by missionaries as the medicine of Christendom even though the medical conceptions and practices did not have Christian theological content. In this respect hospital medicine bore some resemblance to humoral medicine in the Islamic world. Unlike the Muslim clerics of West Africa who turned increasingly to the more strictly religious medicine of the Prophet, the missionaries suppressed spiritual healing for fear of encouraging African enthusiasm for it. The result was that spiritual healing was more easily permitted by the Anglo-Catholic movement in England (from which the missionaries came) than by the movement's churchmen in East Africa.

The essays on twentieth-century African medicine are local studies drawn from a diverse range of settings around the African continent. A central recurrent theme has been mentioned already: the question of a medical system. These studies all recognize the diversity of medical conceptions and practices within the particular locality, and then search for sources of coherence, of system. Individual essays find coherence in very different ways. Prins, for example, argues that the categories by which people understand and control affliction are central, and that it is possible to identify the systematic character of these categories by separating a society's core conceptions from its more peripheral ideas.

Sindzingre and Zempléni (chap. 12) take a very different approach. They explore the terms in which Senufo of the Ivory Coast name a sickness, describe how it happened and the agent that produced it, as well as its place in the life of an individual. They identify recurrent logical patterns in Senufo discussions of cause, agent, and origin, but then emphasize that "We have not described here a medical taxonomy, which would be absurd, but have sought to elucidate the formal principles that underlie this society's tendency to elaborate fragments of an etiological code." The fragmented code can be described, but it is not part of a total cultural system. The authors emphasize that "the specification of cause, agent, and origin is in no way a necessary condition for the treatment of a disease." For the Senufo as described by Sindzingre and Zempléni the process of explaining a sickness and of treating it proceed quite separately from one another, along two different tracks.

Christopher Davis-Roberts (chap. 15), writing about the Tabwa of Zaire, argues that their concepts of illness and transformation form a coherent whole. The central narrative in which that coherence emerges does not, however, claim to be about the whole of Tabwa society and its concepts; it is the narrative of an individual's illness. The illness is a unique event, one with special communicative power. Its meaning is revealed only through the healer's vision, through the therapeutic process of "recognizing illness." "Reality," according to Davis-Roberts's account, "has a fluidity and interactive quality that accords to the eye a status at once profound and powerful." In a sense the whole of socially accepted epistemology unfolds through the individual illness experience.

For Greenwood (chap. 11) also, what happens to the afflicted individual is at the core of the medical system. According to his description of Moroccan therapeutics, the basic shared categories of the medicine of the Prophet and of humoral medicine diverge yet interact. In each case of illness shared experience is related to inner experience, optimizing the conditions for a return to health. The categories of explanation may be diverse, but a system is created by individuals, using the pieces of cultural explanation as in a patchwork. Greenwood explores Moroccan images of sexuality that are evoked by illness categories. The sexual images, among others, tie the individual's experience of illness to societal categories of illness explanation. The cultural experience becomes personal experience, and by so doing becomes efficacious as therapy.

Harriet Ngubane (chap. 14) and Murray Last (chap. 16) both introduce questions about the relationship between the relative power of competing practitioners and the content of their knowledge. Their case studies point to opposite conclusions. Last, writing about medical concepts and practice in Northern Nigeria, ranks competing therapies in a hierarchy of organization and access to government funds. Maguzawa medicine, the medicine of non-Muslim local practitioners, ranks lowest. Because it is at the bottom it has become desystematized. Last argues that both patients and practitioners often "do not know" about Maguzawa medicine, even when they are using it, and also "do not want to know." Local practitioners neither pursue a uniformly accepted set of practices nor adhere to a coherent set of conceptions. Ngubane's description of South African diviners makes the opposite case to Last's. Zulu diviners, who are at the bottom in terms of Last's hierarchy of government funding, form associations to maintain the coherence and the systematic character of Zulu healing.

In the opening essay of the section on postcolonial medicine F. M. Mburu (chap. 17) explores inequalities in the distribution of basic government services in Kenya, especially within Nairobi. The poorest parts of the city have less access than the richer ones to sanitation, to clean water, and to health care.

Carol MacCormack (chap. 18) introduces Weber's analysis of the forms of legitimacy in her reflections on the relationship between "traditional" healers and bureaucratic health services. In doing this she returns, from another angle, to the question of the relative power of competing healers. She explores the possibility of increasing the influence and autonomy of local healers within health care structures that are centrally planned and centrally controlled.

PART TWO

The Decline and Rise of African Population: The Social Context of Health and Disease

INTRODUCTION

The broad curve of the decline and then rise of African population during the past century defines, in the most general way, the health consequences of a complex assortment of historical causes. The decline was drastic between 1880 and 1920 in East Africa and in large parts of Equatorial Africa, including much of what is now Zaire, the Central African Republic, and the Republic of Congo. By the late 1920s the continent's total population was stable, or perhaps growing. It grew rapidly after World War II. The full story will only be told by future scholars in a multitude of local histories, but the broad patterns are so strong and distinctive that we can say that they are solidly grounded. This is particularly true of regional population decline in the early colonial period, and of broad population growth after 1945. The separate essays that follow make a start toward explaining those causes in terms of the social context of health and disease on the continent of Africa.

POPULATION DECLINE

Early Colonial Period

Historians give three basic interpretations of early colonial population loss. The first has a long history going back to the time of conquest. Henderson, in the Oxford *History of East Africa*, states the position dramatically (1965, 123):

> East Africa [before conquest] was ravaged by tribal wars and by the depredations of the Ngoni and the Arab slave traders. The lot of many of the native inhabitants was indescribably wretched. They lived in terror of the slave-raiders; they suffered from malaria, smallpox, typhus, sleeping sickness, and other diseases; their cattle were victims of the tsetse fly and of rinderpest; their

> fields were stripped by locusts. Slave raiding and epidemics increased recourse to witchcraft.

Henderson argues that East Africa had always been a region of horrendous diseases, that the epidemics of the early colonial period were in no way unusual, and that colonial rule was needed to change this situation. The record of East African population history does not support his case.

The second position focuses on changes in population distribution and movement in the colonial period. Urbanization, the building of roads and railways, labor migration, and the movement of armies all increased the possibilities of transmitting communicable diseases. Dawson, for example, in his disease-by-disease account of Kenya in the early colonial period, attributes the greatest burden of mortality to labor migration (1981, 134; see also 1983, 7). Hartwig and Patterson, in their introduction to *Disease in African History* (1978, 12), combine the argument on mobility with a second that improved communications "disturbed the relative tolerance which many rural Africans had developed for local strains of the parasites causing malaria, dysentery, trypanosomiasis, and perhaps other indigenous diseases." Good's chapter (1978) provides an especially clear example of this sort of localized tolerance. His approach is a useful variant of a much less defensible position taken by others: that Africa as a whole had been isolated in the precolonial period, and that diseases, newly introduced from overseas, swept across the continent in much the same way that Old World diseases swept across the Americas after Europeans first crossed the Atlantic. Breaching Africa's isolation, in this view, was necessary even though costly in human life (Azevedo 1978, 188).

The third explanation of population decline under early colonial rule indicates that conquest was a political event that deprived Africans of the capacity to control their own environment. The European conquerors forcibly instituted new patterns of settlement, labor, and land use despite their own ignorance of African ecology, and thereby destroyed the basis of survival. This is the essence of the position John Ford takes in his book on trypanosomiases (1971). Helge Kjekshus (1977), in a book on East African ecology that owes much to Ford, makes the same case.

It is unwise to evaluate the overall worth of the three interpretations without first looking at regional differences. The population trends that define the early colonial experience in East Africa did not exist in the west, and the health problems of the equatorial forest were different from those in either East or West Africa. The crucial comparative questions—why regions differed from one another—have not been studied carefully.

The Eastern African Region

The literature on East Africa offers a rich selection of interpretations of disease history along with a dearth of population figures. But all recent scholars agree that the population of Kenya, Uganda, and Tanzania declined sharply during the years between colonial conquest and 1920.

Marc Dawson, in his valuable recent work on the history of disease in Kenya (1978, 1979, 1981, 1983; see also Dawson's essay in this book [chap. 3]), attributes an especially significant role to smallpox epidemics that raged in the aftermath of the major famines of 1892 and 1899–1900. According to Dawson's interpretation, famine led to population movement and concentration because the search for food drove people out of their homes. The new patterns of population concentration then aided the spread of the disease.

Helge Kjekshus, writing about early colonial Tanzania (1977), asks whether the famines of the 1890s were natural events, or consequences of colonial conquest. He argues that the region's population had been growing in the nineteenth century only to suffer disastrous decline after conquest. This interpretation underemphasizes the destructive impact of international trade in the years before conquest. It is more likely that warfare and insecurity drove people into dense defensive settlements where they were forced to intensify their agriculture. The density of population would then have been a result of population movement, not of population growth. Hartwig (1976, 1979) gave a reasoned rebuttal to Kjekshus's claims of population growth, showing that in the precolonial decades famine, cholera, and smallpox took a great toll.

Sleeping sickness brought some of the most substantial population losses in early colonial eastern Africa. This is the subject of an important book, John Ford's *The Role of the Trypanosomiases in African Ecology: A Study of the Tsetse-Fly Problem* (1971). Ford, who had a long career as a colonial scientist, argued that African societies had developed effective ecological controls for trypanosomiasis. They had succeeded in isolating the most dangerous forms of trypanosomiasis in what Ford called *Grenzwildnisse*—wilderness areas at the borders of populated territory, arranged so that people and cattle did not come into frequent contact with tsetse flies. The European conquerors destroyed a whole range of controls and unleashed a plague on Africa. Ford wrote (1971, 9):

> It is a curious comment to make upon the efforts of colonial scientists to control the trypanosomiases, that they almost entirely overlooked the very considerable achievements of the indigenous peoples in overcoming the obstacle of trypanosomiasis to tame and exploit the natural ecosystem of tropical Africa by cultural and physiological adjustment both in themselves and their domestic animals.

Later in the book (p. 143) he wrote:

> Like their British neighbours across the Kagera in Ankole the Germans looked upon themselves as saviours of people sunk in centuries of barbaric misery. Few realised that they were the prime cause of the suffering they were trying to alleviate.

These are rare expressions of opinion in a massive work of detailed ecological analysis. Its central point is that the conquest destroyed African control of the ecosystem and thereby let loose diseases that had long been held in check.

Ford emphasizes the role of two disasters in the breakdown of control—the rinderpest panzootic, which wiped out cattle and wildlife, and smallpox, which together with famine reduced the human population. These two sets of events, together with the colonial wars that brought them, upset the ecological controls that had long contained the threat of trypanosomiasis. Once this happened, tsetse-fly belts continued to advance. Colonial boundaries rigidified the *Grenzwildnisse*, and a host of ecologically ignorant authoritarian measures, many of them intended to control tsetse, led to the expansion of tsetse-fly belts.

One of the core images of Ford's book is of the Semliki Valley, whose residents were forced to move from the upper hillsides to certain death of sleeping sickness in the valley bottom. It is no wonder that some Africans of the region saw colonial actions as a form of biological warfare (Nayenga 1979).

The Equatorial African Region

Large regions of Equatorial Africa, under French and Belgian control, experienced population decline more extreme than East Africa's (Coquery-Vidrovitch 1977, 341, 346). Trypanosomiasis played a role here, too. In addition, the colonial disruptions of local economy and society were among the most sweeping and intense on the continent. The regime of enforced rubber collection, for example, won notoriety even at the time (Coquery-Vidrovitch 1972; Harms 1975). Infertility also threatened long-term survival in Gabon, Congo, Central African Republic, and parts of Zaire and Cameroon. In some of the region's societies, even in recent times, 20 to 40 percent of fifty-year-old women have never had children (Belsey 1976, 320–322).

Romaniuk (1980; 1967) and Retel-Laurentin (1974*a*, *b*, 1979*a*, *b*) agree that sexually transmitted diseases were the major cause of infertility. Retel-Laurentin emphasizes the role of syphilis, but gonorrhea is a more likely cause of infertility (Belsey 1976).

Sexually transmitted diseases appear not to have spread widely before the nineteenth century. Harms describes how syphilis, spreading from the coast in the 1880s, was so deeply feared that local African judges could impose the death sentence on women who slept with Europeans (Harms 1981, 181–183). The problem of infertility could not have been one of long standing, because the population could not have sustained itself over the long term while threatened by late-nineteenth-century levels of loss (Caldwell 1985).

No one has written a serious analysis of patterns of sexuality in the transmission of disease. Such an analysis would need to take account of the economy, work patterns, and sexual division of labor for the period both before and after colonial conquest. Dennis Cordell (1983*a*) points to the works of Thomas (1963) and Dupré (1982) as examples of studies working along these lines (see also Lux 1976).

The areas of Equatorial Africa that tended to suffer high levels of infertility were those occupied by concessionary companies: private enterprises to which European governments granted the right to govern large tracts of African territory for their own profit. It is unclear why infertility was common in those places. Perhaps military forces played a role in spreading sexually transmitted diseases. Scholars could illuminate the problem by mapping military forces in the early colonial period in relation to the distribution of venereal disease and of infertility. In any event, population decline in that period was not solely a result of infertility, for extremely high infant and child mortality also played a role. Belsey (1976) cites infant mortality figures ranging from 30 to 80 percent for nine villages in Zaire, as reported in 1911 (p. 326). This would have been one additional consequence of the upheavals brought by early colonialism.

The concessionary companies of early colonial Equatorial Africa did not have sufficient capital to make long-term investments in their African holdings. They aimed at short-term profits even if these could only be won by brute force. The agents of concessionaires terrorized or killed people unless they brought goods for export. Undercapitalization of privately owned colonial territories, combined with a drive for short-term profits, created some of the worst health conditions in the past century. Undercapitalization was also an important part of the reason for the terrible health conditions in the mines of Southern Rhodesia at the same time (Van Onselen 1976).

West Africa saw few signs of the population decline that was so significant a part of the early colonial period in Equatorial and East Africa. In this region as in other parts of the continent the statistics of the period are unsatisfactory, but scholars seem generally to agree at an impressionistic level that West Africa's population was relatively stable, possibly suffering small losses in some places, enjoying gains in others, but in no way similar to the drastic declines of Uganda or French Equatorial Africa (Ajaegbu 1977; Caldwell 1977, 8; Frishman 1977, 277; Hill 1977; Inikori 1981, 299; Patterson 1977, 1981*a*, 87, 96; Perrot 1981; Wilks 1975, 90–93; Wrigley 1979, 128).

If African surrender of control over the local environment led to disastrous population loss in East Africa, why did it not have the same effect in the west? Inikori (1981) explains later population patterns with reference to the slave trade which, in his view, served as the equivalent of the later shock of conquest in eastern and equatorial Africa. He relies on Cissoko's description of sixteenth-century and seventeenth-century epidemics at Timbuktu (1968) to argue that the slave trade led to political upheavals, which, in turn, caused demographic disasters. As a result West Africa suffered its period of demographic decline long before the colonial period. This interpretation does not pass the test of comparative analysis across regional lines. Angola suffered intense slave trading from an early date, yet this did not protect it from population loss in the nineteenth century when colonial pressures became intense (Dias 1981; see also Thornton 1977 and Miller 1982).

Perhaps disease adaptation in nineteenth-century West Africa was less localized than on the eastern side of the continent. The peoples of West Africa had probably never been as narrowly restricted geographically as East Africans to particular zones. "By 1800," according to Patterson and Hartwig, "West Africans had many generations to build up defenses to cope with their more complex disease environment" (1978, 8; see also Patterson 1981*b*, 2–3).

West African populations were in movement over centuries, especially in the savanna and at the desert edge. People living in the driest zones have always moved southward into the wetter savanna during the dry season and in dry years, with many returning northward again with the rains. This was more significant for biological adaptation than the movement of traders because it meant that whole populations interacted with one another and with alien environments. Pilgrimage to Mecca by way of Sudan may also have been significant, for it was a form of movement in which West Africans left their homes, were exposed to alien disease environments over long periods, and then returned home. Al-Naqar estimates that 15,000 West Africans accompanied King Mansa Musa to Mecca. Even if the figure is not precise, it is clear that large numbers of people were involved. Other pilgrimages were also substantial (al-Naqar 1972, 12; personal communication, Ismail Abdalla).

The picture is less clear in the forest zone of West Africa, except for the effects of interaction with aliens at the coast, and the consequences of trade-induced warfare. The distribution of the sickle-cell gene is one piece of evidence showing that West African populations were less localized in their adaptations to their environment than the peoples of East Africa. The gene confers some resistance to falciparum malaria. In parts of East Africa where falciparum malaria is a significant problem a much larger percentage of the population has the gene than in malaria-free areas. The equilibration of gene and disease is much less precise in West Africa (Livingstone 1967), showing that populations were probably not tied as narrowly to particular micro-environments as on the eastern side of the continent.

The final disastrous event that marked the end of early colonial population decline struck all the regions of the African continent. This was the influenza pandemic of 1918/19 which, according to Patterson and Pyle (1983), took between 1.5 and 2 million lives in sub-Saharan Africa. Wartime movement of soldiers and laborers helped to spread the disease, which moved rapidly along newly constructed lines of rail.

POPULATION GROWTH

At some point in the 1920s population began to grow. Since then, the rate of growth has increased rapidly. Gregory and Piché (1982) estimate the continent's population as 164 million in 1930, 219 million in 1950, 352 million in 1970, and 458 million in 1979.

The high rates of population growth do not, however, indicate that people are healthy. The crude death rates of the 1970s varied between 15 and 40 per 1,000. These were among the highest in the world, as was the infant mortality rate of about 200 per 1,000 (Cantrelle 1975; Gregory and Piché 1982; Vallin 1976). Another sign of poor health is the prominence of infectious disease among causes of death. This was characteristic of western Europe mortality patterns before life expectancy began to increase, at which point degenerative diseases such as cancer and cardiovascular disease became more important. In Africa today the great killers include malaria, diarrheal diseases, measles, tetanus, and respiratory diseases. Maternal mortality is also a significant cause of death (Cantrelle 1975; Ware 1978) and increasingly stress-related diseases such as heart attacks.

The great growth in African population must be understood against a background of poor health, and cannot be taken (without more specific evidence) as a sign of generally improved conditions. The precise determinants of population growth are largely unknown. We do not yet have the detailed regional population histories, which must precede works of broader synthesis.

Caldwell writes that a decline in mortality caused the population explosion. His argument grows inexorably out of his assumption (1975*a*, 1977, 1985; Pool 1977*a*, *b*) that precapitalist modes of production in Africa require high fertility, which is then unlikely to rise further as conditions change. The fertility levels recorded in the 1950s were, in his view, typical through the long span of African history. For Caldwell it was high fertility that sustained precolonial population despite the very high mortality, caused by an unhealthy environment made worse by the dangers of warfare.

Caldwell's assumptions about precolonial population have been challenged. There are two problems. First, warfare was not a major direct cause of mortality (Kjekshus 1977; Wrigley 1979). Political upheavals may have had an impact on population, but it was through disruption of food supplies and the impact on disease transmission. Second, precolonial populations probably did not share midtwentieth-century fertility patterns (Cordell et al. 1987; Ganon 1975, 697; Iliffe 1989; Manning 1981; Swindell 1981). The Caldwells themselves (Caldwell and Caldwell 1977) showed the importance of the duration of postpartum sexual abstinence. A survey of historical change in postpartum practices (Schoenmaeckers et al. 1981) shows that in scattered places on the African continent abstinence continued for extended periods in the precolonial period but became shorter as the twentieth century unfolded.

We do not have comprehensive data on fertility and mortality, even in the twentieth century. In some countries nationwide censuses were carried out during the colonial period, but in others national governments made the first censuses only in the 1970s. At that late date a large proportion of censuses collected no information on fertility and mortality (Tabutin 1984). Even when it is collected, the information is often inaccurate. In most cases the interviewer collects mortality data retrospectively, asking about all deaths within the preceding twelve months. This procedure almost invariably underestimates the number of deaths. In the Kombol survey zone in Senegal, for example, a retrospective survey in 1963/64 counted 126 deaths among one- to four-year-olds, whereas continuous observation over the following three years showed the same zone averaging 233 deaths each year in that age group (Cantrelle 1975).

It is likely, nevertheless, that mortality has in fact been declining over the past sixty years, even though the causes of the decline are largely unknown. One possibility is that improvements in transportation reduced famine mortality by making it easier for people to move away from famine zones (Caldwell 1975*b*). Yet people do continue to die during major famines (Watts 1983). The question is whether the number of deaths has declined. The most common baseline for answering this is the early colonial period, a time of unusually high mortality.

A second possibility is that population has grown since 1945 because medical interventions have saved lives. Some places are well endowed with medical care, but for the majority of the continent's population even today biomedical care is usually a brief encounter between patient and doctor—rarely a matter of thorough diagnosis, treatment, and follow-up. Nevertheless, a few innovations have contributed to twentieth-century population growth. In one of the rare local case studies of the colonial period, Patterson (1981*b*) estimates that colonial Ghana's mortality declined because of chemotherapy for malaria, vector control and therapy for trypanosomiasis, sulfa drugs and then antibiotics for pneumonia, vaccination for smallpox, and treatment of traumatic injuries. Today antibiotics, antimalarials, and immunizations continue to make a contribution.

Geographic variations in mortality give some clues on the long-term mortality decline. Rural mortality is consistently higher than urban. Some of the most precise estimates are for Senegal, where Cantrelle placed infant mortality in Dakar at 57 per 1,000, while it reached 247 per 1,000 in rural Thienaba. Sanders (1982) estimates similarly drastic urban–rural differentials for Zimbabwe. In Kenya, life expectancy for women in Nairobi in 1969 was 63.8, compared to 47.5 in Rift Valley Province, and 50.0 in Western Province (Monsted and Walji 1978, 69).

These differentials show that mobility and urban crowding, which are sometimes taken as the major causes of disease and mortality, are less important than other factors. But which ones? Clean water supply is a possibility. Patterson (1979) shows that Accra's piped water supply expanded rapidly in the years after World War I, at a time when the city made few advances in the disposal of human waste. Access to clean water makes diseases of the gut less likely. These are major killers and major causes of malnutrition.

Political and economic power, which is concentrated in Africa's cities, shapes the distribution of water supplies. World Bank and bilateral donor loan policies also contribute to the preference for urban areas. Kenya in the late 1960s, for example, spent 2 dollars per capita on urban water supplies, and 2.5 cents per capita on rural water in a country where the vast majority of the population was rural (White et al. 1972, 13–14).

It is possible that nutrition, too, is better in the city, although urban food supplies have worsened recently with the intensification of economic crisis in many countries. Possible reasons for the differential in nutrition, aside from water supplies, include a softening of the effects of seasonal hunger for city-dwellers who purchase food in all seasons, and a shortening of women's workdays, making it possible for them to cook more frequently. Benyoussef et al. (1974) compared rural and urban samples in Senegal with respect to a number of health indicators. They found that city women were heavier than their rural counterparts, and city-dwellers had higher hematocrits (indicating less anemia). The only indicator on which the urban sample was worse off, because higher, was cholesterol.

City people also have easier access to medical care, which might make some difference because of immunizations, antimalarials, antibiotics, and some surgical interventions. Orubuloye and Caldwell (1975), in an attempt to demonstrate the effects of medical care, studied two towns in Ekiti Division of Nigeria's Western State, one with biomedical facilities and one reliant only on popular healers for care. They found that children were much more likely to survive in the town with a hospital. But they ignored several possible explanatory factors. People in the hospital town drew water from shallow wells, as opposed to water in the other town from streams in which people defecated. Most important of all, men from the hospital town were more likely to live at home with their families, whereas many of the other town's men migrated to find work. In studies around the continent absent fathers and child malnutrition often go together.

The assumption that declining mortality is the only source of African population growth in this century needs to be questioned. A number of writers on African historical demography now challenge the argument that fertility on the African continent was consistently high in the precolonial period. Jay O'Brien (1987) and Marc Dawson (1987) show that decisions on birth spacing and on the desired total number of a woman's children are influenced by a wide range of social and economic factors which change through time. O'Brien's comparative study of two villages in the Sudan is suggestive, for he shows that in the village that lives by wage labor, birth intervals are shorter than in the village where labor is coordinated by extended kinship groups, as it would have been in the precolonial period. Dawson cites statistics showing an increase in children per woman in central Kenya between 1922 and 1977/78. John Iliffe (1989), reviewing these articles as well as the more general discussion of African population change by Cordell et al. (1987), says that the larger issue has not yet been decided, that we do not yet know whether fertility has in fact increased over the past century. The final judgment will be a long time coming, for it must be built on a number of detailed local studies.

While research and debate unfold, it is clear that the explanation of African population growth based on continuous high fertility cannot be accepted. Systematic support has not been offered for the hypothesis that fertility on the African continent was always high, and that population grew as a result of declining mortality.

A continentwide literature search on postpartum sexual practices shows that the period of abstinence grew shorter in a number of places (Schoenmaeckers et al. 1981). Where this happened, it is important to know why women's reproductive lives changed. Understanding the patterns may help us to understand more general changes in fertility. Could the decline of postpartum abstinence in these cases mean that patriarchal social groups lost some degree of control over women, who then chose to have more children? If this is so, why did they choose more children? The answer is not clear. Another possibility is that in the nineteenth century, when patriarchal kinship groups still held together, people were relatively secure in the knowledge that their kinship groups would provide them with adequate support in old age. With the decline of these groups the old people needed more children and grandchildren to increase the probability that one or another, acting as an individual, would provide support. If this is what happened, then the desire for maximum fertility grew with time alongside the decline of patriarchal groups.

An altogether different possibility is that the increase in fertility grew out of needs for labor. The colonial economy made great labor demands on each domestic group, either by taking migrant male workers out of the household, or by requiring the production of export crops (Meillassoux 1975). Perhaps husbands and wives tried to increase the household's future supply of labor by shortening abstinence periods. In this case maximum fertility is not a precapitalist survival, as Caldwell would have it, but rather a creation of colonial capitalism intended to meet labor needs (Turshen 1984). The problem with this explanation is that it makes colonial capitalism sound like a conscious individual, and that it would likely sound alien to those who abstain. (See the broad surveys by Schoenmaeckers et al. [1981] and Caldwell and Caldwell [1981]) The most common justification for a long period of postpartum sexual abstinence is that it is essential for the health of the infant, or that it is a sign of the mother's morality.

To reach a full understanding of the decline in abstinence we would need an extended analysis of change in domestic and community organization in the twentieth century. This would take account of the changing labor needs of the economy and would also give due emphasis to the ideology and organization of domestic groups.

ESSAYS ON THE SOCIAL CONTEXT OF HEALTH AND DISEASE

The following essays make a start toward explaining the historical context within which the population of the African continent declined and then rose. Dawson's essay (chap. 3) on Kenya, for example, analyzes the history of smallpox, one of the major diseases implicated in early colonial population decline.

Cordell, Gregory, and Piché (chap. 1) explore the social determinants of morbidity and mortality over the whole of the period since colonial conquest, using illustrative materials from the Central African Republic (called "Ubangi-Shari" during the colonial period) and from Burkina Faso. They discuss two very different patterns in the relationship between political control and morbidity, mortality, and fertility. One pattern characterized the years of conquest and the early years of colonial rule—the years that were, in this region, the era of population decline. A second pattern characterized the period from the 1930s onward—the time of the continent's general population rise. The early period was one of upheaval, violent deaths, the direct appropriation of labor and its products, the disruption of African agriculture, and the rapid spread of disease. During the later period the violence ended and some health services improved, but the pattern of mortality, morbidity, and fertility showed was not uniform. The later period is characterized by differentiation according to class and according to residence. By the years after World War II in Burkina Faso, as in many other parts of Africa, city-dwellers were likely to live longer than their rural counterparts, and it is presumed that those better off had an easier time surviving than the poor.

The differentiation of health conditions for different segments of the population during the years of population growth is of general importance for many parts of Africa. Megan Vaughan (chap. 2) pursues this theme in her essay on the 1949 famine in colonial Malawi. She discusses famine in terms of the differential entitlements to food of different segments of the population. Skilled workers and substantial businessmen survived most easily; some even profited from the famine. Small farmers who cultivated their own inadequate plots and did casual labor for other African farmers were very hardpressed. Among the worst off were women in female-headed rural households. The aggregate picture of population growth in the postwar world conceals great variation: prosperity and satiety for some, starvation for others.

Randall Packard explores the association between mining labor and the spread of tuberculosis in South Africa. In some parts of Transkei by the early 1930s, 90 to 95 percent of men over the age of twenty tested positive for tuberculosis. Yet despite the ubiquity of this infection in some parts of South Africa, where racial politics pushed blacks toward shared poverty, even there inequities among Africans were important. People who are infected and well nourished show few symptoms of the disease, which becomes active at times of stress and malnutrition. Significant nutritional differences among individuals therefore had significant health consequences. As we can see, the history of tuberculosis is a broad history of nutrition, or rural differentiation, of migration, and of urban work.

Marks and Andersson continue the discussion of health in South Africa, surveying a broad range of health problems and policies from the time of the mineral revolution until the years just after World War II. Like Packard (chap. 4), they document the tragic toll taken by migratory labor. They provide an extended analysis of the interplay between fundamental social change, disease, and health policy in the 1930s and 1940s. By the 1930s the economy of the overcrowded African reserves was breaking down. These were the areas where women were expected to farm so that they could feed their children whose fathers were away at work, and at the same time the areas to which workers were expected to return for their livelihood if there were no jobs, or to be cared for if they were ill. The breakdown of the reserve economy created a health crisis. Governmental authorities needed to respond to it, either to end the migratory system or to meet minimal health needs so the system could survive.

In 1942 the government, struggling to respond to the crisis and also to the increasing militancy of blacks who had moved to the cities during World War II, appointed a National Health Services Commission, which ultimately recommended that the country be divided into a grid of 400 health centers that would emphasize prevention, nutrition, and health education as well as curative treatment for whites as well as Africans. The Commission's recommendations were never carried out, for a number of reasons. Some of the pressure for health reform came from a health crisis in the 1930s among poor whites. Changes in the economy and in the structure of racial privilege improved health conditions for the poorest of the whites, thus decreasing the government's sense of urgency concerning health reform. The South African government's movement toward apartheid after the election of the nationalist party in 1948 was built on the assumption that the migrant labor system would be preserved in something like its old shape, and not transformed. The white electorate decided that the mines and farms were to continue to have sources of cheap labor. The period since then has been one of drastic inequalities between Africans permanently resident in the cities, and Africans living under the most difficult conditions in the reserves or "homelands." These inequalities are perpetuated in the health care system as in most other spheres of life. The racial politics of South Africa thus created inequalities in health that are at their most extreme between blacks and whites, but which also divide black people from one another.

ONE

The Demographic Reproduction of Health and Disease: Colonial Central African Republic and Contemporary Burkina Faso

Dennis D. Cordell, Joel W. Gregory, and Victor Piché*

INTRODUCTION

The extremely high levels of mortality in Africa are no secret. By way of introduction,[1] we note two indicators of mortality that dramatically reveal the differences—between Africa and other so-called developing regions, and between Africa and the industrialized "West." First, in Africa life expectancy at birth in 1988 was 85 percent of that of Asia and 79 percent of that in Latin America. Moreover, the expectancy of fifty-two years in Africa is less than three-fourths of the rich world's average of seventy-three years. Infant mortality rates (deaths under 12 months of age per 1,000 births) are a second indicator that dramatically emphasizes the differences in risk. The aggregate figure for Africa is 110 per 1,000 for 1988, compared with 72 for Southeast Asia, 89 for the Middle East, 57 for Latin America, and 41 for East Asia. For the world's "more developed regions," the rate is 15 per 1,000 (Population Reference Bureau 1988).

Equally important by way of introduction is the wide variety of mortality conditions within Africa: between regions and countries, between rural and urban areas, and between social classes (Gregory 1982; Ruzika 1983, 70–71). Research in the 1960s and 1970s focused on geographic differences in mortality. In West Africa, for example, Senegal displayed the most striking regional variations for which data were available. In the 1960s child mortality in Dakar varied from 16 per 1,000 children (from ages one through four inclusively), to 48 in semiurban Khombole, to levels ranging from 81 to 141 (!) in some rural areas (Cantrelle 1979, 6).

*Joel Gregory, lifemate, close friend, and colleague, died of AIDS in Montreal in the summer of 1988. Dennis and Victor would like to dedicate this revised version of our text to him.

More recent multiple-round studies in the region such as the Enquête de mortalité infantile au Sahel (EMIS), as well as the Demographic and Health Survey (DHS) in Mali, have permitted the identification of intervening medical, health, and social factors. The impact of social class is clear. Another survey in Bobo-Dioulasso (Burkina) suggests that maternal education, identified for some time as a very important explanatory variable in infant mortality, is most influential when accompanied by higher income and better housing, along with greater use of health services (Mbacke and Van de Walle 1990). An overview of mortality over the past two decades hence suggests increasing differentiation by region and social class. Compared with other regions of the world, however, it can be said that rates remain extremely high for all but the upper classes.

Understanding the reasons for such dramatic rates of human wastage should rank among the most urgent priorities for scientific research and political intervention. It is urgent to do so, for in Africa the situation is as socially unacceptable and politically unjust as it is in Latin America—so eloquently described by Hugo Behm (1980, 15):

> When the *Titanic* was sunk, in 1912, 3 percent of the female passengers in first class were lost, 16 percent in second class and 45 percent in third class. In . . . Latin America there are 345 million passengers, subject to differential risks by social class, just as cruel, or even more cruel than those of the *Titanic*. Annually almost a million bodies of children less than five years old are thrown overboard; they come mostly from the "third class" and, above all, they should not have died. Our responsibility is to show to those at the political levels of decision-making, and to the people themselves, with scientific objectivity, the magnitudes of this monstrous genocide and the deep causes which lie behind it.

Fellow third-class passengers include the four-fifths of Africans who live in rural areas and the vast majority of the urban population.

Although death rates have declined in recent decades, the single most important political and scientific question may well be "are mortality levels going to continue to decline?" From a global perspective it is clear that since the eighteenth century, and particularly since the nineteenth century, mortality levels in Europe and North America have declined steadily, and sometimes dramatically. More recently, and especially since the war of 1939–1945, a similar trend began in the Third World, first in Latin America, and then in parts of Asia and Africa. But the trend has not continued (Ruzika 1983, 61; our italics):

> In all three major regions of the [Third] world a slowing of the improvement was noted in the late 1960s and the early 1970s. . . . The deceleration and even stagnation of mortality occurred at levels that were all far too high not to be amenable to further rapid reduction. . . . *The reasons for the slowing of the improvement of life expectation are not yet fully understood.*

This trend continued in the 1980s. Although differences from one region to another have grown, Africa nonetheless remains the continent with the highest mortality rates; indeed, the gap between Africa and Asia has widened. More specifically, the number of African countries whose mortality levels are falling farther and farther behind world averages increased over the period 1970–1985 as compared with 1955–1970 (Waltisperger 1988, 283–285).

In the remainder of this section and the one that follows we would like to look at the demographic and social context within which changes in mortality and morbidity levels occur (or do not occur). The third part of the chapter presents two historical case studies—Ubangi-Shari (today's Central African Republic) and Burkina Faso (formerly Upper Volta)—as illustrations of our analysis.

MORBIDITY AND MORTALITY AS PART OF DEMOGRAPHIC AND SOCIAL REPRODUCTION

In Africa, as elsewhere, mortality cannot be studied in isolation from other demographic phenomena. Such a statement may seem self-evident. However, conventional demographic analysis usually disaggregates demographic change into separate studies of fertility, mortality, and migration. This compartmentalized approach is reflected in the conceptualization of each parameter and the development of quantitative methods. The classic demographic formulation of population change is:

$$\text{Births} - \text{deaths} \pm \text{net migration}$$

This can be disaggregated in various ways. Births minus deaths is natural increase. Immigration minus emigration is net migration. Births plus immigration is growth; deaths together with emigration, loss. Demography as a discipline continues to *add* births, *subtract* deaths, *add* immigrants, and *subtract* emigrants. However, the way(s) that these phenomena combine to assure population renewal (or not)—the unified process that we term the "demographic regime"—is seldom analyzed holistically. In addition, this equation is simply arithmetic, and does not tell us anything about the social processes tying these phenomena together. Demographic behavior, and attitudes about health and illness, are a function of social norms, which in turn reflect the material reality of social production and reproduction (Cordell et al. 1987; Gregory and Piché 1981). Reproduction is used in a holistic sense, referring to the dynamic processes of the entire demographic regime; reproduction does not only refer to fertility and fecundity, which is only one part of the processes, and which can more accurately be defined as procreation.

To illustrate the interrelationships among demographic processes, we note one frequently accepted hypothesis about the impact of infant mortality on fertility. High-fertility societies are also those with high mortality. The most commonly suggested link between infant mortality and fertility stresses the replacement hypothesis, that high fertility attempts to compensate for the probable loss of a substantial fraction of offspring at very young ages. But the relationship is not unidirectional. High fertility in and of itself can contribute to higher infant and fetal mortality, through diminished maternal health and repeated risks associated with pregnancy and childbirth. Reduced birth intervals can also contribute to increased mortality at young ages.

Yet the dynamic relationship between fertility and mortality goes much further. In particular, mortality decline does not always produce fertility decline. In fact a major excess of births over deaths in cases of declining mortality is central to the contemporary preoccupation with rapid population growth in much of the Third World. The explanation for this apparent independence of fertility and mortality lies beyond the demographic regime, and must be sought in a more holistic analysis of demographic behavior as part of social reproduction (see Cordell et al. 1987; Dawson 1987).

An appropriate starting point for the more comprehensive approach we advocate is to ask how social units—households, families, villages, and societies—reproduce themselves demographically; how do they make sure that additions are sufficient to make up for the losses? Part of the answer lies within the boundaries of the demographic regime itself; part, in the analysis of the larger processes of social reproduction.

Within the context of the demographic regime, social units have reproduced themselves in the face of substantial mortality and emigration. The demographic quality of the process, and in particular the age and sex structure of the population, has frequently been pushed to its limits. The crucial ratio is probably the dependence burden, or the number of physically productive individuals relative to the number of unproductive or marginally productive ones. Many units and some entire societies have disappeared, given their inability to offset losses and burdens. Slavery, war, epidemics, famine, and other catastrophes have intervened, producing discontinuities in the process of demographic renewal (see, e.g., Cordell 1987*b*).

Migration provides a short-term answer to major discontinuity, either by the incorporation of new people into a threatened community through forced or voluntary immigration, or by emigration from one unit to another that is more viable. In the longer term, fertility has often proved to be surprisingly resilient. The limits of sexual imbalance in a population are not known (Guttentag and Secord 1983), yet the social and biological necessity of reproduction means that the sex ratio of people old enough to form procreative unions must be kept in reasonable balance as long as high mortality and high fertility characterize the demographic regime.[2] The necessary flexibility to adjust to long-term as well as to short-term and seasonal imbalances has often been provided by the relatively rapid adjustment of the socially appropriate age for marriage for both men and women, and the grouping of a fraction of women (or exceptionally, men) in multiple partner unions (Manning 1981; Thornton 1980). Beyond altering marriage, a threatened population may respond in other ways, by telescoping the calender of births, or increasing their intensity. Coming full circle, the morbidity and mortality characteristics of populations condition the capacity to emigrate, to procreate, and even to attract (or capture!) immigrants.

Part of understanding *how* demographic reproduction occurs requires inquiry beyond the demographic regime itself. People and societies react to morbidity and mortality, for example, not only by replacing individuals, but also by attempting to regulate, and reduce the threat of illness and death. They derive therapeutic practices from observed experience and metaphysical interpretation. On the preventive side, they also attempt to improve survivorship and the quality of life. These same practices also aim at improving fecundity, reducing sterility and ameliorating maternal health, thus enhancing the conditions of fertility. An understanding of migration likewise lies for the most part beyond the confines of the demographic regime—in the political economy of rural and urban residence, of regional and national space, and the links between origins and destinations.

If *how* demographic renewal occurs is difficult to analyze precisely, *why* it happens is a question so general that it could lead to an attempt to explain human existence. At a more "mundane" level, the survival strategies of household, families, and communities are central to explaining why social units reproduce themselves. For example, the rationale of high fertility for social groups dependent on labor-intensive production is clear (Gregory 1986*a*; Gregory and Piché 1981): many children provide needed labor for agriculture, herding, and craft activities. The demographic regime encourages this strategy as a way of responding to the threat of high mortality and the permanent or temporary loss of household members through migration.

The wider realm of social reproduction also dictates this logic. Demographic reproduction cannot be isolated from the larger institutions of social reproduction, and particularly those that participate in the reproduction of the labor force: the household, the family, the workplace, informal and formal education, and local and cosmopolitan health care. A materialist analysis of the demographic regime stresses this perspective. Only a fraction of a population that is being renewed participates in the active labor force at any one time; the rest is maintained during periods of inactivity (sickness, injury, old age) or being reproduced for the longer term (children) (Meillassoux 1975). And while orthodox labor-force demography excludes domestic labor from its analysis, feminist critiques permit the reintegration of the domestic and the public spheres, both in terms of the labor produced and reproduced, and in terms of the ideology that conditions reproduction (Anker et al. 1982;

Ferguson and Folbre 1983). Recent research on women and work in the Caribbean at the University of Montreal has incorporated such a feminist perspective (see Gregory et al. 1988; Neill 1988; Poirier et al. 1985, 1989).

Up to now we have raised many theoretical questions about the place of mortality and morbidity in an overall analysis of demographic renewal. Answers must be found to as many of these questions as possible. The challenge, of course, is to develop an analytical framework that can be applied to the diverse experience of African societies.

A FRAMEWORK FOR ANALYSIS

The social production and reproduction of health and disease and of local and cosmopolitan health practices affect morbidity and mortality both directly and indirectly. Health practices have a significant direct impact on mortality because of the important biological component of illness and death.[3] But other components of social reproduction, the reproduction of the labor force, and the reproduction of the demographic regime also affect morbidity and mortality indirectly.

In our analyses we identify four levels of causality depicted in columns I–IV of figures 1.1 and 1.2. This flowchart format does *not* suggest that one level is more important than another. The formulation simply structures the way in which factors of health and illness affect death and identifies some of the direct and indirect paths of explanation. We do not attempt to operationalize the model, although the case studies in the following section illustrate some aspects of it.

Four sets of assumptions shape the model. First, the study of the impact of mortality on a society begins demographically because the phenomenon cannot be separated from fertility and migration. Second, the direct causes of death can be described by a relatively small number of categories. Most of these have significant and observable biological components; however, suicide and violence are different. Third, these categories are directly conditioned by the mental and physical health environment. And fourth, the health environment is *primarily* determined by the prevailing political economy. These assumptions give rise to the four levels of the model (see figs. 1.1 and 1.2). The levels also influence each other: II affects I directly, III affects I through the intermediary of II, and so on.

Two points need to be reemphasized. First, the genuine determinants of mortality are *not* diseases or disease states (II). Rather, the medical "cause of death" only serves as an indicator of the broader social determinants (III and IV) that are at work (see Mosley 1983, 26–27). Second, the "cause of death" is seldom discrete; for the young, Mosley observes that, "in most cases (death) is the result of a long series of individually minor biological

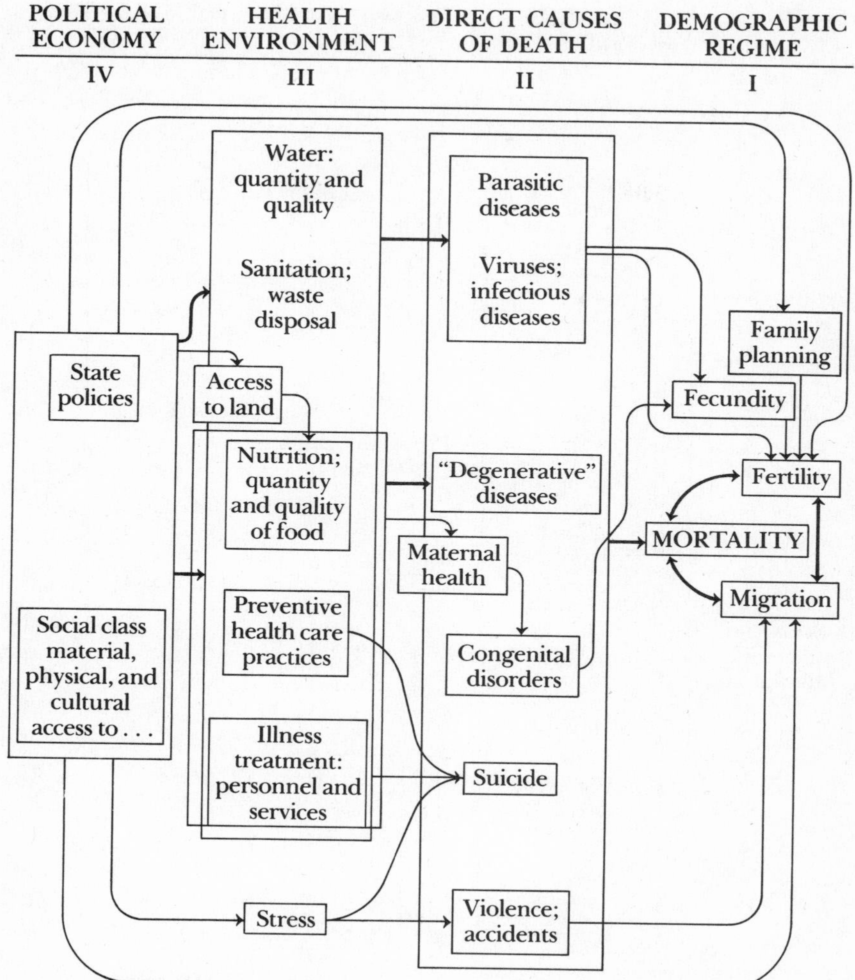

Figure 1.1. The social reproduction of health and disease: factors conditioning mortality and the demographic regime.

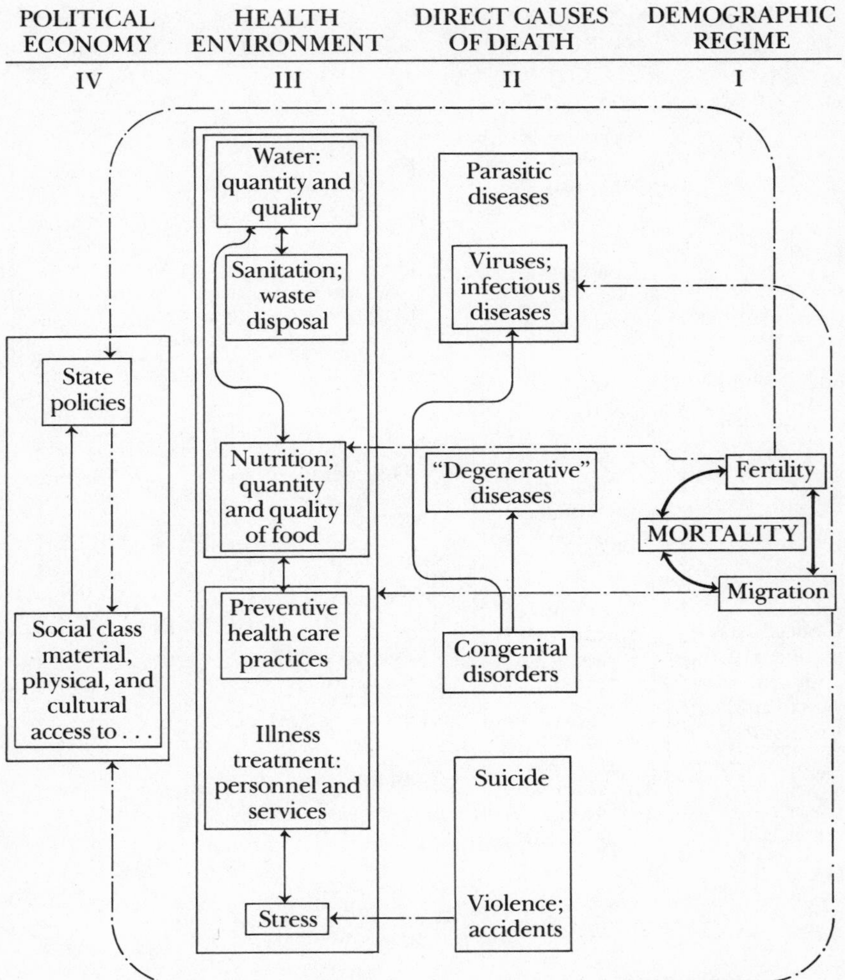

Figure 1.2. The social reproduction of health and disease: interrelationships between factors and feedback mechanisms.

insults which cumulatively retard growth, lead to wasting, and progressively wear down the resistance of the individual" (1983, 27).

We propose a framework that is similarly multicausal, but suggest a slightly different hierarchy of analysis emphasizing the difference between factors in the health environment (III) and the political economy that conditions them (IV). Figures 1.1 and 1.2, which should be read as if superimposed one on the other, schematically depict these relationships. The first column on the right (I) in both figures places mortality in the context of the demographic regime. The second (II) identifies direct causes of death and illness, while columns III and IV illustrate the indirect impact of the health environment (III) and the political economy (IV).

The holistic analysis of mortality presented in the figures requires detailed comment. First, column I suggests the complexity of analyzing mortality as part of the demographic regime. For example, direct causes of death can also be indirect causes of fertility change and, sometimes, of migration. The replacement hypothesis mentioned earlier illustrates such a situation; because people in populations with high infant and juvenile mortality rates wish to maximize the chances of having adult sons and daughters, they do nothing to restrict fertility. Secondly, it should be pointed out that while column II depicts the direct causes of death, it does not systematically include the direct causes of fertility or migration. The depiction of the demographic regime would be much more developed than shown in column I if column II were expanded to include such variables.

Third, column III examines the "health environment" and summarizes the major ways in which it conditions the causes of morbidity and death.[4] In a simplified way, we have identified some of the major variables that affect the health of individuals, social classes, and communities. Food and nutrition, and health care practices (both preventive and curative) obviously play a major role. Column III does not assign relative importance to conditioning factors. That is a question for empirical verification, which varies considerably according to the age and sex structure of mortality; it depends, therefore, on the historical specificity of a particular society (Behm 1980, 3). The elements included in column III, however, do permit us to formulate hypotheses about both local and cosmopolitan health practices. Column III does not suggest priorities for health policy. The importance of factors conditioning the health environment, and their responsiveness to social intervention, are the subject of considerable debate (Mosley 1983; Ruzika 1983). Our emphasis here, however, is on the relationship between these factors (III), defined in a generalized way, and the direct causes of morbidity and death (II), in order to explore changes in the rates and structure of demographic variables, including deaths (I).

Column IV suggests elements of the political economy that determine the health environment. Political economy is depicted in terms of state policies, and the ways that an individual's access to and participation in, a healthy environment is conditioned by social class. An analysis of access must proceed on two levels: the physical or material access to a healthy environment, conditioned by public policy and social class; and the ideological accessibility of healthy practices. Column IV does not include at least two additional elements of the political economy that condition the quality of the health environment and the potential for healthier lives: the role of external and international factors, and the role of private capital. We have purposefully excluded these factors for two reasons, even if they *must* be considered in the study of the social reproduction of health and disease in contemporary Africa. First, they are difficult to separate. Second, the links between international public "aid" and private capital in the health sector are not only very strong in themselves, but they are intimately tied to the interests of the governing class; external factors and private capital have both played a fundamental role in the production and reproduction of all social classes in Africa (see Gregory 1986*a*).

A final level of causality must be mentioned. Like figure 1.1, figure 1.2 suggests some of the interrelations among causes, but it also illustrates the feedback mechanisms that influence the social reproduction of health and disease. Particularly noteworthy is the multifaceted impact of migration on the entire system. Population movements can quite directly influence the spread and intensity of parasitic, viral, and infectious diseases (see, e.g., Prothero 1968). Even more dramatic is the fact that migration itself probably conditions each and every parameter identified as a conditioning factor (see column III). Specifically, migration almost always changes an individual's or a family's *access* to water, sanitation, food, and health services. Likewise migration is accompanied by stress, for both migrants and nonmigrants, and, therefore, for both receiving and sending populations. Finally, the significance of migration for the transformation of social class cannot be overemphasized (see Gregory 1984; Gregory and Mandala 1987).

While perhaps less striking, the interrelationships among causes of mortality are probably as important as these feedback mechanisms. This comes as no news to epidemiologists and other medical personnel, but it implies that hypotheses about demographic processes must be multidimensional. The most noticeable set of interrelationships is among the factors conditioning the health environment (III). What is commonly identified as preventive health could easily be reformulated as the key element in the production and reproduction of a positive and healthy milieu. The fact that preventive health is central to causality also underscores its vital importance for public policy (Jelley and O'Keefe, in press; Gregory 1986*b*).

Thus far we have discussed the reproduction of health and disease in purely theoretical terms. In the pages that follow we attempt to apply our framework empirically. We analyze morbidity and mortality, the larger demographic regime, factors conditioning the health environment, and the political economy in two territories in two time periods: the French colony of Ubangi-Shari (today's Central African Republic) from the 1870s to the 1950s, and the independent country of Burkina Faso from the 1960s to the 1980s. The choice of these regions and periods is somewhat arbitrary, reflecting our own particular knowledge and interests, but it allows us to illustrate our perspective.

TWO CASE STUDIES

Earlier parts of this chapter emphasize the need for a holistic approach to the study of health in Africa, placing morbidity and mortality in the larger context of the demographic regime—the way that patterns of birth, death, and migration combine to enable a society to renew itself (or not). We suggested that the demographic regime is partially determined by "factors conditioning the health environment" (the elements included in columns III and IV of figs. 1.1 and 1.2). Although the availability of water, for example, partly depends on nature, we suggest that most of the factors listed in column III are profoundly shaped by a society's social relations of production (IV) (see Gregory 1985). In the pages that follow we apply this analytical framework to the evolution of morbidity and mortality levels, demographic regimes, and the social relations of production in two case studies. Throughout the text we have included Roman numeral references to identify the various levels of our model.

Ubangi-Shari, 1870–1900: Economic Integration, Violence, and Demographic Change

Social formations in Ubangi-Shari in the late nineteenth century ranged from hunter-gatherers in the tropical forests of the far southwest, to small-scale agricultural societies throughout the central savanna, and larger-scale, centralized states in the southeast and the north (for a survey, see Cordell [1983*b*]). By the 1870s the entire region was more open to external influences than ever before, with important direct and indirect consequences for health, patterns of demographic renewal, and the social relations of local societies.

During the nineteenth century northern and eastern Ubangi-Shari became integrated into the Muslim world. Relatively peaceful initially, the process became increasingly violent. Apart from ivory, Ubangi-Shari had little that northern Muslim traders wanted in the way of material wealth. But the demand for slaves was increasing in the Islamic world; Muslim traders and the Muslim states on the fringes of the region subsequently came to regard Ubangi-Shari as a source of slaves. Isolated raiding parties from the outside were succeeded in the 1860s and 1870s by organized and seasonal campaigns from within as states within the area expanded their own slave-raiding operations (Burnham 1980; Cordell 1985*a*, 52–75, 103–12; 1986; 1987*b*; Prins

1907, 139, 141; Santandrea 1957, 151–155). Raiders captured more people while a proliferation of trade routes to the north made it easier to export them. In addition, Ubangi-Shari's growing role as a provider of slaves to the Islamic world ultimately brought a great expansion in slave-holding in the region itself.

This shift affected African mortality (I), morbidity (II), and demographic regimes (I) in several ways. First, the increasing violence (II) caused more death. Data are scarce, but during one set of attacks in 1903, villages lost between 10 and 60 percent of their populations (Cordell 1985*a*, 110).

As for those enslaved, increased demand for labor (IV) lowered standards of living (III), and malnutrition (III) probably increased morbidity and mortality. And, as with many slave populations, fertility rates probably declined as well. The health environment (III) differed, depending on the way slave labor was organized. Slaves who worked in large groups on plantations, such as those owned by the sultan of Dar al-Kuti in north central Ubangi-Shari, probably fared less well than those resettled in slave villages who organized their own labor. In general, however, it is our hypothesis that the political economy of slavery (IV) brought an increased tempo of work. (This was certainly true in other regions; see Lovejoy [1986, 184–246, passim]). Given limited technology, additional labor was necessary to produce surpluses for the ruling classes, maintain the instruments of violence necessary for continued raiding, and sometimes, support a more elaborate state apparatus to keep slaves in check.

But slave-raiding and slavery affected the mortality and morbidity, and demographic regimes of nonslave populations as well. Raiding provoked flight, which directly caused death from starvation or exposure. Concern for security frequently overrode concern for proximity to water; many refugees settled in the high rock outcroppings scattered through this part of the savanna (Dybowski 1893, 286; Prioul 1981, 136–141). Flight, therefore, probably precipitated higher rates of diseases (II) from both inferior nutrition and insufficient or contaminated water supplies (III). In addition, the loss of people made it difficult for those who remained to mobilize the labor necessary to maintain earlier agricultural practices. Many people abandoned the customary, but demanding, cultivation of millet and sorghum. They resorted to gathering and hunting and/or less intensive agriculture—planting patches of more easily maintained, but less nutritious, cassava (Prioul 1981, 116–18).

Integration and slave-raiding also brought important changes in the disease environment (II). Early in the century intensified contact with the Sahara and the Nile valley encouraged, or may even have introduced, diseases such as smallpox and syphilis (Browne 1806, 355; Patterson and Hartwig 1978, 8, 9). Largely as a result of the changes wrought by slavery (IV)—an expansion in the scale of production and the need for protection from spiraling violence—the last half of the century witnessed the emergence of larger, more densely populated settlements (III). Endemic diseases such as smallpox appeared in virulent epidemics; in Ndele, the capital of Dar al-Kuti, for example, three smallpox epidemics broke out in the first decade of the century (Cordell 1985*a*, 110; 226, n.60). Other epidemics struck the Banda settlement at Grimari in 1904, and in Bangassou, the capital of the Nzakara state on the Mbomu, one-fifth of the population died of the disease between 1903 and 1905 (Dampierre 1967; Kalck 1980, 123; Serre 1960, 24).

Southern and southwestern Ubangi-Shari, the "river region," experienced a parallel expansion of contact with the outside world. However, these regions were opened to capitalism by way of the Great Congo Trade to the southwest and the Atlantic economy beyond. Central Africa also became a source of slaves for this network, but the dynamics were different. First, the end of the Atlantic slave trade had the greatest impact: a drop in slave prices and an expansion in slave-holding on the southern rivers (Harms 1983, 95–110). Riverain societies became wealthier, with important consequences for reproduction (IV, I). Participation in the trade enabled these societies to acquire increasing numbers of slaves, from the interior or from downstream in exchange for ivory (Cordell 1987*b*; Samarin 1984*b*, 213; Serre 1960, 60), thereby altering the political economy (IV).

Penetration of capitalism brought changes in mortality and morbidity in southern and southwestern Ubangi-Shari in the late nineteenth century, just as the expansion of slavery signaled changes in the east and north. Greater mobility brought new diseases (III); moreover, forced and voluntary migration fostered large fortified settlements along the rivers (Cordell 1986; Dybowski 1893, 156; Samarin 1984*b*, 213), which probably promoted epidemics. These changes encouraged some societies to alter the way they renewed themselves. Fertility may have dropped, but not necessarily as a result of pathological problems (see Cordell 1987*b*). Economic opportunities and changes in social relations made it advantageous to import slaves rather than have children. Bobangi villages that participated in the trade, for example, tended to have few children, a characteristic of their demographic regime extended into the present century.

Ubangi-Shari, 1900–1930: Primitive Accumulation and Health

The "Scramble for Africa" brought the French to Ubangi-Shari. The early colonial period witnessed a brutal effort to restructure the political economy (IV), through the redirection of production, and the extraction of labor from African societies (IV). European activities may be grouped under two headings: exploration and conquest, and "pacification" and development. Both types of activities continued throughout the period, although exploration and conquest were more characteristic of the earlier years, and "pacification" and development dominated the years following World War I. Both provoked higher levels of mortality and morbidity, as well as important changes in demographic regimes.

Some of the consequences of the first three decades of European intervention resembled those associated with the slave trade. Arriving from the Atlantic by way of the Congo and Ubangi rivers, French expeditions often responded with violence (II) to the reticence or refusal of Africans to supply their needs; hence the familiar refrain of death and flight (Cordell 1983*b*, 71, 1987*a*; Prins 1907, 156–159). Later campaigns of "pacification" produced similar effects.

European *missions*—of exploration, conquest, and "pacification"—also frequently requisitioned food by force of arms; in addition, almost all required African canoe paddlers or porters, either recruited in the southern river region or supplied by local authorities along the way (Cordell 1987*a*; Prioul 1988, passim; Samarin 1984*a*, 357–359; 1984*b*, 193, 196–198, 203–205, 208, 210, 211–212). Along established itineraries such as the *route du Tchad* linking the Ubangi and Shari rivers, the repeated requisition of food and porters made it impossible for African societies to feed themselves adequately. Lowered nutritional levels (III) made people more susceptible to many diseases (II) (Cordell 1987*b*).

During the same period, the policies of the colonial state (IV) reflected French efforts to encourage the so-called *mise en valeur* of the colony. In 1897 France offered the lion's share of Ubangi-Shari to private concessionary companies, which thereby obtained rights to all natural resources as well as a monopoly on trade. In theory, the companies were to make investments in the infrastructure necessary for capitalist development: roads, administrative posts, and markets. In fact, they inaugurated an era of brutal primitive accumulation. The companies imposed head taxes payable in gathered and hunted products—mainly rubber, ivory, and wax. At first, these tasks required only a minimum of labor, since such products were found nearby. But as time passed they became more difficult to find; this was particularly true for rubber vines, which were usually slashed to collect the latex faster. People thus traveled farther, further reducing the labor time available for subsistence production. Simultaneously, the companies and the colonial administration raised taxes (Cordell 1987*a*; Coquery-Vidrovitch 1972, 51–57; Coquery-Vidrovitch and Moniot 1974, 199–200). René Maran (1983, 15–16) describes the devastation produced by such measures:

> This region was very rich in rubber and very populated. Fields of all sorts covered the area, which had many chickens and goats. Seven years sufficed to ruin it from one end to the other. Villages disappeared, fields disappeared, chickens and goats were wiped out. As for the people, burdened by unceasing and unremunerated work they could not devote the necessary time to their fields. They saw illness descend, famine invade, and their numbers diminish.

These policies had both direct and indirect effects on mortality and morbidity. Death (I), either from violence inflicted by company police, or from physical suffering (II) accompanying forced collection, was not uncommon. Men who refused to collect rubber, or who did not collect sufficient quantities, were often punished; sometimes their wives and children were taken hostage (Coquery-Vidrovitch 1972, 179). Other effects (II) may have included ill health during pregnancy, producing weak infants; poor postpartum health; and a cycle of low fecundity and depressed fertility. The absence of many men also meant that women were, as a group, less exposed to the chances of becoming pregnant, resulting in lower birth rates (see Cordell 1987*a, b*). As for the children a smaller labor force translated into less food, with a negative impact on infant health.

Forced collection of rubber and other products, like the forced and "recruited" labor that succeeded it, also degraded the health environment (III). For example, the absence of men for longer periods led to diminished agricultural production, undermining nutrition (Kalck 1970, II, 521). Furthermore, the burden of labor on women probably increased in the absence of men—with a consequent reduction of time available for child-care, food preparation, water collection, and sanitation—all essential elements for a good health.

As time passed, capitalist development (IV) increasingly required a less haphazard and more regular supply of African labor and its redirection, with adverse effects on health. Labor was of two types—forced and recruited. Forced labor was produced by the intervention of the colonial state which required that African males provide a specified and constantly increasing number of days each month to the administration. Tasks ranged from porterage—a major burden for villages along major itineraries such as the *route du Tchad* (Cordell 1987*a*; Goutalier 1979, 133–153)—to the construction of administrative buildings.

The precise impact of forced labor on African health cannot be measured, although among the Manza, conscripted as porters and workers along the *route du Tchad*, forced labor undermined the health environment (III) in several ways that indirectly increased mortality and morbidity. A decade of work on the *route* began in 1901. The total number of porters and workers recruited is not known, but in 1912, the year of its completion, 50,000 "volunteers" provided 236,388 days of work (Cordell 1987*a, b*; Goutalier 1979, 138–142). Although population figures were admittedly subject to error, estimates suggest that 35,000 people lived along the route in 1900; by 1905 their number had dropped to 18,000 (Gaud 1911, 259). One observer concluded that the frequent famines among the Manza stemmed from their inability to mobilize labor for food production (Van Overbergh 1911, xx, xxii–xxiii): "In earlier days, say the Mandja [*sic*], slave raids were terrible, but it was a trouble that passed. . . . Today the crushing burden is regular, systematic, monthly, annual—recurring" (Gaud 1911, xxi). Over the long term, frequent famines nurtured disease levels (II):

> they abandoned their villages and plantations, preferring privation to taking another load. Sleeping sickness, finding a fertile field, has terribly afflicted this exhausted, hungry, miserable, and naked population. The afflicted make up 18 to 40 percent of these villages (*décembre 1921*).

Labor recruitment operated somewhat differently. First, apart from providing workers for the public sector, the policy supplied workers for the private domain—for the forestry companies of the southwest, and, after 1921, for the construction of the Congo-Océan Railroad between the Atlantic coast and Brazzaville, the capital of French Equatorial Africa. Second, although it was theoretically voluntary, the colonial administration supported recruitment campaigns and encouraged villages to respond with workers. Third, such labor was remunerated, although at a very derisive rate. While its consequences paralleled those of forced labor, recruited workers were not nearly so numerous.

Such policies also brought higher levels of death and disease (I) among the laborers themselves. The development projects (IV) of the colonial state and private capital were not located in the most densely populated parts of the colony. Consequently, workers had to travel to their place of employment. Such migrations were taxing on health. Recruitment often entailed movement over greater distances—down to the Ubangi River in the 1910s and even farther with the construction of the railroad (Azevedo 1976, 247–248; 1981, 1–20; Cordell 1987*a*; Sautter 1967, 245) Laborers often lacked the necessary clothing and food supplies, and shelter was inadequate (III). As a result many railroad workers died of respiratory diseases such as tuberculosis and pneumonia (II), contracted on the work sites but aggravated by very poor housing (Sautter 1967, 273–285). Others died in the course of the long return to their villages.

Capitalist development, like slave production, also brought the reorganization of space (III), with increased mortality and morbidity, and migration. In the 1910s the French initiated a program of *regroupment* (Burnham 1975; Dampierre 1967, 533; Sautter 1966, 1018–1020). Relocation along streams, paths, and later, roads, facilitated the recruitment of porters, the collection of head taxes, and the conscription of labor for the construction and maintenance of infrastructure. Transportation routes were drawn to the perceived needs of the colonial administration, often disregarding African needs; and people often found themselves living in villages far from the best agricultural land. Access to water sometimes posed problems as well.

Regroupment created a longer-range threat, however. Precolonial agriculture was itinerant, an adaptation to abundant land with soils of limited fertility (Guillemin 1956, 61; Prioul 1981, 165–166). Settlement in one location longer than a few years was fraught with problems. Exhausted soils produced smaller yields with consequent nutritional decline (III). At the same time, in the late 1910s and 1920s, an increasingly well-implanted colonial state (IV) initiated more development projects requiring more efficient tax collection and more African laborers.

The direct and indirect consequences of forced *regroupment* for mortality and morbidity are by now familiar: some death, and considerable flight, with people adopting itinerant lifestyles, and paying the costs of freedom in vulnerability, diminished nutrition, and heightened susceptibility to disease. There were exceptions—the Ndri, who lived just north of the Ubangi River on the *route du Tchad*, for example, seized the opportunity of more regular communication to increase cassava production for sale to their neighbors (Prioul 1981, 96). But this was the exception rather than the rule.

Up to now most of this discussion has focused on changes in the health environment (III) and the impact on mortality and morbidity levels in Ubangi-Shari. But the immediate causes of death (II) also shifted. The redistribution of population, greater mobility, and intensified intercommunication created a new disease environment. Goods moved and people migrated; diseases, spread more widely as a result of increased mobility, found larger population reservoirs, and took on epidemic proportions. The most sobering of these outbreaks was the great sleeping sickness epidemic that spread through Central Africa in the early years of French rule. Noticed by the French as they moved up the Congo River and its tributaries in today's Gabon and the Congo before the turn of the century, the disease spread inland with the implantation of the colonial and concessionary regimes (Austen and Headrick 1983, 64). In Ubangi-Shari it appeared in the forest regions of the south and southwest around 1900 (Headrick 1981); communities on the southern rivers were afflicted next, followed by population living along the new colonial routes of communication—the case of the Manza has already been noted (Coquery-Vidrovitch 1972, 495; Headrick 1981, 4–5).

The great influenza pandemic of 1918/19, estimated to have killed 20,000 people in Ubangi-Shari, is another example (Huot 1921, 443–462). The worldwide outbreak of this disease was not uniquely associated with colonial rule, but it spread more quickly and widely in the colony as a result of the reorganization of population and space (Coquery-Vidrovitch and Moniot 1974, 169–170). We suggest that, as in the case of sleeping sickness among the Manza, the weakened state of the population contributed to higher rates of morbidity and mortality from the disease (for a survey, see Patterson [1981*a*]).

The French were aware of the threat that higher mortality, depopulation, and disease posed to the ability of African societies to renew themselves. Nor was the colonial regime oblivious to the low fertility rates of many societies. With the appearance of sleeping sickness they sent medical missions to Central Africa to assess the impact of the disease and recommend measures to combat it (III) (Leboeuf et al. 1909). However, an aggressive, systematic campaign against the disease came only in the 1920s. The campaign revealed that, while sleeping sickness was a major problem, other diseases were also widespread; in the 1930s the effort to combat sleeping sickness was expanded to include other infectious diseases. These initiatives paralleled those in the other territories of French Equatorial Africa (Austen and Headrick 1983, 63–70).

The impact of these efforts is difficult to assess. While taking measures to combat diseases, the colonial state intensified policies (IV) that had contributed to a deterioration of African health in the first place—encouraging the recruitment of ever larger numbers of workers for a colonywide road network and the Congo-Océan railroad. In addition, even though some medical personnel were sincerely concerned with the state of African health, most administrators couched health problems in the context of depopulation. The importance of the head tax meant that the government often perceived health problems as fiscal ones, interpreting death in terms of lost taxpayers. When not interpreted as fiscal problems, disease and death were seen as threats to the labor supply (Rondet-Smith 1911, 229).

French failure to lighten tax and labor burdens on African populations during the 1920s, a time of increasing morbidity and mortality, strikingly underscores the preoccupation with revenue and workers to the detriment of African health (see Cordell 1987*a*, *b*). In fact, the colonial administration made African survival still more difficult by introducing forced cotton cultivation. Not only was each village to raise cotton on a certain portion of its cultivated land, but special fields were to be grown for local chiefs and administrators. Cotton cultivation, like the other policies described above, extracted labor from a subsistence economy where the labor force was already stretched to its limit. The additional time necessary for cotton was subtracted from labor devoted to food crops, a juggling act made more complex because intense periods of work in cotton fields coincided with peaks in the labor required for millet and sorghum (Guibbert 1949, 2; Stürzinger 1983, 222–223). Cotton revenue offered little compensation for reduced food production because prices to the producers were minimal, and quickly returned to the coffers of the colonial state in the form of head taxes. And because forced cultivation of cotton applied to women as well as men, the demands on female labor increased, with consequent decline in energy devoted to maintaining a healthy environment.

But nutrition (III) did not decline only because of a lack of food. As in the slave-raiding era, less nutritious cassava replaced sorghum and millet in large parts of Ubangi-Shari. The shift represented an effort to change the agricultural calendar to meet the needs of cotton cultivation, since cassava requires less labor and has a less rigid agricultural schedule. It is our hypothesis that this era marked the emergence of famines during the *période de soudure*, the months just before the harvest—a shortfall often cited by French administrators to illustrate their views of Africans as incapable of planning and as irresponsible.

By the 1920s the precarious reality of African health and the reduced ability of African societies to renew themselves demographically had become clear. But the fact that forced labor recruitment and cash cropping remained the centerpieces of colonial economic policy (IV) reveals that the administration was primarily moved to increase investments in health by material necessity rather than by humanitarian concern. More complete demographic data in the 1920s had revealed a much smaller population than earlier estimates; administrators saw that the viability of the colony, not in the distant future but in the short term, required a commitment to lower mortality and morbidity not just among laborers but among the population as a whole. Partly as a result of this realization, a more extensive health service emerged (III). However, despite increased concern for African health, and perhaps even a more sophisticated understanding of the demographic regime (I), French colonial policy did not slow efforts to reshape Ubangi-Shari to fit the needs of capitalism (IV). By the early 1930s, the most brutal phase of labor extraction had passed. But accumulation went on. By this time colonial policies had so marginalized subsistence rural production that Africans were increasingly obliged to participate in the capitalist economy. The supply of labor and export products could be manipulated more subtly through the adjustment of tax and wage levels rather than by dispatching troops. Such economic transformation continued to impair the ability of African populations to renew themselves. The cost in African health remained high.

Ubangi-Shari, 1930s–1950s: Health and Class Differentiation

Whereas Africans, individually and collectively, frequently resisted the requirements of capitalist development schemes through the early 1920s, by the end of the following decade strategies shifted to working out a way to survive by producing in both the subsistence and capitalist spheres. The depression of the 1930s abetted this shift. As prices paid for raw materials dropped—cotton prices paid to Africans, for example, declined by 50 percent between 1927 and 1933/34 (Kalck 1974, 241, 245)—Africans were pressured to expand production to earn sufficient cash to pay the head tax. At the same time, the administration, anxious to preserve revenue during the crisis, increased the levy; greater numbers of Africans were thus forced more completely into capitalist production as producers of cash crops or as wage laborers (Coquery-Vidrovitch 1976, 402, 408, 410–412, 422).

A second change occurred in the 1930s. The era of conquest, "pacification," and the naked extraction of surplus from African laborers came to a close. A basic road network was in place and the railroad had been completed, although forced labor obligations remained. In addition, the lengthy but effective suppression of a series of uprisings by the Gbaya in the west demonstrated the futility of continued physical resistance. (See O'Toole [1984] for a convincing reinterpretation.) The period was marked by the consolidation of capitalist relations and the institutionalization of the colonial presence.

Just as the excesses of primitive accumulation gave way to a more structured extraction of surplus value from a population more or less incorporated into capitalist social relations in the 1930s, so did deaths resulting from direct physical violence (I) decline. Some people continued to migrate to escape the French, but their numbers dropped markedly because the colonial state exercised tighter control than before.

In Ubangi-Shari, the increased infrastructure and activity in the health sector in the 1930s (III) brought both a greater understanding of the direct and indirect causes of African mortality and morbidity, as well as more elaborate strategies for dealing with them. Annual medical reports through the 1930s trace the campaign to combat sleeping sickness (Austen and Headrick 1983; 68–69; Suret-Canale 1964, 508–513). This effort was the centerpiece of health strategy, but these documents also report on other problems in great epidemiological and geographic detail. They identify the major chronic diseases—respiratory ailments, leprosy, and yaws, in particular. During this period the debate also emerges over whether the low number of children in the south and the east was a result of low fertility or high infant mortality (see Cordell 1983*a*, 1985*b*, 1987*b*).

Even though the administration came to understand mortality and morbidity somewhat better, it is nonetheless very clear that the French did not perceive the broader contours of the demographic regimes (I) of African societies and the ways that colonial economic policies (IV) affected the capacities of African populations to renew themselves. During the late 1920s and 1930s, policies of labor recruitment for the final phase of railroad construction, and increased cash-crop production that resulted from heavier head taxes made it harder for African populations to renew themselves. In the western part of Ubangi-Shari, for example, age pyramids found in the 1946 health report show small proportions in the fifteen- to twenty-year-old age group, made up of people who would have been born between 1926 and 1931. Such high infant mortality may well have been the result of the major epidemic of sleeping sickness (II) that raged in the region just at this time. While the reports treat the epidemic as a product of chance, we can ask to what degree the dislocation occasioned by the suppression of the Gbaya revolt in the same region, and the diversion of labor from food crops were not major causes of the high mortality. It is known that susceptibility to infectious diseases (II) is greatly increased by malnutrition (III); moreover, sleeping sickness reaps high mortality among infants in particular. African recollections suggest just such a connection: "The people also speak of a period when infants died in large numbers because of the lack of food."

This failure to see the larger problem was, in part, the result of a poor understanding of the limits of the demographic regimes (I) of African societies to produce the labor needed for both subsistence and capitalist production. Blindness to the limits of village reproduction and production was illustrated particularly well in the early years of recruitment for the railroad when authorities planned for each local community to produce the food required by local recruits and to transport it to collection points (Sautter 1967, 264–266). Ironically, at a time when the administration seemed to have some appreciation of the problem of infant mortality and low fertility, it was explicitly acknowledged that the policy would increase the burden of women: "because it was the women who worked the fields, it seemed normal that they could produce enough for the absent men" (Sautter 1967, 264–266).

Thus far this essay has treated Central African societies as homogenous, at least in terms of the risks of mortality and morbidity that they incurred. The 1940s, however, marked the increasing differentiation of the African population. The criteria were two—region of residence, and class. By the late 1940s, campaigns against endemic disease waged by the colonial health service had given birth to a basic health care system, with facilities concentrated in the south and southwest. In addition, a skeletal system of primary education in these same regions provided a context for health education and preventive care. However, these services were unequally distributed geographically; and, with a few exceptions, they tended to be concentrated in the emerging urban centers. Thus geographical location of health services (III) translated into differential access to health care.

In the same period, class differences (IV) were exacerbated by different social groups' living health experiences, and probably different demographic regimes. This process had important consequences for mortality, morbidity, and health. Earlier in the colonial era chiefs were appointed (Weinstein 1970) and became a rural elite. They were not only exempt from the vicissitudes of forced labor, but they also benefited from the income of fields of cotton worked by villagers. Less forced labor, we suggest, translated into lower mortality and morbidity; moreover, a greater wealth sheltered such groups from shortfalls in food. They were also more successful in protecting themselves from disease. As health facilities were implanted, they benefited more from them than their villagers, either because such facilities were built in the settlements of loyal agents of the colonial state, or because chiefs could more easily take the time to travel to the nearest clinics.

Petty traders made up the second group of privileged Africans. The colonial administration began quite early to encourage the immigration of Bornoans and Hausa, who, by the 1940s, had become important agents for the distribution of European imports. In some cases they also acted as agents for European firms that purchased African peasant production. Such traders tended to live in the small urban centers most likely to be endowed with medical facilities; in addition, they had the means to pay for care. Little comprehensive research exists on this class (Bradshaw, personal communication); none exists on its health history. But we hypothesize that petty traders, too, were healthier than the local populations among whom they lived.

A third group of privileged Africans was made up of the urban, Western-educated class. Shortly after the conquest, the French established schools to educate a few Africans to serve the administration. With the end of conquest and pacification in the late 1920s, they expanded efforts to create a parallel class of Africans associated with the administration. In addition, the state had integrated Central Africans, often Yakoma from the river region, into the colonial military and police forces. Such groups often enjoyed privileged access to medical care. By the late 1950s the government employed nearly 5,000 African functionaries in Ubangi-Shari, many of whom were of local origin (Zoctizoum 1983, 1:209). As in the case of the chiefs and traders described above, these individuals also enjoyed privileged access to health facilities and possessed greater means to pay for care.

The Central African peasantry also produced a group of wage earners. By the 1950s salaried workers numbered between 45,000 and 55,000 (Zoctizoum 1983, 1:209; Kalck 1974, 293). They were employed in a dozen sectors of the colonial economy. Kalck suggests that roughly 275,000 people lived on the salaries of 55,000 administrative employees who earned 1.9 billion Central French African (CFA) francs. In contrast, 900,000 rural people had a combined income of 4.1 billion CFA or 4,500 per person. The difference in income becomes more marked when on further examination it becomes clear that a large part of rural income went to a small group of coffee planters (Kalck 1974, 293).

The diversity of occupations and wage levels suggests that patterns of mortality and morbidity were not homogeneous within this group; nonetheless, we suggest that their demographic behavior, as a group, differed from that of the peasantry. For one thing, they probably were healthier than the general population since they were younger and often had to undergo physical examinations. They were part of a work force that reproduced itself primarily through migration with the advantages and the disadvantages that mobility entailed. Because they were mostly males recruited as adults, we hypothesize that employers were probably more concerned with their ability to reproduce their labor on a day-to-day basis than with fostering biological reproduction. As such they may well have received better care in the event of a short-term illness or a minor accident. The care of chronically ill workers, however, was probably not guaranteed; these individuals were returned to their villages to be maintained by the domestic economy.

By the final decade of the colonial period, then, we suggest that capitalism had produced differential demographic regimes among the people of Ubangi-Shari. We hypothesize furthermore that class and regional differences increased during the independence period of the 1960s through the 1980s in West and Central Africa. The data are not sufficient to confirm this proposition in the case of Ubangi-Shari (which became Central African Republic after independence in 1960). We do, however, have ample information for Burkina Faso during this period. Hence we illustrate our hypotheses regarding the political economy, the demographic regime, and health in the independence era with reference to this Sahelian francophone country of West Africa.

Burkina Faso, 1960s–1980s: The Era of Independence

The political economy (IV) of Burkina Faso at the time of independence in 1960 was characterized by extreme economic dependence on France—partially mediated by neocolonial Ivory Coast, precariously managed by a minuscule national bourgeoisie, yet effectively administered by a well-entrenched rural chieftaincy. Economic and social infrastructure compared with the weakest in Africa, with hospital services available only in the two largest cities—Ouagadougou and Bobo-Dioulasso—and a few scattered, poorly equipped, unstocked clinics in secondary towns. Much as in Ubangi-Shari, the production of food crops had suffered from fifty years of neglect and competition with cotton.

The most significant feature of the Burkinabè political economy in 1960 was the country's well-established function as a reservoir of labor for the larger regional economy, and for Ghana and the Ivory Coast in particular. A temporary, circulatory proletariat had been created by colonial violence and capitalist intervention (Cordell and Gregory 1982). Yet this was a part-time proletariat, moving back to the domestic, peasant economy (IV) of rural Burkina Faso at the end of six months, or a year or two of wage labor. Migrants found employment on coffee and cocoa plantations in the south, in the ports, and in the lowest-paid jobs of the informal sector of the rapidly growing urban economies of Abidjan, Bouake, Accra, and Kumasi.

Despite deep crises in the Sahelian region subsequent to the droughts and famines of 1971–1975 and the mid-1980s, and the debts incurred as a result of increased petroleum prices, the Burkinabè political economy (IV) has not been stagnant. Since 1960, Burkina has experienced six different governments, all of which came to power by military coup. Despite numerous heads of state and a parade of different executive institutions, this period may be divided into two phases, a neocolonial era from 1960 to 1983 characterized by the continuation of preindependence development policies, and a revolutionary era that began in 1983 with the arrival of the "Conseil national de la révolution" (CNR). Founded and headed by Thomas Sankara until his assassination in October 1987 as the result of an internal power struggle, the CNR is presently guided by Blaise Campaoré.

Although they made little effort to intervene in the well-established system of circulatory international labor migration, successive governments to 1983 expanded the social infrastructure of the country, including schools, clinics, and a vaccination campaign (III). In staffing these programs, they also fell into the seemingly inevitable pattern of a rapidly multiplying civil service. Indeed, the growth of the administrative sector accounted for the vast majority of jobs created in the first twenty-five years of independence (Sanagoh 1977, 195–200). While the rhetoric of governments from 1966 to 1983 emphasized the primacy of the rural sector, agricultural development, and the need for rural transport, marketing, and hydraulic infrastructure (III), the sad reality is that successive regimes failed to attract substantial funds for genuine rural development (Gregory 1974). This crisis stimulated the growth of rural class differences (Reyna 1983) and deepened conflict between men and women over changes in the rural sexual division of labor (IV) (Conti 1979). The rural economy was unable to provide a decent level of survival for the vast majority of the Burkinabè population living in villages. A notable exception to the sad tale of failed rural development is the relative success of an effort to increase productivity in the Volta Valley in southwestern Burkina by eliminating onchocerciasis (river blindness).

Meanwhile, the mushrooming growth of Ouagadougou, the capital and largest city, reflected the concentration of state expenditures on civil service salaries and on urban amenities. From a population of 58,000 in 1961/62, Ouagadougou grew to 177,000 in 1975 and to 440,000 in 1985 (Haute-Volta 1962, 13; 1979, vol. 2, table 1; Ouedraogo 1988). This population growth (I) has been generated by high urban birth rates, probably higher than those in rural areas (Pool 1977*b*); slightly declining urban mortality rates (Harrington 1977), and rapid rural–urban migration (Coulibaly et al. 1980, 38–51). Perhaps most important, and the least studied at the present time, is the expansion of the informal sector in Ouagadougou, creating a vast lumpenproletariat (IV). According to a recent survey, over 70 percent of the people of Ouagadougou worked in the informal sector (Van Dijk 1986). Living well below the poverty line and dependent on multifarious and ingenious strategies of survival, these people rely on the domestic sphere for day-to-day and longer-term reproduction of the labor force (IV). To a lesser extent, Bobo-Dioulasso, the next largest city, and several secondary towns, have experienced the same dynamic (Gregory 1976; Haute-Volta 1979, vol. 5; Ouedraogo, 1988).

In this extreme context, it is hardly surprising that most health indicators place Burkina Faso near the top of mortality lists and near the bottom of survival lists (I). In 1988, the crude death rate was about 19 per 1,000 and the infant mortality rate was 145 per 1,000; these levels of mortality produce a life expectancy of forty-six years at birth, among the lowest in the world (Population Reference Bureau 1988).

But mortality is only part of the picture. Levels of morbidity are also pathetically high—many of the causes of death (II) having been exacerbated by colonial exploitation (IV) and national neglect (IV) of the health of the peasantry and the marginal urban classes. For example, malaria grossly reduces the chances of survival to ages one and five. The multiple varieties of diarrhea that weaken infants, children, and adults alike account for a substantial fraction of infant and juvenile deaths, and render adults more vulnerable. Measles and cholera frequently sweep through the population. And beyond the direct causes of death, malnutrition (III) is reinforced by drought and the perverse and subtle effect of age and sex discrimination. On a more positive note, it must be underscored once again that genuine efforts to eliminate river blindness through the Onchocerciasis Control Program in the Volta River Basin area have succeeded quite dramatically (see, e.g., Thylefors and Tonjum, 1980; Vangelade, personal communication).

Studies over the last quarter-century provide more detail about the demographic regime indirectly produced by patterns of disease (II) and the health environment (II) in the extremely peripheralized political economy of Burkina Faso. The 1960/61 demographic survey (Haute-Volta 1970) revealed a crude death rate of 32, and an infant mortality rate of 182; when adjusted for underreporting, these rates are considerably higher, 36 and 262 per 1,000 (Coale and Lorimer 1968, 158). These rates are high by any contemporary and most historical standards; they are further dramatized by the exceptional level of juvenile mortality (deaths between ages one and five), estimated at 234 per 1,000 (Demers 1981, 10; Haute-Volta 1979, 2:262).

Since independence these high levels of human loss have dropped, although at an irregular rhythm, with substantial geographical differences, and probably characterized by significant discrepancies among social classes (IV). The only synthesis of Burkina mortality data over the period 1960–1975 suggests a decline of 28 percent in the infant mortality quotient (Demers 1981, 10). Although this decline may be exaggerated, given the difficulty in assessing the quality of data on mortality in the 1976 postcensus sample survey, careful consideration of the existing demographic information and an analysis of socioeconomic trends leads Demers to suggest that infant and juvenile mortality probably did decline between 1960/61 and 1976. Adult mortality, however, remained stable. The combined effects of these changes at a national level produced an overall crude death rate of 24 per 1,000 in 1976, down from 32 per 1,000 fifteen years earlier; life expectancy at birth would have increased from thirty-two to thirty-eight years (Demers 1981, 17–20).

To what factors can we attribute this improvement? First among most hypotheses is the effect of the massive and universal vaccination campaign of the Service de Grandes Endémies, conducted in the 1960s and early 1970s. The program aimed at children and some of the major threats to early survival: measles, whooping cough, tetanus, and diphtheria. These preventive measures (III) by themselves would have significantly increased chances of infant and juvenile survival. This hypothesis is consistent with the 40 percent decline in deaths between one and five years (Demers 1981, 10). Relative stagnation of adult mortality at high levels would also be in accordance with this explanation.

A second hypothesis suggests that the provision of services, including piped water in the cities, more numerous wells in rural areas, a minimum of maternal health care in the largest towns and cities, and rudimentary curative centers in a scattering of villages across the country, might have improved some children's chances of survival (Demers 1981, 72–95). Confirming this explanation requires more study.

In addition to the changes over time in health and mortality, the distance between social groups has been stretched by growing class differences, and by the ability of urban populations to exert direct political pressure on the national government (IV) in favor of increasing their access to social services and the income necessary to improve survival levels. Some abbreviated mortality data confirm these hypotheses. For example, the 1960/61 survey showed a substantial gap between urban and rural mortality. Among women thirty to thirty-four years old living in Ouagadougou, for example, 73 percent of children born alive had survived to the time of the study; among women of the same ages living outside the two largest cities, only 59 percent of their children had survived (Haute-Volta 1979, 2:262).

Crude infant mortality rates show the same pattern: one-third lower in urban areas sampled, as compared with rural areas. A survey in 1969 also detected an urban advantage in survivorship, even when comparing the fairly well-served Mossi rural population with Ouagadougou and Bobo-Dioulasso (Harrington 1977). The most recent survey, covering the period 1981–1984 and carried out in the four cities of Banfora, Bobo-Dioulasso, Koudougou, and Ouahigouya, yielded infant mortality quotients of around 85 to 90 per 1,000 (after adjustment for underestimation); these are substantially lower than the rate of 140 per 1,000 still prevailing in most rural areas of the country (EMIS-Burkina Faso 1988, 79).

Differences among rural areas are also probably substantial. The chances of survival in a Burkinabè village depends partially on where one is born. Levels of mortality in 1976 in Mariatang, a village in Dagara country in the southwest (Benoît et al. 1982, 41–54), for example, were substantially lower than in a Mossi village in central Burkina at about the same time (Smith 1977, 264). Rates from the valley of the Volta Noire in central-western Burkina from a few years earlier are still slightly higher (Retel-Laurentin and Benoît 1976, 281). These variations reflect the complex levels of causality and substantial differences in the factors that condition the health environment (III) from one village to another.

Almost no empirical work has been conducted on differences in mortality by social class in Burkina Faso; in fact, very little work has been done on social class at all. One indicator that we have is that provided by the 1969 survey of Pool and Associates (Pool and Coulibaly 1977; Harrington 1977). Class distinctions are intimated by statistically significant differences in survivorship between children of mothers who had had formal schooling, and offspring whose mothers had not had such an opportunity. Survivorship was 12 to 19 percent higher among children in the first category: 12 percent in the Mossi villages in the sample, and 18 and 19 percent in Bobo-Dioulasso and Ouagadougou (Harrington 1977, 222). A more recent survey confirms these findings. It was found, for instance, that infant mortality was lower when mothers were educated and/or engaged in remunerated activities, and when household incomes were higher (EMIS-Burkina Faso 1988, 128–135).

Excessive morbidity, ill health, and malnutrition condition this high mortality. For infants, the three most important diseases, accounting for 54 percent of all identified causes were, in descending order of importance, malaria, measles, and abdominal infections (Haute-Volta 1979, 2:268). A study in rural Mossiland in 1972–1974 of mortality at all ages identified diarrhea and dehydration as the number one killer, and malaria and fevers as the second. The same study reported monthly rates of morbidity where 50 persons per 1,000 had normal activities curtailed by fevers, 10 per 1,000 reported daily coughing with sputum, and 6 per 1,000 had their normal activities affected by diarrhea. Perhaps the most disturbing observation concerned the physiological data for children zero to six years of age: 22 percent measured were below 90 percent of the median Stuart-Meredith height-for-age measurement, and another 29 percent were between 90 and 95 percent of the median. Nearly 9 percent were below 80 percent of the median weight-for-height measurement, and another 43 percent between 80 and 90 percent (United States, Agency for International Development [USAID] and Centers for Disease Control [CDC] 1975, 18, 23–24).

A study in Bobo-Dule country in central western Burkina compares infant and juvenile mortality, suggesting not only differential morbidity by age but also different strategies for improving health at various ages. The most frequent cause of death in the first year of life was tetanus, followed by diarrhea and vomiting associated with fevers. These causes accounted for 55 percent of infant deaths. In the next four years of life, diarrhea and vomiting took over first place (34 percent), followed by measles and smallpox (16 percent), and fevers (10 percent) (Retel-Laurentin and Benoît 1976, 283). Finally, the 1981–1984 EMIS survey identified three main causes of infant deaths (before age two): diarrhea, measles, and endogenous causes; medical intervention seems to have eliminated tetanus. The study estimated that if diarrhea were eliminated, the probability of surviving from one to two years of age would double; the infant mortality rate would decrease from 82 (unadjusted) to 68 per 1,000 (EMIS-Burkina Faso 1988, 100).

Hence a sketchy, and yet not inconclusive, picture emerges for the period between 1960 and 1983/84; high general mortality in a context of high morbidity; extremely high infant mortality matched by almost equally high juvenile mortality; slowly rising life expectancy and mortality rates that are declining but still as high as those of any other country; and, finally, greater risks of death among rural and uneducated populations.

This dramatic wastage of Burkinabè infants and children, and the chronic dissipation of the human capital of the country as a result of generalized ill health, must be considered in relationship to the entire demographic regime (I). Labor power is not only lost to early death and to ill health, but also to international emigration. While much of the migration is temporary, a fraction of the labor power of nearly every rural Burkinabè household migrates to capitalist zones beyond the rural household economy (Saint-Pierre et al. 1986).

These demographic losses can be compensated in only one way, through continued high levels of fertility. Indeed no changes have been detected in birth or fertility rates since the 1960/61 demographic survey. All studies point to the reality and logic of fertility levels of between six and seven live births per woman (Pool and Coulibaly 1977, 33–35). There is little immigration into Burkina Faso, and return migration to rural areas does not compensate for losses. As a result Burkinabè households produce a large number of children to offset the heavy toll taken by mortality and emigration and to compensate for the reduced productivity caused by high morbidity. Early marriage and the exchange of children among kin and even nonkin are additional survival strategies.

The price is high, and is probably borne most by women and children; Burkinabè mortality, morbidity, and emigration increase the labor burden for women who try to offset losses to male emigration, as well as care for the sick, the feeble, and the aged. Children are probably incorporated into the household labor force at the earliest possible moment and are faced with emigration as a social responsibility, or as an escape from the patriarchal control of their fathers, uncles, and grandfathers. The migration of many young people has turned into flight and has probably had the unfortunate effect of diverting intergenerational conflict, which might have provoked change in productive and reproductive strategies among the rural population.

Ending this case study on a speculative note is appropriate, for Burkina Faso and the Burkinabè population embarked upon a new phase of national development (IV) in 1983. For the first time in this century, development objectives took a new turn, with the coming to power of a radicalized second generation of military officers led by Sankara and Compaoré. The sweeping policy changes proposed and partially implemented by the new regime can be neither dismissed as empty rhetoric nor glorified as a revolutionary dawn. Experiments in radical social transformation in other parts of Africa suggest that in Burkina, as elsewhere, such changes imply sacrifices as difficult as the day-to-day sacrifices that have been imposed by neocolonial regimes and international institutions such as the International Monetary Fund.

During his years as head of state, Sankara reiterated his observation that previous development policies had been unfair to the rural population; women, girls, and youth in general; and the lowest paid parts of the urban population (see, e.g. Sankara 1983). As far as is now known, Compaoré's regime still adheres to this point of view.

Despite this new vision, it is still too early to determine whether the CNR has improved the health environment of the vast majority of Burkinabè. Early indications are nonetheless promising. According to a recent evaluation report of the United Nations Fund for Population Activities (UNFPA), health is improving. Maternal and child health and family planning services are increasingly available, although overall coverage remains low; for example, complete vaccination of children aged six months to six years for diphtheria, whooping cough, and tetanus was estimated at 42 percent in 1984 (UNFPA 1986). The report went on to identify three crucial positive factors in health intervention in Burkina: a strong government commitment, mass mobilization, and a genuine concern for women. Many studies identify these factors with decreasing mortality (see, e.g., Caldwell 1986). Whether Burkina will ultimately succeed in this noble endeavor depends on the government's ability to restructure state institutions and the social relations of production and reproduction (IV) over the long term.

CONCLUSION

Our case studies have proceeded from an analysis of the political economy (IV) to the demographic regime (I). We begin this conclusion by emphasizing a major point—that mortality can be understood only in relation to fertility and migration, the other demographic parameters that make up the demographic regime, and beyond that, in relation to the larger political economy of a society. Demographic regimes alter over time with the changing political economy (see Cordell et al. [1987] for an extended theoretical discussion of this point). From the case studies, it is possible to identify three distinct demographic regimes in Ubangi-Shari and Burkina Faso, each relating to a specific period in the transformation of African political economies.

At the end of the nineteenth century the demography of Ubangi-Shari was characterized by high and increasing mortality, by what was probably the manifestation of low fertility and some sterility, and by new patterns of more intensified migration. Morbidity, and the health environment in general, probably suffered rapid deterioration, particularly with the introduction of new diseases and the epidemic outbreak of old ones. Violence and insecurity reinforced these tendencies.

This late slave-raiding regime characterized northern and eastern Ubangi-Shari. Southwestern and southern regions were characterized by similar mortality and morbidity, higher levels of sterility, and, therefore, lower fertility, and equally disruptive migration. In both regions demographic renewal was severely threatened by the extraction of a significant fraction of the labor force. In the north and the east, the losses were heavily female, while in the southwest and the south, they consisted primarily of young men. In all zones, losses of labor jeopardized production as well as reproduction.

European penetration around the turn of the century was a major demographic watershed. The demographic regime, already severely undermined, suffered further erosion. Slave-raiding reached its height in the ten years after 1900. Its pernicious effects were reinforced by the colonizers' appropriation of substantial amounts of labor and their extraction of raw materials—both accompanied by violence and depopulation. The epidemics of sleeping sickness and other diseases further contributed to the decline of the health environment, finally alerting the French to the risks of destroying the reproductive capacities of their exploited populations. The effects on the early colonial demographic regime replicated and intensified those described for the end of the nineteenth century. During this period the population of Ubangi-Shari declined dramatically.

Faced with the threat to their labor supply, the French were obliged to react, and in the following period, from 1930 to 1950, systematically pursued preventive and curative health programs. At the same time, violence became less necessary as a mode of labor recruitment, given the thirty years of systematic integration of Africans into the colonial system (Cordell 1987*a*). These two changes probably reduced the threats to survival. The first awareness of the seriousness of sterility and subfertility also dates to this time (Cordell 1987*b*). Migration was characterized by the circulation of labor between peasant production and the incipient capitalist sphere. Class differentiation became apparent along with differential demographic strategies. The restructuring that culminated in this period produced a demographic regime specific to peripheral capitalism (Gregory and Piché 1981; 1986*a*).

A well-documented example of such a regime is Burkina Faso in the national period (1960s–1980s). Over the past quarter-century the peasant sphere has been effectively articulated to the needs of the expanding capitalist economy of Ivory Coast and of urban Burkina. Mortality, and infant mortality in particular, remain high because of the persistence of infectious and parasitic diseases. Until the advent of the CNR in 1983, investment in the health infrastructure and a massive vaccination campaign in the early years of the period produced only a slight improvement in life expectancy, especially for the more privileged urban classes. Throughout the independence era, both permanent and circulatory labor migration to the coast and to the larger cities of Burkina Faso drained the peasant sphere of a major fraction of its productive forces and of its reproductive vitality. This draining of the rural labor force increased pressure on households to maintain, and perhaps even to increase, fertility.

We set out in this paper to demonstrate that the demographic reproduction of health and disease is intimately related to the social reproduction of African societies. Indeed, all demographic change is a product of social change, and not the result of some primordial urge to reproduce, as is suggested by the all too common neo-Malthusian scenarios depicting humanity's demise as a consequence of mindless reproduction. By means of a model and case studies, we have systematically illustrated the components of the demographic regime and the political economy and health environment that produce it. The exercise clearly shows that mortality is a social phenomenon. Why it is high or low, increasing or decreasing, or unevenly distributed is intimately linked to the larger efforts of societies to reproduce themselves socially, from one day to the next and from one generation to another.

NOTES

1. We would like to express appreciation to Mona Wildman, formerly of the Department of History, Southern Methodist University, who typed early versions of this manuscript, along with Jay O'Brien, Gail Israel, Bruce Fetter, and Steven Feierman for their comments on the original paper. We are also grateful to several institutions: the Social Science Research Council of New York, which partially financed travel to the African Studies Association conference in Boston in 1983, where we first presented our ideas; to the National Endowment of the Humanities, whose Travel to Collections Program provided funds for research in the French archives in Aix-en-Provence and Marseille; and to the International Development and Research Centre (Ottawa) for supporting a trip to a conference at the Institut du Sahel in Bamako, where our model underwent scrutiny by people associated with various Health and Development projects in the Sahel (see Gregory and Piché 1986*a*, *b*). *Editors' note*: Research materials from the following archives were utilized in this chapter: in France, Archives nationales françaises, Depôt d'outre-mer, in Aix-en-Provence; Archives du Service de santé colonial, Institut de médecine tropicale, Service de santé des armées, in Marseille; in the Central African Republic, formerly Oubangui-Chari, Archives de la Kemo-Gribingui, Bibliothèque de l'Ecole nationale d'Administration, and the Archives du Musée Boganda, both in Bangui.

2. When demographic replacement is more easily assured, in cases of low mortal-

ity and/or net immigration, sex ratios can swing more widely away from unity, and procreative unions can be bypassed by a fraction of the adult population.

3. Biological causes and limits have dominated the thinking of many demographers about mortality and have profoundly influenced demographic methods of analysis. For a seminal article see Bourgeois-Pichat (1952).

4. Ibid.

TWO

Famine Analysis and Family Relations: Nyasaland in 1949[1]

Megan Vaughan

In 1949 a serious famine occurred in the Southern Province of Nyasaland. In this chapter I describe the course of that famine in the area in which it struck with greatest severity—the Lunzu and Lirangwe sections of Blantyre district.[2] In analyzing the descriptions of events I am concerned with two main questions. First, which sections of the community suffered and died during the famine, and is it possible to provide a model that could "predict" the differential impact? Second, what were the responses of the community to the onset of famine, and how did these responses in themselves condition its course? Bound up with both questions is the issue of how far this was a famine structured by the particular circumstances of the late colonial period in Nyasaland.

The analysis of famine has undergone radical revision. In the last few years. The simple and long-standing notion that famine was the result of "food-availability decline" seems not to accord with the facts about contemporary and past famines and has been largely rejected in favor of the theories that stress the role of the market and of government intervention (Cutler 1982; Seaman and Holt 1980; Spitz 1980). As long ago as 1952 Josue de Castro, in his book *The Geopolitics of Hunger*, attacked simplistic Malthusian theories of famine causation in favor of a more complicated model: "essentially world hunger is not a problem of production limited by the coercion of natural forces . . . but of a politics that is based on the premeditated division of the world into ruling and dominated groups" (Castro 1977).

More recent analyses of African famine also stress the global political and economic origins of hunger (Ball 1976; Bryceson 1980; Cliffe 1974, Lofchie 1975). Along with this recognition of the political and economic origins of hunger has come the increased awareness of the differential impact of famine within any given community. The writer who has highlighted this most and the only one who has successfully united the analysis of "cause" with that of "effect" is Amartya Sen (1981; see also Ghose 1982; Oughton 1980).

Sen's "entitlement theory" is concerned primarily with understanding how different sections of the community obtain their entitlement to food in normal times, and how and to what degree these entitlements might be affected by changes in the market economy. His analysis of access to food thus relates directly to the ownership structure of any given society and the position of each individual within this, and it emphasizes the class basis of suffering in any famine. In passing, Sen also acknowledges that distribution *within* the family may also be of relevance, and in a recent article in *New Society* he has given this more emphasis (1983*a*; see also 1983*b*). However, the influence of family and kinship relations on the pattern of famine is not part of his entitlement model, but simply a footnote that shows recognition of the attention now being paid to the problem by nutritionists.

What evidence we have for the 1949 famine points to the need for a closer examination of the issue of food distribution *within* the family, and of how this and marriage relations affect the pattern of suffering in a community struck by famine.

In the first section of this essay I describe the course of the famine. There are few written accounts of this, and therefore the description draws heavily on oral sources.[3] Where written sources do exist, however, I have incorporated them.

Famine was not a new phenomenon to the people of Blantyre district, and food shortage was for some households there an annual event. But when the rains failed in the 1949 season there was a general feeling that this was a calamity beyond most people's experience. In retrospect, older people who had lived through the 1922 famine in the same area said that they could have predicted the disaster of 1949. The year 1947 had been the "year of the locusts," when many crops were destroyed, and in consequence there had been very few full granaries in the area in 1948. Furthermore, the rain failed in a way that indicated that the drought was not amenable to traditional remedies. In November and December, when it was apparent that the rains had stopped, people gathered in many villages to pray for rain. They sang the songs that they had always sung to call the rain and appease the ancestors. But despite the prayers, and the taboos and sanctions that accompanied them, the rain did not come. Christians were meanwhile exhorted by their churches not to join in the heathen prayers in the villages but to pray for rain in the church instead. Both Catholic and Protestant churches held rain-calling ceremonies, and the Protestants served tea and biscuits after them.

When prayers of all types failed, some people looked around at their neighbors to see who might be "holding the rain" for their own ends. The usual suspects were old men with gray hair or bald heads, but people who were making bricks were also in line for accusation—after all, they would be the first to suffer if the rain fell. One man working in Blantyre at the time heard stories of such accusations being made in his home village. The people accused there were those who had long been labeled as "lazy" and who, even in favorable conditions, never had enough food to feed themselves. The accused were made to drink water and hot pepper, and if they were men (as they generally were) they had chili powder rubbed into their testicles. Some were taken off to see the famous Doctor Bwanali, a soothsayer and healer who lived in Lunzu, but he invariably looked into his glass and found them to be innocent, saying that the drought was beyond human intervention. Others were taken by their neighbors and brought to the office of the District Commissioner in Blantyre, but he took a line on this similar to that of Doctor Bwanali and sent them home. Quite quickly the consensus seems to have emerged that this drought, unlike less severe ones, was the work of God and could not be attributed either to human action or to the anger of ancestors:

> No black cloud could be seen, and no thunder was heard. According to our belief, when people are "holding the rain" an expanse of dark cloud is seen and thunder heard, but suddenly all the clouds get swept away and the sky clears. This did not happen in '49. The drought was too serious to blame on any human being. Some believed that the territorial spirits were angered and needed a sacrifice to cool them down. Some believed that it was God's work. The two camps used their means to ask for rain—but still no rain came.

Most people did not replant their maize, both because the seed was difficult to obtain and, more crucially, because the rain with which to replant never fell. There were some people in the area, however, who did have maize in their granaries left over from the previous year. These lucky ones generally had large gardens that stretched down to the riverbanks. On such land they were usually able to harvest something, as the soil retained moisture from the river or could be irrigated from it. There were also those men who had married into the area but who had retained gardens in their own homes. One man had a garden in his home at Chiradzulu, an area much less severely affected by the drought, and he had fetched food from there. One woman recalled that her parents had a full granary when others had nothing because her father had land at his home in Ntcheu (in the central highlands to the north of Blantyre district) and he brought food from there. She said that every day there were at least ten people queuing up outside their home to beg for food, including old people who had been brought by *machila* (a kind of stretcher). Other people who, according to oral accounts, were privileged under these circumstances were urban workers and local businessmen. Urban workers were lucky in that their employers invariably either gave them free food, food on credit, or food at a price lower than that on the open market. Tenants living on estates were usually entitled to the same privilege. Of course within this group there were wide variations in wage levels and incomes, but the main advantage of being a regular employee during the famine was that it entitled one to easier access to food. There was a lot of theft and some unrest in the towns of Blantyre and Limbe, and mindful of this, the government had instructed employers to make sure that their workers were fed. Some employers gave out free food, others gave salary advances. One man interviewed worked at an Indian-owned store in Limbe and earned only 10s.6d. (ten shillings, six pence) per month. However, in January 1949 his employer started giving him an advance on his salary of 7s.6d. to enable him to buy maize. In general, this man said, the people of Blantyre and Limbe had little difficulty in getting maize, as long as they had money (see Walter and Wrightson 1976). One young woman was working as a domestic servant for an Indian family and earning a meager wage of 3s.6d. a month. However, her job had the advantage of allowing her to eat with her employers, and during the famine this was worth a lot in real terms. Another man also earned 3s.6d. a month, working as a watchman for an African store owner, but on top of this he received a ration of flour and beans which was enough to feed his family throughout the famine. Another was a storekeeper in an Indian-owned shop in Limbe, whose wife and children lived at home in Lirangwe and farmed a garden there. His employer gave him a small basket of maize flour every Saturday which he took home to his family, and he also bought maize from a government depot in Chirimba, near Blantyre. The price was high and everyone complained, but they also recognized that they were better off than their relatives at home in Lirangwe and Lunzu, who could not get maize even if they had money. These four people were members of the lowest-paid group of employees, with wages far below those published in the official government statistics, and in normal times they must have been living on the margins. During the famine, however, they became members of a relatively privileged group, and their families considered themselves lucky.

Government and mission employees received the most privileged treatment of all. Employees of the Blantyre Mission of the Church of Scotland, apart from being given maize flour on credit, were also allocated gardens on which to plant sweet potatoes and cassava (*chilingano*), and were given time off work to cultivate. Government employees were allowed to buy maize at a price half of that on the open market. Although this supply was supposed to be strictly rationed, people found ways around the rationing system and could sometimes accumulate quite large stocks. Depending on the individual, these stocks were then either distributed to family members at home or sold to villagers in the famine area at a handsome profit. One man had been employed by the government as a driver, taking stocks of maize from one place to another. As a government employee he could buy maize at the price of 3s. per four-gallon tin, and sell it in the villages for 6s. or more. Futhermore, as he said, so much maize was exposed to him in his job that he was able to "play monkey tricks with it."

Right from the start of the famine, then, there were those who had privileged access to food supplies and could use this in a number of ways. Traders and businessmen with motorized transport were in a particularly advantageous position, for although the government initially tried to prevent the movement of maize from one district to another, this soon proved to be impossible and against their own interests. One businessman "found himself" with twenty bags of maize (each weighing 200 pounds) at the beginning of 1949. People came from all over the area to buy from him. He sold the maize at the price of 1d. per plate, and the twenty bags were exhausted after a month. Another businessman, who owned a truck, had thirty bags of maize at the end of 1948, and sold it at the same price of 1d. per plate. Those who had no money performed *ganyu* labor[4] for him—molding bricks and cutting down trees—in order to earn the money they needed to buy food. Another family, whose business normally consisted of buying and selling fish and vegetables, switched to maize-trading in 1949 because it was so profitable. One aspect of the African businessman's trade did not do well in this period, and that was maize-milling. As one woman said, "Before the arrival of the government relief maize, one could scarcely hear the sound of a maize mill." Stories abounded of how hungry people gathered at the mills to sweep up the flour that had fallen from the mill and take it home in handfuls, and of how the maize mill owners soon put a stop to this practice and began selling the sweepings instead.

By March or April 1949 the famine looked really serious in the Lunzu and Lirangwe areas: "The situation had started as a small joke, but it turned into a bad joke, and a serious issue." The main features of this second stage of the famine were (1) the extreme mobility of the population (especially the men) in search of food to buy, earn, beg, or gather and (2) the progressive breakdown of whatever community support and family solidarity had existed earlier. Some aspects of this stage of the famine are recalled vividly in the pounding songs of women of the area. These songs, and other forms of recollection, indicate the uneven distribution of food both within the community and within the family (see Campbell and Trecher 1982; Jelliffe and Jelliffe 1971; Pankhurst 1966). They also show how long-standing links between different geographical areas could be brought into play at times of crisis. Foremost among these links were marriage ties.

As things got worse and as local supplies of food became completely exhausted, people began looking farther afield for places where they could obtain food, either with cash or in return for goods or labor. Men (and sometimes women) went off in groups to search for food in the Ngoni highland areas of Ntcheu and Dedza, in the highlands bordering Mozambique to the west, and in the Mulanje area to the southeast. Many of the men who went on these expeditions were making use of family ties in these areas. There was a long history, for instance, of Ngoni men migrating south for work and marrying in Blantyre district.[5] So at a time of crisis these men went back to their own homes expecting, and usually getting, help from their relatives there. It was seen as a husband's duty to find food for his wife and family, and those men who did not do this were chided in the women's songs:

> What type of husband are you,
> Staying at home with the women?
> The other men are off to Mwanza now,
> Why not you?
> You just stay here and your only "work"
> Is to fondle women.

Men were aware of the praises they could earn from their wives' families if they succeeded in finding food for everyone. Women sang the praises of their husbands to their skeptical mothers, and the men replied realistically that they did not expect this new-found popularity to outlive the famine.

The journey on foot to the highlands or to Mulanje was long and arduous, and some people died on the way. While traveling they lived on wild foods that they gathered in the bush, and of which there seems to have been a general communal knowledge. There were varieties of yam-like tubers, wild cassava, banana roots, edible grass, fungi, and fruits, but collecting and processing these foods was time-consuming and had to be done with extreme care as many of them were fatally poisonous if not cooked correctly. The women and children left at home also collected these wild foods, and often grandmothers would take their grandchildren off into the bush to collect them. As time wore on, many people developed severely swollen limbs, "famine edema," and this they attributed to the eating of these wild foods (see Keys et al. 1950).

When they reached the Ntcheu-Dedza highlands, the men were usually greeted with generosity from their relatives. They were given a meal to revive them and a place to stay, and then they either bought food if they had cash or worked for it. Sometimes they exchanged beads, plates, and clothing for maize flour. In the early months of the famine they also sold their domestic livestock (mostly chickens and goats), but the supply of animals was quickly exhausted. In any case it is said that the people of Mwanza began to refuse to accept the animals in exchange for grain because of their disturbing tendency of turning into snakes as soon as their owners had departed.

Men bought food in varying quantities, at a price comparable to that paid by the urban workers of Blantyre and Limbe–that is, 3s. for a one-gallon tin. The demand was high and there was no bargaining. One man who had money remitted from a son working in Southern Rhodesia walked to Ntcheu and bought two bags (of 200 pounds each) that lasted him and his family for about two months. He returned to Ntcheu several times during the year.

Another man was a tailor whose business was naturally suffering with the famine, but who did have some money saved up. He walked to Ntcheu as well, diverging into the hills on the way to collect wild foods. One woman whose husband was insane joined a group of people traveling west to Neno and Mwanza. She had no money so she worked in people's gardens in order to earn a small basket of maize. Not everyone met with immediate sympathy in the areas in which they sought food, as one man recalled:

> One day I went with my friends to look for food in Ntcheu, but when we got there a certain woman asked us rudely to "produce the serious famine for her to see", and after failing to produce it she told us to go back to Lirangwe and wrap the famine in big leaves and bring it to her!

At home the women waited for their husbands to return, which they usually did at night so that their neighbors could not see how much food they had with them. But if the oral sources are to be believed, often the men did not return at all, but stayed away in their own homes until the famine was over, or married other women in the areas to which they had gone for food. The year 1949 is thus remembered as one of "many divorces," and this aspect of the famine features in many pounding songs:

> We have suffered this year,
> Our men are divorcing us,
> Oh what shall we do with this hunger?

Those marriages which survived the famine were said to be "good and strong ones" that could outlive any disaster, but for many women the famine proved the fragile nature of marriage ties with men from a different area, and many of the songs sung by the women during the famine were critical of men and skeptical of marriage. For those women whose husbands were labor migrants in Southern Rhodesia or South Africa. the famine was also a test of their marriages. Some of these women were better off than most—if their husbands sent regular remittances then they had a steady source of cash with which to buy food. But if their husbands sent nothing they had to rely on the help of relatives, and this tended to dry up as the famine progressed. As well as being remembered as the year of divorces, 1949 is also recalled as a year of few marriages and few conceptions. Women did not conceive in this time, and this they attributed to a lack of desire for sexual intercourse (though amenorrhea probably played a part) (see Jelliffe and Jelliffe 1971, 57; Le Roy Ladurie 1979). In one song a young woman laments the fact that she is without child:

> I am the nurse of the sun,
> I am nursing the sun
> While my friends are nursing babies.

Those babies who were born in 1949/50 were said to be sickly and weak, and nursing mothers were anxious that without enough food to feed themselves they would not have enough milk for their babies. One woman recalls how her milk supply became insufficient to feed her three-month-old baby and how she had to make her drink a thin porridge instead. But it was probably the small children who had already been weaned who suffered more than the babies, and their constant wailings were heard everywhere. Stories were told of how some mothers unable to quiet their children or to find food for them secretly murdered them, while others were simply abandoned along with the very old and the disabled:

> I can hear the crying of the child,
> He is crying continuously,
> He is crying like a bird.
> He has slept out there in the bush.
> Because he has nowhere else to sleep.

As the custom of *ubombo*[6] progressively broke down, so increasingly each family, and then each individual, paid attention only to its own food supply. Families ate only inside their houses, not outside and in public as was usual. Children had to be kept inside at mealtimes, otherwise they would go and beg at every house in the village. It was recognized that everyone had to look after their own immediate family problems, but it seems that this situation was nevertheless regarded with some embarrassment. In general it was the women who had the strongest ties at home and who were more or less obliged to stay there and care for the children. However, some women decided that the only way to obtain food was through prostitution in the towns. According to male informants, many women from the famine-stricken areas came to Blantyre and Limbe and slept with any man who could assure them of a meal. To some extent this evidence is reinforced by the women's own songs, which associate the famine with prostitution.

For many months people survived on a combination of food-earning strategies. In some places a small harvest of sweet potatoes relieved the situation in May and June, and those who had planted the fast-maturing variety of cassava could harvest something of this in August and September. More importantly, however, the government finally opened maize distribution centers in the area, from September onward. One of these was at the Lunzu Native Tobacco Board market, and another was near the railway station at Lirangwe. Here people could buy a ration of maize at the price of 3d. per pound. This distribution system is well remembered by people of the area. A few of them had experienced something similar but on a smaller scale in 1922, but for most this kind of government intervention was a complete novelty. The food distribution system was organized with military precision and relied heavily on the village headmen to ensure that the supply was fairly distributed. Each village headman was allotted certain days of the week when he should come to the center with his people. Each family head was allowed to buy maize to the value of 5s. per family, although some people managed to get around this regulation and secured more. People who were completely without cash (usually women) had to work for food by collecting large stones, which were then used in the building of a road to the railway line. The really old and destitute were given free food, but these issues were kept to the minimum. One regulation strictly adhered to, and well remembered by the women, was that all married people had to pay for the food. This applied equally to women whose husbands had abandoned them or whose husbands were migrants but did not send any money home. Most families, if they contained more than one adult member, used the government distribution as one arm of their overall food-procuring strategy. Urban workers would continue to get food from their employers while their wives queued for food at the government centers; other men would continue to walk to Ntcheu, Dedza, Neno, or Mulanje while their wives worked on the road to earn food.

According to official reports, it was around December 1949 and January 1950 that people in the Lirangwe-Lunzu area began to show signs of severe malnutrition. People had been suffering from famine edema for some time, but now there seemed to be a sudden and severe deterioration in their condition. Both oral and written sources confirm that it was the very old and the very young who suffered most notably, and oral accounts also mention pregnant women as being vulnerable. Many old people were abandoned and either died in their homes or collapsed on the way to the distribution centers. The oral accounts of both men and women indicated that it was men who lost most body weight and who died most often of starvation (although there is no confirmation of this in the written sources). Male informants say that men died most often because of the burden of anxiety placed on them by the responsibility they had to feed their families—but some women say that it was those men who had remained sexually alive who died (Carter 1982). Men were also thought vulnerable to dying at the mere thought of food. Several accounts exist of how men would put stones in a pan and pretend that they were frying dried maize, and then would die at the sight of the stones in the pan.

In January, feeding camps were set up to deal with the worst cases of malnutrition. One of these was on the tobacco estate of a European named Binson, near Lirangwe. Here the old and the destitute were kept behind barbed wire and fed twice a day on thin porridge. Their faces were haggard and their eyes protruding, and they all suffered from *matenda a njala* ("the famine disease"). They wore labels around their necks ("like dogs that have been vaccinated against rabies"), and the woman in charge of feeding them made them dance when they had eaten "so that the food would reach all parts of their bodies." The really bad cases were taken to the Blantyre Mission Hospital for further "food treatment." (The disease was hunger and the medicine was porridge—so the one who gave out the porridge was known as "doctor.")

In the meantime the more able-bodied were working hard to weed their gardens. Some people had obtained maize seeds and cassava cuttings free from the government, but most preferred to find their own "local" seeds and traveled long distances to obtain these. Some people got around the suspension on beer-brewing and held work parties to ensure that a maximum area was cultivated. Women complained that they were too weak to both cultivate their gardens and to pound the relief maize (by now no one had money for maize-milling). In some distribution centers the government began to issue ready-milled maize (*ngaiwa*) when they realized that some women were simply unable to pound.

At the same time the government was attempting to enforce more strictly the conservation measures that it had introduced into the area in the 1940s. The assumption was made that people would be more willing to follow these now that they had experienced the famine. This link was not so clear in the minds of those who had endured the famine, but the famine and the more strictly enforced measures *are* directly linked in many people's memories. Some people viewed the fines and arrests of people who infringed the laws as being direct punishments for having caused the government so much trouble with the famine. The fact that a 2s.6d. "famine tax" was levied on all adult males reinforced this impression that the government was punishing them.

The 1950 harvest was a good one despite the physical weakness of many people at the critical times and despite the difficulties of obtaining seeds. But many people died when they began eating "real" food again. As one person put it: "This was because their bodies had got used to 'bad food' so that when they started eating good food again this caused reactions in their bodies, with fatal results." The situation was complicated by a smallpox epidemic that had started in the highlands of Ntcheu, where many people from the south had gone to get food. The medical authorities found it difficult to control the outbreak because of the extreme mobility of the population during the famine. However, according to oral reports, people from the south were well acquainted with smallpox and of their own accord many went to be vaccinated, so that when the disease reached the famine area its results were not severe.

By the next planting season (1950/1951) people were in a better position to respond to the lessons of the famine, although in many cases their responses were conditioned by government policies and regulations, as well as by the communal memory of this famine and previous ones. Most people apparently planted more cassava and sought out varieties that they had sometimes not grown before. The Lomwe people, whose history was marked by famine, were experts on cassava, and some of them returned to Mozambique to collect cuttings of the varieties that were particularly useful in times of drought.

How the society adapted itself back to "normality" after the famine we do not know. There are stories (told by women) of how husbands who had fled during the famine returned afterward to attempt reconciliation with their wives, but were uniformly turned away. There are songs, too, which indicate that even during the breakdown of social norms at the height of the famine people were half-conscious of how their behavior might be judged afterward. One song warns young girls to behave with propriety during the time of hunger, or afterward they might face harsh judgment:

> Be careful girls when speaking.
> This famine will one day end,
> And then we will see [recall] your pride.

In this second section I analyse the available background written evidence in an attempt to construct a "Sen-type" model of the famine. I then consider how far this model accords with the evidence from oral sources.

The immediate postwar period in Nyasaland was one of rapid economic change and the marked growth of African capitalist activity. In the area affected by the famine, long-term changes such as the growth of population combined in the postwar period with the increase in wage employment (both at home and abroad), the enforcement of government conservation measures, and the increased circulation of money in the villages. We certainly need to look beyond purely agricultural factors if we are to understand the nature of the famine in Blantyre district, because by the late 1940s a majority of households there relied for their income on a combination of wage-earning and agricultural production, and sometimes on what would now be termed "informal sector" activity.

About half of Blantyre district was occupied by privately owned estates, and this had been the case since massive land alienation of the late nineteenth century. Although by the 1940s there were about seventy estates in all in the Blantyre district, the greater part of this land was owned by two companies—the British Central Africa Company and the Blantyre and East Africa Company. Both companies had histories of inertia and nonexploitation of their vast land reserves. However, by the mid-1930s they were beginning to attempt greater control of the African residents on their land, and in particular they were enforcing more strictly the rental obligations of their tenants. An agreement dating from 1943 between one estate and its tenants indicates that these obligations, when enforced, could be very demanding. When they were not complied with, the estate owners could apply to the District Commissioner to evict tenants. In 1937, for instance, the British Central Africa Company made application to evict 1,200 tenants for failure to fulfil obligations. Of this number, only 150 finally received eviction, but the threat of eviction was enough to discourage further settlement on privately owned land. Successive District Commissioners reported that this insecurity led to congestion on Native Trust Land (the unalienated, customary land), where holding sizes were becoming progressively smaller in the 1940s.

Another feature of the 1940s was the growth of the twin towns of Blantyre and Limbe, and the increase in the number of public works in the area. This growth was allied to the postwar "tobacco boom," which resulted not only in the expansion of estate tobacco production but also in generally higher levels of investment in urban property. For the people of Blantyre district this meant that there was an increased demand for labor in the area—both skilled and unskilled—and wage levels rose. To some extent, then, the increasing congestion on Native Trust Land around Blantyre was compensated for by an increase in employment opportunities. According to the Labour Report for 1949, in March of that year there was a total of 67,630 people employed by European and Indian-run enterprises in the Southern Province, the vast majority of which were male laborers working in tea and tobacco industries. The wages for unskilled labor had risen to an average of £1.2s.6d. a month (inclusive of a food allowance), compared with the average wage in 1939 of 6s. to 10s. (Nyasaland Government 1940, 1950). Hand in hand with this growth in wage employment went the growth of craft and service industries—this group included butchers, dairymen, traders in fish and vegetables, knife-makers, charcoal burners, lime burners (supplying the building industry), carpenters, canteen owners, shoe-repairers and, most importantly, women beer-brewers (Nyasaland Government 1932). Beer-brewing became a major industry around Blantyre in the 1940s and an important means by which families residing on congested Native Trust Land could make up some of their budget deficit. For although wages had risen fast in the 1940s, so had the urban cost of living. Calculations made in 1947 estimated that in the years between 1939 and 1947 the cost of living for an African urban resident had risen by 100 percent, unless he was in a position to provide most of his food supplies, in which case the estimate was of a 50 to 60 percent rise. This fact would help explain why in the course of the 1940s labor emigration from Blantyre district to South Africa and Southern Rhodesia increased very markedly. As estate owners effectively prevented their male tenants from emigrating (the penalty was family evictions), we must assume that most of the emigrating men came from Native Trust Land. This leaves us with a picture of Native Trust Land around Blantyre which can be summed up as one of increasing land congestion, increasing low-paid wage employment of men, and increasing long-term male absence.

Living in the same areas, however, were the families of a different economic group consisting of skilled employees (artisans, teachers, clerks, and the like) and the wealthier of the African self-employed craftsmen and businessmen. This was a relatively small group. We have no figures for the self-employed, but in 1949 of the total of 83,054 people employed by European and Indian enterprises in the whole of the Protectorate, some 4,694 were classified as clerks and artisans. Although a small group, it was an important one and becoming more significant both economically and politically in the 1940s. What little evidence we have points to the fact that members of this group had larger than average landholdings, as well as higher than average earnings from their employment or trade. These were the employers of *ganyu* labor, who do not show up in the official statistics. There are a number of reasons for thinking that the fortunes of this group rose during the immediate postwar period. First, the rise in tobacco prices meant that the earnings of some Africans had increased (as well as their own earnings if they were themselves involved in tobacco production). This money in African hands from cash-crop production was combined with the earnings of disbanded soldiers who had fought in the war, creating what many Europeans saw as a glut of money in African hands. As imports were restricted and expensive, in the postwar period a much smaller proportion of this wealth than normal was spent on imported cloth and other goods. The government concluded that money was actually being hoarded in mattresses and under floorboards. When Phyllis Deane investigated this question, however, she came to the conclusion that the money *was* being circulated, but in the African sector where there was an increased velocity of trade. Unable to buy imported items, people instead spent what cash they had on building better houses and enjoying a more varied diet—hence the growth in the African building industry and the growth in the service sector in Blantyre. European officials also remarked on the increasing number of African traders who owned motorized transport and maize mills, and who thus capitalized on the increasing demand for food from the growing urban or periurban population in the south.

The picture that seems to emerge when one looks at the changes of the 1940s is one of increasing differentiation among the African population of Blantyre district. If we now return to the famine, we should be able to see how these different groups fared.

The first group were the upper ranks of the skilled workers and businessmen. These personally suffered very little during the famine. They had not only cash and other assets at their disposal but also privileged access to food supplies, either because they were themselves food-traders, or because they received food from their employers at very favorable rates. Some members of this group undoubtedly profited from the famine.

The second group to emerge consisted of the smaller self-employed traders and artisans. Most members of this group must have experienced a drastic fall in income—as the famine took hold fewer and fewer people had money to spend on luxury foods and on services such as laundering, shoe-repairing, and tailoring. Furthermore, as these people were self-employed they did not have the easy access to food supplies enjoyed by urban employees of government missions and European and Indian-owned businesses. Whether or not they suffered personally in the famine would depend on whether they had cash savings to spend on food.

The third group were the families of men in low-paid wage employment in European and Indian sectors of the economy—such as agricultural laborers, tobacco-graders, road laborers, and so on. These people were drawn from the Native Trust Land around Blantyre. In general they would not have had large holdings of land or significant savings. Many of their wives will have been employed part-time as beer-brewers, but this aspect of the family income came to a halt during the famine. Some of this group will have been laid off work when the famine struck and thus left to fend for themselves, but the evidence indicates that many of them, along with the resident tenants on estates, were either fed free or given privileged access to food supplies by their employers. Thus although this was generally a group of disadvantaged people, during the famine the fact of their employment in the "formal" sector of the economy carried a definite advantage.

The fourth group, and the one that is least visible in the sources, consisted of those households whose members were involved both in cultivating their own plots of land and in doing *ganyu* labor for more fortunate peasant households or craftsmen in the area. These people suffered during the famine because they were not employed in the formal sector of the economy and thus were not eligible for the help that those employed there received. What is more, their employment by other African households must have ended fairly early on in the famine. One suspects that many members of this group ended up as recipients of free government issues, but only after many of them had died or suffered greatly.

This, then, would be the classification of the population emerging from the written sources, and to some extent it accords with information from oral testimony. The first group—the wealthier traders and businessmen and skilled employees—emerge as the avaricious mill-owners and self-confessed hoarders of the oral testimonies. The second group—the self-employed craftsmen and smaller traders—are also represented in the testimonies, as in the case of the tailor who shut down his business and used his savings to buy food in Ntcheu. The third group—those families of men in low-paid employment in European and Indian sectors of the economy—also emerge clearly in the oral sources as having benefited from a "legitimate" foothold in the privileged urban sector, with easier access to food supplies. The fourth group, and probably the largest of all, is the least well-defined in oral sources—they are simply "the poor" of every village, and as such have little to distinguish them.

But a further consideration of the oral sources shows that there are drawbacks to the model constructed above. To begin with, women are virtually invisible in a classification based on written sources. These sources assume that all women can be classified and identified with their husbands. The oral evidence, however, shows clearly that many women were abandoned during the famine and that others were already living in households without resident husbands. Some but not all of these female-headed households constituted a group that was very susceptible to starvation during the famine. Most women who earned cash did so in normal times through their involvement in beer-brewing or *ganyu* labor, and both of these activities came to an end with the famine. If they had young children, their mobility was severely restricted, making it less possible for them to travel in search of food. The oral testimonies emphasize that whether women and their families suffered often depended on unquantifiable factors of marital breakdown, affection, reliability, and so on. For instance, some of the women whose husbands were labor migrants were relatively privileged in having cash remittances at their disposal. Those women whose husbands sent nothing, however, were among the more vulnerable groups in the community when the famine struck. Also emerging from the oral sources is the fact that for biological and social reasons the elderly and the very young were more likely to suffer than other age groups. Of course, the degree of hardship faced by these groups would depend to some extent on the economic classification of the households to which they belonged—so that, for instance, the young children of a businessman were less likely to die than those of a low-paid laborer—but it is also the case that social attitudes and family relations had a part to play here. The oral evidence shows conclusively that divisions within the family could be just as significant as divisions within the community as a whole. The evidence on marriage patterns highlights this issue most vividly. Any classification of the population that attempted to predict which groups would suffer during a famine would certainly have to take these factors into account. In other words, if Sen's "entitlement theory" is going to be used practically to define the target groups for famine relief in a given society, then "entitlements" based on marriage, on age and sex need to be fed into the model along with those based on production or exchange. The politics of the family may emerge as being an important factor in defining who suffers in any food shortage.

Also emerging from the oral sources is the fact that both long-term and short-term adaptations to food shortage could actually affect the course of a famine. The evidence indicates that the twentieth-century pattern of marriage ties between the Ngoni of the central highlands and the Nyanja, Yao and Lomwe communities of Blantyre district provided some kind of "insurance policy" for those communities. Presumably the validity of these ties was strengthened by the experience of the 1949 famine. But the women's recollections also show that there were conflicts inherent in such marriages which could come to the fore during a crisis. While on the whole the people of

Blantyre district benefited during the famine from the policy of "out-marriage," for some women the famine simply proved the fragility of marriage with men of a different ethnic group (Bloch 1973). These particular marriage ties were a product of patterns of employment that had their origins in the early colonial period, although the practice of "out-marriage" in general was also a feature of societies in this area in the nineteenth century. A more recent modification to the nature of marriage ties, however, had come about with the growth of labor emigration from the Southern Province in the 1940s. This quite sudden growth in the absence of men for long periods may well have caused a disequilibrium in family and social relations which came to light during the famine. Clearly further research needs to be done on the nature of labor migration in the 1940s and its impact on these societies, but it is probably fair to say from the evidence that the famine struck at women more severely because of this recent change in the economic orientations of the area.

Some "responses" to the famine were conditioned by the actions and expectations of the colonial state. Several accounts show that people actlvely petitioned the government for famine relief via their headmen and chiefs. Although generally the famine reinforced the structures of order and authority, it did occasionally and briefly place colonial authority in a hazardous position. Rumors of cannibalism by Europeans were common, and there was a rash of petty theft in 1949 and 1950 which remained largely untouched by the small police force of Nyasaland. The police had no food with which to feed the prisoners, so even when a culprit was caught, he was usually released.

Adjustments after the 1949 famine were severely affected by government action. For instance, some of the "traditional" agricultural responses were inhibited by current policy. The one crop that survived the drought well was the perennial ratooned sorghum, and one would have expected the cultivation of this crop to have spread after the famine as a result of this. However, there was a prohibition placed on its cultivation by the Department of Agriculture, which was worried about its role in spreading crop disease. Likewise, during the drought those people who had wet *dimba* (marsh) land and gardens along the riverbanks had been able to harvest something—but riverbank cultivation was also being actively prevented by the Department of Agriculture, so that further expansion of cultivation into wet areas was severely restricted. In 1950 the government doubled the producer price for maize, thus encouraging people to grow a surplus if they had the land available. However, this action also meant that the urban employees who had been protected against the greatest hardships of the famine now had to pay a higher price for their maize. The already existent pattern of spreading one's risk between a rural and an urban livelihood must have been reinforced by the experience of the famine and the price changes afterward.

In conclusion, a background knowledge of the economic divisions existing in Blantyre district in the 1940s allows us to make a Sen-type classification of "entitlements" that would in part predict which sections of the population suffered most in 1949. The group that emerges as most disadvantaged in this model is that consisting of households that even in a normal year are not self-sufficient in food, who are short of land, and who make up their food deficit by performing casual labor for other peasant farmers. These households would be the first to suffer in a situation in which the local demand for labor fell drastically and when the price of foodstuffs was high. Unlike those households with employees in the "formal" sector, these casual laboring households were not cushioned by privileged access to food supplies or the paternalism of employers. The oral evidence, however, shows that there are added dimensions to the pattern of suffering. First, it draws attention to the fact that in all groups some family members may have suffered disproportionately, and the poorer the group, the greater the disproportion likely. Both young children and the old suffered more than other age groups. In part this can be seen as a biological rather than a social factor, but it is clear from the testimonies that not only were they less able physically to withstand food shortage, but they were also the first groups to be abandoned by their kin. Second, the oral evidence draws attention to the plight of women in the famine—to the fact that there were large numbers of women who were without the economic support of a husband even before the famine, and many more who found themselves in this position in the course of the famine. Again, the poorer the household, the more likely a husband was to abandon it, but this phenomenon cannot be fully understood without an understanding of marriage and kin ties in the area.

It is clear that the society's immediate and long-term responses to food shortage did affect the course of the famine, and in ways not predicted by the colonial authorities. In particular, the activation of long-distance kin ties and the communal knowledge of famine foods delayed the necessity for famine relief by about six months. On the other hand, the action of government in feeding the urban population and in eventually providing relief for rural families must have been fed into the community's own "model" of famine and would have conditioned many families into expecting the government to take on this role in the future.

There is no doubt that the 1949 famine was an event structured by the conditions of the postwar period in this area. By placing emphasis on the role of family relations and social structure I am not aiming to deny the role of economic analysis, but rather to indicate that these social aspects of famine are an integral part of the economic analysis. Family and kin relations were also affected by the conditions of the 1940s—by land shortage, labor patterns, government agricultural policies, wage levels, and community prices—as well as by older and less tangible factors such as marital relations and obligations and attitudes to children.

The story of 1949 in Nyasaland shows that if we are going to understand the impact of famine, we must see it in the context of the whole web of economic and social relations, from the level of the household to that of the state.

NOTES

1. World Copyright: The Past and Present Society, 175 Banbury Road, Oxford, England. This article is reprinted with the permission of the Society and the author from *Past and Present*, issue no. 108 (August 1985), pp. 177–205. An extended account of the research presented here is given in Megan Vaughan, *The Story of an African Famine* (Cambridge: Cambridge University Press, 1987).

2. I wish to acknowledge in particular the contribution made to fieldwork by John Yesaya and Humphrey Chindenga and gratefully acknowledge the financial support provided by the Research and Publications Committee of the University of Malawi. This chapter was first presented as a paper to the American African Studies Association Conference in Boston, December 1983. I am indebted to the following people for their detailed comments and suggestions: William Beinart, Andrew Butcher, John Iliffe, Terence Ranger, Amartya Sen, and Lan White. (*Editors' note*: In addition to the published and informant sources, several types of sources from the Malawi National Archives were consulted for this chapter, but could not be referenced in the text because of space constraints in this book. These include Blantyre District Court documents; documents pertaining to the 1949/50 famine; correspondence from the District Commissioner of Blantyre; agreements between landlords and tenants; Annual Reports for the Blantyre and Central Shire Districts, 1937/38; Village Surveys, Blantyre District, 1944; and various other documents.)

3. The oral evidence used in this chapter was obtained from nearly 200 interviews conducted in March–June 1983 in the Blantyre, Chiradzulu, and Zomba districts of southern Malawi. These interviews were conducted by the author and aided by students of Chancellor College, University of Malawi. Interviews were concentrated in areas known to have been severely affected by the 1949/50 famine, but within these areas selection was random. Those quoted or referred to in this chapter include Adam Diliza, Machinjiri village, Traditional Authority (hereafter TA) Machinjiri, Agnes Siwetela, Nkawajika village, TA Machinjiri, Anderson Fred, Malunga village, TA Kapeni, Baloon Kachere, Masulani village, TA Chigaru, Bekana Saimon, Masulani village, TA Chigaru, Beyadi Misomali, Malunga village, TA Kapeni, Mrs. Chomboko, Mpira village, TA Lunzu, Christine Somba, Somba village, TA Lundu, Dawa Somba, Somba village, TA Lundu, Donald Mpira, Mpira village, TA Kapeni, Mrs. Dorofe Jemusi, TA Machinjiri, Dorothy Kabichi, Mpira village, TA Kapeni, Elizabeth Gomani, Malunga village, TA Kapeni, Flackson Madyera, Somba village, TA Lundu, S. Ganet, Kandio village, TA Kapeni, Village Headman Gulani, Gulani village, TA Chigaru, Herbvert Peter, John Kwadya village, TA Kapeni, Ida Jemusi, Mtendera village, TA Kapeni, Jameson Chisala, Kamlenga village, TA Machinjiri, John Njoka, Machinjiri village, TA Machinjiri, K. Kalemba, Lunzu Trading Centre, Mrs. F. Kamowa, Mbera village, TA Kapeni, W. Kumpanda, Lunzu Trading Centre, Lapken Moses Kanyenga, Padoko village, TA Machinjiri, Layiti Rabson, Malunga village, TA Kapeni, Mai Malita Gulani, Gungulu village, TA Chigaru, Mai

Nambewe Joni, Chitima village, TA Kapeni, Mrs. N. Mandauka, Somba village, TA Lundu, Mayani Ngolo, Chitima village, TA Kapeni, Mrs. F. Michael, Kandio village, TA Kapeni, Michael Phiyo, Chitima village, TA Kapeni, Michael Pote, Kandio village, TA Kapeni, J. Manyazi, Gulani village, TA Chigaru, Mr. Mubulala, Chikande village, TA Kuntaja, Nabanda Gomu, TA Machinjiri, Mrs. Nabanda, Somba village, TA Lundu, Mrs. Nkupumula, Chimpira village, TA Machinjiri, Village Headman Nyani, Nyani village, TA Malemia, Zomba district, Rabson Frank, Gulani village, TA Chigaru, Salima, Masulani village, TA Kapeni, Salome Alfred Solomon, Mthini village, TA Machinjiri, Village Headman Somba, Somba village, TA Lundu, Thomson Chapimpha, Gulani village, TA Chigaru, Victor Misonje, Malanga village, TA Kapeni, Virginia Yotana Nansato, Kaludzi village, TA Machinjiri, Walter Chotha, Nkamajika village, TA Machinjiri, Wilfred Kampazaza, Mananani village, TA Machinjiri.

4. *Ganyu* is casual labor performed in the peasant agricultural sector.

5. Here and at a number of other points the argument is based on materials from the Malawi National Archives. This chapter relies on the following files, among others: AFC 3/1/1, AFC 3/2/1, AFC 7/2/1, AGR 3/7, BA 1, 1909–1936, LB 4/2/1, LB 5/4/1, MP 12324, NSB 3/12/1, NSB 7/1/4, NSB 7/1/5.

6. *Ubombo* is a word expressing the custom of people helping one another at times of trouble, such as dearth.

THREE

Socioeconomic Change and Disease: Smallpox in Colonial Kenya, 1880–1920[1]

Marc H. Dawson

Smallpox is an ancient disease in both Kenya and the rest of Africa, but the patterns of transmission, the rates of endemicity and epidemicity, and the measures employed to control the disease changed in the early twentieth century.[2] In Kenya the socioeconomic changes of the colonial period had significant effects on the way in which smallpox was spread and controlled. In precolonial Kenya, the disease maintained a low level of endemicity with periodic epidemics, but at times of ecological stress smallpox flared into devastating pandemics. These outbreaks resulted from famine-related population movements and the impact of the drought on the seasonal nature of smallpox. The socioeconomic changes of the early colonial period caused the disease to appear more frequently in small local outbreaks with sizable epidemics being uncommon. Thus the endemicity of smallpox changed from low rates before the twentieth century to higher rates during the early years of this century, while widespread epidemics became infrequent.

In order to study the impact of early twentieth-century socioeconomic changes on smallpox, an understanding of the epidemiology of the disease in nineteenth-century East Africa is essential. Some recent works on the history of disease in Africa have revived the notion that many diseases, including smallpox, were newly introduced into the continent during the nineteenth and twentieth centuries (Hartwig and Patterson 1978). These works argue that the impact of epidemic diseases on isolated nonimmune African populations was comparable to the terrible mortality suffered by the peoples of the Americas and Oceania. The argument is false, particularly for smallpox, which has a long history in Africa.

Smallpox was endemic on the East African coast early in the nineteenth century, but some historians doubt that it reached the interior (Hartwig 1979, 664). How could it have existed at the coast and not in the interior?

The old assumption that coast and interior had no contact is untrue. Recent studies of the relations of coastal societies and their immediate inland neighbors reveal that they had rather early extensive and intensive contacts (Feierman 1974; Spear 1978; Ylvisaker 1979). Coastal hinterland societies had contacts with their inland neighbors, who communicated, in turn, with more distant peoples. Smallpox introduced into such a network of contacts would have spread rapidly among completely nonimmune populations with devastating results. Thus, Europeans or foreign long-distance traders were not needed for smallpox to be carried into the interior. Nor had smallpox needed European carriers to spread into the interior of sixteenth-century Central and South America. The disease raced southward from the Spanish settlements in Panama through the intervening Indian populations eventually reaching the Inca empire in Peru. Pizarro and his companions, the first foreign contacts, arrived in Peru to find smallpox had already devastated the Incas (Crosby 1972, 51–56; Dobyns 1963, 493–515).

Historians have misunderstood the behavior of smallpox in nineteenth-century Africa by basing their analyses on twentieth-century epidemiological experiences (Hartwig 1979, 665–666). While the use of modern medical data can be misleading when applied to the past, recent studies reveal important facets of the epidemiology of African smallpox. There is a growing body of evidence that Africa had an indigenous strain of smallpox, which was found in all parts of the continent. Until the mid-1970s physicians had distinguished only two clinical forms of smallpox, variola major and variola minor (alastrim). Variola major was the more severe and frequently fatal form of the disease and the type of smallpox usually found in Europe and Asia. Alastrim or variola minor was a mild and nonlethal form of the disease found in South America and southern Africa (Benenson 1975, 288–290; Dixon 1962, 43).

Studies by British virologists in the 1960s and smallpox-eradication workers in the 1970s revealed the presence of an intermediate strain of smallpox in Africa, which they named *variola intermedius*. The disease had a mortality rate around 2.8 to 10.9 percent compared to variola major's 20 to 40 percent and variola minor's less than 1 percent. In any outbreak most clinical cases appeared to resemble variola minor, but cases resembling variola major were also found (Bedson, et al. 1963, 1085–1088; Conacher 1957, 157–181). The disease had slow transmission rates, and similar epidemic and endemic cycles for the disease emerged from all regions of the continent (Breman et al. 1977; Dumbell and Huq 1975, 303–306; Fofana et al. 1971, 175–179; Henderson and Yekpe 1969, 423–428; Hopkins et al. 1971, 689–704; Imperato 1972, 983–994; Imperato et al. 1973, 261–268). Clearly, if Africa had its own strain of smallpox found in all parts of the continent, the smallpox virus could hardly have been introduced and spread or have undergone the very same change throughout the continent in recent times.

In nineteenth-century East Africa, smallpox was a disease characterized by a low level of endemicity. The African strain of smallpox appeared to have required intensive contact for transmission. Because of the need for close contact for transmission and the frequently mild nature of the disease, smallpox was contained in relatively small populations (Foster et al. 1978, 831–833; Henderson and Yekpe 1969, 427–428; Hopkins et al. 1971, 696; Imperato 1972, 991).[3] Most outbreaks were very local, probably confined to households or small villages. Overnight visitors, such as trading partners, blood partners, or distant relatives, could be infected and carry the disease to their homes. Casual contacts with foreign traders or people in markets would have had little significance in transmission of the disease.

The long-distance trade caravans were not responsible for introducing "foreign" smallpox into the interior, but they may occasionally have carried variola major into the interior during imported epidemics on the coast. They could, however, spread the endemic African strain of the disease to new areas. Smallpox was a problem for long-distance traders, posing the same threat to their caravan members (leaders, porters, or slaves) that was faced, for instance, by eighteenth-century European and American soldiers (Duffy 1979, 78–79). The concentration of a large number of nonimmune rural young men and women in daily contact created ideal conditions for smallpox to erupt. The terrible toll in lives of African porters and slaves from smallpox reported by various European travelers probably occurred, but the rates would have been higher than those normally found in an outbreak in any small African village. Young adults (fifteen to thirty-five years old), those most likely to be found working as caravan porters or seized as slaves, suffered a significantly higher mortality rate than children or older adults (Burnet and White 1974, 83, 99–101; Dixon 1962). Porters and slaves were often marginally nourished, which possibly increased their mortality rates.

The Indian Ocean trade occasionally carried variola major to the East African coast and probably on into the interior. This strain made fearful appearances on the coast in the nineteenth and twentieth centuries (Dumbell and Huq 1975, 304).[4] Precolonial East Africans were aware that "foreign" smallpox was not only more virulent but also had a higher mortality rate. Richard Burton reported one such epidemic when the disease had been introduced to Zanzibar by a dhow from Muscat. The disease was very virulent, and there were numerous cases of confluent smallpox with its usual fatal results (Burton 1872, 195). Another, possibly imported, variola major epidemic occurred on Pemba in 1899, when smallpox swept the island, killing at least 20,000 freemen and 10,000 slaves. An Arab from Zanzibar had introduced the disease, but a British official reported that a dhow had brought the disease to Zanzibar from Arabia. He went on to note that the disease was normally endemic in the islands and that the indigenous form did not greatly worry the inhabitants. If the disease was imported from Arabia or India, the islanders feared the inevitable severe and deadly epidemic that followed on both the islands and on the mainland.

Periodic epidemics of the African strain of smallpox also occurred. In Ethiopia W. C. Plowden stated that smallpox was always present and periodically broke out in epidemics. Other observers reported that approximately every ten years an epidemic struck Ethiopia. In 1819 J. L. Burckhardt noted that smallpox occurred in the Sudan every eight to ten years. This epidemic periodicity was also found in twentieth-century West Africa (Bayoumi 1976, 2; 1979, 194–205; Breman et al. 1977, 758–759; Burckhardt 1819; Fofana et al. 1971, 176; Hartwig 1981, 5–33; Hopkins et al. 1971, 691; Pankhurst 1965, 344; Plowden 1868, 100).[5] In East Africa, however, drought and famine struck approximately every ten years. During and in the wake of famines, smallpox usually ravaged East African, Sudanese, and Ethiopian populations. The problem for the historian is which strain of smallpox caused the widespread epidemics and high mortality. Unfortunately, this determination is not possible in most cases. In 1898–1900 in Kenya, smallpox broke out simultaneously on the coast and in Ukambani, which means probably the endemic African strain was spreading. The possibility cannot be excluded, though, that variola major was later introduced and spread alongside the African strain. The temptation to explain every major smallpox epidemic as being the result of imported variola major should be resisted but cannot be totally denied. The nineteenth-century European travelers and colonial authorities always sought outside sources for epidemics. The African strain of smallpox was capable of erupting into an epidemic form and causing high mortality.

Several historians have noted the relationship between famines and disease, particularly smallpox (Ford 1971, 140; Ford and Hall 1947, 21). They assume that sudden starvation weakens populations' resistance to disease, thus causing the endemic form of smallpox to become epidemic. This assumption, however superficially reasonable, is not true. Malnutrition and many diseases do interact, frequently synergistically. Nutritional status is also an important determinant of the immune response of the host; however, in regard to smallpox, an individual acquires immunity only by contracting the disease or through vaccination or variolation. Therefore, in the case of smallpox, malnutrition undoubtedly determined the fate of many smallpox sufferers, but could not act as the cause of widespread epidemic (Scrimshaw et al. 1968). Rather, the most important cause of precolonial epidemics was the social reaction to famine.[6]

Several types of famine relief measures caused the massive epidemics. Raiding, trading, and population movements were departures from daily routines and provided an opportunity for endemic disease to become epidemic. The population movements, not malnutrition, led to the spread of the disease. Endemic smallpox did become epidemic during famines, although historians have not understood the actual dynamics. For instance, Ford and Hall wrote concerning the pastoral Bahima of Ankole and Karagwe in 1892: "It is a reasonable assumption that the sudden starvation of the pastoral people so weakened their resistance to disease, that the endemic form of smallpox rapidly became epidemic and of course, also afflicted the agricultural population" (Ford 1971, 140; Ford and Hall 1947, 21).

Pastoral populations could maintain smallpox endemically, but the disease probably was not common. The surrounding agricultural peoples had higher endemic rates due to their higher population densities. When in 1892 rinderpest wiped out virtually all the Bahima cattle, the pastoralists were forced to get food from the agriculturalists. When the lesser immune pastoral population came into extended and intensive contact with the agriculturalists, an epidemic inevitably resulted owing to the increased number of nonimmune people both pastoral and agricultural in the infected agricultural villages. In Kenya, the Maasai crowded into Kikuyu villages in search of food in the wake of the 1882–1884 and 1892 cattle epizootics. The Kikuyu harvest had been poor, however, and famine soon broke out. The group of Kikuyu young men circumcised in 1892 called themselves *mũtung'u* (smallpox) after the disease that broke out. The agricultural Kamba and Kikuyu both had sufficiently large and dense populations to keep smallpox at higher endemic rates. In West Africa Imperato noted a similar pattern of smallpox outbreaks, when Sahelian pastoralists came into contact with agricultural populations in Mali (Imperato 1972, 984, 993).

A closer look at raiding and trading will illustrate the process. Raiding characterized famine periods. In the 1898 famine, raids occurred on caravans, European railway camps, other people (e.g., Kamba raids on the Mbeere), and even on one's neighbors.[7] Raiding provided very limited opportunities for passing an infection between raiders and victims, but the sources reveal one example. A European missionary related that once while traveling on the Athi plains he came upon a "heap of human bones." He was informed that they were the remains of Maasai who had built camps there. During a smallpox epidemic among these Maasai, Kamba from Kangundo raided them capturing their cattle (and probably some women) but also caught smallpox and spread the disease upon returning to Ukambani.[8]

Another effect of the increased raiding was the gathering together of warriors in compounds for either defensive or offensive purposes. As noted above, this age group (fifteen to twenty-five years old) suffers a greater mortality from smallpox. Thus when the disease was introduced among the warriors, many died. In fact, some sources specifically state that the mortality was greatest among the young in 1898 (Dixon 1962, 8; Kershaw 1972, 170; Muriuki 1974, 122–123). Also, families probably banded together for protection, thus increasing the size and population density of villages, and hence their vulnerability to epidemic disease (Mwaniki 1974, 238):

> Trading was a normal activity, but famine saw a substantial increase in its frequency. A Chuka informant told Mwaniki: People exchanged goods all the time, but the period of famines saw the intensification of the exchange and even the creation of more meeting places for exchange.

Kikuyu informants made similar comments concerning the food trade (Muriuki 1974, 250). The increase was both in internal and external trading. Merritt reported Taita testimony describing the way men moved from village to village to buy food during a famine in the mid-1880s. In 1898 in Taveta, as food became scarcer the men were forced to travel more widely to find food, as were the Kamba and Kikuyu (Jackson 1976, 193–216; Merritt 1975, 101, 103, 127; *Taveta Chronicle* June 1899, 158). External trade increased dramatically in famine periods as well, creating the need for new special markets. All the people in the region knew where these famine markets were held and large numbers of people came to trade. The need for food even overrode political differences at times, and Mwaniki's Embu informants claimed that hostilities were stopped in order to begin trade relations (Mwaniki 1974, 12–13, 58, 101, 139, 273). Similarly, the Kikuyu and Kamba traded heavily in 1898–1900, even though Kamba slave-raiding and stock-raiding activities had seriously strained some local relations.[9]

The increased population densities in nonfamine areas were the result of two famine relief practices, pawning and migration. In pawning a man placed himself and his dependents, or only his dependents, in a servile position with a patron who, in turn, provided food and protection in exchange for labor. The man could redeem his dependents by paying a fee or by working the fee off if he had pawned himself. The Maasai and Kamba in 1892 and 1898 sent many women and children to the Kikuyu in this way (Jackson 1976, 193–216).

Migration of individuals, families, or larger social units was usually directed to areas where kinsmen or blood partners lived or where any food could be obtained. Many Kikuyu families charitably took in Kamba famine refugees without any preconditions or expectations of payment. These famine refugees were free to leave at the end of the famine, settle permanently, or could be adopted by their hosts, which occurred frequently among the Embu and Kikuyu (Mwaniki 1974, 12–13, 139, 304; Saberwal 1970, 44). Usually people moved in small groups, but the total number of people involved was considerable. The Kamba seeking shelter with the Mbeere became numerous enough to overwhelm their hosts militarily. The sources describe large numbers of Kamba leaving their homes for Kikuyuland, and the number of Kikuyu going to the highlands was numbered in the thousands (Munro 1975, 47; Muriuki 1974, 106; Mwaniki 1974, 217; Tate 1904, 135; *Taveta Chronicle* 1900, 182).

Another reason for the massive smallpox epidemics was the breakdown during famines of the traditional means of dealing with the endemic form of the disease, the practice of variolating during epidemics, and in the case of the Kikuyu, the traditional ceremonies to drive away epidemics. The Kikuyu, Embu, and Taita all practiced isolation of smallpox victims. The Kikuyu did not permit people to leave or visit homesteads afflicted by smallpox. During famines the maintenance of isolation was impossible. People traveled anywhere at any risk to obtain food. Thus, numerous reports can be found of smallpox victims roaming in search of food and spreading the disease (Leakey 1978, 889–890; Merritt 1975, 122–123; Mwaniki 1974, 304; *Taveta Chronicle* 1899, 169).

The Kavirondo reportedly practiced variolation (inoculation) into the colonial period. A person who is inoculated usually contracts an attenuated form of the disease, and the risks of dying are fairly low. If the inoculator penetrated too deep or the pus came from a person who had not yet passed the critical stage of the disease, the risks of death were great. The major problem with variolation as a public health measure was that inoculated people could infect other people with full-blown smallpox. Hence, a man could protect his family through inoculation, but unless they were all isolated they could infect the rest of the community. During famines, population movement made such isolation almost impossible (Dixon 1962, 108–110; Langer 1976, 112–117; Livingstone 1858, 141–143; Owen 1925, 333–335).

When an epidemic of smallpox or any other disease was approaching or struck, the Kikuyu held two different types of ceremonies to drive the disease away. The first ceremony involved the gathering of all the women of one ridge (*rũgongo*), who would then sing and yell to drive the disease on to the next ridge. The women of the neighboring ridge would in turn gather and drive the disease on to the next until the disease had been driven from the land. The second ceremony involved the sacrifice of a goat by the head either of a homestead or more commonly of a lineage. After prayers to *Ng'ai* (creator god), old men cooked and ate parts of the goat. Then the stomach contents (*taatha*) were taken and sprinkled around the borders of the lineage's territory, and other parts hung from special arches, *mariigĩ*, constructed over the main footpaths. These actions would prevent the disease from entering their homes (Cagnolo 1933, 87; Crawford 1906, 87–88; Kenyatta 1937, 250–253; Leakey 1978, 903–905).[10]

The epidemiological significance of these actions is the gathering of all the members of a lineage at one place and time. These ceremonies would have allowed individuals in the incubating and infectious stage of the disease to come into contact with members from different homesteads. Given the nature of African smallpox the importance of these casual contacts at a ceremony for transmission of the disease is unclear. Similarly, Africans who insisted on visiting sick relatives may have been at risk of contracting the disease.

Finally, the drought itself may have contributed to the heightened incidence of smallpox. Studies of the pattern of smallpox endemicity in the tropics have revealed a particular seasonality to the disease. Smallpox is a disease of the dry season. This pattern partially results from the increased intercommunication possible during the dry season but also to the virus. High humidity tends to kill the smallpox virus very quickly, thus shortening the time it can remain viable outside the body and infect a new victim. Therefore, as the dry season sets in, the number of smallpox cases begins to rise until the rains set in and the numbers begin to fall (Breman et al. 1977, 759; Fofana et al. 1971, 180; Henderson 1976, 25–33; Hopkins et al. 1971, 692). If the rains do not fall, the number of cases probably continues to rise and combine with the famine related changes, both of which would result in an epidemic.

The early colonial period saw increased movement of the sort that spread epidemic diseases, but without famine. Trade expanded greatly with the introduction of cash crops; labor migration caused larger and more frequent population movements; and urbanization created larger and denser population. The introduction of vaccination did help prevent epidemics, but the British vaccination campaigns were beset with problems of chronic underfunding, vaccine shortages, ineffective vaccine, and African resistance. The result was that local outbreaks of smallpox appeared frequently with only occasional widespread epidemics.

In the colonial period the disease seemed to Europeans to have changed its nature. The colonial medical officers commented on the "mild" nature of the disease as compared to the virulent and deadly disease observed during the 1898–1900 famine-epidemic. The nature of endemic African smallpox did not change. The major strain of smallpox remained variola intermedius, which required intimate contact for transmission, was slow to spread, and compared to variola major was a disease of "mild" nature—specifically, low mortality and less severe clinical manifestations. Thus, colonial medical authorities trained to diagnose and treat variola major would find cases of rural African smallpox puzzlingly mild. Similarly, almost all Kikuyu informants claimed *mũtung'u* (smallpox) never returned after the devastating epidemic at the turn of the century. Clearly, then, *mũtung'u* cannot be translated simply as smallpox, but as severe smallpox resulting in a large number of victims and deaths. With this definition, *mũtung'u* never returned to central Kenya. The real change was the rising morbidity of smallpox in the early colonial period.

After the 1897–1900 famine, smallpox did not appear in rural central Kenya on an areawide scale until 1916. Between 1900 and 1912, most district and medical reports refer to smallpox occurrences as "sporadic cases," or appearing in a "mild form." In 1913 the incidence of smallpox increased with serious outbreaks reported in Nyeri and Meru and many scattered cases around Fort Hall. Again in 1914 and 1915 smallpox was quiescent, appearing in isolated cases or small local outbreaks. In 1916 with many African soldiers and carriers returning from the war, smallpox broke out again on a large scale with 100 outbreaks in Kenya Province alone. The disease died down again in 1917, but when the 1917/18 famine began the incidence increased, particularly around Nairobi. Again the disease appeared in rural areas in sporadic local outbreaks through 1920.

Nairobi's experience with the disease was somewhat different. With its denser population the city had frequent large outbreaks. The disease struck on a significant scale in 1909, 1913, and 1915–1918. The occurrences in Nairobi were usually several months long and the reported cases numbered well over 100.

Before 1920, Nyanza Province suffered more heavily from smallpox than did central Kenya. This area had been devastated in 1899–1900 by famine and smallpox. After that, the disease appeared sporadically in the area until 1909/10, when an epidemic struck every district in the province. As in central Kenya, the disease was quiescent from 1910 to 1915, but was a serious problem from 1915 to 1918. In 1915 and 1916 the disease swept through the entire province and Kisumu district alone reported 3,000 deaths due to the disease. Smallpox remained at epidemic levels until 1919, when the number of reported cases finally dropped to lower levels.

Increased population mobility was an important factor in increasing the frequency of smallpox. This is not to say that in the precolonial era there was not trade or travel to different areas. Some of the precolonial Kikuyu markets were held regularly and attended by over 1,000 people, some of whom traveled great distances to attend. Interethnic trade—specifically, Kikuyu-Maasai, Kikuyu-Kamba, and Kikuyu-Ndia—is well documented (Leakey 1978, 19, 44; Muriuki 1974, 2, 153, 237, 253). Rather, the number of people involved in colonial labor movements was far greater than in precolonial times, and the distances traveled were much longer. As early as 1905 the Kisumu Provincial Commissioner reported "Kavirondo" coming to work in Kisumu in substantial numbers, and by the outbreak of World War I over 20,000 registered and many unregistered laborers passed through Kisumu. As early as 1901, Kikuyu traveled to Nairobi to sell their crops. In addition to the thousands involved in produce trade, thousands of Kikuyu, Embu, and Meru were heading for Nairobi and Mombasa in search of work. With the improved road network, railways, and active labor recruitment, the number of laborers and traders moving between their homes and work had reached the tens of thousands by 1914.

Labor migration and increased trade had two effects on the epidemiology of smallpox: (1) on the laborers themselves and (2) on the population in the reserves. Men leaving the reserves and traveling to Nairobi, the coast, and other areas exposed themselves to infections in a new environment. Several witnesses before the 1912/13 Native Labour Commission testified that returning laborers had contracted diseases while working away from home.

Smallpox was often mentioned. Travel conditions were usually conducive to the spread of disease with men crowded into rest camps or locked into railway cars. Once on the job, living conditions were no better, as men were forced to live in cramped and crowded accommodations. On inspecting one estate Hobley found that fifty Kikuyu were housed in seven huts, none of which was tall enough to stand in. On some plantations men were forced to remain living in huts with people suffering from leprosy or smallpox, and medical attention was usually nonexistent (Orde-Brown 1970 [1925], 182). Hence, many laborers were stricken with the disease.

The returning infected laborers or traders represented a threat to the populations in the reserves. Numerous instances can be found of local epidemics originating from a returned traveler. A typical example was a smallpox outbreak that raged for three months in Mukokoni (Ukamba Province) in October 1918. The original case was a man who had gone to Nairobi to sell his chickens; while there he stayed in a house where a Kikuyu had smallpox. Ten days after returning home, he fell ill and infected sixteen of the twenty people in his homestead. The other four people had already had smallpox. During the next three months, the disease spread from there to five other homesteads, eventually infecting fifty-one people, with six fatal cases.

The most clear-cut example of this threat to public health was the havoc wrought by the returning survivors of the Carrier Corps in 1916. The men were simply returned to their home districts and released regardless of their suspected medical condition. The result in Kenya Province was 100 different outbreaks of smallpox, as well as several other diseases (Patterson 1919). This example was repeated in many other areas of Kenya.

The creation of a city like Nairobi, which in twelve years grew from a group of tents to a city of 19,900, had a significant impact on the epidemiology of smallpox. The city with a large and dense population developed as a business and transport center and constant attraction to labor, providing an environment where disease would be constantly present. As a commercial and transportation center, Nairobi also functioned as a disseminator of disease to the surrounding countryside. The medical records give numerous examples of rural outbreaks of smallpox starting from a person just returned from Nairobi. In fact, some migrant Kikuyu workers regularly traveled back and forth between their rural homes and Nairobi on a weekly basis. The area in Nairobi most frequently lived in by migrant Kikuyu workers was the Indian Bazaar, one of the most densely populated areas of the city. Returning labor migrants from the coast and other areas along the railway visited the Bazaar in order to buy goods before returning home.[11] Consequently, every smallpox epidemic in Nairobi either originated in the Bazaar or quickly spread there, due to the presence of a large number of nonimmune rural people.[12] These people, when infected, spread the disease after returning to their rural homes.[13]

Colonial vaccination campaigns helped, but lack of funds, the difficulty of maintaining an effective vaccination system, and African resistance hampered the efficacy of the campaigns. The funding for medical care for Africans was not a high priority in the colonial budget prior to 1920. As a result, shortages of lymph for vaccination at critical times often plagued health officials. The director of Nairobi's Bacteriological Laboratory claimed his staff and facilities were insufficient to keep up with the demand for lymph, and more funding was needed desperately. The small medical budget also restricted the number of vaccinators who could be trained and employed. The second problem was the lymph itself. The vaccination returns from any area (indicating number vaccinated, etc.) for the period under discussion were anything but complete. In most areas, the physician or vaccinator followed up less than one-quarter of the people he vaccinated. Thus, it was difficult to know whether the vaccinations "took." Many times they probably did not, owing to poor technique but also as a result of the loss of potency of the vaccine. The lymph was easily ruined if poorly stored during transportation to and at the rural outstations. In 1916, colonial medical authorities discovered that the strain of smallpox used for lymph production at the Nairobi laboratory was completely ineffective. This fact came to light only when they received numerous reports that "vaccinated" Africans had contracted smallpox.

The last problem was African resistance to vaccination campaigns in colonial Kenya. Many Africans refused to be vaccinated for fear of being poisoned by the European or African vaccinator, or they were simply afraid of what appeared to be a painful experience (Cagnolo 1933, 254). The manner in which vaccination campaigns were carried out did little to elicit cooperation. African vaccinators would travel to the camp of the local chief, who would send out his unpopular administrative police to order all his subjects to assemble at his homestead for vaccination. Fines were levied for noncompliance, but it is unclear how attendance was noted. The people were not told why they were being vaccinated other than to prevent some disease. This failure to communicate and educate inevitably led to both opposition and indifference. Some anticolonial movements, such as the Mumbo cult in Nyanza Province beginning in 1913, seized on the vaccination campaigns as a vehicle to express their discontent (Ogot 1963, 257). In 1916 when smallpox was spread widely by the returning survivors of the Carrier Corps and the lymph was discovered to be ineffective, those "vaccinated" Africans who contracted smallpox were convinced that vaccination was responsible for spreading disease. Sores sometimes became septic. All these factors led Africans in some areas to oppose vaccination. Nevertheless, the vaccination campaigns appear to have been partially effective among the Kikuyu. In Nyanza Province, however, the disease did not appear to have responded to vaccination campaigns. In fact most of the complaints about the efficacy of the vaccines, as well as the most ardent indigenous opposition, came from that province.

The major reason for the lack of colonial smallpox epidemics was improved famine relief. With the railway, new road network, and increased emergency expenditures, colonial authorities were able to deliver food quickly to famine-afflicted populations, which had the unintended effect of preventing an epidemic. For instance, the first major famine of the colonial period began in 1917 when the long rains fell very heavily, ruining crops. Then in late November the short rains failed completely in central Kenya. The "Famine of Kimotho" began to afflict the Kikuyu and others by early 1918.[14] Food was already short because men had been away in military service. Additionally, a new variety of weed, called *karigei*, had infested many fields. The government quickly began to import large quantities of South African maize and shipped it to the new railhead at Thika. Many Kikuyu, Embu, and Meru went to Thika to purchase the food, while some southern Kikuyu and Kamba traveled to Nairobi. European settlers brought some famine relief food to Fort Hall at the request of the district commissioner (Savage and Munro 1966, 322). Other Kikuyu and Kamba used their traditional famine-relief measures and sought aid from friends in nonfamine areas. Colonial authorities attempted to prevent this kind of population movement. The famine continued through August, and the roads to all government centers were reported lined with corpses. In early 1918 smallpox appeared in Nairobi and southern Kenya Province, but the epidemic was not extensive. In Fort Hall District, smallpox was not reported and informants claimed that only a few people died of starvation, and none due to disease. They credited the food supplies brought by the government for limiting the number of deaths.

Smallpox did not erupt into a massive epidemic following the Famine of Kimotho even though everyone had to go to Thika or an administrative center to receive relief supplies. Colonial officials sold the grain very cheaply, and many Kikuyu bought grain there at least once. Cases of smallpox would have been found there and isolated, and their companions vaccinated. This action would have effectively reduced the incidence of the disease, but not completely as the outbreak in Nairobi showed. Also, as the morbidity rate of smallpox rose in the early colonial period, the level of immunity to the disease would rise in the population as a whole. This higher level of immunity would mean that there would have been fewer susceptible individuals and decrease the possibilities of a widespread epidemic as seen in 1899, when immunity levels were probably much lower.

The epidemiology of smallpox in Kenya underwent a significant change as the result of new economic and demographic patterns during the early colonial period. In the precolonial period the disease was characterized in its endemic state by sporadic cases and minor epidemics, but could erupt into widespread pandemics in the wake of famines. As intercommunication increased with the growth of trade, population movements, and urban centers the incidence of smallpox during the colonial period increased giving rise to many local outbreaks. With the more frequent outbreaks of smallpox in the colonial period, the level of immunity in the population rose and, when combined with a partially effective vaccination campaign, reinforced the already mild nature of smallpox in Africa. In central Kenya, the disease in the early colonial period was usually of a mild, nonfatal variety, except for the major outbreaks in 1916 and 1917 brought by the Carrier Corps. Smallpox, despite more frequent endemic occurrences, appears to have followed its seven- to ten-year epidemic pattern with major epidemics occurring in 1898–1900, 1909/10, and 1916/17. In sum, in most of colonial Kenya, smallpox retained its less virulent characteristics, but the morbidity rate rose and consequently widespread epidemics became very rare.

NOTES

1. An earlier version of this chapter appeared as "Smallpox in Kenya, 1880–1920," *Social Science and Medicine* 13B (1979) (4): 245–250. Revised by the author and published with the permission of Pergamon Journals Ltd.

2. I wish to thank Steven Feierman and David Henige for their comments and the Social Science Research Council and Fulbright Hays Programs for the funds to conduct this research. (*Editors' note*: In addition to the references cited, research on this chapter was based on the following sources: the Great Britain Foreign Office; the Kenya Land Commission testimonies at the Rhodes House Library at Oxford University; Church Mission Society of London archives; the Holy Ghost Fathers Archives, Paris; District and Provincial Political Record Book and Annual Reports for Fort Hall, Nyeri, Ukamba, Nyanza, Kiambu, Dagoretti, Meru, Kisumu, and Kenya; East Africa Protectorate Annual Medical Reports; Coast Province Archives; Kenya National Archives, including Medical Department Files; Nairobi Bacteriological Laboratory Reports; interviews in Kenya with Wakairu Njauini, Kiguro Thuo, Kiberenge Thuo, Wairire Mbogo, Kimani Kamuti, Kamau Kamuti, Thiga Gacanja, Muhia Mundu, Nduati Kaguamba, Ellias Thegeyia Miruri, Mukuhi Karari, Kiuru Kamau, Peter Njane Wamwere, Charles Njanja Kabera, Kiberenge Githua, Jacob Itotia Kung'u, and Kimau Mwangi.

3. For example, in 1977, smallpox remained undetected by medical authorities and was transmitted for five months among a group of forty-six Somali nomads, thirty-seven of whom were susceptible and nineteen of whom became infected.

4. In Kenya Dumbell and Huq found twenty-five instances in which variola major broke out in Kenya, more, in fact, than the African strain. This was probably due to Kenya's large Asian population and the use of Mombasa and Nairobi as the main shipping centers for East Africa. The situation would have been very different in the nineteenth century.

5. Bayoumi shows the importance of population displacement due to famine and war in creating conditions for endemic smallpox to explode into epidemic smallpox.

6. The relationship between famine and smallpox could be shown just as well by studying the reactions to famine of the Giryama and their flight to coastal towns in the 1880s and 1898–1900 (Letterbooks, Church Mission Society of London, 1898–1900).

7. Boyes (1912) states that the Kariara Kikuyu were raiding the people from Kabete, who were coming in search for food. Thuo (see note 2) stated that people from Gatundu and Kabete came there to steal food, hence all people from there were suspect and raided.

8. This was during the 1892 smallpox and rinderpest outbreaks.

9. The Kikuyu also traded heavily with the Maasai in 1892 and 1898 in reported special markets they had for the Maasai.

10. Kenyatta describes another ceremony to deal with epidemics in which the entire community is called to arms with sticks. Everyone then proceeds down to the river that borders every ridge beating the bushes to drive away the evil spirit causing the disease. When the river is reached, all the sticks are thrown into the river and the disease is thus carried away.

11. On the centrality of the Bazaar, the governor wrote in 1914: "The bazaar is the centre of the native trade. To the native generally speaking, Nairobi means the bazaar: and the bazaar exists in virtue of the native trade, the volume of which is enormous. There is a daily influx into it of thousands of natives, of whom the greater number come by road from Kyambu" (Great Britain Colonial Office, Confidential Print Series. CO.879, vol. 114, no. 58. February 3, 1914). Philp noted that not only did thousands move between Nairobi and the reserves, but that in Kenia Province all the outbreaks of smallpox could be traced to Nairobi. Therefore, he believed that Africans should be prevented from detraining at Nairobi, as they all get off and go to the Bazaar to buy clothes and also contract infections (letter from H. R. A. Philp, November 11, 1916).

12. The 1909 epidemic broke out in the village on the Nairobi River, which had a population density of 6,000 people per square mile, and then spread to the Indian Bazaar area. The 1916 epidemic originated in the Bazaar and spread rapidly to the River Road area.

13. The fact that Nairobi acted as a disseminator of disease to the rural areas cannot be doubted, but whether Nairobi was being infected from other rural areas and then passing the disease on is still an unresolved issue.

14. The "Famine of Kimotho" was the local nickname in Fort Hall District for the famine of 1918/19. The name derived from the name of the District Commissioner, who was left-handed. Kimotho is the Kikuyu term for a left-handed person and the District Commissioner's nickname.

FOUR

Industrialization, Rural Poverty, and Tuberculosis in South Africa, 1850–1950[1]

Randall M. Packard

At the beginning of the nineteenth century, tuberculosis was a rare disease in South Africa. By the 1920s, however, it had reached epidemic proportions. As in Europe, the rise in tuberculosis in southern Africa was a product of industrialization. It was, in the words of Rene Dubos, "perhaps the first penalty that capitalistic society had to pay for the ruthless exploitation of labor" (Dubos 1953, 207). Yet in contrast to the European experience, tuberculosis did not descend on the working class of southern Africa as a whole. Rather, it fell heaviest on the black and colored portion of the working class, who, within the peculiar confines of racial capitalism, were the most exploited segment of the labor force. Of all reported cases of tuberculosis in South Africa today, 82 percent are black, 15 percent colored, 1.5 percent Asian, and 1 percent white (Disler and Oliver 1984, 28). Moreover, while tuberculosis in Europe was primarily an urban-based disease, under the system of migrant labor, which became the norm throughout South Africa, and in association with the impoverishment of rural areas, which frequently resulted from industrialization, tuberculosis by midcentury was firmly established in the countryside.

While tuberculosis has been all but eliminated among whites in South Africa, it remains a major cause of morbidity and mortality among blacks. In 1979, the Medical Officer of Cape Town estimated that the incidence of tuberculosis among whites was 18 per 100,000, while that for blacks was a staggering 1,465 per 100,000 (WHO 1983, 120). A prevalence survey conducted in the Transkei in 1977 estimated that 4.3 percent of the population had active tuberculosis, a figure that ranked among the highest in the world. Current official estimates put the prevalence of tuberculosis in the Transkei at 2.3 percent (Fourie et al. 1980, 71).

The high toll that tuberculosis continues to take among blacks, despite concerted efforts by health officials in the region to control the disease, reflects the continued existence among blacks of living and employment conditions that provide an ideal breeding ground for the disease—overcrowded housing, malnutrition, concurrent parasitic diseases, physical and mental stress associated with the workplace, and inadequate general health care. Understanding these conditions, but more importantly the political and economic forces that have created them and continue to foster their existence, is a necessary first step in any realistic attempt to cope with the disease.

This chapter examines the history of tuberculosis in South Africa in an effort to clarify the complex interplay that has occurred between the country's developing political economy—the growth of urban and industrial centers, the development of migrant labor patterns, and the impoverishment of rural areas—and the changing incidence and pathology of tuberculosis among blacks from the middle of the nineteenth through the middle of the twentieth century.[2] It is necessary to stress at the outset, however, both the preliminary nature of the analysis and the difficulties involved in reconstructing the history of disease in Africa. These difficulties arise out of the near absence of reliable statistical data on morbidity and mortality among blacks; from the necessity of employing more indirect data collected from hospital records and medical reports; and from the impressions of medical officials, employers of labor, missionaries, and administrative officers. These types of data clearly do not permit one to achieve the degree of statistical exactitude demanded of epidemiological studies. Yet the data that are available for South Africa are strongly suggestive with regard to certain patterns of interaction between social and economic processes on one hand and changing patterns of disease on the other hand.

THE ETIOLOGY OF TUBERCULOSIS

To understand the causal factors associated with the spread of tuberculosis and the connection between tuberculosis and industrialization in southern Africa overall, one must first understand the etiology of the disease (Comstock 1975; Dormer 1943). While tuberculosis results from a person being infected by tubercle bacilli inhaled into the lungs or, more rarely, ingested into the alimentary canal, infection by itself does not necessarily produce active tuberculosis. In many, if not most cases, an otherwise healthy individual will experience only a slight malaise at the time of infection and may not be aware of having been infected. In such cases the invading bacilli are limited to a primary focus in the lungs and mediastinal glands, which may heal completely, although more frequently the foci fibrose, calcify, or ossify. When the infection is contained to these primary foci, the host experiences little in the way of physical symptoms.

If the primary complex does not heal, however, the disease may become progressive, spreading in the lungs and through the lymphatic channels to the systemic circulation to set up new foci in other parts of the body. If this process goes unchecked, the patient gets what is known as "progressive primary disease," an acute infection common to urban blacks with tuberculosis, and frequently ending in death if untreated.

Not all cases in which the infection spreads beyond the primary complex become progressive. In some cases, the disease will heal and result in a calcified primary complex and a few unidentifiable scars in other organs as a result of healing of the disseminated foci. Such individuals exhibit no clinical symptoms of active disease but react positively to tuberculin testing. It is not uncommon to find over 90 percent of the adult black population of the South African Homelands tuberculin-positive.

Yet this healing is but a remission. Under certain conditions, associated primarily with stress and malnutrition, the primary complex within such individuals becomes unstable and begins to break down. When this occurs, the disease once again becomes active, leading to long-term and often chronic disability which, if left untreated, can cause the host to die.

In short, infection does not necessarily lead to active disease. The course that the infection follows—regardless of whether a person develops symptoms, the length of the incubation period, and the speed at which the disease progresses—is determined by the level of host resistance, which, in turn, is shaped by both biological and environmental factors.

Biologically, the ability of a host to resist the activation of infection is determined by heredity. Certain individuals are born with a higher genetic susceptibility to tuberculosis infection. This fact should not be confused with the now-discredited theory of racial susceptibility, which asserted that certain races, and especially blacks, exhibited a high, racially based, vulnerability to tuberculosis. This vulnerability was said to account for the high rate of primary progressive tuberculosis and tuberculosis mortality among urban blacks in South Africa at the beginning of the century (Packard 1990). In actual fact, this vulnerability was due in large measure to the absence of any experience with tuberculosis in childhood. This inexperience meant that the more genetically susceptible members of the urban black population had not been killed off in childhood by the disease. In epidemiological terms, urban blacks at the beginning of the century represented an "unseasoned" population with regard to tuberculosis and thus experienced high rates of morbidity and mortality from the disease.

Environmental factors play an equally important role in determining the ability of a host to contain an initial tuberculosis infection or prevent a reactivation of the disease, and the experience of urban blacks in South Africa with the disease was as much a product of the conditions under which they were forced to live as of their lack of experience with the disease. Perhaps the most important of these conditions was malnutrition. While the link between malnutrition and disease has come under serious scrutiny of late (Aaby et al. 1983), there is strong evidence that deficiencies in both the quantity and quality of host nutrition reduces the ability of the host to contain tubercular infections (Dubos 1959). Stress, both physical and mental, has also been shown to reduce host resistance to tubercular infections. So, too, a number of studies suggest that the concurrence of other infections may reduce host resistance and lead to the breakdown of tissues and a reactivation of disease in those previously infected.

To understand the epidemiology of tuberculosis among blacks in South Africa and its relationship to industrialization, therefore, one must look at two sets of factors: those that contributed to the spread of infection among the black population and those that reduced black resistance to infection and thus their ability to control the effects of tuberculosis.

PREINDUSTRIAL SOCIETY AND DISEASE

Evidence for the presence or absence of tuberculosis among the black population of South Africa prior to the middle of the nineteenth century is extremely limited in both quantity and quality. There were very few trained Western medical professionals within the region, and those that visited or settled there had very little experience in treating nonwhites and almost none with black Africans. Moreover, the reliability of their observations must be questioned, given the limited nature of medical knowledge concerning the causes and pathology of tuberculosis and of the technology available for diagnosing the disease.

Despite these limitations, it is significant that the reports of early medical and nonmedical observers are nearly unanimous in asserting that tuberculosis or "consumption," as it was then called, was almost unknown among blacks prior to the 1860s.

While references to consumption among whites, "coloreds," and Khoisan peoples appear as early as the eighteenth century, the first published reference to consumption, rightly or wrongly diagnosed, among blacks in South Africa occurs in J. W. D. Moodie's *Ten Years in South Africa 1820–1830*. Subsequent literary references up through the 1850s indicate that the disease, while present among blacks, was rare, indeed (South Africa, Union of, Tuberculosis Commission 1914, 25).

The early absence of tuberculosis among blacks in South Africa was confirmed by medical men and missionaries who lived in various districts of the Cape Colony during the second half of the nineteenth century and whose opinion as to the prevalence of tuberculosis among blacks was solicited by the 1914 Tuberculosis Commission. For example, Archdeacon Turpin, describing his experience with the disease in Grahamstown, stated that when he came to this country in 1857 "there were very few cases among the natives, and these only occurred among young 'School Kaffirs.' It was not until fifteen or twenty-five years ago [i.e., the 1880s] that he ever saw the disease among raw natives, after which it became prominent" (p. 29). Dr. R. G. Lamb, District Surgeon at Uitenhage, expressed the opinion that when he began his work in 1874 there was no tuberculosis there: "It was the rarest thing to come across a case of tuberculosis among the Natives" (p. 30). Similarly, Dr. W. A. Soga of Elliotdale wrote, "My own impression of twenty years' work among them [blacks] is that phthisis is a new disease among them." By and large the cases that were seen by these observers occurred among blacks attending mission schools or working for Europeans (McVicar 1908, 20).

A similar picture emerges from early Natal records. In the areas along the coast with the longest history of European settlement, tuberculosis appears to have become initially established during the 1860s though the Zulu claimed to have known the disease for a long time, it having perhaps been introduced by early European traders and then spread in the densely settled regiment barracks established by the Zulu king Shaka and his successors. On the other hand, information provided by Europeans living in the interior of Natal suggests that tuberculosis was a relatively rare disease among blacks as late as the 1880s. Dr. E. Niemeyer of Utrecht, The Netherlands, reported that tubercular disease was originally unknown among the Zulus and added that while vaccinating some 13,000 Zulus in 1892 he had not seen a single case of tuberculosis (McVicar 1908, 199).

As one moves further into the interior the evidence indicates that even as late as the 1890s tuberculosis was rarely, if ever, seen among blacks, reinforcing the picture presented in Cape and Natal records of a disease whose prevalence was related to the extent of European contact. The district surgeon at Lydenburg in the eastern Transvaal reported in 1904 having seen only a few cases, and Dr. B. O. Kellner of Bloemfontein in the Orange River Colony reported in the same year that the disease was until recently unknown among blacks (McVicar 1908, 198). Finally Dr. Neil McVicar claimed to have not seen a single case of tuberculosis among blacks in the Shire Highlands of Malawi during his four years of work there between 1896 and 1900 (McVicar 1908, 201).

The evidence that exists, therefore, points strongly to the conclusion that tuberculosis was either unknown or a rare occurrence among blacks in South Africa prior to European settlement or, perhaps more precisely, at the time of European settlement, and that the extent of the disease was closely related to the length of European contact. The evidence is, of course, open to question, given the limited nature of medical knowledge and technology and the uneven distribution of medical practitioners. Still, the unanimity of opinion and the clear contrast between the picture of an early low prevalence with that of an epidemic found in similar records from the 1870s onward lend a certain credence to the albeit subjective opinion of earlier observers. Thus the 1914 Commission concluded, "the belief in its comparatively recent appearance and especially in its recent increasing prevalence is too widely held to be disregarded" (p. 35). It is also worth noting in this regard, that the southern Africa data correspond to that collected elsewhere in Africa in pointing to a relatively recent introduction of tuberculosis or at least to a relatively low prevalence of this disease prior to European settlement (Collins 1982, 789).

If blacks were relatively free from tuberculosis in the 1850s and 1860s, the disease had reached epidemic proportions among those blacks living in the major urban centers of South Africa by the turn of the century and had begun to make inroads among blacks living in rural areas. While statistical data remain of questionable reliability during this period, they do give an impression of the dimensions of this epidemic.

Health records from the Cape Colony, where notification of all forms of tuberculosis became mandatory in 1904, reveal that the mortality rate from tuberculosis for blacks living in the major towns of the Colony was 6.8 per 1,000 in 1904 and 6.22 per 1,000 in 1911. In comparison, the European rates for these two years was 1.55 and 1.05 per 1,000, respectively (Tuberculosis Commission 1914, 54). The mortality rate for blacks living in the Ndabeni Native Location outside of Cape Town from 1915 to 1918 was 5. 31 per 1,000 while that for New Brighton outside of Port Elizabeth for the same period was 6.29 per 1,000 (Allan 1924, 10). Even higher rates were reported for the native locations of Uitenhage (11 per 1,000) in 1911 and King Williamstown (9.7 per 1,000) in 1915 (Laidler 1938, 659).

It must be noted that, given the migrant nature of black workers and the frequently noted fact that blacks who became ill in urban areas frequently returned home to seek treatment, blacks who contracted tuberculosis and subsequently died from the disease often did not appear in urban mortality figures. We may, therefore, assume that even the relatively high rates of mortality noted above underestimate the actual mortality rate experienced by blacks living in urban areas, although the magnitude of the difference is unknowable.

Statistics from the Transvaal reflect a similarly high mortality rate among urban blacks, particularly in the towns of the Witwatersrand, where the mining industry contributed significantly to the overall incidence of tuberculosis among blacks. For these communities, the mortality rate from tuberculosis per 1,000 persons in 1903/04 was 3.22 among blacks and 1.44 among whites. In 1911, the black rate had risen to 5.88, while the white rate was 1.70. Again the black rate is certainly too low (Tuberculosis Commission 1914, 67). The mining industry's practice of repatriating any worker who became ill meant that a large number of blacks did not appear on the mortality lists. In the late 1920s when Dr. Peter Allan investigated the fate of repatriated mineworkers with tuberculosis, he found that between 50 and 60 percent had died within two years of repatriation (South African Institute of Medical Research [SAIMR] 1932, 240). Thus, the actual mortality rate for blacks contracting tuberculosis in the mines in 1912 was probably closer to Gorgas's calculation of total wastage (deaths plus repatriations) from tuberculosis 10.87 per 1,000 than to the official mortality figure of 6.02 per 1,000 (Gorgas 1914, 36).

While the mortality figures for urban areas are of questionable reliability, those for rural areas are of almost no value statistically during the first two decades of the century. As the 1914 Tuberculosis Commission Report noted, even in the case of Europeans, it is likely that only two-thirds to three-quarters of the deaths were recorded, and most of those were uncertified (p. 59). The percentage of nonrecorded deaths was undoubtedly much greater among rural blacks. Nonetheless, one gets the impression from the reports of European physicians, missionaries, and administrators working in the so-called native Territories that tuberculosis, while not as extensive as amongst urban blacks, was on the rise during this period, and that the rise corresponded to increases in black involvement in various aspects of European society and most importantly, involvement in the expanding capitalist economy of white South Africa.

EUROPEAN SETTLEMENT AND THE SPREAD OF TUBERCULOSIS IN SOUTH AFRICA

The fact that tuberculosis occurred earliest among blacks living in close association with white settlement areas—in towns, ports, prisons, and mission stations—and fairly late among those living in more distant rural areas suggests that the rising epidemic of tuberculosis among blacks resulted at least in part from their contact with Europeans. This was certainly the opinion of most medical professionals in South Africa at the time; and there can be little doubt that while there were other causal factors involved in the rising tide of tuberculosis, the coming of European settlers during the nineteenth century, and especially during the last quarter of the century, greatly increased the pool of infected individuals in South Africa and thus the risk of infection for native-born whites and blacks.

Given the high levels of tubercular infection that existed in Europe during the nineteenth century, it is reasonable to assume that a significant number, if not all immigrants, carried with them tubercular infections (Dubos 1953, 96; McVicar 1908, 205). Although it is equally probable that, at least initially, most of these settlers showed no symptoms of the disease. They were thus little threat to the black populations with whom they subsequently came in contact. For those settlers who made a successful start and subsequently were able to prosper in their new life at the Cape and Natal, the sunny temperate climate of South Africa proved beneficial, and they remained free of disease and did not become sources of infection to others. However, there were a good many immigrants who were less fortunate and who found life in Africa difficult. In this category were the large numbers of East Europeans who flocked to the Rand during the 1890s. Unable to make a reasonable living, forced to live on the margins of white society, and unable to properly house or feed themselves and their families, these less fortunate settlers often suffered a reactivation of their tubercular infections and became open sources of infection (Van Onselen 1983, 74–75).

Thus, under any circumstances a certain proportion of the immigrant white population was likely to develop tuberculosis and become potential sources of infection to non-Europeans as well as to other whites. Even members of the British Army serving in South Africa during the first half of the century experienced a mortality rate from tuberculosis of 2.4 per 1,000 (McVicar 1908, 205).

This apparently "natural" pool of European-borne infection was increased dramatically during the last quarter of the nineteenth century by the immigration of hundreds of Europeans, primarily from England, who were suffering from tuberculosis and who came to South Africa because its climate was reputed to be beneficial for tuberculosis. At the time, the threat that these tuberculosis cases represented for the native-born white and black populations of South Africa was not appreciated. This was, in part, because the infectious nature of tuberculosis was discovered only in 1884 and even then was not widely accepted. Of equal importance, however, was the fact that there was no mandatory registration of deaths in the Cape Colony or elsewhere in South Africa until 1895. There was thus no way to accurately assess the force of tuberculosis on mortality rates. Consequently, medical journals of the Cape Colony extolled the virtues of various health resorts for consumptives within the Colony, and particularly in the drier areas of the Karoo, in towns such as Burgersdorp, Cradock, and Beaufort West, to which consumptives from Europe had been coming since around 1880 (McVicar 1908, 204–205; Tuberculosis Commission 1914).

Unaware of the potential consequences of the immigration of tuberculosis, town officials in the Cape Colony made no effort to curtail the spread of infection among the towns' noninfected inhabitants. Thus the Chairman of the 1914 Tuberculosis Commission remembered seeing at Beaufort West during the early 1890s "the consumptives at the chief hotel, and of whom there were a number, sitting all day on the stoop, expectorating into an adjacent open water furrow which was the only source of water supply of many dwellings and of the extensive coloured location just below" (Tuberculosis Commission 1914, 36).

The spread of infection by immigrant consumptives in Cradock is clearly described in the testimony of Dr. J. McCall Fehrsen to the 1914 Commission. He noted that when he first began practice in the town in 1874:

> There were no cases of tuberculosis among the indigenous white population, and there were few scattered cases among the Hottentot and Bastard races in the town location. At the time, consumptives began coming pretty frequently from England, travelling up to Cradock by coach. There were about six such cases when he arrived, but twenty years later there was always an average of thirty or forty in the town and the disease had also increased enormously among the coloured population of the location.

He remembered at least one instance in which the disease had been spread to members of the family of a farmer giving shelter to such consumptive immigrants (Tuberculosis Commission 1914, 28). A good number of male immigrant consumptives, in fact, made a living by serving as tutors for the children of local European farmers, while some women found employment as governesses, thereby becoming sources of infection within these families (Russell 1906, 214). Infection was also spread among the colored and black residents of the towns through the common practice of servants taking leftover food from their consumptive employers and using it to feed their own families.

With the establishment of compulsory death registrations, medical authorities in the colony came to recognize the high toll that tuberculosis was taking among both the native-born white and black populations of these resort towns. Writing in the Annual Report for 1905, the Medical Officer of Health for the Cape Colony noted (Medical Officer, Cape Colony 1906, 2):

> It is a significant fact that the centers in the Colony, such as Beaufort West, which we formerly knew to be free from disease and which, owing to their peculiarly favourable climatic conditions, have been chosen as health resorts by immigrant consumptives, should at the present day be the most severely affected by the disease, its incidence falling not only on the native but also on the European portion of the population.

The death rate among Africans and coloreds in Beaufort West in 1896, the first full year of registration, was 8.7 per 1,000. By 1903 it had reached 18.5 per 1,000, while the average between 1903 and 1906 was 14.3 per 1,000 (Medical Officer, Cape Colony 1906, 2). While some of this increase can be attributed to increased compliance with registration regulations, the observations of medical men at the time leave little doubt that a good part of the increase was caused by an actual rise in the tuberculosis death rate.

THE GROWTH OF TOWNS AND THE SPREAD OF TUBERCULOSIS

The rapid growth of urban centers following the mineral discoveries of the 1870s and 1880s increased opportunities for the transmission of infection between European immigrants and blacks. Until the early 1870s South Africa was primarily an agrarian society, and there were no more than twenty towns with a population exceeding 1,000. The major towns included the ports and commercial centers of Cape Town, Durban, East London, and Port Elizabeth and the administrative centers of Pietermaritzburg, Pretoria, and Bloemfontein. Scattered throughout the hinterland were isolated smaller towns and hamlets such as Worcester and Uitenhage in the Cape and Ermelo and Lydenburg in the Transvaal. While African locations were established in a few towns such as Uitenhage (1836) and Grahamstown (1856) prior to 1870, the black population of South African towns was relatively small. In fact, the Transvaal Volksraad decreed in 1844 that no African could settle near a town without official permission (Welsh 1971, 72).

By 1880, however, there were nearly 22,000 blacks working on the diamond fields at Kimberley and by 1899 roughly 97,000 Africans working on the gold mines of the Witwatersrand (Marks and Rathbone 1982, 12). The latter population had grown to over 200,000 by 1910, eliminating, for the moment, any hope that the Transvaal whites had of keeping blacks out of urban areas. The black population of all the major towns and cities swelled during World War I as a result of wartime demands for labor and the consequences of restrictions on land usage by rural blacks stemming from the Native Land Act of 1913.

During the early years of urban growth, there were few restrictions on the movements of Africans and coloreds within the major towns of the Cape Colony, with the exception of Kimberley, where closed compounds for African workers were established between 1882 and 1886. This lack of restrictions facilitated contact and social intercourse between the members of different racial groups, and especially among the working classes, to a degree that was not permitted later in the century (Swanson 1979, 300; Van Onselen 1983, 39; Welsh 1971, 174). In addition, the mines brought black workers into close contact with their white counterparts. During the early years of the gold-mining industry nearly all of these white miners came from Cornwall and, like other Europeans of the day, were infected with tuberculosis. Under mining conditions and in association with silicosis their infections were reactivated, making the white miner an early source of infection for black mine workers (Burke and Richardson 1978, 147–171).

The relatively open nature of social relations no doubt contributed to the spread of tuberculosis between racial groups and specifically to the infection of newly arrived blacks by whites and coloreds. Ironically, when white municipal councils began to segregate urban housing, they did so, in part, to protect the white population from what they saw as the more disease-prone black population. It could be argued, however, that in terms of disease blacks had more to fear from integration than did whites.

While there can be little doubt that the dramatic rise in tuberculosis among South African blacks during the last quarter of the nineteenth century and beginning of the twentieth century can be traced initially to increased contact with tubercular whites, this contact alone does not explain the epidemic that occurred. Of equal, if not greater, importance were the conditions under which blacks lived and worked within the urban centers where contact occurred. These conditions were marked by extreme overcrowding, which facilitated the spread of tuberculosis among the urban black population, inadequate diets, lack of sanitation, and work-related physical and mental stress, which lowered black resistance to infection and produced a highly susceptible black population. In addition, restrictions on urban residence and employment meant that black workers were mostly temporary sojourners in the urban areas and that there was a constant flow of workers, and thus of infection, back and forth between the workplace and the rural areas from which the workers came.

TOWNS, MINES, AND TUBERCULOSIS

The squalid housing conditions under which most black workers lived in the growing urban centers of South Africa during the 1890s and early twentieth century have been described elsewhere. It need only be noted here that the majority of blacks, living on inadequate wages and faced with the unwillingness of employers and urban authorities to provide sufficient housing, were forced to live in extremely unhealthy conditions marked by overcrowding and that these conditions contributed to the spread of tuberculosis as well as other diseases (Bonner 1982; Koch 1983; Swanson 1979; Van Onselen 1983). As the 1914 Tuberculosis Commission concluded with regard to black housing, "Altogether one could hardly imagine more suitable conditions for the spread of tuberculosis" (p. 126).

The housing provided for black workers in the mining compounds of the Rand and Kimberley, while generally of better quality than that found in the municipal locations, was also marked by serious overcrowding. At Kimberley during the early years of compound construction, the authorized space per inhabitant in a barrack was 600 cubic feet and the minimum space required for good health was estimated to be 330 cubic feet. However, the actual space was often much less and was identified as a primary cause of the extraordinary high mortality rates from disease experienced by black workers in the compounds (Turrell 1982*a*,*b*, 64). By 1913, when members of the Tuberculosis Commission visited the DeBeers Diamond Mines at Kimberley, the situation had apparently not improved despite claims to the contrary by compound managers. The Commission noted that there were more inmates than bunks in the barracks they visited, "so that many had to sleep on the floor or else outside in the open" (Tuberculosis Commission 1914, 151). At the Jagersfontein Diamond Mine in the Orange Free State, the Commission found that the compounds were in extremely bad condition (p. 169):

> A large portion of the boys have to sleep outside in the yards, but even then they could not accommodate all of the boys, but for the fact that there are

always a third or a half, as the case may be, out on shift. Thus day and night they are always overcrowded.

The official capacity of the mine compound was about 1,600, whereas the actual number of workers housed was 3,900. The mine managers noted that the overcrowding of the mine compound resulted from the commencement of underground mining following the exhaustion of surface deposits in 1910. As an underground mine, Jagersfontein was subject to labor regulations that reduced the length of shifts from twelve to eight hours. In order to maintain production, the mine owners simply hired more workers so that they could run three shifts of eight hours instead of two of twelve hours each. This resulted in a one-third increase in the work force without any increase in compound space (p. 168). There was a significant jump in the incidence of tuberculosis, pneumonia, and other respiratory diseases following these changes. While part of the increase may have been due to the changed nature of work, it was no doubt also related to overcrowding (p. 75).

In regard to the gold mines of the Rand, the Commission report noted that the requirement of 200 cubic feet per inhabitant, while generally adhered to, was inadequate, and that the space should be increased to 300 cubic feet. The Gorgas Report made a similar recommendation in the same year (Tuberculosis Commission 1914, 211). Yet even this was often inadequate, for as Cartwright notes, cubic airspace per occupant measurements were a product of a pre-bacteria-era theory of contagion and were of little relevance when, as was the case with black miners, the occupants slept in close proximity to one another in stacked bunks, or huddled together for warmth on cold nights because the barracks were inadequately heated (Cartwright 1971, 21).

While overcrowding and inadequate ventilation in the compounds played a significant role in the dissemination of tubercular infection among black miners on the Rand, the conditions in the mine itself also played an important role, especially after 1910 when axial water-fed drills began replacing dry reciprocating drills. The change was designed to cut down on atmospheric dust and thus the incidence of silicosis, which at the time was a major killer of white mine workers although it was rarely seen among blacks. The moist spray from the drills, however, facilitated the dissemination of tubercule bacilli in the mines and increased the incidence of tuberculosis among both black and white mine workers (SAIMR 1932, 74). A review of the history of silicosis on the Rand presented to an International Labor Organization (ILO)-organized conference on silicosis in 1930 noted that there had been a change in the type of silicosis present in South Africa between 1900 and 1930 "viz. an increasingly early tuberculosis infection became observed as the volume of water underground increased, turning simple into infective secondary cases of miners' phthisis" (Burke and Richardson 1978, 161; Irvine et al. 1930, 183). Thus measures designed primarily to reduce disease among the white labor force contributed to the prevalence of tuberculosis among both the black and white labor force.

While inadequate housing, overcrowding, and atmospheric conditions in the mines encouraged the dissemination of tubercular infections among black workers, improper diets and physical stress lowered black resistance to infection and thereby contributed to the high levels of active disease among urban blacks during the first decades of this century.

Changes in diet associated with urban employment was perhaps the most important condition that lowered black resistance to tuberculosis during the first decades of this century. While little research has been done on the nature of urban black diets at the beginning of the century, there appears to have been a noticeable shift in the types of food consumed by urban blacks in comparison with their rural counterparts. The variety of vegetables which were a common feature of most rural diets at the end of the nineteenth century was more limited in the diets of city-dwellers. Fresh fruits and vegetables, peddled by black women in the locations, were seen by many blacks living on limited food budgets, and especially those at the lower end of the black economic spectrum, as expensive luxury items (Phillips 1938, 120). While some early locations provided garden plots on which blacks could grow their own vegetables, these plots were converted to house plots as the locations became increasingly crowded (Bonner 1982, 130; Phillips 1930, 109–110).

Urban blacks also tended to substitute relatively nonnutritious white bread (containing bleached flour) in place of maize and other grains. In addition, coffee (which was relatively cheap) frequently replaced milk (which was expensive), especially among the poorest urban households, as a staple beverage (Phillips 1938, 33–41; Tuberculosis Commission 1914, 130). The corresponding loss of both animal protein and vitamins may well have lowered black resistance to tuberculosis infections. Since, as Dubos (1957) notes, "Inadequacies in protein and ascorbic acid retard healing and thereby become one of the determinants of the exudative type of disease through their interference with the production of fibrotic tissue." While the extent of these deficiencies is impossible to measure, given the absence of additional nutritional and medical data on locations, malnutrition, and especially scurvy, was a common phenomenon among blacks working on the land and in the diamond mines at Kimberley, as well as on the mines in Southern Rhodesia (Van Onselen 1976*a*,*b*) during the early years of this century.

Black mine workers in Kimberley were not provided with food provisions by the mining company even after the creation of closed compounds, but were permitted to purchase their own provisions from company stores, which, in turn, were supplied by local merchants. This pattern established by the Labor Wage Regulation Act of 1887 was the result of a compromise between the mine owners' desire for closed compounds and the interests of local merchants who feared that closed compounds would reduce their market as the mines developed their own sources of food supplies to feed their workers (Turrell 1982*b*, 62–64).

The average cost of food for a black miner at Kimberley was estimated to be one shilling per day. This represented, at the time, roughly one-third of a black worker's wages and many mine workers spent less than this, choosing to reduce their consumption in order to save money for other uses. The unwillingness of mine workers to allocate income for food is indicated by the failure of an attempt by the superintendent of compounds to offer "well-cooked meat-meals" for six pence. The compound restaurants had to be closed down for lack of patrons (Tuberculosis Commission 1914, 151).

The impact of reducing outlays for food on the health of miners is difficult to determine without more information on the composition of diets and on the cost of various items in the diets. However, there does appear to be a correlation between the unwillingness of certain groups of workers to allocate money for food and the incidence of scurvy. Thus the 1914 Tuberculosis Commission Report indicates that the three groups that were "meanest" in regard to purchasing food supplies—blacks from Bechuanaland, Basutoland, and the Cape Province—were also the three groups with the highest incidence of scurvy. Moreover, this overall incidence of scurvy amongst underground workers in the DeBeers mines was 478 per 100,000, while that for the surface workers, who were paid less, was 510 per 100,000 between 1903 and 1912. The higher incidence of the disease among surface workers almost certainly reflects their lower wages and a corresponding reduction in their food consumption (Tuberculosis Commission 1914, 157, 164).

The diets of black gold miners were more regularized than that of workers on the diamond mines of Kimberley, since food rations were supplied by the mines. The diets of gold miners were not, however, necessarily more nutritious. Dr. William Gorgas, who was invited to advise the Chamber of Mines on sanitation measures in the face of extremely high mortality rates among black workers, criticized the standard food ration provided to the workers (Cartwright 1971, 33):

> I have never seen so large a portion of the ration supplied by one article as is here supplied by mealie meal. The two chief components of the daily ration are 2 lb. of mealie meal and 6.85 oz. of meat. This I think a great deal too large a portion of carbohydrates for men doing the hard manual labour that the natives do.

The near absence of fresh fruits and vegetables in the diet accounted for an extremely high incidence of scurvy among black miners, and as noted above, reduced resistance to tuberculosis. While this deficiency was largely corrected following Gorgas's report, the diet remained heavily dependent on cereal protein as noted by Gorgas's protegé, Dr. A. J. Orenstein, who was engaged on a permanent basis as Superintendent of Sanitation by the Chamber in 1915. Orenstein noted in 1923 that "The value of cereal protein for restoring tissue loss in the human body is only a fraction of milk protein, and mealie protein . . . is a rather poor protein for restoring tissue waste" (Orenstein 1923, 131). The composition of the mine diet was further criticized in 1932 by the South African Institute of Medical Research's report on tuberculosis among black mine workers (p. 71) for lacking adequate levels of vitamin A. Like vitamin C, low levels of vitamin A in diets has been correlated with the development of tuberculosis (Getz 1951, 681).

Aside from the nutritional content of the standard mine ration, the distribution of food within the mines was uneven and created additional nutritional problems. In order to prevent the loss of shift time, it was common practice to serve only one big meal a day following a worker's shift, supplemented by a smaller meal, which frequently consisted of no more than coffee or cocoa served prior to the shift and bread issued on some mines to be consumed during the shift (SAIMR 1932, 70–71). This meant that much of the work being done by mine workers was being performed on a near-empty stomach. Thus even where the general diet was adequate, its distribution meant that the high energy demands of mine work, especially toward the end of the shift, were not being adequately met, causing physical stress. In addition, favoritism on the part of "compound police-boys" who supervised the distribution of food meant that "certain boys—probably weakly ones who most required nourishment and are least able to obtain it from outside sources—go without their full ration" (Tuberculosis Commission 1914, 212).

Along with dietary deficiencies, working conditions affected levels of resistance to tuberculosis among black workers. The impact of working conditions on the resistance level of black workers in the townships is difficult to assess, since the tasks performed by them were highly varied. We have a much clearer picture of the relationship between work and health among mine workers at Kimberley and on the Rand.

Aside from the generally arduous nature of mine work, often carried out in excessive heat and humidity, simply getting to the mine face on the Rand could be a taxing experience (SAIMR 1932, 73):

> The transportation of a large number of natives underground takes a considerable time, and a certain number may have to wait an hour or even two before they can enter the case which will carry them down. On a cold winter's morning this waiting, which is often done in the open, or practically in the open, may make a serious inroad into the native's vitality, which if one takes into account a long walk on the surface and perhaps a climb underground, may *in toto* represent a serious drain on his energy, so that he may reach his work already in a tired condition.

Returning from the shift created additional hardships. The clothes of the miners completing a shift were frequently drenched with perspiration and from the heavy use of water in the drilling process. There were no changing rooms available for black miners prior to 1920, but only shelters, and these only from 1911 (Katz 1980, 202). The miners, therefore, had to proceed to the compound without an opportunity to change or wash off. During the winter months this could easily result in a severe chill. Even as late as 1932, by which time the mines had provided changing rooms to reduce the effects of exposure, the Tuberculosis Committee noted that "there has not been an equal appreciation of the risk of chill run by natives during the time spent (which may be an hour or more) after knocking off work in a hot, damp place, in waiting to be hauled up to the surface" (SAIMR 1932, 73):

> The waiting places are near the down-casts are comparatively cool and dry. The contrast between one's temperature sensations in the slow-moving air of most working places and the gales blowing down the underground main roads must be experienced to be appreciated.

The combination of exhaustion, hunger, and chill could not help but contribute to the ill health of all but the most robust worker. The exact relationship between these conditions and susceptibility to tuberculosis is unclear; however, the 1932 report suggested that these conditions contributed to an annual spring "flare-up" of influenza, which, in turn, "lit up" existing tubercular lesions, producing an annual rise in tuberculosis losses during the summer months (SAIMR 1932, 135).

The importance of silica dust and of silicosis in predisposing mine workers to tuberculosis has been frequently noted, and there can be little doubt that silicosis contributed to the overall incidence of tuberculosis among black mine workers. Yet mine statistics from the early 1930s on the incidence of pulmonary tuberculosis among black mine workers with various years of service reveal that the highest incidence (58 percent in one mine) occurred among miners who were in their first year of service and who showed no signs of silicosis. The incidence dropped dramatically from 20 per 1,000 during the first year to under 5 per 1,000 by the second year and remained relatively low until the fifth year, when it began to climb again, the rise being attributable in large measure to the complicating effect of silicosis resulting from long-term exposure to mining conditions (SAIMR 1932, 142). Thus silicosis, while contributing to the overall incidence of tuberculosis in the mines, was only one of a number of mine conditions that contributed to the high incidence of tuberculosis among black miners during the early decades of this century.

The high toll that tuberculosis took among black miners in their first year of service, in fact, suggests that the initial exposure to the combination of adverse factors described above, overwhelmed whatever natural resistance the new recruit brought to the mines and resulted in either a reactivation of existing tubercular lesions or an inability to localize a new infection acquired in the mines. Yet this conclusion raises an interesting problem. Why were mine workers who survived the first year, or who were on subsequent contracts, able to resist the combination of adverse factors better than the new recruit? The 1932 Tuberculosis Committee attributed this increased resistance to physical acclimatization, without really defining what this process entailed, especially with regards to the reengagement worker. One would assume that if the conditions of housing, diet, and working conditions described above were deleterious to the health of miners, they would affect all miners equally. Yet this may not have been the case. To begin with, as noted above, resistance or susceptibility to tuberculosis is to a certain degree hereditary. There are individuals who are biologically more susceptible to the disease and less able to resist infection. Such individuals would likely have succumbed to the disease during their first year of service. Those who survived their first year of exposure made up a population which was then biologically more resistant, or "seasoned."

Yet the experienced mine worker may not simply have been biologically more resistant, he may also have learned skills of survival which lowered his vulnerability. He may have learned how to increase his energy by rationing bread during his shift, by saving food from the big meal to eat before the next shift, or by allocating money to supplement his diet with food purchased outside the compounds. He may also have learned when to leave the shaft face in order to reduce waiting time in the shaft and thus exposure to drafts. In these and other ways, for which a great deal more research on the experiences of mine workers is necessary, the experienced mine worker may have simply learned to survive on the mines. A knowledge, however, which could not protect him from repeated exposure to silica dust.

In summary, the creation of large-scale urban centers at the end of the nineteenth century and beginning of the twentieth century and the massive movement of blacks to these centers exposed the black workers to conditions that facilitated the spread of infection and reduced their ability to control infection. Together, these conditions led to the tuberculosis epidemic among blacks living in the towns and labor centers of South Africa described above.

MIGRANT LABOR, RURAL POVERTY, AND THE SPREAD OF TUBERCULOSIS

While an increasingly permanent urban black population began to emerge in South Africa following World War I and was well established by the 1940s, blacks were often temporary sojourners who out of choice or necessity moved back and forth between their rural homesteads and the urban locations and mines. This migratory pattern, which benefited the employers of labor by reducing their labor costs, together with the desire of black workers to seek treatment at home and the mining industry's practice repatriating all miners found to have contracted tuberculosis, meant that the urban-based tuberculosis epidemic eventually spread to the rural areas from which the black workers came.

While urban locations and missions undoubtedly produced a considerable number of tubercular migrants, it was the mines which were seen by medical authorities and administrators as the primary producer of infected migrants during the first two decades of this century.[3] Thus the Public Health Report for the Cape Colony for 1906 notes, "Noticeable, and singularly coinciding with the figures given us from Johannesburg, is the general testimony of district surgeons that the disease is mainly spread by Natives returning from the mines" (Medical Officer, Cape Colony 1907, 311). An even stronger claim concerning the role of returning mine workers was made by Dr. Grant Millar, District Surgeon in Pondoland in 1908 (Millar 1908, 380):

> Pondoland is one of the chief recruiting fields for the gold mines of the Transvaal . . . and I have no doubt that this is the primary cause of tuberculosis amongst the Pondo.
>
> A young man goes up from this district to work in the mines at Johannesburg. After working there for some six months or a year—where it must be remembered that conditions of life are totally different to what he has been accustomed to . . . he happens to contract phthisis, as likely as not from a fellow worker, after which he returns home to Pondoland where the manner of living is preeminently calculated to favour the spread of the disease. . . . Time and again one native returned from the mines infects almost the entire occupants of a hut previously quite healthy.

While there is general agreement that returned mine workers played an important role in the spread of tuberculosis in rural areas of South Africa, the rapidity with which the disease spread, once introduced into rural areas, varied considerably from area to area and within a single area over time. Thus, in contrast to the Pondoland experience, tuberculosis in Portuguese East Africa, Swaziland, and Basutoland spread slowly at first, emerging as a serious medical problem only in the late 1920s and early 1930s (SAIMR 1932, 41–42, 91–102). Conversely, tuberculosis was very extensive among Zulus at Eshowe in Natal by the beginning of the century, with as many as five cases per day being seen at the Native dispensary in 1914, but had become much less frequent by the early 1920s (Allan 1924, 19).

While the reasons for these variations are both diverse and difficult to sort out, the rate at which the disease spread in the rural areas of southern Africa was clearly affected by the same two sets of factors that determined its spread in urban areas—conditions that increased opportunities for infection and factors that lowered the ability of the host population to cope with infection.

Looking first at the factors affecting the rate of infection, the extent of a society's involvement in migrant labor played a significant role in determining the speed with which tuberculosis spread among its members. Thus, the relatively low rate at which tuberculosis spread in Zululand, Swaziland, and Basutoland in the 1910s and 1920s, in contrast to its more rapid spread in the Transkei and Ciskei during the same period, resulted in part from the more extensive involvement of men and women from the latter territories in migrant labor. Similarly, the rise in tuberculosis among the Basuto in the 1930s reflects, at least in part, their increased involvement in migrant labor at that time. The proportion of men and women absentees to the total population in Basutoland jumped from 8.7 percent in 1921 to 15.3 percent in 1936 (Murray 1981, 4). While the rising incidence of tuberculosis in Swaziland during this same period does not appear to correspond to any increase in Swazi involvement in labor migration, regional variations in the incidence of tuberculosis within Swaziland did reflect different levels of participation in mining. The 1931 Annual Medical Report for Swaziland indicates that a larger number of reported cases of tuberculosis and syphilis occurred in the southern areas of the country than in the central and northern areas and attributes this difference to the greater involvement of men in the south in migration to the mines (Swaziland Annual Medical Report 1931, RCS 22/32 SNA). Similarly, the 1933 Annual Medical Report from Bechuanaland contains the following observation (Schapera 1947, 176):

> The distribution of pulmonary tuberculosis was fairly even in the Southern districts of the territory while in the Northern districts (Mangwato and Tati) it was lower than in the South. The distribution may be of some significance in that up till the end of 1933 native labourers have not been recruited from north of Latitude 22 for work on the Gold Mines in Johannesburg.

Differences in the risk of infection and thus in the pace at which the disease spread in rural areas was also affected by living conditions within various districts, and particularly housing conditions. Thus in Pondoland, where the disease spread very rapidly among the families of returned mine workers, Millar describes excessive overcrowding (Millar 1908, 381):

> One may see some twenty people—men, women, and children—crowded into a small hut, the door of which is carefully blocked up and which contains no other opening or ventilation of any kind. This overcrowding is very much the rule, it being quite the exception to find a hut not overcrowded. Now imagine a phthisical patient one of this crowd, constantly spitting on the floor and on the walls of the hut, and can it be wondered at that the disease spreads.

Millar ascribes this condition to the imposition of a tax of ten shillings per hut upon the Pondo by the white authorities. In order to reduce their tax burden, the Pondo built fewer huts, leading to the overcrowding of existing structures. Ironically, a taxation policy designed in part to generate labor may have undermined the social reproduction of labor in Pondoland.

Opportunities for spreading infection were also great in Bechuanaland, where large aggregations of people in villages made the transmission of infection relatively easy (Schapera 1947, 77). In contrast, Swaziland medical authorities commented frequently on the role played by the Swazi's dispersed settlement pattern in forestalling the spread of all infectious diseases. It is worth noting also that Swaziland taxes were based on the number of wives a man had, not on the number of huts and thus did not encourage overcrowding.

The pace at which tuberculosis spread in the rural areas of South Africa was also determined by the ability of members of the rural population to resist the spread of the disease once infected. A population whose members are able to control their infections will produce fewer open cases of tuberculosis and thus fewer sources of infection. As in the urban setting the most important factor in determining whether a rural inhabitant was able to control the infection was nutrition or, rather, the absence of an adequate diet.

Given the general equation between malnutrition and tuberculosis, so frequently cited in the medical literature, one would expect that the rapid spread of tuberculosis in the Ciskei and Transkei areas during the first two decades of this century would have been accompanied by widespread malnutrition. Yet the studies of Beinart (1983) and Simkins (1981) seem to counter this assumption. Beinart found that in Pondoland, at least up to the 1930s, increasing migration to the gold mines went along with increasing agricultural production. Wage labor enabled young men to acquire cattle for homesteads and slowly accumulate productive capital. Simkins argues that total production in the reserves was stable and met a constant proportion of requirements from 1918 to 1955.

While these studies are perhaps correct in terms of aggregate production, they disguise patterns of social and economic differentiation within the reserve areas as well as shifts in the composition of diets which are not necessarily reflected in calculations based on the overall production of subsistence crops.

The incorporation of rural areas of southern Africa into the expanding capitalist economy of South Africa led to considerable economic stratification among rural homesteads (Bundy 1979; Kimble 1982; Slater 1980; Webster 1981) . This is reflected most clearly in the distribution of livestock. An investigation into the nutritional levels of blacks in Transkei in the 1930s revealed that in Umtata district 25 percent of all households had no cattle, and 58 percent of the remaining households had herds that were too small to meet household milk requirements (Fox and Back 1938, 129). In another district three out of 1,000 stock-owners owned 70 percent of the sheep and 50 percent of the cattle (Fox and Back 1938, 45; Webster 1981, 23). Similarly, in Swaziland, 70 percent of the households had no stock at all in 1914 (Crush 1983, 443). Inequalities in grain production were also frequent. Judith Kimble (1982) has shown that while Basutoland was a net exporter of grain up to the

1930s, this surplus production was dominated by chiefly groups, and a landless peasant class had emerged as early as the 1890s. Similar disparities occurred in household grain production in the Transkei at this time. Inequalities of this type meant that while overall productivity within the reserves may have been stable, some families were much better off than others. This would account for the discrepancy that exists between optimistic descriptions of productivity in the reserves and the frequent references by medical officers and administrators to malnutrition within these areas, and for the general decline in the physical condition of black mine recruits, noted by mine medical officers during the early 1930s (SAIMR 1932, 63).

This significance of economic stratification for the distribution of tuberculosis among the Transkei and Ciskei populations is impossible to measure in the absence of detailed data on the economic status of tuberculosis cases during the period in question. However, a recent epidemiological study into social and economic factors associated with tubercular infection among young children between three months and ten years of age in the Ntshiqo location of the Transkei found that in families with a monthly income of five Rands or more (35 percent of the families sampled), 9 percent of the children were infected. Whereas in families with a monthly income of less than R.5 per month (65 percent of sample), 14 percent were infected (Burney and Shahyar 1980, 346).

Overall production of food-supply figures are also deceptive in that they disguise important shifts in dietary patterns and the loss of important elements in the diets of rural inhabitants. In terms of nutrition, the ability of reserve populations to produce an adequate grain supply may have been less important than their increased dependence on grain and a decline in the consumption of milk and other animal fats and proteins from the end of the nineteenth century through the first three decades of the twentieth century. This pattern and its nutritional consequences were described by numerous European observers during the late 1920s and early 1930s. Thus a physician from Queens Town concluded that "The Ciskei and Transkei Natives are deteriorating through diminution of stock and resultant loss of the traditional occupations of a pastoral peoples and a loss of milk from the dietary. The custom of making and using 'amasi' (sour milk) has almost ceased for want of milk" (SAIMR 1932, 262–263).

The decimation of native herds by the rinderpest pandemic of 1896/97 and the consequent loss of milk supplies coinciding as it did with the opening of mine recruitment in many areas of southern Africa no doubt contributed to the early spread of tuberculosis among rural black populations. In fact, Dr. Allan, in his Tuberculosis Survey of 1924, concluded that the early epidemic of tuberculosis among the Zulu was directly related to the rinderpest epidemic and to the inability of the Zulu to get "amas" (*amasi*, sour milk). This situation was worsened around 1910 by the onset of East Coast

Fever among the Zulu herd. "The children born during the years following the Rinderpest were then attaining puberty, and by not getting sufficient nourishment, fell easy victim to tubercular infection." The reestablishment of Zulu herds following World War I may conversely have contributed to their relative freedom from tuberculosis in 1922 (Allan 1924, 19).

Yet the reestablishment of herds did not occur everywhere. Moreover, even where the cattle population increased, as in certain parts of the Transkei and in Swaziland, where the cattle population quadrupled between 1911 and 1936, land alienation and restrictions on land usage enforced by the colonial authorities led rapidly to overgrazing and to a sharp deterioration in the quality of native cattle. Thus the Union Director of Native Agriculture reported in 1933 that (*South African Medical Journal* [*SAMJ*] 1936, 29):

> The native cattle in many parts are the worst for conformation that can be seen anywhere in the world. They are very bad, both from the trek-ox point of view and the milk and beef point of view. Milk is essential unless it is proposed to abandon any attempt to protect the child life of the areas.

The reestablishment of herds and milk supply was further restricted in the Transkei by the introduction of sheep. From 1912 to 1936, the number of sheep rose from a few thousand to 3,000,000. This led Fox and Back (1938, 44–45) to observe that

> from the point of view of food supplies, the introduction and encouragement of wool production is nothing short of suicidal when we consider the density of population and consequent shortages of fresh milk and oxen for draught purposes. It is the sheep which are driving the cattle off the land.

The authors go on to note that only a small portion of the African population of the territory benefit from the raising of sheep:

> there is such unequal distribution of small stock that it is true to say that a small minority, consisting of Bunga Councillors, headmen and chiefs are gaining a small income from wool at the expense of the food supplies of the many.

In general, the unequal distribution of livestock including cattle meant that many families went largely without milk supplies at this time. Dr. E. Joki, in a manpower survey of the Transkeian territories in 1942, found that only 25 percent of the cattle were capable of producing milk above the amount needed for their calves and that of 663 children examined in Flagstaff, only 54, or 8 percent, consumed milk (Joki 1943, 6).

The limited milk supply available to rural blacks was reduced further by the policy of establishing "Native Creameries" to which the blacks were encouraged to send their milk, beginning in the 1930s. The policy designed to relieve some of the economic problems faced by rural blacks, without at the same time investing substantial government resources into rural development, was highly successful from the point of view of the creameries. Many blacks, and especially poorer blacks with few alternative sources of income, sent what little milk they had to the creameries. From a health and nutritional viewpoint, however, the creameries were widely decried by medical authorities as a disaster, which contributed to the ill health of the reserve populations. In Swaziland, where a number of creameries were established during the 1930s, the chief medical officer, discussing the Swazi diet, noted, "If the native is going to depreciate still further his already defective diet by sending his milk to the creamery and either doing without or using it in the condensed form he will be establishing just those conditions that are most favorable for the development of the tubercle bacillus" (Swaziland Annual Medical Report 1932).

In addition to the loss of milk supplies, the existence of markets for grains and pulses grown by rural blacks and the creation of new demands for the limited incomes of rural inhabitants such as for school fees, taxes, dipping fees, and for the purchase of European-manufactured goods, encouraged rural inhabitants to sell their subsistence crops as well as their milk so that even where subsistence production was adequate, nutritional needs were often not met. It was common among the Swazi, for example, to find families selling off their maize supplies early in the harvest season to pay taxes and then being forced to purchase food at higher prices toward the end of the year, often resulting in food shortages. As rural impoverishment and dependence on wage labor increased during the 1930s, the practice became more frequent and nutritional vulnerability more widespread, contributing to the rising tide of tuberculosis in Swaziland during this period.

In short, despite evidence of stable crop production levels in the reserve areas of South Africa, patterns of economic stratification and shifts in consumption patterns created conditions of malnutrition for a sizable portion of the rural black population. This, in turn, contributed to the spread of infection within these areas. It not only lowered the ability of rural blacks to resist the infections introduced by returning wage earners but also created conditions in which workers who had been infected while living in an industrial environment but had not developed active symptoms, broke down and became active sources of tuberculosis once they returned home (Schapera 1947, 177).

The introduction of tuberculosis by returning migrant workers into rural areas in which overcrowding, agricultural impoverishment, and dependence on wage labor had been established among a sizable portion of the population, created conditions conducive to the spread of tubercular infection. In areas in which these conditions were widespread, such as in the Transkei and Ciskei, infection spread rapidly, creating a plateau of self-sustaining cross-infection that was no longer dependent on the introduction of externally derived sources of disease by the early 1930s. Tuberculin testing carried out in these areas in the late 1920s and early 1930s revealed extremely high levels of infection. In the southern areas of the Transkei and in Pondoland, men over the age of twenty had a positivity rate of between 90 and 95 percent. In addition, the rate for women was the same as that for men and 60 percent of the children under ten years were positive reactors, indicating both the extent and the self-sustaining nature of infection and distinguishing this region from rural areas elsewhere in Africa where the rates for women are normally substantially lower than those for men and where children below the age of ten seldom experience an infection rate of over 20 percent (Paviot 1967; SAIMR 1932, 199–202).

In areas such as Basutoland and Swaziland where involvement in migrant labor grew more slowly and where dispersed settlement, the absence of overcrowding, and a slower rate of agricultural impoverishment delayed the spread of infection, lower levels of infection had been reached by the early 1930s. Thus the same survey revealed that while Basutu men over the age of twenty had a positive rate of 81 percent, the rate for women in the same age group was 68.5 percent, while children under the age of ten had a rate of only 9 percent (SAIMR 1932, 203).

These rates of infection suggest that it was unlikely that migrants returning with tuberculosis contributed significantly to the spread of tuberculosis among rural inhabitants in the Transkei and Ciskei after 1930, although they may very well have continued to be a threat to rural Basuto and Swazi. Moreover, they certainly continued to contribute to the tuberculosis mortality figures for all areas.

The prevalence of active cases among rural blacks is difficult to assess. Hospital data on the proportion of tuberculosis cases to the total number of cases seen, while suggestive, is of little use for determining the prevalence of the disease in the wider population. Allan calculated that there were some 450 cases of tuberculosis among the 23,000 blacks living in the Butterworth area of the Transkei in 1929. That works out to a prevalence rate of just over 2 percent (SAIMR 1932, 208). A much lower figure emerges from a study conducted by B. A. Dormer in Natal in 1938. Dormer (1943, 82) estimates that the prevalence rate among rural blacks was 250 per 100,000, or .25 percent. These figures represent at best rough estimates. However, they conform to the informal observations of medical authorities working in these two areas. Moreover, they correspond to the divergent experiences of these two areas with regard to the conditions described above.

In general, the prevalence of tuberculosis in the rural areas of southern Africa in the 1930s was probably less than that in the urban areas and was certainly less than it was to become following World War II.

World War II marked the beginning of what B. A. Dormer (1948) has termed the "second act" in South Africa's tuberculosis epidemic. The war and its increased demand for labor combined with deteriorating conditions in many reserve areas to draw thousands of blacks into the cities and industrial centers of South Africa. In a sense, the experience of World War I was repeated on a larger scale. However, in contrast to World War I, the army of black workers that moved from the rural areas into the cities during World War II was highly tubercularized and as a result had a higher susceptibility to tuberculosis, even if their case mortality rate was lower as a result of "seasoning." The result was a massive urban epidemic of tuberculosis (Dormer 1948, 53):

> The rural Bantu, most of them positive tuberculin reactors, poured by the hundreds of thousands into urban areas to seek work at a time when housing was at a standstill. . . . The result was a vast killing epidemic of TB. The environmental stresses—malnourishment, crowding, and a lack of hygienic amenities—could not have been more classically arranged to demonstrate that it is not racial susceptibility but these very stresses that cause a major epidemic.

The official tuberculosis mortality rate for blacks in the major urban centers of South Africa shot from just over 400 per 100,000 in 1938 to over 900 per 100,000 by 1946.

The return of infected and active cases of tuberculosis to the rural areas launched a second wave of infection and disease in these areas, especially in those areas in which infection had been limited prior to the war. The wave grew larger as nationalist attempts to remove blacks from urban residences and return them to the reserves during the early 1950s not only reintroduced sources of tuberculosis to the rural areas but contributed to overcrowding and to the declining agricultural productivity of these areas following 1955 (Simkins 1981). Thus not only was there an increase in the risk of infection and in tuberculosis mortality rates but also a lowering of nutritional levels and resistance to disease among rural inhabitants, leading to the extremely high rates of active disease. Prevalence rates in the Transkei rose to over 4 percent in some areas to 8 percent in Kwazulu (Arabin et al. 1979) and to 1 percent in Swaziland, Lesotho, and Botswana.

CONCLUSION

Since the early 1950s the South African government has made extensive efforts to control the spread of tuberculosis and lower tuberculosis morbidity and mortality rates. Yet years of treating patients with antitubercular drugs and vaccinating children with BCG (bacille Calmette-Guérin) have had little impact on the overall prevalence of the disease. Moreover, there are indications that in certain areas, such as the western Cape, where record keeping and medical services are most efficient, the incidence of tuberculosis is rising, with a virtual epidemic afoot among coloreds.

In a paper presented to the First Symposium of the South African Medical

Research Council's Tuberculosis Research Institute, in August 1985, Drs. P. B. Fourie, G. S. Townshend, and H. Kleeburg (1986, 386) posed the following problem, reflecting their growing frustration over the failure of tuberculosis control measures to effectively eradicate tuberculosis: "Since the disease [TB] is totally curable and available control measures are sufficient to combat the disease effectively, the natural course of the epidemic can be altered to a rapid decline. Why then does the problem remain such a serious one?"

In trying to understand the persistance of tuberculosis in South Africa, the Tuberculosis Research Institute (TBRI) has conducted extensive research on the epidemiology of the disease and evaluated existing treatment and control programs. Although this research is important, it has failed to either explain or halt the continued onslaught of tuberculosis. This is because neither TBRI officials, nor the state that employs them appear willing to address the foundations of black poverty, malnutrition, and disease upon which the current epidemic of tuberculosis is based. This is not to say that these officials are unaware of these problems and their impact on health among blacks. They have rather chosen to place their faith in the ability of medical science to solve health problems in the face of adverse social and economic conditions. Thus the director of the TBRI observed in 1982 that "Proof that one can control tuberculosis without general uplift of the people and change in their socio-economic situation is everywhere" (Kleeburg 1982, 23). This conclusion is contradicted by the history of tuberculosis in Europe and America, where much of the decline in tuberculosis mortality occurred before the development of effective treatment for the disease and was achieved through the elimination of the conditions of malnutrition, physical stress, and overcrowding that had been associated with early industrialization. Until these conditions are eliminated among blacks in South Africa, it is unlikely that the current high prevalence of tuberculosis among them will be lowered.

NOTES

1. This chapter was written in 1983. Subsequent research in South Africa was conducted in 1984 and 1985. The completed study is published in my book *White Plague, Black Labor: Tuberculosis and the Political Economy of Health and Disease in South Africa*.

2. Research for this study was carried out in South Africa and Swaziland during 1982 and was supported by research grants under the Fulbright-Hays Program administered by the Department of Education and the Council for the International Exchange of Scholars. Subsequent research was supported by the Social Science Research Council. I wish to thank all three agencies for their support. I wish to thank Drs. Shula Marks, Philip Curtin, and Steven Feierman for their comments on earlier drafts of this study.

3. Given both the early conditions on the mines and the large numbers of blacks traveling to the mines, there is no doubt reason to attribute the spread of tuberculosis in rural areas to the return of infected mine workers. Yet one also suspects that a certain amount of this attribution reflects economic jealousies felt by Cape Authorities over the booming economy of the Transvaal and the threat that this represented in terms of the Cape's labor supply. Thus the 1906 Public Health Report cited here goes on to note how the resulting spread of tuberculosis among Cape blacks is "decimating the Colony's most valuable labour asset," and questions whether, "from a human life point of view . . . we ought to waste our Bantus over mine labour."

FIVE

Industrialization, Rural Health, and the 1944 National Health Services Commission in South Africa[1]

Shula Marks and Neil Andersson

INTRODUCTION

Advances in the field of medicine are at the heart of a great deal of South African government propaganda. Pictures of smiling doctors (white) and nurses (black) and chubby babies adorn the glossy pictorials celebrating the "independence" of its "new black states" or Bantustans. In 1977 the Secretary for Health proudly claimed that "after painstaking research all endemic diseases of Africa have been eradicated in South Africa" (South African Government 1977, 9). The statement is misleading; parasitic and vector-borne diseases are still prevalent in South Africa, and in some cases have been given a new lease of life through policies of uprooting and "resettlement" and overcrowded urban squatter camps. If the boast is a half-truth, the propaganda pictures are grotesque. In 1979 a black child was believed to die every twenty minutes of malnutrition; and this was before the recent devastating drought began to take its toll. Since the late nineteenth century, the major killers in South Africa have not been the "endemic diseases of Africa" but the diseases of industrialization: malnutrition and the nutritionally related infectious diseases, particularly tuberculosis. We are, of course, not arguing that preindustrial South Africa was in some miraculous sense free of disease; the "endemic" diseases of Africa were both debilitating and probably limited population growth, as did periodic famine and epizootics. Nevertheless, contemporary patterns of morbidity and mortality for the black population are probably closer to those of early industrial Britain than precolonial Africa.

These patterns are not new. By the 1940s South African medical professionals and state health officials clearly recognized the social production of much disease; they saw the connections between ill health and social change, between industrial development and dislocation in the countryside. Ironically at that time a number of South African health workers were in the forefront of medical advance and were poised to make important interventions in the field of preventive social medicine. During World War II, in response to dramatic economic change, the disintegration of the rural economy, the intensity of class struggle in town and countryside, and a growing sense of crises on a number of fronts, the South African government appointed a National Health Services Commission to explore the possibilities of establishing a unified national health service. This was to be based upon the most "modern conception of health," specifically, promotive and preventive community health services. Its findings and recommendations were, in the South African context, revolutionary and in line with, if not in advance of, those of similar commissions and inquiries both in the United Kingdom and the rest of the Commonwealth. Yet, after a promising beginning, the recommendations of the Commission were all but buried and forgotten for more than thirty years. Recently, its rhetoric has been revived in the 1977 Public Health Act, legislation that rationalizes and perpetuates the urban–rural divide in health care in the very different context of a balkanized South Africa.

The reasons for the appointment of the 1944 National Health Services Commission, the reversal of its recommendations and the revival of its language in the 1970s further our understanding of the articulation of class power, politics and health, the implications of social inequality for health care systems, and the ideological and political struggles that accompany developments in the health field. This chapter shows how South Africa's disease pattern resulted directly from its specific form of industrialization and capitalist development, and traces its implications for mortality and morbidity in both town and countryside. It then explores why and how the National Health Services Commission addressed the crisis in health which was produced and examines the reasons for its failure.

THE IMPACT OF THE MINERAL REVOLUTION ON HEALTH

South Africa's contemporary health pattern is rooted in the social changes that began with the discovery of minerals in the last third of the nineteenth century: diamonds in Kimberley in 1868 and vast seams of gold at very deep levels underground on the Witwatersrand in 1886. The industrial and agrarian revolution which followed the development of the mining industry, the new concentrations of population on the mines and in the rapidly developing towns and the special hazards of the mining operations as well as growing impoverishment in the countryside were to have swift and devastating implications for the physical well-being of workers, both black and white.

Although today the Chamber of Mines runs fine modern medical facilities and has developed sophisticated techniques to deal with mining accidents, the early days of the industry—as in most places—were characterized by a total disregard for human life. At Kimberley, in 1883, a smallpox epidemic raged unchecked for ten months because of the silencing of local medical men by the mine owners. The magnates feared that recognition and notification of the disease would lead to a diminution of their labor supplies. It needed the intervention of the Cape Parliament and the passage of the Cape's Public Health Act, which made notification of the disease compulsory, before the disease was brought under control (Burrows 1958, 259–262; Merriman 1960, 207–208; Turrell 1982*b*, 258–261).

A similar disregard for human life was revealed in the inordinately high accident rate, once the mines moved from open-caste to underground mining. Both at Kimberley and on the Rand, this transition was accompanied by an enormous increase in the accident rate: 9.5 per 1,000 between 1881 and 1889, and 6.2 per 1,000 over the next ten years. On the Rand it averaged a little over 4 per 1,000 between 1896 and 1905 (Turrell 1984, 3).

Even more serious in the long run than the accident rate were the ravages of disease that followed in the wake of both uncontrolled urbanization and deep-level mining first at Kimberley and then more extensively and more pervasively after the opening of the mines on the Witwatersrand. In the 1870s Kimberley was described by one medical man as "among the most unhealthy towns in existence" (Matthews 1879, 5) with a death rate among Africans of about 80 per 1,000. Ten years later it was over 100 per 1,000—and this in a predominantly young adult male population. In the early years this was probably largely the result of dysentery and diarrhea, and a similarly high death rate through the lack of adequate water supplies and sanitation was to characterize the black locations of other South African cities in the twentieth century (Turrell 1984, 59–75). In Kimberley the introduction in 1886 of closed compounds for housing black mine workers probably diminished morbidity from lack of sanitation through the introduction of waterborne sewage and clean water. The confined space in which large numbers of men were forced to live, however—the poor food and the sharp changes in temperature that characterize underground mining, together with grueling working conditions—led instead to the spread of tuberculosis and other infectious respiratory diseases (Turrell 1984, 6–8). Chest disease was to be the most enduring legacy of the mining industry to black southern Africa.

On the Rand, the nature of deep-level hard-rock drilling and the recruitment of huge quantities of migrant labor from a vast region of southern Africa led to an even higher incidence of respiratory diseases: miners' phthisis, nonpulmonary tuberculosis, and pneumonia. In addition, scurvy, enteric fever, and meningitis were also rife among Africans. Initially, it was the mainly British skilled workers, recruited from the international mining frontiers, who bore the brunt of miners' phthisis: in 1904, for example, it was revealed that the average age of death of Cornishmen who had worked on rock-drills in the Transvaal was 36.4 years with an average period of rock-drill employment of only 4.7 years (Burke and Richardson 1978, 141–171). Of eighteen leaders in the 1907 white mine workers' strike, all but four had died of miners' phthisis ten years later. Of the remaining four, three were suffering from the disease (Walker and Weinbren 1961, 23; Yudelman 1983, 93, 119).

Through their struggles, white miners gained state intervention on their behalf and both inspection and compensation schemes were implemented by the second decade of the twentieth century—twenty-five years after the first exploitation of the gold mines. In a series of acts known as the Prior Law, the state laid down the basis for a comprehensive system of compensation for white victims of miners' phthisis between 1912 and 1918. After 1916, white and black miners were periodically examined for phthisis by a government-appointed dust inspectorate. Certainly after 1912 the worst effects of the disease for white miners were controlled, if far from eliminated (Walker and Weinbren 1961).

Black workers were by no means so fortunately placed. Deskilling, job fragmentation, and labor substitution led to a protracted struggle between white workers and the mine magnates which need not concern us here. As the costs of employing white skilled workers rose, so the incentives increased for the mining industry to employ more blacks at the rockface and for longer periods of time. For these workers the health costs of this process were high. According to Burke and Richardson (1978, 169):

> the changing proportion of migrant European labor in the white workforce and the declining numbers of European miners, both relative to black miners and absolutely, meant that the costs of compensation measures . . . could be effectively controlled. Perhaps even more important in this respect was the increasing control of the African labor market after 1907 which facilitated the passing off of the major burden of phthisis onto the black work force. . . . In line with this trend by 1910 tuberculous phthisis was the second largest killer of African labor, representing no less than 18 per cent of all African mortality [on the mines].

Between 1902 and 1911, the tuberculosis mortality rate for Africans in the Transvaal mining areas virtually doubled (Report of the Tuberculosis Commission 1914).

Africans from northern Mozambique and British Central Africa (Malawi) suffered most heavily as a result of respiratory disease on the Rand. In the first decade of this century, the death rate was staggering: in 1903, for example, of 28,669 Africans from the east coast, 490 had died within the first month, and a further 270 within two months, mostly from pneumonia and other respiratory diseases. For the year ending June 1905 the figures were 130 per 1,000 for Mozambiquans, 118 per 1,000 for Africans from British Central Africa—and this was probably an underestimate (Cartwright 1971,

17–23). In part this may have reflected the extremely poor health of Africans in Mozambique and British Central Africa at this time: the 1890s had seen a variety of natural disasters in the region, drought, rinderpest, smallpox, locusts, and an invasion of chiggers. The earlier depredations of the slave trade had been replaced by the dislocation of colonial rule. Colonial settlement and game-preservation policies had led to shifts in cultivation patterns and the spread of sleeping sickness, which reached epidemic proportions in some regions. These factors together with the imposition of colonial taxation ensured a flow of labor to the enterprises of the white south, but may have also meant that the health of those who left was already undermined (Vail 1977). Climatic change and especially the extremes of temperature on the highveld increased the vulnerability of these particular workers on top of a long and arduous journey. Conditions in the mining compounds undoubtedly aggravated their initial debility: inadequate food, overcrowded compounds and the prevalence of respiratory diseases among the existing mine work force.

The shortage of labor after the South African war (1899–1902) and the recognition by the Milner adminstration, which governed the Transvaal between 1902 and 1907, of the need to temper the frantic exploitation of labor by the mines in the interests of longer-term conditions of production, led the state to lay down minimum standards of airspace, better food, and medical provision. So long as the Chamber had access to an infinite labor market, however, there was little incentive for them to change. The importation of 60,000 Chinese laborers between 1905 and 1907 solved an immediate labor shortage for the mines in the years after the South African war and obviated the need to look more fundamentally at the problems of ensuring a future African work force.

The ending of the Chinese labor experiment, the heightened militancy of the white working class and the undiminished mortality among "tropical" Africans led the state to intervene more forcibly. In 1913, the South African government eventually banned the recruitment of Africans from north of latitude 22 degrees south. In the same year, the richest of the Mining Houses, Rand Mines, brought Colonel Gorgas out from the United States of America to advise them on health conditions. Gorgas, who had built up a remarkable reputation through his contribution to the control of yellow fever during the building of the Panama Canal, produced a scathing report on conditions in the mining industry and made a number of recommendations on nutrition, accommodation, and medical facilities (Cartwright 1971, 31–37). Although these were not fully implemented, his report did lead to some improvements for black gold miners. The appointment of J. A. Orenstein, one of Gorgas's assistants in Latin America, as Medical Officer of Health (MOH) for the Rand Mines and the establishment of the South African Institute of Medical Research jointly by the state and the Chamber of Mines facilitated this process.

The accident rate began to drop and food and shelter for Africans actually on the mines probably improved over the next few years, as the mining regulations were supervised by an inspectorate responsible to the Director of Native Labour of the Native Affairs Department. This provided some check on the activities of mine doctors. The richer mines, under pressure from the state began to improve their medical services, to build up-to-date hospitals to deal especially with accidents, and to train African medical orderlies (Cartwright 1971).[2] By the 1940s the Gold Producers' Committee of the Chamber of Mines could boast (Fagan Commission 1948):

> The mining industry has through the course of the years steadily built up complete medical services for its Native labor force. At this stage for approximately 300,000 laborers there are 37 well-equipped mine hospitals with over 7,000 beds providing accommodation on any one day for a little over 2 per cent of the labor strength. . . . There are more than 60 medical officers. The nursing staff consists in the main of qualified male European nurses and probationers with trained and training Native orderlies.
>
> The system of medical care of the mine Native labor force provides an example of an objective which medical authorities agree should be the goal for every community, i.e. a good diet and a periodic examination for all members of the population, no matter in what work they are engaged. The mine Native laborers, from whatever source, undergo two or even three separate medical examinations to determine whether they are fit to work on the mines at all and to differentiate them for different forms of labor on the mines. . . . Their daily diet is ample and well-balanced and the physical condition of the great majority of Natives improves as a result of it.

This evidence, produced by the Chamber of Mines in order to justify continuing the migrant labor system, ignored the rather wider repercussions of capitalist development in South Africa for African health. For, if by the 1940s actual conditions on the mines had improved out of all recognition, it is clear that at the same time the health of the majority of blacks had been dramatically transformed as a direct and indirect result of the mineral discoveries.

Thus as George Gale, then Secretary for Health in the Union Government, pointed out in a long and important memorandum to the same commission (Fagan Commission 1948):

> The migratory system of labour (which, of course is not limited to mine labor but also extends to secondary industries and to domestic service) has far-reaching effects upon the health of South African Natives. These are: (a) direct—upon the individuals and their families; (b) indirect—by way of the effects upon the general economy of the Native rural areas, which in turn affects health.

While he agreed that the individual mine laborer was "hygienically housed, well-fed and medically cared for while on the mine," he continued:

> the mine medical services protect the mine-worker only so long as he is on the mine. They do not extend to the rural area to which he returns when his health breaks down *owing to the conditions of migratory labour*. Obviously they cannot; but the point is that the mine medical services do not meet the really serious detrimental effects, with regard to health, of the migratory system.
>
> To begin with, the mines recruit only physically fit persons. Among those whom they reject are many who have become unfit through venereal disease, tuberculosis, and muscular-cum-articular "rheumatism"—chronic degenerative diseases of which the principal initial cause is conditions of mine labour. . . . The migrant labourer returning with untreated or inadequately treated venereal disease may infect his wife (and other women) in the rural area. . . . Gonorrhea in women is a principal cause of sterility. Syphilis in women causes miscarriages and still-births, and even when living children are born they are frequently congenital syphilitics. Sterility, miscarriages and the birth of sickly children are a frequent cause of unhappiness and even divorce. . . . In many areas the incidence of syphilis among child-bearing women is 25 per cent or over.

Isadore Frack, a general practitioner who later became the Superintendent of the Baragwanath General Hospital, put it even more pithily when he noted in 1943 (Frack 1943, 69):

> In South Africa we have produced the most up-to-date and scientific means of producing this disease [TB] in natives. Raw natives are recruited from native territories, brimful of health and natural vitality, and sent down the mines in skips. After a period varying from two to six years they develop silicosis and contract tuberculosis. They are then withdrawn from the mines and, after a few months spent in a native mine hospital, are repatriated to the territories [i.e. the reserves]. A natural reservoir of tuberculosis is being established in healthy country natives. The town native becomes infected in the same way and the native population is becoming tuberculized.

Yet not all malnutrition, venereal disease, or tuberculosis were simply the result of migrant labor to the mines. South Africa's dependence on mineral extraction and position in the world economy meant that the effects of uneven development were felt also in the towns which developed in the wake of the mineral discoveries. The most spectacular growth was in the port towns and on the Rand, where industries were heavily dependent on the demands of the mines. Housing and sanitary conditions in the urban areas concerned Medical Officers of Health from the beginning of the century, and the fear that infectious disease was no respecter of class or racial boundaries led public health officials to be the foremost advocates of urban segregation. As elsewhere, the "metaphoric equation" of blacks with infectious disease, and the perception of urban social relations in terms of "the imagery of infection and epidemic disease" provided a compelling rationale for major forms of social control, and in particular the segregation of African "locations." There was, however, little amelioration in the conditions giving rise to poverty-based disease: the low-wage urban economy and the underdevelopment of the countryside (Swanson 1979). Even the passage of the 1923 Urban Areas Act, which imposed segregation on urban areas and gave central government powers of intervention in the provision of African housing, proved inadequate to force municipalities to take requisite action. Rate-payers were not prepared to foot the bill for African housing, which they felt was the responsibility of industry; industry unless faced by working class organization saw no reason either to subsidize African housing or raise black wages (Andrews 1984).

Thus in the first decades of the century unhealthy working and living conditions, long hours of work, and inadequate nutrition made an increasing proportion of the new African urban population susceptible to infectious and nutritionally related diseases. Epidemic diseases such as influenza, measles, typhoid fever, and dysentery took a frightening toll in the slums. Infant mortality was particularly high: according to the MOH of Johannesburg in 1926/27, it was recorded at the startling figure of 922.74 per 1,000 live births "which if it were correct would amount to a calamity, but which actually, as Euclid would say, is absurd" (Unterhalter 1982, 625). While this figure was almost certainly a reflection of the gross inadequacies of birth registration procedures, at the very least they suggest that a large proportion of the population was not recognized by the state notification procedures until its infants died. In 1929/30 infant mortality rates per 1,000 live births in Port Elizabeth, East London, Pretoria, Bloemfontein, and Johannesburg were said to be 213, 370, 388, 583, and 705, respectively. Large numbers of infants died from diarrhea caused by "cheap, inferior, and often contaminated condensed milk," in part because traditional breast-feeding practices broke down in the face of grinding urban poverty (Unterhalter 1982, 626). The absence of sufficient food, clean water, decent shelter and sanitation meant that in the 1920s crude death and infant mortality rates were probably even higher than the mortality rate in the rural areas (Unterhalter 1982, 625).

That the increased segregation in South African cities made little difference to the incidence of disease among Africans was indicated by a report on the conditions in Durban by the Joint Council of Europeans and Natives in 1931. At that time, they maintained 90 percent of blacks were unsatisfactorily housed and only 10 to 25 percent had adequate water supplies. Their report concluded (Durban Joint Council 1931):

1. Infectious diseases such as measles, whooping cough, chicken pox, etc. such as are spread by herding [i.e., overcrowding] are relatively more common among natives than Europeans.
2. Diseases attributable to defective diet such as scurvy and rickets are relatively more common among natives than Europeans. The opinion was ex-

> pressed that defective diet is not as harmful in directly causing diseases such as these mentioned as it is in predisposing to disease through lessening the body's powers of resistance.
>
> 3. Diseases attributable in large part to exposure such as pneumonia and rheumatism were deemed relatively more common among natives.
> 4. Diseases due to improper ventilation such as Tuberculosis and other respiratory diseases are far more common among Natives than Europeans.
> 5. Diseases largely due to improper sanitation such as dysentery, intestinal parasites and enteric fever were considered far commoner amongst Natives than Europeans.
>
> These questionnaires showed that the extremely unsatisfactory conditions under which Natives live in the peri-urban areas are reflected in their illnesses.

Far from improving in the 1930s, these years saw a further deterioration in urban health conditions, as the 1936 Native Lands Act and Trust pushed more people off white-owned lands just as the effects of the world depression further undermined both black peasants and the more marginal white farmers. With South Africa's recovery from the depression and the tremendous spurt in secondary industrialization that accompanied her leaving the gold standard, there was a new demand for workers in the towns. The number of urban Africans increased from about a half a million in 1921 to nearly 1,500,000 by 1946. One-third of these were now women. The influx of African families into the towns further strained the inadequate housing and welfare facilities and immense squatter camps grew up on the outskirts of the main cities—especially Durban and Johannesburg.

As George Gale pointed out in the statement in 1946 we have already quoted, living conditions in the urban locations were far worse than in the rigidly controlled compounds. Although wages in industry were considerably higher than on the mines and rose more rapidly during the war years than at any other time except for the late 1970s, the average wage was still only £40 a year: and this disguised enormous inequalities, with many receiving far less. Evidence presented in the *Report of the Interdepartmental Committee on the Social, Health and Economic Conditions of Urban Natives* in 1942 (South African Government, *Report* 1942) revealed a state of "appalling poverty." Scurvy, rickets, and pellagra were prevalent and lowered resistance to infectious diseases. The ravages were particularly noted amongst African school children: according to a contemporary survey, in Durban over 40 percent suffered from clinical signs of malnutrition, while the Lovedale mission doctor, Neil McVicar, wrote of a procession of African school children at the time, "It seems to me that I had never before seen such a collection of miserable-looking objects. One could only suppose they were the victims of mass undernourishment" (South African Government, *Report* 1942, 5). Adults were not immune, however. In 1938/39, the Superintendent of the Edward VIII Hospital recorded that (ibid.)

> nearly all the Native patients, quite apart from the disease or injury for which they were admitted, were undernourished. One can safely say that about half of them were grossly undernourished. . . . Symptoms of pellagra and similar diseases were quite frequent and in children, conditions such as nutritional oedema were common-place.

The majority of Africans were living in houses that were "injurious or dangerous to health." Sanitation and clean water were often nonexistent and the disposal of garbage "rarely satisfactory" (*Report* 1942, 9):

> The dust which blows about the average location must . . . form . . . various sources of pollution, harbour an exceptionally rich flora of septic and other pathogenic germs; and it is not surprising that sore eyes, skin diseases, tuberculosis and bowel infections are as common as they are.

THE IMPOVERISHMENT OF THE COUNTRYSIDE

In other ways, too, the interaction between disease in the mines and locations, the migrant labor system and the spread of ill health, especially tuberculosis, in the countryside was more complex than either George Gale or Isadore Frack allowed for. For it was not simply the return of the migrant from the unhealthy towns and mines that led to the alarming spread of disease which was noted in the interwar period. The diseases were not automatically transferred to the rural areas. The accelerating spread of tuberculosis, malnutrition, and venereal disease in the "reserves" from the 1920s resulted from the conjuncture of the health hazards of the mining industry, the migrant labor system and low-wage urban economy with the simultaneous and connected impoverishment of the countryside.

The decline of African agriculture is usually associated with the effects of the Native Lands Act of 1913, which set aside under 8 percent of the land in South Africa for some 70 percent of the population and increased the powers of white landlords over their tenants. In fact the Lands Act simply accelerated processes of impoverishment which were already under way. Following the mineral discoveries, the increased capitalization of white agriculture displaced growing numbers of Africans from the land. Reserves became overcrowded as Africans were removed from settler land. And as the state stepped in to support settler agriculture through the building of roads and railways—which almost invariably bypassed the African areas—the extension of credit to whites through cooperatives and landbanks, and selective taxation both to push out labor and to hamper small producers, so black peasants found it increasingly difficult to compete with state-subsidized white farming. At the same time they had to cope with epizootics such as rinderpest and east coast fever (1897/98 and 1911–1920) and periodic drought, often followed by floods (Beinart 1983; Bundy 1979; Cooper 1981;

Palmer and Parsons 1977; Ranger 1978*a*). Although white farmers suffered losses, unlike Africans, they were partly protected by the state and private credit from the vagaries of world prices. The starvation wages being paid Africans on the farms and in the towns and their increasing dependence on the market, which made them even more susceptible to the ups and downs of the international economy, aggravated the situation.

From about the 1920s (although in some areas it had already begun, as we shall see, in the nineteenth century, while in others it was only to become manifest in the 1930s and 1940s) people who had been able to produce an adequate subsistence and a surplus for the colonial markets were now having to purchase their food. By the time of the 1930–1932 Native Economic Commission, falling yields, scarce resources and a heavy dependence on labor migration, which in itself further undermined agricultural production and reflected its underdevelopment, were in evidence almost universally in the eastern Cape, particularly the Ciskei; the reserves in the rest of the Union were moving in a similar direction. The Depression may have been the turning point for the rural areas. Despite the "betterment" schemes of the late 1930s, by the mid-1940s government reports were showing that the production of African staples such as maize and sorghum had declined in the reserves throughout the country.

For the Chamber of Mines, conditions in the eastern Cape were of direct concern as, under the impact of the 1929/30 world depression they began to recruit a greater proportion of their labor internally. The effects of the depression and the devastating drought that began in 1929 and dragged on in many areas until 1933 on top of the existing poverty, indebtedness, and overcrowding in the rural areas was revealed in the Chamber's hospital statistics. As the 1932 SAIMR Report on Tuberculosis revealed (p. 63):

> A certain proportion of the Natives admitted to the hospital on arrival at the [mines] depôt are admitted because they are physically below par, and they are kept back for rest and feeding up before being distributed to the mines. In 1928 this quota accounted for 4 per cent of the B.S.A. [British South Africa] admissions, in 1929 for 5 per cent, and in 1930 for 23 per cent. It must be understood that these figures deal with Natives other than those applicants who are definitely rejected as being unfit physically for employment on the mines.

By the late 1930s, when 40 percent of their mine labor force came from the eastern Cape, the Chamber of Mines was sufficiently alarmed by the evidence of rural decline to send its own nutrition survey under Fox and Back (1938) to the Transkei and Ciskei: it was paralleled by a Department of Health Survey conducted by Sidney and Emily Kark.[3] Their findings were uniformly grim. Fox and Back maintained that records from different parts of the "Territories" suggested that 25 percent of children died during their first year, 33 percent before reaching two, and about 50 percent before reaching eighteen. Deficiency diseases were common among small children (Fox and Back). The preoccupations of their paymasters are perhaps best revealed by two quotations from the report (Fox and Back 1938, 2, 5):

> Regarded merely as the condition of a primitive people, their present condition might perhaps be accepted as problem for gradual improvement by a well-disposed European administration. But regarded as the condition of one of the many reserves of labor on which the future prosperity of the Union must partly depend, the problem at once becomes one for urgent attention, too costly for the nation as a whole to be allowed to drift.
>
> *We wish to put on record our emphatic disagreement with the generally accepted idea that any increase in food production will, in the long run, result in a fall-off of labour supplies.* Such an idea is short-sighted and pernicious. In brief, the policy of building up a labour supply on the basis of economic pressure and semistarvation, merely means that immediate requirements are being met at the expense of future supplies.

THE SPREAD OF TUBERCULOSIS AND OTHER EPIDEMIC DISEASES

It was, above all, tuberculosis that was the barometer of poverty in both town and countryside. We do not, of course, have very conclusive evidence on the health of Africans in South Africa until after the mineral revolution. Nevertheless, it is clear from eyewitness accounts of the African population in the first half of the nineteenth century and from the recollections of Africans and mission doctors recorded in the early twentieth that outside of periods of warfare, epizootics, and drought, malnutrition was rare and tuberculosis virtually unknown in precolonial African society (Collins 1982). It is revealing that in the early nineteenth century, the diseases of poverty—especially tuberculosis—were first noted among the proletarianized "coloured" population of Cape Town, and some of the tuberculosis in the eastern Cape was undoubtedly spread by infected individuals from Europe who came there to recuperate; as early as the 1820s, John Tshatshu, son of the chief of the Ntinde, one of the most westerly Xhosa groups, had contracted the disease. Significantly the chief was a Christian, and his people were among the first to lose their land in the Cape frontier wars that began in the late eighteenth century.

It was only subsequent to the late-nineteenth-century mineral discoveries, the widespread annexation of African territories and the inception of the migrant labor system that diseases of poverty were noted on any scale, however. As the 1932 Report of the Tuberculosis Research Committee remarked in inimitably bland fashion, although the disease "may be fairly well tolerated under natural or tribal conditions, . . . susceptibility is fraught with extreme danger when exposure to danger is accompanied by a sudden change in occupation, food, housing and mode of life" (SAIMR 1932). Thus, widespread tuberculosis was noticed earliest in those areas that were the first to feel the impact of land and cattle loss and internal stratification: the Ciskei and Transkei. Within ten years of the opening of the Kimberley diamond fields, medical men in the eastern Cape began to remark on the alarming increase in veneral disease and tuberculosis and by 1895 the MOH for the Cape Colony was sufficiently concerned to agitate for an inquiry and some kind of action.

The conjuncture of increasing landlessness and the loss of cattle in the frontier wars, the 1857 cattle-killing, and the 1897 rinderpest, together with early labor migrations and the presence of individuals suffering from the disease at resorts in the region, rendered the Ciskei especially vulnerable. Africans more remote from contact with Europeans and who had managed to retain their hold on the land were far less affected. In the late nineteenth century a great deal of labor migration was the response of still viable peasant households to the new markets and new opportunities in Kimberley and the Rand. Young men would be sent to the mines and towns to earn money to invest back in the countryside in ploughs, fertilizers, and cattle. Among the Mpondo, who were only recruited for the mines after the rinderpest epidemic in 1897, tuberculosis was first noted as a problem in 1908 (Beinart 1979, 199–219). As late as 1907, Neil McVicar, the mission doctor at Lovedale who made a special study of the subject, found no evidence of tuberculosis in either Botswana or Lesotho. McVicar noted the greatly decreased mortality from the disease among those Africans still living in "the still largely 'tribalized' Bantu communities." As late as 1906 a conference of the Principal Medical Officers of health in southern Africa regarded tuberculosis as a particular menace "among Natives adopting civilized customs and those frequenting large centres of labor" and in the towns, although they agreed it was also on the increase in rural areas. In 1914, too, the government's Tuberculosis Commission noted the highly differential spread of the disease (SAIMR 1932, 8):

> Speaking generally, it is found to be least prevalent in Zululand and the Northern Transvaal, more so in Basotuland, still more in the Cape Native Territories [Transkei] and most widespread among Natives in the settled districts of the Cape Province.

Nevertheless, it concluded,

> Owing to the extent to which the disease occurs on the mines and the large number of natives employed thereon, together with their frequently changing personnel, the mining industry is one of the most important of all the factors in the cause and diffusion of the disease among the Native population.

By the mid-1920s, a number of concerned voices were being raised about increasing poverty in the countryside and the spread of tuberculosis. In 1924, a survey by Dr. Peter Allan, for the Public Health Department, established that 60 percent of the known cases of sufferers returning from the mines had since died. The high mortality and rapid fatality, both of the returned migrants and of their contacts in the rural areas, was taken as further evidence of the relative novelty of the disease. More ominously, as the 1932 Tuberculosis Report of the South African Institute of Medical Research pointed out, whereas in earlier years there had been a good recovery rate once sufferers returned to "tribal conditions"—specifically, adequate food, uncrowded and well-ventilated housing—by the 1920s these conditions clearly were no longer the norm in the eastern Cape (Bundy 1979, 221–223). Tuberculosis was now "common and widespread" in the Transkei and Ciskei (Allan 1924). In the mid-1940s, it was estimated that 75 per cent of Africans in the southern Transkei were "tuberculized" (Allan 1924).

RURAL EPIDEMICS

If, in South Africa as in nineteenth-century Britain, tuberculosis was "the social disease, perhaps the first penalty that capitalistic society had to pay for the ruthless exploitation of labor" (Dubos 1953), it was by no means the only disease to be given vast extension as a result of the economic transformation of these years. We have already looked at some of the health implications of rapid and unequal urban growth; in the countryside, the undermining of peasant agriculture not only helped to spread tuberculosis but also led to increased rates of other infectious diseases and high levels of malnutrition, including chronic scurvy and actual starvation. Diseases such as typhus and malaria periodically took on hyperendemic proportions. Louse-borne typhus was prevalent in the nineteenth century in the eastern Cape, present-day Lesotho and Botswana, the Orange Free State maize belt, and northern Natal, apparently in a mild form. It became a major killer in the twentieth century, especially during times of economic depression and drought.

Typhus was hyperendemic between 1917 (when the disease was first officially recognized) and 1923, and again during the early 1930s and 1944–1946, which were also times of economic stress. Africans on farms in Orange Free State and the eastern Cape reserves appear to have been particularly hard hit. In the Transkei and Ciskei, for example, the annual number of cases reported between 1920 and 1923 was over 8,000, while in 1922 the Public Health Department maintained that "on a conservative estimate, the disease is killing not less than 2,500 Natives, most of them of working age, annually in the Union." Although typhus came to be regarded as endemic in the Transkei, and therefore somehow "natural," its increased incidence in the late 1920s and early 1930s was the result of "the increasing poverty of the Natives resulting from various causes such as prolonged drought and over-population," as the then Secretary for Public Health, Dr. E. H. Cluver, pointed out in 1935 (Cluver 1935). He continued, "It is possible that immunity acquired during the previous epidemic period was wearing off; but the excessive lousiness of the Bantu population [*sic*] and their malnourishment resulting from the widespread financial depression seem sufficient to account for the rapid spread of infection." According to the Assistant Medical Officer of Health, the concentrations of destitute people on the Free State farms in search of food and work disseminated the disease, especially as (Fourie 1934):

> many employers . . . did not take early steps for the early discovery of cases of illness among their natives, nor did they worry themselves about the condition of temporary labourers entering their employ. The result was that deverminisation had to be carried out on a very much larger scale and with less prospect of eradicating the disease than would have been the case had primary outbreaks been reported promptly to the magistrate.

As a disease, typhus was preeminently fitted to play a "metaphoric role" because of its concentration among blacks from the reserves and the degree of social control that it enabled the state to exercise in the name of prevention. The fear that the disease would spread from the rural areas both among mine workers and in the densely populated towns had led to draconian and highly discriminatory deverminisation (deworming) procedures for the time of the diagnosed epidemic in 1917 which were bitterly resented by the black population and provided a focus for political action by the African petty bourgeoisie (Andersson and Marks 1983). When in 1943/44 an epidemic of "unprecedented dimensions" broke out once again in the Ciskei and Transkei in the context of drought and famine, and possibly spread by returned soldiers, the scale of the disease, fears of its spread to whites and accusations of "almost criminal" neglect fed into the parliamentary and popular demands for speeding up the National Health Services Commission, which was already compiling its report.

If typhus was the scourge of the eastern Cape and parts of the highveld in times of economic distress, in the subtropical lowveld and Natal-Zululand, malaria, again a disease regarded as "endemic," also reached hyperendemic proportions as a result of destitution, climatic conditions and the ruthless exploitation of labor. Its periodicity was remarkably similar to that of typhus in the eastern Cape and on the highveld. As Randall Packard has recently shown in relation to the malaria hyperepidemics in Swaziland, contrary to belief at the time that they were due to excessive rainfall, there appears to be a direct correlation between the outbreaks and the shortage of food as a result of drought followed by rain. The search for work by migrant laborers, carrying the disease in their blood from the lowveld to the highveld, where the local populace had less immunity, was a major contributor to malaria's high mortality (Packard 1984).

In Natal, the general underlying causes were much the same, but in the epidemics of the 1920s, labor exploitation played an even more direct role. Thus, in the 1920s, disregarding the warnings of medical men, labor recruiters for the railways and sugar plantations brought nonimmune labor into the malarial areas, without taking even the most basic health precautions. Sick workers were simply returned home on the railways, many without money or food. The total disregard for elementary public health measures led to a prolonged tussle between the Public Health Department and the Railways and Harbours Board, over the proper precautions to be taken. As the Natal MOH pointed out in 1930, the spread of malaria into areas it had never been known in before, such as southern Natal and Pondoland, as well as its escalation to reach hyperendemic proportions by the late 1920s and early 1930s, was "a preventable malaria disaster." It was directly related to the expansion of sugar plantations in the region in response to world demand. Although Max Gluckman engaged in anthropological field research in Zululand in the 1930s somewhat contemptuously dismissed the notion that malaria had been introduced by the white man into "a Zulu arcady," it is perhaps not entirely surprising that many Africans believed that the epidemic which raged in the late 1920s was "due to the fact that the waters of certain rivers . . . have been poisoned by the white people" (Gluckman 1968).

Malaria prevention was undoubtedly taken in hand in the 1930s in Natal, through the training of African health assistants, who were successful to a certain extent in both administering quinine and controlling mosquito-breeding, while the Public Health Department tightened up its control over the actions of employers of labor in malarial areas. Dealing with the roots of the problem, the appalling poverty resulting from the low wage economy and the undermining of peasant agriculture, was rather more intractable.

TRAINING SCHEMES AND HEALTH CARE SERVICES FOR AFRICANS

In the 1930s it became increasingly clear that underlying the burden of disease was the fact that the reserve economy was breaking down: it could no longer act to subsidize the welfare costs of low-paid labor on the mines and farms or in the towns. As Colin Bundy remarks, "There was in the 1920s a shocked, and in the 1930s a widening realization of the state of the Reserve areas; a series of graphic descriptions (and rather less precise prescriptions) appeared" (Bundy 1979, 221). Both the Commission of Inquiry re Public Hospitals and Kindred Institutions (the Vos Commission) and the Commission on Medical Training for Natives (the Loram Commission) noted the rapidly deteriorating health of the African population in both town and countryside and the urgent need to organize medical services and hospitals to remedy the situation. The Loram Commission proposed a state-subsidized training program for African doctors and the establishment of rural health units which would consist of "one or more medical men, a small hospital [and] four or more 'health stations' in remoter parts of the native reserve," staffed by African health assistants and nurses (Loram 1930). In 1930 the annual scientific meeting of the Medical Association of South Africa (MASA), held in Durban, noted the pressing need to improve health conditions among Africans and adopted two resolutions proposed by Dr. A. J. Orenstein, of the Chamber of Mines and SAIMR, that (Loram 1930, 520–521)

> this meeting, whilst convinced that there is a great need for medical, nursing and health services in the Native Territories and other rural areas of the country, reiterates the view already expressed by the Branch Councils and Federal Council of the Association that no distinction on ground of colour be made in the qualifications of medical men, nurses and health visitors;

and that

> this meeting requests the Federal Council [of MASA] to take immediate steps to formulate proposals for a rural medical, nursing and health service to be submitted to the government on behalf of the Association.

Despite the increasing agitation of the Chamber of Mines, whose views Orenstein was in large measure representing, and the recommendations of the profession and the Loram commission, as well as the widespread recognition of the necessity, the Hertzog government took no further action on the training of black medical practitioners. An offer from the Rockefeller Foundation of £65,000 to establish a parallel medical school for blacks at the University of the Witwatersrand was rejected for political reasons and perhaps as a result of the opposition of the then Secretary for Public Health, Sir Edward Thornton, who was the ardent champion of a scheme along the lines of the Auxiliary Medical Officer in French West Africa. What lay behind Thornton's reluctance to take action was well revealed in his own words to the special conference called by the meeting of the South African Medical Association on the subject (Xuma 1931):

> The proposals, if given effect to, would add enormously to the difficulties of European practitioners in making a living in South Africa if the resources of the State are to be utilized for producing native medical practitioners in the manner proposed. . . . This is the further difficulty . . . that the native practitioners would be deemed by certain sections of the European population to combine the wisdom of medical practitioners with the art of witch-doctoring, as has already happened in the past in South Africa.

Thus, the alleged costs of training fully qualified black practitioners in South Africa, fears of competition between black and white doctors and "the menace of Native practitioners attending European patients which is already looming on the horizon" were potent spurs to inaction (Xuma 1931).

The idea of training paraprofessionals received slightly more attention. In 1933 an Interdepartmental Committee under Thornton's chairmanship recommended the training of medical aids. The scheme was close in intention both to the Loram concept of Health Assistant and Thornton's idea of a medical auxiliary: African men with at least a Junior Certificate were to be given four years' training at the black college at Fort Hare, followed by a final year at the American Board of Mission's McCord Hospital in Durban. When the "liberal" Jan Hofmeyr became Minister of Health in 1934 (a portfolio he held with several others in the Smuts-Botha "Fusion" government) he persuaded the Chamber of Mines to contribute £25,000 toward the scheme, on the grounds that

> in a few years' time there will be an acute shortage of native labor on the mines and elsewhere. It is not therefore merely from a humanitarian but also from an economic point of view that it is essential . . . to try to reduce the appalling amount of preventable disease in the native territories.

By 1935, the industry was giving nearly £85,000 to the Union and Protectorate governments for the establishment of medical and hospital services in African areas. As W. Gemmill, General Manager of the Gold Producers' Committee of the Chamber of Mines, delicately put it:

> This payment is, in effect, a recruiting charge, inasmuch as it is made with the object of promoting the welfare of Natives in South Africa so that there shall be an ample supply of Native labourers for the mines.

In fact, the medical-aid scheme soon ran into difficulties. Fort Hare changed the minimum entry qualification to matriculation and Africans quickly realized that they were being offered a training that was almost as long as the full medical qualification but gave them no right even to prescribe drugs (Schapiro 1987). Dr. A. B. Xuma, one of the few Western-trained black doctors in South Africa at the time, and later to become President of the African National Congress, had pointed out the dangers of this as early as 1931. The program became extremely unpopular among the black intelligentsia. As George Gale, initially a teacher on the scheme and later one of its most bitter critics, pointed out, it fell between two stools. It provided neither fully qualified medical professional training for Africans nor the large cadre of paraprofessionals that could have made an impact on the ill health of the rural areas. It was abandoned by the state in 1943 after some three dozen African medical aids had been trained—about half the number originally anticipated (Gale 1938) and several hundred less than the nurses required to make any substantial contribution.

By the turn of the decade, the existing health services, particularly in the rural areas, were widely acknowledged to be wholly inadequate. In the late 1930s, the ratio of physicians to patients varied from 1:800 in the Cape

Peninsula to about 1:35,000 in many black rural areas. Of the 2,000 practitioners in the country, over half practiced in the main towns; the rest were scattered over an area of 462,000 square miles. In addition to about a dozen African doctors, the only African health care workers were a small but increasing number of nurses (nursing was already becoming an extremely popular profession for daughters of the black elite), medical aids, a handful of malaria and public health workers in Natal and a small army of "deverminisers" in the Transkei. In the urban areas, according to the Interdepartmental Committee on the Social, Health and Economic Conditions of Urban Natives in 1942, few local authorities had carried out their obligations under the 1919 Public Health Act in relation to African areas, despite some sporadic pressure from the Public Health Department and the Native Affairs Department. Few local authorities were prepared to spend more on the black areas than they raised from the black population itself. A system of fiscal segregation was developed which led to the poorest areas being most neglected, despite a widespread recognition and fear that epidemic disease "knows no colour bar" and increasing alarm over the future of the labor force:

> Thus, as the Department of Public Health put it in 1938: With a national agricultural and industrial economy based on cheap Native labor, the health conditions of the non-Europeans have become of paramount interest to the Europeans. Further the fact has been stressed that disease knows no colour bar and the European community is continually paying the penalty for tolerating reservoirs of infection among the Bantu population. In spite of such utilitarian arguments, widespread apathy or even opposition to efforts to provide for the fundamental health requirements of the Native are still encountered. It is only in the last year or two that serious thought has been given to the non-European health problem as a whole. This revealed immediately the deplorable lack of knowledge of the Natives's health and social conditions.

The increasing cost of this ill health both for industry and for the overburdened municipal hospitals concentrated the mind wonderfully. According to the Medical Inspector of the Transkeian Territories in July 1938:

> There is no doubt that if the Natives of the Transkei are to have at their disposal the medical facilities which should be provided, if the principal labor reservoir in the Union is to be is to be preserved, if the segregationist policy of the Government is to be at all practicable or successful, if the Europeans in the Union are ever to be free from the ever present threat of communicable diseases . . . then the state will need to undertake a far greater responsibility in connection with medical and health services both financially and in regard to personnel than is at present the case.

In 1938/39 the Natal municipal and provincial authorities clamored for assistance as their medical services threatened to break down under the increasing African demand for hospital services. Thus, in 1938 a special meeting was held of a subcommittee of the Provincial Consultative Committee to discuss "Native Health and Hospital services." It referred to the "desperate position of hospital treatment of Natives and the dangerous lack of preventive and health services in Native rural areas." It appealed to the Public Health Department to see "hospital provision and rural health services" as a "single problem," and for financial assistance from central government for provincial hospital services as well as for rural "convalescent homes" and clinics. The health authorities were now also under pressure from the Native Affairs Department, which argued that the 1936 legislation which empowered the South African Native Trust to buy up European-owned farms was "a most favourable and opportune time for inaugurating a State medical service for the Native areas: a reflection of the increasingly urgent demand from capital for much needed state assistance to secure the reproduction, and subsidize the welfare costs, of its labor force." It was in this context that the Public Health Department invited George Gale to join its ranks as an expert on African rural health[4] and members began to advocate preventive rather than purely curative measures in the rural areas.

As A. de V. Brunt in the department argued in a memorandum compiled in response to the Provincial subcommittee's proposal:

> The problem is becoming extremely acute because of the deterioration of the Native communities, their increased desire for European medicine, the demand for more Native labour and the establishment of large segregated Native communities by the Native Trust and Land Act 1936 . . . unless an adequate and organized service is instituted on the basis of "prevention is better than cure," then the hospital problem will become impossible.

It is somewhat ironic that the health centers that were to become South Africa's showpiece in the field of preventive medicine in the 1940s and the keystone of the recommendations of the National Health Services Commission took their origin in a drive by the government for a cheap formula for African health needs in the context of segregation. Thus, in 1939, the Secretary for Public Health, Cluver, wrote to the Deputy Chief Health Officer in Cape Town:

> Government is definitely opposed to *any* increase in Native hospital beds. All increased demand for treatment of illness among Natives must be met by cheap clinics. Such clinics must be set up in rural areas where the bulk of patients could be treated on out-patient lines.

To the Secretary of Finance he put the matter even more bluntly:

> The deterioration in health and the greater hospital-mindedness of the Natives are responsible for the rapid increase [in demand for hospital places by Afri-

> cans]. The position has already been reached where the provinces are unable and unwilling to carry on with their present financial resources. . . . In order to control expenditure on Native hospitalization and to reduce the demand in a manner which will ultimately result in a considerable saving to the Government a scheme has been evolved to establish inexpensive clinics in rural areas for the early treatment of disease among Natives. . . . The proposal is to establish in each area a central clinic and a few subsidiary clinics. . . . The subsidiary clinics will consist of inexpensive huts where patients can be treated and examined. It is anticipated that very little will be spent on buildings. Hospital equipment will be of the cheapest.

In response to the dramatic deterioration in African health and the absence of an adequate service, the Department of Public Health proposed establishing three health centers or clinics in African rural areas headed by a doctor assisted by ten African nurses and health assistants at a total cost of £12,000. Even this meager provision was whittled away after the outbreak of war, and it was only the health center at Polela in Natal under the inspired direction of Sidney and Emily Kark which really got off the ground. With the support of Harry Gear and George Gale in the Department, they were able, despite the inauspicious origins of the experiment, to pioneer a new form of community and preventive health that established South Africa's reputation for progressive medicine over the decade.[5]

To many observers it was clear that far more would have to be done to resolve the health crisis that had developed by the late 1930s. Moreover, the problems went beyond simply those of health to affect every aspect of African social, economic, and political life. The early war years saw an unprecedented level of militancy and trade-union organization among black workers, while the African petty bourgeoisie, led by Dr. A. B. Xuma, significantly, as we have seen, one of the few overseas-trained African doctors, was also increasingly dissatisfied and embittered. The need to gear all resources to the war effort heightened the necessity to improve the labor supply and mollify African opinion: hence the number of commissions of inquiry and conciliatory gestures. Then, as now, however, the carrot of promised reform was accompanied by the stick of increased coercion, as in the case of Emergency Regulation 42, which outlawed African strikes. Moreover, the challenge to the state at this time did not only come from Africans. The declaration of war, as is well known, had split the Smuts-Hertzog United Party, and the government's decision to join the allies was made on a narrowly won majority in parliament. The war years saw violent extraparliamentary actions by Afrikaner nationalists against the Smuts government, and it was clear that the Smuts government was losing control both among urban Afrikaner workers and even more crucially among the white farmers in the countryside (O'Meara 1983).

THE IMPACT OF CAPITALIST DEVELOPMENT ON AFRIKANER HEALTH

From its formation in 1934 the Purified National Party had attacked the inadequacy of the government's attempts to deal with the welfare needs of the Afrikaner *volk*. Although health was of concern only to a relatively small handful of medical men in the party, it seems clear that through the 1930s there was a rising tide of popular concern with white social welfare, and increasing demands for some form of national insurance, if not a national health service, for whites. Although it was the deterioration in the health of their African workers that most concerned capitalists, South Africa's white population had also felt the impact of the processes of industrialization and proletarianization. Through the first half of the twentieth century, the stream of African workers making their way to the towns had been paralleled by newly proletarianized Afrikaners, pushed off the land largely as a result of the capitalization of agriculture. The process was accelerated by the rise in land prices and in the effects of the Anglo-Boer war and natural disaster. Unlike Africans, whole families were pushed off the land and were dependent on their meager urban earnings. Unskilled and barely literate they could compete as equal neither with the skilled English-speaking workers who were drawn to South Africa from an already advanced industrial proletariat, nor with the Africans who still had access to some elements of a rural subsidy for the support of their families. With their access to the vote and their not infrequent kinship and local ties to the Afrikaner establishment, they constituted a serious problem for the South African state. Their presence in the towns and the dangers of a cross-color class alliance with equally poor and exploited blacks fueled demands for urban segregation, the so-called civilized labor policy and the populist anticommunist appeals of Afrikaner nationalism. By the late 1920s, it was estimated that one in five Afrikaners was a "poor white" (O'Meara 1983, 82).

As among Africans, so the patterns of morbidity and mortality among poor Afrikaners also resulted from South Africa's capitalist development. In both town and countryside, accounts of public health officers and school medical inspectors revealed the high incidence of preventable disease, while the Carnegie Commission, which inquired into the position of poor whites and issued a five-volume report in 1932, painted a truly deplorable picture of Afrikaner health. In the malarial Bushveld of the Transvaal and on the alluvial diamond diggings in the northern Cape, whites suffered from malaria, schistosomiasis, and tapeworm, while in town Afrikaners suffered from tuberculosis and rickets. Maternal and infant mortality, although not at this time as high as among Africans, were higher than in other industrial countries (Unterhalter 1982, 631–632). As late as 1939, a nutritional survey revealed that over 47 percent of Transvaal school boys suffered from malnutrition; while the statistics for the remaining provinces were not quite as high, they were far from satisfactory. According to Henry Gluckman (1939), who became Minister of Health in 1946, in the early 1940s:

> Typhoid fever, the incidence of which is a most sensitive index with regard to the standard of environmental hygiene in any area or country is probably ten times as high for all sections of the people compared with other civilized countries in the world. The incidence of diphtheria in 1939 was 125.8/100,000 of the European population in spite of the fact that medical science has discovered how to eliminate this disease almost entirely.

Tuberculosis rates were rising even among the European population from 24.8 in 100,000 in 1922 to 46.2 in 1942. Venereal disease, malaria, schistosomiasis and dental caries were all major problems for whites as well as blacks. And, as for the vast majority of blacks, for many whites, especially in the rural areas, there were no available services within their means: in many parts of the country, the 1942–1944 National Health Services Commission was met by the cry, "*Hulle word siek, hulle gaan dood en hulle word maar net begrawe.*" ("They get sick, they die and they are just buried.")

It was clear too that the organization of South Africa's health services was totally inadequate. Largely as a result of the compromise at the time of union, where matters of health and public health were largely ignored, the responsibility for health was divided in a bewildering fashion among provinces, municipalities, and the central government. The result for patients could be disastrous as they were shuttled between the different authorities. As Dr. H. S. Gear, Assistant Health Officer in the Department of Health, remarked in 1936, "Confusion, inefficiency, inertia and extravagance are all to be laid at the door of this illogical division of public health duties in the Act [of Union]" (Gear 1938, 137). Health took a low priority in these years, except at times of epidemic among whites as in 1919; the first Minister of Public Health was appointed only after the influenza epidemic and the passage of the Public Health Act, passed in its wake, and even then the portfolio was combined—usually with Interior, Welfare and Education—until Gluckman became Minister of Health in 1946.

Largely as a result of their militancy—or agitation as the Chamber of Mines would have it—white mine workers had secured a certain degree of protection from the worst ravages of miners' phthisis and tuberculosis, as well as reasonably adequate compensation; in certain industries, unions had organized sickness benefit funds but relatively few workers and an even smaller number of the total population were covered. With the advent of the Pact Nationalist and Labour Government in 1924, various forms of state insurance schemes were discussed for the first time. In 1928 an inquiry was instituted into old-age pensions, workers' compensation, and health insurance, although it was only as South Africa began to recover from the depression that these discussions were given any effect. In 1936 a Departmental Inquiry again recommended the establishment of National Health Insurance for the urban areas and improved medical services for the rural areas and African territories. These were never implemented, however, despite the advances in terms of general welfare for whites in the second half of the 1930s with the general economic recovery—the introduction of old-age pensions, unemployment benefits, widows' pensions, and the establishment of a Department of Social Welfare.

In the rural areas, the District Surgeon was supposed to take care of the health of paupers, but in fact this left large numbers of ordinary wage-earners and rural families crippled financially by medical bills. At the time of the 1929/30 debate on national insurance schemes, one or two medical men began to call for a national health service in the columns of the *Journal of the Medical Association of South Africa*, but they were largely ignored by both the state and the profession, although the call for a national health service seems to have been a part of the political platform of the South African Labour Party. Despite the centrality of the issue for Afrikaners, there were surprisingly few demands from Nationalists for a national health service. It is true that at the Volks-kongress of 1934 and the government's conference on Social Work called in 1936 there were appeals for a form of national health insurance and the Vrouevereenigings (Nationalist Party Women's Organizations) were also in the forefront of demands for improvements in health and nursing services: among their concerns was the very high rate of maternal and infant mortality. Among the politicians, the notable exceptions were Drs. A. J. Stals and Karl Bremer (Botha 1950*a*; 1961, 72–133) who were the Nationalists' front-bench spokesmen on health, although one has the impression that their appeals fell on deaf ears among their fellow politicians on either side of the House and perhaps more generally.

THE NATIONAL HEALTH SERVICES COMMISSION

In 1939, when Gluckman once again called for a form of national health insurance, he was supported by the Nationalists and especially Bremer, who demanded an improved service in the rural areas; the Labour Party went further in demanding a national health service. All their proposals were almost contemptuously dismissed by the then Minister for Public Health Harry Lawrence as "impractical." In 1939 the nationalist Member of Parliament (MP) Karl Bremer proposed to establish a state medical service; the idea was again given short shrift by the government. Yet within two years when Gluckman once again brought up the subject, this time appealing for the appointment of a National Health Services Commission, the response was very different. In the context of the war demands and the political strain on the state, there was greater preparedness to think and talk of social reform. To the consternation of the medical profession, public dissatisfaction with the existing state and expense of health care led many to turn to "practitioners outside our [i.e., the medical] profession" for advice and treatment, and there were even calls in parliament for the official recognition of what the MASA was pleased to term "such cults." At the same time, the clamor against the high cost of medical care led them to fear "unguided, hasty legislation . . . drafted by laymen" (*Journal of MASA* 1941, 4). The response of the profession, both in the columns of their *Journal* and in the publication by the Medical Association of South Africa of *Planning for Health in South Africa*, a scheme for a nationally organized health service, led the Department of Public Health to fear it was losing the initiative. As the Department saw it:

> A "democratic health service" as outlined in the pamphlet is in essence a proposal that the health services of the country be handed over "lock, stock and barrel" to the medical profession. . . . It is inadvisable that any [such] scheme be allowed to crystalize since once it is put forward as the considered view of the M.A.S.A., it will be infinitely more difficult to secure general acceptance of any alternative scheme which may be within the capacity of the Government (from political and financial angles) to give effect to.

Officials recommended the adoption of the Gluckman proposal as the lesser of two evils, and in 1942 the Commission was appointed under the chairmanship of Gluckman himself and with broad representation from public life, including the trade unions and the medical and nursing professions.

The Commission's brief was "to inquire into, report and advise upon the provision of an organized National health service in conformity with the modern conception of 'health' [which was carefully defined in the report] which will ensure adequate mental, dental, nursing and hospital services for all sections of the people of South Africa." It took evidence from more than 1,000 witnesses all over South Africa and from all walks of life, and collected over 12,000 pages of evidence.

Its wide-ranging and remarkably innovative recommendations involved the total reorganization of South Africa's current health care system. Its principal objective was stated to be the establishment of a national health service that would reach all the people of South Africa, regardless of color, and which would be paid for out of a health tax that would be assessed as part of general taxation according to means. Crucial to its plans was the rationalization of the complex set of existing structures dealing with health into a unified system under central state control, but with local answerability. The aim was to establish preventive health services rather than to perpetuate high cost private practice which failed to reach the poor and the state-funded high-technology, hospital-based curative system currently in operation for whites and a small minority of urban blacks. These objectives would be ensured through the division of the country into a grid of some 400 health centers based on the model established by Sidney and Emily Kark at Polela, which had been drawn to the Commission's attention by George Gale, one of its most ardent proponents.

A significant shift in thinking had occurred, however. Whereas in the original conception of the health centers, as we have seen, the main motive was to establish a cheap and segregated service for blacks in the rural areas, under Gluckman and Gale—who was clearly in large measure responsible for the thinking behind the Commission report, and who had been greatly influenced by the success of the Karks's experiment at Polela—the health center was to provide the model for all of South Africa, regardless of race, and for its positive preventive and democratic possibilities.

As George Gale explained in an article in the *South African Medical Journal* (22 June 1946, 326) the health centers were to be based on an acknowledgment of the social origins of much disease:

> Its approach to health needs is entirely different from that of ordinary private practice. It places in the field not an individual medical practitioner, but a team. . . . They are trained to observe, in the homes of the people, the environmental, including the social, factors which are working for or against health. These they record, and the record is available to the team at the health center when dealing with individuals from these homes.

While recognizing the wider reasons for ill health, it was hoped that the health centers would also prompt research into the social causes of disease and advise government departments in such areas of labor, social welfare, nutrition, and health education. Clearly the health centers could be successful, however, only if the more fundamental premises of the Commission were accepted—and this demanded more than an organizational change in the nature of health services.

A number of the recommendations of the Commission were embodied in the National Health Act of 1946, which was piloted through Parliament by Gluckman. Even before the full report had been published at the end of 1944, however, the Smuts government showed its unwillingness to undertake the action necessary to fulfill its central tenets. On October 9, 1944, in a public statement, the Prime Minister undertook in advance not to impinge on the constitutional rights of the provinces by interfering with their control of hospital services. The idea of a health tax was also jettisoned as financially impractical. Thus Smuts surrendered any idea of a central state service. The best that could be achieved was the establishment of a central coordinating body to try to reduce the overlap in functions. A Central Health Council was also set up to advise the government on health matters. The government did nonetheless decide to go ahead with the establishment of the health centers on the Polela model, and within five years some fifty new health centers had been formed in both rural and urban settings. A new center, the Institute of

Family and Community Health, was established under Kark's direction at Clairwood, Durban, to provide a comprehensive system of health care for all sections of the Durban community, through the work of interdisciplinary teams of health workers—physicians, nurses, health educators, social workers, and other auxiliaries, to be drawn from the local community. It also aimed to train cadres to work at the other health centers (Gale 1970, 495–517).

Despite some initial enthusiasm for the Gluckman report, it is clear that almost immediately the health centers roused the opposition of the medical profession, which feared competition and insisted on a more conventionally based curative health service. The government's failure to implement key aspects of the report gave the profession its opportunity to stiffen its resistance to the health centers. Clairwood became the focus of much of this discontent. For a few years the health centers and the Clairwood Institute survived on their own momentum. With the accession of the National Party to power in 1948, however, the climate became far less propitious for experiments in the health field. Although both the first two Ministers of Health, A. J. Stals and Karl Bremer, were proponents of preventive health care, Stals had little clout in the Nationalist cabinet and Bremer, too, was constantly frustrated by his cabinet colleagues. Neither had any sympathy for the colorblind form of health care service being pioneered at Clairwood. Despite Bremer's criticism of the Smuts government for reneging on the idea of a National Health Service, his own efforts to persuade the provinces to give up their powers were no more successful. He had little support from a cabinet more concerned with the needs of wealthy farmers and Afrikaner entrepreneurs than with the ill health of the mass of the populace. The general transformation of the position of the "poor whites" as a result of South Africa's industrial expansion into secondary industry during and after World War II made issues of welfare for whites of far less urgency than they had been in the 1930s. And it was certainly not part of the Nationalist Party's brief in the 1950s to worry unduly about black health.

For a few years the health centers and the Clairwood Institute survived notwithstanding a government inquiry into their alleged communist tendencies that was never published. While not overtly hostile, Stals and Bremer, who were not particularly enthusiastic about the health centers, soon promoted the technologically based curative services demanded by the medical profession (Botha 1950*a*, 104). Nor was the Department of Health uniformly in favor of the new centers. Initially both the health centers and the Clairwood Institute were able to continue, and the institute's training program of preventive and family medicine was in fact integrated into the undergraduate medical degree course of the Durban Medical School (for black students), which was opened in 1951. It was supported financially by a grant from the Rockefeller Foundation, and politically defended by George Gale, who had become Secretary of Health in 1946. From 1948 onward, however, Gale found the political position in the Department increasingly uncongenial, and in 1951 he resigned as Secretary to become the first Dean of the Durban Medical School. Even there he faced numerous political battles, and when in 1956 the Rockefeller grant, which subsidized both the Clairwood Institute and his deanship, came to an end and the state refused to take it over, Gale left South Africa to become Dean of the Medical School at Makerere. Nor was he alone. From the mid-1950s on, most of Kark's students and disciples left South Africa—to attempt the establishment of similar preventive community health centers in more sympathetic parts of the world. Kark and his followers undoubtedly went on to influence the international development of social and community medicine through the World Health Organization and their new teaching commitments. In South Africa, however, by 1960, both the Clairwood Institute and most of the health centers had died because of a lack of funds (Gluckman 1968).

In retrospect, it is perhaps not surprising that the recommendations of the National Health Services Commission were dropped after 1948. The central dictum of the Commission that "unless there were drastic reforms in the sphere of nutrition, housing, health education and recreation, the mere provision of more doctoring would not bring more health to the people of the country" demanded a drastic restructuring of the social order, which went well beyond the white consensus. Perhaps it also exceeded the capacity of the political economy, which was still so heavily dependent on the primary sectors of farming and mining. Despite the idealism of the war years and the reformist tendencies of elements in the United Party, it is clear that they went too far even for the Smuts government; the mining industry, for example, still depended on unorganized low-wage migrant labor from impoverished reserves and, like the white farmers, adamantly opposed any notion of urban stabilization. Dominant classes in the state were simply not prepared to sustain the welfare costs involved in a National Health Service. The Afrikaners who gained power in 1948 were even more dependent on a low-wage migrant labor economy. Once the immediate problems of poor white health were resolved and improved and expanded benefit societies and insurance schemes were able to take care of white working and middle-class health, the impetus for a more radical solution of South Africa's health problems evaporated. The medical profession rapidly retreated from its wartime position, while continuing to pay lip-service to notions of community service and preventive health care for a few years. Later this was reduced to an insignificant subsector of formal medical education.

From the 1950s onward, National Party ideology dictated that problems of African welfare be transferred to the newly created "Bantu homelands" or Bantustan authorities. Africans were to be made to pay for their own health and welfare costs. The result was the continued neglect of preventive medicine, and continued high levels of infant mortality from malnutrition and infectious diseases. Tuberculosis claimed 100,000 new victims each year, and cholera and typhoid raged in the rural areas (WHO 1983). The attempt to transform all urban African labor into rightless migrant labor and the failure to recognize African rights in the urban areas sharpened the effects of the low-wage economy, resulting in poor living conditions and high disease rates.

Ironically, since the early 1970s, in line with international health thinking, the South African government has begun to revive the rhetoric of the 1944 Health Commission. In response to black worker militancy of the early 1970s, the Soweto uprising and continued African resistance, international pressure, and transformation in the economy, which increasingly demand a stabilized urban work force, the welfare concessions first made available to whites have now been extended to the black petty bourgeoisie in the towns and the black elite in the Bantustans. Health has become part of a wide-ranging but not particularly successful strategy of co-option.

The late 1970s saw a revival in the Bantustans of some of the ideas of the social medicine of the 1940s, with an emphasis on the role of local clinics, health teams and the training of paraprofessionals. In the so-called white areas—the towns and white farming districts—health services were brought under the provisions of the 1977 Health Act (No. 63) which replaced the 1919 Public Health Act and its various amendments. In keeping with the Bantustan policy, a dual health structure for blacks has been fostered, with one kind of medical practice for the rural areas and another in the "common areas"—a division that was not envisaged in 1944. Responsibilities in the "common area" remain divided between state, provincial, and local authorities, with limited attempts at coordination. Complaints at the inefficiencies of the system continue from the medical profession. Despite the verbal commitment to preventive medicine, the continued emphasis on private medical practice and large hospitals suggests that high technology, curative personal health care remains the norm for the white population, and perhaps for a section of the blacks with rights in urban areas. The estimates for expenditure on preventive health amount to at best about 5 percent of the total state health budget, while the annual maintenance and running costs of the Johannesburg General Hospital exceed the total health budget of all the Bantustans (WHO 1983).

The dualism both replicates and legitimates existing power relations in South Africa. The rhetoric of reform couched in the language of international development and health care agencies has a certain utility in the attempt to convince world opinion that "apartheid is dying in South Africa." A limited number of changes have been made, and there is an increasing emphasis on more effective and lower-cost medical strategies for blacks, both in the urban areas and in the Bantustans. In Cape Town and Soweto there have been reports that maternal and child health care clinics have brought about dramatic reductions in infant mortality rates, although the effect of this on longer-term morbidity and mortality rates remains to be seen. In the Bantustans, health budgets have been increased, although this increase is minute in relation to the need. Nor is it clear how much of the increase is spent on the needs of the poor. In the absence of far more fundamental changes of the kind envisaged by the planners of 1944, the recent reformism is unlikely to have much impact on the "health of the people" (Laurence 1977, 89–94).[6]

NOTES

1. *Editor's note*: This chapter was written in 1983 and reflects the conditions in South Africa's health services at that time. In addition to the sources cited in the text, the work is based on a number of other primary sources that could not be fully spelled out here because of space constraints. These include the South African Government Native Labour Bureau; the Native Laws Commission; the South African Institute of Race Relations Archives, University of Witwatersrand; the South African House of Assembly Debates in *Hansard*; reports of the South African Railways; reports of the South African Public Health Department; reports of the South African Department of Native Affairs; reports of the National Health Services Commission; archives of the Rockefeller Foundation, South African region; and editorials and statements in the *South African Medical Journal* addressing the topic of this chapter.

2. *Doctors of the Mines* contains the mine-owners' account of these reforms: it was "a commemorative volume published in 1971 to mark the 50th Anniversary of the Mine Medical Officers' Association of South Africa." The blurb on the dust-cover provides a splendid example of the official version of medicine in South Africa:

> It tells the story of how primitive tribesmen from the most remote corners of Africa have come to the mines and have been taught that the White man's medicine is more powerful than the witchdoctors. The wonderful health record of this army of men most of whom work underground has been achieved by the scientific studies of diseases that once decimated the tribes.

As this chapter shows, this is almost the exact opposite of the truth.

3. "The thin, round-shouldered, flat-chested, pot-bellied child with spindly legs was such a common sight that it can only be concluded that many were on the borders of starvation. The problem is thus not only one of providing this or that particular food factor, but rather a need for a general increase of all foodstuffs that will tend to build up a healthy Bantu population" (Report of the National Health Services Commission 1944).

4. Gale was appointed in December 1938. According to his widow, Mrs. Audrey Gale, "They appointed George because he was supposed to know about 'the natives.'" (Oral interview June 21, 1983). We are grateful to Mrs. Gale for the interview, a delightful tea, and access to George Gale's papers. Gale, initially a mission doctor, had worked with the Fort Hare scheme for training medical aids before resigning on account of its inadequacies, and had recently written a privately published pamphlet, *A Suggested Approach to the Health Needs of the Native Rural Areas of South*

Africa (Gale 1938), which was to greatly influence the Karks after they established the health center at Polela. He was probably the key person in the Department of Health encouraging the health center idea and played a major role in the formulation of the *National Health Services Report*. He became Secretary of Health and Chief Health Officer for the Union of South Africa between 1946 and 1952. In 1952, he resigned from a government service increasingly unsympathetic to his views to become Dean of Durban Medical School. The importance of Gale's role was also confirmed in oral interviews with Sidney and Emily Kark, August 1979 and September 1982.

5. At Polela, for example, between 1942 and 1946, in the area of "intensive health visiting," the death rate fell from 38.33 to 13.11 per 1,000; the infant mortality, from 275 to 155 per 1,000. Scabies and impetigo (both of which were widespread in 1942) were almost eliminated (G. Gale, "Government Health Centres in the Union of South Africa," SAM).

6. South Africa spent a vast amount of funds on propaganda boasting its fine medical services for blacks in the1970s. Among the glossy hardbacks produced was a volume entitled *The Health of the People. A Review of Health Services in the Republic of South Africa in the Mid-Seventies* (Johannesburg, Department of Health, 1977.)

PART THREE

Therapeutic Traditions of Africa: A Historical Perspective

INTRODUCTION

The focus of this section is on Africa's "multiple streams of healing traditions, each with its own distribution in time and space," to bring forward a phrase from this book's introduction. *Traditum*, the Latin root, refers to that which is "handed down," either orally, or in written text or other strict codification (Janzen 1989; Marty 1982, 3–4; Sullivan 1988). This use of the term is similar to that by archaeologists and culture historians to account for sets of cultural features that remain recognizable over time and space, although not static. Thus a health and healing tradition would reveal characteristic ways of identifying and classifying disease, organizing treatments, and expounding its teachings. The elements of the healing traditions are, however, not disembodied and free-varying. They are embedded in the logical and ideological contexts of living communities; they are shaped by economic, social, and political forces.

Some writers of the present section, notably Zempleni and Sindzingre (chap. 12) and Greenwood (chap. 11), portray traditions as finely integrated systems of ideas and practices. However, others, especially Murray Last (chap. 16) on the "Maguzawa" Hausa, acknowledge the system, but argue that it may lack salience, or as in Ranger's account (chap. 10) of mission medicine that it may reflect internal contradictions. The notion of a "medical system," introduced a decade ago (Janzen 1978*a*; Leslie 1976; Twumasi 1975) and still used (Good 1987; Yoder 1982), is by no means universally accepted, be it from the "ethnomedical" or from the "ecological" perspective (Janzen and Prins 1981; Press 1980).

The degree and basis of system or structure in health care may thus vary a great deal. One source of this range concerns the extent of conceptual or ideational ordering in a therapeutic tradition in a given setting. Murray Last's contribution in this regard is the very helpful notion of "medical culture" as a way of speaking of the substance of ideas, without absolutizing "system." Essays by Greenwood on Morocco (chap. 11), Abdalla on Islamic medicine (chap. 6), Sindzingre and Zempleni (chap. 12), and Prins (chap. 13), describe theories of causality and classification of disease, axioms about misfortune, and concepts of anatomy, infection, and human functioning as the bases of order in medicine. Carol MacCormack (chap. 18) introduces "legitimacy" of a health care practice, in the sense that Max Weber understood it, as a further variable in the way medical ideas and practices may cohere. Janzen's chapter (chap. 7) on precolonial Kongo coast utilizes the touchstone of corporate organization in medicine as a basis for order and system.

The political dimension of medical institutions establishes the bases and the criteria by which resources will be channeled into definitions of illness, related therapies, and specialties. Centralized polities have long been the force providing shape to explicit health care practices. The reforms of Uthman dan Fodio and Muhammad Bello in the Hausa states provided support to the *malams* and *sharifas* (Abdalla, chap. 6); the king of Swaziland reinforced *isangoma* diviners (Ngubane, chap. 14); the colonial states sponsored yaws and smallpox eradication campaigns, and the primary health care and public health campaigns of the postcolonial Kenyan state and city of Nairobi—all these represent focusing policies to achieve particular health goals and priorities.

Less clear-cut, but as important in the equation, are the decentralized applications of political energies in achieving particular health goals. The implications for health of the West African associations such as Sadoho (Sindzingre and Zempleni, chap. 12), Poro and Sande (MacCormack, chap. 18), the cults of affliction of Bantu-speaking Africa (Lemba in Janzen [chap. 7]; Nzila in Prins [chap. 13]; Isangoma in Ngubane [chap. 14]), the healing rituals and practices of independent Christian churches and Muslim Sufi congregations; the local campaigns of mission churches; the primary health care campaigns scattered across a countryside—all these equally reflect the political dimension of gathering resources and focusing their application through policy. Of late there has been a growing awareness of the need to coordinate the efforts by African medicine specialists to establish their role in postcolonial national society through professionalization (Last and Chavunduka 1986). This, too, is an example of the political ordering of medicine.

In the general (part) introductions of this volume and in the chapters in part II, the role of the modern state in structuring health care has been shown abundantly. Policies and practices endorsed or promoted by the state have been shown to be instrumental on health, both for good and for ill. Early colonial Ubangi-Shari's labor and taxation practices (Cordell, Gregory, and Piché, chap. 1) had disastrous effects on the health of its people, typical of most early colonial practices. Similarly, the failed reforms in South Africa in the 1940s (Marks and Andersson, chap. 5), demonstrate the impact of state policies on health (or illness). Curtin's contribution (chap. 9) pointedly looks at the impact of colonial state policies in shaping health care and public health. Mburu (chap. 17) shows how state policy in Kenya was related to the decline in infant mortality and to overall public health in Nairobi.

The pervasiveness of the political dimension in shaping and ordering health and healing requires that an honest portrayal of a therapeutic tradition also builds into it the recognition of historical change. Healing traditions in Africa have often been called on to provide interpretations of a rapidly changing reality, to find answers to new questions. As seen in part II, disease challenges have often shifted rapidly, and so have the therapeutic responses. An early example of this is found in Janzen's chapter (chap. 7) on Western Equatorial medicine. In response to the eighteenth-century collapse of the Loango kingdom during the coastal trade, medicines and ritual techniques arose to come to terms with the growing level of conflict and witchcraft suspicion in the society. Whereas previously the *nkisi* mode of treatment had often reflected royal and ancestral power, it now began to reflect the power of more aggressive and uncontrolled water and nature spirits. Appropriate research on change and continuity in African therapeutics has barely begun. Long-term and large-scale continuities may be punctuated by equally far-reaching changes and local variations. There may be continuities in some realms of the therapeutic tradition, such as explanatory ideas, while the social and political, or ecological, reality changes. The essays that follow thus explore historical avenues of inquiry.

The chapters, in accordance with the above perspective, are organized into a loosely historical framework to address the changing face of therapeutics in Africa. We have purposefully grouped chapters on varied therapeutic traditions into similar eras—precolonial, colonial, postcolonial—to demonstrate that all are equally "historical," that is, changing, and that all have been utilized to alleviate disease and improve health.

THE AFRO-MEDITERRANEAN MEDICAL TRADITIONS: CLASSICAL ORIGINS

The histories of Western medicine and African medicine are intertwined in numerous ways over millennia; there have been currents of influence in both directions. Some early basic features of Greek medicine derive from the medical learning of dynastic Egypt (Steuer and Saunders 1959). Imhotep—vizier, architect, and physician of King Djoser who united the two kingdoms in 2600 B.C.—was later identified by the Greeks as Asklepios, patron god of healing (Westendorf 1978, 141). Although only about a dozen manuscripts of explicitly medical nature survive from the early dynastic period, these suffice to show that early Egyptian medicine was highly developed for the then-known world. Pathologies recognized and treated included a wide variety of disorders either given pragmatic explanation and treatment or considered to be caused by spiritual or magical forces. The channels or elements of the body, as well as the central importance of the heart, were recognized in this system, although the blood, later an important element in Greek medicine, was not an important fluid central to bodily functioning.

The extent to which ancient Egypt's medicine reflected significant dimensions of the healing arts of Africa, or represented independently developed knowledge, remains an open question. Some of the characteristics of ancient Egyptian medicine are suggestive of more recent African medicine. For example, the anatomical interest in the abdomen (El-Nadoury 1981, 164–166), as central bodily passage undifferentiated in its functions as digestive tract and reproductive organ (Westendorf 1978, 118–119), echoes emphases in some African systems of the nineteenth and twentieth centuries. Similarly, the role of the healing arts as a function of central authority, as illustrated by Imhotep's role in the unified kingdom, utilized to maintain order and health in the society, reflects certain Central African relationships between chief or king and healer.

These ancient layers of African science and art are, at least in North and East Africa, buried beneath later features of the early medicine of Mediterranean classical antiquity, of the humoral medicine of Hippocrates and Galen, and as filtered through Islamic thought and practice (Tempkin and Tempkin 1967). Three chapters in the present part reflect different directions of this medical tradition. Greenwood describes the present-day character of Greco-Islamic medicine in Morocco, emphasizing it as a basis for food and health classifications, as well as its synthesis with "medicine of the prophet." Abdalla (chap. 6), in a historical account of medicine in Hausaland in northern Nigeria, describes the supplanting of humoral medicine by "medicine of the prophet" and synthesis with Hausa healing arts. Curtin shows how the late-nineteenth-century European colonial assumptions about health and illness, as well as early policies of urban planning in Africa, were based on Greek humoral medicine. This medical learning may be traced from Greek antiquity, and is based on ideas about the interaction of the natural elements fire, earth, water, and air with the four humors—blood, phlegm, bile, and black bile. Codified somewhat in writings of Hippocrates and Galen, humoral medicine explains health and disease as the outcome of balance and imbalance, of hot and cold, and the combinations of humors. The system also serves as the basis of food classifications; its therapies include bleeding, cupping, and purging.

With the expansion of Islam into Africa in the seventh century, this classical "Greek" medical learning spread across the regions penetrated by Arabic-speaking Moslem conquerors, traders, and scholars. Centers of medical learning prospered in Cairo, Alexandria, Tripoli, and Rabat and as far south as Timbuktu where, in the twelfth century, university-training included medicine and philosophy.

Alongside this expansion of what is in Africa often called "Arabic" or "Islamic medicine"—problematic, according to Abdalla, since its practitioners are not necessarily Arab nor Islamic—there arose another emphasis known as "medicine of the prophet," consisting of Bedouin rules about hygiene, baths, food and drink, and social relations, many of which were attributed to legends from the Prophet or the Qur'an. As in the Near East, the secularized medical learning of antiquity did not rest easily alongside Prophetic Medicine. Conservative Muslim movements and leaders promoted strict Koranic practices at the expense of humoral medicine and classical philosophy, with a marked effect on the diagnosis and treatment of sickness. This Prophetic Medicine stressed purity in the framework of a strong moral code, and in some settings, exorcism of spirit possession. These latter have been strongly represented across the Sahel in Senegal, Mali, and the Ivory Coast, and as far east as Tanzania and Kenya, often embedded in the local congregations or orders of Sufism, or even in more indigenized form. In these places where Prophetic Medicine is found, it is visible in rules about circumcision and hygiene, the performance of prescribed purification rituals, the making and wearing of Koranic charms, as well as the exorcism of *jinn* spirits in the diagnosis of misfortune and disease. Specialized healers in the tradition of Prophet's Medicine have been named *marabout* and *sogo*, *sharif*, *malam*, and *shaykh* (in West Africa), *fgih* in Morocco, as well as in a few cases that of the Bantu-speaking African healer, *mganga* (as in Tanzania).

COLONIAL MEDICAL TRADITIONS: MODERN ORIGINS

The medicine that entered Africa from the West in the late nineteenth century and early twentieth century derived in Europe from the same humoral Hippocratic and Galenic teachings as had been adopted by North African and Near Eastern centers. In Europe this medicine remained the mainstay of physicians and barber-surgeons for nearly two millennia before giving way to "modern" Allopathic medicine. Whether this transition is considered from the standpoint of the humors of the Galenics or the elements of Paracelsus' cosmos, the locus of disease changed from rather broad to more narrow causal and classificatory domains. Vesalius, in the sixteenth century, defined the person in terms of a physical anatomy, thereby taking an important step away from the humoral or cosmic force view of Galen and Paracelsus. By the eighteenth century, Morgagni had rejected "fluids," the focus of humors, as the seat of disease, and emphasized organs and organisms instead. Virchow, in the nineteenth century, further localized anatomy in the study of tissue. This narrowing of the unit of focus in anatomy and physiology continues into the present as medical scholarship and practice concentrate on cells, molecules, and atoms (Ackerknecht 1982). The history of disease conceptualization follows a similar "narrowing" course in European medicine, from seeing the person afflicted as a miniature cosmos, to seeing the disease as an alien intruder within the body. Sydenham, seventeenth-century physician and friend of empiricist philosopher Locke, is credited by some with this transformation—in his case, malarial "recurrent fever" (Dewhurst 1966)—whose historical path culminates in the nineteenth-century bacteriology of Pasteur, Koch, and Jenner that played a prominent role in the isolation of the active agents of the great contagious diseases in medical history.

Although Allopathic medicine is based on the ancient doctrine of contraries, its modern meaning emphasizes reaction to, or assault on, a pathological condition or agent by its opposite. In antiquity, treatment introduced a "counteracting procedure" (allo) to the disease or condition (pathy), such as bleeding to drain away turgid blood, or enema to purge constipation, or heat for excessive cold. With the discovery of germs by nineteenth-century bacteriologists, Allopathy found a new scientific explanation for the doctrine of contraries. Drugs could be found or created that counteracted diseases carried by outside agents. Since that time, the Allopathic approach has become the dominant theoretical mode of Western medicine. Drugs destroy germs; surgery removes pathological tissue. Electronic and mechanical devices serve to find and destroy the pathogen within the physical body. A less influential, although still significant, paradigm of Western medicine is "homeopathy" ("same as pathogen") which, in areas such as immunization through live disease organisms, develops antibodies that repel the disease.

It was this narrowly focused Allo(counter)pathic (disease) paradigm of medicine that, at the point where it was becoming dominant in European medicine, was brought to Africa to wage the battle against the famous scourges: sleeping sickness, malaria, smallpox, typhus, cholera, and others that gave the continent the reputation of the "white man's grave," and which needed to be conquered in the name of civilization and progress. Curtin's contribution in this volume (chap. 9) describes the role of growing medical knowledge in the fight to create cities in colonial Africa of the 1880s that were free of malaria, and the juggling of several treatments, including the physical removal of people from malarial zones and the discovery of quinine as a cure and prophylaxis.

The several medical paradigms brought by emissaries of Western civilization to Africa also included Christian spiritual healing (Comaroff 1981, 1985). In their zeal to cure Africa's diseases with Allopathic medicine, Western medical practitioners, especially the Christian medical missionaries, emphasized the role of Christian compassion in their work, as a prelude to winning converts to the Christian gospel. As Terence Ranger shows in his contribution on mission medicine (chap. 10), the narrow physical emphasis of mission Allopathic medicine, coupled with the tacit holism of Christianity and the prominent display of Christ the healer in the scriptures, laid the basis for the independent African churches that emphasized spiritual healing, divination, and celebrative dancing in their liturgies. This was doubly ironic because Christian missions usually took a critical stance toward the holism of African medicine, arguing that it was superstitious, and that true healing could occur only in hospital-based Allopathic medicine.

The Mediterranean medicoreligious influences in Africa in the past three millennia—beginning with that of ancient Egypt, its legacy in the medicine of classical antiquity via Islam and Europe, Prophetic Medicine, and Christian Faith Healing—have all left their mark in the African continent. They have not, however, been adopted uncritically or without change. They have been selectively received and integrated within, or alongside of, the continually changing African ideas, practices, and institutions.

INDIGENOUS AFRICAN THERAPEUTIC TRADITIONS: AN OVERVIEW OF THE CLASSICAL FORMATIONS

The prevailing African ideas, practices, and institutions regarding therapeutics that have over the centuries confronted and often absorbed external medical influences are best understood in terms of the broad, integrative patterns of African civilizations, whose origins and stages of florescence are well known and need only brief review here. The status of research into the health and healing dimension of these civilizations is not as far along as areas such as the history of food production (Harlan et al. 1976) and metallurgy, linguistics (Greenberg 1955), art (Vansina 1984*a*; Willet 1971), or music (Arom 1985). Some of these patterns reflect continentwide regularities. Simha Arom, in his impressive review of the history of scholarship on African music, suggests that distinctive polyrhythmic and polyphonic structures are widespread, from Algeria to the Cape. It is not improbable that some of the features of healing and adaptation in ancient hunting and gathering societies were common across the continent, and have been the basis of regional or local therapeutic traditions that arose around distinctive food-production and settlement traditions.

In West Africa, the domestication of plants and animals was well under way by 1000 B.C., giving rise to numerous localized cultural traditions. Urban centers began to appear in the savanna by the early centuries of the first millennium A.D. Stratified social systems predated the arrival of Islam, as did trade tying together the zones of West Africa. By the early years of the second millennium A.D. Islam began to grow in importance in the life of the savanna zone, but it never completely supplanted pre-Islamic ritual or therapeutic practices. In the West African savanna, local and Islamic traditions have evolved and interacted. Abdalla's and Last's contributions (chaps. 6 and 16) show the indigenous Maguzawa culture of the Hausa of northern Nigeria being gradually supplanted by the reformist Medicine of the Prophet. Zempleni and Sindzingre (chap. 12) present Senufo concepts and practices of illness diagnosis and therapy, which are representative of the savanna zone. Public health and African medicine in Sierra Leone, as portrayed by MacCormack (chap. 18), reflect elements of the Guinea Forest context, to the south of the savanna.

The spread of food cultivation and sedentary society southward through and around the equatorial rainforest has come to be associated with the spread of the Bantu languages. These languages began to spread, perhaps as early as 1000 B.C., from the northwestern corner of the current territory of Bantu-speakers, in what is now the border area of Cameroon and Nigeria. They ultimately came to be spoken throughout the whole of central, eastern, and southern Africa. Food production and ironworking spread rapidly through this area during the first millennium A.D. The close overlap of the expansion of agriculture, of ironworking, and of interrelated languages has led scholars to hypothesize that in most cases the three processes were a single one—the spread of the Bantu-speakers (Birmingham and Martin 1983; Ehret and Posnansky 1982; de Maret 1980; Vansina 1984*b*). The languages and cultures, which evolved in the relatively recent past, are closely related to one another, and therefore the peoples of this region share interrelated healing practices.

The present collection of papers has been selected to show the broad outlines of the historic therapeutic cultures that Bantu-speaking societies created. Janzen's chapter about the Loango coast of western Equatorial Africa, and Waite's contribution (chap. 8) on East-Central African precolonial public health map the western and eastern limits of the *nkisi* complex, a characteristic feature of "western Bantu," that is, the complex that spread from the Cameroons through the forest and along the coast. Ngubane's portrayal of healers' networks in the Zulu region of South Africa, and Janzen's account of the Lemba cult of the Atlantic coast, sketch the contours of the collective "cult of affliction" (*ngoma*, *isangoma*) institution found in East, Central, and South Africa.

Ecological settings have shaped ideas and practices in African therapeutics. Both the West African and the Bantu-speaking civilizations, defined primarily by sedentary agriculture, have articulated with pastoral nomadism throughout their histories. Where the tsetse fly has been absent—as in the Sahel, across the eastern Sudan, in the lake region of East Africa, and into moderate South Africa—pastoralism has conveyed a distinctive set of ideas about health, sickness, and medicine. Similarly, other environmental zones of desert, tropical rainforest, and savanna, have exerted their influences on health and healing. Over the centuries, both the ecological settings and the cultural traditions have slowly and surely evolved distinctive therapeutic ideas, practices, and institutions, well adapted to local dictates. These distinctive features have also determined how the therapeutic traditions from the Mediterranean north, the Islamic East, and from the Christianized and scientized West, would be received.

AFRICAN THERAPEUTIC TRADITIONS: CENTRAL ORIENTATIONS

If musicological research has discovered distinctive structures in African music, linguistic research has demonstrated major distinctive language families, archeologists and culture historians have laid bare the history of a unique agriculture, it is plausible, although at this stage of research largely "guesstimation," to propose a set of distinctive characteristics common to African therapeutic traditions. These are introduced as: empirical therapies based on careful—although not necessarily "experimental"—observation of sickness and the appropriate means of intervention; "ritualized" therapies that purposefully entail heightened affect by the therapist within an extensive symbolic framework of singing, dancing, and the metaphoric uses of natural and cultural objects; collective therapeutic rites conducted by associations of those formerly afflicted who have become healers; divination, the systematic scrutinization of misfortune within the rubric of distinctive etiologies and epistemologies, or orders of ideas; and, ideas of adaptive order, that is, general cultural values and concepts that promote health in the lives of ordinary people in society.

An inventory of empirical therapies in the African setting would need to include bone-setting, midwifery, and a host of specific interventions for such ailments as fever, rheumatism, intestinal disorders, parasites, lactation deficiency, earache, toothache, headache, epilepsy, menstrual disorders, and more. The medications would be based on a wide array of mineral, animal, and especially vegetable substances reflecting the desert, savanna, and rainforest ecologies. Although this volume does not focus extensively on this level of African medicine, instances of it are given in Zempleni and Sindzingre's account of Senufo medicine (chap. 12), Prins's account of Lozi medicine (chap. 13), and Janzen's account of Kongo medicine (chap. 7), and other writers may be noted on this subject (Ampofo 1977, Banghawe et al. 1972; Harjula 1980; Keharo 1972; Kokwaro 1976; Watt and Breyer-Brandwijk 1962).

As important as an extensive summary of works on empirical research in African medicine, for a volume such as this, is an appropriate presentation of ritualized therapeutics, because these, in the African setting, have too frequently been ridiculed and misunderstood. Rather than to see this as misguided science, or merely magical, as Malinowski might have seen it, we would prefer to see it as the purposeful amplification of mundane or empirical therapies with highly charged affective symbols. Where and when these therapies are invoked depends on the understanding of the cause of the misfortune, and what may be seen as an appropriate handling of it. Two levels of analysis are required here. First, the commonality of divination, and the ideas that go into it. Second, the nature of the social context deemed to require ritualized therapy.

The shift from mundane to ritualized therapy is analyzed by Gwyn Prins, in his chapter on Lozi medicine of Zambia (chap. 13), as a switch from "low density" to "high density" disorders. These latter are fraught with tension, anxiety, and fear of being polluted by both human and superhuman conflict. They may be focused on the individual, or on the collectivity. The stakes are higher, thus the symbolic realms of human relations need to be reordered, worked out. Appropriately, only consecrated individuals are capable of handling such powerful therapies as the purification of polluted persons and settings, or sacrifices to ancestors, or the neutralization of menacing spirits. The social context of misfortune is highly appreciated in the African setting. Analysis of this setting is often the first item of the therapy management group's agenda, or of the diviner's to whom they may pass a case.

Divination is reflected in a number of the chapters, either in case studies as those reported by Sinzingre and Zempleni (chap. 12), Davis-Roberts (chap. 15), Ngubane (chap. 14), Janzen (chap. 7), and Prins (chap. 13), or indirectly in the study of ideas that inform the need for expert social diagnosis. In the progression from narrow to more inclusive, ritualized modes of treatment, a more general level of thought and representation is sought that ties together the many approaches available to African therapeutics. Over a wide region of societies in Africa, etiological imputation of misfortune allows for that which "just happens" (Gillies 1976). This has been translated by some as "natural," although this is perhaps overly laden with problematic epistemological implications. Many African terminological glosses of this etiology are translated as misfortune caused "by God." This is not the God of divine retribution of Islam or Christianity . In any event, the same perspective moves readily on to the contrasting etiological pole which interprets misfortune by its "human" causes—*matuku a sintu* (Lozi, in Prins [chap. 13]), *kimbevo kia muntu* (Kongo, in Janzen [chap. 7])—which may include simple error in judgment, excesses of various kinds, inconsistencies and contradictions, as well as willful gossip and witchcraft of a more sinister variety.

A worldview that emphasizes the human cause of misfortune, including disease, has its therapeutic counterpart in a range of institutional and cultural health support systems, to use a neologism of Western welfare. Corporate ritual and healing orders are widespread in Africa, and are described in contributions by Sindzingre and Zempleni ("Sadoho" and "Poro"), MacCormack ("Sande"), Abdalla ("Bori"), Janzen ("Lemba" of coastal Kongo society), Prins ("Nzila"), and Ngubane ("Isangoma") (chaps. 12, 18, 6, 7, 13, and 14, respectively). The latter describes the remarkable network of diviner-healers of southern, and particularly South, Africa who provide support and clarity to a region torn by the strife of apartheid, divided families, and chaos described in several essays of parts I and II of this volume.

The ideas of health that inform the associations and the social order they grow out of, include such notions as "coolness," to combat the "heat" of conflict, witchcraft, greed, and envy; "purity" to replace the "pollution" of confused social roles, transitions, and foul settings; "balance" among people, and between humans and the natural order.

That these indigenous institutions and perspectives are not more frequently marshaled to build upon, when planners and developers enter African countries, is unfortunate. The final essays by Mburu (chap. 17) and MacCormack (chap. 18) suggest ways in which the structures of health care can be aligned, and built within, community realities.

SYNTHESES AND TRENDS IN POSTCOLONIAL AFRICAN MEDICINE

In the postcolonial era there is widespread awareness of the multiplicity of healing traditions available to sufferers and their families. Sinzingre and Zempleni (chap. 12) suggest that for the Senufo the introduction of alternative therapies such as those offered by a dispensary or hospital may not change the etiological ideas over disease. This "medical pluralism" is not so much a wished policy of governments as a de facto result of the continuation of social and religious traditions, and of the lack of resources for the achievement of health through means of clean, adequate quantities of water and other public health measures. Thus, as has already been discussed in the introduction to this volume, the resource of health care has been shaped at the national policy and program level, as well as at the level of users, by the combined exercise of often complementary and competing strategies. Mburu describes this process in Kenya with respect to the government's attempt to come to terms with a rapidly growing capital, Nairobi. From the post-World War II years until 1980 the city grew from about 100 thousand to a million, with large sprawling suburbs and the chronic health problems that such living conditions bring on. Mburu (chap. 17) shows the city of Nairobi being served by a combined set of governmental, private, and traditional resources. A major problem in the achievement of improved health care delivery remains the uneven distribution of resources in Kenya.

MacCormack's contribution (chap. 18) is based on the efforts of Sierra Leone's health workers and officials to combine, or at least coordinate, all sectors of health care resources. Sierra Leone, having concentrated on the improvement of a high infant mortality rate, has succeeded in largely eliminating neonatal tetanus from births presided over by the Sande society midwives through the introduction of sterilization of razorblades used to cut the umbilical cord of infants (personal communication, Carol MacCormack 1988). MacCormack, whose writing has been informed with extensive firsthand health care training as well as anthropological research, offers in her essay (chap. 18) avenues toward the legitimation of new knowledge for the traditional practitioner, as well as better cultural and social legitimation for the Western-style practitioner and for primary health care programs.

As the general introduction to this work suggests, the juxtaposition of diverse therapeutic traditions in the lives of many people today has highlighted the process of "therapy management" on the part of a sufferer's kin and a circle of significant others, including at times practitioners. Whether the process of diagnosis and decision-making occurs informally within a family or kin group, or involves elements of a wider kin or ad hoc consultant group, or even specialized diagnosis and divination procedures, it is a very widespread practice in African countries. Since having been described in Janzen's *Quest for Therapy in Lower Zaire* (1978*b*), the practice has been confirmed and further assessed by a number of other researchers (Feierman 1981, 1985; Good 1987). Speaking of the therapeutic quest as the "itinéraire thérapeutique," Marc Augé (1985) has also identified the significance of seeing the medical culture as embedded in the social categories and crisis contexts of ordinary people rather than only specialists and experts. Therapy management is described in several essays. Ranger (chap. 10) describes it in the Tanzanian Christian community of Masasi; Davis-Roberts (chap. 15), in an extended case from the Tabwa of southeastern Zaire. Sindzingre and Zempleni (chap. 12) find it in Senufo therapeutics as well.

These essays are intended to offer, in one volume, a well-rounded introduction to varied therapeutic traditions in the African continent both as evolving sets of ideas, practices, and tools for achieving health, and as the elements of a pluralistic health care kit that reflect the diversity, and the richness, of the continent.

Precolonial Medicine

SIX

Diffusion of Islamic Medicine into Hausaland

Ismail H. Abdalla

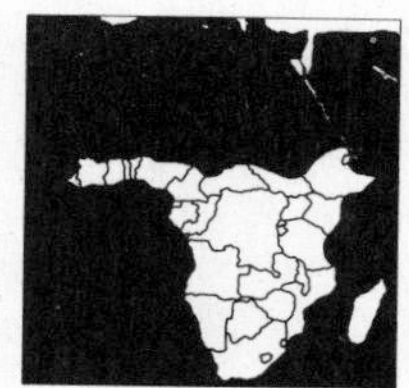

INTRODUCTION

The history of Islamic medicine in Africa encompasses the interaction of multiple streams of therapeutic tradition: Greco-Islamic medicine based on the theory of the four humors, the medicine of the Prophet Muhammad based on religious precedent and inspiration, and the local African medical traditions with which these interacted in each particular locality. This essay will sketch the character of medicine in the Islamic heartland and then go on to discuss the process by which it diffused into Hausaland of what is now northern Nigeria. It will examine how and when Islamic medicine interacted with local therapeutic practices, and explain the historic significance of these important developments.

That an "Islamic medicine" has existed in Muslim countries from early times to the present is indisputable. The real problem for the historian is defining what we mean by the term *Islamic medicine*. The problem is not new. Historians of science and orientalists of different disciplines have long disputed the appropriate terminology to describe the experience through the centuries of men and women in the field of medicine in the Muslim world (Browne 1921; Sarton 1927–1948; Ullman 1978, xi). Some orientalists who started as litterateurs, felt contented with the term *Arabian* or *Arabic* on the grounds that the Arabic language was the medium in which literature on medicine was written (Leclerc 1876; Brockelman 1902, 1937–1942, 1947). Others, mainly historians of science, generally preferred the other term, *Islamic* (Hamarneh 1962, 1965, 1968, 1970*a,b*, 1971, 1974, 1977; Meyerhof 1926, 1928, 1929, 1931, 1935). However, on closer examination, neither term proves satisfactory. While admittedly the argument for calling this medicine "Arabic" has its attraction, the term fails to account for the many works and treatises on medicine compiled by Muslims and non-Muslims alike in languages other than Arabic: Hebrew, Turkish, Persian, Urdu, Wolof, Hausa, Fula, Somali, Swahili, and a host of other languages in the Middle East, Southeast Asia, and Africa.

As early as the twelfth century of the Christian era physicians in *Dar al-Islam* (the world of Islam) began to write in the vernacular tongues of the non-Arabic-speaking populations in Persia, Turkestan, and the Maghreb. This tendency grew stronger as time went by, and as the political hegemony of the Arabs was gradually replaced by that of other nations; Persians and Turks in the east, and Berbers in the west (Hodgson 1974, 3). The increasing use of local languages in writing on medicine as well as on other subjects was a natural consequence of the diffusion of Islam and Islamic culture in lands far removed from the Arab core area. It also explains the comparative ease with which the new faith was accepted by many non-Arabic-speakers in different parts of the world (Gilliland 1971, 216ff.). To apply the term *Arabic* or *Arabian* as a definition of the phenomenon of therapy and therapeutic practice in *Dar al-Islam* from early times to the present is therefore untenable.

The other term, *Islamic*, is not adequate, either. Neither in theory nor in practice was the medical experience of Muslims truly or exclusively Islamic. The *Qur'an* (Koran), whose word for Muslims is final in all other aspects of life, has little to say about medicine or healing. In fact, the word *medicine* (Arabic *tibb*) itself does not appear in the 114 chapters that make up the Muslim holybook. Furthermore, many physicians who flourished in *Dar al-Islam* and who contributed a great deal toward establishing the medical profession were Jews, Nestorian Christians, Sabaeans, and Zoroastrians. Again, Islamic medicine relied heavily on Greek, Persian, and Indian medicine, but especially on the Greek, so much so that many historians of science barely incorporate it in their otherwise comprehensive works of world history of medicine (Ackerknecht 1982; Sigerist 1961; Walker 1955). Unlike the designation *Arabic* or *Arabian*, the term *Islamic medicine* does include in its wider spectrum all writings on medicine and allied sciences in all languages of *Dar al-Islam*. Like it, however, it fails to be comprehensive, and as far as the religious affiliation of the main contributors in the medical field is concerned, misleading.

It appears that, all said, we are still left without a satisfactory terminology for that branch of science usually called *Arabian medicine*. To resolve this problem of definition one must first exclude the term *Arabian*. It is incorrect on both linguistic and ethnic grounds. But more importantly, it has not been used in the Islamic sources to describe the medical literature and medical experience of *Dar al-Islam*. Muslim historians and physicians generally preferred the other term, *Islami* or *Islamic*.

For the purpose of this study, therefore, I will use *Islamic medicine*, but with a qualifier. When used here, the term *Islamic* must not be restricted to, in

Professor Hodgson's words, "of or pertaining to Islam, the religion." Rather it should be understood to mean "of or pertaining to Islamdom; to the social and cultural heritage historically associated with the faith called Islam, and with those who flourished under its banner, be they Muslims, Christians, Jews or Sabaeans" (Hodgson 1974, 58).

Thus defined, Islamic medicine logically includes the medical experience of all the peoples of the Islamic world, wherever they might be. But to define Islamic medicine in this way makes it difficult to sketch the interaction between the local sources of Hausa medical practice and the elements brought in from the heartland of the Islamic world. For the sake of clarity the term *Islamic medicine* used in this work means the total medical experience of the peoples of *Dar al-Islam* proper—those portions of Asia and Africa that once constituted the Islamic Caliphate. It hence excludes the whole of sub-Saharan Africa.

This geographic delimitation is further reinforced by a chronological differentiation as well. The Hausa medical practices of which we have records seemed to have evolved much later than Islamic medicine—probably after the fourteenth century, when Islam itself and the Arabic language first came to this region. Hence, from a historical point of view, it is distinct. Furthermore, the slow but steady assimilative and adaptive process that followed the contact between Islam and local tradition left its imprint on Hausa medicine as practiced today in northern Nigeria or preserved in manuscripts. Hausa medicine retained many of the characteristics of pre-Islamic therapy, as exemplified by its emphasis on indigenous *materia medica*, on *bori* rituals for healing, and the association of pre-Islamic spirits with certain ailments. At the same time it availed itself of the imposing Islamic medical literature and heritage of which it often strove earnestly to be a part. Hausa medicine is thus a continuum of medical practice and theory, at one pole of which is the Maguzawa traditional pre-Islamic therapy, and at the other, Islamic or Greek medicine.

There remains the question of defining the term *medicine* or *tibb*. Modern dictionaries define medicine as "the science and art of dealing with the maintenance of health and the prevention, alleviation, or cure of disease." This definition sounds very much like that of many physicians who flourished in *Dar al-Islam* after the ninth century. Al-Razi (A.D. 865–925), for example, described medicine as the "art concerned with preserving healthy bodies, combating disease and restoring health to the sick" (al-Majusi n.d.).

On the surface it appears that there is no difference between the classical Islamic concept of medicine and the modern Western idea of the same, especially among certain hygienists who emphasize a total environmental, social, and pathological approach to medicine. However, they are not similar. Since what constituted health or the lack of it in classical times in *Dar al-Islam* and in many traditional Muslim societies today is not necessarily the same as the modern Western definition of these two phenomena, it follows that what the Muslim physicians of old deemed as medicine may more logically be described in modern Western terminology as medicine, hygiene, nutrition, psychology, divination, astrology, and even sports and business. Thus, when I use the Arabic term *at-tibb* or its English equivalent, *medicine*, in this discussion, I mean the composite body of knowledge of Islamdom that came down to us in extant works that deal with the ever-lasting physical and mental problems of human existence, not only with regard to the more immediate problem of maintaining health and combating disease in human and beast, but also the problem of guaranteeing success, and avoiding failure or misfortune in love, business, travel, marriage, education, war, or politics as well as in all other situations in life in which humans face anxiety or uncertainty and for whose resolution or containment their unaided means and endeavors are considered inadequate or inappropriate.

MEDICINE IS FOREIGN

Arab historians divided the sciences into two branches: those considered native and Arab, and those regarded as foreign. The former were connected with the traditional, religious, and linguistic sciences: Qur'anic exegesis, the science of the apostolic traditions, jurisprudence, scholastic theology, grammar, lexicography, rhetoric, genealogy, and literature. Philosophy, goemetry, arithmetic, astronomy, music, medicine, magic, and alchemy were foreign sciences, knowledge of which was acquired through translation and assimilation (Nicholson 1964, 283). What interests us here is that medicine was included among foreign sciences, even though medicine men were known in Arabia long before Islam. Ibn Abi 'Usaybi'a in his celebrated *Uyun al-'anba'* or the "Classes of Physicians" (Ibn Abi 'Usaybi'a 1883, 200–206) mentions ten practitioners who flourished in Arabia before or imediately after the advent of Islam. The most important among these were a certain al-Harith and Kalada al-Thaqafi whose medical advice the Prophet Muhammad sought on several occasions (Leclerc 1876, 28). It is significant that although the Prophet administered medicine to needy followers, and that some 300 or so *hadiths* or traditions and anecdotes attributed to him deal with medicine and related subjects, the Prophet was not considered a practitioner, and his medical advice, exhortations, or recommendations were not regarded as part of medicine, at least not during the high period of Islamic civilization. Nevertheless, the "medicine of the Prophet" or what is believed to be his, was destined to have a great influence on the medical profession not only in *Dar al-Islam*, but in many parts of Asia and Africa where Islam established itself as a religion and a way of life for hundreds of thousands of people.

Although foreign in origin, medicine and medical practice soon occupied an important position in people's lives. It developed into a well-defined and established profession. The apparent increase in wealth in *Dar al-Islam* and the tendency to urbanize, with the concomitant demand for drugs and medical care, helped to enhance the profession. The manufacture of paper in the second half of the tenth century, moreover, facilitated considerably the dissemination of medical knowledge. But above all it was the transmission of intellectual and medical legacies of earlier Greek, Roman, and Persian civilizations that laid the foundation for the development of Islamic medicine.

Under the benevolent and enlightened patronage of the Abbasid Caliphs of Baghdad many important medical works of Hippocrates (fifth century B.C.), Paulos Aeginta, and Galen (d. 59 B.C.), and others were translated into Arabic or Syriac by the end of the ninth century (Ibn Abi 'Usaybi'a 1883, I:200–206). Caliph al-Ma'mun (A.D. 813–836) established *Bayt al-Hikma* or the House of Wisdom as a bureau of translation and appointed Hunayn b. Ishaq al-Ibadi (A.D. 803–873), an accomplished physician, linguist, and scholar, to head it (Hodgson 1974, 289). Hunayn, his son Ishaq, and his nephew and student Habish, not only translated Greek medical compendia but also wrote medical treatises of their own on different topics (Ibn Abi 'Usaybi'a 1883, I:198). Medical schools and hospitals were established in many towns in the Caliphate which were provided with well-stocked libraries and teaching halls. Medical practice became highly respected and often very lucrative. The practitioner was held in high esteem by the public, but especially by the members of the ruling families on whose bounty he usually depended (Hamarneh 1970*a*, 39). It was during this period—the ninth to the eleventh centuries—that Islam's most celebrated scholar-physicians flourished: Ibn Masawayh (d. 857), al-Tabari (d. 855), Razi (d. 925), and Ibn Sina (d. 1036).

With Ibn Sina, Islamic medicine as a science and as a profession reached its zenith. By this time were not only its principles, theory, and ideals determined but also its subject matter and its content established. These theories, ideals, and contents of Islamic medicine were expounded in many classical works: *Firdaws al-Hikma* of Al-Tabari, *Kamil al-Sina'a* of al-Majusi, *Al-Hawi* of Razi, and *Al-Qanun* of Ibn Sina, to name just a few. According to these and other classical works on medicine, healing and every therapy is created by God. In its Islamicized version the Hippocratic oath reads, "I swear by God—Lord of life and death—the giver of health and the creator of healing and every therapy" (Ullman 1978, 30). But although God may well be, according to the authors of these compendia, the originator of all health and healing, medical practice seemed very early to have a life of its own, independent of Allah, and clothed in its Greek naturalistic philosophy, often despite Him.

To be sure, Allah did not disappear altogether from the medical writings of the period. Physicians in *Dar al-Islam* still reminded their patients and readers that no cure could be achieved without the Will of Allah. Apart from this conventional reminder, their commitment to Greek medicine and Greek philosophy was on the whole complete. The Greek humoral theory, which will be considered in more detail later, triumphed, in its Galenic eclectic spirit, over the traditional Bedouin and Prophetic Medicine. Nevertheless, this victory, as we shall see later, was not total, or lasting.

As a result of the influence of the Greek legacy, medicine and medical practice in Islam became rational and lay. This is not to say that the medical system that existed before—the Bedouin and the Prophetic—was completely irrational. What the Greek medical and philosophical legacy did was to sharpen those elements that were rational in the Bedouin and Muhammadan therapy and to suppress its magical or religious components. Muslims in the ninth century and after managed to separate medicine from religion. Unlike the Persians before them whose priest was also a physician (Elgood 1962, 13), Muslims eliminated priesthood almost completely from the medical profession, at least during the high period of Islamic civilization. The pragmatic empirical approach to healing made it possible for physicians not only to detach themselves from medicine but also to treat it as a science pure and simple, rather than as a ritual or an avenue for communication with the supernatural.

The Muslim medical system was divided into two branches: the theoretical and the practical. The first category includes the knowledge of the six common principles that determine health and sickness: (1) the quality of the air people breathe, (2) the intake of food, (3) work and rest, (4) sleep or lack thereof, (5) vomiting and the use of enemas, and (6) people's emotional states (Hunayn ibn Ishaq, cited in Hamarneh [1970*a*, 46]). A seventh principle, in keeping with the importance of the number seven in the Muslim belief system, was later added: accidental injuries such as fractures (al-Tabari 1885, 121–123). Almost all compilers of medical works followed Hunayn's classification of medicine and his identification of the six principles of health and sickness.

Disease, in contrast, is described as what injures the organs of the body or interrupts or disturbs their function. It is caused by the collection of superfluous matter or wind in the diaphragm, hot and bitter matter or disorder of any of the other four humors (al-Tabari 1885, 11). It falls into three categories: disease of the homogeneous elements such as blood, disease of individual organs such as arms or legs, and that of the whole organism (Siddiqi n.d., 93). No longer is disease classified on the basis of the natural and the supernatural; rather, it is now understood in purely naturalistic, mechanical terms. It can be caused mechanically, as when superfluous matter collects in the diaphragm, thereby disturbing the natural function of the organ in the body. It can be caused ecologically, as when the air is contaminated and polluted. It can also take place as a result of malfunction, as when the four humors are out of balance in the body.

These theoretical positions taken by the physicians and scholars of *Dar al-Islam* who were trained in Greek medicine and Greek philosophy, were opposed to the popular and religiously oriented Prophetic therapy, which emphasized the supernatural element in disease causation, and thus cure.

The other brand of medicine, applied medicine, was considered equally important. In fact, no practitioner would deserve the name before he could establish his reputation as a successful healer, no matter how well-versed he might have been in the medicine of the Ancients. So important was practice for aspirant physicians that hospitals and medical schools invariably became teaching schools where students could start administering medicine under the supervision of their professors. Ibn Abi 'Usaybi'a mentions that Razi allowed his students to administer medicine in his presence, and interfered only when they showed incompetence or ignorance (Ibn Abi 'Usaybi'a 1883, 310). Able physicians, in addition to their diligent study of Greek sources, compiled medical manuals based on their own experience for their own use, or for the benefit of their students. These compilations proliferated under titles such as *mujarrabat* (experimentation) and *nawadir*, (anecdotes, marvels, unique experiences).

There were those among Muslim physicians who were so taken by Greek medicine, especially the authoritative and definitive Galenic school, that they simply denied the existence of knowledge outside the works of their Greek masters. Mikha'il b. Marawayh (midninth century), for example, was asked once about the banana and whether it was edible. He replied that since it was not mentioned in the Greek sources he would neither eat it himself, nor recommend it to others (Ibn Abi 'Usaybi'a 1883, 183). However, this was the exception. Many physicians of *Dar al-Islam* experimented with new medications and drugs, whether indigenous or imported from far-off countries such as India or China. Al-Razi in Iraq, Maimonides in Egypt (d. 1204), and Ibn al-Baytar in Spain (d. 1248) are good examples.

Nor were these physicians hesitant to apply inductive methods in diagnosis and treatment. This process of reasoning was an established method of scholarly research used in Islamic law by the ninth century, and was applied with great success by jurists like al-Shafi'i (d. 820) for formulating legal opinions on matters about which the *Qur'an* and the traditions of the Prophet Muhammad were silent (Hodgson 1974, I:330). It also appealed to the philosophically minded physicians like Ibn Sina (d. 1039) whose meticulously organized *Canon* (Arabic, *Al-Qanun fi Al-tibb*) bears witness to his therapy, which was deduced logically, almost mathematically, from Galenic and Aristotelian medical theories (Playfair 1958, 369).

In addition to inductive and deductive methods physicians in *Dar al-Islam* were on occasion bold enough to point out the errors of the Greek physicians. Abdel Latif al-Baghdadi (A.D. 1162–1231), after examining many skeletons, came to the conclusion that the lower maxillary consisted of a single bone and not two, as described by Galen, while the sacrum was a single bone also, instead of six (Sarton 1927–1948, 2:599).

Nevertheless, physicians in *Dar al-Islam* were faithful students of the Greek sages, and the philosophical and intellectual framework that shaped medical practice in Islam remained largely unchanged from that of the Greeks. For Muslim physicians regarded Greek knowledge as something permanent, of unalterable value, demanding only elucidation and expansion, but not criticism, much less refutation. There was, therefore, no revision of Galenic medical thought and practice. Physicians in *Dar al-Islam* assiduously adhered to the theory of the four cardinal elements and the four humors, a theory originally put forward by Hippocrates but developed and systematized by Galen, to explain health and disease. According to this theory, blood was hot and moist like air, a cardinal element, and phlegm was cold and moist like water, the second element. Yellow bile was hot and dry like the third element, fire, while black bile was cold and dry like earth, the fourth element. A human being was part of nature which consisted of the four elements, and, likewise, the human body was constituted by the four humors. Elements and humors had common qualities, and as such, they formed the bridge between the microcosm and the macrocosm (Siegerist 1961, 151).

The humoral theory was not only adopted by physicians in *Dar al-Islam* but was also highly elaborated and minutely explained, especially by Ibn Sina in his *Al-Qanun fi Al-Tibb*. Since that time it determined the understanding of physicians of how disease could be diagnosed, and what principles were involved in treatment. This, in turn, influenced the attitude of physicians and pharmacists alike toward medicaments and herbs and the different healing powers and properties attributed to them.

The main theory that characterized the response to disease of physicians, pharmacists, and the public in *Dar al-Islam* in medieval times was "*Contraria contraris*," an age-old Greek and also universal concept that was the foundation stone of Hippocratic medicine. It emphasizes polarity, interaction between opposite poles to bring about cure, such as the Chinese primordial forces of the male Yang (positive, active) and female Yin (negative, passive), the left and right of Muslims, light and darkness of Zoroaster, and bush and city of the Maguzawa Hausa, to name a few examples. Disease due to the predominance in the body of any of the four humors should be treated by its opposite. "Hot" medicaments for "cold" diseases, evacuation for plethora, indigestion, or stomach overfill, and rest for exhaustion-caused diseases (al-Tabari 1885, 5). The sole responsibility of the physician was not to effect cure as such but rather to help nature bring about relief, for nature always took care of itself by itself.

For the treatment of diseases affecting the organs, five general rules are enumerated: (1) bringing the affected organ back to its natural temperament; (2) removing the matter (of disease) from the higher to the lower parts of the body, and from the left to the right, and from the "noble organs" (heart, liver) to the accessory ones; (3) the treatment of the noble and sensitive organs differently from other organs; (4) the treatment of the external parts with mild medicine; and (5) the evacuation of superfluous matter from the intestines by means of purgatives, from the stomach by the use of emetics, from the chest and lungs by gargles and expectorants, and from the liver, the spleen, and the bladder by diuretics. The superfluous blood contaminating the whole body should be released by bleeding (al-Tabari 1885, 132).

As much as possible, suitable diet should be used as treatment. Only when it fails to produce results would simple drugs and even compound drugs be used, the latter when the simple medicines fail. The idea is that a certain drug may cure one sickness, but may have side effects that may harm the organ in another way (al-Tabari 1885, 90). So important was the idea of monotherapy among Muslim physicians that many eminent pharmacists and doctors compiled books on simple drugs, including Razi, Ibn Juljul, and Ibn Baytar.

Like diseases, drugs and herbs were classified according to their assumed temperament and powers. Following Galen's steps, Muslim physicians listed eight conditions for the identification of the power of a drug (Ullman 1978, 104):

> (a) The drug must be pure, (b) the illness for which it is prescribed must be simple and not complex, (c) as a control, a contrary illness must be treated with the same drug, (d) the drug must be more powerful than the illness so that its effect can be seen, (e) time for experimentation with the drug must be short so as to eliminate any possible outside accidental effects or illness, (f) the effect of the drug on several people at different times and seasons should be noticed, (g) its effect on animals must be observed, (h) the difference between foods and drugs on the sick person must be taken into account: the first warm the body by their entire substance, the latter by their quality.

These ideas about drugs and herbs and how their powers could be identified and their medicinal value determined filled many a volume. Indeed, there developed a voluminous technical literature on medical botany that far outstripped that of the Greeks, especially in toxicology. A division of labor emerged between physicians and apothecaries as a result of progress in pharmaceutical techniques and accessibility to countries like India and China, which were known for their advanced science of *materia medica*.

PROPHETIC MEDICINE TAKING ROOT IN HAUSALAND

Islamic medicine as outlined above never reached Hausaland. Like most other aspects of the Islamic civilization in medieval times, it weakened with the decline of an urban and imperial civilization. These changes were accompanied by a thorough-going change in the philosophical orientation of Islamic medicine. Its approach to disease and cure was almost totally replaced by one that emphasized dependence on supernatural elements in diagnosing and treating illness.

The fourteenth-century sociologist-historian Ibn Khaldun made the following statement about the medical profession in his time in *Dar al-Islam*: "In contemporary Muslim cities, the craft of medicine seems to have deteriorated, because the civilization (population) has decreased" (Ibn Khaldun 1900, 3:149). Ibn Khaldun saw the deterioration of the profession of medicine as directly related to the decline of population in the urban communities of plague-stricken North Africa and the Middle East in the fourteenth century (Ibn Abi Dinar 1967, 147). His observation is correct, for as he himself argued, "medicine is a craft required by sedentary culture" (Ibn Khaldun 1900, 1:149). When the sedentary community disintegrates, the medical profession based on it, likewise, degenerates. Such an argument is, of course, in conformity with Ibn Khaldun's thesis in his *Muqaddima* that *'Umran* or "civilization" with its various crafts, professions, and specializations can flourish only with urbanization and sedentary culture (Ibn Khaldun 1900, 3:301).

By the time Islam reached Hausaland in the fourteenth century, urban civilization in the Middle East and North Africa was declining (Ibn Khaldun 1900, 2:386). The hegemony of Muslims as a world power was successfully challenged in the West by the now rising Christian Europe, and in the East by the steppe peoples of Central Asia. As early as the eleventh century Spanish Christians took the offensive against Muslims in Spain, capturing Toledo in 1085, Cordova in 1236, and Seville in 1248 (al-Maqarri n.d.). In 1492 Grenada, too, fell to the Christians, who lost no time in taking the battle into the Maghrebian territories (Hitti 1951, 556). The early years of the sixteenth century saw the Portuguese establishing themselves securely in one fortress after another along the coast of North West Africa (Knapp 1977, 262).

The political situation was not much better in the east. The Mongols, who for a long time had been advancing against the Caliphate, finally captured and destroyed Baghdad—the Abbasid capital—in 1258 (al-Din 1911, 284). With the destruction of the capital of the Islamic empire, even the symbolic unity of the peoples of *Dar al-Islam* was lost forever.

More serious than the political and social disarray of the Islamic peoples in this period was the intellectual transformation of *Dar al-Islam*. The creative liberalism and rationalism of the Mu'tazilites, which reached its highest point during the reign of the sixth Abbasid Caliph al-Ma'mun (A.D. 813–833), had, during the time of his immediate successors, been suppressed. Slowly but steadily religious fundamentalism established itself, in the east, through the conservative Ash'ari movement of the tenth century, while in the west, it manifested itself in the two puritanical *jihads* (religious laws or revival movements) of the Almoravids (1053–1147) and the Almohads (1147–1169)

(Ibn Abi Dinar 1967, 120). Creative scholarship, whether in theology, law, mysticism, literature, or science, suffered most. Before this intellectually conservative phase of Muslim history, all major issues in the different disciplines had been openly and freely discussed and all points of difference debated in the main centers of learning of the Caliphate (al-Ghazali 1967, 13). But this period of free thinking and debate came to an end when Muslims came to believe that all the main issues of their belief system were clearly and satisfactorily explained by the *'ulama* or jurists. Hence no urgent need was felt for further investigation or independent judgment, especially if these pertained to dogma and law. Even Ibn Khaldun found no room for fresh investigation in certain branches of learning. "The traditional legal sciences," he says, "were cultivated in Islam in a way that permitted no further increase" (Ibn Khaldun 1867, 344). All that was needed from the point of view of the Muslim relationship with Allah or with fellow-beings was contained in the major *Shari'a* law books, which were considered complete and final.

This stage in Muslim intellectual history is generally known as the closing of *bab al-Ijtihad* or "the door of independent judgment." No scholar, however eminent, could henceforth qualify as *mujtahid*, an authoritative interpreter of the law (Gibb 1965, 97). While the freeze on intellectual freedom was originally intended only to safeguard the law against unorthodox innovations, it developed to preclude almost all innovations. Despite his unique scholarly achievement in social science, Ibn Khaldun reflects this basic conservative attitude when he explains the main function of literary composition. The main purpose of literary composition, he maintains, "is to make a summary of, or to elucidate works of earlier scholars, or to rearrange topics and divisions therein; to correct mistakes overlooked by earlier writers or to add a point here or there where necessary so as to render the treatment of a particular subject more comprehensive or its meaning more clear, or finally to compile in one tract related topics that are dealt with separately in different works" (Ibn Khaldun 1900, 3:284). "All else," he adds, "is unnecessary and a mistake, a deviation from the road all intelligent scholars think must be followed" (p. 285).

The analogy of "closing the door," as John Hunwick rightly noticed, is significant. The implication was that what was shut in was complete and perfect or as perfect as man could hope to make it. What was left out was irrelevant and unwanted (Hunwick 1974, 26). It was natural that the period that followed the closing of the door of *ijtihad* was characterized by a "rechannelling of scholarly efforts from the creative to the imitative" (Hunwick 1974, 26). The genius of Muslim scholars during this middle period (1200–1800) with the exception of men like Ibn Khaldun, was directed mainly toward consolidating the works of earlier generations, "in compiling lexicons and encyclopedic works, or writing commentaries on the works of earlier masters, or in abridging them for the use of students, and then, having made them almost incomprehensible through such compression, again writing commentaries to elucidate their terseness" (Hunwick 1974, 27).

This process of consolidating and imitating the scholarly achievements of the ancients, not only preserved these sciences for posterity—which is important—but gave them a force of legitimacy and authority that could only grow stronger as time went by. By the time Islam made its first inroads into Hausaland, this intellectual traditionalism and conservatism was already three to four centuries old in the lands further north. The West African societies whose Islam was introduced by the puritan Malikite Almoravids in the eleventh century (al-Idrisi 1971, 130) were disposed to be conservative, and to accept as a matter of course the closing of the door of *ijtihad* on all issues, religious or otherwise. The implication of this acceptance will become clear as one considers the Hausa medical treatises.

Of immediate relevance to the history of Islamic medicine in West Africa and Nigeria was the predominant Malikite School of Law. This religious rite was named after its founder Malik Ibn Anas, an accomplished *hadith* scholar who died in 795 (Ibn Khalikan 1948, 201). Malik's celebrated book, *Al-Muwatta'* (The Path), became the foundation document of the Malikite school in the Maghreb, and many commentaries on it, like *Al-Mudawwana Al-Kubra* of Sahnun (d. 854) and *Al-Risala* of Ibn Abi Zayd (d. 928), are still popular in Nigeria.

In formulating legal opinions on many issues affecting the life of Muslims, Malik depended, after the *Qur'an*, solely on the *hadiths* current during his time in Medina, preferring these to any other *hadiths* that might have been in circulation elsewhere in *Dar al-Islam* (Ibn Khaldun 1900, 3:6ff.). The Medinese community, he argued, was not corrupted by the tribal feuds and the luxury of life of the garrison towns in Iraq, Syria, or Egypt. When no *hadiths* or anecdotes were available to support a certain opinion, he chose to take the Medina way as normative (Hodgson 1974, 1:321–322). Unlike the complex Muslim communities that flourished in towns like Damascus, Baghdad, or Cairo, the pristine Medina community was homogeneous and simple. Malik's dependence on the norms of this community for legal purposes not only idealized these norms but also made simplicity and even conservatism look religiously valid, a fact that had important consequences in the history of Muslim jurisprudence. The Prophetic *hadiths* and anecdotes as well as the practice of the Medinese themselves assumed an increasing importance in all parts of *Dar al-Islam* where Malikism prevailed. It is no accident, therefore, that the *hadiths* dealing with medicine and related topics were and still are in great demand among the Maghrebians and West African Muslims.

Beside Malikism, Shi'ism, which is, after Sunnism, the largest sect, seemed to have emphasized dependence on and veneration of things Prophetic among Muslims. The Shi'a teachings dramatize and sanctify not only the life and deeds of the Prophet but also of those who claim descent from him.

Their propaganda originally started late in the seventh century for purely political goals, to regain the office of the Caliph from its unlawful occupants, the Umayyads and later the Abbasids (al-Tabari 1879–1901, 509ff.). Eventually the Shi'a succeeded in establishing their own independent governments in many provinces, in Fez (788–974), in Tunisia, and later in Egypt (909–1171) as well as elsewhere, only to be wiped out, in due course, by Sunnis (al-Tabari 1879–1901, 396). Nevertheless, the impact of Shi'a philosophy and ideas on Sunni Islam was enormous (Ibn Khaldun 1900, 2:156ff.). As a result, the deeds, the sayings and anecdotes of the Prophet Muhammad began to assume greater significance in the political, religious, and social life of Muslims. From the twelfth century onward, those traditions that dealt with medicine and similar subjects were extracted from the larger body of the *hadith*, compiled in separate "medical" books under the title *Al-Tibb Al-Nabawi* (Medicine of the Prophet) and were hence given wider circulation in *Dar al-Islam*.

But Shi'ism influenced Sunni Islam in yet another way. Almost as a reaction to Shi'a teachings, a natural development of the Shi'a idea of the legitimacy of the Imam's religious power derived ultimately from the Prophet himself, popular Sunni Islam also established its own order—Sufism—to closely associate itself, for the purposes of legitimacy, with the founder of Islam. From the twelfth century onward Sufism, especially the *turuq* or religious orders, won over traditional Islam. There were developments in the intellectual life of Muslims conducive to this change. First there was the Ash'ari conservative movement mentioned earlier. But more important were the relentless and vicious attacks of the celebrated Muslim theologian, al-Ghazali (d. 1111) on philosophy and on the position taken by philosophers with regard to certain issues of dogma (al-Ghazali 1947, 35). Sufi orders proliferated in many parts of *Dar al-Islam*, more especially in the Maghreb, where they often harbored covert resistance against central authority.

The importance of conservatism as far as the history of Islamic medicine is concerned lies in the fact that it emphasized dependence on tradition to the exclusion of speculative thought or innovation. This tradition connects with the Prophet or his immediate companions through the *silsila* or chain of the religious or Sufi way from the *murid* or disciple to the Prophet. Consequently, the *shaykh* or head of a Sufi order or *tariqa* is believed to be always inspired in his actions, religious as well as temporal, by the *silsila* and directed and controlled by this invisible mystical bond (Ibn al-'Arabi 1809, 59). The *shaykh* could, if he wanted, cause himself to have dreams in which he could meet and communicate with the Prophet Muhammad and receive from him direct answers to any problems. Ibn al-Hajj of Qairawan (d. 1336) relates the story of one such *shaykh* who always communicated with the Prophet in dreams every time he was asked to give medical advice to a sick person (Bello n.d., 65–66).

As the head of his *tariqa* the *shaykh* was frequently asked for and dispensed medicine and medical advice to the members of his community who were in need (Westermarck 1926, 153). Such medical advice and treatment, especially that which the *shaykh* took from the *Qur'an* or *hadith* became doubly significant in the eyes of believers; on one hand because of the supernatural force it had as the actual word of Allah or his Prophet and on the other hand because of the mystical power, or *baraka*, that came down from the Prophet through dreams or through the *silsila*. A medical pronouncement of the *shaykh*, whether verbal or in writing, became an important part of the medical experience of the Islamic peoples in the Maghreb and West Africa, where religious orders, first the Qadiriyya and its many offshoots, and later the Tijjaniya, flourished (Gibb 1965, 202ff., 593ff.). By the late medieval period Islamic medicine and religion, which had remained more or less separate during the high period of the Abbasid Caliphate, drew much closer as time went by, and as Islam expanded further afield from the centers of Greco-Hellenic influence in the Middle East. The writings of the famous occultist of Islam Ahmed b. Ali b. Yusuf al-Buni of Algeria (d. 1225) (Sarton 1927–1948, 2:596) in which he emphasized the powers and the secrets of Quranic verses and Allah's attributes became increasingly popular, and are still highly esteemed in northern Nigeria, especially among practitioners with background in Islamic education.

The *shaykhs* of the *turuq* were not alone in the profession of health, and in the Maghreb, not even the most important factor in the spread of the knowledge of Islamic medicine among people. There were the *shurafa* (sing. *sharif*), an exclusive class of religious elite who possessed *baraka* by virtue of descent from the Prophet Muhammad (Westermarck 1926, 1:36). Through this power the *sharif* is able not only to communicate with the supernatural but to manipulate its forces for the benefit of the sick and the needy (Westermarck 1926, 1:155).

There is a difference, however, between the way the *shaykh* and the *sharif* effect healing. The former, and any other religious scholar, for that matter, heals mainly through the power inherent in the word (Greenwood, chap. 11 in this volume). The latter brings about cure because of the mystical power possessed by him as a descendant of the Prophet, that is, power from within. The distinction between the two is important for this discussion, as both existed in Hausaland. Indeed, the former, or his equivalent the Hausa *malam* or religious scholar, is the only medical specialist of any importance among Muslim Hausa to this day. In the case of the *shaykh* or the *malam* the freedom to innovate in medical practice or to incorporate new techniques of healing, although not circumscribed completely, was significantly limited by the Islamic medical tradition to which the *shaykh* or *malam* became heir, and on whose authority and sanctity his own were dependent. The *sharif*, in contrast, was very much on his own, and his authority as a practitioner depended not so much on the written word as it did on his own charisma. Westermarck, for example, reported that members of a certain Sharifian family who were blacksmiths cured swelling (*nufakh*) in any part of the body by "moving a burning oleander twig toward it but without touching the skin, and then spitting on the skin" (Westermarck 1926, 1:156). Unlike the *shaykh* or the *malam*, the *sharif* brings about relief without recourse to either the *Qur'an* or the *hadith*, if he wishes to do so. It follows from this dichotomy that the continuity of medical knowledge and practice was guaranteed in the case of the *shaykh* of the *tariqa* or the *malam* by the *Qur'an*, the written tradition of the Prophet, and by the pseudomedical literature that became abundant from the twelfth century onward. In the case of the *sharif*, medical practice and expertise was acquired and even maintained by his own *baraka*, which is inheritable. Hence, where he ceased to have descendants, as was probably the case with many *sharifs* who settled in Kano and Katsina in early times, the medical practice contingent on his own personal power might not be transmitted and consequently might disappear.

There are some people in Kano who claim descent from Sharifian families. There is even a quarter in the old city by the name "Sharifay." But none of the people interviewed in this quarter claimed *baraka* of the type explained here.

A number of factors thus influenced Islamic medicine and later its development in Hausaland: the establishment of Sufism and religious orders; the proliferation of *sharifi* families and the role they played in medical practice; the uncontested control by the conservative Maliki school of law of the religious, social, and intellectual life of the Maghrebians, and later West Africans; and finally, the general stagnation of creative scholarship in all sciences in *Dar al-Islam* from the thirteenth century onward.

Islamic medicine became religiously oriented and highly supernatural, thanks to the writings of men like al-Buni and al-Suyuti. The empirical and clinical approach to medicine exemplified by physicians like al-Razi, Ibn Sina and others in earlier centuries had disappeared (Hamarneh 1971, 1097). Instead, emphasis was laid on the medicine of the Prophet, on the assumed numerical healing powers of verses of the *Qur'an*, the names of angels, prophets, and saints as well as on magic and divination. It is mainly this type of medicine we encounter when we consider Hausa Islamic medicine.

DISSEMINATION OF ISLAM AND ISLAMIC MEDICINE IN HAUSALAND

The earliest surviving document on the history of Hausaland, the *Kano Chronicle* and the seventeenth-century manuscript *Asl Al-Wangarayyin Al-Ladhina ma-a al-Shaykh* ([1968], 7–42) tell us that Islam was brought to this region in the reign of the ninth *sarki* or king of Kano, Zaji, son of Tsami (1349–1385), or later. Half a century after this date, during the reign of the twentieth *sarki*, Yakubu (1452–1463), "The Fulani came to Hausaland from

Melle, bringing with them books on divinity and law." Kano began very early, it appears, to attract settlers from the western Sudan as well as from the north and the east, mainly Bornu (Rattray 1953, 10).

Like Kano, Katsina also pulled in emigrants from other parts of West Africa, especially the Wangarawa (*Asl* [1968], 10) and the Fulani (Palmer 1967, 79) as well as North Africans, Saharan peoples and people from Bornu. Some of those who came from North Africa were *shurafa* (*Kano Chronicle*). In addition, a few scholars came with their students from Egypt, settled in Kano or Katsina, and started teaching (*Asl* [1968], 10).

Other towns in Hausaland, like Zaria in the south, must have attracted similar settlers, although perhaps in much smaller numbers, and more likely at a later date. At any rate, Islam began to take hold in Zaria when its *sarki*, Muhammad Rabbo (midfifteenth century), was converted to Islam (Smith 1975, 196).

At least four centuries elapsed between the time Islam was first implanted in Hausa soil and the date when the Fulani in Nigeria launched their revival movement or *jihad* in 1804. This intervening period witnessed three distinct phases of the Islamization of the Hausa people. First, an initial comparatively short period of the separate coexistence of Islam and local cults (*Kano Chronicle* n.d. [1908], 97), or what Fisher calls "quarantine." During this phase Islam was practiced only among the newcomers from North Africa, Mali, or Bornu: traders, clerics, or refugees. This was followed by a period of gradual but slow acculturation and conversion characterized by mixing of Islamic and non-Islamic beliefs and practices. This intermediate phase triggered the last, that of reform, or militant Islam. For only a reformer could mobilize public opinion against those pagan practices irreconcilable with Islam, and which through force of circumstance were allowed to continue (Trimingham 1961, 41). It must be observed, however, that these three phases did not occur in all places concurrently, nor did "mixing" necessarily always precede "reform."

Islamic Medicine in Hausaland

If we accept as correct the view that Islam spread progressively among the Hausa from the time it was first introduced, what does this tell us about the dissemination of Islamic medicine in Hausaland? From the very beginning, Muslims in Hausaland exploited, as they did elsewhere in Africa, the "medicinal powers" of Islam in order to propagate it. Unfortunately, we hear of no medical books or treatises being brought into Hausaland—not, at least, in this early period, although books on the traditions of the Prophet Muhammad, on divinity and etymology are reported as early as the fifteenth century if not earlier (*Kano Chronicle* n.d. [1908], 111). However, it is reasonable to assume that Muslim settlers, whether coming from Songhay, Air, or Bornu, must have brought with them medical writings and medical knowledge, if only for their own use. The fact that they were coming to a strange land in which they might encounter diseases and problems of a different kind would certainly make the newcomers acutely aware of the perils facing them, and hence they would take additional precautions to protect themselves against all possible contingencies. As it turned out, they used whatever expertise they had in medicine to the advantage of their new patrons—the Hausa kings—and consequently to their own advantage.

As early as the time of Yaji (1349–1385), the Wangarawa who brought Islam to Hausaland practiced medicine. The *Kano Chronicle* informs us that when the Muslim congregation in Kano prayed all night long Allah received their prayer and struck blind *sarkin* Garazawa, one of Yaji's pagan chiefs who was opposed to the building of a mosque under the sacred tree (*Kano Chronicle* n.d. [1908], 104). Furthermore, Yaji sought and obtained the prayer of the Wangarawa which enabled him to conquer his enemy—the men of Santulo (*Kano Chronicle* n.d. [1908], 105). Later, in the reign of Rinfa, when it was decided to cut down the sacred tamarind tree to build a minaret in its place, Muslims once more resorted to prayer. The *shaykh* of the Wangarawa "took an axe . . . and recited some secret incantations which the Lord had taught him. He repeated this three times and every time he spat on the head of the axe and then struck the Tamarind tree." Only through prayer and the "secret incantation which the Lord had taught him" was he able to prevent the tree from growing back to its original shape during the night when laborers stopped cutting it (*Asl* [1968], 12).

Again, during the reign of the seventeenth *sarki*—Muhammad Zaki (1582–1618)—when Katsina fighters threatened to take Kano, the *malams*, or religious elite, intervened and saved the city. "Shehu Abu-Bakar the Maghribine said (to the king) if you wish to repel the men of Katsina I will give you something to do it with." The king agreed and the *shaykh* gave him the "medicine" by which he was able to drive away the enemy (*Kano Chronicle* n.d. [1908], 116). It appears that by the late sixteenth century the influence of Muslim clerics in the political and religious life of Kano had become considerable. Already the practice of *Dirki*, a ritual centered around the *Qur'an* and for which sacrifices were offered, was established (*Kano Chronicle* n.d. [1908], 116). Zaki's successor, Muhammad Kukuna (1652–1660), offered many gifts of silver and gold to the *imam* of Kano and asked for charms that would guarantee the continuation of his rule (*Kano Chronicle* n.d. [1908], 121). These examples illustrate that Muslim clerics started as early as the fifteenth century to intercede with the supernatural, in this case Allah, on behalf of their Hausa overlords, pagan as well as Muslim, and not without success. One would assume that such services were also extended to other members of the royal families, as well as to those individuals in Hausa society who needed them and were able to pay for them. Muslim practitioners could apparently bring about victories, defend cities, assure rain, protect property, and ward off calamity and misfortune.

Nor was such a situation in which Muslim prayer and medicine had proved beneficial to political leaders unique to Hausaland. Similar episodes and experiences were reported by Muslim geographers like al-Bakri and historians such as al-Sa'di, Alfa Mahmud, al-Umari, Muhammad Bello, and al-Hajji Sa'id. Early in the eleventh century al-Bakri reported that the conversion to Islam of the chief of Malel in Upper Senegal was the result of the successful plea of a resident *malam* to Allah to send rains to the drought-afflicted province (al-Bakri 1960, 178). In a similar situation, in Sokoto, al-Hajji Sa'id describes how his *shaykh* Umar, on the request of *sultan* Bello, prayed for rain on behalf of the town of Gharnaq. Rain fell that same night after prayer, and "just on the desperate town and its vicinity but on no other" (al-Hajj Sa'id 1966, 202). More recently, European explorers, travelers, historians, and sociologists described comparable situations in which Muslims customarily mediated between their pagan clientele and the High Deity; Bowdich and recently Wilks (1964, 330–332) report experiences among the Ashanti and Goody, with the Gonja of northern Ghana (Goody 1968).

Unfortunately, the *Kano Chronicle* and *Asl* are silent as to that prayer or "medicine" these early practitioners in Hausaland used. However, we are told (*Asl* [1968], 12) that the *shaykhs* spat when they recited their incantations—an act typical of ritual healing in Hausaland even today. Although these two sources do not mention a type of healing common in contemporary society in Nigeria that involves drinking the water in which the ink used to write chapters from the *Qur'an* on a slate is washed, undoubtedly such a practice was known. The *Qur'an* itself, as we have observed earlier, became a symbol that the indigenous population venerated in much the same way as they did their pre-Islamic ritual symbols. To "internalize" the potency of the sacred symbol for the purpose of cure by drinking "its" water is a logical step from the application of that symbol externally through incantation and spitting.

In summary, Islam was brought to Hausaland in the fifteenth century or earlier by emigrants and traders from western Sudan, from across the desert or from Bornu. During the long period of Islamization that followed, Islam existed side-by-side with local cults and traditions influencing them and being influenced by them. It competed with them at times, and at times tolerated them, while it was steadily and slowly gaining new ground. This phase of coexistence was characterized by syncretism, which manifested itself in the medical field. The Hausa kings and Hausa people in general shifted back and forth from one medical system to the other in order to maximize their own interest in the continuously changing socioeconomic conditions of Hausaland after the sixteenth century.

SEVEN

Ideologies and Institutions in Precolonial Western Equatorial African Therapeutics[1]

John M. Janzen

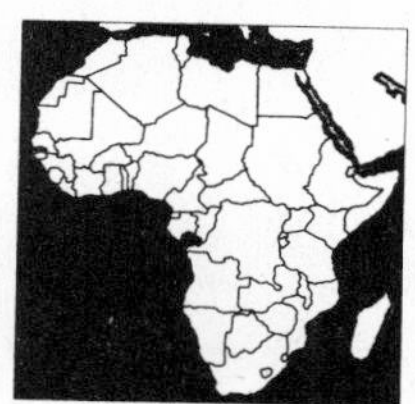

INTRODUCTION

The history of precolonial Equatorial African medicine will be examined here as a series of transformations at several levels: successive classifications of medicinal taxonomies over time; the shifting base of corporate social structures of healing organizations; and the changing legitimating ideologies of particular medicines with respect to background cultural worldviews. Such a rendering of Equatorial African medical history is possible perhaps only in one locality of the wider western Equatorial region, the Loango coast, because of the wealth of archival material from ledgers of visitors to that port city and region during the sixteenth to nineteenth centuries, and as a result of the German Loango Coast Expedition in the 1870s, one of the earliest systematic ethnological expeditions.

In order to make the most of the Loango archival materials, they may be interpreted on one hand against the backdrop of larger-scale archeological and linguistic-historic evidence, such as has been used increasingly in African history (Ehret and Posnansky 1982; Vansina 1978, 249–318; Waite 1986), and on the other hand, the "foreground" of contemporary ethnographical studies, extrapolated back to interpret institutional features. Linguistic and historical evidence places the Congo coast societies in the "Western Bantu" stream (Vansina's "Atlantic" 6ii subgroup 1984*b*, 134; also Guthrie 1967–1971), thus related historically to coastal and forest societies northward to the Cameroons.

The medical culture of Lower Congo-Zaire shares with the entire Bantu-speaking region of central, eastern, and southern Africa common cognates (Guthrie 1967–1971)[2] for such terms as sore or wound (*puta*, *pute*), to become ill, or to suffer (*duad*, *duadi*), to bewitch, curse, or use power of words to heal or harm (*dog*, *doga*, *dogo*), the concept of the person, and source of some afflictions (*ntu*), the main role for doctor (*ganga*, *nganga*), plant medicine (*ti*), consecrated medicine, powerful charm (*pingu*), or curse (*ping*, *pingo*), the drum, drumming, and dance often used in major therapeutic rituals (*goma*), and the concept of the "cool," to "cool down," to "become well, cured" (*pod*).

Within this general medical culture reflected in the common cognates, the Kongo-Atlantic coast reflects, further, the more limited Western Bantu lexicon. Although *nganga* is the common term for doctor or healer, *mbanda* or *mbuki* are frequently used to refer to more specialized types of diviners or healers. In addition to the generic Bantu term for plant medicine (*ti*), Kongo medicine also uses the Western Bantu *kay*, or *kag* to refer to leaves, or forest plants. The use of kaolin, or white clay, is widespread in Bantu-speaking Africa; however, the term *luvemba* or *pemba* is limited to western Bantu languages; it is the only term in Kongo languages for this substance often used as the basis of medicines and ritual. And, although the wider Bantu cognate *pingu*, powerful medicine, appears as a class of charm (*pungu*, *mpungu*), the wider concept of consecrated medicine in western Bantu is *kiti* or *kici* (*nkisi* or pl. *minkisi* in Lower Congo/Zaire). As we will see, Loango coast archival and ethnographic records demonstrate the central role of the *nkisi* in the response to disease and social conflict, as well as the buttressing of roles of authority such as the Loango kingship.

The outlines of this verbal dimension of a health culture mesh with the more recent ethnographic picture of Kongo society. The proto-Bantu cognate *dog*, or *dogo*, *lok* in western Equatorial African languages, labels the pervasive assumption that human relations and human society can cause sickness. It is too narrow, and misleading, to translate this cognate, and its derivatives, as "witchcraft" as some have done. It is rather "the power of words and thoughts" that is the common denominator behind all of the applications of this term: *lokila loka*, to speak an oath, *ndoki*, witch, or possessor of mystical power; *kindoki*, mystical power. The course of working out a diagnosis for sickness or misfortune thus may, at some point, entail research into whether conflict or mystical connections lie behind a sufferer's lingering sickness. A range of therapeutic or ritual actions exist in coastal Kongo society to deter such causation, or to deal with it if it occurs.

Although in modern Kongo society explicit *nkisi* solutions are rarely used, the care with which interpersonal relationships are integrated with physical treatments, and the ways in which kin or friends keep in touch or share with sufferers' decision-making in the therapeutic quest, reflect the historic culture of consecrated ritual techniques known as *nkisi*. It is thus possible to map out points of societal and individual focus in twentieth-century life that reflect some of the *nkisi* emphases in earlier times (Janzen 1971, 1977; Janzen and MacGaffey 1974; MacGaffey 1977, 1986).

Research on contemporary Kongo therapeutics (Janzen 1978*a*, 1982, 1987) has revealed a pattern of management of individual cases by a combination of individuals around the sufferers, including their lay kin and the practitioners consulted. Taken as a whole from episode to episode in each case, and cumulatively across cases, the "stress points" or highlights of the medical culture emerge (Janzen 1975, 1978*a*). At an earlier time, for comparative purposes, this work had spelled out the several dimensions of a constellation characteristically found in Kongo medical culture: (1) the indigenous taxonomy's conception of a problem in need of a solution; (2) a technique—social, pharmaceutical, symbolic—regularly utilized in response to the problem; (3) a practitioner or set of practitioners who take the technique in hand, whether they are laymen or consecrated specialists; and (4) the social context of the decision (in the "therapy managing group") to utilize one or another, or a series of, therapeutic options (Janzen 1978*b*, 121). These points of emphasis correspond to levels of transformations in Loango and coastal Kongo precolonial history that are taken up here.

The therapeutic history of Loango and its hinterland may be seen through three types of transformations. The first is the variations and shifts in the classifications of *nkisi* medicines over time, identifying those that disappear and the new ones which emerge; the second is the relative degree of corporate strength such medicines possess at particular eras, thereby judging their influence, command of resources, and role as representative of political and economic forces; finally, transformations will be examined in the ideological and mythological rooting of the major *nkisi* associations—especially Lemba—in the conventional belief culture, so as to understand the selective legitimating emphases that were built up and defended by particular institutions.

TRANSFORMATIONS IN THERAPEUTIC TAXONOMIES

The excellent Loango coast documentary record permits an accounting of replacements and shifts of emphasis in the inventory of *minkisi* over several centuries. Read alongside changes in political, social, and economic history, this ritual or therapeutic history provides a "barometer" of the perception of change and responses to it in the manner suggested by Prins in chapter 13 of this work.

Although earlier observers mentioned Loango medicines, Dapper's 1668 *Naukeurige Beschryuinge der Afrikaensche Gewesten* (Dapper 1668) was the first scholarly work to present a systematic view of Loango's *minkisi* medicines and their practitioners. Almost certainly Dapper's inventory misses some major medicines or shrines, for example, Bunzi, the earth shrine of the region. Yet the presentation suggests a ranking from most important or central to the kingdom to more peripheral in importance.

Tiriko, a shrine near Loango in Boarie, is made of a house whose roof is held up by four anthropomorphic pillars. Tiriko's priest, accompanied by a boy acolyte, daily prays for the health of the king and the well-being of the land, the growth of crops, and the luck of merchants and fishermen.

Boessi-Batta, another *nkisi*, is specialized in the task of bringing trade goods home without contaminating one's household domain. It is thus pertinent to the merchant's life. Boessi-Batta consists of many objects distributed in two separate parts: a shelf-like construction at the door of the merchant's house, and several movable containers. One of these, a large lion-skin sack, is filled with many kinds of shells; iron bits and ore; herbs; tree bark; resin; roots; seeds; feathers; claws; rags; fish bones; and horns, teeth, hair, and nails of albinos and other "unnatural" creatures—a veritable depository of cosmic representations. To this satchel are added two calabashes decorated with cowrie shells, iron hooks, and topped with a bush of feathers and colored with red *tukula* wood powder. The opening of one of the calabashes is carved to resemble a mouth-like orifice, into which wine is poured to activate the *nkisi*. When merchants go abroad to trade, they take these movable parts weighing ten to twelve pounds with them. On returning, they are met by the priest of Boessi-Batta, who, with lines drawn on body, incants in rising tone of voice as he unpacks the *nkisi* ingredients, in parallel with the merchant's actions. Presently the priest's eyes exorbit as he becomes possessed with the spirit of Boessi-Batta. Drinking a liquid to calm himself, he declares the wish of Boessi-Batta, the fee, and measures to be taken or other medicine to be utilized. Boessi-Batta thus deals with the problems of the merchant, his passage outside of his household and locality, and his return home.

Another *nkisi* in seventeenth-century Loango is Kikokoo, which resides in an anthropomorphic wooden shrine in the seaside village Kinga, at the site of a large cemetery common to Loango Bay. Kikokoo protects the dead against witches (*doojes*, *ndoki*) who in their nocturnal craft are said to drag off the souls of the dead to slavery and forced labor. Kikokoo also assures the arrival of ships with fish and merchandise.

Nkisi Bomba is celebrated in a special feast associated with the coming out of Khimba initiates who are dressed in a head garb of feathers and skirt of palm raffia, and who wave a red-and-white hand-shaker. Their frenzied drumming and mock-mad behavior is the final public phase of the initiation. Later accounts of Khimba indicate that Bomba is Mbumba Luangu, the rainbow serpent.

Lemba, in Dapper's recital of Loango coast *minkisi* of the seventeenth century, is a Moquissie of great importance, worthy of being honored by the king, for whose bodily health it serves. As long as he does not become ill, it is noted, he is surely kept well by it. Lemba, in this account, consists of a small four-cornered mat one and a half feet large, with a drawstring at the top (making it a satchel), in which are placed several small calabashes, cuttlebones, feathers, dry shells, iron bits, bones, and the like, all colored with red *tukula*. In the Lemba ceremony, the distinctive Lemba drum is played by a boy, and is accompanied by rattling shell whistles. Consecrated kola is spit into a small pot filled with *tukula* and consecrated water, and this is then sprinkled with an asperge onto the *nkisi*, the body of the priest, and that of the king, to the accompaniment of singing and chanting. Nobility in attendance receive the special Lemba anointment of stripes of red *tukula* on their bodies, thus absorbing the honor of Lemba. After this, the *nkisi* is hung, with its small pot, asperge (sprinkler), and satchel, in its appropriate place in the house of the Lemba priest or a special Lemba house behind his residence.

Other medicines noted by Dapper include Makongo, consisting of rattles, drums, small sacks, and red fishhooks; Mimi, a small house shrine in a banana grove with a throne holding a basket of objects including a "paternoster" of seashells and a wooden statue of Father Masako; Kossi, a sack of white snail shells filled with white clay and used in rites of crawling between one another's legs, eating, washing, donning bracelets and bands of protection against lightning, thunder, and sickness; Kimaje, a pile of potsherds on which priests deposit old ragged caps and other worn-out ritual paraphernalia and dedicate replacements, so as to assure the new moon and new year's coming, as well as protection on the seas; Injami, a shrine found in a village near Loango, represented by a huge statue in a house; Kitauba, a huge wooden gong used in swearing oaths or sending sickness to another; Bansa, another statue covered with red powder; Pongo, a "wooden" calabash or container covered with cowries, filled with many carved symbols, used in "black magic"; and Moanzi, a partially buried pot between two dedicated trees, containing an arrow and a string on which are hung green leaves, and whose adherents wear copper armrings and avoid eating kola.

This seventeenth-century inventory of medicines reflects accurately what we know through other sources about the Loango kingdom and society. The kingdom is still intact, as repeated references to the well-being of the king suggest. Passing reference in connection with *nkisi* Tiriko to trade, alongside the health of the king, prosperity, the soil's fertility, and good fishing situate it in a way that it is not perceived as a great threat to the kingdom's structure. However, in the symbolism of Kikokoo and Boessi-Batta there is a hint of more serious problems resulting from the trade, especially the slave trade.

Kikokoo's characteristics are laced with slave-trade attributes, including the forced labor of kidnapped souls and the acquisition of trade goods. The *nkisi* appears to reflect the ambiguity felt over desiring trade goods while wishing to be protected against slavery. Boessi-Batta as well reflects a concern for the protection of the household from defilement of goods brought from afar, but with the same ambiguity over the attractiveness of these goods. Boessi-Batta's importance is indicated by the fact that it was exported with slaves to Haiti where the symbolism of the household versus the beyond remains in the Bosu shrine of voodoo. Lemba's presence in the hands of the nobility reflects a trend that increasingly took control of trade out of the hands of the king and his ministers of trade (*mafouk*).

Historical conditions in Loango in decades and centuries after Dapper's midseventeenth-century account have been documented and analyzed in great detail (Janzen 1982). The international trade, initially controlled in the coastal kingdoms of Loango, Kakongo, and Ngoyo by the king's trade ministers (*mafouk*), had begun with copper and ivory exports in the sixteenth to early seventeenth century (e.g., forty tons per year of copper from the Loango coast). However, this "legitimate" trade was gradually replaced by trade in slaves, so that by 1680 4,000 slaves were being exported annually from the three ports of Ngoyo, Kakongo, and Loango. By the early eighteenth century, this climbed to 15,000 slaves per year (Martin 1972, 86). Not until the early nineteenth century did this volume in slaves begin to taper off, being replaced by "legitimate" trade by the last quarter of the century.

During this period, the tight control of trade by the kings had given way to a trade flow controlled by an increasing number of *mafouk* who no longer represented the kings, but their own or clan interests, and who transacted trade directly with European merchants and companies. The kings themselves were reduced to dealing increasingly as private parties with traders, rather than on behalf of their polities. By the early nineteenth century the structure of royal succession in Loango had collapsed and was replaced by a succession of interregnum officers, the "cadaver priests" (*banganga mvumbi*). Not only in the hinterland, on the trade caravan routes to interior markets (like Mpumbu), but right in the coastal capitals, power was taken over by an indigenous mercantile élite. This élite was synonymous with the Lemba priesthood, whose mercantile prowess supported the recruitment of new priests and the exchange of ceremonial wealth.

A third development in the coastal societies needs to be mentioned, pertaining to the structure of shrines. Loango was held to be the most prominent of the three kingdoms in a political sense; its ruler held semidivine status as supreme ruler (*ntotila*) and supreme judge (*ntinu*), with a close relationship to Nzambi the Creator. Rituals for first fruits, rainmaking, and eating and drinking in isolation were his charge; a state flame was maintained by him and distributed regularly to the region's hearths. But in one respect Ngoyo was most prominent, for its territory contained the major shrine Bunzi, to the earth goddess. The relationship between the three kingdoms was described by analogy as that between husband Loango (*nunni*) to wife Kakongo (*mokassi*) to priest Ngoyo (*itomma*) (Bastian 1874, 160–163, 238). During the period from 1700 to 1850 Bunzi's shrine slipped out of the control of the royal families or their priests and came to be represented in the dispersed chiefdoms of the interior who controlled the trade; these derivative Bunzi shrines were called "pseudo-Bunzi" by the late nineteenth century scholar Bastian (1874,

160–163, 238). In the Teke kingdom a similar transformation occurred, in that the *nkobe* lords claimed major power in about 1650, and generated movable shrines derived from the central earth shrine, leaving king Makoko a mere ceremonial figurehead (Vansina 1973).

By the midnineteenth century, for which there is again excellent documentation on Loango's *minkisi*, provided by Pechuel-Loesche (1907, 380–385) and Bastian (1874, 160–163, 238) of the German Loango expedition of the 1870s, there is no mention of the king and his well-being. Rather, central concern is expressed for control of trade, adjudication and retaliation, thief-finding and witch-finding, and fertility.

Bunzi, the traditional earth shrine, is now held to be an important palaver oracle, as well as a rainmaking oracle related to the wind that brings rain. Pechuel-Loesch considers this male "pseudo" Bunzi to be an aberration from the original female earth shrine in which kingdoms were legitimated (1907, 380).

Now-extinct Kikokoo has been replaced by female Gombiri, protector of Loango Bay, hunter of witches and murderers. Mansi, already an ancient *nkisi* mentioned by Dapper, continues to serve as a protective shrine on the ocean coast near Loango, rising to great popularity as oracle in the decade from 1840 to 1850, before its main shrine was demolished. Ngombo, the widespread *nkisi* of divination, continues in use.

In addition to these fixed shrine *minkisi* (except Ngombo) there is, in Loango of the midnineteenth century, a long series of adjudicatory and retaliatory *minkisi*, necessitated no doubt by the collapse of formal appeal courts of the kingdom. These include Tschimpuku, a woven bag, Mpusu, a four-cornered basket with tightly fitting lid, companion piece to Malasi, two-headed hippopotamus-shaped sculpture, Mboyo-zu-Mambi, a pot lid resting on three legs, and Mpangu, a wooden block wrapped tightly with a chain; these are all juridical medicines whose songs, techniques, and symbolisms concentrate on the task of bringing clarity and justice into the tangled and chaotic port city. Mboyo is held to be a direct successor of the ancient *nkisi* Maramba, mentioned by a sixteenth-century English sailor (Battel 1814; Pechuel-Loesche 1907, 382). Other seemingly adjudicatory techniques betray private motives of self-defense and aggression. For example, Simbuka can "kill with a quick strike"; Kunja lames; Kanga-i-kanga creates a headache in its victim, causing him to run off wildly into the wilderness; Mabiala Mandembe, sometimes given human form, drives its victims, especially thieves, mad (Bastian 1874, 163; Pechuel-Loesche 1907, 381).

Against these methods of overt aggression, there are many protective devices. Mandombe, embodied in an iron chain, protects its devotee in war and fighting; Imba, a bracelet with a shell affixed to it, protects its wearer from drawing blood in a fight and reaping the wrath of the opponent and the judges. These and others are all individualized *minkisi*, suggesting that collective institutions are less and less able to render satisfaction, or security. Related to the theme of seeking security is *nkisi* Njambe (Dapper's Injami), used to make its devotee alert and to achieve ecstasy or possession by taking its white seeds to the accompaniment of music.

Possibly because of the combination of insecurity due to slave trade and the appearance of venereal diseases, the medicines of the nineteenth century reflect an increasing attention to fertility. Whereas in the seventeenth century generalized medicine had included fertility of crops and women, along with successful trading, now there emerges a proliferation of medicines for pregnancy and childbirth. Mpemba (also Pfemba, Umpembe) consists of one or more treatment centers that draw scores of women seeking advice and admission to its rituals, founded by a famous midwife using specialized techniques (Pechuel-Loesche 1907, 385). This movement has left its historical evidence in the famous Mpemba maternity figurines of women holding a child on their laps, a breast in one hand (Lehuard 1977). The *nkisi* and its clinics were off-limits for men; its activities were carried out only on a moonlit night. In a related function, Mbinda supported marriages and cured women's problems. It, too, was strictly a woman's affair carried out in the moonlight, with subjects shaven and naked. Men, hair, tobacco smoke, liquor, and water under some circumstances were prohibited to its adherents. Sasi, a drink administered by a female priest, fostered health in pregnant women in childbirth or their newborn offspring. Kulo-Malonga stopped excessive menstrual bleeding; Bitungu treated sterility in women; Dembacani and Cuango-Malimbi treated impotence in men (Bastian 1874, 164).

A variety of individualized "secular" treatments could be added to this partial array of nineteenth-century Loango medicines, suggesting a closer resemblance to Occidental medicine. Treatments existed for a variety of stomach ailments. Mpodi, the cupping horn, was accompanied in use by skin incisions and used for many complaints. Bone-setting was done by the Lunga doctor, using massages and splints of bamboo or some equivalent material. Infections and swelling were handled by skin punctures with a knife, upon which was put powder of the kola nut and other seeds. There were snake-bite remedies and many more herbal and manipulative treatments.

The largest category of public medicine evidencing expansion in the nineteenth century, together with adjudicatory, aggression and fertility medicine, is that pertaining to trade and entrepreneurial endeavors. Mangossu (Dapper's Kossi?) is lord of trade, travel, marriage, or any other general enterprise. The priests of this famous oracle-*nkisi* were easy to recognize, because they were forever moving about, seeking a shrine home, their patron spirit being a restless wanderer. Tschivuku, a man's *nkisi*, was embodied in a woven ball kept in a rack-like shrine in the village to ensure successful trading. Its observation consisted, among other things, of the men, returned from their trading journeys, playing a sort of kick-ball with the *nkisi*, laughing and carrying on, while the women remained hidden out of sight. Mpinda was a large bust, three-quarters human size, which although an *nkisi* of the land, protected river trade. Pechuel-Loesche mentions an unnamed trading *nkisi* that consists of a red trunk kept in a "factory"—trading warehouse—containing all sorts of medicinal objects (Pechuel-Loesche 1907, 374, 377).

Lemba is the "major" medicine of the era because it reflects in its makeup and function a combination of all the above-mentioned areas of taxonomic growth: fertility, marriage, adjudication, and trade control. Its shrine was situated mostly in a movable *nkobe* box, a drum, and a copper bracelet, or, alternatively, on the coast in a few places, in a backyard fixed household shrine or house. Its membership was made up of prominent merchants, judges, chiefs, and healers and orators of the vast region that extended along the trade routes inland to Malebo Pool and Mpumbu market. Its functions emphasized alliances between key landed families, peaceful trading in markets, and matrilineage continuity through mutual solidarity of patrifilial sets of intermarried "fathers" and "sons."

This inventory of Loango coast medicines from the seventeenth to nineteenth centuries suggests that there are some categories of relative permanence—for example, local shrines like Bunzi, or Ngombo divination; protection against witchcraft kidnapping—and other areas of expansion or shifting, including techniques of adjudication and retaliation embodied in such *minkisi* as Mabiala Mandembe. More important than these "surface" transformations are shifts and alternations in the way a given function or experiential domain is anchored in a cosmological category such as the sky/land/water classificatory trichotomy, the domestic/beyond dichotomy, or any of the transitory zones between these categories, or other cyclical processes seen in color symbolism, day/night contrasts and the like (Fukiau 1969). The point is that functions, techniques, and ingredients known in daily experience are shuffled and recombined within existing cosmological or classificatory categories, and only rarely are the more abstract categories dissolved or invented.

At the level of daily life, techniques and insights of sacred medicines are closely tied to social interaction and the skills of individuals in responding to perceived areas of problems. Frequently ingredients or techniques are combined because of the punning or rhythmic quality of the ingredient's name; for instance, *luyala*, a fruit, might be included to affect the power of ruling (*yala*); *lusaka-saka* leaves, with a pungent incense odor, would effect a blessing (*sakumuna*), and so on (Nsemi 1974). This suggests that assemblages of medicines within fixed cosmological taxonomies, as presented at various intervals in the documentation of the Loango coast or its hinterland, demonstrate the presence of empirical observations related to the effect of plants on the physical body, or of symbols and rhetorical techniques on the social or political body. Where such information is compiled from medicinal functions, their names and the names of ingredients or constituent elements—symbolic, chemical, behavioral—and the categories to which they relate, it is possible to understand and anticipate taxonomic changes in a therapeutic system and thus understand the changing perception society's members have of their condition. Where particular medicines harbor multiple functions, or are situated in several taxonomic slots, they often address major social issues and become public corporations.

TRANSFORMATIONS OF CORPORATENESS IN THERAPEUTICS: LEMBA, MAJOR DRUM OF AFFLICTION IN NORTH BANK LOWER ZAIRE, 1650–1930

In this history of medicine in western Equatorial Africa, the "drums of affliction" deserve special attention because they demonstrate the ascendancy of a particular *nkisi* genre to the status of a dominant social form: the transformation of corporateness. My discussion of this issue is couched here in an analysis of Lemba, the major drum over several centuries in the region between the Teke-dominated markets of Malebo Pool (e.g., Mpumbu near the present-day Kinshasa) and the Atlantic coast, between the Congo-Zaire-Nzadi River and the Kwilu-Niari River.

Corporation theory has rarely been applied to Bantu-speaking Africa's healing associations. One account of Central Africa's religious culture couches its discussion of healing in terms of "religious movements" led by charismatic leaders, lasting no more than a few decades (MacGaffey 1970, 27). Emphasis is on the "ephemerality" of these movements, especially during the colonial period, when, of course, the colonial state was the dominant corporate body of the region, harassing all others out of existence or into subordination. However, as was seen in the above review of the history of Loango therapeutics, not only did some *minkisi* endure several centuries, but they could be extremely influential in shaping regional institutions and ideas. The Bunzi shrine, for example, embodied the insignia of leadership of coastal kingdoms—Loango, Kakongo, Ngoyo, Vungu—as well as lesser chiefdoms of the region. Bunzi constituted the symbolic legitimacy of most political organizations during a major historic era. I do not wish to develop here the implications of linking *minkisi* with the origins of the corporate traditional state, although it is apparent that when the somewhat artificial religion/government or medicine/politics dichotomies are put aside, the historical analysis of cults of affliction, medicines, and forms of therapy takes on a more significant stature.

Lemba's emergence in the seventeenth century as a regional network astride the international trade routes had the effect of eroding the territorially defined entities such as the coastal states. The same effect is reported with regard to the *nkobe* reform of the seventeenth-century Teke kingdom, which brought the twelve *nkobe* lords into prominence and autonomy and reduced the effective power of the central regent Makoko (Vansina 1973). The corporateness of ritual or healing orders (*minkisi*) may thus be described either in terms of the territorially fixed or bounded entity, including certain states, or in terms of other transterritorial entities that appear to have been uniquely suited for the control of trade and the resolution of social problems resulting from the sudden upsurge of wealth, mobility, and the unrest linked to trade, especially the slave trade.

In corporate theory, as formulated by Maine (1960), Smith (1974), and in Equatorial Africa by MacGaffey (1976), the characteristics of a corporate body include (1) being a presumptively perpetual aggregate; (2) having a unique identity; (3) having a determinate set of social boundaries and memberships; and (4) possessing the autonomy, organization, and agreed-upon procedures to regulate a given social structure around a diversity of (e.g., therapeutic, trading, alliance) affairs, so as to indicate political "clout" through the development of leadership roles, delegated authority, administrative coordination, and the existence of a constitution, origin myth, or body of special lore. The corporate category, by contrast, is an agglomeration lacking the power and authority of the corporate group, although like it, it possesses presumptive perpetuity, determinate social boundaries, identity, and membership. In contrast to the corporate group, the corporate category has a single function or criterion (Smith 1974).

The distinction between a corporate category and a corporate group would nicely differentiate the simple *nkisi* (MacGaffey 1970, 27) from the *nkisi* "drum" (*ngoma, nkonko, nkonzi*), the fully public corporate ritual healing association. A further distinction in corporate theory between the corporation sole, a leading role through which a series of individuals pass in succession, and the corporation aggregate, which multiple role-holders may simultaneously possess, describes the difference between the chiefdom or kingdom on one hand, and the equally powerful healing association on the other.

Lemba membership consisted of the region's prominent merchants, priests, chiefs, judges, and their wives. *Lemba i luyalu*, "Lemba was the government," said one clan head. *Lemba i nkisi wangyaadila*, "Lemba was the sacred medicine of governing," suggested another. *Lemba i luyaalu lwa niekisa*, "Lemba is the government of multiplication and reproduction," stated an elderly Lemba wife. Elsewhere, Lemba's role was described as that of "calming the villages," or "calming the markets," "perpetuating the family," and so on, covering a diversity of functions we now see is typical of the major corporate drums of affliction.

As a therapy, Lemba functioned similarly to other Central African healing associations in that the sufferer participated in a healing ritual, paid entrance fees, and if successful, in due course emerged as a fully accredited "doctor" (*nganga*) in the order. In the case of Lemba, he and his wife or wives together held the status of being a Lemba household. Lemba's illness has in the literature been variously described as "any illness affecting head, heart, abdomen, and sides" (i.e., any illness at all), "respiratory illnesses," "near-mortal illnesses from which one recovered miraculously," or "possession by Lemba's ancestors." These are all individual symptoms mentioned in connection with the initiations of particular individuals. A stronger case may be made for relating these individual symptoms or illnesses to collective class symptoms in the body politic of the region. As suggested, little of the Lemba region was effectively ruled by centralized polities: an acephalous society of segmentary lineages covered the territory. The volume of trade that crossed this region required some form of social control so as to assure the flow of goods in markets and caravan routes without breaking the redistributive system found in the lineages. In other words, the major problem was how to maintain the productive system set in motion by the trade without creating a separate class of wealthy merchants, in violation of the prevailing egalitarian lineage ethic. Also, feuds that could and did break out needed to be adjudicated. Justice needed to be meted out where crime, violence, and grievance were experienced. All this was required without the benefit of centralized or appeal courts, armies, and tribute systems found in surrounding kingdoms. Lemba's total "medicine of government" operated somewhat as follows to solve these problems, couched in the prevailing mode of affliction—the Lemba illness.

The Lemba system identified the wealthy and obliged them to enter its roles. Although the ideology of access to Lemba—dreaming of Lemba, being possessed, and so on—was populistic, suggesting that anyone could, in theory, join, the final stages of the initiation were very costly. In the central area around the Mboko-Nsongo copper mines at the turn of the century, full initiation cost twenty-five pigs plus all other feast items. This is comparable to the price of three slaves near the end of the international slave trade, or to one large boat at Mpumbu market in 1885, or to 200 to 300 pounds of ivory at the same time. On the periphery of the Lemba area initiation was less costly, but even that cost was such that only the wealthy, or those with extensive patronage, were able to afford admission.

Lemba's stance toward those wealthy who did not wish to join was aggressively inclusive. They were invited, cajoled, harassed, and even mystically threatened and forced to join. Herein lies an important characteristic of the Lemba medicine. Social marginality or peripherality was transformed into legitimate leadership. For example, the "upwardly mobile" slave running a trade caravan, was likely to become a Lemba priest; and his wife or wives, priestess(es). A skilled orator who held in his hands the techniques of social solidarity and of division, was actively recruited for Lemba. A reputable healer was obliged to join. Comparable to a modern single party state in some ways, Lemba sought to control, or capitalized on, the major human and material resources of the region.

As suggested, this "estate" of resources was nonterritorial. Markets were controlled not by single local chiefs, but by committees of representatives from surrounding lineage settlements including Lemba priests who could "calm" the markets. Lemba initiations were presided over by shifting proximal bodies of priests and priestesses from the region surrounding the neophyte couple, not by a fixed local chapter. Unlike the territorially fixed chiefdoms and kingdoms, Lemba's estate derived from the nonterritorial fabric of social exchanges and regional trade.

A key feature of each initiation, therefore, was the marriage ceremony between the neophyte priest and his spouse or spouses from other prominent lineages. Lemba marriages often embodied the patrilateral cross-cousin marriage form or some functional equivalent, a form encouraging egalitarian exchange relationships between corporate descent groups over time (Leach 1965; Lévi-Strauss 1949). By contrast, matrilateral cross-cousin marriages, if generalized, would lead to hierarchic endogenous enclaves. In the Lower Congo-Zaire, these latter were widely practiced, and contributed to isolated small-scale polities. Lemba's marriage politics, as a countermeasure, maintained the egalitarian transregional network of kinship exchanges.

Lemba's characteristics so far might be thought to describe a feudal aristocracy, except for the major fact that Lemba membership was not inheritable. On this key criterion, Lemba differs notably from all chiefly or state systems surrounding it. Often fathers initiated their sons, and had them marry nieces along the patrilateral cross-cousin marriage form. But the insignia of Lemba membership—the *nkobe*, the copper bracelets and the drum—went with the Lemba priest and priestess(es) to their graves.

In general, then, Lemba generated its authority and power in a stateless setting through the cognitive, emotional, and socioeconomic incorporation of the Lemba "sick," specifically, prominent orators, healers, merchants, clan leaders, and prosperous slaves. A key aspect of this incorporative process in Lemba was the father–child relationship in which the initiation was couched. The patron *nganga* who healed and sponsored the initiation was a real or fictive "father" (*se*) to the neophyte. Fictive paternity in Lemba made possible the use of patrifiliality as a cognitive mode of ordering special integrating relationships in the region's matrilineal society. Just as true fatherhood was important in a person's identity, its absence implied the stigma of slavery. Where slaves were admitted to Lemba, the emphasis on paternity gave alienated persons a ritual "father," an opening to a legitimate title or pedigree. Lemba's etiological myths, as shall be seen in the next section, return again and again to the problems of legitimacy, foundership, independence, and the reconciliation of the "child" to his "father" or of the father' s "recognition" of his true son.

By extending Lemba to those who demanded it (felt possessed by it), and could afford it, Lemba transformed social, economic, and cognitive marginality and centrifugality into integrative order. The ethos of healing, exchange, and paternity resolved important structural contradictions in the society. It joined isolated communities through its notion of the pure marriage; it permitted a strong figure in the community to retain a close association with his (or "a") father while becoming an adult member of his own matrilineal village. In the case of the slave "son" residing with his master "father," Lemba permitted him to become a prominent member in the same community—a "founder"—without having to sever lines of legitimacy. Finally, Lemba created the social form whereby the lineage, the major local base of economic (human and material) productivity, might be integrated into the regional and international economic system. It insulated the productive élite from the envy of their kinsmen, yet required them to periodically redistribute their accumulated wealth to their local dependents. The sickness of the prominent who were drawn to Lemba thus consisted primarily in the psychological vulnerability and breakdown before the clashing interests of lineage egalitarianism and mercantile affluence to be derived from the long-distance trade. Viewed thus as both a means of individual therapy and regional trading association, the fusion of "cult of affliction" and government makes sense.

Lemba's rule continued until the end of the nineteenth century. Then the railroads built by Belgian and French colonialists from the Pool to the ocean—one south of the Zaire River to Matadi, the other along the Kwilu-Niari Valley to Pointe Noire—usurped trade control and the operation of caravans. Pressure upon chiefs to participate in colonial rule divided the ranks of the order. Missions fought for the rejection of all *minkisi*. Colonial taxation and *corvée* labor diverted the social investments that Lemba had previously held. Lemba's final initiations were held in the 1920s and 1930s. Although little remains today of Lemba the institution, three centuries of Lemba thought have left a major impact on the regional culture's values.

TRANSFORMATIONS IN IDEOLOGY: LEMBA'S ANCHORING IN REGIONAL MYTHOLOGY

Regional mythological structures were not fundamentally changed by three centuries of corporate Lemba dominance, however. Lemba was everywhere derived from the "conventional" cosmology of heroes, deities, and categories. This led one observer to suggest that Lemba was "more recent," or "less primordial" than earth shrine Bunzi. In the process of anchoring the *nkisi* to a pantheon of existing deities, two types of transformation occurred in the case of Lemba. First, local deities differing from locale to locale were incorporated into etiological myths of Lemba. Second, these narratives, if examined as a set, reflect uniform shifts reflecting a pervasive Lemba structural emphasis.

Typically Bantu, Lemba's etiological myths move in their narrative flow from a unity of power to a diversity of powers and functions embodied in *minkisi*. The upper level of oneness is embodied in Nzambi-God or a dual pair who are not given material representation in medicines. Lemba's ultimate origins are ascribed to Nzambi, but the relationship to humans is always made through a mediating deity. In the coastal areas this figure is earth deity Bunzi, her male partner Kanga, and their daughter Lusunzi (the violent storm); in the Mayombe forest it is Moni-Mambu, the trickster; in the north it is Mahungu, androgynous double figure; eastward in Teke country, it is the hierarchy of Nga Malamu, Kuba, and Mahungu.

Comparison of the narratives inside and outside Lemba reveals that Lemba is everywhere cast in a problem-solving, mediatory charter myth. Outside of Lemba the same heroes run afoul of structural and situational contradictions, or semantic ambiguities. For example, in a Lemba charter myth from Kivunda in the Manianga, Mahungu dances around the palm tree of God; through this act, Mahungu's "male" and "female" selves are separated. God's Lemba solution is for the two to "marry in mutual harmony" in Lemba (Fukiau 1969). Outside of Lemba, Mahungu is cast as a tragic hero. A text from Mayombe portrays Mahungu as two brothers, elder and younger, who part ways over a deep misunderstanding akin to that between Cain and Abel in the Bible. In another set of "conventional" texts outside Lemba, Mahungu is a father–son dyad comparable to the father–son pairs in Lemba. The son is led by a dream to discover a mermaid in the belly of a python who promises him great wealth in trade at the ocean if he will leave home forever. He accepts, and enjoys great luxury in this arrangement, but longs for contact with his father. A hunter, seeking his father's stray pigs, finds the son. Father and son are reconciled, the son loses his fortune and finds himself a pauper at his father's home, where, in grief, he dies.

The trickster cycles in Lemba and outside Lemba reveal a similar contrasting set of harmonious and tragic narratives. In the Lemba-related etiological narrative, Tsimona-Mambu overcomes many obstacles to gain recognition of his father, Nzambi-God, and to seek a solution to his wives' problems. Nzambi invents the Lemba *nkisi* and bestows upon him the Lemba medicine and rings and sends him home to live in peace. In conventional trickster narratives, the hero blunders through a host of crimes and errors. At first forgiven for his naïveté, he is ultimately, however, held accountable for his actions and executed for his sins, a wretched, tragic antihero.

These transformations in the common mythic culture of the Lemba region suggest that despite local variations, even variations in characters, a common Lemba structure is present. At least one student of Lemba argues that this manipulation of rhetoric was an intentional ideology of social and political control (Malonga 1958, 45). Part of Lemba's popular front, according to this view, was the populistic panacea cure-all for ills. But the genuine Lemba therapeutic insights and political mechanisms operated in secret learnings, instruction, and behind-the-mask analysis and intervention in current events.

CONCLUSION

The historical reconstruction of a dominant cult of affliction such as Lemba, with its role in governing, alliance-building, trading, as well as the more familiar attributes of healing, and designing a mythic charter of the good society, should contribute to a better comprehension of African therapeutics. Too much writing on the subject has arbitrarily been limited to the individualistic, the pathological, the disorganized, and the ephemeral—thereby verifying the colonial stereotype of Central African humanity. What are the implications of a revision of such views to include the corporate, the normative, the organized, and the permanent?

Certainly African therapy has in many ways also considered individuality. Victor Turner's assessment of Ndembu drums of affliction in his now-classic work speaks of "ritual assemblies" that take the afflicted individual and incorporate him into a moral community (Forde 1965). He warns his readers not to think of these assemblies as organizations in a conventional sense; they are, he says, "categorical" rather than "corporate," cross-cutting territories and kinship units. Probably most drums and medicines in the recent history of Central and Equatorial Africa have been like this. But the case of Lemba should give us pause.

One remarkable characteristic in African drums of affliction is the transformation of the sufferer into the healer. This process permits social and cognitive control without recourse to the total and centralizing institutions characteristic of Occidental medicine. A Lemba song puts the transformation thus: "That which was a 'stitch' of pain, has become the path to the priesthood." Implicit in such a therapeutic attitude is the idea that the solution grows out of the problem through its becoming the focus of community. The range of applications of this mode of thinking are broad, ranging from hunting troubles, fertility concerns, trade, beauty, social structural issues, justice, to the more philosophical issues such as the "two-in-one" of twinship, purity, and pollution, and more. It is apparently open-ended in its application, proving a viable model for some social problems in modern industrial society as Corin's study of Zebola in Kinshasa (Corin 1979), Ngubane's of Zulu *isangoma*, or Prins's account of Nzila, elsewhere in this volume.

Most intriguing of all is the prevailing ideology of therapy that grows out of a dominant drum of affliction. One gets the picture not of a society indulging in its weaknesses, sicknesses, miseries, and woes, but of a society that has, at least historically, known how to construct functionally specific as well as more general institutions to overcome philosophical, social, and perhaps ecological threats. The underlying tenet of this worldview is an appeal to life-force: *ngolo* in Kongo, *mpolo* for the Tio and their immediate western neighbors, *karamo* among the eastern rainforest Nyanga, *poloo* with the Kuba, and so on (MacGaffey 1970, 27). In a careful analysis of Lemba-related texts, verbal categories appear that characterize other properties of a system of wholeness: purity, order, access to spiritual energy, clarity, and redemption (Janzen 1982, 144, 315–321). Harriet Ngubane, writing on Zulu therapeutics, suggests that the notion of "metaphysical balance," summed up in the term *lungisa*, is central to any definition of health in Central African and general Bantu-speaking culture. *Lungisa* is a positive morality that includes "the people's sense of responsibility, their good intentions toward others, their responsible decision-making, helping others to discard harmful substances and influences, and their duty to the ancestors and dependents. Anything less than this gives rise to lack of balance in the natural, human and mystical realms, and dire consequences" (Horton 1967, 155; Ngubane 1976, 318–357).

NOTES

1. An earlier version of this chapter appeared in *Social Science and Medicine* 13B (1979) (4):317–326. Revised by the author and published with the permission of Pergamon Journals Ltd. Research for this chapter was conducted in Lower Zaire in 1964–1966, 1969, and 1982; and in archives and museums in Europe and North America. It was funded by the Foreign Area Fellowship (1964–1966), the Social Science Research Council (1969), the Canada Council (1971), the Alexander von Humboldt Stiftung (1977), the U.S. National Endowment for the Humanities (1978), and the Fulbright Senior Research Fellowship (1982).

2. These terms are taken from Malcolm Guthrie's useful proto-Bantu lexical compendium in his *Comparative Bantu*. For the sake of simplicity we have not used Guthrie's symbols for reconstructed cognates. Despite its usefulness for historical linguistic reconstruction of cultural domains such as medicine, Guthrie's hypotheses about the historical migrations of Bantu languages have been invalidated by more recent research. His program of reconstructing proto-Bantu languages from existing lexica, is being updated and expanded continuously.

EIGHT

Public Health in Precolonial East-Central Africa[1]

Gloria Waite

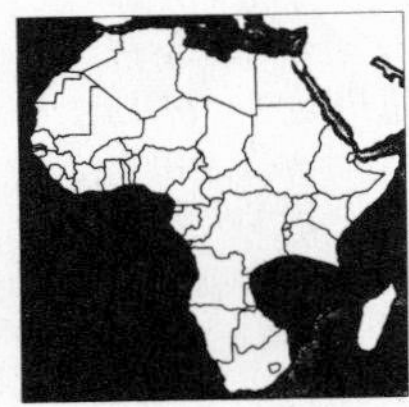

INTRODUCTION

This is a study of public health institutions in precolonial east-central Africa. This region encompasses modern-day southern Tanzania, Malawi, northern Mozambique, Zimbabwe, Zambia, and southeastern Zaire.

East-central Africans, and other people who were historically nonliterate, have received scant attention in studies in public health history. The history of medicine, and by extension the history of public health, tends to be confined to European, Egyptian, Chinese, and Indian societies because they have written records that date from early times. All other peoples have been placed in a category called "primitive." While there is some recognition of the "origins" of public health in so-called primitive societies (Rosen 1958), there is a tendency to dismiss these societies altogether in studies in public health history (Burton et al. 1980; Wain 1970). Thus, east-central African public health history has invariably meant the changes and developments in the European institutions that were introduced in the colonial period (Baker 1976, 296; Beck 1977; Clyde 1962; Gelfand 1976; Sabben-Clare 1980; Webster 1972, 244; 1973, 7, 27, 48).

This study breaks with that tradition by focusing on the precolonial period, before European rule and the advent of most recorded history for the region. The central thesis of this study is that a certain amount of public health existed in African societies prior to the colonial period and was not, therefore, newly introduced by Europeans in the twentieth century.

Several cases are presented of a number of societies in the region whose public health institutions underwent change at various periods between about the eleventh and twentieth centuries. The evidence is based mainly on oral traditions, linguistic and ethnographic data. Although there are still some scholars who doubt the credibility of unwritten source material for historical reconstructions, in the main it is generally accepted that such sources can be very useful, whether in the absence or presence of written documents (McCall 1969; Vansina 1968, 1985). Indeed, much of what we know about the precolonial political history of this region is derived from such evidence, and there is no reason why our knowledge of institutional change cannot be expanded to include the medical system. Nevertheless, such data are very difficult to work with. Therefore, the only changes in public health institutions that are discussed here are those that resulted from contacts between the ruling strata of immigrant and autochthonous groups, because the historical evidence for this kind of interaction—for example, loan words and imported artifacts—are the easiest kind to uncover in linguistic and archaeological records and are the safest kind from which to draw historical inferences in the absence of written sources. All of the immigrant groups originated within east-central Africa, with the exception of the Ngoni people from the Zulu kingdom in South Africa, who entered the region in the nineteenth century. Externally derived materials are not, of course, the whole of any people's traditions, but they are very useful clues to cultural change and social interaction.

A useful working definition of public health that includes the features found in preindustrial, nonliterate societies was put forward some time ago by Charles Hughes, who defined public health quite simply as all illness that affects the public as well as all activity that it undertakes to influence its health status (Hughes 1963, 157). This definition is broad enough to include illnesses and other ill-health concerns from the ancestors or caused by violation of taboos, as well as illnesses brought on by congenital or environmental conditions. The activities it covers can include rainmaking, identification of sorcerers, and control of infectious diseases, as well as public sanitation works and health education. The definition provided by Hughes can be expanded even further. As indicated in this study, public health is the meeting ground between politics and medicine. Thus, public health services are those that ruling elites provide, at least theoretically, on behalf of the public for particular illnesses and other ill-health conditions. These elites may be priests, chiefs, and kings, or presidents and ministers of health.

PRECOLONIAL SOCIETY, MEDICINE, AND PUBLIC HEALTH

The people of east-central Africa who are the focus of this study are Bantu-speaking agriculturalists whose ancestors settled in the region at least 2,000 years ago. Using agricultural techniques known as "shifting cultivation," they had by at least 1,000 years ago settled in most of the ecological niches in the region, growing tuber, pulse, and grain crops. They kept small livestock and raised cattle where tsetse flies did not prevent that. Their production unit was the family or household and they produced for their own consumption and for some limited exchange. Several families lived together in villages that were headed by senior lineage heads. Above these lineage heads were clan heads and minor chiefs who ruled over several villages. By the eleventh century, if not before, they began to form kingdoms in the region, particularly where there were extensive resources, such as cattle, or deposits of minerals, such as copper, gold, iron, and salt, around which commercial networks were established.

Throughout the centuries a set of diverse medical traditions emerged in the region. This diversity stemmed from cultural nuances rather than from any structural or substantive differences (Waite 1981). Thus, at a general level, the medical traditions of Bantu-speaking east-central Africa, somewhat but not altogether with those of the rest of Bantu-speaking Africa, constitute a single medical system that is distinct from those of non-Bantu-speakers in the region and beyond. The description that follows is a generalized account of the medical system of the people under discussion, highlighting the features in that system that are significant for this study. It draws upon earlier work carried out by the author that involved extensive field collections in parts of the region (Waite 1981).

Contrary to what is commonly believed in the West, all illnesses in Bantu-speaking Africa were not attributed to spirits or witches, even in the past. Several causations of illness and disease were known (Waite 1981). Many people even now can identify and treat common ailments and endemic diseases such as malaria, sleeping sickness, and measles. There is an extensive pharmacopoeia derived from barks, leaves, roots, saps, and other natural products. Historically, most individual health problems were taken care of in the household, but two medical conditions required the intervention of ruling elites. These conditions were illness (and other calamity) that were caused by spirits and those caused by sorcery.

Spirit causation is a significant part of the premodern or traditional medical system. Hence, this system is best described as a medicoreligious one, as distinct from the modern-day biotechnical system. In the traditional system, spirits are believed to bring certain kinds of illnesses and other afflictions to individuals, to families, and to whole communities. When illness is of unknown origin or calamity strikes the whole community, people consult doctors who divine the cause of the problem by using their own spirits for inspiration or by using mechanical devices. If the doctor diagnoses the problem as being caused by neglect of ancestral spirits, then people generally undertake propitiation of those spirits by going to specially selected sites where they place items such as food or manufactured goods that they offer as gifts to the spirits, whom they call upon to hear their complaints.

There are two kinds of ancestral spirits. Some represent founders of the individual family, while others represent founders of the community, such as chiefs and kings. The spirits of founders of communities are called "territorial" or "tutelary spirits" in the literature for the region. Tutelary spirits cut across family lines because they belong to the community and are evoked on its behalf (generally only for rainmaking). They are associated with public proscriptions, and their propitiation is controlled by chiefs, kings, and priests. Propitiation for family spirits, in contrast, is done in private, generally only for familial illness and other trouble, and under the direction of the family elders. In some societies in eastern-central Africa familial propitiation is done inside the home, while in others it is done away from the home. But in no case does the ceremony involve the whole community. Therefore, propitiation for family spirits is not a public health service.

Nor does activity for spirit possession illness fall within the definition of public health given above. Spirit possession illness is somewhat intermediary to the illnesses and calamities caused by family and community spirits (Waite 1980). This illness is caused by family spirits, not tutelary or community spirits, but placating these spirits is a public activity. The afflicted person undergoes public dancing. The community, consisting of neighbors and family, gathers around the possessed person and provides the choruses and instruments for the songs sung by the possessed while the person dances. The participation of the community gives spirit possession a public character, but people gather voluntarily, not because any authority compels them to do so. Unlike propitiation for tutelary spirits, spirit possession activity is not under the control of ruling elites. Dancing is done at the behest of the possessed (and that person's spirits), and not by order of ruling elites. Thus, because ruling authorities do not control spirit possession activity, it, like family spirit propitiation, is not a public health activity. The propitiation of community or tutelary spirits is the only public health activity involving spirits that will be discussed in this study.

A second area of public health in the precolonial health sector is sorcery—its incidence and control. Sorcery involves antisocial, nefarious acts. Generally, sorcery is suspected when people die suddenly or have an illness that is unexplainable and progresses rapidly. From the outset sorcery accusations are made in public. Sorcery is not a family matter, but during colonial rule the public nature of sorcery accusations and control was sharply curtailed. Historically, ruling elites, whether priestly or chiefly authorities, intervened and "medicalized" the conflict. "Medicalized" seems an appropriate description because the various techniques used by the authorities to identify sorcerers (whether by inspiration from the spirits, by poison ordeals, or whatever) and the medicines used to counter the sorcery were also used in strictly medical contexts.

Besides tutelary spirits and sorcery, a third area of traditional public health is public taboos. Historically, when epidemics such as smallpox and other catastrophic events occurred, the authorities prohibited people from engaging in certain everyday activities, such as conjugal relationships and house-to-house visitations. These prohibitions were practical as well as symbolic since nuclear-family and extended-family contacts were important in nonindustrial societies. The suspension of normal activities reminded the community that it was in a dangerous state. Public taboos, however, are seldom discussed in this chapter, for their change and development are more difficult to track. Sanitation control is not discussed either. However, wastes were disposed of, houses were burned down following deaths from certain illnesses, and villages were periodically relocated in order to free them of vermin. The only public health activities discussed in this study are sorcerer identification—or sorcery control—and tutelary spirit propitiation.

The authorities who controlled traditional public health institutions were priestly, chiefly, and kingly figures, or they combined both chiefly and priestly roles. These authorities, like the spirits they evoked, were "guardians of the land" and all that dwelled therein (Schoffeleers 1978). They derived their power and authority from their ancestral spirits and from their knowledge of medicines. There are some accounts of competition and even conflict between priests and kings because they claimed the same power and authority, as some cases below will indicate. Nevertheless, the control exercised by elites over health care institutions and other resources set them apart from the rest of the population.

Within this generalized tradition of the traditional medical system there arose a variety of customs over the centuries, in part the result of various historical events including the rise of several local expansionist groups from about 1,000 years ago (Waite 1981). Several of these groups are discussed below. Their histories demonstrate how health care was affected by political developments. The evidence for these cases is drawn from oral traditions, archaeological findings, and linguistic and ethnographic data. These sources are less abundant for some periods and parts of the region than for others. Therefore, more is known about some of the immigrant groups than about others. But it is apparent that while some immigrant groups had only local impact, the influence of others was more far-reaching. Some of the immigrants left a record of their political entrance into an area and also of their public health traditions. Occasionally, though, the immigrants were compelled by circumstances to adopt the traditions of the people over whom they claimed sovereignty, as will be indicated below.

The earliest case for the study of the influence of politics on medicine in precolonial east-central Africa is based on evidence that emanated from the Luba-Lunda kingdoms of southeastern Zaire. Luba-Lunda influence on central Africa was widespread. In the east, the area covered in this study, they impacted upon peoples as far away as northern Mozambique and Zimbabwe.

Luba-Lunda Influences

In the Shaba (Katanga) region of southeastern Zaire archaeologists have found remains dated to at least 1,000 years ago of densely settled sites with considerable commercial and cultural activity associated with large-scale workings of salt and copper deposits (Van Noten 1982). In the eleventh century descendants of the builders of these sites may have begun a series of migrations out of the area to a number of places, including Zambia, Zimbabwe, Mozambique, and Malawi in the east. These migrations are attested to by archaeological evidence and supported by oral traditions (Phillipson 1977). The immigrants did not significantly alter the basic culture of the societies in which they settled, but they did introduce new ideas and expand upon others in government and public health.

The period that ushered in southeastern Zairean influences in east-central Africa may simply be called "Luba-Lunda," after the two systems of kingdoms known to have emerged in the Shaba region and to which the new ideas have been traced. This period is still obscure, although it may have been a very formative one in eastern-central African history. Certain items in the political culture of societies in the region originated among the Luba and Lunda peoples (Hoover 1978; Reefe 1981; Vansina 1966). These include kingly insignia (such as iron bells), ideas about royal descent (*bulopwe*), and fictitious kinship ties (perpetual kinship and positional succession) between those who ruled major and minor divisions of the kingdoms. *Bulopwe* conferred on a man the inherited right to rule by his descent from the original possessor of *bulopwe* (Vansina 1966). A small royalty was thereby created, determined by real kinship links. Perpetual kinship and positional succession, however, were principles that created fictitious kinship links and provided other integrative mechanisms that led to an increase in the number of elites, for these also now included those in incorporated chiefdoms. *Bulopwe* is thought to be a Luba innovation, while the Lunda, who emerged after the Luba kingdom was well established, are credited with originating perpetual kinship and positional succession, which they used along with *bulopwe*. All of these institutions became known in the east, but the dates of their introductions are not known, nor whether *bulopwe* and perpetual kinship came together or separately. Nevertheless, the elites from Luba and Lunda who introduced these new political ideas may have also built new shrines and may have created a more prominent role for the *mwavi* poison ordeal in sorcery control.

The evidence for these developments is linguistic. The Chewa in Malawi and the Lamba in western Zambia call their shrines for tutelary spirits, *kachisi* and *akacesi*, respectively (Doke 1963; Scott and Hetherwick 1970). *Kici*, the reconstructed root from which these names are derived, is found throughout southern Zaire, where it means a certain class of esoteric medicines and the "spirits" evoked by practitioners of these medicines (Burton 1961; Guthrie 1967–1971; Janzen 1975, 1979, 317). Among the Chewa *chisi* also means the use of medicines in a special context (Scott and Hetherwick 1970). For unspecified Shona-speakers in Zimbabwe *chisi* has a narrower meaning. There it is not the name for shrines. Instead, it means the "day on which work (in the lands) was forbidden by the tribal tutelary spirit" (Hannah 1959). These are the only known distributions in east-central Africa of words derived from this southern Zairean root. *Chisi*, then, means sites for tutelary spirits, public proscriptions concerning these spirits, and special medicines. It may have been introduced by the authorities who brought Luba-Lunda political institutions to east-central Africa. Although associated with kingly elites, priestly ones also have a role in the establishment of *chisi*, for they keep the shrines, declare the days of rest, and generally are the possessors of the *chisi* medicines. The creation of stronger political units during the Luba-Lunda period may have strengthened the position of priests (also called "mediums"), for they would now enjoy the patron of kings and great chiefs.

In support of their own increased power, or in an attempt to decrease priestly power, chiefly and kingly authorities may have begun making greater use of ordeal poison for identifying sorcerers, instead of continuing to rely on the metaphysical techniques employed by the mediums. Until then the mediums may have been the main or only source of authority that controlled sorcery.

Ordeal poisons were widely used in Africa before the colonial era and are probably very old. Nevertheless, with phonological variations, *mwavi* is the name people gave the poison ordeal that they used to identify sorcerers in eastern Zaire, throughout Zambia, in Malawi, in most of Tanzania, and in parts of Mozambique (Retel-Lauretin 1974*b*). Almost without exception, *mwavi* in east-central Africa meant any ordeal, including trial by fire and boiling water, but most importantly the poison ordeal. The poison ordeal was a drink made from the bark of certain trees that was drunk by suspected sorcerers on the order of secular authorities. Outside of east-central Africa, the name *mwavi* is known only in Uganda, where it is used for ordeals in general, but where specific ordeals are known by other names. In Kenya, other parts of Tanzania, and from Zimbabwe to the furthest extent of Bantu-speakers in South Africa, *mwavi* is not known at all, neither as a generic nor as a specific name for ordeals. *Mwavi*, in its preeminent role as a name for an ordeal poison, is limited to east-central Africa. Its distribution correlates with the distribution of Luba-Lunda political institutions, with some exceptions. These exceptions are the various Shona-speaking people in Zimbabwe, the Pogolo, Ndamba, and others in south-central Tanzania, and the Nsenga in eastern Zambia. The Shona appear by linguistic and archaeological evidence to have received some Luba-Lunda materials and ideas, but their ordeal is called *mteyo*, a name limited to Shona-speakers and thus probably of origin among them. In southern Tanzania and in eastern Zambia the ordeal name *mwavi* is probably of secondary distribution, for there is no evidence of direct Luba-Lunda influence there (Waite 1981).

In any case, whether called *mwavi* or *mteyo*, poison ordeals were controlled by chiefs and kings whose powers over an important institution—sorcery control—have been enhanced by this technique. Kings and chiefs now possessed a material device in the form of a naturally occurring poison. By possessing this method of sorcerer identification, they were in a position to challenge the authority of priests, whose ability to control sorcery depended on inspiration from their spirits, a method that they alone possessed. Conflict arose between kings and priests over the control of sorcery because they each claimed that their technique was the correct one. For instance, such a conflict arose in the Kalonga kingdom of the Chewa in Malawi (Schoffeleers 1978). This kingdom had an infusion of Luba-Lunda ideas and materials in its political and public health institutions. By the fifteenth century it was composed of a number of subkingdoms and tributary chiefdoms. In that century, tensions arose within the ruling network and accusations of sorcery were lodged against M'bona, the official medium in the Kaphwiti tributary chiefdom. M'bona was said to have withheld rain, and his accusers demanded that he undergo the poison ordeal trial in order to establish his innocence or guilt. M'bona refused, saying that he alone had the infallible power to uncover sorcerers, and he denounced the ordeal as being unjust. But his protest was in vain. M'bona was forced to leave the Kalonga kingdom for refusing to drink the ordeal, and the Kaphwiti chiefdom that supported him was also forced to relocate (Schoffeleers 1972, 73).

Undi's Kingdom and the Nsenga

The history of Undi's kingdom, another scission of the Kalonga kingdom, provides further evidence of the relationship between politics and health care. From around the seventeenth to the eighteenth century the first Undi and his successors (all of whom took the title Undi) built a kingdom that stretched from southern Malawi into central Mozambique and eastern Zambia (Langworthy 1969). Among the peoples over whom Undi established hegemony were the Nsenga, who lived along the Zambezi River in central Mozambique and on the eastern plateau in southeastern Zambia. The river Nsenga was the first to come under Undi's hegemony. The extension of Undi's authority over the plateau Nsenga was a later development. Chiefs from both groups paid tribute to the Undi kings. In the area of public health care, however, an important difference existed between the two Nsenga groups. Those on the plateau did not adopt Chewa traditions, while those along the river did.

The Chewa's principal institution of public health revolved around their guardian spirit, which was variously known as *Chiuta* (*Chauta*) or *Chisumphi*.

Chiuta seems to be the older of the two names. Although *Chiuta* may have been a tutelary spirit at some remote time, by the time of Undi's expansion over the Nsenga it had become a supreme deity. The central shrine for *Chiuta* was at Kaphirintiwa in the core Chewa area in central Malawi (Schoffeleers 1978, 147).

Even before the rise of Undi, the worship of *Chiuta* had spread south of Malawi into Mozambique, where some Chewa were already settled (Rita-Ferreira 1966). However, the proximity of these Chewa to the river Nsenga was not a sufficient condition for the diffusion of *Chiuta* to the latter. Political inclusion was necessary, and this came with Undi's expansion. Undi took control of *makewana*, the mediumship for *Chiuta*, and relocated its shrine at Msinja, not far from Kaphirintiwa (Rangeley 1952, 31), probably around the same time that his kingdom expanded over the Nsenga along the river. It must have been in this way that *Chiuta* came to be known by these Nsenga, whose descendants today consult this spirit, not only for rainmaking, but also for identifying sorcerers (Williams-Myers 1978).

The Nsenga on the plateau in eastern Zambia, however, had a different experience. Undi's expansion into eastern Zambia occurred after his expansion along the Zambesi. Tradition has it that when Undi lost control of the mediumship of the *Chiuta* shrine, because a restored Kalonga dynasty was able to appoint its own mediums, Undi went west (Schoffeleers 1978, 147). The westward expansion led to an alliance with the Kalindawalo chiefdom among the plateau Nsenga. The relationship between them was based on perpetual kinship, which created real and fictitious kinship links between the progeny of the Undis and those of the Kalindawalos (Langworthy 1971, 1). Nevertheless, despite this relationship, Nsenga identification with the political charter of Undi's kingdom did not lead to an adoption of Chewa public health services. The supreme deity of the Nsenga continued to be known as *Mulungu*, which was the name given the supreme being by many Bantu speakers, and was probably of proto-Bantu provenance. *Mulungu* was a remote being and seldom assumed the significance of *Chiuta* and *Mwari* (to be discussed below for the Shona). In most Bantu societies ancestral spirits were more important than *Mulungu* in the daily affairs of men. The plateau Nsenga continued to consult their ancestral spirits, *mizimu*, when rain was needed, and these *mizimu* were consulted at shrines called *kawimba*, which the Nsenga built at special trees (Waite 1981). These plateau Nsenga did not adopt the Chewa god *Chiuta* or the Chewa shrines, *kachisi*, which were generally located in hills, not at special trees. On the plateau the Nsenga continued to identify sorcerers through the *mwavi* poison ordeal that was under the control of their chiefs.

Thus, although traditions of the plateau Nsenga and the Undis indicate a political relationship between them, it was probably a weak alliance, or else we should expect that the plateau Nsenga would have adopted Chewa public health traditions just as the river Nsenga did. Harry Langworthy, who carried out extensive investigations on the history of Undi kingdom, believes that Chewa authority was only established on the plateau when Undi's power was waning (Langworthy 1969). As a result, strong political ties were never forged there and the weakened kingly authority may have been unable to implant its own sacred authority. Matthew Schoffeleers, the leading authority on east-central African spirit mediumships, has noted several occasions in east-central African history when immigrant rulers were unable to impose their traditions and instead had to defer to the institutions of the people they conquered (1973, 47). In the cases cited by Schoffeleers the imperial leaders themselves settled among the conquered. This did not happen in the case of the Undi kingdom, though the Undis may have settled some colonists among the plateau Nsenga (Langworthy 1969). Still, an analogy may be drawn from Schoffeleers's work in that the inability of the Undis to affect the public health traditions of the plateau Nsenga may have been because of a weakened authority, perhaps because the Undis no longer controlled the important Chewa shrine at Msinja in central Malawi. Among the Nsenga along the Zambesi, however, the Undis' authority was established at the peak of their power and when they were still in control of the *makewana* mediumship of *Chiuta*. Political change was not, therefore, in and of itself a sufficient basis for change in health institutions, as the story of the plateau Nsenga indicates. But without political change health care institutions were unaffected, as the case of the river Nsenga suggests.

The Rozvi Kingdom and Mwari

In the seventeenth and eighteenth centuries a new development also arose in public health traditions among some of the Shona in Zimbabwe and Mozambique, when the Changamire dynasty of the Rozvi kingdom introduced the *Mwari* rainmaking institution to them. The evidence is drawn from oral traditions and ethnographic accounts.

The Rozvi kingdom of the Changamires was the successor to the old Torwa kingdom of the Kalanga in southwestern Zimbabwe. The first Changamire, a man named "Dombo," originated in the Mutapa kingdom in northeastern Zimbabwe. Tradition has it that he was expelled from Mutapa for refusing to drink the ordeal (probably *mteyo*). Once established in old Torwa, Dombo and his successors are said to have used the ordeal to intimidate and control recalcitrant tributary kings (Bhila 1982), but there is no information at present as to whether Dombo Changamire introduced the use of ordeal poison to the people in Torwa. What is known, however, is that the Changamires adopted the Torwa institution, *Mwari*, used for rainmaking. *Mwari* was the guardian spirit of the Torwa kingdom and was propitiated through a well-developed priestly organization. According to tradition, *Mwari* invited Dombo to intervene in the civil war that was tearing Torwa apart and that is how the Changamire dynasty arose. Yet the relationship between the Changamires and the *Mwari* mediums was not always harmonious, for there is at least one tradition of unspecified clashes between them (Fortune 1973, 1).

However, as the Changamires built their own kingdom, known as "Rozvi," by expanding their hegemony over several peoples in southern Zimbabwe and central Mozambique, the influence of the *Mwari* institution also spread. People such as the Manyika and Ndau in the east began sending delegations to the *Mwari* shrines, which are found only in the Matopo Hills in the core Rozvi area. For the diffusion of *Mwari* influence under the Changamires, the most extensive information comes from the history of the Manyika who live in eastern Zimbabwe.

The Manyika were apparently politically subordinate to the Changamires, for they say that they sent tribute to the Rozvi kings on an annual or semiannual basis (Bhila 1982). The Changamires confirmed their kings, although they did not choose them. Then, about 100 years after it began, this political relationship ended. The Manyika stopped sending tribute and stopped allowing the Changamires to confirm their kings. However, important links remained. One of these was the tradition of sending delegations to *Mwari* shrines in the Matopo Hills, a tradition that persists to the present day. The Manyika say that they go to the *Mwari* shrines when their own tutelary spirits prove inadequate for rainmaking.

Mwari is only discussed in the ethnographic literature in relation to rainmaking (Bhila 1982; Bucher 1980; Daneel 1970). Nothing has been recorded about the role of this spirit or its mediums in sorcery control, past or present. During the Rozvi period *Mwari* became a common source of power for rainmaking over a wide area of southern Zimbabwe and central Mozambique. Even today the *Mwari* shrines link people across boundaries of traditional kingdoms (Fortune 1973, 1). Activities associated with the spirit supersede all other rituals in these kingdoms. And the shrines are staffed with priests, dancers, consecrated women, and messengers who have been drawn from the diverse groups that have over the centuries been introduced to *Mwari*.

There will be reference below to further developments involving *Mwari* in the nineteenth century. In addition to that case, several others are presented for that century, that show the influence ruling authorities had on health care services. The first of these cases is that of the Hehe and the Ndamba in southern Tanzania. The evidence is drawn mainly from linguistic data.

The Hehe and the Ndamba

In the first half of the nineteenth century the Hehe-Bena people of the southern highlands of Tanzania began wider hegemony in the region between the highlands and the coast. In the Kilombero Valley a Hehe subchief established authority over the Ndamba (Waite 1981). This suzerainty over the Ndamba lasted only for one or two generations. Some informants say that it ended with the coming of the Mbunga in the mid-1800s, who are said to have driven out the Hehe subchief. Other traditions claim that the Hehe had retreated before the Mbunga came because of climatic conditions (Waite 1981). Whatever the case, the Hehe made an enduring cultural impact on the Ndamba. In the core vocabulary of the Ndamba and that of their neighbors, the Pogolo, there are several Hehe loan words that indicate either long-standing or intensive contact between them (Waite 1981) that probably occurred prior to Hehe hegemony over the Ndamba. There are still other words that are shared only by the Hehe and the Ndamba, but not by the Pogolo and others beyond the highlands, and which probably arose during the period of Hehe dominance over the Ndamba. What is especially significant about these limited shared words is that they refer to items that are important in public medicine. They form part of the terminology used in rainmaking and sorcery control.

For rainmaking, any one of three terms is used by the Ndamba to describe their activity. Two of them need not concern us here for one is found throughout much of Bantu-speaking Africa, and the other term is restricted to the Ndamba (Waite 1981). The third term, however, *kumluwa Mlungu*, has probably been adopted from the Hehe. The Hehe high god is called *Mlungu* and his mediums are known as *iluungu*. For the Ndamba, *kumluwa Mlungu* literally means "to make prayers (take gifts) to the person (medium) of *Mlungu*." Related to this borrowing may be another loan word, *ndonya*, which the Hehe and Ndamba use for "rain" (Waite 1981). No significance for this term has been uncovered in Ndamba culture, but in the second half of the nineteenth century immigrant Mbunga elites, who incorporated a section of Ndamba, began to use *ndonya* centrally in their terminology for rainmaking activity, as will be indicated below. Although neither the highlands nor the valley suffer from want of rain, for both are in high precipitation zones, too much rain at the wrong time can ruin the agriculture. Perhaps the Hehe claimed superior knowledge of rainfall patterns, or claimed access to a superior spirit—possibly *Mlungu*. It may have been under these circumstances that *ndonya* entered the Ndamba language. Perhaps two generations of Hehe domination were insufficient for giving *ndonya* institutional significance in Ndamba life.

The same may be said for the word *libiki*, which the Hehe and the Ndamba use for "tree" and "stick" (Waite 1981). Again, no information is available on the cultural application of this loan word in Ndamba society. It appears today to be only associated with "tree" and "stick" and used in no other context. However, in the branch of the Ndamba people that came under Mbunga domination, *libiki* became central to the activity of identifying sorcerers.

The Mbunga-Ndamba

The original Mbunga were some of the dislocated peoples created by the Ngoni wars around Songea in southwestern Tanzania in the mid-1800s

(Waite 1981). More will be said below about the origin of these conflicts. The Mbunga leader, Lipangalala, took his people into the Kilombero Valley, where they subjugated some of the Ndamba. The Ndamba language predominated in this new society and the Mbunga in fact became Ndamba, biologically and culturally. Nevertheless, comparative data collected from the Mbunga and those they subjugated or came to live near indicate that the Mbunga rulers transformed some of the public health traditions of the Ndamba they incorporated, and also that they introduced an institution from outside the valley that was adopted by several peoples in the valley (Waite 1981).

The Hehe word for "rain," *ndonya*, that the Ndamba as a whole apparently adopted in an earlier time, now became expressly associated with rainmaking in Mbunga society. On one hand, the Mbunga call the activity *kuluwa ndonya*, "to make prayers for rain," and have no other term for this activity; the Ndamba proper, on the other hand, have a variety of terms, as noted above. Unlike the Ndamba, the Mbunga are very centralized, and this may explain their singular term in comparison. The Mbunga may have been asserting themselves as inheritors of the earlier Hehe domination by making *ndonya* part of their traditions, and making it more central to their activities than the original Ndamba may have. However, the Mbunga did not keep the Ndamba institution for rainmaking, *kumluwa Mlungu*, possibly because they introduced a new institution, the *mbuyi* mediumship.

The *mbuyi* mediumship originated among the Ndwewe people. The homeland of the Ndwewe lies in the path the original Mbunga travelled en route to the valley. Tradition has it that the Mbunga incorporated some of the Ndwewe because of their skills in rainmaking, for they possessed the *mbuyi* mediumship.

The *mbuyi* lives at the shrine where a Mbunga royal spirit is found; namely, the burial site of a king. The *mbuyi* enjoys royal support and is consulted by all the societies in the valley. Like the Rozvi kings in Zimbabwe in an earlier time, the Mbunga ruling elite introduced a unifying public health tradition to the peoples in the valley. All of the societies in the valley consult the *mbuyi* for rain, but only the Mbunga consult the medium for sun, an activity they call *kuluwa luyuwa*. No people in the valley other than the Mbunga have a term, and probably not even an act, for making sun. Nor can this practice be traced to southwest Tanzania, from whence the original Mbunga hailed. It appears to be a Mbunga innovation. It is a technique for getting the rains to cease when they began too early in the valley. Even as the Hehe in an earlier time may have been introducing a better technique for rain control with *kumluwa Mlungu*, which the Ndamba adopted, so might sunmaking have been the Mbunga rulers' way of offering a better technique to the Ndamba they conquered and incorporated. In both cases the rulers may have enhanced their status over conquered peoples with these techniques.

The *mbuyi* is also consulted when sorcery is suspected. Although the *mwavi* poison ordeal is known in the valley, it is a minor technique for sorcery control. The *mbuyi* uses two other methods. One of these, *kutunga*, is probably of Ndamba-Pogolo origin because it is used by them and the Mbunga and is not known outside the valley. Another technique, called *libiki*, is limited to the Mbunga, for only Mbunga informants report its use. *Libiki* means "stick" and "tree." It is also the term used for the process whereby a family goes to the *mbuyi* with a bundle of sticks that represent suspected sorcerers, when sorcery is alleged. The *mbuyi* then discards the sticks one-by-one until he comes to the alleged sorcerer. The word *libiki*, if not also the technique, was introduced to the valley during the Hehe period, as noted in the case above. However, the Ndamba today use *kutunga*, which does not involve sticks at all. Thus *libiki*, like *ndonya*, was implanted in an earlier time but only took on institutional significance under the Mbunga rulers.

The Mbunga people came into being as a result of the *Mfecane*, the period of conquests and dispersals of peoples in South Africa that resulted from the formation of the Zulu nation under Shaka in the early nineteenth century (Omer-Cooper 1969). When Shaka destroyed the Ndwandwe kingdom around 1818/19, in the process of building his own, remnants of the defeated Ndwandwe fled north. They joined other refugees fleeing Shaka and crossed the Limpopo River with them. They sojourned for over a decade among peoples in western Mozambique and in Zimbabwe. Then, moving north, they reached the Zambesi River in the mid-1830s, where the party split into two. By now the name "Ngoni" had been attached to them. One party of the Ngoni was led by Mputa, who took them northeast into southern Tanzania, where their conquests contributed to the rise of new refugee groups, such as the Mbunga. The other Ngoni followed Zwangendaba, who took them directly north until they reached western Tanzania, where Zwangendaba died in 1848. Succession disputes followed his death and his following split into five sections, with each section moving south. The story of only one section is told here, that of the Ngoni under Mpezeni I, who eventually reached eastern Zambia, where they settled around 1860 near the present town of Chipata near the Malawian border.

Mpezeni's Ngoni

Mpezeni's Ngoni were few in number when they arrived in eastern Zambia. Like the Mbunga who were settling in the Tanzanian Kilombero Valley around the same time, the Ngoni built their society anew by incorporating a significant number of the local people, in this case the Nsenga. The offspring of this union learned the Nsenga language and culture of their mothers. Politics and public health matters, however, were under the control of men, and in particular those of the royalty. Since the royalty was distinguished from the commoners by its adherence to Nguni (Zulu and Swazi) customs, this meant that politics and public health reflected Nguni customs. Although borrowings from the Nguni culture are found in all areas of the Ngoni health care system, they are most pronounced and abundant in the public health sphere, since the royalty that controls this area claims descent from the original followers of Zwangendaba, who were Nguni (Waite 1981). The evidence for the Nguni borrowings is based on ethnographic data.

For rainmaking and other occasions for praying to founding spirits, the Ngoni evoke the name of the Zulu ancestral spirits. Senior men, chosen by the Mpezeni to represent the various parts of the kingdom, sacrifice cattle at the base of *Pseudolachnostylis maprouneifolia* ("msolo") trees. Cattle are traditionally the mainstay of all Nguni societies and women are not supposed to go near cattle, hence they do not participate in these ceremonies. The Ngoni are more centrally organized than the Nsenga and therefore the Mpezeni delegates authority for this and other public matters. The Nsenga proper, however, take cultivated products as gifts for their sacrifices, and men and women participate in their ceremonies. They go to shrines they call *kaimba*, which they build at certain trees, either *P. maprouneifolia* ("msolo"), *Adansonia digitata* (baobab and "mkuyu"), or *Trichilia emetica* ("msekisi"). The Ngoni thus departed greatly from the Nsenga propitiation customs that they inherited.

For control of sorcery the Ngoni came to share with the Nsenga the tradition of using the *mwavi* ordeal. The Ngoni, however, administered the ordeal according to their own political traditions, which were closely patterned on Nguni practices. Thus, a lieutenant of the Mpezeni ordered all adults in a village to assemble and drink the ordeal when sorcery was suspected. The Nsenga practice, in contrast, was to have one suspect at a time drink the ordeal. The Ngoni assembly has also been described for the Swazi and their neighbors, the Thonga, of southern Mozambique. In these societies the villagers were assembled and a diviner passed in a trance in front of them, identifying sorcerers through inspiration (Junod 1962; Kuper 1963). The only difference between this southern African practice and that of the Ngoni is that the latter used the Nsenga ordeal. The Ngoni mass gatherings for identifying sorcerers may be the forerunners of the witchcraft-eradication movements that emerged in the twentieth century in east-central Africa, and will be discussed in a later section. If these movements are a later manifestation, then the Ngoni can be said to have made an enduring contribution to traditional public health in east-central Africa.

The Ndebele and Mwari

The final people considered here, the Ndebele, also arose during the *Mfecane* (Omer-Cooper 1969). They were originally known as the "Khumalo" and their leader was Mzilikazi, a general of Shaka who fled with his kinsmen from the Zulu kingdom around 1821. The Khumalo went into the area that is now called the "Transvaal," where they received their present name, Ndebele.

They stayed there until they were driven out by Boer commandos and Zulu *impis* (warriors) in 1837. In that year they crossed the Limpopo River into southwestern Zimbabwe, where they settled as conquerors over the Rozvi empire that had come into being two centuries earlier (Omer-Cooper 1969). Although the Ndebele incorporated a large number of the Kalanga, their offspring speak the Ndebele language, not the Shona language of the Kalanga. Yet, despite the apparent prestige of Ndebele culture and traditions among the Kalanga, the latter did not adopt the Ndebele public health institutions. The evidence is again ethnographic, but now also includes eyewitness accounts.

The original Ndebele public health institutions were controlled by the royalty and centered around their kings and their (Nguni) spirits (Cobbing 1977, 61). To the Kalanga, however, these institutions were inadequate. They preferred their own *Mwari* rainmaking institution. There is a highly organized network of priests centered around *Mwari* (Schoffeleers 1978b, 267). The techniques that the *Mwari* mediums use for rainmaking are perhaps better suited to the climate of the plateau than were the Ndebele rainmaking techniques (Bhebe 1979). Or perhaps the Ndebele rulers had to concede the dominance of *Mwari* in the area. In the preceding Rozvi period that was discussed above, the Changamires had probably found it expedient to make the *Mwari* spirit a part of their traditions. The evidence for the Ndebele kings who followed them certainly indicates that they found it to their interest to consult *Mwari* priests (Bebe 1979). A Jesuit missionary visiting the area in 1882 wrote the following about Lobengula, Mzilikazi's successor (Bhebe 1978, 287):

> Lo Bengula . . . wants the influence of [*Mwari*] with the natives. As long as he gratifies them he can easily rule the Matabele [*Ndebele*] and tributary tribes. Without their support his prestige and authority might indeed be considerably diminished in the opinion of many people; their opposition might destroy his power.

Lobengula was also observed working closely with *Mwari* priests, and he even had the reputation (among Africans and Europeans) of being a rainmaker himself (Bhebe 1978, 287).

Thus, for at least 500 years, from when the Torwa state arose around the fourteenth century, to the coming of the Ndebele, the *Mwari* tradition was deferred to by all political authorities who ruled the area around the Matopo Hills. This deference was discontinued when the British established colonial rule there in the late nineteenth to early twentieth century.

THE COLONIAL PERIOD AND ITS AFTERMATH

The period of European colonialism was foreshadowed by the Portuguese, who settled in east-central Africa in the sixteenth century. The Portuguese built trading posts along the Zambesi River and small estates called *prazos* in northern Mozambique (Isaacman 1972; Newitt 1973). Although the Portuguese impacted on African society through their encouragement of the external slave trade and by their introduction of firearms, there is no evidence that they had any influence on traditional institutions of health care. The period of colonialism, in contrast, left a permanent impression on public health in the region.

Colonial rule was established through a series of conquests that began in the late nineteenth century and continued into the twentieth century. These conquests were carried out in east-central Africa by the British, Belgians, Germans, and Portuguese, each of whom lay claim to sections of the region. As various chiefs and kings were conquered, they lost control over their lands, considerable parts of which, in some areas of the region, were taken over by European settlers. Chiefs and kings also lost control over the productive forces, for most African men in the region were forced out of the villages through various coercive measures, to go to the mines and industrial centers in order to earn cash, first for colonial taxes and then eventually just to feed their families in the villages, since less and less food production was occurring there.

Colonial rule brought new institutions and cultural formations to eastern-central Africa: new technology and its organizations; new social relations and ideologies. Colonial administrators, police, missionaries, traders, industrialists, and other modernizing agents represented and upheld the new order. New health personnel were introduced and others were trained locally in the new biotechnology.

The public health programs that were introduced during the colonial period reflected the socioeconomic and political changes. In the first place, just the force of European conquest and subsequent demands for monetary taxes and cash crops led to population dislocation and disequilibrium in the disease environment between people and animals. Therefore, some of the earliest public health measures that were introduced by the colonialists were attempts to control the epidemics that were created by the wars of conquest. But a comprehensive system of public health care in east-central Africa, by all accounts, developed with the colonialists' rising concern for increased African worker productivity (Baker 1976, 296; Beck 1977; Clyde 1962; Gelfand 1976; Sabben-Clare 1980; Webster 1972, 244; 1973, 7, 27, 48). Beginning in the 1920s, the principal public health programs that were instituted were physical examination of workers (mainly to eliminate the impaired), control of vector-borne diseases (such as sleeping sickness and malaria), maternal and infant care, urban sanitation, and health education. These programs were not altogether successful, nor even widespread. They received only minor portions of colonial budgets, with the funds decreasing over time. They did not include disability allowances, for only the productive periods of the colonized workers were of interest to the colonizers.

As new medical institutions were introduced, existing ones were suppressed. African medicines were denounced as quackery and superstition. In Zimbabwe (Southern Rhodesia), where priests may have posed more of a threat to impending colonial rule than elsewhere in the region, many of them were jailed on suspicion of helping the movement of resistance to colonial rule. As a result, a number of *Mwari* and other shrines ceased to operate because there were no longer priests to staff them (Bourdillon 1972, 112; 1974). The British also sought to suppress sorcery control. In Southern Rhodesia the government passed the Witchcraft Suppression Act of 1899, which made it a crime just to accuse anyone of practicing sorcery (Daneel 1971). In other British colonies similar acts were later passed and "witch-finding" of any kind was banned (St. J. Orde-Browne 1935, 481). Public control of sorcery thus came to an end, but not the public's belief in the existence of sorcery.

Nevertheless, in adapting to the new order, the Africans brought into it some of the old. Syncretic forms of medicoreligious activity arose, influenced by the newly introduced Christian religious practices. One form of syncretism can be seen in the witchcraft-eradication movements that emerged in the region in the 1930s and beyond. Not only do these movements represent the changing times, they also appear to be a continuation of the earlier tradition of not only uncovering sorcerers, but of uncovering them in mass assemblies.

The first of these movements occurred in Malawi among the Chewa and Ngoni peoples. Subsequent movements occurred as far away as southeastern Zaire in the west and southern Tanzania in the east (Larson 1976, 88; Marwick 1950, 100; Richards 1935, 448). Each movement was led by a charismatic leader who claimed to have power to uncover sorcerers, and who used mechanical devices of various kinds to do this. The witch-finding, as it was called, took place in mass assemblies, where the witch-finder called on people to confess their acts of sorcery and throw away not only their sorcery medicines but also any medicines that were mixed with mineral and animal products, for these ingredients were believed to be "magical." Such medicines, to the witch-finders, were unscientific and therefore unacceptable (Larson 1976, 88; Marwick 1950, 100; Richards 1935, 448). These witch-finders were "modernizers." They accepted the Christian and Western models of medicine. However, they imposed these beliefs into the traditional structure. Their use of mass assemblies to identify sorcerers is reminiscent more of the old Ngoni antisorcery campaigns than of the modern-day camp meeting revivals. Moreover, the "medicine" that these witch eradicators used, which was called *mchape*, became a replacement for the traditional witch-finding substances, principally the poison ordeal, that the colonial rulers had banned. But like earlier witch-finding activity, the eradication movements were outlawed during the colonial period and remain so under independent African governments. Since public control of witchcraft is now forbidden, witchcraft identification has become a private matter between the patient's family and the traditional doctor it consults, although judges do occasionally adjudicate cases in which sorcery is alleged.

The relatively complete replacement of the African traditional public health system by the Western, European system was due to the integration of the African peoples into what had truly become, by 1920, a world-system. Africa had come to resemble the West, insofar as its kin-based and tributary modes of production were replaced by industrial capitalist production which created new health concerns and new health services. When colonial rule ended in east-central Africa after the middle 1960s, European introductions remained. This development was not unlike what happened in earlier times. As indicated above, Hehe traditions continued among the Ndamba, and Kalanga traditions (through the Rozvi Changamires) continued among the Manyika and Ndau long after Hehe and Rozvi political authority had declined among them. So, too, the African rulers in the postcolonial period continue to give legitimacy to Western goods and services. They import technology from the West in the form of hospitals and pharmaceutical products, primarily for use by the elites and urban-dwellers (Elling 1981, 89; Glucksberg and Singer 1982, 381; Yudkin 1980, 455), and they use scarce foreign exchange to go to Western capitals for advanced medical care (Frankenberg and Leeson 1974, 255).

However, unlike the European colonialists, the postcolonial African rulers are interested in expanding health services to the rural areas and have a more accommodating attitude toward African medicine. As a result of this interest in African medicines and practitioners, some countries in east-central Africa are using traditional health personnel in public health services (Bibeau et al. 1980; Borrell 1981; Msonthi 1983, 40), and some are also researching the use of indigenous medicine in national (i.e., public) health services (Baker 1983, 59; Chhabra 1984, 157; Hedberg et al. 1982, 1983; Janzen 1976/77, 167; Msonthi 1983, 120; Tomé 1979, 13).

Traditional doctors are somewhat reluctant to share their herbal knowledge with the modernists. In Zimbabwe, for example, some traditional healers have formed an organization called The Spirit Mediums' and True *Ngangas'* Association of Central Africa in opposition to the government-sponsored organization of African healers, ZINATHA. The True *Ngangas* say that ZINATHA lacks the religious and political substance of traditional medicine (Carver 1983, 57). Their opposition suggests that national governments are only incorporating traditional medicines and personnel in a truncated form. Nevertheless, even the little that the new elites are doing is probably important. Through this co-optation they can justify their rule, expand health care under their control, make it less expensive and culturally more acceptable. In this respect, the modern rulers are behaving like their counterparts in the precolonial period. Those earlier rulers also expanded and innovated health services, as the numerous cases cited here indicated.

CONCLUSIONS

The definition of public health that was used in this study did not require the east-central Africans to conform to models based on the European or Western experience. It was general enough to encompass rainmaking and sorcery control, two principal areas of public health service in the African tradition. Rainmaking was a service provided through propitiation of tutelary and supreme spirits; sorcery control was undertaken through identifying sorcerers. These activities were done in public, for the common good, and under the direction of ruling authorities, who were either priests, chiefs, or kings.

Unlike earlier studies of the history of public health in east-central Africa, this one was almost exclusively concerned with the precolonial period. In order to cover that period the study had to utilize evidence derived from unwritten sources, which are practically all that are available for that period. The principal sources used here were oral traditions, linguistic and ethnographic data. Since the most rewarding evidence comes from data on cultural contact between peoples, the cases that were discussed involved interactions between groups with immigrant and autochthonous status.

A further study of public health in precolonial societies might consider the extent to which there were improvements in people's health status under new rulers. Services alone are not a sufficient basis for improved health. Even in the modern period it is believed that good health has resulted more from better nutrition and higher standards of living than from the increase in or improvement of health services (Illich 1977). To what extent, we might ask, did agricultural innovation or improvement form part of the success of new rulers who introduced new institutions involved in rainmaking? Also, there is evidence that shows the role of social change in sorcery accusations. We know, too, that during the colonial period witchcraft eradication movements were merely a new method of controlling sorcery (Lee 1976, 101). We might ask, therefore, to what extent social change in the precolonial period also threatened the well-being of communities and paved the way for the creation or diffusion of new methods of sorcery control? Some data are already available toward answering these questions, but more could still be collected.

NOTE

1. An earlier version of this chapter appeared in *Social Science and Medicine*, 24 (1987) (3):197–208. It is republished here as revised by the author, with the permission of Pergamon Journals Ltd.

Colonial Medicine

NINE

Medical Knowledge and Urban Planning in Colonial Tropical Africa[1]

Philip D. Curtin

Europeans conquered most of tropical Africa between 1880 and World War I. This was also a period of rapid advance in tropical medicine. Malaria was by far the most serious threat to Europeans living in the African tropics, and the mosquito theory made its appearance just when colonial administrations were struggling to keep soldiers and administrators alive in a difficult environment. New currents in European thought regarding urban planning flourished in these same years—the key period for city planning in Africa, when colonial capitals were either founded or redesigned. The play of these cross-currents of thought during a period of crucial decision-making offers an interesting example of ideas in action, one with implications for our understanding of human behavior both in Africa and beyond.

THE HUMORAL PARADIGM OF EARLY COLONIAL MEDICINE

Europeans had been applying their medical ideas to the African scene since at least the early nineteenth century. Through midcentury they were especially concerned with medical topography—studies of particular locations, soils, temperature, and rainfall to determine what makes a place healthy or unhealthy. Some of the things they concluded were true; others were not. They had known for centuries that high altitudes meant cooler weather, and they associated heat with putrefaction and hence with disease. In India, officials had retreated to the "hill stations" in the warm season since the beginning of the century. But they also sought protection at much lower elevations, in the belief that malaria in particular was caused by emanations from the soil, which crept "assassin-like close to the earth" (Rankin 1836, 147–148). One solution was simply to put houses on stilts, elevating them ten to fifteen feet above the ground. That was a common prescription for tropical housing in India and the West Indies as well as in Africa. So was the idea of putting military camps in high places whenever possible.

In 1863, following the Sepoy Mutiny of 1857 and the sanitation scandals of the Crimean War, a royal commission gathered evidence and issued detailed recommendations for sanitation reforms in India. These and other reforms reduced the death rate from disease of British soldiers serving in India from about 50 per 1,000 mean strength in the 1850s to less than 16 per 1,000 by the early 1880s—before either the mosquito vector for malaria or the germ theory of disease had come into play. One aspect of these reforms was full development of the cantonment system in the 1870s and 1880s, permanent military camps located away from the noxious odors of "native" habitation, preferably to windward. Segregated residential areas for civilians followed the same patterns, with priority given to ventilation and separation from the Indian towns (King 1976). In the decades after the mutiny, this residential segregation also satisfied an intensified racism among the English in India.

The hill stations of India and malaria-free barracks, such as Newcastle in Jamaica, were 2,000 to 4,000 feet above sea level. Authorities in British West Africa also considered, somewhat uncertainly, the wisdom of moving to higher ground. In the 1840s many thought that 400 feet of altitude sufficed for safety. Others recommended 3,000 to 5,000 feet, which was more realistic if the purpose was to get above the range of *Anopheles* mosquitoes. One of the earliest radical suggestions came from MacGregor Laird, the pioneer builder of iron steamboats. He thought safety could be found only above 5,000 feet and recommended settlements above that altitude on Mount Cameroon, which rises more than 13,000 feet, and on the off-shore island of Fernando Po, where the peak comes to 10,000 feet (Laird 1842, 350–351). The British did nothing at that time, but before the end of the century, the Germans built their colonial capital for Cameroon at Buea, high on the side of Mount Cameroon.

Elsewhere administrators more often thought of shorter moves. In 1872 the governor of Sierra Leone wanted to relocate the colonial government in the Sierra Leone mountains, where a 1,000-foot altitude was available. In 1884 the governor of the Gold Coast was allowed to move his personal residence from Accra on the coast to Aburi on the Akwapim Ridge, about twenty-five miles away and 1,000 feet higher. In 1897, however, when the governor of Lagos also wanted to move to higher ground, he advocated a site north of the Lagos lagoon, about four miles away but only fifty feet higher (Spitzer 1968, 49–61).

Avoidance of disease was not the only motive for moving administrators to higher places. It also satisfied the need to segregate the governors from the governed, following the Indian precedent. Furthermore, Europeans with power and wealth naturally looked for building sites with a breeze and a view—segregated or not. ("The big house on the hill" was not merely an American phenomenon.) Long before the end of the century, the well-to-do in Bathurst (now Banjul) came to live along the riverfront. At Dar es Salaam in German East Africa, the earliest "European" quarter, only informally segregated, lay on land a little higher than its surroundings, with a possible view over both harbor and ocean. Nor was it necessarily a matter of sanitary planning that the European sections of Brazzaville, Dakar, Pointe Noire, and Abidjan were all called *le plateau*, while the equivalent sections of Accra and Lusaka were "the ridge" and countless *bomas* or district headquarters in East Africa occupied the highest point around.

Just as the nineteenth-century British drew on Indian precedents, the French drew on their experience in North Africa, where urban segregation of foreigners had ancient roots. Separate Greek trading settlements in the Levant go back at least to 800 B.C. About 700 B.C. the Egyptian government allowed a separate Phoenician and a separate Greek town, Naucratis, in the lower Nile delta. The practice reappeared in a slightly different form during the Middle Ages, when Muslim powers on the south shore of the Mediterranean permitted Christian and other foreign merchants to maintain shore establishments, called *funduq*, under strict government control (Curtin 1984, 38, 78–80).

In Algiers the French had a segregated settlement even before the conquest of 1830, and much the same was true in all important cities of North Africa. After the occupation, settlers streamed in, and the French, following ancient custom, built a European-style city alongside the existing Muslim town to accommodate them. In most cases, they simply called the French city *la ville nouvelle*. The old city was sometimes called the *medina*. In the twentieth century the pattern became triparite as Muslim migrants from the rural areas built shanty towns for themselves on the outskirts—the *bidonvilles* from the French word for oil drum, a favorite construction material (Berque 1958, 5–42).

Urban segregation received new impetus from medical changes toward the end of the century. From the 1790s onward, medical investigators struggled with a group of associated problems concerning the transmission of disease—indeed, with the nature of disease itself. To begin with, two assumptions were universally recognized as empirically proven: some diseases, like smallpox and plague, had the power to spread from one person to another; others, like malaria, appeared to be endemic in certain parts of the world but were not clearly transmittable by personal contact. The first of these modes of transmission was often discussed as "contagion." In the terminology of the time, the second was sometimes called "infection," sometimes "miasma." Nineteenth-century usage of these terms can be confusing. The words are familiar, but the meanings were often different. "Contagion" was not thought of as an organism that moves from one person to another nor was it necessarily a specific cause of a particular disease. Rather, it was an emanation from the body of a person who had the disease, or from that of a person who had died of it, or from the bodies of people who were not even ill, if they were crowded together without sufficient ventilation.

Health and disease were thought of as part of a set of dynamic interactions between the body and its environment. When nineteenth-century Europeans wrote about the dangers of a tropical climate, they meant literally that temperature, humidity, and emanations from the soil were the sources of danger. They also believed that every part of the body was related to every other part, so that the disposition of the mind could, for example, affect the stomach. Health and disease were general states of the whole organism. Many people in the medical profession believed that one set of symptoms could be transformed into another without a specific cause. The body was seen as governed by inputs and outputs—water, air, and food balanced against perspiration, respiration, and excretion. The classical humoral theory suggests that these have to be kept in balance, and underneath was a persistent belief that disease was associated with immorality in a way that was more sensed than explicit. Ventilation and the quality of the air were important, not because air might contain dangerous organisms but because generalized contagion might build up to dangerous levels without a constant change of air (Rosenberg 1979, 116–136). By the 1870s, however, some of these ideas began to change. Louis Pasteur and Robert Koch had discovered bacteria that caused specific diseases by invading an organism and living on it as a parasite. This germ theory opened up a whole new world of possibilities for the cure and prevention of disease, but it was not assimilated immediately by the public mind or even by the medical profession.

GERM THEORY AND TROPICAL MEDICINE

The application of the germ theory to tropical medicine began in 1881, when Carlos Finlay in Cuba presented his first paper arguing that yellow fever parasites were carried from person to person by mosquitoes. In the same year, Alfonse Lavernan in Algeria discovered malaria parasites in the blood of their victims. During the next decades, new work appeared in France, Italy, England, and the United States leading to a general breakthrough in 1897/98. It was then established that the *Plasmodia*, the malaria parasites, were carried by various *Anopheles* mosquitoes and that they passed through one stage of development within the mosquito and another within the human host. Up to that time, it had been assumed that black people had an innate protection. But Koch found that non-Europeans also contracted malaria, although once past the age of five they rarely showed the normal clinical symptoms. Those who survived developed an apparent immunity as long as they were otherwise healthy and as long as they were reinfected at intervals by the bite of infected mosquitoes (Scott 1939, 151–159, 355).

By 1900 these ideas were fully formulated and ready for practical application in Africa. Indeed, in 1899 Ronald Ross, who is usually credited with the discovery of the mosquito as a vector for malaria, visited Sierra Leone with a group from the Liverpool School of Tropical Medicine to confirm that *Anopheles* mosquitoes were indeed the principal carriers of malaria in Africa. His experience there and in India convinced him that the most effective way to attack malaria was to attack the vector that carried it. Robert Koch took another direction, based on his previous experience in Africa and Southeast Asia. He had first visited Africa in 1897/98 to study malaria and blackwater fever; among other things he experimented on the responses of Africans to various dosages of quinine. He was most interested not in the mosquitoes but in what went on in the blood of the victims (Clyde 1962, 19–20).

In 1899–1900 he continued the malaria investigation in the Dutch East Indies and New Guinea. This brought him to the world center of quinine production. The cinchona tree, whose bark is the natural source of quinine, is native to the Andes, but its various species differ greatly in their yields of effective antimalarial alkaloids. The uneven effectiveness of the bark had contributed to medical uncertainty about its use before 1830, when French chemists first succeeded in isolating quinine and other alkaloids. Thereafter, quinine gradually became available throughout the tropical world then under European control. Naturalists found that the bark of one species, *Cinchona ledgeriana*, could yield up to 13 percent quinine. By the 1870s *C. ledgeriana* was firmly established as a plantation crop on Java, and in the next two decades factories were built, principally in Germany, to extract the drug on a mass scale. At that point, the Dutch East Indian government began to introduce mass quininization in the principal cities, especially in Batavia. By 1899 the free distribution of quinine in Batavia alone totaled more than 2,500 kilograms per year (Bochalli 1954, 125–130). Koch also conducted an experiment on a group of nonimmune estate workers moving into a malarial region. None of those who were given prophylactic quinine came down with malaria, while virtually all of those in the control group became ill. Although some medical people still doubted the value of prophylactic quinine, Koch's experiments convinced many others that newcomers to a malarial region had to protect themselves. Koch advocated that colonial governments in the tropics set out to destroy the source of infection through mass quininization of the entire population.[2]

Between 1900 and 1903 a third approach to malaria control came from Britain's Royal Society, whose malaria committee sent two doctors, S. R. Christophers and J. W. W. Stephens, of the Liverpool School of Tropical Medicine to conduct research in West Africa. They noted the views of Koch and Ross, but they thought that both mass chemotherapy and mosquito control were a mistake (Christophers and Stephens 1900, 3:19):

> So closely associated indeed are malaria and the native in Africa, and so wonderfully constant is the presence of anopheles where natives are collected in numbers, that we doubt whether any operations, now possible, directed against anopheles will do much to diminish the danger of malarial infection. In fact, in Africa the primary aim should be to remove susceptible Europeans from the midst of malaria. To stamp out native malaria is at present chimerical, and every effort should rather be turned to the protection of the Europeans.

They also noted that, because of the Africans' apparent immunity, blood samples from adults rarely revealed actual plasmodia in the bloodstream, but children with clinical symptoms had parasites in their blood. Children were therefore thought to be the prime source of infection, and Christophers and Stephens believed it was imperative to protect Europeans from the vicinity of African children between birth and the age of five. Keeping Europeans at mosquito's range away from African children, they argued, would "render Malaria a comparatively rare disease"—a phrase remarkable for its ethnocentric arrogance, if nothing else (Christophers and Stephens 1900, 3:24). The question then became one of deciding how far the principal species of African *Anopheles* could actually fly. Stephens and Christophers were not bothered by this issue. They took the view that African mosquitoes were race-specific in their taste for human blood, preferring the African to the European variety. The insects could be expected to hover around the Africans' huts, regardless of the distance they might be able to fly (although *Anopheles* can be carried much further by the wind, malariologists now regard two kilometers as sufficient to provide a measure of protection) (Bruce-Chwatt 1980, 122; Christophers and Stephens 1900, 1:56, 4:3–5).

The theories of early malariologists soon became confused with one another and with older medical views that persisted. Ross, for example, was much impressed by the segregationist argument; his previous experience in India convinced him that the cantonment policy worked. In spite of his personal role in discovering the mosquito vector, he at first opposed screening of houses. He much preferred mosquito nets and especially electric fans and punkahs (Hindi, "fans"; the Indian ceiling fan consisting of a cloth-covered wooden framework pulled back and forth by a servant). He thought that a moving current of air would serve not only to drive off mosquitoes but also to keep the body cool and "retain the natural energy." He thought that punkahs and segregation were together responsible for the lower death rates of Europeans in India than in Africa. And, as late as 1902, he still opposed the regular prophylactic use of quinine (Ross 1902, 36–47). Beginning in May 1900, the Colonial Office in London distributed a pamphlet of instructions, prepared by the staff of the Liverpool School of Tropical Medicine, to officers in the colonial service. Ross's influence was evident in the main recommendations: elimination of *Anopheles* mosquitoes, personal protection against mosquito bites (not screening of houses), and residential segregation of the European population (Dumett 1968, 153–197).

The fact that these rules followed so fast after the medical discoveries was significant, but so was the wide variation in the manner of their application. The whims of individual administrators, their residual beliefs about contagion, or their racial and cultural chauvinism were often decisive. Some of these differences can be illustrated from the experience of the five colonies of British West Africa along Gambia, Sierra Leone, the Gold Coast, and Northern and Southern Nigeria.

The government of Sierra Leone responded quickly and with a most elaborate project, based largely on the ideas Ross spelled out after his visit there. Priority was given to the destruction of mosquito breeding grounds, but that turned out to be harder than anyone recognized at the time. *Anopheles gambiae* and *Anopheles funestus*, the most dangerous of West African vectors, were extremely hard to control. They were not confined to swamps or low places or even to the pronounced rainy season. They could breed in any small puddle or even a footprint where a little water might collect. The Caribbean *Anopheles* was somewhat easier to control, and the *Aedes aegypti*, the carrier of yellow fever, was easier still since it bred around villages and houses and had an extremely short range in flight. The success of American public health officers in combating yellow fever in Cuba and Panama helped raise false hopes for mosquito control in Africa. The second priority in the recommendation was residential housing with maximum ventilation, and third was the separation of European from African housing (Gale 1980, 495–508; Ross 1910: 285–286).

The plan that actually emerged in Freetown was based on still another set of priorities. Following Indian precedent, it proposed the building of a new segregated suburb, which was even named "Hill Station," recalling the Indian term. The site chosen was about 750 feet above sea level and four miles from central Freetown. In 1902 the government began constructing specially designed houses, and a fair number were actually available for occupation by 1904, including one for the governor himself. All faced north and were raised on columns to keep them well above the ground—still following the miasma theory. The ground beneath was covered with cement, supposedly to prevent mosquitoes from breeding, but that practice was already a common recommendation to prevent malarial poisons that might rise from the soil. Around Hill Station was a strip of land a quarter-mile wide cleared of all trees, tall shrubbery, and houses. The first zone was reinforced by a less stringent sanitary corridor a full mile wide, in which no African house-building or occupation of land was to be permitted, although tall vegetation was allowed (Spitzer 1968, 55).

The most curious feature was the extent to which Africans were excluded. Servants were allowed to work at Hill Station but not to spend the night there. Apparently the assumption was that mosquitoes would bite only at night—which is not completely true in Africa any more than it is in North America. All African children were rigorously excluded, although Koch's research had established by 1900 that adult Africans were not genuinely immune to malaria, that they were permanently infested with the parasites, and that they occasionally showed clinical symptoms. At such times, they, too, could infect mosquitoes, so that perhaps one-quarter of adult Africans were as dangerous as their children. The chief medical officer for Lagos, Nigeria, pointed this out to the Liverpool Chamber of Commerce in December 1900. The chamber published his lecture, but the information either failed to reach Sierra Leone or was simply ignored (Strahan 1901).

Meanwhile, construction at Hill Station continued at considerable expense to the government, including the cost of a mountain railway that opened for both passenger and freight traffic in 1904. Opposition was inevitable. Freetown had a black mayor, a municipal government, and a class of Western-educated journalists, physicians, and lawyers. They objected, first of all, because the land taken over for Hill Station was confiscated from its African owners. They believed that funds spent to improve living conditions for Europeans might be better spent to improve the urban facilities for all classes, and they soon realized that racial segregation on sanitary grounds would lead to racial segregation on other grounds as well. Later suburbs were, indeed, built and segregated by race without a medical justification. And it turned out that Europeans who lived at Hill Station came down with malaria at about the same rate as those who did not (Smith and Pearse 1904, 278–282; Spitzer 1968, 57–60).

The recommendations for sanitary segregation were carried out somewhat differently in the Gambia. Bathurst, like most older West African towns, had never had even de facto segregation. Fewer than 100 Europeans resided in the whole colony and protectorate, and many Africans were as well-to-do as the expatriates. Some twenty-two European residences were scattered throughout the more prosperous part of the town, so that segregation would have required wholesale rebuilding and redesign of the urban area. Medical authorities thought that was impractical on grounds of expense. In 1911, however, a project surfaced that would have given the Gambia its own equivalent of Hill Station—on the closest approximation to a hill in the vicinity, the thirty-foot cliffs at Cape Saint Mary, where the Gambia River enters the Atlantic seven and one-half miles below the town. That plan died for lack of funds, although a limited segregation of certain desirable streets was achieved during World War I, and some of Koch's ideas ultimately penetrated in the form of free quinine for school children.

The expropriation of land owned by well-to-do Africans in the Gambia raised a problem that has recurred almost everywhere urban redevelopment has been tried—right down to the present, in Africa and out. Either to build a new town or to force people to move within the old one creates windfall profits or unexpected losses. That prospect easily generates both friends and enemies for medical authorities.

Accra on the Gold Coast was another old city, with residential patterns not unlike those of Bathurst, and it had a class of affluent Africans far from eager to spend their money for the sake of European health. The Western-educated African community was already an effective political force, having compelled the government in 1898 to withdraw a proposed lands bill. The government demolished some dilapidated buildings for sanitary reasons, and it tried to eradicate mosquitoes within urban areas. It also set up segregated areas for government officials in Accra and several other towns, but segregation was neither complete nor compulsory in the first decade of the new century (Dumettt 1968, 170–171).

Then Sir Hugh Clifford became governor during World War I. He supported sanitary segregation in principle only, arguing that it was all very well if the government could afford it and if it did no harm to race relations. He knew perfectly well that it was expensive and did harm race relations. He also ensured that his attitude would prevail in the long run by enlarging the unofficial membership in the Gold Coast Legislative Council, which meant that traditional chiefs and educated Africans could make their opposition effective. They immediately took the position that the best medical strategy was to improve health conditions for the African population, thus protecting Europeans as well. After 1913 the issue of segregation—for other than government officials—was effectively dead in the Gold Coast.

Pressure from the Colonial Office continued, however, in spite of improving mortality figures for the European community—largely the result of prophylactic quinine and mosquito control. A conference of principal medical officers for all the British West African colonies met in 1909 and again in 1912. It supported segregation and, in 1912, drew up a plan to complete the segregation of the European population in all African towns within ten years, but the plan was easier to apply in designing new towns than in rebuilding old ones.

In 1907, for example, officials selected a site for a new capital of the Northern Territories of the Gold Coast, the future Tamale. The plan called for a segregated European section upwind from the African town, following Indian precedent, and separated from it by an open space. Founding a new town on a vacant site had the advantage of beginning with a clean slate, but there was a complication. What should be done to protect African clerks who worked with Europeans in the same offices? The chief medical officer for the

Northern Territories recommended not only that Europeans be segregated from the local population but also that their clerks be segregated from both (Kimble 1963).

In the separate colonies of Northern and Southern Nigeria (amalgamated to form a single colony in 1914), the situation was again different. In Lagos, Governor William MacGregor was himself a medical man who had followed the recent publications on malaria. He had serious doubts about the new directives from London, especially the idea of demolishing parts of the city to create sanitary cordons—partly because any such move would be unfair to the African population and partly because it had little promise of being effective. If Africans were truly the reservoir of parasites, the thing to do was to attack the disease at its source—among the Africans themselves. In 1900 William Strahan, his chief medical officer, had already pointed out that adult Africans, not children alone, were infested with the parasites, that they could transmit the plasmodia to a mosquito much of the time in spite of their apparent immunity. He, too, thought that the only wise course was to eradicate malaria among the Africans, although sanitary segregation might help in the meantime.

MacGregor himself went further. Although he paid lip-service to Ross's ideas, he made his government's priority quinine prophylaxis, which became compulsory for government officials and was urged on the African population through a publicity campaign and the offer of free distribution of quinine to the whole population of Lagos and its suburbs. The second phase of MacGregor's program was to screen European houses and workplaces, even at the cost of reduced ventilation. Third, he mounted an antimosquito campaign (Dumett 1968, 181).

The Lagos government did nothing to implement sanitary segregation until 1907, when it condemned seven acres of urban land fronting the Lagos race course for conversion into an exclusive European settlement. Houses in that part of Lagos belonged to the most substantial class of African merchants and professional people. They were quick to react as others like them had done in Accra, and the issue was drawn in much the same way. The Africans had allies as well as opponents within the administration. As in the Gold Coast, the "unofficial" members of the Legislative Council were African. They were also organized in the Aborigines Protection Society, which could muster enough political clout to make segregation an embarrassing issue. The European section near the race course came into existence, but the government was unable to get all Africans to leave. The idea of creating a new suburb for Europeans on higher land up the railway toward the interior lingered on, but the immediate solution was to set up newly built segregated suburbs to the east of downtown Lagos, although the actual construction was postponed to the period between the two world wars.[3]

Like the Northern Territories of the Gold Coast, Northern Nigeria also provided a clean slate. Only in 1900 did the government set up an administrative structure. Sir Frederick Lugard, as governor, immediately began to move administrative quarters at Lokoja on the Niger to a new site one mile away from the existing town, and he acted in conscious imitation of the Indian cantonment system, not on Ross's directives alone. He extended segregation to all new district headquarters. Even the "rest houses" built in many villages for the use of administrators on tour were to be built at least 400 yards from the nearest "native" dwelling, and Africans were forbidden to use them under any circumstance. Following outmoded nineteenth-century ideas about contagion Lugard himself criticized the Colonial Office for its failure to say enough about the "predisposing causes" of malaria. He regarded these as, first of all, inadequate housing, and especially the emanations arising from the damp ground. An inadequate diet and lack of exercise were also important causes. Lugard took care to build appropriate tropical housing for the senior European staff. He had tennis courts built and used government funds to subsidize polo clubs—still another reminder of his early experience in India.

Correct house design was a continuous government concern in the early years of the mosquito theory. In 1906 the Colonial Office sent a circular dispatch to West African governors, who were asked for their opinions on the most desirable features of staff housing for the tropics. The governors of Sierra Leone, Southern Nigeria, and Northern Nigeria answered in greatest detail. All three stressed the importance of an airspace under the house. All three wanted a wide veranda on all sides of the house to avoid the dangerous direct rays of the sun. All three disapproved of screened doors and windows—ventilation was more important than keeping out mosquitoes. Once again, the mosquito theory and, indeed, the germ theory of disease had failed to penetrate the ingrained beliefs of administrators in the dangers of miasma. To the extent that the mosquito theory was recognized at all, it was as a justification for segregation, which was desired on racist grounds anyhow. An ingenious doctor in Bathurst left government bungalows unscreened for the sake of ventilation but screened the servants' rooms to protect the mosquitoes and hence the masters from infective bites.

The findings of scientists who visited Nigeria in the early years of the new century appear in retrospect somewhat less "scientific" than those of Governor MacGregor in Lagos. A team from the Liverpool School of Tropical Medicine took as its point of departure the "fact" that "native children," and only native children, were the source of malarial infection. Destruction of mosquitoes and other measures were all very well, but "segregation of Europeans at a distance from all the natives offers itself now as the only measure by which absolute freedom from the disease can be guaranteed." The Liverpool expedition also held that "native servants" were no real danger since, as adults, they were not carriers; the only danger was that they might have

African women and children visit them. There was also the "fact," already expounded by Christophers and Stevens, that mosquitoes preferred African to European blood. Having African servants might well attract mosquitoes to come "swarming after them from the native quarter." Once segregation had been accomplished, these authorities saw no real harm in subsidiary measures like prophylactic quinine or even "mosquito-proof houses in certain circumstances" (Annett et al. 1902, 54–56).

Later medical personnel went further still. In 1912 Dr. M. Cameron Blair, senior sanitary officer for Northern Nigeria, wanted to extend sanitary segregation to commercial districts. There, only Europeans would be allowed to own stores. All commercial premises were to be nonresidential. As usual, Africans other than servants were not to pass the night within 400 yards of a white man's house, although African servants were nevertheless allowed to live in their masters' quarters. Measured against the mosquito theory, this made no sense at all. Its apparent medical basis was much more clearly the theory of generalized contagion emanating from the "native town"—drawn from nineteenth-century medicine and Indian colonial practice. The obvious commercial advantage to white over black merchants also suggests the strong possibility of latent racism in Blair's arguments.

In opposition, Governor Hesketh Bell took the same position Clifford had taken in the Gold Coast. It was all very well to protect the health of Europeans, but the social cost was much too high. He pointed out that a number of Lagos Africans were professional and businessmen of wealth, who lived on the same scale as the Europeans themselves. Such people were clearly no sanitary threat; to disturb them would complicate race relations and disrupt commercial life in a country with an African as well as a European business class. With this defense Bell, too, slipped away from the new medical teachings; if Africans were indeed the main reservoir of plasmodia, rich carriers were as dangerous as poor ones. But Bell's inconsistency shows that his response was more political than medical. Similarly, the proposal to allow servants in the European quarter reflected a desire to be segregated but not inconvenienced.

What actually emerged in Northern Nigeria was more complicated than the early plans had been. In the new townships that were laid out as the railway advanced toward Kano, each urban area was divided into four sections: the official and European section, at least 400 yards to windward of the others; the commercial-industrial section, laid out near the railway line and station; a quarter for African clerks and superior artisans; and a strangers' quarter (*sabon gari* in Hausa) for African laborers and the poorer class generally. This scheme was somewhat modified where an African city was already present, as in Zaria or Kano. There, the *sabon gari* became the quarter for African strangers but not necessarily for the poorest class. In any event, the four-part scheme remained—and still exists in many northern cities.

Although the administration established this plan in response to medical advice, it also resembled an ancient tradition of West African urban planning. For at least 1,000 years, West African rulers had been accustomed to segregating traveling merchants and other strangers in a separate ward or town, where they could enjoy their own customs under the autonomous authority of their own leaders. Sometimes the merchant quarter (*zongo*) was a single section of the larger city, but often it was completely separate and situated as far as five to ten kilometers from the ruler's capital (Curtin 1984, 38–59).

As sanitary segregation advanced in Northern Nigeria, the popularity of the idea grew in official medical circles. In 1911 the medical advisory committee to the Colonial Office approved a proposal by Sir Rupert Boyce and Sir Patrick Manson that the following paragraph be inserted in the next edition of the *West African Pocket Book*: "It has been proved that the separation of Europeans from natives is one of the most efficient means of protection against disease endemic amongst native races. Even partial separation, such as sleeping outside the native quarter at night time, affords a very considerable degree of security." In 1914 Lugard, on returning as governor-general of a united Nigeria pushed for more thorough-going segregation. His Townships Ordinance of 1917 made it possible to impose a fine or imprisonment on Europeans who lived in a non-European zone. In wartime this scheme was impossible, and therefore it was never actually implemented, partly because Lugard's successor in 1919 was the same Hugh Clifford who had opposed segregation in the Gold Coast. Many segregation plans between 1914 and 1919 proposed removal of African merchants from commercial zones, but the economic advantage of such action for Europeans was so blatant as to weaken even arguments based on sanitary grounds (Gale 1980, 503).

This intersection of sanitary and commercial motives was even clearer in the German colony of Cameroon. German colonial medical policy was deeply influenced by Koch's ideas about mass quininization—pursued most avidly in Tanganyika. But, just as quinine became increasingly important for the prevention and treatment of malaria in British West Africa, ideas about sanitary segregation spread in German medical circles. In Cameroon, Dr. Ziemann, the chief government physician, had been arguing since 1900 that the quininization was impractical. The port town of Duala was a case in point. In his view, the Duala people were racially incapable of practicing proper mosquito control. In 1910 he was able to state, with unusual precision, that 72 percent of them were infested with malaria parasites. He therefore proposed to move them away from the seafront, which would become a European zone separated from the African quarter by a one-kilometer neutral zone (Austen 1977, 477–497; Rudin 1938, 349, 411–413; Rüger 1968, 220–254).

The resulting removal was certainly the most massive attempted in West Africa up to that time. If the plan had been fully implemented, about 20,000 people would have been removed from their homes along the Wouri River. By contrast, the German population of Duala numbered only about 400, and much of the Duala waterfront had already fallen into European hands by purchase. No valid administrative reason existed to expropriate so much land—especially in view of an 1884 treaty that guaranteed the Duala their permanent right to it.

The move created a major colonial crisis. The Duala had been mainly a commercial people in the middleman trade between the Germans and other Africans of the interior. For them the loss of waterfront property meant something worse than an annoying inconvenience; their business interests were at stake. European missionaries and town merchants joined them in opposing the move. Compelled to follow their converts, missionaries would lose buildings and other capital investments in the coastal zone. And the missionaries' converts were the merchants' customers. Even more important for German commercial interests, the land along the waterfront was rising in value. If the government expropriated what remained in Duala hands, speculators' profits would go to the government, not to the merchant community. Even the chief government medical officer of this period objected that the scheme made little sense on medical grounds. The government, however, pushed the measure through with official backing in Germany, a clear sign that rising racism was more important than either economic or sanitary considerations.

The leaders of the Duala counterattack were much the same kind of people—using much the same tactics—as the African leaders of the antisegregation movement in the British colonies. The "king" of the Duala was Rudolf Manga Bell, a German-educated descendant of the royal family, who had been put in office by the government in 1908. Under his leadership, the Duala not only petitioned the local government but also tried to reach the Kolonialamt in Berlin—and beyond it, the Reichstag. Manga Bell hired a German lawyer to represent the Duala in Berlin. As the controversy became increasingly bitter, local officials removed Manga Bell from his post. In desperation, he tried to extend his appeal to other European countries he thought might be sympathetic. His timing was bad. In the summer of 1914 increasing tension in Europe made any such appeal appear to be less than patriotic. Just as the war began, the local administration in Cameroon arrested Manga Bell and his secretary Ngoso Din, tried them for treason, and executed them.

German East Africa, on the other hand, witnessed the most thoroughgoing attack on malaria through chemotherapy in all Africa. The future Tanganyika had been a center for Koch's own research, and Dr. Heinrich Ollwig, an official of the East African medical service, had gone to Southeast Asia as part of the Koch team in 1899–1900. In 1901 Ollwig returned to East

Africa as head of a special unit whose name translates as "Expedition for Combating Malaria in the Protected Territory of German East Africa According to the Proposals of Medical Privy Councilor Professor Dr. Koch." This campaign was not limited to the distribution of free quinine to those who could be persuaded to use it. Ollwig divided Dar es Salaam into zones and sent his men with police escort from one zone to another inspecting all inhabitants and prescribing for infected adults two grams of quinine every ten days. Today the dose would be considered low, but at that time the problem was more administrative than medical. Medical authorities could not keep track of people circulating back and forth between village and town, and the quininization program could not be enforced. And yet the attempt continued down to World War I and was supplemented by mosquito eradication, screening, and other antimalarial measures—in line with the eclectic programs emerging in other colonies. Here, too, as in Cameroon, voices favoring more formal segregation were also heard. In 1904, for example, the medical authorities in Dar es Salaam published a city plan providing for a six-part subdivision based on race and race mixture (Beck 1977, 52; Clyde 1962, 23–27).

MALARIA: MOST IMPORTANT SINGLE ARGUMENT FOR SANITARY SEGREGATION

Although malaria provided the most important single argument for sanitary segregation, other diseases sometimes played a role. Older ideas about how to control smallpox and plague through quarantine, including the *cordon sanitaire*, antedated the germ theory by centuries. In early colonial Africa, bubonic plague reappeared, and with it came earlier forms of sanitary segregation. The plague had been absent from Africa and Europe for centuries, but it now returned in a pandemic that began in China, reaching Canton and Hong Kong in 1894, Madagascar in 1898, South Africa in 1901, the Ivory Coast in 1899 and 1903, the Gold Coast in 1908, East Africa by 1910, and Dakar, the capital of French West Africa, in 1914. Whereas segregation against malaria was mainly a matter of removing the Europeans from the African town, the favorite measure against plague was to remove those who became ill. In a racist era, the natural solution was to expel Africans from the European town.

In West Africa, the French followed the North African tradition by building their cities in the European style—sometimes alongside an existing African town, sometimes at an entirely new coastal or transportation point. In Senegal, the oldest colony, the ancient capital of Saint Louis had been built like an eighteenth-century French town, with a central *place*, streets laid out in a grid, and buildings constructed in the European style—but with an African town on the outskirts. Saint Louis, moreover, was racially unsegregated. It had had an African mayor since the eighteenth century. Segregationists found a social setting even more entrenched than that of Accra or Lagos.

In the comparatively new city of Dakar the rise of racism led some planners to suggest legal segregation even before 1901. In that year a sanitary commission recommended the creation of a hygienic village—in effect, a section of the city from which African-style thatch houses would be banned. Others recommended a sanitary cordon around the *plateau*, which was to become the site of a new European residential area. When the plague struck in 1914, the government condemned and burned all thatch-roofed houses in the part of the city where most Europeans lived, as it also burned the houses where African plague victims had died. It ordered their remaining inhabitants to move to a new African town on the outskirts, to be called the Medina following the North African precedent, just as the new suburb of Freetown had become Hill Station following the Indian precedent.

In September and October 1914, 2,900 of perhaps 38,000 people living in Dakar were driven out of the city. The expulsions from Dakar, like those in Duala, provoked a strong African opposition. Feelings had already been aroused by a conflict between the colonial government and the Lebou people of Dakar—a conflict that centered on African rights to urban land. Also in 1914, Dakar and the other Senegal *communes* succeeded in electing their first African representative to the National Assembly in Paris. Like the Africans of Lagos, Duala, and Accra, the Dakarois had influence, if not real power, with the government. As the epidemic weakened, the disturbances died down, and the government stopped moving people to the Medina. But it kept the idea that Dakar should be divided into two sections, one mainly for Europeans and the Medina for Africans. Yet race was not the only criterion. The government resorted to a cultural distinction based on architectural style. The "European" town was to be for Europeans and for any Africans willing and able to live in a European manner. That division lasted through the interwar years, though the European town tended to expand away from the harbor onto the highest available ground. Remnants of the division are still visible today, although the old Medina has been rebuilt in reinforced concrete and a newer ring of *bidonvilles* has grown up still farther out. At the end of the 1920s, the population of the Medina was only about 8,000, while 20,000 Africans remained in Dakar proper (Betts n.d., 143–152; M'Bokolo 1982, 13–46; Seck 1970, 132–133).

Other new cities in French tropical Africa followed the Dakar pattern. The administration laid out a city in European style often with elegant boulevards and government buildings. Europeans tended to live in or near these centers, but some Africans lived there as well, although most lived in the local equivalent of the Medina, sometimes, as in Bamako, under that same name (Cruise O'Brien 1972, 54–55, 94–95, 217; Dresch 1950, 200–230).

In French Equatorial Africa and Madagascar, these African quarters were more often called *villages*, with the suggestion that they were a part of rural Africa brought to the fringes of an urban setting—not a real part of the new city. But even in Brazzaville, a few poor whites lived in the *villages*, and some of the few Africans who could afford to do so lived in the European quarter. In Madagascar, the urban patterns were derived from nineteenth-century precedents—much as in Senegal. The French conquered Madagascar from their existing colony of Réunion in the Mascarene Islands. On Réunion, a local middle class called *créole*, often of mixed descent, had long since come into existence. When the French moved forward to coastal Madagascar, the *créoles* moved with them. At coastal points such as Tamatave, residential customs followed Mascarene precedent. Europeans and the wealthier *créoles* lived in well-built houses in the most desirable part of the town. Poorer *créoles* lived somewhat aside with a few of the native Malgache, but the government made every effort short of legal prohibition to keep the Malgache in a separate *village indigène* some distance west of the town itself. And Madagascar was part of an Indian Ocean as well as an African world. Some medical authorities in Tananarive wanted to move the "natives" at least 1.5 kilometers away from the European soldiers' barracks—citing the Dutch practice in Batavia on Java, rather than any nearer African precedent (Dresch 1948, 3–14; Martel 1912, 528–529; Salanoue-Ipin 1911, 38).

If the French administration failed to push sanitary segregation as far as governors like Lugard had attempted, that was not because its medical advice was different. Medical authorities were well aware of what the neighboring colonial power was doing. As early as 1903, the standard French text of tropical hygiene had picked up the recent works of British antimalarial segregationists like Christophers and Stephens and presented them as the teachings of "science." Just when the British were discussing appropriate tropical housing, the French did the same (Condamy 1906, 21–28; Reynaud 1903, 165–171).

In British East Africa, the government's first steps had something in common with those of the French in North Africa—or with their own urban policies in Egypt. Zanzibar, Mombasa, and Lamu were all small, preindustrial cities, but the British built a *ville nouvelle* alongside the old town only at Mombasa. There, the new port works and the railhead of the Uganda Railway attracted a substantial European community, which soon established its own quarter outside the old town. Zanzibar and Lamu remained unsegregated in spite of government projects to separate African and European living quarters. In Lamu, European residents were too few; all that remains today of the segregation projects is the residence of the district commissioner, located on the highest site in the neighborhood. More Europeans came to Zanzibar than to Lamu, but it remained a protectorate where the sultan was still sovereign, at least in theory.

In the new towns that appeared along the railway to Lake Victoria—Nairobi, Nakuru, Naivasha, and Kisumu—segregation appeared from the beginning, but more from Indian precedent than for medical reasons. Indian influence was important in the main towns, even before British annexation, and British control brought still more settlers from India, alongside European civil servants who had served in India. The first step was to segregate Indian from European quarters, again following the Indian pattern. It was far from clear in the beginning that Africans would eventually become the vast majority of the urban populations.

In East, as in West, Africa the thread of racism became increasingly strong as World War I approached. The most elaborate segregationist proposals, combining racist and sanitary objectives, came from W. J. Simpson of the London School of Hygiene and Tropical Medicine, who, on a tour of Kenya, Uganda, and Zanzibar in 1913/14, made recommendations, followed by an elaborate final report filed in July 1914. Town planning in Europe, he believed, required the separation of commercial, residential, and manufacturing areas, but in Africa different principles were necessary (Simpson 1914, 9–10):

> something more is required where the races are diverse and their habits and customs differ from one another. . . . It has to be recognized that the standards and mode of life of the Asiatic do not ordinarily consort with the European, whilst the customs of Europeans are at times not acceptable to the Asiatics, and that those of the African unfamiliar with and not adapted to the new conditions of town life will not blend with either. Also that the diseases to which these different races are respectively liable are readily transferable to the European and vice versa, a result especially liable to occur when their dwellings are near each other.
>
> In the interests of each community and of the healthiness of the locality and country, it is absolutely essential that in every town and trade centre the town planning should provide well defined and separate quarters or wards for Europeans, Asiatics and Africans, as well as those divisions which are necessary in a town of one nationality and race, and that there should be a neutral belt of open unoccupied country of at least 300 yards in width between the European residences and those of the Asiatic and African.

For Mombasa, he suggested four segregated zones—for Europeans, Indians, coastal Africans, and Africans from the interior—more elaborate than was common in coastal West Africa, but less so than the German practice next door in Dar es Salaam. Although drastic, this proposal was mild compared to another "medical" opinion of the time. An earlier senior medical officer of the East African Protectorate (now Kenya) wanted to remove all Africans from Mombasa islands—at a time when the European population was 148, the African 27,000.

Some of Simpson's recommendations recall the blend of commercial greed and sanitary enthusiasm found in Nigerian and Cameroonian segregation schemes. He believed, for example, that the old Indian bazaar in central Nairobi was unsanitary and should be replaced. But his way of replacing it was to expropriate the land from its Indian owners and reclassify the section for Europeans only. The property was, he noted, among the most valuable in central Nairobi, so that its resale to Europeans would be free of cost to the government. In 1915 Simpson moved on to Kampala, where he recommended ethnic zoning with intermediate green belts, but the principles of sanitary segregation had already been imposed on most district towns between 1907 and 1915. The result was a number of double-centered towns, with one focus on the *boma* or administrative building, surrounded by a European residential neighborhood, and the other on the Indian bazaar, surrounded by the commercial district. The *boma* was typically on a high point southeast of the urban center, cooled and cleansed by the prevailing southeast winds. Today from the air the most visible evidence of the old pattern is the golf course, wrapped around the *boma* quarter in the open space originally intended to protect Europeans from infections (McMaster 1968, 341–342).

Just as Lugard's segregation plans marked the high tide of sanitary segregation in British West Africa, Simpson's plans were its high water mark in the east. Many of his projects were rejected as too expensive, and the medical and social advantages appeared less pressing in the postwar world than they had in wartime. For East Africa, the issue came to a head in 1923 with the political struggle between Kenya's white settlers and Indians. The duke of Devonshire, then secretary of state for the colonies, issued a general statement in Parliamentary Proceedings (1923, xviii:15) from cabinet level. On segregation, it said

> Following on Professor Simpson's report, a policy of segregation was adopted in principle, and it was proposed by Lord Milner to retain this policy on both sanitary and social grounds. . . . It is now the view of competent medical authorities that, as a sanitation measure, segregation of Europeans and Asiatics is not absolutely essential for the preservation of the health of the community. . . . It may well prove that in practice the different races will, by natural affinity, keep together in separate quarters, but to effect such separation by legislative enactment except on the strongest sanitary grounds would not, in the opinion of His Majesty's Government be justifiable.

Other colonial powers responded with different emphases, but virtually all tried to do something about mosquitoes through segregation. The Belgian Congo became the most thoroughgoing practitioner anywhere in Africa. In Leopoldville, Kalina (the original European quarter) was separated from the African quarter by a sanitary cordon consisting of a golf course, a botanical garden, and a zoo. Congolese were not allowed to live in the European town with the exception of a few domestic servants. From 9 P.M. to 6 A.M., Congolese were not permitted in the European town without a special pass, and no Europeans were allowed to visit the African city. The only exceptions were a few *immatriculés* (Africans who enjoyed a quasi-Belgian status), but even they were not allowed to live in the European quarter until 1956 (Comhaire 1953, 22–29; LaFontaine 1970, 19–21).

Although Leopoldville was exceptional, some form of racial, social, or cultural segregation triumphed everywhere in colonial Africa—most fully in South Africa, Rhodesia, and elsewhere in the Belgian Congo—but with a different mixture of racial, medical, and social justification in each case. In southern and central Africa, the mining compound for migratory labor became the precedent for segregation under the influence of the peculiar social and political circumstances of the 1920s, when urban patterns of southern Africa became fixed. But urban segregation appeared even in Cairo, where an English-style *ville nouvelle* began to grow even before the formal colonial period began, although there, as in the Maghrib, segregation was not so much racial as cultural (Abu-Lughod 1971: 98–117; Cell 1982, 46–81; Mason 1958, 238–254; van Onselen 1976*a*: 34–73).

In Western town planning generally, sanitary segregation was only one thread among many. Its rise and importance were exactly contemporaneous with the passage of zoning legislation for North American and western European cities, some of whose features were also ostensibly justified by sanitary goals. Residential areas were to be separated from industrial smells, just as the Indian cantonments were to be separated from the smells of the "native town." Other goals, however, were social or economic. After the late 1890s, suburban subdivisions in North American cities were protected by detailed covenants laying down restrictions ranging from rules for residential construction to those governing the residents themselves (no blacks or Jews allowed).

CONCLUSION

In the broad sweep of African urban history, then, the desire for sanitary segregation played a role in the formation of residential patterns, but the motivation of racial and cultural segregation was no less important than precedents of the Indian cantonment system, the North African *funduq*, the southern African mining compound and "native reserve," and even broader European ideas about governmental and private controls over urban development. Although its influence was strong, medical thought was neither alone nor dominant in giving shape to the cities of tropical Africa. It is perhaps more interesting as an illustration of the way both physicians and administrators tried to solve problems of life and death in an alien environment, with the help of science interlarded with race prejudice, political convenience, and economic advantage—all of this in the middle of an important paradigm change in the history of Western medicine.

NOTES

1. This chapter is reprinted from the *American Historical Review*, 90 (June 1985) (3): 594–613, with the permission of the American Historical Association and the author. *Editors' note*: In addition to references cited in the text, primary sources used in this chapter but not cited because of space limitations, include the following: Great Britain Parliamentary Papers and Army Medical Service Reports; the Public Record Office, London; the British Colonial Office; National Archives of Ghana in Accra; National Archives of Nigeria, Ibadan.

2. The speed with which this new information was diffused is little short of amazing to someone accustomed to academic publication in the social sciences in the 1980s. Koch's reports appeared serially, beginning while he was still in the East Indies. His second report, for example, was dated December 9, 1899, Batavia. It was published by the *Deutsche medizinische Wochenschrift* of February 1, 1900, and in English translation by the *British Medical Journal* of February 10. For the English series, see Koch (1900), "Professor Koch's Investigations on Malaria."

3. The inland site would have been near the present location of Lagos airport. The once-segregated suburbs on the islands remain today, now integrated, as the fashionable districts of East Marina, Ikovi, and Victoria Island. See Walter Egerton to Lord Elgin, December 2, 1907, January 27, 1908, IA, CSO 3/46. Also see Frederick Lugard, "Report on Amalgamation," enclosed with Lugard to Lord Harcourt, May 9, 1913, IA, CSO 3/02.

TEN

Godly Medicine: The Ambiguities of Medical Mission in Southeastern Tanzania, 1900–1945[1]

Terence O. Ranger

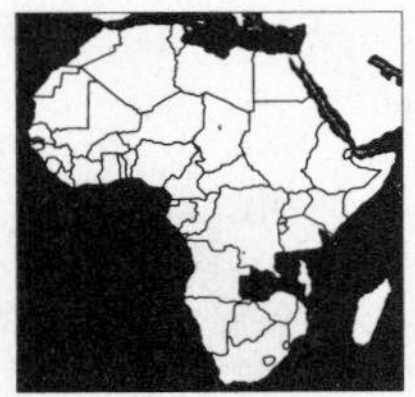

INTRODUCTION

Once upon a time medical histories of colonial Africa were unashamedly triumphalist. They recounted the steady expansion of facilities; the heroic and successful fight against tropical disease. They saw medical provision as perhaps the one totally constructive and benevolent aspect of colonialism. And they saw the practical triumphs of Western medicine as the greatest force for conceptual change, compelling Africans to abandon their unscientific worldview. More recent historians have cast a colder eye on the proclaimed aims and achievements of colonial medical treatment. They have charted colonial epidemics, the ravages of World War I, the rise of industrial diseases, the entrenchment of diseases of poverty and undernourishment. They have stressed the role of doctors as allies of colonial capitalism; the way in which sanitary theory was used to enforce urban segregation or to override African property rights; the high-handed and often misconceived way in which rural populations were shifted and centralized in the name of the war against disease. With its combined aspects of coercion and inefficiency, colonial medicine had ambiguous ideological effects; perceiving it as a key element in white power, some Africans aspired to gain access to its forms; others accepted its ruling with resignation as an aspect of industrial discipline. But there was little prospect that the perceived triumph and benevolence of Western medicine would fatally erode African concepts of disease, treatment, and causation (Phimister 1978, 102–150; Ranger 1978*b*; Swanson 1977, 287).[2]

In this revisionist medical history, the emphasis has shifted away from missionary medicine. As I myself wrote in a recent article (Ranger 1979, 507):

> We have been accustomed to thinking of medical provision for Africans in terms of the missionary doctor, selflessly itinerating the rural areas. In Rhodesia, at any rate, very many more African men encountered doctors at or on the way to their places of employment. . . . They were scrutinized to protect the health of Europeans with whom they might come into contact; they were subjected to authoritarian restrictions and disruptions which reached their peak in times of epidemic or fear of epidemic; and all the time they were kept going as workers on medically advised minimum diets and "running repairs."

It is time, I think, to turn back to missionary medicine. My purpose in this chapter is to examine a missionary case in which many of the factors of coercion, subordination to the interests of industrial capitalism, and so on are absent; in which the theory and practice of medicine were determinedly benevolent, even if paternalist. In such a case the high expectations of the missionaries that Western medical provision would produce profound ideological transformations can be usefully tested and examined. In the particular mission I have selected—the Universities Mission to Central Africa (UMCA) diocese of Masasi in southeastern Tanzania—these conditions certainly existed. The UMCA was hostile to industrial capitalism and did its best to achieve a self-sustaining rural economy. It looked back to a doctor—David Livingstone—as its founder. It had an elaborate Christian theory of medicine and healing. Its clinics and hospitals provided, with those of the Catholics, the sole effective medical facilities in Masasi district. Its second mission doctor, Leader Stirling, is at the time of writing Minister of Health in the Tanzanian Government; Julius Nyerere has described contemporary Tanzanian health policy as a continuation of the "tradition" of rural health care established by the UMCA (Stirling 1977, xii–xiv). Here, if anywhere, one might expect to find a profound penetration of African conceptual systems by the ideas of Western medicine.

THE THEORY OF MISSION MEDICINE

There is no question of the central importance that the UMCA theorists ascribed to mission medical work. "One feels that the medical work is the one solid asset of the missionary work here," wrote G. H. Wilson, "Preaching in a tongue of which one has but an elementary knowledge is discouraging work. . . . But the care of the sick and afflicted without thought of reward or return bears witness to Christ as it did in Galilee long ago" (Wilson 1914, 302).

There were broadly four claims made for medical work. The first and most important was that it carried on the work of Christ Himself. Christ did not, of course, employ the methods of nineteenth-century medicine, but it was assumed by nineteenth-century bishops that doctors were the true successors of Christ the Healer. "How much of the influence of our Blessed

Lord, while on earth," reflected Bishop Smythies of Zanzibar in 1892, "came through healing diseases" (Smythies 1892, 51).

The second claim for medicine consisted precisely in its power to penetrate heathen and even Muslim societies that were resistant to evangelization. Smythies's definition of a medical missionary was "a doctor who uses all his medical knowledge for a missionary end, whose aim it is to use the great influence which his profession gives him to draw his patients to the love of God." In many parts of East Africa, Smythies thought, hostility to Christianity could only be overcome by "sympathy shown for the sufferings of the body . . . together with the power to alleviate them" (p. 51).

But medicine was seen also as a weapon in a more direct and militant confrontation with heathenism. The asserted superior power of European medicine over African treatment of disease was held to demonstrate the validity of Western rational explanation over African superstition. While bishops thought in terms of the continuation of Christ's own ministry and of the penetrating power of sympathy, mission nurses thought more in terms of combat. Thus Mrs. Williams described from Zanzibar in 1880 how she had begun to treat a child "with a horrid skin disease" (Williams 1880, 33):

> I doctored it and the places were healing beautifully when I found that the child was wearing charms. I told (the mother) that I could do no more for it till they were removed. But it was no use; she refused to take them off, so I put the ointment away. . . . Eight months or so have passed since then, during which time the child has worn the charms and has been getting very much worse. Over and over again the mother has begged me to cure it. . . . It has been very hard to see the poor little thing growing worse and to hear its piercing screams when they put on native medicine, and yet do nothing to relieve it. Now, I am only too thankful I did not yield. . . . I told her once more that I could do nothing till she gave up the medicine of the devil. Greatly to my surprise she cried, "Give me a knife" and immediately cutting off the charms from her child's neck gave them to me. I joyfully went in and prepared the ointment. You will be glad to hear that the healing has been very rapid.

Masasi nurses produced nothing quite so formidable as this. But the same idea comes out of Miss Andrews's account in 1918:

> All pain and illness are in African minds the direct action of evil spirits. The power of witchcraft is so great and so overwhelming. Sometimes the whole place throbs with the tom tom wherever one goes. Someone has fever and the devil is being drummed out. . . . Every attendance at the dispensary is a defiance of evil spirits.

Even Masasi African clergy fell into the same idiom. Daudi Machina described in 1910 "a kind of illness which is prevalent at Lulindi," the site of the mission hospital. People called this illness "possession by an evil spirit." Machina continued:

> One man who was seized with it sent for an *Ngoma*, that is for a drumming and dancing to drive out the spirit and nearly all the town heard the noise of the *Ngoma* and everyone thought he was possessed by a devil, even the Christians. . . . (I said) "I don't believe that you are really ill; it is nonsense; a trick of evil spirits. Now every man who has been taken ill, let him be brought to the nurse at the dispensary and she will examine him and if it is not true she will know for she is a doctor and she will also know exactly what medicine to give him!." Well, since that day no one . . . has been possessed by an evil spirit. So the medicine for this illness is to name the lady who is a doctor!

Machina told a woman who was wearing protective charms that he did not believe that Christians could be possessed. "Cut off your charms and I will send you to the nurse to get medicine."

The fourth and final claim for mission medical work was that the hospital instilled time sense, work discipline, sobriety—those invaluable preconditions of rational thought and action. As Dr. Howard wrote in 1914 of medical work in northeastern Tanzania:

> I think there is nothing more striking than the marked difference there is in a patient when he has been with us for a few weeks. We are but human, and at times we admit a man or woman to whom we feel a distinct aversion. At the end of a week or two we forget that we ever had that feeling; the person who roused it is now so improved, not only in health, but in tone and behaviour.

Such were the justifications and expectations of mission medical work. Up to 1945, at any rate, none were fulfilled. I shall seek to show in this chapter that mission medical provision with its scientific rationality was not experienced by Africans as a continuing part of Christ's ministry. They looked for spiritual healing and were not offered it by a church that had compartmentalized healing off into the hospital and the dispensary as a task only for nurses and doctors. Whatever sympathy was shown in Muslim areas by missionary medics, no Christian penetration followed. Nor did African acceptance of the utility of mission medical treatment for certain diseases at all shake their overall belief in the tenets of indigenous philosophies of misfortune. Finally, Masasi hospitals never achieved before 1945 the sort of ordered discipline that Dr. Howard expected to raise tone and behavior. By 1945, as we shall see, every one of these assumptions was being questioned and UMCA clergy and medics alike were calling for a new strategy of healing.

THE BELATED ARRIVAL OF MISSIONARY MEDICINE IN MASASI

The medical work of the UMCA encountered the same problems of credibility everywhere, but they were compounded in Masasi by the fact that medical provision did not begin there until so late in the day. Hospitals and dispensaries were operating at the UMCA headquarters on Zanzibar thirty years before any were opened in Masasi. Medical workers were active in northeast Tanzania and in Nyasaland a good decade before anything began in Masasi. The main reason for this was that UMCA medical provision was largely in the hands of women and Masasi was for long regarded as too dangerous a region for the dispatch of nurses. The Ngoni raids and the later resistance to German penetration deterred mission strategists on Zanzibar from deploying nurses there, and even when the colonial peace was imposed on the area the bachelor clergy of Masasi expressed resolute opposition to the arrival of women workers.

Even after nurses had arrived the upheavals first of the Maji-Maji uprising in 1905 and then of World War I, which in Masasi involved battles and massive dislocation, brought all mission medical work to a close. Mission nurses did not return to the district until March 1919 and it was not really until the appointment at long last of Frances Taylor as mission doctor for Masasi in 1926 that anything like regular and continuous medical work got under way.

DETERIORATION OF HEALTH IN MASASI, 1880–1926

We shall have occasion to notice several consequences of this delayed start, but one was of overriding importance. The theorists of medical mission assumed that Africans would greet the whites as emancipators from disease. The development of mission influence would coincide with gradual but marked improvements in health as a result of the successes of mission medicine. In Masasi, mission medicine could hardly begin to make much of an impact before the 1920s. But by that time Africans had come to connect the dominance of the whites not with an improvement in health but rather with a grave deterioration. New diseases spread—some indirectly the result, some coincidentally with it. Diet was impoverished; famine and death became structural features of the region; the war had a devastating impact. By the 1920s the articulators of indigenous systems of explanation in Masasi district were not faced with the problem of trying to explain away the successes of scientific European medicine. Instead they were faced with the problem of trying to come to terms with, to explain, and to seek to control epidemic disease and sapping malnutrition.

Diseases which appear to have been introduced by the colonial incursion included many that had been the great child-killers of nineteenth-century industrial Europe—measles and whooping cough in particular. Diseases that appear to have become more widespread as a result of the movement of people under colonialism—porters, labor migrants, troops, and carriers—included smallpox, which had certainly been present in southern Tanzania but which gave rise to severe epidemics in the early decades of the twentieth century. Diseases that were prevalent in other parts of East Africa but which had not hitherto existed in southeastern Tanzania were brought back there by migrant workers moving to and from the European plantations on the coast—the outstanding example of such "industrial" diseases in Masasi district was hookworm, which was still quite rare in the mid-1920s but had become a major threat to health by World War II. Diseases that arrived coincidentally with colonialism—although no doubt also assisted in their movement by its widening of communication—included jiggers, the history of which was engagingly spelled out in 1925 for child supporters of the UMCA (*African Tidings* 1925, 34:15):

> Jiggers really have no business to be in Africa. Their real home is in the tropical part of South America, but as they burrow into people's feet they managed to get taken from South America to Jamaica. In Jamaica . . . there are ever so many descendants of the West African slaves, whom we took there in the bad old days. Naturally enough Africans from Jamaica go to see their friends in West Africa and in their feet travels the jigger. Thereafter the jigger flea traveled across Africa—"about the year 1900 it reached the East Coast."

In addition to all this was deterioration of diet. The Masasi area had never been agriculturally rich. Cattle could not be kept there, which deprived people of a key insurance against famine, and except for the dew-drenched Makonde plateau to the east, there was uncertain rainfall. However, there seems no doubt that things got worse under colonial rule, and especially as a result of the war. The relatively diverse economy, which had given some protection against crop failure, gave way under colonialism to a total reliance on cereal and cash-crop cultivation. Demands for tax and the need for cash for clothes and utensils meant that people sold whatever surplus of grains they had at harvest time and had to buy grain back at inflated prices in the hunger months. Hunting became much less important as a supplement to the diet. During the war "the troops in their leisure hours ruthlessly destroyed game," and after it "the government . . . raised the price of a game license to a fancy figure. No longer can one of our men go out and shoot an eland or a gazelle to vary our chicken menu" (*African Tidings* 1920).

The war brought all this to a high point of suffering. The Germans interned the missionaries and commandeered their food stocks, which had in the past been used for famine relief. They also commandeered peasant grain surpluses. The local agricultural economy was left in a perilously fragile state and in 1915 it collapsed into a disastrous famine. "The famine this year," wrote the teacher Obed Kasembe in 1917, "is greater than any famine I have known in my life: perhaps it is equal to the famine in Canaan in the days of Joseph." "I was given very hard work," wrote Edward Abdallah, "the task of carrying food for the Germans, and taking it to their stores. I did this work for the space of a year and in the year 1915 we had a terrible famine, and for the space of four months I buried six to ten people every day. . . . We had no food at all, not even a little, only the insects in the bush." Famine was followed by disease. Deacon Silvano Ngaweje was in charge of Mnyambe parish. "In 1915 there was a severe famine which extended over a wide area, and in many places many people died, and half the Christians who had been baptized at Mnyambe died." Then "from December 1918 until May 1919 Mnyambe and the whole Makonde district was overrun with smallpox and a disease called influenza. . . . As a result . . . very large numbers of people died. The scourge lasted for a period of six months. The Christians and Catechumens who survived the famine of 1915 perished of the smallpox and the coughing."

It was into this disaster that mission Europeans returned in 1919. Their medical services appeared ludicrously inadequate. "We have had sad epidemics of smallpox and influenza, with many, many deaths," wrote Vincent Lucas, priest in charge of Masasi. "Miss Horne carried on dispensary work despite the almost complete absence of any drugs except quinine. Influenza and smallpox claimed a large death toll, but she did all she possibly could."

Of course, the numbers of mission medical personnel thereafter increased and their drug supplies improved. Nor was there again a disaster on the scale of the war. But the district had not recovered from the war when severe economic depression set in—beginning in 1926, the year of Dr. Taylor's arrival. As we shall see in more detail, poverty and undernourishment fostered recurrent epidemics of measles and whooping cough right up to 1945, with consequent heavy infant mortality (Ranger 1978*b*).

It is hardly surprising that the people of Masasi region did not see mission medicine as a liberation from disease! Instead they made various attempts to comprehend these misfortunes. It was reported that the people looked on the influenza epidemic as a judgment upon Europeans for the war, and therefore as being another burden that the Africans had to bear for the sake of their white brothers. As it was a new plague they invented a new name for it, so with a touch of African humor they called it "bom-bom" because the explosive cough reminded them of the noise of the cannon.

On the Makonde plateau, so the Newala district book informs us, people believed in a malevolent deity of epidemic, known as Nandenga to the Makonde and Nayapuru to the Makua:

> Nandenga is a malevolent mythical person who, when not occupied, lives in a large tree, a lonely valley or hill. He is believed to take on human form in various guises, young and old, tall and short, but has the distinguishing characteristic of long hair. His activities are widespread, as opposed to the more localized *uchawi* (witches). Against him the *Mahoka* (departed ancestors) have no power. For example, the great plague . . . of smallpox during the war was attributed directly to Nandenga. He was alleged to have traveled the country from village to village with a large vessel containing the . . . disease, sprinkling it in

> various proportions in the villages. . . . The measles epidemic of 1928 was considered to be the work of Nandenga against whom the clan *mbepesi* (ancestral flour) was powerless. He cannot be supplicated. One must just bear the evil he brings.

The extreme pessimism of this interpretation was, however, modified as it came to be believed that children could be saved from Nandenga's wrath if certain rites were observed. As late as November 1945 Lyndon Harries was recording that "only last year in a non-Christian area I found that children had been shaved on one side of their heads. There had been an epidemic of whooping cough, and it was believed that the tribal gremlin, whose name was Nandenga, would pass over all the children whose heads had been shaved and not afflict them with the . . . complaint." Harries was perceptive enough to remark that such a belief did at last give some comfort in an otherwise comfortless situation.

TRIUMPH AND FAILURE: YAWS AND MEASLES

It would certainly be misleading to imply that mission medicine had no successes at all in Masasi. In fact, it had at least one spectacular success, if a paradoxical one. In Masasi some of the tropical diseases turned out to be relatively easy to deal with; and missionary medics were optimistic about eradicating all of them. It was the familiar diseases infiltrating from Europe which before 1945 defied all attempts at treatment by the medical missionaries.

Tropical diseases had at first seemed a terrifying obstacle to missionary penetration of the East and Central African mainland, and the UMCA had a tragic record of missionary deaths. But by the time that medical work began in Masasi district the mission had come to feel a new confidence in its capacity to overcome African disease. In May 1921 J. G. Christopherson, M.D., F.R.C.P., F.R.C.S., demanded massive government support for mission medical work on the grounds that it was now plain that great victories could be won (Christopherson 1921):

> In no department of medicine has progress been so rapid in recent years as in tropical diseases. . . . There is no branch of medicine where disease is treated with such confidence and exactness nor where the result of the treatment is so satisfactory and conclusive as the diseases of the tropics. It is no exaggeration to say that the treatment of such tropical diseases as ankylostoma, bilharzia, yaws, malaria, dysentery . . . had advanced out of the realm of hope, or even of legitimate speculation. The cure of such tropical diseases is almost a matter of mathematical calculation.

"If only government would provide the necessary money and drugs," wrote Christopherson, the mission could "check and eradicate the many dangerous diseases, epidemic and endemic." After all, "the economic prosperity of tropical Africa depends on the country being made healthy," and "medical science points out the surest way of solving the labour question." Smallpox, hookworm, malaria, yaws, and bilharzia—all were capable of "being stamped out," so that "the vast, unhealthy areas of Africa became habitable, healthy and profitable." Christopherson (1921) continued:

> The medical man is the modern "pioneer of civilization" in tropical countries. No one has the qualifications of a British doctor for liaison work between Government and native—no one has a greater influence; he is in touch with the natives in their homes and he can break down native mistrust of European methods. . . . A doctor's reputation in the tropics radiates for miles; patients walk a considerable journey to consult him. But his reputation is also in proportion to the good he is able to do his patients—and this depends on the medical paraphernalia at his disposal. He cannot perform miracles without money. As the native only judges by results, the doctor should be adequately equipped to make the result successful. . . . Every case cured . . . is placed in the native mind to the credit of the Government.

Christopherson was being overoptimistic; knowledge of most tropical diseases and capacity to treat them had reached a sort of plateau by the 1920s, and little advance was to be made until the development of antibiotics. But at least in *one* area it seemed that miracles were being performed. In August 1923 *Central Africa* rejoices:

> People say that the age of miracles is past. From a mere layman's point of view it certainly is *not* with regard to the work of healing, and still less from the point of view of the African. It is to us and to them miraculous the way in which things are done and the people healed. . . . There are these wonderful injections . . . again to a layman miraculous to a degree—and some of you may have read of that splendid recovery by this means of a man who after suffering for over a year from a painful disease was cured in four days, and who was met on the road shortly afterwards literally dancing for joy.

These miracles of healing were achieved in Masasi with sufferers from yaws, the one tropical disease to which, through a sort of lucky accident of discovery, effective remedies had been found. The treatment of yaws, indeed, was the most attractive service offered by the mission to Africans. Thousands flocked to the clinics from all over the southeast, until the movement of people took on some of the dimensions of a mass pilgrimage. But even here there was remarkably little of the predicted carry-over effect. Readiness to come for yaws treatment did *not* break down a more general "mistrust of European methods." A successful cure did *not* rebound to the credit of government; the pilgrimages receded leaving very few converts. In its intensity, its periodic and spasmodic character, and in its isolation from general notions of misfortune and healing, the movement of yaws victims to the mission clinics resembled nothing so much as an indigenous healing cult, of which there had been a succession in this region (Stirling 1977, 21):

> Yaws, or *mbelegu*, was in the words of Leader Stirling: A horrible disease beginning with a foul ulcer in some part, usually the leg, and continuing with tumid sores all over the body. Later, deep ulcers break out in various parts, bones ache, swell and rot away; sometimes a large part of the nose and mouth may be destroyed. After many years the disease eventually dies out leaving the victim more or less scarred and crippled.

According to mission doctors, "native remedies" were "absolutely powerless" against yaws (Howard 1913/14, 239). The child readers of *African Tidings* were told that "the medicine man's cure is that poor patients should starve and drop red hot charcoal on each sore every day" (1925). At any rate, yaws sufferers were responsive to any immediately effective treatment.

There were four such offered in the sequence of mission dealing with yaws. The first, before World War I, was potassium iodide, applied externally to the sores. "It heals most wonderfully," exclaimed Dr. Howard (1913/14, 239). In Masasi district the first yaws pilgrimages began to Luatala, the headquarters of chief Matola II where Nurse Dunn had opened a dispensary. Used to the timid reluctance of their patients, the nurses were taken completely by surprise by the rush. "They come from such distances now," wrote Nurse Dunn in September 1913; "today three turned up from the other side of the Rovuma. We have seven tribes represented in hospital—Yao, Makua, Nyasa, Ndonde, Mwera, Makonde, and Angoni. Of course, it is the marvelous treatment for *mbelegu* that brings the people. My potassium iodide is finished" (Howard 1913/14, 239). Pressure soon built up on Luatala dispensary and increasing quantities of potassium iodide were sent and consumed. The movement had become a popular one and had escaped all control by the mission. "They are packed like herrings in a barrel," wrote Nurse Dunn, "and there are numbers staying in the villages around and coming daily for treatment. They come and bring their food and *insist* on staying. . . . I am at my wits' end" (p. 274). By the next month she was complaining "they *are* a problem and I feel completely overwhelmed. We talk of sending to the Makonde chiefs to tell them to prevent the people coming! But can one open a dispensary and then tell people to stay away? They come in droves!. . . . I feel so helpless" (p. 304). But the rush continued unabated into 1914. "The hospital at Luatala is a wonderful sight," wrote Miss Andrews in July, "a great camp of some 220 people and 50 or 60 little fires at night. By this time the dispensary at Masasi itself was similarly besieged."

The outbreak of the war and the internment of the nurses brought this first phase of the yaws pilgrimages to an end. In any case by that time the medical limitations of the treatment were becoming apparent to the nurses. The potassium iodide "takes months to really do them good," and the yaws sufferers were not prepared to undergo long-drawn-out treatment. As far as they were concerned, the initial striking improvements in their conditions did not proceed from anything analogous to the craft of the herbalist; nor did they appear as one part of a systematic explanation of disease. They were "miracles," instantaneous cleansings similar to those promised in the period movements of witchcraft eradication. One applied an ointment, one observed for a while the new ritual of the dispensary, and that was or should have been that. "Some of the people are very tiresome about coming regularly," complained the Masasi nurse in 1914, "perhaps they come every day for a week or two and then disappear for weeks. When they do return all the good they have derived from their medicine is entirely undone. Very often they have not the patience to follow up the treatment, but seem to think they ought to be cured at once, and so go off to try all sorts of native treatment." But after all, at the dispensaries it was all ritual and no communication. The nurses could speak Swahili but none of the "tribal" languages, and hardly any women in the Masasi district spoke any Swahili at all.

The war period saw a great recrudescence of yaws among all its other misfortunes. Those "cured" by the potassium iodide relapsed. Once again, this was very like the relapse that inevitably followed the eradication of witchcraft. After the war, people were ready to try another movement of healing. For a while they were offered nothing new. When the nurses got back to Masasi district they still used potassium iodide, although with increasing reluctance because they knew that in those parts of the UMCA territory that had doctors, a new "miracle" treatment of yaws by injection had been developed. In 1924 a nurse at Lulindi hospital looked back on these frustrating years:

> Quite three-fourths of the dispensary and hospital patients are suffering from yaws. We did our best to help them, and nurses and dispensary boys day after day put on a patchwork of gauze and iodoform, and later an ointment over the numberless ulcers. We tied on bandage after bandage, and at the same time they were given an expensive drug which had the effect of cleaning up and healing the ulcer in about six weeks to two months and relieving the pain. If we had had enough of the drug, costing 1 pound a pound, and if the patient had had the perseverance to make visits to the dispensary week by week for three to six months' course of the drug, we could sometimes have obtained a permanent cure; but this did not happen often. The African saw himself apparently healed and went off home to the engrossing job of planting and harvesting. He forgot the nurse's injunction to come regularly. . . . The nurse might perhaps be excused for thinking what was the good of going on in the face of this constant relapse.

Meanwhile in Nyasaland and northeastern Tanganyika injections of Norvarsan (novoaresenobenzol) were being given under the supervision of mission doctors. The nurses in Masasi, where there was still no doctor, read the exultant reports of miracle cures in *Central Africa* with a great deal of envy. "Yaws is the country's enemy," wrote Christopherson in 1921. "It is quite curable; the cure (novoaresenobenzol) is expensive, 10s a dose now, but each case needs only one dose. It should be used energetically on a large scale." "Till recently," wrote a northeast nurse in 1923, "treatment was far from satisfactory . . . now . . . an intravenous injection or two is enough to cure the worst cases and a course of medicine after the injection is given to ensure the permanence of the cure." "I don't wonder these people think that miracles are happening," wrote a nurse from Korogwe, "one is amazed oneself."

Early in 1924 the new injections came to Masasi. The district was visited briefly by Dr. Mary Iles, who introduced the newly developed and cheaper bismuth sodium tartrate solution, which could be injected intramuscularly and could thus be handled by African dispensers as well as by nurses. In a great outburst of delight—printed in *Central Africa* under the heading, "And There Was Great Joy in That City," the Masasi nurses recorded the transformation:

> One injection—sometimes two—quite cures the early form: the horrid sores dry up, often in two days, and the two years of misery are saved. . . . We have been given a means of healing and relieving what was a weight of almost unbearable misery and hopelessness to both patient and nurse.

At once there began again the yaws pilgrimages. "We have simply been swarmed . . . they have come in batches . . . the hospitals at Masasi and Lulindi are more like gypsy camps than anything else." Dr. Iles's medical report for 1924 revealed very clearly that the medical work of the mission was focused almost entirely on yaws. Between January 1 and September 30 of 1924 out of 618 in-patients at Masasi hospital no fewer than 504 were yaws cases and 66 with other forms of ulcers (Iles 1924, 125). The fame of the needle—*sindano*—spread far and wide; people came from very long distances; and as soon as a dispensary was opened in a new part of the district there were at once crowds of yaws patients. The atmosphere was very clearly that of the spontaneous and intense movements of mass cleansing. The nurse at Lulindi reported a patient with a large growth on the leg who had been told that the injection was no use and that only an operation would help: "I have been five days coming here. Lots of people from where I've come from have been cured—and they told me you would cure me. What have I done that you should deny me? Do you know anything about me that you won't give it to me?" (p. 116).

The intense movement was short-lived. By 1927 there was "a very marked decline" in the numbers coming for yaws treatment; for the first time the Masasi dispensaries and hospitals began to treat a wide range of diseases. This decline, so Dr. Taylor hoped, was "due to the success with which hundreds of cases were treated in the three or four preceding years." But there was also a little disillusionment on both sides . It turned out that one or two injections did not, after all, produce permanent cures. As Leader Stirling later wrote (Stirling 1977, 21):

> After one or two injections they would see such a dramatic improvement that they were quite satisfied, and no words would persuade them to continue with treatment until they were fully cured. So the disease smouldered on and infection continued to spread.

The instant, final, miracle cure had to wait until "the use of long-acting penicillin" after World War II. Then there took place the third of the great yaws pilgrimages. It also turned out that, ready as they were to observe the immediate rituals of the dispensary, the yaws patients did not convert to Christianity. As Dr. Taylor wrote in 1929 "from the missionary point of view this part of our work at first sight seems of very little direct value, for the patients rarely stop long and often come from great distances, so that it is useless to try to teach them the Faith" (Taylor 1929, 13).

Conversion to "European methods" was even less likely. It was accepted that the Europeans could treat yaws, but it was observed that they manifestly could not treat many other things. "There are diseases which English medicines cannot cure at once and the African medicines can cure it," wrote a group of African schoolboys in 1928:

> European medicine is very good if a man gets yaws (but) we have some very big diseases and Europeans cannot cure them. They cannot cure elephantitis and they cannot cure snake bites, but African doctors can. If you have been bewitched by evil spirits . . . Europeans cannot cure you, but African medicines can cure these diseases at once.

The schoolboys tactfully ended by remarking that "European medicine can cure them and us, but African medicines cure ourselves only."

For many Africans out of school the analogy with the healing or antiwitchcraft movement seemed the most striking. A series of these occurred in the Masasi district between the wars, a response to, among other things, the recurrent epidemic disease and famine. Such movements were, in fact, antimedicine, commanding their initiates to throw away both African and European medicines. But the attitude of these movements to the yaws injections was significantly different. In 1929, for instance, the *Amanjingo* movement entered Chidya district, where there had been a dispensary treating yaws since 1927. The *Amanjingo* messengers summoned people to a ceremony of purification, of ritual shaving and a communal meal. Disease and misfortune were explained in spiritual terms and were to be dealt with by mutual aid and repentance rather than by medicines or other external means. No one was to bewitch anyone else; "there should not be any quarrels in their house." No one should go to a herbalist. And "no hospital medicine is to be used *except injections.*"

While these ambiguous triumphs over one tropical disease were taking place, Masasi district was being ravaged by epidemics of nontropical diseases, and in particular measles. The problem was not that Europeans could cure only some African diseases as well as their own diseases; it was that they could cure some African diseases but could not cure many of their own. Measles was regarded as a very minor part of the appalling health situation at the end of World War I. "We have had sad epidemics of smallpox and influenza," wrote Vincent Lucas in July 1919, "but things are better and the only local epidemic now is measles" (Lucas 1919, 170). Measles perhaps sounded a childish disease to Lucas. But in the later 1920s, as the economic depression deepened in Masasi and diets grew yet more impoverished, measles came to be the major killer of children. In 1926 there was "a great deal of sickness all over this part of the country . . . whooping cough, measles of a virulent type and influenza also of a bad kind." In Masasi parish itself "there was scarcely a home without at least one or two ill. The children suffered dreadfully, and the death rate among the babies must have reached a very high figure." The *Annual Report* for the year 1928 remarked:

> If 1926 was called a year of famine, 1928 must be called a year of illness, and the two were probably more closely connected together than we can trace. Along the coast road came first an epidemic of measles. This should not be in itself a ground for alarm. But the cases proved almost all of a virulent type and grave complications supervened, with the result that mortality was high and the lines of childrens' graves grew longer and longer.

The next great measles epidemic came in December 1936. It was "followed by serious complications and in many villages there has been very heavy child mortality." There was little that the mission could do to help except to supplement diet. Dr. Taylor wrote:

> In districts near our hospitals and dispensaries we have been able to help. . . . As the epidemic drew to its close in Masasi, it was a common sight in the dispensary to see a row of out-patient children, thin, miserable little things, drinking milk out of large blue enamel mugs! It made all the difference to their convalescence. . . . If we could have sent our dispensary assistant out to the out-stations as we did to the houses fairly near the hospitals, taking medicine and if necessary milk to the children, the mortality could have been decreased everywhere.

In 1938 Silvano Ngaweje reported from Chiwata that "diviners had been going about lately, deceiving many people." It was not coincidental that he also reported "sickness, an epidemic of measles and coughs; many children had died of measles. Through the years of the war there were epidemics of measles, whooping cough and influenza" (Harries 1945, 122). It was only after the war, when the mission had supplies of dried milk to distribute, that the nurses and doctors fully appreciated the chronic malnutrition of the children of Masasi, which made these diseases so deadly (Taylor 1929, 34). As the realization came to them, they wrote of the medical situation in Masasi in terms very far removed from triumphalism. In 1945, after half a century of medical work, Leader Stirling told the annual anniversary meeting that his area "was riddled with disease." Lyndon Harries quoted with approval A. T. Culwick's scathing indictment of the "product of a quarter of a century of British rule in east Africa . . . a native population still riddled with disease, badly housed, poorly fed and living in the most abject poverty" (Harries 1945, 121). "Children suffer from measles, whooping cough and chicken pox, and the first of these is one of the most common causes of blindness" (Stirling 1945, 80).

The missionary medics did not think that all this was primarily their own fault. But it was hardly surprising in view of it that mission medicine had not produced a scientific revolution in attitudes. "So long as the economic life of the people remains as it is," wrote Harries, "a life of deep poverty . . . subject to constant famine . . . there can be no doubt that the old way of life is bound to prevail" (Stirling 1945, 122).

THE LAY THERAPY GROUP IN THE CHRISTIAN VILLAGE

Lyndon Harries believed that the poverty of Masasi district was an inheritance from the precolonial past. "So long as these Africans find themselves dependent on the same low conditions of life as they endured before the days of Dr. Livingstone, there can be no doubt that the old way of life is bound to prevail." The case was in fact rather different. Poverty in Masasi had assumed new forms—there were new patterns of disease; famine had become more endemic; migrant labor and tax demands exercised new pressures. Few of the inhabitants of Masasi district supposed that they were living "the old way of life," and many of them tried to find new ways of coping with misfortune. The treatment of disease lay at the heart of this search.

It lay at the heart of it not only because disease was the most specific of misfortunes but also because decisions about the treatment of disease involved collective discussion and determination. An individual might decide to become a Christian; but when that individual fell seriously ill it was his kinsfolk, his *jamaa*, who determined how he should be treated, whether they were Christians or not. The Masasi evidence for what Janzen has called the "therapy group" is very strong. Dr. Stirling, writing home in June 1935, remarked that "operations are greatly feared in these parts, and often we cannot get consent to do the most necessary operations. The relatives (who have all the say) prefer to take the patient home to die" (Stirling 1947, 20–21). Stirling wrote in 1940 (Stirling 1940):

> The decision rests with the elders of the family and not with the patient himself. The individual is only of importance as a member of the tribe. A patient's leg is not his own property, but a piece of a part of a family, and if you want to cut it off you must ask the elders of that family, and a single veto from an important relative is usually final.

The sole right of the *jamaa* to determine how the patient was to be treated was jealously guarded and periodically reasserted against European medical authoritarianism. In July 1938, for example, Dr. Frances Taylor operated in a difficult childbirth case. The mother died. As the priest in charge recorded in the Masasi parish log-book:

> Akumachinga came to explain business of a woman operated on by Dr. Taylor before her *jamaa* consulted. He says that the only person with any authority, Bartlett's mother, Neema Nakaam, refused to consent all along and her "mjombe" who was sitting outside . . . was not aware that there was any undue danger, until in the last few minutes he was called inside. I said that I did not know all the circumstances of the case but that we Europeans always tried to align our customs with those of the Africans. . . . (The family asked me) to write this down and when the Bishop returns (they) will seek an opportunity to explain the whole matter to him. . . . Dr. Taylor was wrong to operate.

But if the doctors sometimes found the rights of the *jamaa* an impediment, in other ways they were obliged to rely heavily on the action of the family as a therapy group. It was family members who carried in the sick, often over very long distances, and it was family members who remained to tend the sick and to cook for them once they were "in hospital." Since European nurses were behaving like doctors, it was left to the *jamaa* to do the nursing. "We like the patient to have one relative with him," wrote Dr. Taylor in 1929, "for it is difficult to get anyone to cook and fetch water for him otherwise."

The *jamaa* were not merely determining whether a patient should have an operation—and observing it when it took place. They were also determining whether an illness required European medical treatment at all. The log-books often record a Christian father summoned in for rebuke by his parish priest because one of his children had been sick and a diviner had been summoned. Time and time again the father explained that in this matrilineal society it was not *his* responsibility to determine the treatment of his child but that of the matrilineal relatives. Hence illness in a Christian family at once involved the wider society in a series of choices among alternative therapies.

In the 1920s and 1930s there was, in fact, an abundance of alternative therapies to choose from. It certainly was not a simple confrontation of European medicine and "the old way." Apart from mission medical work, there was a steady penetration into the district of Muslim ideas and practices of healing. And there was plenty of innovation outside Christianity and Islam altogether. To the long-established diviner and herbalist were added the emissary of the antimedicine movement and the witchcraft eradicator. The *jamaa* were confronted with a bewildering variety of remedies. They made full use of them. While they were choosing European treatments for yaws, they were choosing Muslim and indigenous treatments for a whole range of other ills.

The log-books of the subparishes enable us to see the process at work in the Christian village as a whole. The log-book of Napacho parish, for example, reveals a series of African teachers trying to combat the villagers' recourse to witchcraft-eradication rituals or to exorcism dances. The teachers urged their fellow Christians to "depend on God only. We should endure our troubles fear and doubt"; they advised them to take their sick to the hospital. They often failed. Villagers took the medicine of the *Mchape* witchcraft-eradication movement in December 1933; they treated children for measles through the *Iyoto* exorcism dance; and when chided by the teacher a defiant parent would reply, "I am not doing this to the teacher's child. This is my own child." A log-book of one subparish states:

> Teacher Mowala of Mkoma village encountered in November 1941 overt opposition from the *jamaa* of a local Christian: In the evening I went to visit one of the Christians who was ill. . . . I advised her relatives to take her to hospital, but they refused, saying that her illness could not be cured by hospital drugs. I asked them why they believed so and they answered that this was a disease of the spirits (*pepo*). They told me that in order to have her cured they would have to play the *Ngoma ya Majini*. I explained to them that since she was a Christian it was improper for her to indulge in such rites. Then *Che* Kuthbert Nayopa (the husband) also said that he too did not like these rites, but his wife's relatives answered: "This is only your wife and not your relative. We are related to that woman and we reserve the right to do what we wish. We don't prevent her from membership of her religion but we also don't like you to interfere with our affairs. It's all our business." Kuthbert kept quiet and never said a word. . . . They insisted on playing the *Ngoma ya Majini* and refused to take the sick woman to hospital.

In such circumstances teachers often felt themselves to be in a position both dangerously exposed and ill-defined. Teachers feared witchcraft used against them by parishioners whom they had rebuked. They feared that their own resort to European medicine was in itself a cause of ill-feeling. "Many people here are Christians," wrote A. D. Mateso in the Tandahima log-book for May 14, 1950, "but they still believe in heathen traditions. I am really worried because the people here are discontented because I took my child to get some medicine for he is sick. Should I leave him without medicine?"

Teachers themselves had little well-founded appreciation of the scientific arguments for missionary medicine. They condemned alternative therapies not because these were bound to be ineffective but because they were outlawed by the mission. In fact many teachers believed that alternative therapies often *were* effective, and there is a good deal of evidence that they sometimes drew upon them when their own families were sick.

In this teachers were at one with some of the most convinced of African Christians. Church elders disliked the professionalization of European medicine, which undercut their own role in the healing of their own communities. In December 1932 the elders of Lukwikwa parish, where a mission hospital had recently been set up, asked the Bishop to allow them to call together all the "older people to discuss the number of deaths recently." They promised that *Chisango* divination would not be used "and said that the only purpose of the meeting was to comfort and encourage one another."

African priests shared many of these attitudes. As late as 1968 one of the students of the University of Dar es Salaam interviewed her uncle, the retired UMCA priest, Petro Ligunda. In his account of medical change we can see all the ambiguities of the process:

> *Chisango* in those days was used by the witch-doctors . . . as we use hospitals nowadays. The witch-doctor used to keep many *chisai* gourds, each with its own medicine inside, just as they keep medicine in bottles at the hospitals. . . . When the missionaries came they tried to convince the people that their new faith was better than their belief in *Chisango*. . . . The setting up of hospitals helped to prove the fact that the hospital's medicine was better than the witch-doctor's. But I don't think the people were wholly convinced that the hospitals could cure everything, because up to this time people are attending the "African doctors' hospitals" and they really do help since there are some diseases that cannot be completely cured at the hospitals. I believe that our doctors' medicine is good as long as it does not bring harm to the people. . . . We parish priests were told to preach on the fact that no Christian was allowed to use *Chisango*. We had to set an example, so we avoided this as much as possible. But . . . people's faith in the African doctor did not die completely since they still go up to be treated and some get cured. We cannot leave our traditional pattern of life—however much the pressure is exerted on us. It is part of us and if we feel something is good we do it.

MISSIONARY ADAPTATION AND MEDICAL MODERNIZATION: THE CLASH OF CONCEPTS

By the 1930s the UMCA Europeans had come to realize that mission medicine had not been triumphant, after all. The white clergy reacted very differently from the white doctors and nurses to this discovery. Vincent Lucas, by now the first bishop of the diocese of Masasi, plumped for adaptation. In July 1935 Lucas expressed his concern "with two great problems." The first was how to provide an adequately "African" education (Canon Spanton 1935, 148):

> The second great problem . . . concerned the medical work of his diocese. Despite all that had been done by white nurses and doctors, there was still a tendency to view medical efforts with suspicion, and with the exception of treatment by injection, to prefer the native charlatans who peddled medicines capable of affecting the most wonderful cures (so they said). The success of such people as the *Mchape* showed that we must discover some way of relating our medicine to their medicine.

The doctors and nurses, however, drew the conclusion that more modernization was needed rather than less; they put their faith in a more effectively scientific education so as to produce African dispensers and nurses who were fully committed to the gospel of Western medicine; they did not wish to relate to African medicine; and they condemned the Christianized initiation rites, of which Lucas was so proud, as dangerously unhygienic.

The master-stroke of Lucas's adaptation policy was his capture of the *Jando* initiation and circumcision ceremony for boys. His Christian version remained a communal rite, taking place out in the bush and involving ordeals and "tribal" instruction, but it was purged of offensive "heathen" elements and firmly controlled by African clergy and teachers. The doctors, for their part, objected to the continued use of "traditional" circumcisers, the unsanitary conditions in which the operation was carried out, and the general health risks of concentrating boys together at times of epidemic. "The circumcisions were carried out in completely primitive and barbaric fashion, the boys lying in the dust surrounded by a howling, yelling mob," wrote Leader Stirling. "I attended a number of these circumcisions but found the conditions utterly impossible for applying any useful treatment. . . . The problem was made much more difficult by the fact that the Mission had given its blessing to these ceremonies . . . and the mission hospital was expected to give full support" (Stirling 1977, 48).

Soon after Dr. Taylor's arrival in 1926, Lucas's first and only synod took place. A medical committee was appointed and duly reported that *Jando* circumcision should be abolished. Lucas vetoed the report. Dr. Stirling arrived in 1935. For five years he tried to clean up the *Jandos*; in 1940 he submitted a report urging that all boys go to the hospital for circumcision. Lucas's "only comment was that when I had been in the mission rather longer I might see things differently" (Stirling 1977, 48).

In his determination to persist with communal circumcision, Lucas was reflecting the whole philosophy of Indirect Rule as well as of adaptation. In 1928, for example, the Provincial Commissioner, Turnbull, had rebutted criticisms of circumcision within the initiation rites from the Director of Medical and Sanitary Services in Dar es Salaam by asserting that "natives have practiced it for generations and it is obvious that were it attended by the dangers . . . (postulated) . . . the system would have broken down. Native physicians are not all fools or rogues; they have excellent remedies and forms of treatment." Turnbull added that he admired Lucas's wisdom in seeking to "retain all that is sound in tribal initiation." He would lend no support to "extraneous influences which sought to destroy tribal and parental discipline without which native society in its present stage cannot hope to progress on sound lines." This chimed well enough with Lucas's wish to find a way of reconciling African and European ideas of medicine—but to the doctors it seemed like a perverse protection of all the forces in Masasi society which resisted the triumph of Western science.

For their part, the clergy who supported Lucas believed the doctors to be at fault in ignoring all sociological considerations. "They were gravely at fault," says Canon Lamburn, "and set us back a very long time." "The medical staff were dead-set against *Jandos*. The opinions of the medical staff took the narrow line that it was contrary to the Hippocratic oath for a doctor to assist in any way an operation performed by an unqualified person" (Lamburn 1970). The medical dangers had been overstated (Lamburn 1970):

> Bishop Lucas had had more experience of these rites than perhaps any.man living, and he declared that he had never known a single boy to die as a result of the operation as performed by an African operator in the dirt and filth of the forest. (God) has given parents the right and duty of bringing up their children.

African parents felt that a hospital circumcision was (Lamburn 1970):

> so far removed from all their traditions that they would not accept it as an initiation rite at all. . . . The secret could not be kept if the candidates went to hospital. More important still, how were the boys to be taught good manners? These are arguments not lightly to be put aside.

African mission staff were polarized on the issue. Some of the African medical assistants made a point of sending their sons to the hospital for circumcision "as converts to science." African teachers and clergy took pride in their sons being circumcised among their *jamaa*, as they said Christ Himself was circumcised.

So the *Jandos* remained a battlefield and often a humiliating one for the mission doctors. Two log-book entries suffice to make the point. The first comes from Lulindi, where one of the two main mission hospitals was situated. In 1942 Harry Dennis, the priest in charge, persuaded the parents of seventeen boys to have them circumcised by Stirling and his assistants outside the *Jando* rite. But the attempt failed:

> The boys were anaesthetized first with novakane [novocaine] but either it was insufficient or else the boys were frightened—a little of both perhaps—for the screaming in some cases was dreadful. I had hoped that this might be the beginning of getting a cleaner and better *Jando* going . . . but I fear we have rather destroyed our chances for some time to come.

The second comes from Masasi, where the other main mission hospital was based and where in August 1944 Dr. Taylor circumcised seven boys in the hospital. The log entry for August 27 reads:

> After Mass *Mwenye* Machinga called the *Wakuu* of the Church and local *wazee* to protest about the hospital circumcision which had been taking place here. He objects to the operation being done by a woman and the whole feeling of the meeting was with him. I explained that I could do nothing to interfere in hospital matters and that if the parents wished to take their children to Dr. Taylor nobody could stop them. They are quite prepared for hospital circumcision if done by a man but even so would prefer them done on the hill so that the customs of the *Jando* may be carried out.

THE CHURCH AND THE PROBLEM OF SPIRITUAL HEALING

In this controversy the perspectives of modern medical anthropology might incline us to be sympathetic to the position of the clerics rather than the doctors. The medical approach certainly was highly individualistic, while the churchmen stressed community. But having said so much about the ambiguities of the medical position we need to close by confronting a central ambiguity of the clerical position. The churchmen were saying that a purely technical medical approach was not enough; they were saying that some way had to be found to relate Christian healing to African healing. But they completely failed to respond to the African demand on them for spiritual healing. Despite all their reservations by this time about the position of the doctors, the clergy was nevertheless left offering only the hospital and the clinic as the contemporary fulfillment of the healing mission of Christ.

This outcome was in many ways odd. The UMCA was a child of the Anglo-Catholic movement, which had done more than anyone else to revive interest in spiritual healing within the nineteenth century Church of England (Gusmer 1974, 78–85). It strongly emphasized the sacraments, which Africans persistently invested with healing power. Time and time again its bishops came slowly to the conclusion that *maybe* in Africa the church ought to make use of exorcism, or the sacrament of unction, or the laying on of hands. As we have seen, the terrible cases of faithful teachers and clergy breaking down under the strain of witchcraft fear prompted some European clergy to argue that this spiritual evil must be contested with spiritual weapons. And all the time African Christians were pressing in on the mission for healing—investing this or that priest with the power to heal by touch, relying on baptism and communion for their power to cure. Yet little or nothing was ever done.

Looking back on his career as doctor and bishop, Hine recounted in 1924 a number of cases in which his episcopal touch had healed people, although without any conscious intention so to do on his part. He concluded (Hine 1924, 172):

> We may ask is it right to follow ancient usages—exorcism, unction—for those who are as they themselves may think possessed of devils, or beyond the reach of medical skill? Is it that in primitive tribes and lands beyond reach of civilization we come more closely into touch with those spiritual powers in which the ancient Church so fully believed?

Frank Weston, Hine's successor as Bishop of Zanzibar, went further than speculation. Weston believed that the "spiritual evil" of witchcraft "could only be met by spiritual weapons"; he believed in the reality of demonic possession. So "he issued careful regulations to his diocese. No one was to be presumed to exorcise but after prayer and fasting, confession and communion. The priest, or other exorcist, may not go to a possessed person alone, but accompanied by devout Christians." I have come across no evidence, however, to suggest that in Masasi district these regulations were ever put into effect—save for the one instance of Lucas's uneasy attempt to exorcise Benedict Njewa. The idea of spiritual healing was so little developed in Masasi that one of Lucas's successors as bishop of Masasi, Leslie Stradling, could still write in 1960 in terms as tentative as Hine's and still place upon the doctors the weight of carrying out Christ's ministry of healing (Stradling 1960, 84–85):

> A Christian hospital is not a bait to catch converts, nor an institution that will so impress patients that they ask to become Christians. . . . Whether or not the hospital brings in any converts we cannot . . . refuse to show to our people the love and sympathy of Christ. In this we are following his own example in Palestine, for he did not use his miracles of healing as a means of winning disciples. On the contrary, he often tried to keep his miracles secret, and wished people to come to him for his own sake, without being drawn by signs and wonders.
>
> On St. Luke's Day, when we were thinking of the healing power of the Divine Physician, I was trying to explain all this to a large congregation in church. I said that, although Christ was no longer visible in his human body after the Ascension, yet we see him still working the same works through his universal body, the church. In the Acts of the Apostles we find St. Peter and St. Paul and others, preaching to great crowds, healing the sick, raising the dead, guiding the conduct of Christians; yet it is really our Lord himself who is working

> through these people. So today the same miracles of healing are performed here, but they are done through the doctors and nurses and their God-given skill. In the Mission hospital here, across the road, it is Christ himself who is healing the sick.

Yet Stradling wondered, "Is this enough? Are we making sufficient use of what is specifically known as spiritual healing?" The church might use unction for the sick; it might institute regular prayers for healing. There was, of course, exorcism—and "though psychosomatic healing has not yet been fully explored, it is difficult for a Christian to argue that our Lord was wrong and that there is no such thing as spirit possession." And there was the laying on of hands. "In England," wrote Stradling, "a great deal of thought is now being given to this matter, but the whole subject has been befogged by quack-healers who often do much harm. . . . In our general uncertainty and ignorance at this time we have to walk carefully: but perhaps we walk too carefully" (Stradling 1960, 91–92).

This protracted "uncertainty and ignorance" in Masasi was all the more remarkable in that the Church of England had been discussing spiritual healing since the Lambeth Conference of 1908 and that a committee of the Conference had published *The Ministry of Healing* in 1924 (Gusmer 1974, 78–85). *Central Africa* sometimes showed awareness of this debate—as in October 1924 when it hailed "the most interesting and inspiring accounts given of the Mission of Spiritual Healing in South Africa" (*Central Africa* 1924, 42:206). But what is most striking about the recent historical accounts of the development of the spiritual healing movement within the Church of England is that the missionary dimension seems to hardly have been considered (*Central Africa* 1924). Bishops in East Africa might speculate that the "spiritual powers" of the ancient Church were especially appropriate there; but in practice spiritual healing was much more extensively employed in England right up to the 1960s than it was in Africa.

This was not really the result of a hard-line insistence on exclusively material and scientific medicine by the mission doctors. Frances Taylor attributed her success in operations undertaken when she was tired beyond endurance to the fact that "my Guardian Angel had taken charge." Leader Stirling developed a devotion to Therese of Lisieux during one of the Masasi retreats (Stirling 1977, 81):

> In the middle of the retreat, I was suddenly called to the hospital and found a child who had been brought in choking. I saw at once that he . . . was dying of aphasia. . . . But this time I had a new weapon. Desperately I called on St. Therese, "Pray for the child." Immediately, breathing began again, quiet and regular. St. Therese has been my great friend ever since.

The bishops wondered; the doctors were open to the idea of spiritual intervention; meanwhile the African Christians insisted on regarding the church as an agency of healing whether the missionaries liked it or not. Certain missionaries acquired a popular reputation for healing power—unknown to him, people used to crowd around Bishop Lucas to receive his blessing and so to be cured. *Jamaa* (kinfolk) carried their sick to receive baptism or communion. The atmosphere of this African church was usually not expressed in written statements for European eyes but rather acted out. Still, we have one fascinating document that brings the world of African Christian therapy vividly to life. In his extreme old age, Kolumba Msigala, one of the African canons on whom Lucas had so heavily relied, wrote in Swahili his reminiscences of the history of Masasi. Unashamedly the old canon described a world of spiritual healing.

Msigala described a journey on the Makonde plateau in the 1890s during which he cured a youth bitten by a *songo* snake. Msigala records himself as replying to his European companion's expressions of astonishment (Msigala n.d., 47–48):

> My father was a native Doctor, not a witch doctor, and he was a true Christian. I have inherited his work but I don't practice it now because I feel my vocation is to teach religion. When the natives are in trouble and need native medicines, I help them. This is our mode of life when we are left to our own devices.

But he plainly did not feel that in choosing to "teach religion" he had in any sense left the field of healing. He described a journey made with Bishop Smythies in 1886 during which Chief Liwengwa was converted and received baptism at the age of ninety. Msigala plainly shared the old chief's belief that he had found spiritual healing (Msigala n.d., 87, 106)

> Oh, what a terrible state the old man was in! He was very ill, almost at the point of death. . . . The Bishop came in and found him on his bed troubling and asked him in a loud voice, "What is troubling you?" He answered in a low voice which could just be heard, "I want your medicine." The Bishop answered, "Which?", and showing his episcopal cross which he was wearing said "This will do you good if you believe in God." Chief Liwengwa said "Give it me, give it me, please; I believe in God." The Bishop gave him another quite big cross and put on him the emblem of a catechumen. Next morning he could speak quite well and asked for baptism, saying "I have heard at Masasi where you come from that people are sprinkled with water three times and recover from their ills, and afterwards go on wearing this sign, abstaining from drink and heathen worship and polygamy. This is what I want and I shall be able to do this."

Msigala also recorded the healing power of Canon Porter:

> I remember that during his life this father performed a wonder—perhaps a miracle. One day I was walking with him on parochial work when he saw a child, called Karowanga, a chronic invalid. He washed his sores, but had no bandage, so he said "Haven't we a purificator in church? Let us bind up this

> child." By chance we had some suitable ones and he split these and bound the wounds of the child with them with medicine. For a time he prayed without uncovering them. When he uncovered them he was quite healed and his arm which had been bent was quite straight. The child was converted by this deed.

It was not surprising that at Christmas 1912 Lucas found that groups of Christians whom he had expected to be admiring the new crib were, in fact, making supplications at Porter's tomb (Lucas 1914, 238).

One might have expected that Lucas could have found here the point of contact he was seeking between African and European ideas of healing. But, in fact, the missionaries devoted a great deal of their time and energy to refuting African Christian ideas about the healing power of the sacraments and the miracles of living holy men. "I preached on the right use of medicines," recorded Canon Faussett in the Masasi log-book in October 1934, "and of the sacraments as against the idea held by some people that Baptism is a charm for curing ills for which people have neglected to seek medical aid, also to counteract the idea that sick people can be baptized whatever their moral state." Bishop Alston May of Northern Rhodesia told his confirmation class at Chipili in 1921:

> Now listen, the strength of Confirmation is not a new kind of "medicine." Understand this well. . . . Perhaps some Christians say in their hearts "I have refused the bad medicine of the heathen; now I will use the good medicine of the Christians. I want to resist Satan; therefore I will get the medicine of Confirmation and Communion, and the strength of God will keep away Satan." They are wrong altogether. . . . It is not medicine that you receive in Confirmation. God the Holy Ghost comes into your heart to help you drive Satan away yourself.

It turned out that the high church tradition of the UMCA made the missionaries less, rather than more, ready to adopt what a recent Anglican writer maintains is the true view that Communion is the essential sacrament of healing. The UMCA missionaries were under constant criticism from their supporters in England for ritual practices that were believed to be dangerously close to Roman Catholicism. "Almost all the clergy seem to be of the ultraritualistic party," wrote a critic, "and to regard the unfortunate African as an appropriate 'corpus vile' for the latest fashion of revived medievalism—fumigations, aspersions, processions, masses, compulsory confessions, etc." The robust Hine found Anglicanism in Zanzibar, with its rosary prayers and the veneration of the Sacrament in Benediction, full of "effeminate teaching and practices such as hysterical emotional females hanker after, but which is contrary to the robust common-sense of the ordinary English churchman." Duncan Travers, the secretary of the UMCA in London, invoked the authority of one of the Cowley fathers—those venerated figures of high Anglicanism—against a dangerous and excessive use of ritual in Africa. Wrote Father Puller:

> To my mind, it is most deplorable that the cults of images and the invocation of the Saints should be instilled into the minds and affections of the infant church of Zanzibar. I consider that practices of that sort are dangerous among European Christians, but they are tenfold more dangerous among newly converted African natives.

Time and time again the UMCA missionaries had to defend themselves against the charge that they were leading their converts into a "magical" view of Christianity.

They accordingly went to great lengths to insist that their sacramental Anglicanism was a religion of freely and fully willed choice of and association with Christ. Bishop Steere, so Chauncy Maples wrote after his death (Anderson-Morshead 1955, 115):

> was of [the] opinion that there was a danger lest many fervent in the adoration of the Holy Eucharist should incline to the error of directing their worship rather to the Presence of our Blessed Lord than to His Person. He feared lest some might even be led to adoration of *Res Sacramenti* and to substitute it for the adoration of the Person of the Divine Master in heaven, to which this mysterious Presence in the sacred elements is intended to lead us.

All this inhibited the UMCA in Masasi from developing a theology of healing that combined a call to repentance with belief in the direct spiritual power of Christ through the sacraments or through the preacher and teacher. Such a theology arose after Tanzanian independence and the transition from a missionary to national church, when Edmund John carried out his extraordinary charismatic ministry of exorcism and healing at Masasi Cathedral (Anderson 1977, 158; Chigunda 1975; Stone 1975). But during the missionary period, healing was left to the doctors—with the single exception of the inaugural blessing of new hospital and clinic buildings. Thus in 1939 Stirling described the opening of the new out-patient block at Lulindi (Stirling 1947, 38):

> The Bishop went all round the building, both outside and in, sprinkling holy water. Then standing in the doorway, he said the traditional prayers, exorcizing any evil spirit and praying for God's blessing on the building . . . finally placing it under the special protection of St. Michael the Archangel. The people here go in constant fear of evil spirits and witches, and even when they become Christians it is one of the hardest things for them to overcome and to realize that the Holy Spirit is stronger than all. So to know that a house has been solemnly blessed in the name of Almighty God, and that therefore no evil spirit can enter in is to give a great increase of confidence.

It was something—but it was not nearly enough to meet the hunger for spiritual healing in Masasi.

It seems clear that the initial high expectations of the effect of medical missionary work had not been realized by 1945. Western medicine had not scored the expected triumphs over disease; its ideological assumptions had not undermined African notionso causality. However, Lucas's policy of adaptation had not come close to Christianizing African concepts of medicine and healing. Together with the resentment that many African church employees felt at salary reductions during the 1930s, the unappeased desire for spiritual healing produced the sort of atmosphere that elsewhere in Africa gave rise to independent churches. This did not happen in Masasi, where the omnipresence of Islam and the abundance of prophetic healing movements appears to have ensured an adequately plural therapeutic environment (Ranger 1971). The UMCA was given a second chance to develop an adequate medical policy after World War II. After 1945 both the old ecclesiastical and the old medical assumptions were abandoned. Lucas's adaptation theory now seemed inert and reactionary; the watchword was now "development." For the doctors the emphasis moved from the individual patient in the hospital and towards community medicine, vitamins, family welfare, preventive medicine. There was a renewed and much more determined attempt to carry European medical ideas into African society. Whether or not this second attempt was any more successful remains for me an open question until I can do the same sort of intensive research for the later period that my sources have allowed for the earlier.

NOTES

1. An earlier, lengthier, version of this chapter appeared in *Social Science and Medicine* 15B (1981) (3): 261–277. The version published here is revised by the author and published with the permission of Pergamon Journals Ltd.

2. This chapter is based largely on four categories of evidence. The Universities Mission to Central Africa (UMCA) published a monthly periodical, *Central Africa*. The tensions among the missionaries were censored out of the magazine, but it provides very useful evidence for mission ideology. The earlier years of the magazine were filled with evangelical triumphs and disasters, but medical expansion constituted the new "pioneer" achievement of the 1920s and 1930s and was given much space. The United Society for the Propagation of the Gospel, Tufton Street, Westminster, has inherited the UMCA archives, in which there is to be found a great mass of missionary correspondence. In Tanzania itself the main source is provided by the log-book diaries that each UMCA priest, catechist, and teacher was obliged to keep. Some 200 of these diaries from the Masasi diocese, kept in English and Swahili, are now in the library of the University of Dar es Salaam. They provide remarkable and detailed material on conceptual interaction. Finally, I carried out a number of interviews with doctors, nurses, clergy, teachers, and clan heads in or from the Masasi area.

Twentieth-Century African Medicine

ELEVEN

Cold or Spirits? Ambiguity and Syncretism in Moroccan Therapeutics[1]

Bernard Greenwood

INTRODUCTION

Two distinct medical systems, the Prophetic and humoral, form the basis of the traditional Arabic medicine that is still predominant in Morocco. In general, the Prophetic system relates illness to psychological and social factors while the humoral system relates illness to ecological factors.

Although they are concerned with different theories of causation and types of illness, there is a profound syncretism where they overlap. Moroccan illness classification shows an ambiguous group of illnesses that refer to either system for their explanation and treatment. The group is made up of chronic and largely incurable organic illnesses—stroke; paralysis; neuralgias; loss of sight, hearing, or speech; and barrenness—and their explanation and management exemplify the society's response to illness for which there is little effective treatment.

This chapter examines how, through the symbols of the two medical systems the inner, personal experience of symptoms and signs is linked to outer, shared psychosocial or ecological factors, facilitating cultural and medical responses that optimize conditions for a return to health.

The analysis is based on a description of the semantic networks around the illness terms in the two systems in order to trace, in Kleinman's words, "the symbolic pathways of words, feelings, values and expectations, beliefs and the like, which connect cultural events with affective and physiological processes" (Kleinman 1973, 206). This approach has been applied to another Islamic society, in Iran, by Good (1977, 25). The conclusions complement those of Crapanzano (1973) and Dwyer (1978), for example, in their Moroccan studies.

Unless otherwise stated, all the data come from fieldwork carried out in the Ain Leuh region of the Middle Atlas Mountains of central Morocco between 1975 and 1977. This followed a year's medical practice in northern Morocco. The population of Ain Leuh is about 4,000, a mixture of 70 percent tribal Berbers, some of whom are pastoral nomads, and 30 percent Arabic speakers, originally from the Sahara. The economy is mainly a peasant agricultural one centered on the village with its artisans, tradespeople and market, and weekly markets nearby.

Information was gathered from informal interviews with patients and healers, small surveys, and attending healers at work. Additional periods of fieldwork distant from Ain Leuh were made because some types of healers were not well represented. These included a healing brotherhood in the western Rif mountains, and two well-known *cherif* (who were also branders), one in the Gharb coastal plain of northwestern Morocco and the other in the southern city of Marrakesh. Brief visits were made to other healers, including the Hamdasha brotherhood of Meknes, the subject of Crapanzano's study (1973).

Although the sources were varied, most were poor rural and urban-dwellers having little access to cosmopolitan medicine. They used herbal and humoral medicine and adhered to the beliefs and practices of the folk level of North African Islam, which is characterized by the presence of marabouts or holy men, religious intermediaries consulted for misfortune and illness. The notable homogeneity of Moroccan culture at this level—referred to as "Moroccan" in this chapter—includes attitudes and meanings around the supernatural, moral values, illness, food customs, and the natural world.

THE MOROCCAN MEDICAL SYSTEM

Arabic medicine[2] was made up of two medical traditions that coexisted during the early Islamic period: the magicoreligious Prophetic tradition, established soon after the Prophet's death; and the secular and empirical Galenic humoral medicine that was introduced by Arab scholars and elaborated as Yunani clinical science (Bürgel 1976, 44–61; Gran 1979, 339).

What contemporary Moroccans call "Muslim medicine" (*dwa musselman*), as opposed to "Christian," i.e., cosmopolitan medicine (*dwa nesrani*), can be shown to have comparable Prophetic and humoral components. Despite European influences and the presence of cosmopolitan medicine, Muslim medicine underlies most of Moroccan beliefs and practice concerning illness and health.

"Prophetic medicine" is used here as a convenient descriptive category and not in its conventional historical sense as "Medicine of the Prophet" (*tibb al-nabi*), which refers to an actual description and practice of Arabic medicine, including humoral and herbal components (Elgood 1962, 33–192).

The present humoral system, largely confined to a hot/cold opposition in foods, physiology and illness, is usually assumed to be a condensed or attenuated form of the full Galenic theory of four humors modified by four qualities, following the decline of Arabic science after the twelfth century. However, it is very similar to what some scholars believe are indigenous folk hot/cold dichotomies in Asia and Latin America, and its wholly Greek origins are debatable (see Foster 1978, 3–19).

Prophetic Medicine

The Bedouin medicine of Muhammad's time included treatment by diet, medicines, and the manipulation of impurity by bleeding, scarificaton, and cautery. These features became crystallized and legitimated by the *Qur'an* and *Hadith*, which affirmed such elements of the Bedouin worldview as spirits (*jnun*; sing. *jinn*), sorcery and the (evil) Eye as agents of illness and misfortune and the use of magic to counteract them.

Two important additions—the healing power possessed by the Prophet and inheritable by his descendants, and the power of the words, letters, and numerology of the *Qur'an* to prevent and treat illness—are perpetuated by the two types of Prophetic medical practitioner: the holy man (called in Morocco *cherif*, pl. *chorfa*), who traces his descent from Muhammad and may inherit practical techniques; and the *Qur'an* expert or scribe (*fqih*, pl. *fuqaha*). Both base their treatment on *baraka* (holiness, blessing), at the same time a social and moral attribute and a mystical and physical force (see Geertz 1968, 32–33, 44–45, 50–51). *Baraka* lies at the positive pole of the moral and medical worldview, opposite the notion of *bas* (harm, misfortune) to which the spirits and spirit-mediated sorcery and Eye belong.

Prophetic medicine is thus characterized by the concepts of illness from spiritual invasion and interpersonal harm, and healing by a power derived from both the Messenger and the Message of God.

The title *cherif* in its widest use describes one of the thousands of men and women claiming descent from the Prophet, who do not necessarily have any special endowment or status in society. It also denotes those *chorfa* (marabouts) who possess *baraka* and are honored and respected on account of membership of one of the holy or powerful cherifian families, a life of piety and religious devotion, or the ability to treat illness (Dermenghem 1954; Eickleman 1976; Gellner 1969). Those who officiate at the shrine of their ancestral saint or are members of religious brotherhoods founded by saints are visited by the sick to obtain healing *baraka* in the form of their saliva or shared food, especially bread, or by attending healing ceremonies and spirit exorcisms. Other *chorfa*, usually practicing alone, have inherited *baraka* specific to one or two illnesses, or possess techniques of cautery, scarification, and bleeding at prescribed points of the body, according to the organs involved in the illness.

While the rationale for these manipulations is the removal of disease-causing spirits, *chorfa* more commonly explain them simply as their inherited *baraka*, or as means of expelling cold. This merging of spirit invasion with humoral cold in the concept of illness from impurity or contamination will be examined later. There are thus three modes of treatment used by the *chorfa*: general healing *baraka* against any illness; technical skills for specific illness; and the exorcism of spirits.

The word *fqih* (scribe, learned person) had the general meaning of someone who has studied the *Qur'an* and *Hadith*, and who works as a school teacher, clerk, or official of the Islamic jural system, and also a particular meaning of a practitioner of Qur'anic magic (*hekma*), which attempts to influence events and relationships by supernatural means. In his ritual role the *fqih* propitiates spirits at births, weddings, funerals, and sacred feasts. He prepares talismans against misfortune for people, buildings, and enterprises; counteracts the Eye and sorcery; exorcizes spirits; and can treat any illness; but his special abilities concern supernaturally caused illness and spirit exorcism.

The medicine of the *cherif* and the *fqih*, then, is broadly of the Prophetic tradition, although both commonly practice herbal and humoral medicine as well.

As well as the *cherif* and *fqih*, the herbalist (*attar*) is commonly consulted. Other healers include the bone-setter, midwife, barber-cupper, market medicine seller, and religious or cult member.

The worldview that supports Prophetic medicine is centered around the spirits, who in Moroccan cosmology are a poorly differentiated race of supernatural beings living, usually invisibly, alongside humans and having a similar social structure. They are characteristically capricious, vengeful, libidinous, obscene, demanding, and violent and are generally respected and feared. A large body of custom relates to their avoidance and propitiation, and to places and circumstances where they are likely to be encountered.

But many Moroccans believe they have to live with the problem of sharing their environment with these beings who, if offended, retaliate by causing illness and madness. The severity of their attack determines in retrospect the type of offense. Insulting or neglecting to propitiate a spirit causes mild or transient symptoms. Treading on or injuring a spirit, especially a malevolent one, leads it to strike back; the victim is said to be slapped (*matruh*), or struck (*madrub*), with symptoms compatible with a blow—localized pain or loss of function, which is prolonged if the spirit enters the body at the point of attack. Sometimes the spirit takes over the whole person, who becomes inhabited (*maskun*) and suffers from depression, madness, epilepsy, or spirit possession.

Thus as conceptual elements in Moroccan cosmology, the spirits provide a medical and moral logic for the causation and treatment of illness. But they are also phenomenal beings that are seen in dreams, delirium, and trance, and by children and the mentally ill, and it is these images that feed common imagination in a society without shamanism or priesthood. Many anomalous phenomena are taken as spirit sightings, particularly animals or people of unusual appearance or behavior in markets, on journeys, or at night. Sometimes men claim sexual encounters with female spirits, or even enduring relationships with them. Such encounters are often blamed for subsequent illness or misfortune.

The circumstances of these spirit encounters confirm the moral element in the etiology of spirit illness. Not only must one avoid accidentally offending spirits in everyday life, but there is danger in thoughts of adultery, and going away from home or out at night without good reason, which parallels the danger to society from such opportunities for mischief. Fear of spirit encounter makes people reluctant to move out of their home and kin environment, a reluctance that is mirrored in the attitude that strangers may be enemies unless made safe by social contact and hospitality. It is not surprising that illnesses caused by spirits are often those that specifically incapacitate the expected social role of the victim.

The two other supernatural causes of illness are mediated by spirits. The Eye, or Eye of People (*el'âin ben adam*) is a glance of envy or ridicule that is retrospectively diagnosed as a cause of illness or misfortune. Most susceptible are new, young, attractive growing or successful things, and unexpected illness in children is often attributed to it. The responsibility for it lies fully with the victim, and fear of it is an effective control against greed, pride, and ostentation.

Sorcery (*es-shor*) is practiced alone or with the help of a professional *fqih* (sorcerer). It is used to harm enemies or their property and to influence affections between men and women. Sorcery substances or *Qur'an*-based formulas, often reversed, are placed near the intended victim, or in food, and as some of these substances contain poisonous alkaloids (especially datura [jimsonweed] and hammaline) and are administered over long periods, food sorcery is often effective. The practice, and more important the accusation, of sorcery is a common element in the conflicts inherent in Moroccan family structure, particularly in sexual relationships and the struggle between a young wife and her husband's mother for economic security (Dwyer 1978; Maher 1974).

Humoral Medicine

While the Prophetic system derives its authority from Islam, is illness-oriented, and relates illness and misfortune to psychosocial factors, the humoral system is its opposite—secular, empirical, health-oriented, and concerned primarily with the inner experience of the body in relation to the environment. It is centered on the opposition of heat (*sxon*) and cold (*berd*).

There are hot and cold foods and environmental factors, whose imbalance in the body produces "hot" or "cold" illnesses that are treated by foods of the opposite quality. There is a marked asymmetry in this opposition: most foods are hot and most illnesses cold, and the position of equilibrium, or health, imparts a negative value to cold foods and climate. Humoral medicines used to treat cold illness are usually doses of the hottest food substances. The qualities of wetness and dryness only concern foods affecting the consistency of the stool, and while the four Galenic humors are known by some experts, in normal practice only excess blood as a feature of hot illness, and excess phlegm as a feature of cold illness are conceptualized.

While there is general agreement on what are hot and cold illnesses, and each person can name at least a hundred food items as hot or cold, with a small number as neutral, in a small survey of twelve subjects there was full agreement on only 25 percent of foods.

Similar differences led Taylor to believe that there was no empirical validity underlying the Indian food classification (Taylor 1976, 293). But in the Moroccan case, analysis of why each item is held to be hot or cold reveals consistent, although idiosyncratic, logical principles derived from a core of empirical practice (Foster 1979; Greenwood 1984, 91–119).

Often no reason was given for a food's quality. Some were classified because their "origin" or "essence" (*âsil*) was hot or cold, and many were learned in childhood. When reasons were given they related to the effect on the body in health and in hot and cold imbalance or illness, as well as to taste, growing and eating season, and nutritional value.

Foods agreed to be hot include garlic, honey, most spices and aromatic herbs, milk, cheese, nuts, game, celery, and spinach. The only foods agreed to be cold are vinegar and turnip, with coffee and sour fruits usually cold.

Table 11.1 shows the agreed features of hot and cold foods, despite disagreement about what foods are hot or cold.

Hot foods make the body feel warm, relaxed and full of energy. The blood rises to the head, giving it a feeling of throbbing fullness; the skin is flushed, and cramps and joint stiffness are relieved. Cold foods make the body feel cold, stiff, and aching; the skin is pale and cold. Often the effects are only felt when a large quantity of the food has been eaten, or the subject is already in imbalance or ill.

It is now possible to see the underlying logic in the food classification. For example, ginger, cloves, and nutmeg contain volatile oils that produce the physiological effects of a warm sensation in the stomach and skin, the relief of intestinal cramps and bronchial congestion, and flushing in the head (Amerine et al. 1965, 236; Wade 1976, 1011). They are perceived as "hot," and are associated with the bodily warmth of summer, a feeling of well-being, and the symptomatic relief of colds, catarrh, and stomach cramps. By association, other piquant or strong-flavored spices are deemed to have the same effects, and are also classified as hot, "in essence."

Vinegar, citrus fruit, turnip, and coffee, in contrast, produce a cold, un-

TABLE 11.1. Features of Hot and Cold in Moroccan Medicine

	Hot foods	*Cold foods*
Taste	Piquant or bitter	Sour
General state	High energy	Low energy
General feeling	Warm, comfortable	Cold, uncomfortable
	Relaxed, sleepy	Restless, sleepless
Blood	Thinner, faster	Thicker, slower
	Rises to head	Weaker
Blood vessels	Full, open	Nil
Blood pressure	High	Low
Skin	Hot, flushed	Cold, pale, blue
Head	Full, throbbing, aches	Nil
Stomach	Warm	Cold, cramps
	Heavy	Light
Intestines	Constipated or nil	Loose, cramps
Joints	Relieve stiffness	Stiff, aching
Menstruation	Relieve cramps	Cause cramps
Nutritional effect	Strength, build body	Weakness, do not build body
Effect in hot illness	Exacerbate	Ameliorate
Effect in cold illness	Ameliorate	Exacerbate
Value for babies	Bad	Good
Value for old, wounded, tired	Good	Bad
General value	Good	Poor
Growing season (where applicable)	Summer	Winter
Eating season	Best in winter	Best in summer

pleasant sensation in the stomach, and sometimes cramps and diarrhea. They are perceived as "cold" and are associated with bodily cold, winter, and the feeling of malaise in common self-limiting illnesses. Any food that is sour or indigestible then comes to be called "cold."

Of the five recognized tastes, piquant and bitter are considered hot, sour is cold, and sweet and salt are neither.

Growing season is another criterion. Foods that can grow in winter are cold. Turnips and citrus fruits are harvested in the winter months and are cold, whereas olives, figs, and dates are harvested in summer and are hot.

With a positive value attached to heat and summer, the season of plenty, and a negative value to cold and winter, the season of hardship, ideas of nutritive value enter the classification. Foods that one can live on, such as meat, bread, and dairy produce are hot, while those that do not satisfy hunger, like lettuce, are cold. This nutritional logic is extended in such ideas as the separation of milk into butter, which is hot, and buttermilk, its watery remainder, which is cold. Egg-yolk is hot and egg-white cold, because "the yolk becomes the chicken and the white the feathers."

This complex food classification, with its related illness classification, is possible because of the marked polysemy of the words "hot" and "cold," which range from the sharpness and bluntness of a knife or human wits to ideas about age, sexual vigor, and fertility, which will be considered later. The whole forms a humoral paradigm that is found in Moroccan natural science, cosmology, and agriculture as well as nutrition and medicine.

The food classification affirms this paradigm. Although only a few "key" foods are pharmacologically active, the other "redundant" foods are classified as well, and they then act as sand strengthening the cement of the humoral theory.

How the latter are classified is less important. The "poor" or economical logic described by Bourdieu that gives symbolic systems practical coherence (Bourdieu 1977, 109) can be found in the way foods are linked to the domains of environmental temperature, inner feelings, and illness by metaphor and metonymy during explanation of their classification. Often a "switcher" is used, a single term that actively relates between two domains and brings its opposite term passively across (Bourdieu 1977, 23).

For example, one informant said that goat meat tasted sour and caused stomach cramps and joint stiffness, and was therefore "cold." Goats, he also observed, were intolerant of winter cold but cows were tolerant, so he reasoned that beef was "hot." In his preference for eating beef rather than goat in winter and for rheumatism, he was using a conceptual link between season and symptoms of imbalance illness which he had established by his perception about goats. "Goat," the cold term, was the active switcher between the domains; "beef," the hot term, was passively brought across as a "therapeutic" food.

By such processes climatic cold and warmth are internalized into viscero-receptive imagery; and illness symptoms are projected onto the ecological domain, the source of preventive and treatment measures.

The two subtle but perceptible states of excess heat and cold—one of throbbing warmth, dryness, flushing, fullness, and energy; the other of cramping cold, moistness, pallor, stiffness, and deficiency—can be quite well correlated to excess parasympathetic and sympathetic activity in the autonomic nervous system of Western physiology (Greenwood 1984, 133–144). The humoral and autonomic theories concern the same areas of physiology. In both there are two antagonistic bodily states whose balance shifts in response to environmental factors to maintain health. The difference is mostly one of emphasis; the humoral system is energetic, the autonomic system is functional, perhaps reflecting differences in worldview of their originators.

TABLE 11.2. Features of Hot and Cold in Moroccan Illness

	Hot illness	*Cold illness*
General state	High energy	Low energy
General feeling	Lethargic, warm	Restless, sleepless, cold
Usually felt in	Head, upper body	Back, lower body
Position	Superficial	Deep
Pain	Throbbing	Dull, constant or spasmodic
Blood	Thin, fast, rising Sometimes dirty	Thick, slow Weak, bad, sometimes poisoned
Blood vessels	Full, open	Nil
Blood pressure	High	Low
Skin	Hot, flushed, dry	Cold, pale, blue, moist
Head	Full, throbbing, aches	Nil
Stomach	Warm, swollen	Cold, cramps
Intestines	Constipated or nil	Loose, cramps
Joints	Nil	Painful, stiff, swollen
Secretions	Reduced or nil	Increased, mucous
Fever (where present)	With rigors, dry	Without rigors, sweating
Illness types	Full head, headache Heatstroke Sunstroke Eye illness Skin eruptions Childhood febrile illness Constipation Specific fevers Some diarrhea with fever	Cold, cough, influenza Ear, nose, throat } Chest, urinary } + secretion Indigestion, stomach Some liver, heart Menstrual, genital Barrenness, impotence Cancer Migraine Paralysis, tremor, wasting Stroke Loss of senses, speech Arthritis, rheumatism Neuralgias
Cause	Sun, heat, hot wind, dust Hot food, especially in summer	Cold wind, water, air, ground Cold food, especially in winter
Predisposing factors	Exertion	Going outside } Getting wet } when warm Cold drink } Discarding clothes in winter
Most at risk	Babies	Old, wounded or tired
Seasonal risk	Summer	Winter
Process in body	Heat enters blood, which rises to head	Cold enters blood and travels toward bones
Treatment	Cooling body Cupping, leeches, bleeding Cold foods, purgation	Warming body, burning Bleeding Hot foods and medicines
Incidence	Less common	Common

Exaggerations of the feelings associated with excess hot and cold foods become the symptoms of hot and cold illnesses, whose generally agreed features are summarized in table 11.2.

The heat or cold is thought to cause illness where it strikes, and also to travel in the body—heat expanding the blood vessels and rising in them to the head; cold penetrating directly toward the bones and internal organs—to produce the most common presenting complaints: "The blood has risen to my head," and "I ache in every joint." The excessive blood in hot illness and mucous discharges in cold illness suggest that the sanguine and phlegmatic humors of Galenic medicine may have become merged with the hot and cold qualities.

The humoral illnesses most accessible to Western understanding are sun and heatstroke, and colds or "chills" of the respiratory system, stomach, intestines, and bladder. Moroccans share the popular Western idea that going out into cold air, cold drafts, and getting wet are a cause of colds and chills (Helman 1978, 107), for which they use the same terminology (*berd*, *bruda*).

But Moroccans extend this folk wisdom to a fear of cold that does not appear to be warranted by the threat of these common ailments. Their concern with cold drafts when coming out of the baths (when they are ritually pure and have entered the liminal state in the cycle of ablution→prayer →return to normal life—and are therefore mystically vulnerable); when going outside at night (mystically dangerous); and the tendency to wear full winter clothes whatever the weather until May 1st, the formal start of summer, suggests that when physical cold enters the body it can become a contamination, in the way it spreads in the body and can be removed as "poisoned" blood from veins, which has an implicit mystical component.

While cold moves downward and inward and lingers there, heat moves upward and outward and is soon dissipated as skin eruptions and head and eye disorders. Although heat sometimes makes the blood "dirty," it is not so much a contamination as an extra fullness and energy of the blood itself. Young children are very hot and prone to hot illness; old, tired, or wounded people have little heat and are prone to cold illness. Heat is thus a symbol of the life-force, only dangerous in excess, that heals cold, the deficiency of life-force in the old and contaminated. It is not difficult to imagine how the symbolic opposition of hot/cold becomes transformed into that of *baraka* spirit invasion between the domains of the natural and supernatural environments.

But Moroccans usually see the humoral system as a theory of diet, oriented toward health rather than illness; as a normative and preventive system rather than a theory of abnormality like the Prophetic system. People bear it in mind in cooking, and meals are prepared according to their own state of health, the temperature and weather, and any special needs of their family. All Moroccans are aware of the dietary rules, whether using traditional terms or ideas about vitamins, protein, and calories. It may be the empirical nature of the system, in which every meal and bodily sensation—not just those in illness—is an experiment, that makes it so viable in contemporary Morocco. Modern foods are incorporated in the system. While home-pressed olive oil is extremely hot, factory-bottled oil is less hot and vegetable oil, of little value. A similar distinction is made between local brown flour and imported white flour. Tinned and packaged foods do not have the humoral value of their original components, and the diet system seems to be reflecting an anxiety that imported or refined foods may not sustain a subtle but important level of health.

ILLNESS CLASSIFICATION

It is now possible to examine how illness is classified in Morocco, leaving aside ideas based on anatomical site, which do not form a coherent system, to concentrate on classification based on causation and treatment. Illness classification is not an explicit system in the minds of Moroccans, except some healing specialists. There is a general reluctance to think or talk about illness in the abstract for fear of bringing it into being; and it is not always necessary for either healer or patient to ascertain cause before a general treatment is given. There are, however, precise names and adequate clinical descriptions for most illnesses in the knowledge of laypeople as well as specialists.

With the above reservations, some idea of illness categories can be elicited by asking "What is the cause of this illness?" and "What illness does this cause?" from which the following divisions can be obtained (fig. 11.1). The first division separates natural from supernatural causation. All illness "from God" has some mechanical explanation and is devoid of spirit involvement; the other three causes are supernatural, and are the province of Prophetic medicine.

Similar divisions are employed by *fuqaha* when they use such diagnostic aids as "the string" (*el xit*), but they divide supernatural cause between

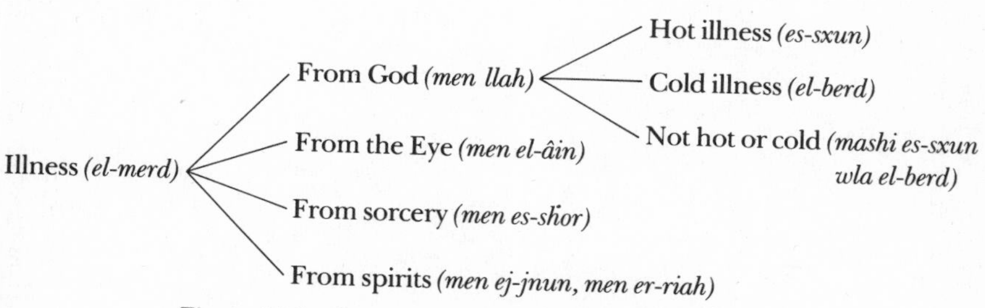

Figure 11.1. Causes of illness in Moroccan medicine.

TABLE 11.3. Illnesses Listed According to Cause

Natural cause			*Supernatural cause*		
	Humoral imbalance			Humans	
Miscellaneous	Hot	Cold	Spirits	Eye	Sorcery
Asthma		Rheumatism	Rheumatism	Childrens' sudden	
Goiter		Neuralgia	Neuralgia	or serious illness	
Diabetes		Sciatica	Sciatica		
Liver		Migraine	Migraine		
Gallbladder		Tremor	Tremor		
Jaundice		Progressive	Progressive	Progressive	Progressive
Spleen		wasting	wasting	wasting	wasting
Kidney		Paralysis	Paralysis	Sudden death	
Salt illness		Face	Face		
Appendicitis		Limb	Limb		
Heart		Stroke	Stroke		
Broken navel		Sudden	Sudden		
Piles		Blindness	Blindness		
Urinary difficulty		Deafness	Deafness		
Cancer		Mutism	Mutism		
Headache		Barrenness	Barrenness	Barrenness	Barrenness
Worms		Impotence	Impotence		Impotence
Eczema		Arthritis	Arthritis		
		Lumbago	Lumbago		
Hives	Acne	Cough	Squint		
Scabies	Skin rash	Sore throat	Tic		
Ringworm	Boils	Cold	Epilepsy		

Impetigo	Full head	Influenza	Madness	Madness
Lice	Headache	Bronchitis	Depression	Depression
Cholera	Red eyes	Pneumonia	Possession	
Smallpox	Sunstroke	Indigestion	Some deformities	Persistant
Scarlet fever	Babies' fever	Stomach cramps		Cough
Leprosy	Rash	Intestinal cramps		Itch
Rabies	Diarrhea	Diarrhea		
Trachoma	Eye illness	Constipation		
Cataract	Ear illness	Urinary pain, discharge		
	Diarrhea	Red eyes		
	Constipation	Earache, discharge		
	Measles	Mumps		
	Tuberculosis	Chicken pox		
	Typhoid	Whooping cough		
	Cholera	Chillblains		
	Malaria	Liver		
		Heart		
		Cancer		

"spirits" and "man." The *fqih* measures with a piece of string from the patient's right elbow to his fingertips, and then reads from one of his texts over the string and the patient. On remeasuring, the string may be of the same length as before, it may fall short of his fingertips, or be longer. If it is the same length there is "spirit illness" or good health; if it is shorter, the illness is "from man" (*men ins*), meaning the interpersonal harm of the Eye or sorcery; if it is longer, the illness is "from God," meaning natural events or accidents of circumstance in the material world, which include hot and cold illness.

Cause of illness thus falls into six categories: three natural—"hot," "cold," and a miscellaneous nonhumoral group; and three supernatural—spirits, the Eye, and sorcery.

While no individual employs an actual classification of particular illnesses, it is possible to synthesize a classification by listing illnesses under their attributed causes (table 11.3). Those that appear more than once have different opinions as to their cause. For convenience English medical and lay terms are used when they appear to be cognate with Moroccan ones; otherwise these are translated literally.

The nonhumoral category contains illnesses each with their own explanation. Thus diabetes ("sugar illness") is caused by eating too much sugar and treated by sugar-free diet, herbal medicines, and beans (some of which have been shown to have hypoglycemic activity) (see Khan et al. 1980, 1044), and insulin; kidney failure ("salt illness") is caused by eating too much salt; asthma is the result of excessive talking and anxiety, or inhaling dust, and treated with herbs; gallbladder illness comes from eating too much fatty and spicy food, but is not a hot illness; jaundice can be treated by yellow medicines. Some illnesses are not cognate with Western ones. "Slipped navel," for example, describes pain and diarrhea resulting from sudden movements on an overfull stomach, and is treated by cupping of the umbilicus, bleeding from the vein above the left heel, or pressure behind the left knee.

The remaining categories confirm the humoral and Prophetic systems as integrated elements in a pluralistic medical system. The classification shows there is a group of longstanding painful or incapacitating illnesses that are commonly attributed to cold, but sometimes to spirits. Although no distinction is made between this group and the remaining cold or spirit illnesses in their explanation of cause, a deeper analysis of these ambiguous illnesses, and especially ideas about their proper treatment, will lead to a second classification of the cold and spirit categories and help to explain this syncretism.

The present question is the nature of the ambiguity surrounding this group. Are they regular cold illnesses that are difficult to treat by humoral means? Or is "cold" used as a euphemistic metaphor for spirit attack, as opposed to possession? Are they a distinct group of illnesses from a contamination that is part mystical, part physical? Is the ambiguity in individual minds as well as between individuals, and does the ambiguity reflect a social change away from traditional beliefs about the supernatural world?

The attribution of spirit cause is complicated by the fear that thinking or talking about spirits may attract or offend them. Embarrassment, euphemism, irony, and protective formulas surround their mention, so that while illnesses such as paralysis and barrenness may be attributed to spirits in abstract conversation, in the face of actual cases people may class them as cold. They may only diagnose spirits when, as in epilepsy, madness, or gross personality change, they "see" the possessing spirit in the behavior of the person.

But there is a genuine distinction, based on the pathology of cold illness. Cold slowly penetrates deeper into the body. While it is still in the skin and flesh it causes coughs, colds, cramps, diarrhea, and discharges, with acute symptoms such as fever and general malaise. But once it has reached the bones or deep organs, perhaps as long as fifteen or twenty years later, it causes deep pain, paralysis, or barrenness, without acute symptoms.

While cold is still superficial, it can be treated with hot foods and medicines and leaves no permanent damage. Once it is deep it is difficult to remove with hot medicines, and needs treatment by a *fqih*, or powerful cherifian *baraka*. The implication again is that cold that penetrates deeply becomes transformed from a purely physical imbalance into a mystical contamination requiring the special medicine of the mystical domain.

"Deep-Cold" Illness

I call this group "deep-cold" illnesses. It includes arthritis, rheumatism, neuralgias, sciatica, migraine, tremor, wasting, stroke, paralysis, sudden blindness, deafness, and mutism. They are in general chronic degenerative illnesses of middle and old age, in contrast to the milder, acute, and self-limiting "simple" cold illnesses.

How are the two distinguished by those who categorize them *all* as cold illnesses? First, in the way they are mentioned: when the word "cold" describes one of the deep-cold illnesses, it is said softly with lowered eyes, expressing anxiety and embarrassment that is entirely absent in the mention of ordinary cold illness. Second, regarding how they are treated: deep cold is "cold that cannot be treated by hot medicines; it needs a *fqih*." The *fqih* himself may make the distinction by his choice of treatment, using for one case of cold, hot medicines and diet and for another case, writing out Qur'anic treatment. Third, how illnesses respond to treatment: hot medicines are usually tried at first, but when they have no effect or provide only temporary relief in, for example, rheumatism and neuralgias (as with the "deep-heat" embrocations used in the West), a *fqih* or *cherif* is sought, and little success is expected.

The most common deep cold is *buzellum*, a sciatic pain down the leg from

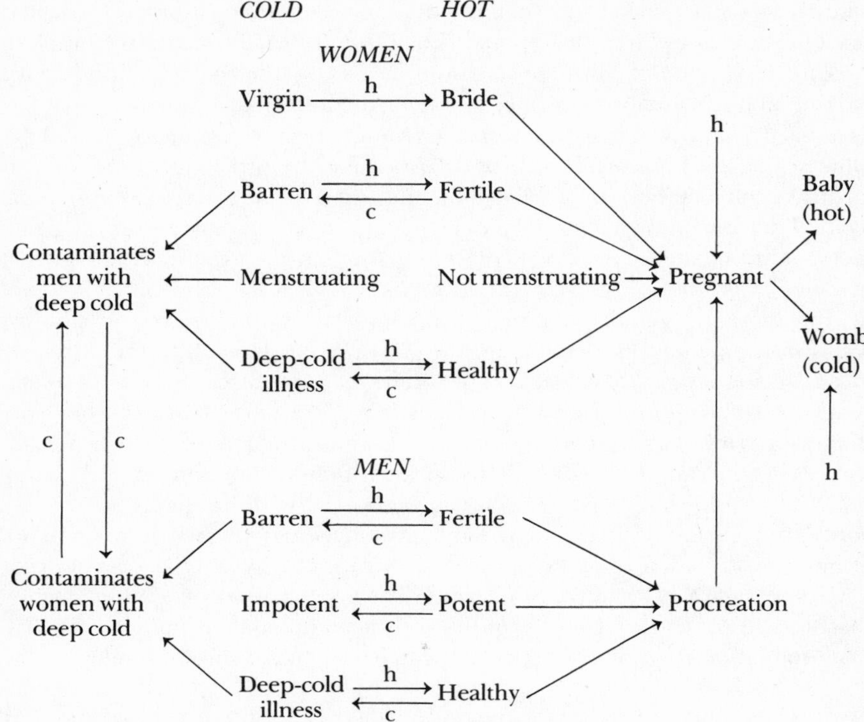

Figure 11.2. Hot and cold in Moroccan reproductive symbolism.

the hip. It is also called *rheumatism*, and the knee may be painfiul and stiff, with weakness or wasting of the muscles. It is usually attributed to cold from drafts or water, but sometimes to sexual contamination. For example:

> *Buzellum* is cold, not from the outside but from women. They can give it to men and catch it from men, but originally it is from Eve's womb. All Muslim women bring this cold.

This idea of the danger inherent in female sexuality is also found in the ritual impurity of menstruating women, with whom intercourse would cause cold illness. But in both sexes barrenness, associated as it often is with pelvic infection, abortion, or venereal disease, is a cold illness that can be sexually transmitted either way. It has a place in the pattern of hot and cold symbolism in reproduction (fig. 11.2). Barrenness is treated with hot medicines or pessaries to "heat up" the sex organs; the Berber bride, at her wedding, crouches over, smoking "hot" incense to heat her womb and make her fertile.

Menstruation is a cold condition, and the cramps are relieved by hot food. At childbirth hot substances are rubbed into the abdomen, "so that the contractions do not cool." The birth leaves a baby that is hot and must not eat hot foods, and a mother and her womb that are cold, and must be revived with a special hot diet. The hottest known substance, ambergris, is taken by old men to restore their sexual vigor when they take young wives, but it should never be taken by those under the age of forty as it produces boils and eruptions.

Deep Cold and Spirit Invasion

It has been established that the deep-cold illnesses imply a mystical and sometimes sexual contamination. A connection can be found between this contamination and the idea of spirit invasion held by some people to be the cause of these illnesses. For example:

> *Buzellum* needs to be treated with hot substances, or by the *fqih*. It results from such things as getting your feet in water. My brother was playing in a fountain when suddenly his feet and legs hurt. They were almost paralyzed with weakness. Perhaps the *jnun* had caused it. Therefore we called the *fqih* to write.

Here water could have been the source of cold. But spirits live in fountains and resent being trodden on by clumsy children; the boy's family thought this the likely explanation.

Spirits live in water; they also travel in winds. The linguistic link between winds and spirits is their common word root, RAH, from which come spirit, soul, self, breath, and wind. The classical word for spirits, *ej-jnun* (night-beings, demons), is often considered insulting to them, and *ar-riah* is the most common term. The word for winds is very similar, *er-reh*, but, as one informant explained,

> The wind does not bring the *jnun*—that is not why they are called winds. We use the word for winds in a slightly different form to mean *jnun* because they move and strike *like* a wind.

Whether illness from contact with winds and water is retrospectively attributed to spirits or cold is a matter for individual interpretation, and may depend on worldview. Two healers—one a progressive and orthodox *cherif* who denied the existence of spirits, the Eye, sorcery, and *baraka*; the other, a traditional *fqih*—gave identical accounts of how illness from draughts is caused, in the one case by cold, in the other by spirits. In both cases the agent entered the body and moved deeply to the bones, causing local symptoms, and spread through the body in the blood to cause a general malaise. Even their diet treatments were the same. In their food classification both were unusual in giving coriander as the only cold herb, but the *fqih* said it had a spirit in it (his only mention of spirits in food). He also said that cold illness predisposes to spirit attack: "When cold has entered, spirits can enter."

It seems that one conceptual structure can serve two worldviews, but not exactly. Advocates of humoral causation look for dietary or environmental indiscretion; while those of spirit causation look for a breach of customary behavior such as treading in a fountain, or suspect immorality by the victim. For them, leaving a house at night while very heated is not dangerous because of cold winds, but because it implies illicit sex. The dividing line, in the group of illnesses under discussion, depends on where, metaphysically, the source of harm that can enter and contaminate the body originates—in the natural world of Aristotle or the supernatural world of the Bedouin tribesman.

CLASSIFICATION BY TREATMENT

Just as the deep cold illnesses are distinguished from simple cold by the way they are treated, when the same illnesses are caused by spirits they are treated as spirit contamination rather than possession. The mechanism is one of attack and invasion rather than inhabitation by a spirit personality, and the spirit is expelled, without ritual or theatre, by a purely *technical* exorcism, using *baraka*, that is *institutionalized* in Qur'anic magic or cherifian manipulations. By contrast, the other spirit illnesses—epilepsy, madness, depression and possession—are seen as inhabitation by a spirit personality, and are treated by *ritual* exorcism, specifically, invocation and expulsion during the victim's trance, using *baraka* that is *personalized* in the state and behavior of the exorcizing *fqih* or *cherif*.

A second classification can now be drawn up, based on treatment rather than cause, in which the humoral category of table 11.3 is separated into "hot," "cold," and "deep cold"; and the spirit category, into "spirit invasion" and "spirit possession," as shown in table 11.4. "Hot" and "cold" illnesses are treated as humoral imbalance; "deep cold" and "spirit invasion," as contamination.

A few illnesses remain separate in the shared category of contamination. Tic and squint were never attributed to cold; nor were impotence, arthritis, and lumbago to spirits in this study.

When comparing classification by cause with classification by treatment, the differences are not always clear-cut. Some of the deep-cold illnesses, the painful ones and barrenness, are treated with hot medicines as well as Prophetic Medicine. So is it justifiable to distinguish two causes—cold as imbalance and cold as contamination—when many people assert that they are causally identical?

Faced with a group of chronic and serious illnesses, the advocates of spirit

TABLE 11.4. Illnesses Listed According to Treatment

Humoral	*Allopathy*	*Removal of contamination*		*Spirit Excorcism*
Hot	Cold	Deep cold	Spirit invasion	Spirit possession
Acne	Cough	Impotence	Tic	Epilepsy
Skin rash	Sore throat	Arthritis	Squint	Madness
Boils	Cold	Lumbago		Depression
Full head	Influenza			Possession
Red eyes	Bronchitis			
Sunstroke	Pheumonia	Rheumatism		
Heatstroke	Indigestion	Neuralgia		
Baby's fever	Stomach cramps	Sciatica		
Rash	Intestinal cramps	Migraine		
Diarrhea	Diarrhea	Tremor		
Eye illness	Urinary pain, discharge	Progressive wasting		
Ear Illness	Red eyes	Paralysis		
Measles	Earache, discharge	Face		
Tuberculosis	Mumps	Limb		
Typhoid	Chicken-pox	Stroke		
Cholera	Whooping cough	Sudden		
Constipation	Chillblains	Blindness		
	Liver	Deafness		
		Mutism		
		Barrenness		

invasion have no trouble explaining the concept of contamination. But the advocates of humoral cold have to imply that physical imbalance has been transformed *inside the body* into mystical contamination, perhaps because they do not admit that the latter is in their external environment. They see spirits as causing only possession, and not as a common danger in winds and water or the cause of the relatively common deep-cold illnesses. They seem to be avoiding the anxiety of attributing these illnesses to supernatural cause, and their explanation fits the symptoms and treatment.

Another use of the diagnostic string shows a similar way of thinking. In the normal person, with the head bent forward as far as possible, a length of string, passed from between the eyebrows over the head to the prominent vertebra at the back of the neck, measures the same as the circumference of his head. But often in someone suffering from "full head," the length taken at the first measurement will not reach around the head. The Moroccan explanation is that the head has expanded. The observer's explanation, knowing that the skull cannot expand by more than a minute fraction, would be that muscle tension and perhaps engorgement of the neck in this condition prevents the head from bending as far forward, so that the first measurement is *less* than the head circumference. But the Moroccan explanation is more satisfying for the patient; his head feels as if it is bursting, and his science confirms it.

As with the reasoning around deep cold, faulty logic has given the facts a better meaning, and meaning is more important than how it is obtained, especially for the patient.

It can be seen from this analysis of humoral medicine that in structuralist terms, symbolic transformations of the hot/cold opposition occur between different experiential domains that link the outer, shared world of the environment to the inner, private world of illness experience. Such a chain of linked domains might be: season → climate → temperature → external perception → food → internal perception → imbalance illness → contamination illness. Meaning is preserved and accumulated along the chain by the processes described.

It is important that the chain is demonstrable in single individuals. For the symbols of the outer world to have real expressive and therapeutic possibility in actual illness, their connection to inner perceptions must be in the actor's mind, not that of the observer or a hypothetical member of the society. Figure 11.3 shows how one informant's network of meanings around hot and cold links his environment to bodily perceptions, illness, and ideas about treatment.

"The Blow of The Bride"

Another chain of meaning that links the inner experience of contamination illness to the domain of mental illness, as defined by Moroccan culture,

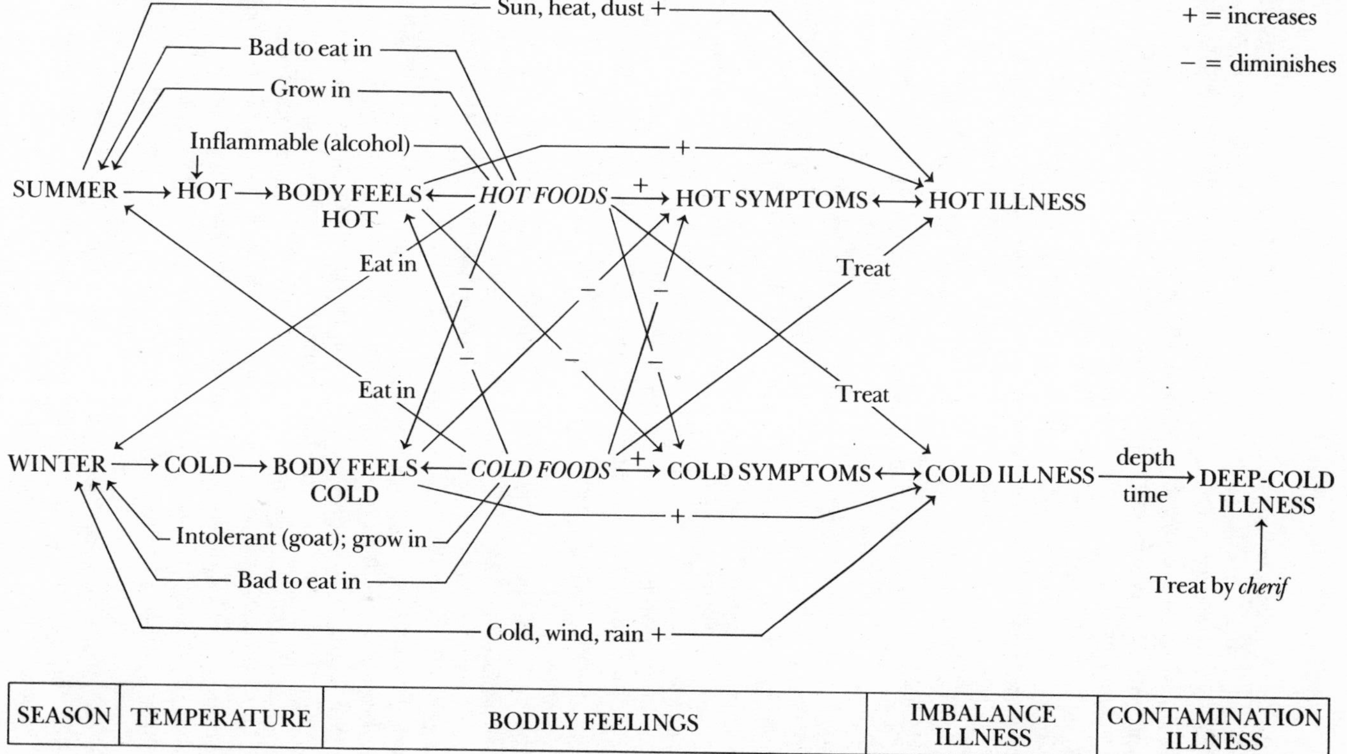

Figure 11.3. One person's network of meaning around hot and cold foods in Moroccan culture.

shows the symbolic transformation between hot/cold and *baraka*/spirits. It is centered around spirits in their phenomenal aspect, and can be traced, although with less methodological purity, by using an illness called *el-ârussa* (the Bride) which spans the categories of cold and spirit illness.

In the Gharb, a coastal plain in northwestern Morocco, a few *chorfa* specialize in the treatment of "the Bride," an illness characterized by the onset of deep pain in one side of the head, face, body, or a limb. After a few days the pain may subside but leave the side of the face or limb paralyzed or contorted. Sometimes the paralysis strikes suddenly and painlessly, and it can also leave the victim dumb, deaf, or blind. Commonly the pain continues without paralysis, in the form of migraine, sciatica, or other neuralgias, or the painful, stiff, or swollen joints of rheumatism.

The cause is cold. The victim has become overwarm in the baths or at home and then gone outside without sufficient clothing, and been struck by a cold draft on the affected part. The cold enters the body and moves in the blood deeply and painfully toward the bones, destroying the flesh if it causes paralysis. No informants knew why it is called "the Bride." When someone is struck by the Bride there is no idea of a blow by a bride; any illness can "strike" (*derb*). Nor is the Bride the wind or in the wind. The Bride is simply the illness.

Treatment, which is difficult, is by a *cherif*, either with the *baraka* of his saliva, rubbed into the skin or eaten in bread, or by letting out the cold through multiple cuts, applying heat with brands, and rubbing in garlic, a very hot substance.

Sometimes another explanation is given in the Gharb for the Bride: a spirit strikes and enters the body, living in the blood and feeding on the flesh of the affected part to cause pain and paralysis. In the treatment, the *cherif's baraka* compels the spirit to leave, or he draws the spirit out of the body through the cuts and its hate of fire and garlic. There is still no reason for the name. The Bride is the illness, not the spirit.

In Ain Leuh in the Middle Atlas, the Bride is not a common term for illness, but it may be heard in three contexts. First as a name for one-sided paralysis of the face attributed to the slap of a spirit, and more commonly called *matrush*, the slap. Second as a name for the paralysis, deafness, temporary blindness, or madness caused by accidentally harming a spirit, through such actions as pouring water on ashes, emptying a hot teapot on the ground, or urinating on the ground without saying "*Bismillah*" (in the name of God); such illnesses are taken to the *fqih*, but are difficult to treat. Third, *el'ârussa*, or the Berber word for bride, *taslit*, is sometimes used for an epileptic fit. It is said that the spirit inhabiting some possessed people craves for meat, and if they see meat they have a fit.

No explanation of the name was offered in this part of Morocco, but in the southern city of Marrakesh, the Bride is the name of a female spirit with flowing hair and the legs of a monkey. If she is inadvertently harmed, she retaliates with blows that cause paralysis.

Again in Marrakesh the Bride is a name for Ayesha Qandisha, a female spirit well known throughout Morocco. The stereotype story is that she appears as a beautiful and seductive girl to men when they are alone in the fields. The man makes love to her, and sometimes even secretly marries her, but then she changes into a hideous hag with long hair, a monkey's body with pendulous breasts, and feet of a goat or camel. She becomes violent and demanding, and her victim may be struck with paralysis, or deteriorate into a shambling, ragged, crazy outcast, wandering and homeless, the typical image of madness.

Naughty children are often threatened with "Behave, or Ayesha Qandisha will get you!"—and she is widely feared by children and adults. People hear the clanking of the chains around her neck and her weird cries at night, and it is said that fear of her "keeps men from seducing women while their husbands are working in France." She is "the defender of women's honor."

To women she can be an ally in their struggle to influence events beyond their control in a male-dominated society. She is thought to live in the unusual trees, rocks, or caves where women go to burn candles or tie knots of cloth as an *'ar*, or conditional promise, such as to sacrifice a chicken if she helps them. But women too can come under her power if they fail to keep these promises.

One solution for men and women made ill or possessed in this way is to join one of the spirit cults common among poor urban dwellers, such as the Hamadsha of Meknes, described by Crapanzano (1973). At their meetings, named spirits, especially Ayesha Qandisha, are invoked and appear to those in trance and demand sacrifice, head-slashing, and other self-mutilations. Healing is sought in attendance, perhaps for life, at these meetings, through a personal relationship with spirits—an open-ended commitment to an often incomplete participational form of exorcism, which Crapanzano calls a "symbiotic cure."

Thus "the Bride" has a number of meanings: as a group of illnesses, practically all of the deep-cold category, caused by cold and treated as deep-cold contamination; as the same group of illnesses caused by spirit attack and treated as spirit contamination; as facial paralysis caused by the slap of a spirit; as spirit possession in the form of epilepsy; as a female spirit who paralyzes if injured; and as the dangerous Ayesha Qandisha.

It seems likely that all these meanings originally derived from the typically ironic epithet for her, which has become a description of paralysis and associated illness, even when they are ascribed to cold. A bride's glance is considered dangerous—during the three-day wedding she is veiled and must not look around at others, for this reason more than her vulnerabiltiy to the Eye—but Westermarck records that her glance provokes accidents, fighting and murder; but never illness (Westermarck 1914, 263).

"The Bride," like hot and cold, is a term whose meanings lie on a pathway between the inner and outer world. The pathway follows spirits from cultural concepts to progressively more phenomenal entities; and types of spirit illness and their causation and therapy depend on this degree of phenomenal reality. Along the pathway can be traced cultural symbols that are hidden or implicit in ideas about deep-cold illness, but explicit in the realm of mental illness, spirit possession, and exorcism. This realm provides the meaning in ordinary illness that is suggested by the name "the Bride." "Normal thought cannot fathom the problem of illness," Lévi-Strauss says, "and so the group calls upon the neurotic to furnish a wealth of emotion heretofore lacking in focus" (1963, 181).

The neurotic realm is the prime concern of the Hamadsha brotherhood as a healing cult. Crapanzano divides the aetiology of spirit illness into the "explicative" and "participational" modes of responsibility. This parallels the distinction already made between spirits as concepts dealt with by institutionalized *baraka*, and spirits as phenomena dealt with by personalized *baraka*. Crapanzano's study concerns the second mode, and Ayesha Qandisha in particular. He notes that the Hamadsha were "able to effect, often dramatically, the remission of symptoms in paralysis, mutism, and sudden blindness, etc." but only when these were symptoms of functional, that is, neurotic, hysterical, or psychotic illness. "They are, in their own fashion, superb diagnosticians, and generally avoid treating those illnesses which are regarded by Western medicine as organically caused. They seldom treat epilepsy" (Crapanzano 1973, 5). Illnesses asociated with participational spirits, at least in the Hamadsha context, can be seen as hysterical paralyses of movement or the senses, and the "social paralysis" of the madness stereotype. The Hamadsha seem to be able to distinguish illness as psychosocial breakdown from organic illness.

Cure is not the only aim of their therapies. By becoming a cult member, the individual is provided with a new social identity, set of values and cognitive orientation. "This new outlook may furnish him with a set of symbols by which—in the case of psychogenic disorders, at any rate—he can articulate and give expression to those particular psychic tensions which were at least in part responsible for his illness. This symbolic set is closely related to the cult's explanation of illness and theory of therapy" (Crapanzano 1973, 5).

AYESHA QANDISHA AND THE SYMBOLISM OF PARALYSIS

In his structural and psychoanalytical analysis of Hamadsha legend and ritual, Crapanzano notes that in men, paralysis, impotence, and sterility all prevent the performance of the male role, and suggests that the hysterical symptoms in men are expressions of femininity and inadequacy in response to the tensions of this role. In Hamadsha therapy the subject's feminization is symbolically completed in his devotion to Ayesha Qandisha, and he is then revitalized through the "male" *baraka* of the Hamadsha saints.

No analysis was made of the treatment of female patients. The broader dynamics of therapy must be assumed to include Ayesha Qandisha as the possible ally of women, as she is for Hamadsha men, dangerous only if neglected. Like the spirit that wrestled with Jacob, she strikes with lameness but also brings blessing to the underdog.

Moroccan men often stereopype women as sexually insatiable, promiscuous, capricious, treacherous, and in league with the spirits, and at the same time weak, inferior, and noncontributory vessels for their children; and these attitudes are used to justify the seclusion and oppression of women. But to some extent they are shared by women about themselves and, perhaps with more reason, about men. At a deeper level these qualities may be the antithesis of the "ideal" Islamic personality, the Constricted Self described by Lerner (1958, 73), and are on this account dangerous for both men and women, as is Ayesha Qandisha, who embodies some of them.

It is in the image of Ayesha Qandisha that the symbolism underlying attitudes to paralysis and associated illnesses must be sought. For it can be assumed that these attitudes, explicit in hysterical cases, are carried over to organic cases because the two are not distinguished—by ordinary people—by appearance or cause. Ayesha Qandisha is desirable and seductive, and at the same time libidinous, quick-tempered, and demanding. She attracts and then dominates men and punishes them with paralysis, barrenness, or madness, undermining their male role (Dwyer 1978, 137–138). More explicity, Fatima Mernissi, a Moroccan sociologist, calls her "the castrating female" (Mernissi 1975, 12).

For a man, Ayesha Qandisha's ambivalence reflects his ambivalence toward women, most acute in the conflicting attitudes of strong emotional dependence but gender and kinship superiority toward his mother. If the "solution" for men's ambivalence is the domination of women, the punishment for this "social crime" may be apparitions of Ayesha Qandisha, the paralyzing female, haunting those who cannot cope with the conflict. It could be said that whereas in Europe spirits are the ghosts of wronged individuals haunting society, Alyesha Qandisha is the ghost of a wronged society haunting individuals.

While these apparitions may be symbols of psychosocial conflict embodied in collective tradition, it is possible to look for their phenomenal origins in remembered real events, whose "traumatizing power is immediately experienced as myth" (Lévi-Strauss 1963, 202). Circumcision is the single childhood trauma that every Moroccan male experiences. Cansever has shown by psychoanalytical testing that Turkish boys after circumcision associated women with aggression and wounding, and represented themselves as feminized and sometimes *with limbs missing* (Cansever 1965, 321). It has been noted that Ayesha Qandisha is used as a threat to naughty children. Are there any features of the circumcision ritual that might imprint in a boy her image as an ambivalent, paralyzing, "castrating" female spirit, and commit him to the Moroccan male attitude toward women?

The word for circumcision, *tehara*, means "cleansing," and its stated purposes are to make the child, aged between four and six, ritually clean, so that he can start going to the mosque and *Qur'an* school and to make him completely male. From this moment he will spend his time more with his father and brothers. Circumcision severs the infant's anomalous ties with his mother's lineage, and places him fully in his patrilineage. Thus the ritual is outwardly oriented toward affirmation of his maleness.

But the boy's experience is of a different nature. Like all major feasts, circumcision is organized by women, but circumcision is called "the women's feast," and they particularly enjoy it, while the men stay uneasily in the background. The boy is traditionally brought by his mother's brother, sometimes ritually "stolen" by surprise to the room or tent where he will be circumcised. One male informant said: "Circumcision is good because it is like what happens to a bride—the deflowering and the blood. It is the same for her as she sits fearfully waiting for her husband."

Sometimes an aunt or old neighborhood woman, the *aguza*, dances and cavorts in front of him as he enters. She is dressed in a long white robe, her hair is loose (a sign of sexual availability) and disheveled, her face is blackened with soot, and her eyes and lips are garishly made up. Sometimes, wearing a chain around her neck which she strikes against a bowl, she chants and makes grotesque faces at the boy. Her purpose is "to amuse him, to keep him from his pains"; and no informant accepted that she represented Ayesha Qandisha.

The circumcision is usually done by barber scissors and the wound traditionally staunched with oleander ointment, the pain of which many adult men remember. On his return home the boy's hair, hands, and feet are dyed red with henna and his head wrapped in a headscarf, both of which are normally reserved for women. He sits where the bride does at weddings; often he is called "the bride of circumcision." Amber beads may be tied to his ankles with red thread, which is also tied around the legs of chickens to treat paralysis. Then he is coddled by his mother and the other women, who all crowd in to admire and touch his penis. His mother feeds him sweetmeats, and may kiss his open mouth and tell him, " Now you are a man."

Crapanzano (1973, 329) has also observed a few of these features of circumcision, and suggests that this single childhood trauma might be at the root of Hamadsha men's feelings of inadequacy and femininity. But for

Moroccan men, the ritual seems structured as if to ensure the psychological effects that Cansever found, to mold the male ambivalence toward women and perpetuate its results, and to engender the symbols of conflict inherent in the male role. Further, it may be relevant to the group of paralyzing illnesses known as "the Bride"; and it may be a continuing source of the image of Ayesha Qandisha as both myth and apparition.

THE "EFFECTIVENESS OF SYMBOLS" IN ORGANIC ILLNESS

The Hamadsha therapy is centered around spirits as features of mental illness and hysterical, or functional paralysis, blindness, and deaf-mutism. According to Crapanzano, through the resolution of the opposition between Ayesha Qandisha and saintly *baraka*, a symbolic transformation takes place that may restructure "psychic reality" sufficiently to resolve the conflict producing the symptoms. Lévi-Strauss has suggested that in organic illness such transformations may also be capable of restructuring "physiological reality" through the inductive property of symbols whose structure is analogous to organic structures (Lévi-Strauss 1963, 202).

In his example of the Cuna medicine song that is recited to facilitate difficult childbirth, there is no evidence for his assumption that the song actually worked on patients.[3] But there are studies from psychosomatic research showing that imagery and suggestion using specific symbols may affect analogous organic structures and processes (Barber 1984).

Whether it is necessary to revive Frazer's analysis of magical efficacy,[4] it is certainly close to the understanding implicit in the therapy of organic paralysis, and so on, when seen as contamination by spirits. But in these mundane organic illnesses the symbols lie dormant, embedded in conventional attitudes and mechanistic treatments, and sealed over by fear of illness and the supernatural. They only become explicit and therefore "potent" in the areas peripheral to organic illness, that is, the functional illnesses and the minor symptoms of humoral imbalance. At these poles ideas about illness are manifest from their experience; in the center they have been drawn in as metaphors, the only available tools in the face of illness that is difficult to treat yet demands some action.

This central position of the contamination illnesses in the continuum of humoral and spirit illness is shown in table 11.4. The illnesses range from transient bodily discomfort through serious physical illness to psychosocial incapacitation; their cause from physical cold through bodily contamination to a mystical marriage to Ayesha Qandisha, and their treatment from physical heat through humoral heat and institutional *baraka* to personal *baraka*, along a chain of progressively expressive and culturally-determined therapies.

CHOICE AND AMBIGUITY AROUND THE CONCEPT OF CONTAMINATION

The central group of illnesses are characterized by a contamination that can ambiguously belong to either the humoral or the Prophetic medical system. Analysis of this ambiguity has shown a profound syncretism between the two historically and philosophically distinct systems at their interface, where an almost perfect homology exists between, for example, the two explanations for the symptoms and treatment of "the Bride" (see fig. 11.4). This syncretism shows the radical divergence from the Galenic theory of equilibrium that is evident in Moroccan humoral theory, and is most extreme in the "deep-cold" illnesses, where cold contamination cannot be removed by humoral allopathic treatment, and resembles the mystical contamination or impurity of the Prophetic system and its Bedouin antecedent.

The choice of spirit aetiology, implicit or explicit, often reflects the gravity of the illness and whether humoral treatment has failed, but more creative use of the choice has been observed in some healers (Greenwood 1984, 219). Choice of humoral aetiology may increasingly reflect a diminishing belief in the immanent quality of spirits and the supernatural, encouraged by social change and the coming of Western medical ideas.

Western medicine is accepted for the simple humoral illnesses, particularly when diets are part of the treatment, and penicillin is a very hot substance because of its success in cold illness. X-rays may be seen as revealing the site of cold, blood sampling as removing it, and injections as inserting heat directly. The humoral system stems from the same philosophical tradition and such affirmations of it may assist the process of change away from the belief in spirits, the Eye, and sorcery. One herbalist, describing how sorcery is dying out, said, "But the feelings still come, so we still sell the remedies."

The internal ambiguity of the contamination illnesses is itself creative for the participants. The illnesses are mostly chronic impairment of the senses, locomotion, and fertility for which the best possible outcome, as in the West, is often coping, adapting, and overcoming, rather than a cure. Decontamination is never complete; pollution can only be contained. The response to them draws explicit symbols from two areas of shared experience—environmental cold as a pathogenic agent of the ecological domain, and spirit encounter as a feature of the neurotic domain—into the implicit understanding of their symptoms and signs. In this way both ecological and psychosocial factors are brought into a response by the patient and society that promotes individual and social rehabilitation and healing. And through the transformation of inner, epistemologically private perceptions of illness into shared social categories of the mystical-moral and physical worlds, the cultural values of these worlds are affirmed during the experience of illness.

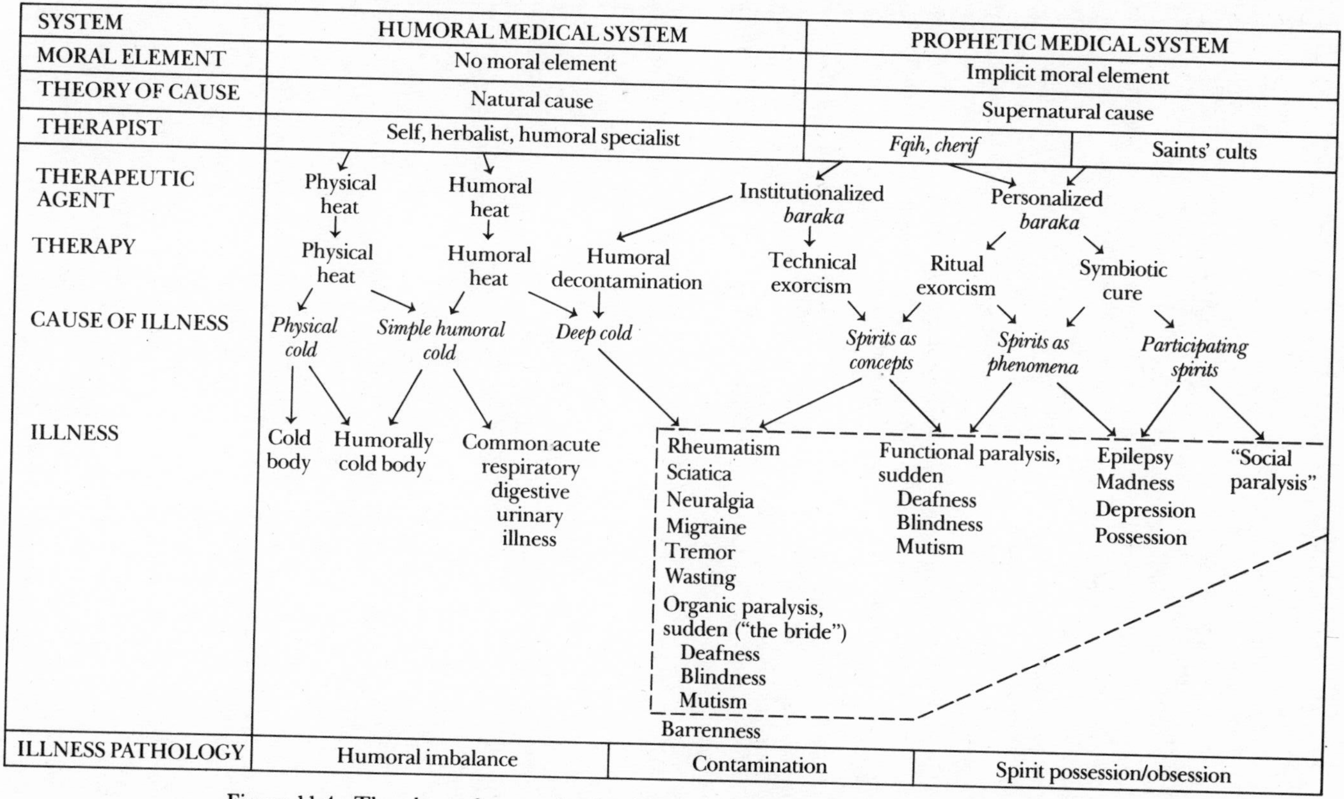

SYSTEM	HUMORAL MEDICAL SYSTEM		PROPHETIC MEDICAL SYSTEM	
MORAL ELEMENT	No moral element		Implicit moral element	
THEORY OF CAUSE	Natural cause		Supernatural cause	
THERAPIST	Self, herbalist, humoral specialist		*Fqih, cherif*	Saints' cults
THERAPEUTIC AGENT	Physical heat	Humoral heat	Institutionalized *baraka*	Personalized *baraka*
THERAPY	Physical heat	Humoral heat; Humoral decontamination	Technical exorcism	Ritual exorcism; Symbiotic cure
CAUSE OF ILLNESS	*Physical cold*	*Simple humoral cold*; *Deep cold*	*Spirits as concepts*	*Spirits as phenomena*; *Participating spirits*
ILLNESS	Cold body; Humorally cold body	Common acute respiratory digestive urinary illness	Rheumatism, Sciatica, Neuralgia, Migraine, Tremor, Wasting, Organic paralysis, sudden ("the bride"): Deafness, Blindness, Mutism; Barrenness; Functional paralysis, sudden: Deafness, Blindness, Mutism	Epilepsy, Madness, Depression, Possession; "Social paralysis"
ILLNESS PATHOLOGY	Humoral imbalance		Contamination	Spirit possession/obsession

Figure 11.4. The place of contamination illnesses in the Humoral and Prophetic systems.

NOTES

1. An earlier version of this chapter appeared in *Social Science and Medicine* 15B (1981) (3):219–236. The present version has been revised by the author and published with the permission of Pergamon Journals Ltd.

2. *Editors' note*: The reader will observe that there is a disparity in the use of the term *Arabic medicine* between Greenwood, who uses the term as a general rubric, and Abdalla, who rejects it in chapter 6 of this volume as unsuitable for those many non-Arabic-speaking societies that use the medical ideas. Similarly, there is a variance between the use of Greenwood's use of the term *Islamic medicine* and Abdallah's use of *Muslim medicine*. We have left both usages because they reflect regional differences and scholarly conventions.

3. The condition is due in some cases to disproportion between the head and the outlet, and in others to mental and physical exhaustion, where it is amenable to general supportive measures, such as nourishment and simple suggestion. Medicines may also have been used by the Cuna.

4. One curious case was the treatment of a Swiss man with a paralyzed shoulder by a Gharb *cherif*, which I witnessed. His condition was certainly organic, with objective evidence of nerve damage that had persisted for a year. A few days after his treatment of "the Bride" by branding, scarification, and diet, he began to make a recovery that was almost complete.

TWELVE

Causality of Disease among the Senufo[1]

Nicole Sindzingre and Andras Zempléni

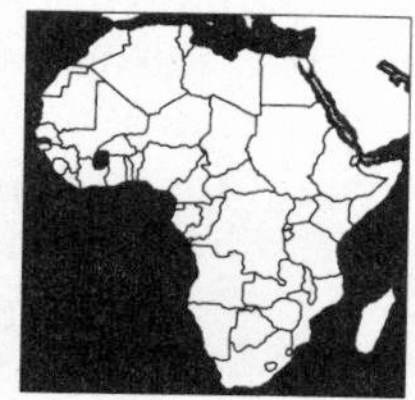

INTRODUCTION

The need to distinguish instrumental, efficient, and final causes of sickness or disease has gradually become established among anthropologists (Glick 1967; Gillies 1976; Foster 1976). These difficult classical terms used to speak of the diagnosis of disease may be translated into other terms for greater clarity. Four questions need to be answered: (1) the recognition of a state of sickness and its eventual naming (Which sickness is it?); (2) the perception or the representation of its instrumental cause (How has it happened?); (3) the identification of the agent that is responsible (Who or what produced it?); and (4) the reconstruction of its origin (Why did it occur at this moment in this individual?). Causality, as we commonly think of it, is therefore the means or the mechanism—empiric or not—by which the sickness is engendered. The agent is that which holds the effective force that produces it. The origin is the set of occurrences that, when reconstructed, render intelligible the outbreak of the sickness in the life of individuals.

Causality in African medicine builds on two further heterogeneous bodies of information. The first is a group of a priori declarations on the necessary connections between the symptom and the disease and the three intervening levels mentioned above. The a priori concept refers here to two distinct things. When ethnographers question their informants about their society's representations, they situate themselves in an objectivizing position vis-à-vis their subjects. The Senufo, the "one" who speaks to the informant as a social or cultural category, is invited to transform into a priori givens a series of etiological accounts learned in the course of individual experiences as sufferer, active partner in sickness episodes, therapist, or an apprentice. The society did not wait for the ethnographer to establish the a priori schemes of causality, unequally spread about. The result is that, at first flush, the inventory of explanatory categories resembles more a bric-a-brac than a neat "taxonomy."

The second body of information is a collection of a posteriori elaborations raised by the outbreak of sicknesses at given moments in given social contexts. In this perspective that includes precedents, the principle of coherence may be found in the sequential chain of interpretive segments of the therapeutic course. The pronouncements must be related to the conditions to which they refer; that is, to pragmatic, subjective, and sociosymbolical conjunctures that confer upon them a contextual meaning in the unfolding problematic of sickness episodes. A priori causality and a posteriori causality are therefore not congruent. Among the Senufo, although certain established connections of the first intervene actively in the interpretive processes of the second, the latter alone renders the a priori etiologies intelligible.

THE ETHNOGRAPHIC CONTEXT

The Senufo live in the Ivory Coast, Burkina Faso, and Mali, numbering about 900,000 persons. The present account deals mainly with the Nafara, Fodonon, Kouflo, and blacksmiths, inhabiting the north of the Côte d'Ivoire (Ivory Coast). Fieldwork has been conducted by the authors over the past decade. The Senufo are mainly farmers whose socioreligious organization is characterized by a strong matrilineal orientation, by the centrality of a secret masculine initiatory institution, the Poro, and by prominent ancestor cults and funerary rites. The principle of seniority that governs relations of subordination at the village, descent group, and age–grade levels, is at the basis of the exercise of authority. If one would characterize the ethos of these groups who have been exposed for a long time to repeated aggression from their Western neighbors, we would—and this is their reputation—speak of conservative and closed societies.

SICKNESS

The ethic of stoical endurance, as it is applied to both daily behavior and the initiatory values applied to suffering, is a first significant element in the Senufo conceptualization of sickness. The state of sickness (*yaama*) is contrasted to that of "freshness of the body" *tyerenyĩmɛ*; *tyere*—body; *nyĩmɛ*—freshness, shade). The verbal set sickness/health is lexically distinguished from that of chance/bad luck, and happiness/unhappiness (*yɛɛfige/yɛɛwuɔ*), as well as white/black. Health and sickness refer to a scale of temperatures, whereas happiness and unhappiness refer more to the color spectrum.

Sickness and unhappiness are not always differentiated. For example, the term *tɔɔrɔ* designates the state, even the mode of existence, of an individual who enters into repeated conflicts. Such a repetition in itself marks a changing state in which troubles cease to be simple events and become the signs of a predisposition—distinguished by the term *nari*—of evil or unhappiness afflicting both individual and group.

These qualifying sets manifest themselves equally in several expressions designating frequent symptoms: fever that is called *tyefuro*, "hot body," also *nyĩmẽ*, humidity, or *weere*, cold (when accompanied by stomachache and vomiting). In a well-known process, one and the same biomedical syndrome can be distributed over different *yaama*, and different symptoms can be assembled into a single nosological entity. Outside current ills, the recognition of the aptitude of designating a sickness may be done by more or less specialized individuals. The layperson often designates the part of the body where the problem is localized: *nyũgo mii yaa*—I have an ache in the head.

The taxonomy carries simple or compound terms. The simple are, for example, *gãguɔli* (cough), *nãmigi* (sore), *kotige* (side pain—when it occurs, "pain in the sides," pneumopathy), *kakɔ̃gi* (rheumatism), *gɔ̃gi* (throat [goiter]), *zããni* (epilepsy), *mɔrigi* (cyst), and so on.

Compound expressions include *yaaŋunɔmɔ* (sleeping sickness; *ŋunɔ*—sleep; to be asleep), *nyɔ̃forigi* (scorched mouth; *nyɔ̃gi*—mouth; *fori*—scorched, ulcers, perhaps vitamin deficiency), *gãguɔfiili*—(white cough; *fii*—white, perhaps a stage of tuberculosis), *laafɛri* (running of the stomach; *laagi*—stomach; *fã*—run, diarrhea); *fũngo nãmigi* (interior [internal] sore; *fũngo*—interior; dysentery, hemorrhaging colitis, amebiasis), *tyewaari* (dry body; *tyere*—body; *waa*—dry; thinning with anorexia), *kubawuɔgi* (black spots; *kubau*—spots on the skin of dogs or cats), *wuɔ* (black; due to the roughness of the first stages of onchocerciasis), and *kubafugi* (white spots; white lesions due to roughness—a stage of onchocerciasis; there is no reference to locality).

EXPLANATORY MODELS

The inventory of Senufo etiological categories demonstrates a number of characteristics common to other African medical systems. A given disease or symptom can be linked a priori or a posteriori to causal categories as shown in table 12.1. We note that what we call "natural diseases" and the Senufo call "diseases of God" are distinguished in this: the first relate the symptom to an empirical factor acting in a "mechanical" mode, whereas the second brings together pathological conditions that neither a common understanding, nor divination, can assign a hypothetical cause.[2] It is thus a negative etiological category, for God (*kulotyɔlɔɔ*) is otherwise the being that the Senufo consider the ultimate origin of things of the world (*dulunya*)—and thus of all sicknesses. "Sicknesses of God" have a significance that is clearly different from that found in the Bantu world, in particular in Lower Zaire, where, as Janzen has shown, the "sicknesses of God" are opposed to "sicknesses of man," which are witchcraft-related (Janzen 1978*b*; Bibeau 1981).

It is noteworthy that Senufo etiological thinking emphasizes neither

TABLE 12.1. Senufo Illness Cause Categories

	Senufo term	Specification
Mechanical factor X	—	"Natural illness"
God ("illness of God")	*Kulotyɔlɔɔ*	Illness without another assignable cause
The of animals killed or of persons who died in bush	*Yawige* (the thing that pursues)	Illness contracted by contamination
The transgression of prohibitions	*Yafũgo*	Prohibitions related to lineage, or individual (objects, statues)
Instrumental magic and fetish objects	*Yasũŋgo. katyɛnɛ*	Illnesses "thrown" or "picked up"
Matrilineal sorcerors	*Dɛɔ*	
Spirits of a place (bush, rivers)	*Mãdebele, tugobele, nakãhãbele*	
Protective aura of matrilineage	*Sãdoho*	Agents who "fall" or "descend" (*tigi*) upon the individual
Matrilineal deceased	*Kuubele*	
Guardian of individual	*ɲinĩgefɔlɔ*	
Matrilineal twins	*ŋãmbele*	

models of mystical aggression nor those of mystical sanction. Its originality consists rather—as is the argument of this work—in a cumulative stock, synchronic and diachronic, of preexisting causalities of which groups and individuals are the identifiers and which are actualized in sickness.

A Priori Causalities

Once evoked, these general traits establish a priori the links between diseases (or symptoms) and causal configurations (cause, agent, origin). We emphasize that these links form a fluctuating set, narrowly dependent on the speaker, rather than a fixed corpus or a definitive code. Nevertheless, they present a series of constant formulas.

The connections between terms and specifications are manifested in two forms. In the first, symptom A is related to cause X through the intermediary of an apparently double linkage expressed as a necessary relation: that of a "reciprocal implication."[3] In the second form, symptom B is enunciated as attributable to one or another element of a set of possible causes—along the

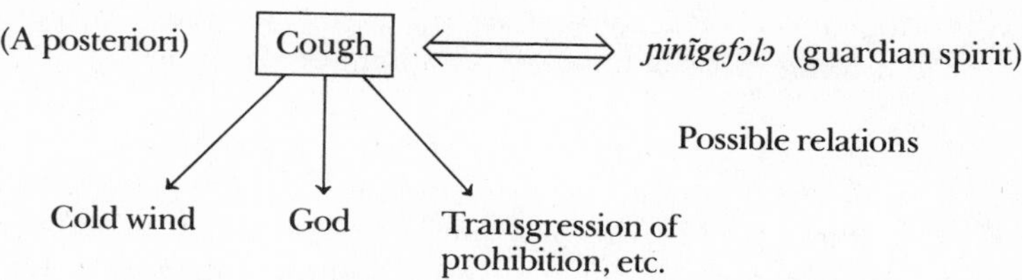

Figure 12.1. Possible causal relations in connection with a cough (⟷ reciprocal causal relations; → possible relations).

well-known model of a "sequence of converging causes" (Gillies 1976; Horton 1967).

These two forms are differentiated under a double rubric: (1) the nature of the causal link (whether hypothetical or not, thus of the type "if p, . . . then q"); (2) the necessity or nonnecessity of the link. The problem in this analysis is in the fact that the content of the terms of the relation per se (A, B, X, etc.) does not permit a characterization of the nature of the causal link: such and such a content (an agent or symptom) can be either a priori a term of a hypothetical relationship, necessary, or uncertain. For example, for the Senufo, a cough is one of the terms for a possible reciprocal relationship with the "guardian spirit" (agent), *ɲinĩgefɔlɔ*,[4] of the individual as much as it is a term of a possible relation with the cold wind or other causes. Thus figure 12.1 shows that the set of a priori causal connections can be divided into two categories: the necessary relations with reciprocal implications—or dualist sets—and those with possible relations. We will first examine the a priori dualist sets enunciated by the Senufo.

A Priori Implications

According to the now classic thesis of Horton (1967, 169), traditional African thought cannot spell out the elaboration of theories that assign an effect to a particular—and antecedent—distinctive cause, or to particular configuration of antecedents. Taking up our analytical language, this would mean that the Senufo do not attribute given symptoms to causes, agents, or origins—which is clearly not the case, and to such an extent that the interpretation offered by the *sãdoho* divination may limit itself to nothing but a pure corroboration of a priori connections established between terms.

It is important to note that the implication—either that effect B leads to antecedent A, or that antecedent A leads to effect B—does not provide a distinctive and pertinent criterion. It is the very existence of the a priori dualist sets and not the direction of the inference that permits us to distinguish two different types of causality. Thus the two following sequences can coexist: this sickness is due to such and such an antecedent; such and such an event will bring on such a sickness. This is a circularity that will appear the most clearly in connections of the sort "symptom ⟷ origin."

Symptom ⟷ Cause

This relationship is often of a "mechanistic" or "deterministic" character, occurring in frequent and benign problems. For example, it is said that *toho* (skin outbreak) is due to skin contact with the grain of the *bolongo* tree. Or, that *fĩnĩge* ("root of urine"; retention of urine) shows up with the individual who urinates on the root of the rice plant. In these simple examples, where the explanatory model is reduced to a singular connection, it is difficult to disjoin cause and origin (the "how" and the "why"). These are clearly differentiated only in cases where all the connections (between symptom, cause, agent, origin) are present, and in which the agent's function is precisely that of distributing the two polarities.

To continue examples, it is said that *binibali* (pestle to pound sauce lying crosswise; *bĩnĩge*—pestle; *bali*—to rest crosswise—i.e., angina) comes from the habit of spitting near excrements. In this case, the representation of the cause carries no link with the metaphor that serves to designate the problem (difficulty in swallowing as if one had the mortar *bĩnĩge* in the throat). The symptom–cause link is not in itself metaphoric.

Also, *nũfũdãhãri* (red worms; athlete's foot with ulcers) is contracted by an individual who walks on the red worms of the same name. In this example, the symptom–cause link is of a metonymic character (the presence of a semantic invariant: the color red).

In a general manner, the set of a priori connections includes a subset specified by the presence of a metonymic relationship between the terms of the configuration (cause–agent–origin) and the symptom. The metonym can be considered from two different perspectives: (1) the invariant recurs all along the causal chain (such as the color red); or (2) the identity is supported organically by the symptom and is the point of application of the causal imputation (e.g., the foot)—a relation of adherence, one might say.

The two preceding examples illustrate well how the stylistic figure (metaphor, metonym), implicated by the denomination of the problem, is independent of the character of the causal link. The metaphoric term has absolute autonomy in the example of *binibali*. In the example of the metonymic chain *nũfũdãhãri*, it is a purely semantic expression of the perception of the symptom. Evidently, as soon as the connection is of a metonymic nature, the invariant element can be present at each stage of the linkage, including the naming of the problem, and in its treatment. It appears that reference to an agent is not a necessary condition of the establishment of metonymic connections. It may be similar in the construction of metaphoric connections as well.

Symptom ⟷ Agent

Numerous a priori etiologies arise from this type of connection in Senufo thinking. They are sicknesses imputed to witchcraft and to magical powers (charms—*yasũŋgo, katyɛnɛ*). The being (witch) or the power constitutes the agent, intention (e.g, jealousy), origin, and by diverse means the causes. A charm can be an autonomous agent or an instrument. An example is *mɛhɛni* (fishhook), sudden dysphagia that can lead to death. This is said to be a sickness that is "thrown" (*yaa wa mi*). All sorts of "thrown" or "gathered" illnesses (benign or mortal, sudden [acute] or chronic) have the common trait of their triple reference to an agent (generally a witch, "the enemy"), a cause (the object thrown), and, of a psychosociological character (the intention to curse, a grudge). Their symptomatological constants are the uncertainty of their initial clinical manifestation and their continual transformation (toward chronicity, eventually) and, if left unattended, their evolution (to rapid death). In this case, the object (the cause) is said to be "inside" the sufferer. Thus *mɛhɛni* (fishhook), in which the sufferer is thought to have swallowed a fishhook thrown into his food or drink, that keeps him henceforth from swallowing and eating. It is the same with *fũngo fĩningi* (interior abscess), where it is said that the sufferer had no initial symptoms, but died at the moment when he began to complain of headache. Sicknesses that are "collected," as *tɔyayi* (foot pain), follow the same scheme: an evil-intentioned agent puts the disease on his enemy's path. These sicknesses have the form of an a priori linked set, but also they have a polyvalent, evolving, dissimulated content that renders impossible their distinctive identification.

Certain diseases such as *yedapɛgi* (foot [sweeper's] pain) permit of an a priori division between agent and cause, which are not necessarily congruent: one contracts *yedapɛgi* when one walks over a "malefic" area or steps on the little *jũŋdu* insect. Two conditional elements are thus juxtaposed on the a priori, pertaining to heterogeneous levels of explanation, but not one and the same moment or type of a given therapeutic segment. "Fetishes" and "spirits" (*mãdebele*) constitute equally a priori agents of a series of symptoms. Among postulated implications, we give the example of "pain in the ears" imputed to the displeasure of spirits offended by lack of attention to them.

All the etiological categories figuring in table 12.1 occupy, by definition, the place of agents, not merely beings endowed with intentionality (such as witches). Otherwise, the postulated origin is not necessarily a psychosocial reaction (such as a grudge), but may be an initial message or reiteration sent by certain agents. For example, it can be persistent skin welts (*sĩgbãhari*), said to be "thrown" by the guardian spirit *ɲinĩgefɔlɔ* (the "creator" of the individual) as a prelude to a demand, which is equivalent to the treatment of the sickness (it carries the signs of *ɲinĩgefɔlɔ*, white shirt with seven bands, cowrie bracelet). This representation of the origin of the sickness as an alliance (with the spirit) is a major trait in the causal chain known as *yawige*.

The Yawige Chain of Causes

A sickness is called *yawige*, the thing that chases or insists (*yariga*—thing; *wi*: follows) when it is imputed to ingestion of, sight of, or contact with, an animal, living or dead, or for a woman's husband to have killed an animal when she was pregnant. Any animal, domesticated or wild, can figure among the agents of these sicknesses. The link between the agent and the symptom operates by the principle *ɲũma*, constituting every living being, and acting here as the cause. Every human or animal cadaver is the resting place of *ɲũma* susceptible of "trapping" (*tyo*) individuals in contact (directly or indirectly) with the body (it suffices to be merely in the same area). This then is, per force, the hunter who killed the animal.

Yawige sicknesses in the strict sense are childhood sicknesses. There is a whole series of a priori sets that link childhood syndromes with a series of animals.

For example, there is *bau* (sheep). The newborn or infant breathes like a sheep. It is said that its mother has eaten mutton during her pregnancy. The treatment is to wash with water used to wash a sheep. Also, there is *kukehere* ("stone dead"), an insect. Neonatal tetanus is caused by the pregnant mother having walked upon the *kukehere* insect that rolled itself up when touched. Also, *pyegi* (the hare), in which the child sleeps with its eyes open like the hare, meaning that the infant's mother is supposed to have eaten a hare during her pregnancy. The treatment is to wear an object representing the *yawige*.

Similar examples include *dekeu*, the cat (all skinny); *kɛwuɔu*, the black monkey (thinning, fingers and toes like those of the monkey); *sɔlɔu*, the water turtle (distended abdomen as in kwashiorkor); *gbori*, the chameleon (large open eyes); *yiriu*, the porcupine (sores over the whole body).

In the majority of cases, there is a semantic invariant common to the agent-animal, the symptom denomination, the perceived organic manifestations, and to the treatment that would relieve the symptom. For example, in the case of the invariant "hare" in the disease *pyegi*, the *yawige* causal chain simultaneously sets into action metaphor and metonym. A first metonymic operation subsumes the animal "hare" under one of its traits such as "sleeping with open eyes." Then, this trait metaphorizes the child's symptom: sleeping with open eyes like the hare. A final metonymic operation includes a part of the animal in the treatment: for example, to carry the hare's foot.

Understood in the narrow sense, *yawige* sicknesses carry a form of common causality based on the idea of contagion, or contamination by the *ɲũma* of an animal. However, every animal intervening either in the naming or in the position of the sickness agent is not thought of as a *yawige* animal. Otherwise, the Senufo can also name as *yawige* (the thing that follows), not just animals, but also instances such as the guardian of the person (*ɲinĩgefɔlɔ*), spirits (*mãdebele*), *nakãhãbele*, or twins *ŋambele*). The term *yawige* denotes a mode of action by an agent and a specific causal sequence in which the agent contracts or "catches" (*tyo*) the disease, the origin of the symptom being not only differentiated, but anteriorized in genealogical time.

Moreover, the extension of the term *yawige* to the instances described above may be explained by its double significance. Although it refers to a single causal chain, it equally designates the other extreme of the process, the treatment that will dissolve the symptom. Again at this point *yawige* animals, *ɲinĩgefɔlɔ*, spirits, twins, even *sãdoho*, spring from the same paradigm. Thus, sucklings or infants affected by a *yawige* sickness wear on their wrists, hair, and hips objects representing in miniature the animal responsible for their ills. In the same manner, the one whose symptom is assigned to twins or to *sãdoho* wears a double ring or a bracelet—the "*yawige*" object of twins, or a bracelet in the form of a python, the "*yawige*" object of the Sãdoho.

The distinctive sign of the agent as the essential part of the treatment is not necessarily a material object. Frequently it consists of a name, for example, of the animal thought to be the cause. Senufo anthroponymy abounds in names such as *Gonão*, *Gotya* (boy- or girl-chicken), *Fotya* (girl-python), and so on. These are all names that attest to a previous event at which the animal "trapped" a forebear of the victim. The extension of the notion of *yawige* is such that a presage (*kaɲɔ̃hɔ̃nɔ̃*) can equally hold the place of a symptom and lead to the occurrence of a *yawige* relationship with an animal. An unusual encounter of one's father with a python will lead to a series of children subsequently born carrying *yawige* names.

To close this section, we note that the pivotal notion of *ɲũma* marks the point of departure of the following reasoning: each individual having been in contact with the *ɲũma* of a living being (through murder or hunt) will fall ill, manifesting symptoms of wasting away or madness, unless he (or she) goes through purification rites. It seems thus that the *ɲũma* is an aggressive and autonomous principle, especially if its original source is death without sickness. The most dangerous *ɲũma* is that of an individual who dies *senɔɔ̃*, accidentally, outside of the village, without having had the time "to be sick," the cause having been anterior to the effect. By virtue of the notion of *ɲũma*, we see that the *yawige* inference operates a priori in both directions (A → B, B → A), either inductively or deductively.

Symptom ⟷ Origin

Most relationships of this type present themselves, as in the previous type, either inductively or deductively. Thus, it is said that a woman who sees the Poro mask *zãgboo* with the stooped head, will give birth to a child with its head stooped. Also, a woman who badly executes a segment of funerary ritual for a *sãdoho* woman will be immediately "joined" by the *sãdoho* power in the form of convulsions. These causal chains occur because of the symptom of an event, in that the symptom is "performed" within the event, via the mediatory focus of a prohibition (*yafũgo*). Thus one speaks of the *yafũyi* of a mask, of a ritual, and so on. It is said, "there will not be a prohibition if a sickness would not result from it." Examples of this show that the causal links can be enunciated in a reversible form, but that only the character of the sequence (symptom → event → symptom) is pertinent. The representation of the sickness *laagbo*, enlarged stomach (*laa*—stomach, intestine; *gbo*—large; bloody amebic dysentery) illustrates this clearly. This malady is imputed to the transgression of a prohibition: of sexual relations with one's menopausal wife, or with a woman whose ex-husband interdicted her menses, or with a widow who has not been ritually separated from her deceased husband. As in the previous examples, the implication here simultaneously operates in both directions. If a woman has a "large stomach," it is because she has had sexual relations of the three types of cases. If she is at risk for such relations, she will get *laagbo*.

The concept of the prohibition is a recurrent element in the expression of the double link symptom ⟷ origin. Before analyzing this essential notion, we should mention that the origin of a symptom may be attributed to acts that do not as such refer to it. These chains bear a greater degree of complexity in the number of links than the simple one (symptom → cause or symptom → origin) noted above. This is the case with symptoms propped up by a certain conception of "contagion" that presupposes contact or relationships. For example, mumps (*gbɔhɔsulɔyi*) are said to happen if an individual makes fun of the swollen face of a sufferer having already contracted mumps. This representation of making fun as the origin of the sickness is found also in the possible etiology of Down's syndrome (*gbahayulogi*; "hanging face") . One treatment for this consists in the sufferer intentionally making himself ridiculous so as to pass the sickness on to the first person who laughs at him. This is an instance of the symptom as a contagious entity with its own autonomy.

The Notion of Yafũgo (Interdiction)

The a priori relations described above conform to a more or less explicit four-dimensional model of causality in which a given element is affected by a later (cause, agent, origin) occurrence. The model of the interdiction (*yafũgo*) has certain particularities. *Yafũgo*, the interdicted thing, is a property that can attach to any object, function, circumstance, moment, or animal. It is a "positive" quality of the substance of these objects or beings that may refer to all possible actions: seeing, touching, eating, walking on, and so on. Thus one says: it is the *yafũgo* of such and such a matriclan of such village to eat *kafa* (dried leg of a small antelope); or, it is the *yafũgo* of *ɲinĩgefɔlɔ* to eat gumbo sauce; or, it is the *yafũgo* of the mortar to sit on it. One will also say "such and such an instance does not like such and such an act." The transgression of a *yafũgo* is supposed to be followed a priori by certain negative consequences such as sickness or misfortune for the actor, or eventually a member of the whole group to which he belongs. The notion of interdiction is an essential point of articulation of possible causalities in both meanings previously stated: symptom → interpretive configuration, or initial event → symptom.

A first type of case of the characteristics of the causal links in the interdiction are as follows. Taken in isolation, the a priori link in which the symptom is related to the *yafũgo* transgression (or the inverse), assigns variable contents to the agent. That is, the symptom is given as a direct effect, without intermediary, of the initial act or event. For example, it is "the *yafũgo* of this *wara*" (medicinal plants not paid for), the sanction being the inefficacy of the *wara* and the occurrence of the symptom. The causal sequence is a direct link from the cause-origin to the symptom. Depending on the perspective adopted, the place of the agent is either empty, or it is held by the support-object of the *yafũgo* (interdiction), or by the individual transgressor. Thus one has the link (symptom ⟷ the thing not to be done), to deal with the "how" question. The "why" question in this linkage refers to a set of symbolic a priori associations that account for certain contradictions and cannot be developed here. The Senufo interdiction has the very general character of a conjunction of negatively marked symbolic poles. For example, mortar → femininity → interdiction upon mortar → men's seating place. Categories of possible and impossible *yafũgo* domains and the symptoms that their transgressions are believed to produce are of the order such as men/women, initiated/noninitiated, and similar. However, specific causal links of the type (symptom ⟷ transgression) are impossible to make.

A second type of case that links the transgression of the interdiction and the symptom does not present itself as an a priori sufficient cause, but is part of a more complex sequence in which it is this link itself that is the origin or the cause. For example, it is said that a *yafũgo* of the *ɲiñĩgefɔlɔ* that women eat in the gumbo sauce, when transgressed (by being eaten by someone else), leads to the symptom *nyɔ̃forigi* (scorched mouth). It is the *yafũgo* of the power of the matrilineage (*sãdoho*), which, when transgressed, reveals that there has been adultery or incest in the matrilineage, whose transgression leads to deaths or infant sicknesses. An agent, specific in this case, upholds the interdictions themselves, in the explanatory model based on transgression.

Yafũgo and Yawige

The *yawige* link is paradigmatic of these complex sequences. The symptom of a *yawige* sickness is followed by the transgression of a *yafũgo* consisting for the future mother in not seeing, not eating, or for the future father in not killing an animal. This produces the following causal linkages:

Yawige being ⟷ transgression of one of its *yafũgo* ⟷ *ɲũma* power ⟷

symptom (sent to a trait of the *yawige* being) ⟷ remedy (part or representation of the *yawige*)

This is a metonymic sequence that presents the essential trait to be differentiated over time. The subject who displays the symptom is not only not the same one who introduces the sequence, but is necessarily a descendant. The symptom is said to be capable of emerging several years after the initial transgression by the mother, but this temporal jump is not pertinent in the extent to which it evokes the symptom as evidence of another temporality, namely, that between two modes of spatially separated beings.

In a general way the action of most of the agents distinguished by the Senufo is conceived as a reaction to specific *yafũgo* transgressions. Since the interdiction is enunciated a priori, its presence is a mute witness that a specific causal sequence has been set loose. It is evidence of a particular etiological scheme at work.

A Priori Models with Complex Etiologies: The Case of Inclusive Disjunctions (Either . . . or)

We have described the set of connections and linkages that is related to a cause, an agent, or a given origin. A priori causalities also constitute models that specify alternative etiologies for a single problem. They tend to circumscribe preferential interpretive bundles that presuppose and orient the paths to be followed.

Thus, a rectal inflammation (*nukũŋgi*—enlarged anus) is a sickness "thrown" by poisoning of food, but it is also a "collected" sickness if the sufferer has transgressed an interdiction of a charm (*yasũŋgo*—a *katyɛnɛ* put in a field to sanction thieves). It is also a sickness transmitted to an infant of a woman who "collected" it during her pregnancy. It is also a complication of the sickness (*fũngo nãmiga*—interior sore), which is rarely "natural."

The case of leprosy (*yaanyɛɛmɛ*—"red" sickness) is somewhat different. Several forms are possible: sickness "thrown" and "sorcerer's shirt," corresponding to the above different syndromes. In "throwing," the sufferer seems completely taken over by the sickness (fingers cut up, many sores, etc.). If the sufferer does not appear to be sick, even if the fingers are cut and the sickness is only apparent, then he (or she) has a "sorcerer's shirt," that is, a shirt that he took off in the morning after he had met with his sorcerer colleagues. It is he himself who is the agent of the "thrown" sickness *yaanyɛɛmɛ*, via the shirt of his victim.

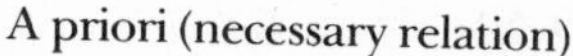

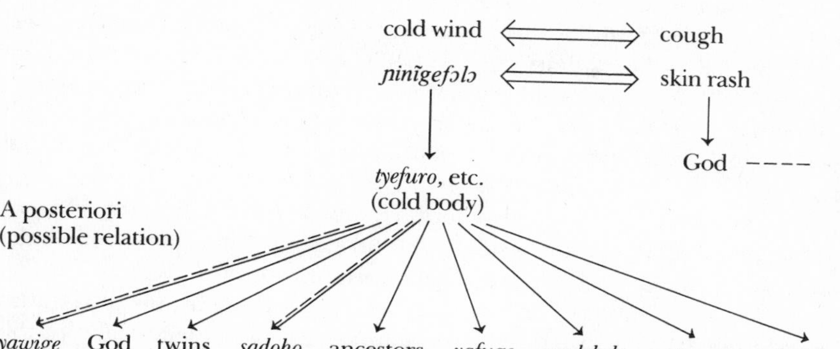

Figure 12.2. A priori and other approaches in Senufo causal interpretation of illness. The horizontal dimension pertains to a priori causality; the vertical, to causalities considered a posteriori, i.e., ex post facto (⟺ reciprocal relations; → possible relations; ---→ preferential causal relations).

Another example is the "sore that endures" (*nɔ̃mkaagi*), a sickness that is either "thrown" by an "individual who knows" (*sityilio*), or wished by the sufferer himself, thus stigmatized as a sorcerer (*dεo*). The reasoning here is of a circular nature: it is a sickness "thrown" if the subject is not a sorcerer; it is a "wished" sore, a "false" sore, if the sufferer is suspected of sorcery. There is also a series of parallels in the case of the sufferer who is "poor." Material misery and the lack of hygiene constitute an empirical explanation of the symptom.

Finally, for a large variety of symptoms or of syndromes, Senufo etiological thinking admits a priori a high degree of commutability, or altering of interpretations, all the while preferred interpretations are given. For example, diarrhea, body swellings, wasting, rheumatism, and so on are attributed to a range of conditions. Thus hot body (*tyefuro*—fever, fatigue, thinning) is attributable—particularly in children—to a *yawige*, a guardian spirit (*ɲinĩgefɔlɔ*), or to the *sãdoho* of the matrilineage. Frequently this pathological condition is the very model of those sicknesses of which the etiology is determined in a manner only a posteriori, despite the preexistence of a bundle of alternatives. Causality is governed here by a principle that is extrinsic to the a priori conditions. Figure 12.2 brings together the relationship between a priori and other approaches to interpreting cause.

The set of connections described here does not constitute a fixed corpus, complete and generalizable to the whole of the Senufo world. We have not described here a medical taxonomy, which would be absurd, but have sought to elucidate the formal principles that underlie this society's tendency to elaborate fragments of an etiological code. Such codes that seem more systematic than among the Senufo, and the reasons for their existence, have been studied by others (Bohannan and Bohannan 1969; East 1939; Price-Williams 1962). Not only do such codes not necessarily reflect medical etiology; they may not direct medical action, for, as Allan Young has noted, diagnosis is never automatic (Young 1976). The diagnostic codes are also not reducible to one of their functions, such as to link the sickness through sanction to certain undesirable social actions. Finally, it is not sufficient to consider these codes as a segment of the local symbolic system, nor as the only product of the human spirit's propensity to transform sensory facts—at the time of sickness—into intelligible categories through the means of connections that constitute a structure. These approaches are all legitimate if they do not misunderstand the heterogeneity between the logic of codes and pragmatic elaborations.

A Posteriori Causalities

The outbreak of sickness can lead to three kinds of reactions: a spontaneous effort to resolve the problem, immediate recourse to therapeutic means, or the establishment of a diagnostic formula that offers etiological instructions. Even if it is a truism, we emphasize that the specification of cause, agent, and origin is in no way a necessary condition for the treatment of a disease. When the Senufo peasants administer their domestic remedies, falling under the panacea of a reputed healer or the local dispensary's various pills or, this failing, the vow of their personal protectors or the *yasũŋgo* of their village, they do not ask themselves nor are they necessarily informed about the "why," the "who," and the "how" of their sickness. Whether or not their action or that of their therapist is founded on a priori causal connections, the therapeutic transaction itself does not necessarily make explicit and, in fact, may even ignore, such a connection. In contrast to other systems—notably Bantu African—these Senufo therapeutic institutions often function autonomously from interpretive institutions.

In effect, a single institution brings together these two functions, that of the *nigmɔ̃* ("borrower of roots"), at the same time diviners, *yasũŋgofɔlɔ* ("owners of charms") and professional therapists. They characterize themselves by an agnostic attitude toward healing of sickness, preferring the explanatory model of magic and sorcery. Senufo divination par excellence, *sãdoho*, is a purely interpretive institution. Its instructions in no way concern therapeutic preparations, nor the operations of other categories, in the majority of therapists (*katyãɔ* of *sityilio*—the one who knows), who possess a partial pharmacological knowledge applicable to certain "ordinary" afflictions. A jar of plants (*wara*) or powder (*tĩm*) serves therapists to treat all sicknesses brought to them. Common folk have a minimal pharmacopoeia, enough to

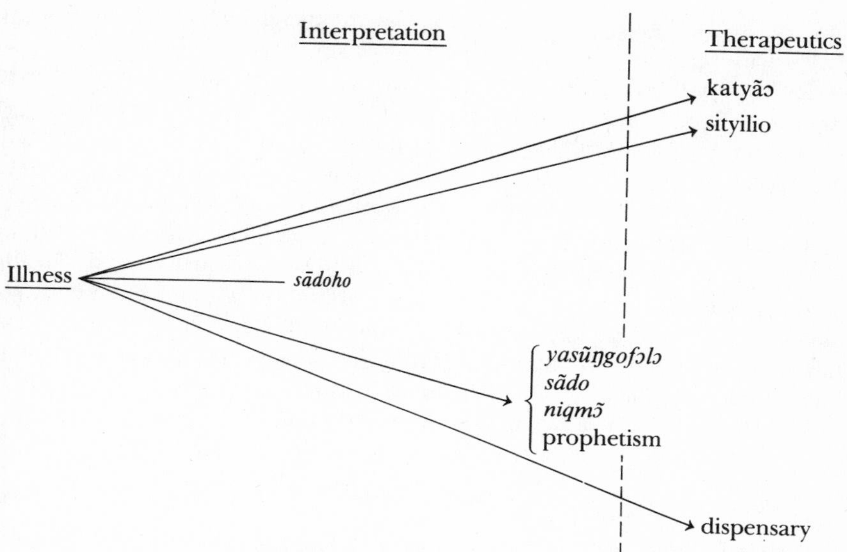

Figure 12.3. An outline of Senufo therapeutics.

"save oneself and one's own." Western medicine, paradoxically, gives rise to therapeutic efforts that are based on Senufo precedents, to the extent that it offers its treatments without sharing the etiological explanations. This is not the case with therapeutic movements introduced by healing prophets or certain "owners of fetishes" in which the therapy goes along with the identification of causal agents, a precondition of therapeutic efficacy (fig. 12.3).

The self-contained nature of the various fields interconnected in figure 12.3 explains, among other things, that the multiplication of therapeutic alternatives does not necessarily bring diversification of causal models. Irrespective of the efficacy of a new treatment (e.g., dispensed by a hospital), the perception of this instrumental efficacy is not a determining factor in the modification of causal thought.

It is the same with Islam's entrance into the picture. Its role in Senufo medical pluralism does not appear in this text. This omission is deliberate. Islam is strongly but unequally present in Senufo country. The groups situated in Mali and in the northwest of Senufo country in the Ivory Coast are largely Islamized, influenced by their Malinke neighbors, who are patrilineal and who do not have the Poro society. Islamization is also more noticeable in the urban than the rural environment. Recourse to the remedies of Muslim healers, often itinerant, is common. In Nafara society, Muslim prophet-healers—who prefer to use the image of the *yasũŋgofɔlɔ*, the interpretation of sorcery, all the while adapting the notion of the sickness as being due to divine will—periodically find a considerable rural clientele among the Senufo. If the importance of Islamic procedures is not emphasized here, this is so for three reasons. This essay concentrates on modes of causal inference and not on the pluralism of therapeutic institutions. As has been emphasized, these institutions among the Senufo function independently of causal models. A Muslim therapist can coordinate his work with an "indigenous" etiology, such as the *sãdoho*, without modifying it. Last but not least, the violence of the historic relationships between the Senufo and their conquerors and Muslim merchants explains beyond a reasonable doubt the strong and persistent ideological tension between the Dioula and the Senufo. In the rural areas, Islam is not a factor in communalization; no social segment claims it. Any ideological appropriation for the Senufo of sickness via Islamic models of explanation would be a calculation doomed to failure.

DIVINATION

Formal etiological interpretation of the sickness event—and as a consequence, the a posteriori determination of its cause—is the domain of divination (*sãdoho*). This is a predominantly feminine work. Senufo *sãdoobele* diviners do not heal nor make pronouncements in symptomatological or nosological matters. They work using a collection of up to a hundred objects each of which represents a lexical or encyclopedic category. With the exception of mechanical factors, these objects include representatives of all etiological categories mentioned earlier: *kulotyɔlɔɔ* (God), *yawige* beings (e.g., python, chameleon), specified interdictions (*yafũgo*), charm-objects (*yasũŋgo* or *katyɛnɛ*), groups and individuals, witches and different varieties of spirits, the dead and the *sãdoho*, the "creator" of the individual (*ɲinĩgefɔlɔ*), and twins. In brief, the diviner's bag contains a virtually infinite series of causes. Sickness is always represented by an object that carries its name and is often identified by means of a named emblem such as "fire" (*naa*), which connotes fever (*tyefuro*), anger, conflict, and so on, all of which "heats the family."

The diviner does not know the identity nor the motives of the client, by definition. So these need to be accompanied by a witness, a consultant, especially in cases of sickness. The divinatory seance always includes three stages followed by a prescription (for sacrifice, avoidance, etc.): (1) interpretation of patterns of objects thrown on the ground by the diviner, who then determines the elementary coordinates of the consultation (identity of the consultant, motives of the visit—visions, sickness, death); (2) the progressive determination of a single cause (principally the agent), by a set of questions with binary responses, by reiterations (yes/no, marked by clapping of the diviner's hand on the thigh of the client or by the open or closed position of an object, *tobɛ*);

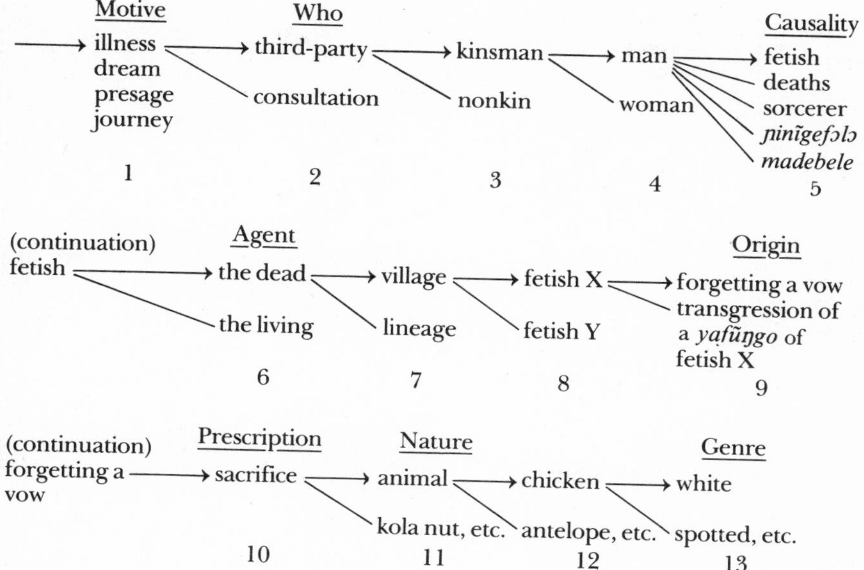

Figure 12.4. Schematic determination of a problem's etiology. (Arrows indicate the path chosen among options.)

and (3) the response by an identical procedure to questions that the client asks at the end of the seance to seek further clarification.

The divinatory procedure rests on the complementarity of two kinds of information: (1) beginning with the juxtaposition of a given number of emblems, limiting the pattern of contents to be combined, the diviner utilizes a group of possible syntagmatic combinations; (2) beginning with a set of enunciations, the diviner traces a unique causal and prescriptive path along a structural tree of possibilities. In the course of the seance, the diviner continues to create feedback loops to verify the correctness of the chosen bifurcations. A schematic example of the etiological determination of a problem is presented in figure 12.4. In this example, the diviner's diagnosis may be summarized as follows. A kinsman of the consultant had been made sick with fetish X of his village, because he had forgotten to make the sacrifice that he had promised it earlier. The diagnosis is particularly perilous for the diviner, insofar as the origin of the sickness—the nonaccomplishment of a vow—is related here to a real and verifiable event that may not have occurred.

Such is not the case when the diviner attributes the problem to a nonempirical fact. If, for example, at bifurcation number 6, he would have taken the branch "fetish of the living," he would have been able to develop the follow-

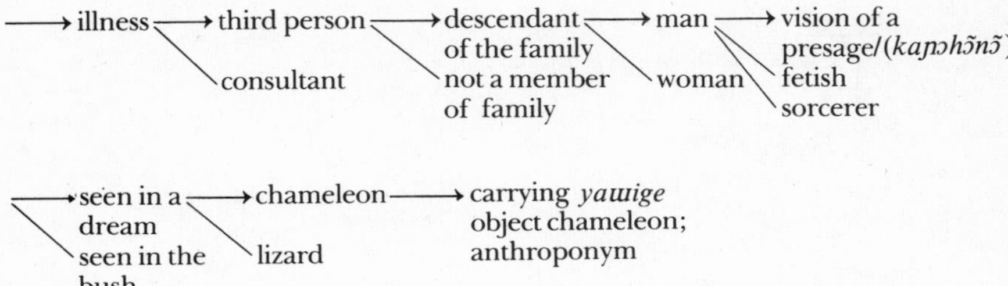

Figure 12.5. Example of Senufo causal sequence of an illness.

ing series. A kinsman of the consultant had been made sick by an act of sorcery by a woman of the Silue matriclan—the agent—living in a locality contiguous to the sufferer. Or, as figure 12.5 shows, another example of the causal sequence is possible.

In this case, the diagnosis may be summarized as follows. A descendant (e.g., son) of the consultant is sick because the *yawige* animal the chameleon has caught (*tyo*) him; the consultant has seen this animal in the bush before (in a vision or premonition— *kaɲɔ̃hɔ̃nɔ̃*). The reality of this event, as well as the memory of it by the consulting person, holds no element of necessity. We emphasize that in the majority of cases, the reality test is not made at the level of the adequacy of the explanatory model against empirical givens, but in the choice of an alternative at each stage of the path leading to the formulation of the explanatory model. If, for example, an individual wishes to know the origin of his repeated migraine headaches, and the diviner engages him in an explanation about an accident that occurred during a journey taken by a woman in his homestead, his competence is by that very fact put in doubt. To take up the terms used by Horton, the fallibility of diviners is a constant preoccupation of the Senufo, who, in the face of serious matters, send several persons—preferably strangers to the affair—to several diviners, preferably at a distance from their residence.

The test of the diviner's veracity lies in the relationship of the speaker to the source of the utterance. In divination the speaker is in touch with the earth spirits (*mãdebele*) residing in carved statues. Cultivated earth is the major interdiction of the *sãdoobele*. Using a divination procedure that formally resembles one previously described, the errors of the diviner are explained either by a transgression of this specific interdiction (to have divided the water or the meal of a cultivator, or to have dug in cultivated soil or gathered termites with a hoe) or to the transgression of other rules, personal or collective, sexual or food-related. These transgressions are believed to be followed automatically by the trickery or dumbness of the spirits, and thus offer evidence of the deceit of the diviner.

SUBSTITUTION

The Senufo know the classic mechanisms of the secondary elaboration that permits . . . to move from one diviner to another, and from one etiological register to another, without putting in question the structure of causality. The schemes spelled out above illustrate that one cannot do better than their divinatory art in using the principle of "converging causal sequences" to make possible certain types of substitutions under certain types of conditions. To introduce this central problem here, we recall the shallow character of the terms "remedy" and "remedial prescription" utilized by Horton (1967, 170) to designate action related to, and flowing from, the divinatory prescription. It is as if, for Horton, the therapy, the remedy, was entirely governed by the divinatory instruction. The Senufo materials, at least, lead one to emphasize the separate divinatory and therapeutic analytical prescriptions. Also, among the Senufo the lack of success of a therapeutic course does not require the reiteration of the divinatory process, nor, as a consequence, the substitution of the explanatory model. For, again, the efficacy of a *wara* (medicinal plant) is not tied to a certain criterion of its composition to the explanatory model. In their therapeutic quest the Senufo substitute easily and with pragmatism among institutions and treatments available to them—whether this be local herbalists, fetish owners, or the dispensary—for problems based on a single identical and unchanging causality along the sufferer's itinerary.

Horton's hypothesis concerning the free substitution of causalities fails to make a sufficient distinction between different elements in the antecedent configuration (cause, agent, and origin). We have described the existence of sets of conditions with reciprocal a priori implications—nonsubstitutable (e.g., skin eruptions—*ɲinĩgefɔlɔ*), parallel to those with substitutable but a priori conditions (e.g., diarrhea, *tyefuro*—hot body, fever).

Divinatory interpretation, an exercise in a posteriori causality, utilizes both substitutable and nonsubstitutable connections. In certain cases, the a priori implication is not lost in the process. For example, the metonymic link "strong" between the sickness *laagbo*, bloated abdomen (bloody amebic dysentery) and sexual relations with a woman suffering from amenorrhea or menopause (who thus "conserves" blood) cannot but be confirmed by the diviner if he knows the facts of the case.

Substitutability can, however, be a quality not of the explanatory model taken as a whole, but of one or the other of its elements: cause, agent, or origin. Thus, if, for a case of infantile sicknesses, the diviner engages the series *kaɲɔ̃hɔ̃nɔ̃*—bush—animal—*yawige*, his freedom of permutations is reduced to a choice between the conditions of causes and of the origin (e.g., father or mother, to see or to touch, and so on). In effect, the a priori metonymic link, known to all, between symptom and agent-animal (e.g., eyes open—hare, sores over the body—porcupine) removes all possibility of permutation in the agent-animal relationship. Everyone knows that childrens' sores are caused by the *yawige* porcupine. Substitution here has bearing only on the determination of the causes ("how") and origin ("why").

In the examples cited of the *laagbo* and *yawige*, the recipients of the sickness constitute determinate categories (e.g., married individuals and children). Is there not a relationship between the predetermination of these objects of sickness and the restriction of the freedom of divinatory substitution? This freedom is the greatest, according to all evidence, for the relatively undefined symptomatic registers, those without specification such as fever, or diarrhea, which are the daily lot of a population totally infected by all sorts of dysenteries. It is here that the model of free substitution advanced by Horton remains pertinent. This, and other issues we have raised around the articulation of a priori and a posteriori causality are raised, it seems, in many other analyses of African medical systems.

SÃDOHO

This is the institution that provides the most coherence to Senufo causal thought. When a matrilineage is confronted with repeated infant deaths, diseases of all kinds, a phenomenon perceived as a persistent "fire in the family" (fever, conflicts, anger), the divinatory diagnosis may identify *sãdoho* as the agent of this state of affairs. This untranslatable term designates at one and the same time a power that is coextensive with the matrilineage, which confers the capacity of divination, and is an initiatory institution.

The Lineage Sãdoho

Sãdoho of the lineage conveys to the Senufo the control under which must be placed all sexual relations of women of the matrilineage by a payment called *yapɛrɛ* (thing with which to sweep, i.e., to purify). This payment, which varies according to the lineage, is made by the men to the *sãdoho* of their partners, at the beginning of conjugal life as well as following the discovery of an illegitimate sexual relationship of the woman (adultery, incest). The paradigm that underlies this is that every sexual relationship, legitimate or illegitimate, leads to the pollution (*fwɔ̃rɔ*) of the matrilineage which only the *sãdoho* can cleanse. When misfortunes are repetitive, when the infants of the lineage have abnormally high "hot body" (fever—*tyefuro*), the head of the settlement makes several divinatory consultations. If the diagnoses converge, this pathological condition will be considered as the effect of the pollution caused by the sexual act of a woman of the lineage who is not under the control of the *sãdoho* of the *yapɛrɛ* payment. Adultery is the most frequent hypothesis. The second stage of the process consists of identifying the author of the defilement. Her confession is essential in the annulling of the *fwɔ̃rɔ*, and the ending of the abnormal signs. The efficacy of all empirical treatment of the sickness is consequent to the confession. For certain sicknesses, the lineage *sãdoho* occupies the place of the a posteriori identified agent.

The sufferer, the basis of the symptom, is not the same individual as the initiator of the problem. Every woman who is submitted to the control of the same *sãdoho* can occupy two positions. The field of action of this force defines the contours of a group. The *sãdoho* is the very substance of the matrilineal descent group; it represents the extension and depth of its corporateness. In the sorts of causality dealt with in *sãdoho*, the individuals of a matrilineage are not considered as discrete units in time and space—as we have seen is the case with the causal chains including *yawige* animal agents.

The continuity of the matrilineage subsumed by this force is illustrated by the mode of election and genealogical inscription of individuals who are active members. In each generation, at least one woman is "taken," "captured" (*tyo*) by the lineage *sãdoho* to attach (*pwoo*) the *sãdoho* carried previously by a uterine ancestress. The principle of a chain of *sãdoobele* is that each place left empty by a deceased *sãdotya*, every unattached *sãdoho*, must sooner or later be filled. For every unattached *sãdoho*, in the meantime, is a potential agent of illness. Widely varying problems can be imputed either to the empty place, or to the refusal to occupy it. Thus, the *sãdoho* has a second type of causality, the origin of sickness here being not pollution, but a vacancy.

This type of causality is organized according to the principle of the reactivation of a genealogy. Whether it is a case of women or of men, the dead *sãdoobele* of the matrilineage constitute a stock particular set of ancestors whom the Senufo—especially the Nafara—distinguish from "ordinary" ancestors. It seems justified to speak here of a tendency to replace specific positions, a tendency found in other matrilineal Senufo societies in other forms. Divinatory diagnostics frequently speak of disease imputations due to preinscribed origins in lineage history, such as ancestors, the *sãdoho* in waiting, twins, fetishes left by the dead, inherited interdictions, spirits with which the dead have sealed personal pacts, tutelary water spirits of the lineage, the *yawige* seen or touched by material ancestors, previous lineage witchcraft affairs, and the like. In this list there are instances constituted by the lineage as a corpus of memories set up by previous events, and particularly the misfortunes or sicknesses that "took" the dead (such as spirits allied to the dead). Inasmuch as we can judge, in the mind of the Senufo, these instances and these memories are dissociated. Diverse in appearance, they are nonetheless homogeneous in their causes. One of the central characteristics of the Senufo matrilineage is its tendency to integrate and conserve events.

This tendency to stock divinatory references according to causal categories may be seen not only in the matrilineage but also in the life of the individual. As an individual, one is the point of convergence of singular marks in one's own history, around such points as interdictions, fetishes, spirits, the *yawige* inherited from one's father, or personal, particular *ɲinĩgefɔlɔ* acquired at the time of a sickness.

One (i.e., the individual) is thus the place in which three series of cumulative inscriptions are superimposed: those of one's own lineage, those of one's father, and those of one's own history—the last of which inaugurate, in their turn, a double series for one's children and uterine descendants.

The reactivation of these inscriptions as terms of sickness causality (agent, cause, origin) is a central characteristic of Senufo etiology. Of course, such a procedure is common in many other African societies, and as such does not exhaust the causal thought of the Senufo. Nevertheless, the reactivation of prior events within a collective body—the matrilineage—offers the principle through which the logic of etiology is most coherent.

The proof of this is the identity of the initiatory process in the lineage *sãdoho* and the divination *sãdoho*. Sickness is the initial point of the sequence; it ends with the taking up of the two forms of *sãdoho*. But the initiatory procedure is begun only when the perception of a saturation threshold of suffering has been reached. Following this, the entire group—with divinatory corroboration—is considered to be sick (a series of deaths, persistent illnesses, repeated misfortunes).

This shift in condition is clearly announced in the words of the rite of initiation. It is no longer a case of resolving an episode of illness, but of "extinguishing the fire in the family," of "cooling off the bodies of the children," to do what must be done to "make the words of the family merely like the wind," to "sweep up (*pɛ*) the accumulated pollution (*fwɔ̃rɔ*) in the family." The point of application of the ritual is the individual who will take, "join," and "wear" the *sãdoho*. The field of action will, however, extend to all of the aforementioned causalities and all of the accumulated events in the matrilineage. At this occasion, sacrifices are performed at each of the lineage "places of sacrifice" (*tɛɛsũŋgi*): to twins, to God, to water spirits, to spirits allied to the dead, to the fetishes of the village, to "ordinary" ancestors such as the founder of the lineage, and, of course, to the *sãdoobele* ancestors, named one-by-one beginning with the one whom the initiated replaces, so as to "place the ashes that recool" to the founding *sãdoho* of the matrilineage.

In sum, all the registered agents in the lineage history are activated, and with them the etiological modalities with which they are associated (e.g., *yawige*, *yafũgo*). The set of these sacrifices is the first "shutter that is opened" in cleansing the pollution of all "bad things" accumulated in the family. The second "shutter opened" is the conferral upon the initiate the distinctive attributes and constraints of the new status of *sãdoo*, which will be kept permanently. This procedure calls forth the image of the scapegoat: it occurs as if the totality of constraints that weigh on the matrilineage—Senufo diviners speak of burdens (*tugoro*), fetishes of the earth—is transferred to the initiate. Resented by the individual as a sanction and a life of suffering—and for this reason obstinately refused at the first divination—the status of *sãdoo* carries a series of specific interdictions of which the most coercive is that of not being permitted to cultivate the earth. In this society of cultivators, not to have the right to touch the hoe, not to seat oneself on one's spouse's stool when the latter comes from the fields, not to be able to walk on freshly cultivated earth, and so forth, puts the *sãdoobele* at the margin of normal socioeconomic affairs. Although given other sexual and alimentary interdictions, the initiate is, however, now integrated into the translineage college of *sãdoobele*, others with comparable specific constraints to those that exist in the Poro initiatory organization.

Although all *sãdoobele* are now linked with the earth spirits—of which fertility is a metaphor of lineage fertility—they are not all diviners. The fact that all diviners are *sãdoobele* shows the coextensivity of the function of mastering causality and the support of all causalities immanent in the social structure. It seems that for the Senufo, the condition of such a mastery resides in their ability to apply these principles to institutional situations.

This is a circular arrangement from which one can deduct a general conception of sickness causality founded on the principle of repetition. That is to say, of conservation. It is a principle that expresses itself in different modalities in the two institutions on which Senufo social order is based: the lineage structure and Poro, the initiatory organization. The sickness event, conceived generally as the reactivation of an anterior event, is thus immediately registered and stocked in the collective memory of the lineage. The machinery of divination seems here to have a function of nourishing this memory with its own moments and memories. It all happens as if the system of causality functions in a closed circuit, to the image of a return to the same point that would not recognize distance and duration.

Taking into account this conception, the phenomenon of medical pluralism has a peculiar status among the Senufo. It is necessary to distinguish between the introduction of alternative therapies and new interpretive models. New therapeutic choices can easily be practiced without notable modification of the traditional interpretive perspective. As for the introduction of new interpretive alternatives, they seem to occur only via the mode of the sharp break with the *sãdoho* as paradigm. This can explain the sociomedical upheavals that periodically engulf the Senufo world in the form of prophetic movements or fetish cults, generally coming from the north—as the wars of old. The common denominator of these is the rejection of all the traditional models of causality, including the restrictions of the *sãdoho*.

NOTES

1. This chapter was published as "Modèles et pragmatique, activation et répétition: Réflexions sur la causalité de la maladie chez les Senoufo de Côte d'Ivoire," *Social Science and Medicine* 15B (1981) (3): 279–294. This chapter was translated by John M. Janzen, and is published with the permission of Pergamon Journals Ltd.

2. The term "hypothetical" is to be understood as it is used in logic: it designates a causal link that is conditional, on the model of "if p, then q."

3. It goes without saying that the "symptoms" relate here to either a singular organic manifestation or to a syndrome (*registre symptomatique*).

4. *ɲinĩgefɔlɔ*, "creator" of the individual; *ɲinĩge*, to cause to come out, rise, create; *fɔlɔ*, owner of, and so on.

THIRTEEN

A Modern History of Lozi Therapeutics[1]

Gwyn Prins

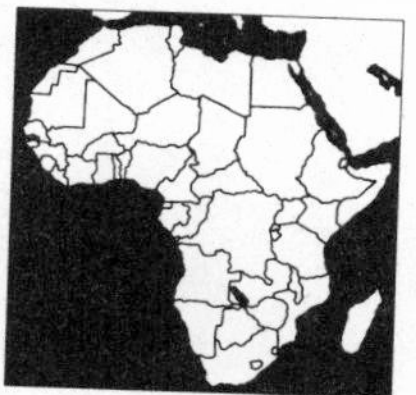

INTELLECTUAL HISTORY AND THERAPEUTICS

The material and intellectual aspects of a society are the warp and weft of its historical canvas. Both are equally essential, and they are mutually interdependent. In studies of "traditional" but contemporary societies, the intellectual aspect is notoriously the most difficult to grasp convincingly. This is even more the case in historical work, where there are daunting problems of evidence. In a study of the Kuba people of Zaire drawn from what must be one of the most extensive bodies of historical cultural data collected for any African society, Professor J. Vansina wrote an entire chapter in order to stress this point. His conclusion poses concisely the underlying problem I want to consider (Vansina 1978, 209–210):

> little can be retrieved concerning religious history and indeed the whole intellectual history of the Kuba. The historian must face the implications of this . . . it is the state of much of the precolonial history of Africa. And I must draw attention to this debility of our reconstruction . . . this particular lack of knowledge will remain a weakness in early African history. And we need to be reminded of that whenever we contemplate trends that are the product of ignorance about both a multitude of events and the motives behind the actions.

This situation has ramifications for the colonial era also because if we are to be able to make best sense of that stream of events, we require good data about both sides in the encounter. The alternative is to presume that we may reasonably infer African motives by analogy, which is not very satisfactory. The long-term solution will be found only when we have many more demonstrably reliable histories of African societies viewed in all their aspects than we have at present.

In the course of doing my other fieldwork,[2] I had come to know a little about healing cults and other therapeutic practices, but only casually. My interest intensified when I went to visit the archives in Zimbabwe, then Rhodesia. There I obtained a copy of a rare book of cultural material collated in the 1890s by a French missionary from Lozi informants under favorable conditions (Jacottet 1896, 1899, 1901). I read it with mounting excitement, for time and again I came across (in recognizable forms) proverbs, stories, explanations of misfortune, symbols whose present-day significance I knew. Given the other enormous turbulences of the colonial experience, the fact of any cultural expression persisting is remarkable enough. What intrigued me, however, was the discovery that it was in the context of affliction and its relief, which included magic and divination, that the historical data made it possible to build up the clearest picture, and thus to enter in detail into the Lozi cosmology of the late nineteenth century and therefore potentially to make the fullest study of the fundamental elements that persisted over time.

Cultural "Core Areas" and the Falsifiability of Knowledge

The preceding subheading is founded on four assumptions that underpin the main methodological suggestion of this chapter, namely how evidence about contemporary therapeutic practice may be usefully employed to historical ends.

1. People place a higher priority on feeling that they understand and control a given situation than on actually doing so. Sometimes the two goals coincide. This assumption has a behavioral consequence that is useful to historians, in that people tend to favor familiar idioms over unfamiliar ones to express things that they consider to be very important.
2. Occam's Razor should be applied to historical explanations and, in the context of all the relevant data, the simplest explanation is to be preferred.
3. In seeking to identify those very important things—the "core concepts" of a society—mentioned in 1 (above), the universal property of perceived affliction rapidly to become a dominant concern until relieved means that recourse is swiftly made to what is considered to be most reliable, which lies in those "core areas."
4. "Core areas" do not behave or appear the same in societies dominated by a scientific way of thinking and those that are not.

These assumptions arise from different sources: assumption 1 is an observation about human nature; 2 is a methodological premise; 3 is like 1; 4 is a bit more abstract, although the ways in which we can employ the other three really hang on what we take it to mean. In the rest of this section, I shall look at each in turn.

The first two assumptions converge to support the hypothesis that "core concepts" will tend to persist and will tend to retain their form. The difficulty with such a hypothesis is that it can be accused of circularity (core concepts persist; what persist are core concepts) and this may be rebutted only by separating convincingly the persisting sheep from the persisting goats, that is, by using another criterion of "coreness." Since there is no reliable way to know where such concepts may pop up—indeed, being so pervasive and therefore vulnerable, part of their defense may be their unpredictable location—we need a guide. For the historian of an African society, the best guide is a thorough working knowledge of the present-day form of the society. In fact, I found that my studies of present-day and past Bulozi were entwined in an inescapable dialectic (Prins 1978, 311). It is one of the rare privileges of the discipline that one has access to that tool, but experience shows that it is often unrealistic to expect historians to use it for to do so involves a long and arduous task. It was then that, for the following reasons, I began to wonder whether the study of therapeutic practices was perhaps a short-cut.

When I first became interested in Lozi therapeutics, I had read none of the comparative anthropological literature. By 1977 when I returned to Bulozi, I had a clearer idea of what anthropologists in Central Africa had said about cults of affliction. I was especially impressed by Turner's work, *Drums of Affliction*, because it appealed to me to be able to read the case material myself and then to see exactly how Turner "cracked the code" of Ndembu rituals and extracted from them a defensible interpretation of the meaning of these powerful dramas within their social settings (Minick 1973; Turner 1968, 8). This work left two forceful impressions. First was the way in which perceived physiological affliction was seen to have resonance in the social and cosmological spheres surrounding the patient. Potential disruption in the first was seen as a likely cause, and drawing on the orderliness and completeness of the second provided remedy, restoring "normality." In fact, it has been this same insight about the acute interaction of these "spheres" that has subsequently struck me as being among the most elegant characteristics of the best recent studies of African medical systems that I know (Janzen 1978*b*; Last 1976, 104–149; Ngubane 1976, 318–357, 1977).

The second impression was a consequence of the first. From an historian's concern with why field data presented themselves in particular forms at particular moments in time, revealing a complex but historically comprehensible pattern of conscious invention and its unconscious side effects, I had become increasingly suspicious of anthropological data collected without apparent awareness of these dangers (Prins 1978*a*, 1980). But the way in which the case materials relating to affliction and its relief, whatever the mode of relief, bored so convincingly to the "core areas" of what really mattered to people in their view of the world as they sought the surest source for remedy, offered such studies the best defense against a charge of historical naivety. So here lies the third supporting assumption.

Norms and beliefs about illness are everywhere culturally "encoded;" the language of symptom and disease is culturally "embedded" and this view underlies the technique of *The Quest for Therapy in Lower Zaire* (Janzen 1978*b*, 7, 191). But we may legitimately assert the converse of Janzen and Arkinstall's proposition: The quest for therapy is about rectifying perceived abnormalities. Ipso facto, it refers back to the notion of "normality"; therefore, the study of this process will serve us well in defining the core and peripheral areas of a culture (core areas are always within but not always conterminous with the area of "normality"). We are defended against the dangers of data manipulated to serve further ends (Henige 1974*a*, 1974*b*, 499; Twaddle 1974*a*, 85, 1974*b*, 303; Vansina 1961, 1974, 109; Waliggo 1976) if we accept our third assumption, which can be expanded thus: because people everywhere are concerned about affliction once it is perceived and seek to be rid of it, and because, as the perceived level of affliction rises, this can rapidly become a preoccupation overriding all others (a point that Turner makes with particular effect), recourse is made to what is most reliable in the quest for remedy. The perception of reliability changes over time as the case history progresses and thus gives us a map of the core and peripheral areas of the entire cultural environment. This offers a valuable specific pathway into intellectual history because of the simplicity of this assumption. So, in a Central African situation of medical pluralism which includes Western medicine, each case history becomes in addition a single minutely detailed guide to the perceived nature of a colonial interaction, an account from the "inside" (Chavunduka 1978; Frankenberg and Leeson 1977*a*, 223–258; 1977*b*, 217; Janzen 1978*b*, 220).

Consciously or by default, all studies of this type adopt a stance on the question of how scientific thought and its material manifestations relate to other modes of thought and theirs. For example, it might be argued that my fourth assumption is incorrect, that there is no real difference because, patently, different modes of thought continue to live side-by-side in people's minds, logically inconsistent perhaps but in practice harmonious because they all stand on the same continuum. This could be a reading of *The Quest for Therapy in Lower Zaire*, but I think that a logic then applied to give the conclusion of basic similarity would be flawed because it confuses two issues. It argues for organized incoherence in patterns of ideas but begs the question of why there is scientific thought at all. In any case, the authors of that work suggest a different intellectual framework for our consideration (Horton 1967, 155; Janzen 1978*b*, 8). Horton offered two central insights. The first helps to explain the tenacity of "core values" even under considerable stress as during a colonial experience as well as the organized incoherence of thought patterns. He distinguished low-intensity and high-intensity situations in life and pointed out that we use common sense in low-intensity situations and mobilize theory only when the stress mounts. It is then that falsification of important beliefs is blocked.

The fact that falsification *is* blocked is a third converging support for our hypothesis of the significance of persisting data, and it means that we should be on the lookout for evidence of this happening. In fact, ever since anthropologists began to think about other societies, the phenomenon has exercised them. Today we have the same range of choices as Frazer, Tylor, and Lévy-Bruhl between basically any "special" theory of primitive mentality or a "general" theory of how anyone blocks falsifiability. Tylor suggested several basic "intellectual conditions for the persistence of magic" which Skorupski has more recently labeled "blocks to falsifiability": means whereby fact and theory lose their ability to collide (Skorupski 1976, 5; Tylor 1873, 133–136). Tylor saw the majority of the successes of magic which he regarded as a "sincere but fallacious system of philosophy" to be the result of "natural means disguised as magic" and/or an "incapacity to appreciate negative evidence." Skorupski observed that both these blocks were the result of *attitude* since they could be removed by the experimental approach. I shall return to this point in a moment. Tylor also suggested a third and different sort of block: failure could be attributed to neglect of conditions or improper execution of rites. Skorupski observed that this was a *structural* block, deriving from the internal logic of the beliefs themselves. Recent thinking about the nature of scientific thought, especially in relation to questions of human behavior, show the sort of scope available for such blocks to operate and suggest motives for them (Hesse 1978, 1–16; Koestler 1959, 227–427; Kuhn 1970). However, the difficulty remains that demonstration of persistence does not explain differences that call up this blocking mechanism in the first place. Why is not the experimental approach mobilized here, particularly when it is clear that in "low-intensity" situations, nonscientific practitioners experiment all the time (Ackerknecht 1971, 17, 95ff.; Janzen 1978*b*)?

Horton's now famous answer is his second insight (Horton 1967, 155):

> that in traditional cultures there is no developed awareness of alternatives to the established body of theoretical tenets; whereas in scientifically oriented cultures, such an awareness is highly developed. It is this difference we refer to when we say that traditional cultures are "closed" and scientifically oriented cultures "open."

However, from one side, case studies such as *The Quest for Therapy* show precisely that people within "traditional" cultures can and do show awareness of alternatives and employ those alternatives without slipping through the looking-glass into a scientific worldview. They do so freely where required in "low-intensity" situations and shielded by selective blocks to falsifiability in "high-intensity" situations. From the other side, work such as Kuhn's suggests that scientifically oriented culture may be less "open" than it once seemed. But this is not an argument for basic similarity in modes of thought. The case studies and analyses presented by Turner, Janzen, Ngubane, and Last and in my own field materials all suggest a different fundamental difference. The case studies reveal that whereas in scientifically oriented cultures, the concentric physiological, social, and cosmological spheres of existence are sharply drawn and discrete so that activity in one need have no implication in others, in traditional societies the spheres are acutely interactive. Gellner has explained this vital contrast and the separation of the spheres in scientific culture as sign and effect, respectively, of the enthronement of truth as the primary judge of data. The real collision, he suggests, is between a world of interacting spheres in which we have a sense of integrated identity and a cold and remote world in which we are able to accumulate vast amounts of effective knowledge (i.e., knowledge that is testable and has predictive potential). His view has been sharply criticized as being romantic. I would merely observe that I find much merit in it for our present purposes because it helps us to organize some of the qualities of this "different difference." Let me distinguish three (Gellner 1974, 158–167).

The first has already been mentioned. When the different spheres of society interact, it is possible that many more aspects of society are involved in supporting the accepted image of understanding and control in that environment. So core concepts (or "entrenched clauses," as Gellner called them) are more pervasive and, because an action or concept may reverberate in spheres other than its own, the converse of core concepts' technically greater vulnerability is their greater importance for social definition than in scientifically oriented society. This should affect the way we examine a colonial encounter. Alerted, we find that for example the history of the primary colonial encounter in Bulozi was essentially the history of how the Lozi defended the core areas in their perception of their world which were in this case entangled with certain aspects of Lozi kingship. But exactly because core concepts are pervasive, the value of any means that may reliably lead us toward them and which is a useful preparation for an approach on a broad front is all the greater.

A second quality of traditional society underlines this point. It possesses a wider and more insistent definition of "normality" than a scientifically oriented society. This "normality" is *moral* in that it defines the social order and is also *cognitive* in that by definition it requires no discussion. To us, this superficially bizarre notion couples closely with the third characteristic, which is that, in Gellner's felicitous phrase, knowledge has no "diplomatic immunity." In other words, the criterion of truth is only one among many, and which criterion dominates in a given circumstance depends above all on the circumstance. Each characteristic has specific implications for the historian.

A "reserved area" of "normality" that requires no discussion sounds like one of the Mad Hatter's propositions. What it means for us in practice is two things. First, we must be prepared to accept that a "core area" may always remain for us a defined area of ignorance. An example would be Evans-Pritchards's explanation of what spirit (*kwoth*) was for the Nuer where he carefully circumscribed what his data could say, excluding the representation of transcendent meaning, but not thereby excluding it from the analysis (Evans-Pritchard 1956, chap. 13). Second, it lays stress upon phenomena that articulate abnormality and thus *refer back* to normality, sketching in the boundary by overstepping it. Affliction and its relief are probably the best phenomena of this kind. But to me, there seem to be clear limits upon what is both semantically and conceptually possible. For example, a cult of affliction which defines a normal state seems to be a contradiction. Either it is not a cult of affliction, or it is not a normal state (Janzen 1979, 317)

The implication of relativity among our criteria and the consequent malleability of our vulnerable data is more directly obvious and better documented, for this is the short explanation of how large-scale invention and manipulation of evidence is possible and why we should be aware of it in assessing any field data. If this suggests the surface agitation that we should expect to find in our data, the two earlier implications suggest the likelihood of considerable long-term stability in core areas (De Craemer et al. 1976, 458).

So, to summarize, if we accept the formulation of assumption 4 which I have sketched out, it suggests that the search for core areas in traditional societies, whether they appear as easily grasped ideas or symbols or only as delineated areas of ignorance, is rather important. This program is supported by assumption 1 and facilitated by the consequence of assumption 1 which I suggested and, from another direction, by assumption 2. The candidacy of medical systems as a vehicle for this search was elegantly supported by assumption 3. Can it be put into practice?

I suggest that there are broadly five types of historical material that we may hope to gather regarding medical systems. Four are illustrated in existing literature to which I have made reference. The first is the most common and is a straightforward description of different therapeutic practices from sources external to the phenomena and which therefore offer good chronological structure to the account. The second is less exploited and harder to obtain. It is the biographical documentation of how individual healers acquired their medical cosmologies. The finest example of this is Janzen and Arkinstall's account of the healer called "Nzoamambu" (Janzen 1978*b*, 161–164).

The third also originates from "internal" evidence but may with luck—which means with high-quality archival data—be tied into an accurate chronological framework. It is a generalized account of disease-causation theories, of diagnostic logic, and of a generalized pattern of which sorts of therapy seem to be appropriate to different degrees of intensity in concern. Ngubane's book lacks the historical dimension, but it is a lucid example of this sort of analysis presented synchronically. The fourth has a limited time-depth within itself but by accumulation will eventually create the best sort of archival source. This is the extended case history, valuable for reasons discussed earlier.

It is important to keep the categories of data distinct in the mind because otherwise there is a danger of illegitimately matching questions to data lacking appropriate characteristics.

A fifth type of material that I want to propose here is the extended case study, which offers us a superb illustration of the way that the spheres of existence interact. To find this evidence, we read the material "horizontally" (diachronically, moment after moment), accompanied by the ethnographer, who points out to us the salient features supporting the analysis as we encounter them. The actors thought and performed the material in this plane. But must the historians wait a generation before they can use such materials—put them into the equivalent of an archive's "closed period?" Can we not impress such material in our pursuit of the history of core areas? Perhaps we could do something analogous to what Lévi-Strauss attempted to do in dissecting myths, namely, read the "horizontal" performance "vertically" (i.e., in a plane not accessible to the performer)? But we should not wish to make an arbitrary code. In the first instance, we might simply hope to isolate recurrent (and therefore arguably important) themes, ideas, and images. Then, on the logic that the "vertical" dissection of a "horizontal" performance protects us against superficial invention and that our assumption (assumption 3) regarding the unique status of affliction protects us against deeper invention, we might reasonably hypothesize that what is causally important in the quest for therapy points us toward core areas in the wider culture. Furthermore, this procedure will also highlight intellectual evidence of how blocks to falsifiability are organized in contacts with Western medicine.

A CENTURY OF THERAPEUTIC HISTORY IN BULOZI

The conceptual and methodological problems that have dominated our concern so far must now recede for a while as I attempt to indicate two perspectives on the history of therapeutics in Bulozi during the last century. After I have done so, we can return briefly to the wider issues to see if and where the account I shall now give helps us with our specific needs.

The two perspectives converge upon the difficulty of distinguishing superficial change and underlying continuity from underlying change and superficial continuity. The first one looks at Lozi theories of disease, visible especially in therapeutic techniques and in the generalized pattern of therapeutic options available. This is the heart of any therapeutic system and therefore is the logical place to begin. I shall demonstrate stability over the century in these areas. During most of this schematized description, I put the question of Western medicine into abeyance, but introduce it at the end.

The second perspective takes up the theme of pluralism; it has two parts. The first of these proposes an "external" history of medical pluralism in Bulozi, suggesting the outline of a chronology for the changing pattern of therapeutic options. I take each major sort of option in turn, and we observe the attraction of structural explanation for one of them. But in that case—the cults of affliction—"external" evidence also exists to question the dramatic structural contrasts. This skepticism grows when we approach the history of the cults "internally," trying to read case material "vertically." I conclude that in trying to understand cultural interaction it is perhaps too easy to be unduly influenced by the visibility of phenomena as we decide how to allocate weight in our analysis.

I propose a rider to this second (narrative) perspective because unavoidably it projects an image of a roughly constant spectrum of physiological illnesses confronted by changing configurations of therapeutic options. In fact, preliminary findings suggest that in Bulozi we may have to conceive of the colonial experience as having specific effects that widened the spectrum of disease as well as of therapeutics. As already stated, this chapter concludes with a reconsideration, in the light of the Lozi evidence, of the suggestion that a study of pluralistic medicine might help us toward reliable knowledge of wider intellectual systems.

Two notions dominate Lozi thinking about disease. The first is of its circular passage through the world which sets conceptual limits on its behavior; the second is that there are two distinct but related ways of encountering disease which thus give direction to the momentum from diagnosis to remedy.

All the good and all the evil in the world are ultimately the creation of the High God Nyambe. In the world he placed a fixed quantity of disease and so all that an individual who is afflicted can hope to do is to be rid of his affliction through the exercise of *butali* (skill, cunning). However, in so doing, he unavoidably places someone else at risk, consciously or not: the devils cannot just be cast out; they do not evaporate, but will find the unfortunate and innocent Gadarine swine. The notion of circularity is most evident in the treatment of more serious afflictions.

In the Nzila cult treatment instituted by Katota Chana, which is now common in Bulozi, the patient is first diagnosed to be suffering from *Nzila* through an interrogation by the *ñaka* (healer). The patient sits on a chair facing another chair or stool covered with a white cloth on which are laid a knife, a fly-whisk (or a small hoe and a small grass broom) and a *cuptea*—a china cup filled with bone paste that has a cross molded in the top, like a hot-cross bun. The cross is called *Mbilingwa*. Bells are rung around the patient's head and if he indeed suffers from *Nzila*, the diagnosis established, he runs off wildly into the bush where, guided by the spirit Moya, he collects plants, leaves, and roots, collectively called *tusenge*. Meanwhile a small shelter (*hupa*) is constructed by relatives outside the village following a prescribed ritual involving the slaughter of chickens. If the cure is successful, the bones of these fowls are crushed to make the patient's *cuptea*. The patient returns with a *tusenge*, enters the *hupa*, and remains there, washing each day with an infusion from the *tusenge*. After different tests by the healer, the cure is confirmed with the destruction of the *hupa*, and the remains of the medicine, now containing the disease, are thrown away. The safest form of disposal is to place the disease in a miniature hut of twigs at a crossing of paths and then to avoid passing that way again since the disease will enter into the next passerby. Now cured, the patient returns home, makes his *cuptea*, and then is a potential healer himself, able to repeat the cycle for other sufferers.

This method of disposal, which makes my point, is common to other forms of therapy than this relatively recent and highly visible cult. Here it is in 1887, described by the founder of the Paris Evangelical Mission in Bulozi (Coillard 1887):

> At the crossing of two paths in the wood I noticed three stakes with magic grasses where someone had boiled medicines and close by a *sefunda*, a circle traced in the sand with the foot. Nguana Kwai (Mwana Kwai: literally "son of tobacco") and Libonda let out a shout of fear seeing me put my feet inside the magic circle, touch and examine the little shelter. "Teacher! You'll die from it! Here is where the *ñaka* has disposed of someone's disease and if you even only approach it, you are sure not only to catch it but to die from it! When we see such things, we make a large detour."

Why such consistency in this persisting idiom? It is central in Lozi medical cosmology and is protected by the "attitude" type of block to falsifiability.

Affliction of an individual may come from one of two sources: "disease of God" or "disease of humans." A person is vulnerable to diseases of God if out of balance with the physical world. Each of the four elements—fire, air, water, and earth (which includes vegetable and animal matter)—contains harmonious and discordant potential. Loss of equilibrium unleashes the discordant potential. Therefore, the aim of therapy for diseases of God is to restore the balance.

Since, in this view, the human body belongs to the "earth" elements, but is animated by the others, symptomatic treatment of body problems calls forth response from a large stock of "folk" remedies and, in more acute cases, specialist remedies, within the pharmacopoeia. In the 1890s Adolphe Jalla, second-in-command of the Zambezi Mission, observed that while physiological knowledge was rudimentary, there being no concept of the function of the organs, the circulation of the blood, and so on, the Lozi possessed a wide range of effective symptomatic treatments, especially purgatives and emetics (Jalla n.d., 127). It is a significant emphasis, for painless digestion and regular daily defecation are important indicators of health and balance; their interruption is an early warning of incipient illness. I do not have information from analysis of the active principles and properties present in the treatments prescribed for specific symptoms, although I do possess details of such treatments collected in the 1930s (Mataa 1935) and by myself in the 1970s, as well as published compendia for two neighbouring areas sharing basically the same botanical resources as Bulozi (Gilges 1955; Symons 1956; Trapnell and Clothier 1937).[3] But simply to look at these lists is to gain several impressions. First, they would not be recoverable in these forms if much of this medicine has not worked, an observation similar to that which Ackerknecht made for primitive pharmacopoeia in general (Ackerknecht 1971, 17). However, second, while there seems to be a stable group of constant therapies, there is a shifting penumbra where change and experiment appears to happen. Third, with no proper notion of dosage, even if the active principle was correct, the chance of failure had to be increased (De Vente, personal communications); finally, the first of Tylor's blocks to falsifiability (that by association with natural recovery) was probably as important here as in any medical system (Shapiro 1960, 109). In figure 13.1, these types of therapy mostly occupy the left-hand area, bounded by the axes "symptomatic treatment" and "individual" to "*ñaka*." They concentrate upon the physiological sphere of the patient's existence—his body.

However, disease could also come from humans. Employing the same image already used, this occurred if harmony ("normality") in society was perceived to be disrupted. This could come about in three main ways: through breach of social norm, through infringement of taboos (*miila*), and through witchcraft (*buloi*). I place these in increasing order of seriousness. Each threat elicited an appropriate sort of response.

Disease as a result of human agency can range from infringing a *sifunda*, that is ignoring a warning, to bewitching, which is qualitatively different. Again to illustrate the durability of these notions of causation, I shall use a nineteenth-century case. The worst *sifunda* to ignore was that established after a successful curing, the one so feared by Reverend Coillard's companions in 1887. However there were other types. Illness could come from breaking the menstrual taboo—a man doing so would be afflicted with a serious cough; this has remained a common folk diagnosis of tuberculosis. Similarly, to break the postpartum taboos incurred grave risks. In late March 1890, the wife of Kanoti Nalumango (himself a skilled "symptomatic" healer and assistant of the Zambezi Mission's white artisan) miscarried in their village, Nakonga, close to the Mission Station at Sefula. To avoid illness, she was immediately taken and confined in a small hut outside the village. Her husband had to remain within the village, but had to avoid crossing the tracks of cattle lest they miscarry, or going near to growing crops. After the next new moon, his wife was entirely shaved, her cooking pot and calabash bowl broken, the hut where she had been, destroyed and then everything burned. Another *sifunda* that has proved remarkably durable concerns property. A thief might become ill with colic if he ignored the warning of a line drawn in the sand to make a charmed circle (*lishengo*), or knotted grass near a field of grain (the most common *sifunda* that I have seen). The unfortunate Nalumango infringed a *sifunda* shortly after his wife's miscarriage and told Coillard that only the person who had made the charm could give him medicine to cure it (Coillard 1890). The idea parallels that of God as source both of affliction and its cure.

Bewitching is most serious because it is the result of conscious endeavor to create abnormality. In these circumstances, the arsenal of divination is mobilized—*ngombo* (divining basket), *litaula* (knuckle bones) and the twentieth-century addition, *sikuyeti* (a gourd filled with latex with a small mirror set into it in which the future is seen; a television set is also *sikuyeti* in siLozi). The outcome of divination may be recourse to any of a range of nonsymptomatic treatments involving individual specialists more frequently than group therapy. But while I do not wish to enter into a further description of witchcraft in Bulozi, it must be said that here too, the idea of a deliberate inversion of norms in order to create "dark" power fits into the basic dualism of the theory of causation. This conceptual integrity is presented in three dimensions in the story of Mwendanjangula or Muba. It shows the common conceptual matrix of group and individual therapies' theories of disease causation; it shows the basic dualism of those theories and it shows how any sort of power possesses "positive" and "negative" potential, waiting to be activated. Furthermore, the myth anchors all this in detail at either end of our chronology.

Mwendanjangula or Muba was and is a monster who inhabits the deep forest. He is described as a man made half of wood and half of wax, divided vertically, or just half a man—one arm, one eye, one leg, one buttock (Jacottet 1899, 122–124, 138–139; 1901, 133–135). He sang like a bird in the 1890s and his victims were drawn irresistibly toward him. Once they saw him, then and in the 1970s they were lost, for like his human brothers, the witches (*baloi*), Mwendanjangula enslaved their spirits (Jacottet 1901, 133–135). He possessed many valuable medicines that could affect behavior of animals and humans. In the 1890s attention was drawn to his possession of "ruling medicine" that could make one a chief. The implication of this is that power to control both nature and humans—to be healer or chief—was linked to "dark" power. The old and modern versions continue; they tell that a man fights with Mwendanjangula and forces him to give up his secrets of power. From this battle comes the Muba healing cult. However, the version of the

1890s stressed the Promethean strain latent in it. After his victory, the man went home, but fell very sick: while power could make men mighty, it could also break them. Nemesis is never far from hubris (Jacottet 1901, 133–135).

Symptomatic treatment characterizes "low-intensity" situations (fig. 13.1). It has been within this sphere that Western medicine has been easily incorporated. Lozi enthusiasm for penicillin injections and courses of chloroquine coupled to the liberal distribution of these drugs from bush dispensaries may soon pose in itself a serious medical problem, while in 1977, testosterone injections were rapidly becoming a new craze. Western medicine is of course very good at setting broken bones, cutting and stitching inside and outside the body, stopping infections, binding up wounds, and successfully concluding difficult deliveries. It is in these sorts of circumstances that ever-increasing numbers of villagers as well as townspeople converge upon the hospitals of Bulozi.

Reputations of individual medical doctors spread rapidly on the bush telegraph, and the size of the clientele is a reliable measure of this, for people travel huge distances to seek the attention of a famous Western physician. I saw this happen dramatically in a mission hospital in 1977 where there had been a succession of mediocre young physicians until, in August, a new surgeon arrived. He had recently retired as chief of surgery from a group of California hospitals. He and his wife spent a fortnight scrubbing the theater and improvising equipment (for example, suction and instant incineration was provided by attaching an airline to the carburetor air intake of a Land Rover parked outside the theater). He then began to operate, and when I visited the hospital on September 12, I found the local government hospital virtually empty while the new surgeon had wards overflowing with patients not only from that district, but from elsewhere in Bulozi as well as guerrilla casualties from the Angolan civil war.

It would not be fair to suggest that Western medicine is appealed to only in "low-intensity" situations. The essence of "shuttling" as described by Janzen and Arkinstall (Janzen 1978*b*) or by Chavunduka (1978) is precisely that it is not. In Bulozi there is a distinction between *matuku a sintu* (African diseases) and *matuku a sikuwa* (white man's diseases). It is based on the perceived diagnosis of a case at any given moment, so a patient may find himself being moved from system to system as the diagnosis of his affliction alters over time. The distinction is basically between afflictions that have reverberations beyond the physiological sphere and those that do not. Of course, a major indicator that a simple fever, swelling or headache has such reverberations arises when it is not fairly quickly alleviated by whatever type of symptomatic treatment is first tried. Therefore, as a case increases in intensity, the first part of that pathway will usually be parallel to an increase in severity of symptoms. But useful discussion of this sort of complex interaction is only possible in the presence of case histories that at the moment I do not possess.

		Symptom	Therapy	Symptom	Therapy	Symptom	Therapy
Low intensity	Symptomatic treatment	*Minor body aches*	Herbal infusions, drunk and applied	A skilled *ñaka* would have available similar types of treatment for any case listed to the left where the condition became more serious than village lore could handle, or if village applied remedies seemed to produce no response. Especially likely to go to the *ñaka* were:			
		Wounds *Swelling* *Skin-scaling*	Animal fat and plant preparations, usually applied				
		Snake and dog bites	External washing, wound suction, emetics				
		Accidental poison	Emetics				
		Leprosy *Smallpox* *Measles*	Herbal infusions used to wash external symptoms			*Depression* *Evil dreams* *Insanity* *Body pains* (often in conjunction with depression) *Severe headaches*	*Liyala* *Siyoya* *Maimbwè* *Muba* and modern derivatives Involve inhalations, washing, sweating
		Constipation	Purgatives				
		Colds, minor coughs	Inhalation of steam from boiling herbal medicines				
		Headache	Cupping with horns				
		Evil dreams	Herbs chewed, spells recited, sitting in the sun	*Abcesses*	Lancing		
		Mild aphrodisiac	Herbs chewed	*Love potions, stronger aphrodisiacs*	Herbal and animal preparations, spoken spell		
		Abortion	Abortifaciant suppositories	*More difficult obstetrics*	Vaginal incisions		
		Simple obstetrics	Uterine contractant, postpartum vaginal anaesthetic from herbs	*Venereal diseases*	Infusions applied and taken, applied via steam or smoke, scarification		
		Gynecological complaints	Various suppositories				

Intensity	Treatment	Individual	"Folk"	Ñaka	Cause (*muloi*)	Communal	
	Divination and symptomatic treatment	*Headaches*	Standing in the wind of a felled tree as it falls				
				Difficult obstetrics	Bewitching		
				Infertility	Taboo breaking, bewitching		
				Pediatrics	Ancestor unquiet, spirit enslavement		
				Severe coughing	Sign of cannibalism		
				Poisoning	*Muloi*, direct action		
				Depression, *Evil dreams*, *Insanity*	Attempts at spirit enslavement		
				Control of wild animals	Evil metempsychosis, familiar		
				Acute forms of common complaints (e.g., indigestion)	Taboo infringement, etc.		
	Divination and nonsymptomatic treatment					*Depression* *Evil dreams* *Insanity* *Body pains* (often in conjunction with depression) *Severe headaches*	*Liyala* *Siyaya* *Maimbwe* *Muba* and modern derivatives Involve inhalation, washing, sweating Disease disposal as described in text
High intensity							

INDIVIDUAL ⟶ "FOLK" ⟶ ÑAKA ⟶ COMMUNAL

Figure 13.1. Low intensity and high intensity (*matuku a sintu* = African diseases) disorders in Lozi treatment.

However, I believe that there is one more helpful observation to be gleaned from generalization.

Figure 13.1 also includes *matuku a sintu*. Severity of symptom moves diagonally across the diagram, but it is the form of diagnosis that determines the status of superficially similar cases. Thus similar types of communal therapy can be mobilized for "low-intensity" problems, or for more severe afflictions of God or of humans. Off the chart lie the largest scale form of appeal, the royal graves (*litino*), to which recourse can be made in times of national crisis, for example, the smallpox epidemic of the early 1890s or the serious droughts of the mid-1970s. The logic of this progression of increasing scale is clearly visible. Also clear is the simple division among therapeutic options in Bulozi. Consistently during the last hundred years, there have been four: Western medicine; the specifics of "folk" medicine; different sorts of specialist *liñaka* (specialists in different symptomatic therapies; in protective medicines against witchcraft; in divination and witch-finding); communal treatment of afflictions called "cults of affliction" by outsiders, *ku folisa mwa milupa* (to cure with drums) by Malozi. One could add various *rites de passage*, which, like the postparturition ritual mentioned above, have a protective function, but here I prefer to leave them aside. Now I shall take each type of therapy except "folk" specific treatment and give thumbnail sketches of how *likalafo za sintu* and *likalafo za sikuwa* (African and whiteman's medicine) have fared during the twentieth century in Bulozi. This is the first part of the second and narrative perspective.

François Coillard, founder of the Zambezi Mission, was the first person to try and apply Western medicine in Bulozi on any scale. Travelers from Livingstone onward had used their medicine chests, of course, but Coillard set about making and using smallpox serum during the epidemic of the early 1890s. He vaccinated people near his Mission Station at Sefula, but was soon summoned by King Lewanika to vaccinate the inhabitants of the royal capital instead (Coillard 1892, 9, 22, 31). In retrospect, the vaccination campaigns instituted during the period of British South Africa Company rule, which ended in 1924, were the biggest single Western medical intervention (with the building of hospitals which began in the 1900s). In 1912/13, 27,000 people were vaccinated against smallpox throughout the country; in 1923/24 a severe smallpox epidemic even closed the mission school at Sefula; 20,000 vaccinations were carried out in the regions adjoining Angola to the northwest and 17,500 in the Sesheke district to the southwest. Smallpox was still rife in the south in 1929/30 and during those years, virtually the entire population of Sesheke district (insofar as the Native Commissioner could judge), was vaccinated. The agents used were the members of the District Messenger Service, the body of men who actually made colonial government work (*Barotse Annual Reports* 1929). A different sort of mass campaign to cure venereal diseases between about 1925 and 1931 met with little success, despite the Medical Officer's optimism at the time (Jalla 1931, 28).

In 1899 the Mission received its first major reinforcement of fourteen white missionaries, among them Dr. Roderic de Prosch, who, with his wife, joined Coillard at Sefula. By the end of 1901, nine of the new arrivals were dead. When this news reached Switzerland, it horrified Dr. George Reutter, who volunteered to go to the Zambezi to look after the missionary community. He arrived in 1902 complete with a portable mosquito-proof house, the first seen in Bulozi, which was erected at the southernmost mission station of Sesheke.

In 1903 de Prosch, now a widower, moved to Mabumbu, twenty miles north of Sefula up the edge of the flood-plain and there, in 1907, was erected the first brick-built hospital in Bulozi. By that year also, mosquito-proof housing had been provided at all the main mission stations, paid for out of a special building fund that had been set up for that purpose at the instigation of Dr. Reutter. At about the same time, a hospital and dispensary for the Lozi were built at the administrative center, Mongu, using receipts from the newly imposed poll tax. In 1910 Dr. Huntley Pelly became the first government medical officer to be stationed there, also conducting out-patient clinics in the royal capital, Lealui, three times a week. He was soon succeeded by Dr. Stanley Colyer.

In Sesheke, Reutter was disappointed with the Lozi response to Western medicine during the early years (as was Pelly in Mongu). However, Reutter saw a change by 1909 that he attributed to the increasing numbers of Lozi who had experienced life in the south through labor migration. In 1910 de Prosch left Bulozi and subsequently died of malaria on the upper Nile while en route to Europe. Reutter replaced him at Mabumbu for two years, but because of family pressure, left Bulozi himself in 1912. However, he could not settle in the Jura again and in 1925 returned to Sesheke and there opened Mwandi hospital. He conducted surgery and inaugurated attempts to treat venereal diseases on a wide scale, although, like the government campaign, since he had no antibiotics, he had little success. Until he left Bulozi in 1931, he was the dominant Western physician. Indeed, Western medicine was a charismatic affair for much of the colonial era. In this, government doctors could scarcely compete since in fact a good deal of their time was taken up in examining potential recruits for the migrant labor organizations before the depression of the 1930s (Gelfand 1961, 43, 50–53, 185, 187). Understandably, it has been the long-serving mission doctors, almost all fluent siLozi speakers, who have entered popular memory: Drs. de Prosch and Reutter of the medical pioneering generation, Dr. Casalis of Senanga district, Dr. Vila of Sesheke district, and Dr. Birkenstock of Kalabo district in the later colonial period.

When we begin to find tabulated returns in the archival sources they reveal that hospital treatments in the early years were overwhelmingly in those "low-intensity" specific categories where Western medicine was conspicuously powerful: malaria, conjunctivitis, some peripheral venereal diseases, diarrhea, and wounds. But medical reports echoed a constant refrain about the puny scale of effort against the mass of visible disease—syphilis, eye ailments, leprosy, and smallpox.

As a result of the money made available under the wartime Colonial Welfare and Development Act, all aspects of colonial government in Bulozi received an injection of new vigor in the 1950s. The system of mission dispensaries attached to mission stations, which had been a feature since very early days, was complemented with new bush dispensaries staffed by "hygiene assistants"; the mission hospitals received increased grants, the Mongu hospital was expanded, and more medical officers were posted to Bulozi. However, it was only really after independence that the Western health system was extensively expanded: new hospitals in each district township, more bush clinics, rural health centers, and more personnel in large numbers. As the long-serving mission doctors slowly disappeared through retirement, they were replaced with an ever changing and very international assortment of physicians. The people rapidly learned to discriminate in the way I illustrated earlier, for while the technical provision of facilities and drugs is now greater than ever before, the Health Service staggers from severe bureaucratic sclerosis, uneven standards of competence among all levels of personnel, irregular supply of consumable stores, and, fundamentally, of cash. At one stage in 1977, the Zambian Ministry of Health became technically bankrupt.

Although there is a move at present afoot to regularize "traditional healers" throughout Zambia by compilation of a register, *liñaka* have not yet encountered problems of organizational paralysis in Bulozi. Among the various specialists, some have been more conspicuous in "external" sources than others. From the earliest visits we know of rainmakers and diviners. Livingstone's famous conversation with the rainmaker was both a good illustration of Tylor's blocks to falsifiability at work in both parties and an illuminating statement of the logic of *muliani* (medicine): it is a trigger fashioned in the tangible world to produce reaction in the cosmological spheres where the real power resides (Livingstone 1960, 240). Livingstone also observed a form of divination using a small axe that gives a yes/no answer by remaining fixed on the ground or being able to be lifted freely which I have observed in use in the 1970s. Similarly, the divining mechanisms with baskets and knuckle bones extensively described in early Mission literature remain in common use (Jacottet 1901, 165; Livingstone 1960, 48). Another category of *ñaka* whose power, like that of the diviner, borders on that of the witch, is the specialist who can control animals. Of these the most important are the crocodile doctors, frequently documented by traders and officials because for a fee they would ensure that livestock swam the Zambezi River in safety. All these specialists, the animal-controlling doctors, could be involved in diagnosing affliction if it were suspected that the patient was suffering a temporary metempsychosis of spirit as a result of witchcraft.

However, the history of *liñaka* during the colonial era was not of simple stagnation, but rather more of entrepreneurial verve. The major growth areas have been in the sale of protective medicines to avoid bewitching on the one side and in new and, it was claimed, ever more effective paraphernalia to bewitch, poison, or affect behavior on the other. On the "protection" side, there has been a snowballing effect since the 1950s and today two individuals, Bo Saasa and Bo Ndopu, who live several hundred miles apart, dominate the market, each catering for clientele from the other's area. This is because there is always the danger that a specialist who gives protective medicine may actually be a covert witch, hoping thus to trap the patient and to enslave his spirit (*silumba*). But enslaved spirits like to remain close to home, so to travel far is additional insurance. Again, as with Western doctors, the bush telegraph provides case histories of successes that hearten the timid who therefore seek safety with the multitude. These two men also sell medicines for luck and success in examinations and job-seeking, but there are also many small men active in this less dangerous part of the market.

The offensive side of the trade tends to be less conspicuous. Two circumstances have affected it during the twentieth century. The first was labor migration, especially to the Transvaal gold mines after the mid-1930s. Within the southern African market for effective poisons, the Malozi have a high reputation among Lozi, especially those people from the Nyengo part of Kalabo district. During the heyday of migration to the Rand, a very extensive trade in dangerous substances developed, with Lozi migrants taking their wares down to South Africa and selling them in the compounds for cash or kind. Among the objects that came into Bulozi in exchange was the *kaliloze* or night gun.

The *kaliloze* gun came in two models. One was fashioned out of a human arm bone. One joint head was cut off, the marrow removed, the outside decorated with the red and black seeds of the *munjindu* tree (*Erythrina abyssinica* or "kaffir boom") set in wax, and then it was loaded with medicine and fired at the rising sun, sending a curse (*siposo*) upon the victim. The other was also decorated with *munjindu* seeds but was more direct in its action, being made out of a length of gas-pipe and firing a 0.303 cartridge, iron filings, and so on. We know all this because it came to light during the great government-initiated witch-hunt of 1956–1958, which is the second circumstance, for it drove the traffic deep underground.

The mine compound market also provided other types of special medicines appropriate to the odd social situations created by migrant labor—for example, *lunyoka*. In 1929, Bo Kamui of Sinumanyambe (near Sefula) was brought to court by his neighbors accused of murdering Mutaluka with *lunyoka*. This was a medicine that Kamui had obtained at Sinoia in Rhodesia and which he had compelled his wife to take on his return. Its effect was that any man not possessing the antidote (i.e., the husband) who had intercourse with the woman would be unable to urinate or defecate and would swell up and die. This, it was alleged, happened to Mutaluka. The consensus of the Chief Messenger and the Chief Adviser to the Native Commissioner was that this medicine first was heard of in the early 1920s. To the fury of his accusers, Kamui was released. The Native Commissioner's elegant logic was that since the Medical Officer assured him that no medicine could produce this effect, not to release the accused was tantamount to a confession that he believed in the medicine, which he did not. In fact *lunyoka* was not new. There is evidence (personal communications, MacGaffey 1979) of it under a different name in nineteenth-century Kongo. It was new to Bulozi and therefore it illustrates a sensitive response to market demands there. One could multiply examples of this sort, but this must stand as illustration of that general point. It was matched in the low-intensity area of specific treatments where healers adopted tablets and especially syringes into their rituals of treatment.

In all these areas of specialization, there is a strong impulse, even today when the prevailing government attitude is not hostile, to keep everything hidden. This is the residual effect of the Great Witch-Hunt of the late 1950s when large numbers of healers were arrested as witches (including Katota Chana of *Nzila*). These events only strengthened the presumption of hostility between Western medicine, especially as practiced by missionary physicians, and African healers. The witch-hunt has also left a specific technical problem for the historian fieldworker because it is popularly believed that the real cause of the witch-hunt was an anthropologist who asked questions about African therapeutics in the 1940s and then gave lists of names to the colonial authorities, on which they subsequently acted. I know of no evidence to substantiate this opinion, but that is not what matters to potential informants.

The way in which people are cured with drums has not changed in method since our earliest observed sources. But while those aspects expressing the theory of disease causation have been stable, change has occurred in two other respects.

Early reports usually called all group therapy "Liala" (Jacottet 1901, 1560–1577; Jalla 1931, 122). Subsequently, other names began to be mentioned—*Siyaya*, *Muba* (originating in southern Bulozi), *Maimbwe* (from the Nkoya to the east), and then, during the midcolonial era, *Bindele* or *Makuwa* from the Luvale. These later arrivals used words and artifacts that aped the Europeans, incorporating ways of handling new problems within established idioms (Colson 1971; Ranger 1975). However, the result was not a proliferation of autonomous cults but rather a sedimentary accretion, offering a constantly updated range of appropriate idioms from which the eventual diagnosis could be drawn.

The second sort of change appears to contradict this explanation. During the winter of 1931, Bo Mulemwa, who lived at Kaande, near Mongu, began to preach in the name of the Watchtower movement. He did so without requesting permission from the Lozi traditional hierarchy who therefore regarded his movement as a threat and infiltrated it with fifth-columnists who provided information that led to his arrest and conviction for seditious teaching. Upon Mulemwa's arrest, one Josias Nyanga came from Fort Jameson to take over, but was removed, and the movement subsided except for a recurrence in east Senanga district when Luka Milimo, one of Mulemwa's assistants, returned home (he was the local chief's nephew) after release from prison in 1934 (personal communications, Francis Suu 1975). The Watchtower movement has not disappeared in Bulozi, although it never subsequently recruited members in such numbers so quickly. Officials at the time noticed that Luvale people resident in Bulozi, and people in rather remote areas, like Lumbe, provided the most fertile recruiting grounds. The episode has been seen both as an expression of popular discontent with the Lozi ruling class and as millennarianism (Caplan 1970, 146; Ranger 1968, 228), and there are elements of truth in both views. But what is relevant here is that the Watchtower episode presented a new paradigm, taken up in the later colonial era movements whose charismatic leaders' minds were formed by the experiences of the 1930s.

In the case of Chana, his affliction began in 1928 and lasted until 1940. His family considered him to be mad. After hospital treatments failed, he eventually cured himself with *tusenge* (medicinal plants, leaves, roots) under the guidance of Moya and then in the later 1940s began to treat others. The first twelve patients he treated became like disciples and his movement rapidly expanded, becoming a registered sect with an English written constitution by 1966 and claiming 80,000 followers throughout Zambia. By this stage, the Nzila Sect was drawing large numbers of people away from the established Christian churches although its constitution (Rule III[c]) stated that there was no conflict of loyalties. One of Chana's senior assistants defected to the Paris Mission founded by Coillard and wrote an exposé of the Nzila Sect (Sefula Book Depot) which represented it as a direct challenge to the churches. Meanwhile, the sect itself was experiencing schism. Lingomba Mululu fell sick in 1953 and entered Chana's Nzila. However, his Moya did not like Chana's treatment and led him away to treat himself with water in bottles from which arose his alternative Nzila therapy, a biography very similar to Chana's own. Clearly the notion of a *cana*, or charismatic individual as focus of each movement, was an idea whose time had come. The old Muba complex of afflictions was also updated into the new Mumatuke version by Mutumwa in the 1960s.

The structural differences between the "old" and "new" affliction complexes are indeed striking, and van Binsbergen has drawn from them a contrast between "nonregional" (old) and "regional" (new) cults which is obviously correct. I look at the situation rather differently. In the first place we must wonder whether the Nzila Sect (as distinct from Nzila) is still a cult of affliction in the sense defined at the beginning of this chapter. It seems to me that the defector's instinct was right, for the sect had become a syncretist church, fulfilling through its regular church-like services different sorts of needs.[4] It is conspicuous that even in the largest congregations, such as that of Mukwae (Princess) Isikanda near the brickfields in Mongu, the "service" and therapy sessions are divided. Furthermore, most people experience Nzila at a remove from this formal structure, in contexts where it clearly deserves the title of cult of affliction.

If we adopt this viewpoint, the structural contrasts appear much less important, the complex interweaving of the Nzila canon of diagnostic songs with others involved in communal therapy, much more striking. Reading the case studies "vertically" gives us a different insight. We can see borrowing of known and durable themes: the *ngombo* (divining basket) is prominent, involved with the idea of fire and the imbalance of elements. We find appeal to the legitimacy of chiefship, a sharing with other cults of important idioms, for example that of the galloping whiteman's horse, which is also Moya's horse, or that of the unquiet spirit. We see Nzila employing old and well-known symbolisms, like that of the chameleon and also evidence of its parentage from Bindele in the consistent use of European themes. There are the powers expressed in writing, the telephone (Moya is alerted in some of the Chana Sect hymns by a cry of "hello, hello, hello"), the white man's church through baptism, catechism, the idea of the charismatic prophet and, indeed, by direct association: dead spirits = air; air = Moya = Christ. Then there is the Europeans' strange diet, celebrated in the *cuptea* and explained as a source of abnormal power, power associated with that of inversion of normality. Cleanliness is central to Nzila thought, which emphasizes being rid of *malabishi* (rubbish) and filth, both moral and physical. Filth is in one place identified directly as a source of "dark" power, and most European things qualify as rubbish.

I offer the impressionist outline of the preceding paragraph as a suggestion of how even from limited observed data one can proceed in order to counterbalance the forcefulness of "external" evidence. But even such a brief set of indications is sufficient to stress a point frequently lost from "external" evidence: we see that while the colonial culture is blocked from damaging core beliefs, it is simultaneously a source of reinforcement by association. To use and to handle is to control. So this is, in fact, evidence for a hypothesis of circular logic to help block falsifiability not by withdrawal into millennarianism, but by vigorous and selective adoption of the threatening forces. I suggest tentatively that in this case the regional/nonregional distinction, while correct, is not as illuminating as an approach from this hypothesis because I find that it offers a potential historical answer, while the other only at best describes an enabling mechanism.

THE EPIDEMIOLOGY OF MAJOR DISEASES IN BULOZI

An iron cooking pot such as is used in Bulozi stands upright only because it has three legs; the same goes for a narrative of affliction and its relief. The first two "legs" I have indicated—Western and African modes of therapy—the third is epidemiology, for the changes in therapeutics that I have suggested did not occur against a static background of unaltering diseases.

Inspired largely by John Ford's example, historians of Africa have recently begun to turn to the study of ecological disruption with great enthusiasm for the theories, even if the data have sometimes not been there in equal proportion (Ford 1971; Kjekshus 1977; Palmer and Parsons 1977). In Bulozi, the particular ecology makes a "catastrophe" interpretation of the late nineteenth century unavailable. The successive smallpox epidemics mentioned from Livingstone's time until the midtwentieth century, and possibly sleeping sickness, were the only major examples of diseases of God that exceeded the capacities of the established therapeutic options (although in the 1890s, there were rumors of primitive vaccination). But during the twentieth century, the particular form of the colonial economy that affected Bulozi—that of migrant labor to the mines of the south—may have widened the spectrum of disease in the country with effects still apparent today.

Venereal diseases were described as a serious affliction by early travelers, and in early administration reports, syphilis was, with leprosy, consistently at the top of the table. However, Lozi make clear distinctions within the generic name *manansa* between *maondo* (the "indigenous" strain), *kashewenge* (syphilis brought back by carriers who went to the 1914–1918 war), and *machangane* (venereal disease strains brought back from the South African mines—"machangane" = Shangaan, the Mozambique people blamed for this). But while this relationship was seen, understood and to a small extent attacked at the time, the expansion of tuberculosis in Bulozi was not.

Here I can only set out the barest lines of a hypothesis. Three converging lines of evidence point toward a direct link between the Rand mines and the epidemic proportions of tuberculosis to be seen in the villages of Bulozi today. The first is documentary.

The death rate among African laborers from north of the 22-degree-south line of latitude was especially high on the Rand, so between 1913 and 1934, the Witwatersrand Native Labour Association (Wenela) was not permitted to recruit above that line (Gelfand 1953, 136; Schapera 1947, 70–71). The connection between tuberculosis and deep mines was openly stated in Botswana in 1936 (Schapera 1947, 176–177), but it had been pneumonia that had worried officials before 1913; so when in 1938 the May and Baker 693 sulfonamide antipneumococcal drug was pronounced to have a significant effect in decreasing the risk to "tropical natives," and in the light of the

Central African Territories' favorable Royal Commission recommendation of 1937, the Northern Rhodesia (now Zambian) government gave permission for Wenela to enter the country. In fact, since the South African government, under pressure from a rapidly expanding mining industry, had lifted the 22-degree-south ban in 1933, Lozi had been crossing into Botswana to engage in migrant labor, but not in the numbers that were to go during the "Wenela era" of the 1950s and 1960s (Wilson 1972, 68–69).[5] During the interwar years, medical reports, the administration, and Lozi informants all agreed that tuberculosis in Bulozi was uncommon. We possess enough information from informants and district health sources about other health matters to be reasonably sure that the contrast between the prewar and postwar situations is not an optical illusion between poor early and better later reporting.

The second line of evidence is from timing. Lozi migrants always sought all the time to go further south to seek work because wages and conditions on the Rand were better than those in Southern Rhodesia (which was not saying much) (Van Onselen 1976*b*, 116–119). Roughly, before the mid-1930s they were discouraged from doing so, after the late 1930s and especially after the war, greatly encouraged. The 1949 Northern Rhodesia Silicosis Commission rehearsed fairly damning evidence that the hot, deep Rand mines were indeed breeding grounds for tuberculosis and that the Wenela control and monitoring system of that time was inadequate; that it was entirely possible for seemingly healthy repatriates to be infected, to carry the disease home undiagnosed and for it to become active when for example their diet deteriorated. Streptomycin was not in regular use until the early 1950s, individual x-rays were conducted before, but mass miniature x-ray screening began only in 1955, first with 35-millimeter, then 70-millimeter, and since 1971, 100-millimeter film. It is, in any case, a technique of uncertain efficiency (Thomson 1974, 155). But before even these facilities were available, recruiting, of course, took place, and as a Wenela doctor explained to me: "the policy, although I didn't agree with it, was that when TB positives were located, Wenela fattened them up and sent them home where, of course, they died, but goodness knows how many others they infected before they did" (Wenela Hospital 1975).

The third line is close to the second, but is from observed data. I have collected statistics of about 1,000 patients at one tuberculosis sanitorium, Yuka Hospital in Kalabo district, and conducted village surveys elsewhere in that district. A preliminary reading of the figures and the evidence of one's eyes are support for the hypothesis. Today we see a population with tuberculosis present *right across the age range*. I take that as a good a priori suggestion of a population that was effectively open, that received large scale infection and that has now attained a "plateau" of self-sustaining cross-infection in villages before widescale immunity begins to develop.

If it is eventually established that this hypothesis has substance, it will be a bitter irony because Wenela contract labor to South Africa was always extremely popular (Armor 1962, 5). Ex-migrants recall the good side of it with a wistfulness perhaps made more poignant by the deep sense of grievance that was and is still felt about the abrupt termination of this opportunity for wage-labor soon after independence. Most swords are double-edged.

The successful diagnosis and treatment of tuberculosis by Western medicine in the Zambian bush has placed demands upon the Health Service where it has been and is least able to meet them in the form of x-ray and laboratory diagnosis facilities, lengthy hospitalization, and/or very accurate out-patient administration of the streptomycin-based regimens. Since independence, Bulozi has fairly consistently reported more cases of both pulmonary and nonpulmonary tuberculosis than other provinces of Zambia (i.e., cases entering the attention of the Health Services); and awareness of the presence of the disease, but absence of good technical support in diagnosis, seems to have led to overdiagnosis of tuberculosis in hospital cases. This, coupled with irregular or incomplete administration of treatment leading to relapse and perhaps further incomplete therapy on another hospital visit, has shown up in random tests on drug-sensitivity where Bulozi returned the highest figures of resistance to streptomycin in the country.[6]

The spread of tuberculosis in the postwar years has also presented African modes of therapy with severe problems. While none possess an effective cure, the way in which the symptoms of tuberculosis first present and slowly develop offers ample scope for divergent low-intensity and high-intensity diagnoses. I have the impression that tuberculosis sufferers tend to "shuttle" a great deal between therapeutic systems, although this will bear much more systematic investigation. The fact that the chemotherapy cure is not instantaneous means that absconding from hospital is very likely and that the long-term result will be death and more people infected. But tuberculosis poses a serious threat to the conceptual viability of African therapeutics and therefore the fact that these premises have not been falsified and that these systems still thrive is an indication of the strength latent in the blocking mechanisms. In this respect, the inefficiency of Western medicine in its local form contributes to that end.

CONCLUSION

Thus, circuitously, we have returned to the starting point of this chapter. How far has our outline of affliction and therapy in Bulozi also offered us reliable guidelines into the wider intellectual history of the people?

We may judge our success in two directions. First, what were the central pivots of medical cosmology? They were five: the notion of the circular passage of disease, the notion of dualism in disease between those caused by God and those caused by humans, the notion of balance between the physical elements as reflected in the social and the wider cosmological spheres, the notion of inversion of "normality" as a source of power, and the notion of the acute interaction of the physiological, social, and cosmological spheres. The value of our third initial assumption (that affliction when perceived caused rapid recourse to what was considered most reliable) seems to be supported. Each of these pivots either is in itself a core concept in the wider culture, or is closely connected to one: the circular passage of power, the fundamental dualism of Lozi cosmology in general (stretching from the account of the High God through theories of kingship and of equity to the image of "proper" diet), the goal of social balance that informed the structures and procedures of government at the center and in the periphery, inversion as a source of "dark" power and the acute interaction of the spheres of existence.

However, we may approach from the opposite direction. What evidence do we find of appeal for legitimacy to other specific areas of the culture? What we see in the case studies interlocks with the evidence from the first approach and sharpens it. There is appeal to the heart of the most powerful cultural statements encapsulating core values, those emanating from the kingship. There is evidence of appeal to spirits in the cosmological sphere using powerful idioms common to the largest scale of ritual apparatus, that of the royal graves. There is a detailed guide to how social imbalance is diagnosed and rectified and to how communication between the spheres is effected. But is this a *self-sustaining* answer to our need, a true short-cut into intellectual history? In the end, it cannot be.

Turner wrote in strong terms against the "cardinal error" of trying to explain case material without first "cracking the cultural code" (Prins 1978*a*, 311). But I would alter the sense of his obviously correct opinion, for "code-cracking" is a fully dialectic process. What I have tried to show here is that even if, beyond itself, a study of therapeutics is not a complete remedy to what Vansina called "this debility of our reconstructions," at least in the case of Bulozi, where I can check our findings with other sources, it looks like a rather reliable guide.

NOTES

1. An expanded version of this chapter appeared in *Social Science and Medicine* 13B (1979) (4): 285–315. Revised by the author and published with the permission of Pergamon Journals Ltd. In addition to sources that are referenced in the bibliography, this work is based on the following archival and personal sources cited in full detail in the original publication: from the National Archives of Zambia—the Resident Magistrate's Reports; the Barotse Annual Reports; the Medical Officer's reports; the Mongu Hospital reports; the Mwandi Hospital reports; the Senanga District Notebook; the Kalabo District Notebook; the Mongu-Lealui Native Commissioner's Court reports; the Provincial Commissioner's report; the Lumbe Silalo File;

from the National Archives of Zimbabwe (then Rhodesia)—the historic manuscript collection; Zambia Nzila Sect files; Livingstone Museum, historic manuscripts collection, including Sefula papers; Wenela Mining Company Hospital, Eloff Street, Johannesburg, depot reports; and many Lozi informants.

2. I gratefully acknowledge a (British) Social Science Research Council project grant and additional financial support from Emmanuel College, Cambridge, in 1977 when fieldwork contributing to this chapter was conducted.

3. Western Zambia is dominated by *Brachystegia isoberlinia* and related woodlands.

4. This is abundantly clear from examination of the Nzila Sect's catechisms, the key parts of which are typed and mimeographed (*lituto za tolo*—dream lessons, etc.), the standard form being taught at the annual convention (which I attended in 1977).

5. Information from W. Gemmill, ex-General Manager, Wenela, Johannesburg, April 23, 1975. Gemmill (Senior) has been instrumental in obtaining Low Grade Ores Commission recommendation of 1933, which opened the way to renewed recruiting in the north.

6. Isoniazid-based regimens have been introduced in the last ten years, but there have been severe supply problems. The sociological problems of lengthy treatments remain.

FOURTEEN

Clinical Practice and Organization of Indigenous Healers in South Africa[1]

Harriet Ngubane

INTRODUCTION

Significant differences in medical practice may be noted between Western-trained and indigenous healers in South African society, particularly in terms of the doctor–patient relationship, the preparation of case histories, diagnosis, and referral to other types of practitioners. A further distinction may be noted, within indigenous medicine, between the *inyanga*, who is usually male and uses African medicines in a nonclairvoyant manner, and the *isangoma*, who is usually female and uses medicines and techniques in a clairvoyant manner. The former observes and examines patients directly and ministers to the whole patient; the latter usually consults with a patient's family and relies on spiritual insights to interpret the causes and consequences of suffering. The networks of *isangoma*, spanning the Nguni-speaking societies of eastern South Africa, are given special attention here because of their role as "morality custodians," maintaining a meaningful worldview in a society beset with rapid changes and deep contradictions.

DIFFERENCES BETWEEN WESTERN AND INDIGENOUS MODES OF MEDICAL PRACTICE

An African in South Africa who requires medical attention has available both Western-trained physicians (with accompanying health institutions such as the hospital) and indigenous healers of two main kinds—the *inyanga*, who is male and uses African medicines but has no clairvoyance, and the *isangoma*, who is usually female and has clairvoyant powers as well as a comprehensive knowledge of African medicines. As I have mentioned elsewhere

(Ngubane 1977), there are in addition specialists in particular disorders, and faith healers.

From the patient's point of view, choosing between Western and African forms of medical treatment entails rather more than differences in assumption about the causes of illness and the appropriate mode of cure. As a matter of common observation in most parts of southern Africa (including Swaziland, Lesotho, regions of Mozambique, Zimbabwe, and South Africa), the two kinds of practice contrast strikingly in at least four major aspects of the doctor–patient relationship, namely, communication, preparation of the case history, information about diagnosis, and the view taken and expressed of resort to other practitioners.

Communication between an African patient and a Western-trained doctor is hampered especially by the common need of the latter to use an interpreter, since rather few such doctors have any command of African languages. The risks of wrong translation or inappropriate phraseology are obvious.

In Western practice, further, the patient is expected to give the history of the illness and describe the symptoms before being examined by the doctor. After the examination the doctor prescribes or dispenses medicines with very little explanation, if any at all, of what the diagnosis is, or of the possible cause of the illness. Often the doctor is not entirely sure on these points, since taking specimens for laboratory examination is rare in private practice.

Last, a particularly striking tendency in Western medical practice in South Africa is for the doctor or the nurse-interpreter to reprimand the patient at some length for wasting time with African healers instead of coming straight to the Western practitioner and institutions. Little thought appears to be given in these harangues to the likelihood that a patient must travel a long distance, or would have difficulty in finding ready cash to pay the doctor, or finds other obstacles to using the Western-trained doctor. Generally the patient is treated in a condescending manner, which reinforces the lack of mutual understanding and makes the patient feel ill at ease, rather like an inmate in one of Goffman's total institutions.

It is important to realize that the effects of this distance and tension in the relations between patient and practitioner are not confined to discomfort or unease on the patient's part. Patients are seldom deterred by any such reprimand from seeking the services of an *inyanga* or an *isangoma* when they consider that circumstances warrant this. What happens is simply that the patient does not tell the Western-trained doctor about whatever resort might have been made to an indigenous healer—nor even about consulting or receiving treatment from another Western-trained doctor. This means that not uncommonly the case history of the patient is inaccurate, omitting crucial items of information, and a patient can even be taking a double and therefore perhaps harmful dose of a given medicine, by virtue of obtaining treatment from two different doctors without informing either of visits to the other.

Problems of communication are obviously less from the start when an African consults an indigenous healer sharing the same language and general culture; but the relationship established between practitioner and patient is very different in other significant ways from that just described. *Inyanga* and *isangoma* do not have identical approaches and techniques by any means, yet they have in common an effective view of the patient as a complete person rather than an example of a particular disorder, as well as a disposition to regard the work of other kinds of medical practitioners as complementary to their own.

Usually an *inyanga* visits patients at their homes, where he is told about the symptoms and can, in fact, observe them for himself, as he spends more than a day with one patient and the patient's family. This period gives him an opportunity to determine whether he understands the particular ailment and is capable of handling it, or whether the family needs to consult a diviner who will diagnose the cause of illness. He may alternatively suggest that the patient be taken to a Western type of medical agency first, before he administers his own treatment; or he may recommend the removal of the patient from existing home social conditions while he administers treatment.

In short, the *inyanga* gets to know as much as possible about the patient and the patient's social situation, and thereby is in a better position to determine the illness of the whole person, physically and socially. By recommending removal of the patient from the home surroundings to the home of a relative of the patient's choice, or even to his own (the *inyanga's*) home, he may well be relieving the patient of the effects of a tension-laden atmosphere.

A diviner (*isangoma*) is consulted by the relatives of the sick person, who remains at home. She is not given the history of the illness or symptoms, as she is expected with her second sight to see beyond what ordinary people perceive and so to be able to know who is ill, what the nature of the ailment is, what has caused it, and how it should be treated. The diviners are graded according to the techniques they employ or the methods of communicating with the spirits which give clairvoyant insight. Every diviner has the private qualification of being able to enter a trance and communicate with her spirits; if she is of a more advanced grade, she can throw bones and interpret their meaning according to how they fall. A diviner of the highest grade has ancestral spirits who speak directly to clients by whistling from the rafters of her house. She only intervenes in person when clients are unable to decipher the whistled words. (Commonly, however, the words are clear, as I was able to hear myself at the two sessions, by different diviners, which I attended.) Diviners of this grade are quite few in number, and have gone through the lower grades. It is up to the clients themselves to choose the method of divination they want.

Apart from their clairvoyant powers, diviners have a comprehensive knowledge of what are known as African medicines comparable to that acquired by an *inyanga*. A diviner therefore can operate at two levels—as a diviner and as an *inyanga*—and at the latter all the rules that govern the behavior of an *inyanga* apply to her. The two roles are kept separate, and a diviner is consulted first and foremost as a diviner; it is up to the patient's people to engage her to heal the patient by using African medicines. Even when approached in this capacity, it is not unusual for a diviner to decline the role and to encourage the family to make use of their *inyanga*, perhaps with a suggestion of the type of medicine to be included in his treatment. Alternatively, she may recommend another *inyanga* who is an expert on the particular disorder from which the patient is suffering.

Moreover, a diviner may advise a patient to visit a Western-type clinic or hospital, or recommend some combination of Western and indigenous treatment. Thus, the patient may be told to visit the hospital and then make a sacrifice to any ancestors who are angry at such-and-such an act of omission or commission; or perhaps to consult the diviner again or visit the regular family *inyanga* to obtain treatment for the "African form of disease" while at the same time getting attention at the hospital for the *physical* ailment, such as by undergoing an operation.

The point to be noticed here is that the diviner—far from objecting to the patient going to another practitioner of a very different kind, such as a Western-trained white physician—often actually recommends a combination of her services with those of others. To a certain extent the same applies to an *inyanga*, who may want the patient to see a diviner first or to visit a hospital or a Western-trained doctor first, and then return to him, the *inyanga*, for further treatment. However, an *inyanga* hardly ever refers a patient to another *inyanga*, except where the case concerns a member of his own family; here it is said that "a doctor does not cure himself" (*inyanga ayizelaphi*).

All this, of course, contrasts sharply with the habitual disposition of the Western-type health agencies to look down on practically all indigenous methods of healing—not surprisingly, since the training provided in medical schools disregards the existence of African methods of cure. African patients, in contrast, see these an alternative or as providing a complementary contribution to a sensible combination of methods for curing a given trouble. In short, whereas Western-type medical agencies embodied hostility toward African agencies, these for their part accepted the Western-type agencies of cure as additional to their own or even as providing an alternative in certain instances, as I have explained elsewhere (Ngubane 1977, chap. 2).

The *inyanga* and *isangoma*, then, are able to communicate far more easily and readily, and to establish mutual confidence, with those who seek their services, than is normally the case with the Western-trained physician and his health agency. Initial ease of communication is reinforced by methods of obtaining case histories which take much wider account of the relevant circumstances of a patient's life and do not discourage the patient from revealing certain opposite medical facts by expressing hostility toward alternative healing practices. Diagnosis also is much more comprehensible to the patient, as is commonly the nature of the cure.

In one further respect the Western-type and indigenous agencies differ in a manner that is favorable to the patient—namely, fees. In the Western-type agencies the fees vary according to the type of treatment given, and so are unpredictable. The *inyanga* and *isangoma* however charge fixed fees, although for the latter these depend on her grade. An *inyanga* charges about £1 in the first instance to enable him to prepare his medicines, and on recovery of the patient receives a cow or its equivalent in monetary terms (about £10 to £25). Thus his services do not come cheaply, and they are therefore sought in cases of long-standing illness and not, say, for a mere cold or a stomach upset. What matters, though, is that the family can budget for the treatment as the fees are known.

A diviner of the highest grade, with whistling ancestral spirits, charges anything from £10 to £20, a bone-thrower about 50p. to £2, and one who merely listens to her spirits and gives her clients her findings gets from 25p. to £1, or a chicken. A top-grade diviner has of course qualified for that rank by going through the lower grades, and it is open to clients to choose what grade of diviner to consult, so that here again they know what to expect in terms of fees.

THE DIVINER NETWORK

I now want to consider more closely certain significant aspects of the diviner's role in Zulu society, which resembles in several ways that of a priest. To attain her status, she undergoes various forms of abstinence and withdrawal from society, avoids contact with sources of pollution such as death, and passes through other experiences that likewise enable her to achieve contact with the sacred realm of the ancestors. She thus reaches a state of purity that she maintains by recurrent observances, and endeavors to live up to the general expectation that she will behave in a moral and upright manner. She must keep confidences, and she has heavy judiciary responsibilities in various cases of conflict, such as accusations of sorcery. It is this very figure, probably the most responsible in the traditional community, who has been and still is treated, by missionaries in the first place and hence by physicians and administrators and others, as the embodiment of superstition, backwardness, and ignorance among supposedly benighted people.

The particular point to which I aim to draw attention, however, is that this highly responsible status is not just left to chance but is maintained by a form of social organization serving to control and discipline them, rather as

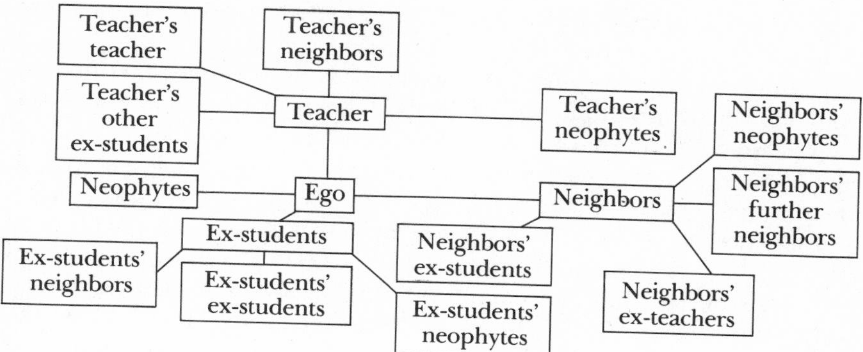

Figure 14.1. Schematic diagram of a Zulu diviner's network (diviner is "ego").

churches control and discipline priests or professional bodies perform similar functions for doctors and lawyers. It is important to realize that the diviners' form of organization is not derived from Western models but is quite indigenous, with historical depth.

Although there is no formal association of diviners, they are kept in frequent contact with one another by meetings that all or most of them arrange from time to time. The occasion for such a meeting is slaughter and sacrifice, beyond or in addition to the frequent sacrifice of a goat that every diviner makes as a matter of course in order to maintain contact with her ancestors. Depending on her affluence, a diviner once a year, or once in every two or three years, becomes hostess to other diviners. These guests are of four categories: neighboring fellow-diviners; ex-students of the hostess, whether from nearby or more distant areas; the diviner who trained the hostess; and neophytes who live with her and are undergoing apprenticeship (fig. 14.1). What counts is that the neighborhood varies from diviner to diviner; in the locality where I did my research I knew twenty-seven diviners well, but according to their proximity to her homestead, some eight to ten of them would be invited from the vicinity of a hostess, in addition to the other categories just mentioned.

This kind of arrangement means that a whole series of meetings is held, over, say, a period of three years, at each of which there is a different set of diviners. A given diviner has the opportunity to meet the ex-students, teacher, and neophyte of each of her neighboring diviners—as well as several diviners who are neighbors of her neighbors but not of herself. As guest of each of her ex-students, she meets their diviner neighbors, and the ex-students and neophytes of each ex-student; and when her former teacher is the hostess the other guests include the teacher's diviner neighbors and her other ex-students and her neophytes. This means that altogether she is part of a very widespread network and visits many different localities in the course of attending these meetings.

It is quite possible for the four categories to overlap in the sense that, for example, neighboring diviners can be ex-students of the same teacher; indeed, it would be a major research undertaking to map out the networks of even a few diviners in the same locality. Nevertheless, at least a rough estimate can be made of the number of other diviners one is likely to meet over a period of, say, three to five years, by making some assumptions of an arbitrary but conservative nature. If every diviner has eight diviner neighbors to whom she is hostess from time to time, seven of whom are also neighbors to one another, and if also every diviner has ten ex-students and five neophytes, then she will be in contact with over 400 fellow-diviners, all over southern Africa.

Such a diviners' meeting is far from being just a social gathering. In many ways it acts as a professional conference and disciplinary or supervisory body at one and the same time. From information I was given and from my own observations at a meeting I was able to attend as a matter of special favor, I would pick out five aspects of such occasions that seemed to me of particular importance. The first is the exclusiveness of the meeting, which emphasizes the solidarity and distinctiveness of diviners. Normally when there is slaughtering and feasting, among the Zulu as among other African peoples, all and sundry can join in as a matter of course; but when diviners meet and feast together, other people keep away, likewise as a matter of course, respecting the diviners' right to their exclusiveness and solidarity. As well as eating together, they sing and dance together, thereby enhancing their fellow-feeling.

Second, the meeting affords opportunities for communication of several kinds. Newly qualified diviners are welcomed in a spirit of fraternity (or, strictly speaking, sisterhood) and news is exchanged about the particular localities from which the various guests have come, about problems posed by the occurrence of particular diseases or of diseases that are unfamiliar where they live, or by new laws that impede diviners. Innovations in dealing with specific problems are also discussed, as is any marked conflict among particular families.

Third, mutual assistance takes the form of a session where each diviner may be requested to divine for another, in line with the saying that *inyanga ayizelaphi*, "a doctor does not cure his own."

Fourth, every such meeting is conducted according to the hierarchy of grades and statuses among diviners. The hostess is never in charge of the ceremonies at her feast, for example. I was not able to study adequately the rules governing the structure of the hierarchy.

Fifth, and especially important, these meetings serve to maintain and emphasize Zulu cosmology, above all in that any diviner who is believed to be getting out of line with the basic principles is disciplined and made to conform.

I remember vividly one particular case of a diviner in the Nyuswa area of Natal who was inclined to attribute her clients' troubles to a desire by their children who had died young and had grown up in the spirit world for due recognition of their senior status, whence they caused misfortunes as a means of bringing pressure to bear on the living. This was considered (by the others) to be utterly incompatible with that part of Zulu cosmology that details that any one who dies unmarried remains a minor and so is associated with the ancestral group of senior spirits who died after marriage. Any such minor spirit could express discontent with the conduct of the living only through or in conjunction with the senior ancestors.

The point here is not just that the cosmology does not provide for a young deceased person growing up in the world of spirits, but that to suggest that such a spirit can act independently is to imply that it can also get married—for seniority as an ancestor is achieved by those who died as married people. In the cosmology there is no allowance for the marriage of spirits. Hence the diviner who propounded this deviation was strongly reprimanded by the other diviners at the meeting in question. What they stressed was that such a serious departure from the Zulu worldview could undermine the credibility of diviners in general. She was told in no uncertain terms that she would not be recognized as part of the diviners' sorority if she continued in error.

What this means is that if there is to be a drastic shift in interpretation of the Zulu philosophy, it must be done by consensus and the effect of the particular shift on other aspects or parts of the whole structure of concepts must be analyzed and assessed.

This complex series of meetings, taking place all the time all over southern Africa, thus maintains a well-structured network of diviners that not only brings each of them into contact with many others but also works to familiarize each with other parts of the subcontinent, both directly by travel and indirectly by meeting fellow-diviners from elsewhere. Thereby a diviner not only becomes able to cite a precedent in a crisis or problematic situation but acquires a store of information about what is going on in many other places. Without casting any slur on the "spiritual revelation" that diviners experience, it is not too much to say that whatever clairvoyance a diviner may possess is greatly assisted and supported by this remarkably well-organized network that keeps her up-to-date or continually in touch with events and human affairs pertaining to her profession.

I have laid all this emphasis on the diviner network, as a major aspect of indigenous healing practices, for several reasons. First, the diviner's position, all things considered, is superior to that of the *inyanga*, who is not possessed by spirits and so does not enjoy clairvoyant powers. Hence the diviner, while possessing the same knowledge of medicines as the *inyanga*, may have further knowledge revealed to her while possessed.

Second, since the diviner reserves the right, after diagnosis, to advise clients to consult a particular *inyanga* and even to tell him what additional medicines to use, it is in the interest of an *inyanga* to maintain good relations with the diviners and even to refer some of his patients to a diviner from time to time, as a form of "scratching one another's back." More importantly, since generally people tend to consult a diviner first, she is in a much stronger position to refer her patients to a particular *inyanga* than vice versa.

Third, whereas an *inyanga* is capable of using his medicines for malevolent purposes the diviner is regarded as a custodian of morality. She must be pure, as this is the condition of her intercourse with the ancestors.

Fourth, as the diviners are guardians also of cosmology, the religious ideology or worldview of the Zulu, they are in a position to innovate or modulate or modify that ideology consistently with what is possible in the context of Zulu philosophy (Ngubane 1977).

Fifth, and following on the previous point, the diviners can set aside certain kinds of ailments as being capable of cure only by the diviners' remedies, as with *ndiki* possession and *igobongo* infant cure (Ngubane 1977, chap. 8).

Last, the diviners are in a position superior to that of the *izinyanga*, as I have shown at length, in having an age-old organizational network and thereby access to a much wider range of contacts and information.

CONCLUSION

I would offer an observation on all this by way of conclusion. What I have tried to describe is the traditional healing practice of the Zulu countryside, in several of its aspects. The urban situation is in a sense derivative from the rural one, in that what happens in the towns among the African population in respect of health care is hardly possible to understand without reference to the rural traditions and customary practices. However, the big difference is that the control and discipline of diviners provided by their traditional mode of organization has scarcely any parallel in town. There, a confused and turbulent situation is prevalent, conducive to the operation of a variety of self-appointed healers, including not a few charlatans. In view of this and in view of recent and continuing hostility toward the diviners in official and Western-oriented medical circles—which has fostered some clandestinity among the diviners and their clients—there is a need for careful and extensive research to ascertain how Africans, especially those in town, nowadays go about meeting their health needs. It would be most inadvisable to take any immediate steps to remedy the neglect and scorn of traditional medicine without first doing the utmost to obtain as precise and reliable a comprehension as possible, sensitive to major nuances, of the present state of indigenous practice and of the activities of its imitators and others who seek to profit from its continuing popularity. Otherwise, yet another disaster of development could result all too easily.

NOTE

1. Reprinted from *Social Science and Medicine* 15B (1981) (3): 361–366, with the permission of Pergamon Journals Ltd.

FIFTEEN

Kutambuwa Ugonjuwa: Concepts of Illness and Transformation among the Tabwa of Zaire[1]

Christopher Davis-Roberts

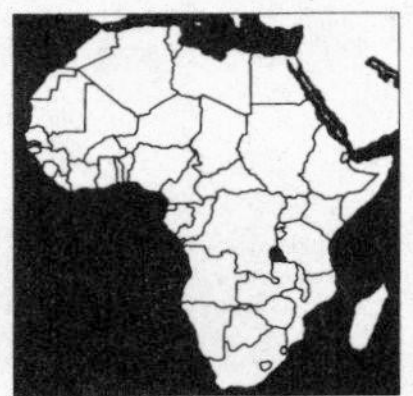

INTRODUCTION

The Tabwa are a matrilineal, virilocal people who live primarily by farming manioc and fishing the rich waters of Lake Tanganyika. They are culturally similar to their southern neighbors, the Bemba, but share other cultural characteristics with their neighbors to the north, the Luba.

Beginning with the description of a single instance of problematic illness, this chapter moves toward the comprehension of Tabwa therapeutics by placing them in their most complete conceptual context. Decisions made regarding methods of treatment, the locus of therapy (both physical and social), and the means of assessing therapeutic effectiveness reflect an epistemology that includes the overlapping domains of physiology, diagnosis, divination, and religious and magical practices, domains whose different contents are nevertheless tightly interwoven by a relatively small number of underlying principles. The articulation of these principles makes clear that Tabwa concepts of illness and transformation form a coherent whole within which both traditional and European medicines take their appropriate and complementary places.

In Tabwaland, as elsewhere, the medical system exists and is experienced not as the discursive, analytic prose of the specialist or the observer, but rather as the narrative or saga of specific illness occurrences, episodes that cut to varying depths across the normal flow of life. For this reason, it is appropriate that we begin our study of Tabwa medical thought with the telling of one such tale. Embodied within it are the concepts of process, of materiality, and of transformation which underlie not only the medical system but also the definition of reality itself. Through an examination of these, we will be able to accurately locate within the epistemological system the therapeutic alternatives from among which BaTabwa regularly choose.[2]

KAPUTA'S DAUGHTER'S ILLNESS

Early in 1977, Malaika, the three-year old daughter of a close friend, Kaputa, developed two fluctuating swellings on the back of her head. These first emitted pus, and then developed lesions that would not heal. During the course of the succeeding months Malaika's parents, her extended family, and my husband and I applied all the therapeutic means at our collective disposal in an attempt to effect cure. Creams, ointments, and penicillin injections were alternated with the application of powdered plant substances and herbal washes, but to no avail.

By the end of six months' time, Kaputa and Kalwa, his wife, were beginning to ask themselves what sort of illness could be so resistant to treatment with both traditional (*ya nchi*) and European (*ya Kizungu*) medicines (*dawa*). Although they felt they should seek divinatory insight into the cause of their daughter's affliction, they postponed doing so because the illness was not life-threatening and they had many other social and financial obligations.

In June 1977 I acquired some tetracycline capsules, and with these, again attempted treatment of Malaika's illness. After five days, the pus and swelling stopped; and although the medication ran out shortly after this, by the end of the month the child's lesions had closed. At about this same time, however, Malaika began to manifest other symptoms. Every morning upon awaking, she would begin to scratch, and swellings would appear all over her body, sometimes especially affecting her eyes and face. Although the swellings would disappear after an hour or so, the itching would remain, a sequence of events characteristic of the illness *masoli* ("urticaria" or "hives").[3] In addition, Malaika began suffering nocturnal fevers that were so severe that they caused mild convulsions (*kustuka-stuka*) and prompted her parents to sit up all night (*kukesha*) watching over her.

Though the fever would remit during the day, the child's temperature was never normal, and my initial efforts to treat the fever with chloroquine were only partially successful. This limited response, coupled with the presence of the hives and the character of the fever led me to eliminate malaria as a possible diagnosis and to instead suspect that Malaika had contracted bilharziasis when visiting her mother's natal village in the mountains.[4] My diagnosis was all but useless, however, for the dispensary was without medicines, and I myself had none of the niridazole required for treatment.

On July 6, 1977, a message was sent to Kaputa while he was at our house, to the effect that Malaika had just been stricken with "convulsions" (*ndege*) while playing at home. What he found when he got there was that his daughter had suffered a series of particularly violent shudderings or tiny seizures that had been controlled on the spot by his mother, who had used the traditional medical treatment of throwing herbal infusions over the child with a broom (*kumusampula*). Against the background of Malaika's ongoing nightly fevers, this incident precipitated Kaputa's decision to seek divination immediately, and also to search the village for itinerant traders who might have niridazole to sell or to exchange for dried fish.

By the next day, fortunately, both problems had been resolved. In the afternoon, Kaputa had located people from Kalemie who were selling niridazole at a price that, although expensive, was still within his reach. He bought ten tablets and began administering them to his daughter that night, following the dosage indicated by my physician's manual.

In the evening Kaputa decided upon a diviner and sent him the "arrow" necessary to begin the process of divination. In choosing a diviner, he employed at least two significant evaluative criteria. First, he selected the type of divination (*tulunga*) considered to be the most accurate and the most likely to reveal deadly etiological agents such as avenging ghosts and sorcerers. Second, he selected a practitioner to whom he was unknown and who was himself relatively new to the village of Mpala. In this way, Kaputa structured the situation so as to increase the veracity of the diviner's insights into his case, for, as he told me, numerous seances with the same diviner or seances with a person who knows one tend to result in the repeated emergence of a few problems, while the real causes of the illness remain unknown.

The "arrow" (*mshale*) by which the divination was begun was a small coin (a one-likuta piece), which had been placed on the ground and prepared by invocations made first by Kaputa, and then by Kalwa. In their statements, each of the pair had cited all possible causes of illness (adultery, thievery, breach of familial obligations, quarrels with neighbors), and instructed that the cause, whatever it might be, present itself to the diviner for the sake of the child's health. Although such invocations have a standardized structure, their statements were nevertheless direct reflections of the many and complex relationships of which Kaputa and Kalwa were part, each of which might have been the precipitant of their daughter's affliction. After its preparation, the "arrow" was given to the diviner, who placed it at the head of his bed, and during the next two nights dreamed of the cause of Malaika's illness.

On the morning of July 9, 1977, Kaputa, Kalwa, and I went to the diviner together. As is customary with *tulunga* divination, a pot of freshly drawn water was prepared and set to boil, and when it was hot, a *lukusu* seed was dropped into it by the diviner. For some time the practitioner completely ignored us and concentrated on the oracular device. He silently questioned it, intently scrutinizing the steaming pot as he shook his rattles, and then plunging his hand into the boiling water and retrieving the seed each time the oracle's answer was no. Finally, he gave us a parable and then a pronouncement that ended in a question.

He said that in his dream he had seen a woman whose husband had died.

She had not been inherited by a successor, but another man had nevertheless entered the house. Then a third man had come, the two men had fought, and the woman was also beaten. Kaputa and Kalwa were to apply this to themselves and their families and to determine who these people might be.

After some discussion the young couple revealed that the features presented by the diviner corresponded to the situation of Kalwa's mother. When Kalwa's own father had died, her mother had been given a successor, as is the custom (*bupyani*) in Tabwaland. However, when this man died, his lineage group had refused to provide the widow with another, saying that she was destroying their line. Others claimed that the husband had been killed by an avenging ghost (*kibanda*) deriving from his family's own evil deeds, and that they were abusing Kalwa's mother in an effort to conceal the truth from the outside world. Eventually, the widow was inherited by a man from another, related lineage group; but, as Kaputa put it, he came "like a thief in the night," performed the necessary ceremony and then left, leaving the widow improperly cleansed.

Shortly after this, Kalwa's mother began to have episodes of "lunacy" (*wazimu*). These were attributed to attacks upon her by the avenging ghost made under the mistaken impression that she was still attached to her deceased husband. Her children sought redress of grievance from their paternal kinsmen in court, but were denied it because they lacked sufficient political weight in the village. Privately the judges told them that they had justice on their side, although they could not be openly granted it. During the succeeding months, Kalwa's mother's condition worsened, until she finally became incurably mad. Harmless, she wandered from village to village, sometimes living with Kaputa and Kalwa, sometimes staying with others, and sometimes sleeping outdoors, naked and isolated from the intercourse of reason.

With the completion of the progress of their mother's illness, rupture in relations between Kalwa's group of siblings, their lineage group, and their affines was such that juridical resolution became impossible. The only release from the avenging ghost was therefore to be sought in the ceremony called "throwing the person in the bush" (*kumutupa mutu mupori*). In this, the diviner would mediate between the afflicted group and the etiological agent responsible for their sufferings. Much of the short discussion after the diviner's pronouncement was devoted to consideration of the details of this therapeutic alternative and to the ways in which it might be carried out.

After the seance concluded, I spoke with Kaputa about the diviner's hypothesis and found him to be in essential agreement with what the practitioner had said. Such a result had been obtained years before after the death of his first child. At the time, Kalwa's stepfather had admitted to having an avenging ghost, but had refused to do anything about it. Since then, however, other problems had intervened, and had been repeatedly cited by local diviners as the cause of illness in Kaputa's house.

Kaputa and Kalwa thought to consult with her siblings, to go with them to another diviner, and, if the same result was obtained, to undertake the ceremony. This, however, was going to take a minimum of some weeks. In the meantime, the effect of the pronouncement itself, were it accurate, would be the remission of Malaika's symptoms. When Kaputa returned to our house that evening, he brought with him the news that Kalwa had arrived home to find Malaika playing, and with her skin cool for the first time in weeks.

For presentation here, this episode has been denuded of much of its detail. Nevertheless, in this, the skeleton of its barest structure, are visible many of the principles that shall be explored below. In this hypothesis, the diviner brought together into one explanatory whole many different domains or levels of experience. These included the nature of the illness itself, both as physiological symptoms and as an event occurring in the life of a three-year-old child. Included as well were the personal history of that child's parents and grandparents and a category of etiological agent that contains implicit within itself a prognosis and a nonbodily therapy.

This interweaving of illness, history, and etiology is more than the simple coordination or correspondence of somewhat disparate factors. Rather, the varied domains are tightly interconnected by an epistemology that constructs and explains reality on the basis of certain significant premises. Among those are:

1. The transposition of a single process from one experiential domain to another (e.g., physiological, social, physical, verbal).
2. An emphasis on the unique event as that which has special communicative power, and the concomitant privilege accorded to the *witness* whose understanding unites with clarity what other's blindness leaves unconnected.
3. A relation between hidden processes and manifest appearances such that the latter can be construed as artifacts of the former, artifacts that are, nonetheless, the only means by which these processes can be known.
4. The concept of time as a developmental process and ideas specifying a complementarity of relations among words, events, and objects in such a processual reality.

Each of these can be examined more completely in relation to a different aspect of the Tabwa medical system as a whole.

CONCEPTS OF ANATOMY AND BODILY PROCESSES

The concepts of anatomy that form part of the Tabwa medical system include not only the delineation of external body parts, but also the itemization of internal organs and the specification of their functions. For BaTabwa, organs work in relative isolation from one another, and do not constitute structures organized into systems that operate as wholes. In addition, organ function is primarily of significance in discussions of the body as atomized and as in a state of health. With the exceptions of the spleen (*safura*), whose enlargement causes "anemia" (*kukosa damu*), and "dropsy" (*safura*), and the heart, whose rapid beating indicates critical illness, BaTabwa do not consider that organs can function pathologically or be subject to attacks by disease. Conversely, the vocabulary of pathology employed in the Tabwa medical system is drawn from the domain of nature, and the human body considered as a whole or thought of in illness can be said to occupy an intellectual space that is in some sense quite different from that occupied by anatomy per se.

The important, normal bodily processes of hunger and gestation result from the actions of the two "snakes" (*nyoka*) or "insects" (*wadudu*) that occupy the body of every human being. Although these creatures are essential, they are also capable of pathological action. It is they who cause certain types of abdominal illness and reproductive difficulties. Others of their kind are responsible for inflammations of the limbs or joints, some of which result in permanent disability. Through the image of the "insect," the BaTabwa effectively conceptualize a series of transformations that are simultaneously systematic in their progression and yet alien to the consciousness and/or well-being of the person in whose body they exist.

In other medical settings, particularly those that have to do with the preparation of herbal medicines, strong analogies are made between the body and trees. The upright stance of the one is comparable to the vertical position of the other: feet, torso, and head correspond to roots, trunk, and branches, respectively, and the runners or roots by which some plants propagate offshoots are comparable to the umbilicus, which is both the materialization of a woman's fertility and the cord uniting one generation of people to the next.

Further, several important deviations from health are directly attributable to the entrance into the body of cold, external winds (*pepo*). Certain types of dizziness (*zungu-zungu*) and diarrhea (*kuendesha tumbo*) are the results of cold winds entering the abdomen via the anus and the fontanels, respectively. Fever (*homa*) is due to the penetration by the wind of one's pores, a penetration one senses as the chills or coldness (*baridi*) that precede the onset of the hot stage of the illness.

Finally, digestion and coitus constitute bodily processes whose functions have complementary meanings in Tabwa medical thought. In contrast to other Bantu groups, such as Gikuyu and Zulu, for whom digestion functions as a model of ritual and social transformations (Kenyatta 1937; Ngubane 1977), the BaTabwa regard the process as the archetypal reduction of something to nothing. When one has expended the usefulness of an object or has illegally diverted funds for one's own benefit, one says one has "eaten" the thing in question, and this brings to an end others' efforts to retrieve it. Similarly, people often underscore the futility of selfishness by pointing out that food is ultimately nothing more than "feces in the bush" (*mavi mu pori*) and therefore not worth denying another. Finally, the latrine is a wasteplace into which magical medicines and amulets may be thrown, that their powers be irreversibly neutralized.

The amoral, profoundly transforming capacity of coitus stands in sharp contrast to the mundaneness of digestion. Uncontained, as in adulterous sexual relations, coitus can cause mortal illness of infants and the death of women in childbirth. Similarly, excessive conjugal intercourse, or intercourse begun too soon after the birth of a child, can result in a reversal of the child's normal developmental processes, occasionally leading to death. Coitus must also be isolated from certain "hot" (*moto*) illnesses, such as "measles" (*suruba*) and "smallpox" (*ndui*) and others, such as "lunacy" (*wazimu*) and "epilepsy" (*kifafa*), whose progress also must be carefully kept on its most benign course by means of medicines. In addition, cultural transformations such as beer-brewing, potting, and the manufacture of oil from peanuts and/or sesame seeds must be protected by abstinence from coitus if they are to yield satisfactory results.

Finally, coitus that is ceremonially "framed," as it were, that is, intercourse that is either interrupted or performed under special conditions, results in the fabrication of "new" cultural entities. In their first sexual contact after the birth of a child, a husband and wife perform a ceremony by which the infant is "matured" (*kumukomesha*). To accomplish this, they practice coitus interruptus with the infant between them. The parents then arise with the child, to whom they then administer a warm infusion of herbal fertility medicines and around whose waist they tie a protective string that has been dipped in these medicines. By means of this procedure, the child's body is closed to disruptive environmental forces and becomes capable of responding to treatment with medicines fabricated by those who have had sexual relations the night before.

Similarly, in the *bupyani* ceremony whereby a widow or widower is cleansed of the coldness deriving from the death of the spouse, the transformation is accomplished by ceremonial intercourse between the survivor and a kinsman of the deceased, after which the couple may remain married or separate, as they wish. Without such a ceremony, the survivor may not approach a fire, may not wash with hot water, and may not marry again.

With the practice of incest (*kisoni*), individuals employ ceremonial intercourse to fabricate amulets that will bring them great wealth. Such an amulet is first compounded by a practitioner, and then taken home by the client, who has intercourse with his sister or daughter in the presence of the object. The amulet is then returned to the practitioner for completion. The use of incest in this way is an act of sorcery.

Coitus, then, is the physiological analogue of fire. Uncontained by the bounds of marriage and disciplined abstinence, coitus works to the detriment of bodily integrity and of cultural processes involving the use of a controlled amount of heat. In this respect it is comparable to the destructive burning that can be the result of a fire that is out of control.

Inversely, by appropriate control and containment, the power of coitus can be prevented from the short-circuiting of other, more delicate cultural transformations, that these come to successful conclusion. Beyond containment, it can, as ceremonial intercourse, have its power directed toward purely cultural ends. Similarly, the capacity of fire to burn can be controlled through the use of objects such as pots and media such as water or oil, so that its transformative capacity can be fully directed toward the fabrication of new entities. Connecting the two affecting powers is the warmed water set out in the evening by a woman for her husband when she desires him, and the warmed water that it is a husband's prerogative to receive every morning on arising.

In the biosocial domain, as well, there is a structure of relations comparable to that which obtains for fire and coitus. Health is an unmarked, balanced state in which an individual "feels nothing" (*hasikii kitu*) other than hunger. The apertures and boundaries of his body are closed to alien environmental forces, and he suffers no excess of either cold (as chills [*baridi*]) or of heat (as fever [*homa*]). With illness, the situation is reversed. Bodily integrity deteriorates as symptoms become ascendant. With the ending of life in critical illness, the body becomes cold and the blood stops circulating, while the pulse becomes rapid and weak. Death is an extinguishing (*kuzimisha*) of life, and those who have been tainted by it must refrain from contact with fire or with hot water until they have been appropriately cleansed.

Life, coitus, and fire are thus transformative powers that are identified with one another in very important ways. They take the *shapes* of entities but are really *processes* whose materializations as the body, semen, and the flame, are not the static, reified objects they might seem to be. Instead, each contains a constant potential for transformation and self-transformation, rendering the unmarked or steady state a fundamentally dynamic condition.

The manifest continuity of the imagery of bodily events with that of natural occurrences has a similar effect. What goes on inside a human being is not different in kind from transformations unfolding without.

Hence, one can meditate on the ordered processes of nature, and thus come to know something of physiology. Inversely, one can meditate upon bodily events and come to know something of the world.

DIAGNOSTIC CATEGORIES AND DIVINATION

The Tabwa medical system provides some 203 diagnostic categories in terms of which specific instances of illness can be described and classified. Of the total, approximately 26 can be distinguished as simple categories, corresponding superficially to the "symptom" of the Western biomedical system, and referring exclusively to a single, physiological deviation from health (e.g., coughing, fever, chills, nausea). The presence of any one of these is sufficient to constitute an instance of illness; and inversely, deviations from a normal state which do not fall into one of these categories are not instances of being sick, but are "conditions" (*hali*) (e.g., blindness, crippledness, pregnancy).

Simple diagnostic categories can be combined and recombined as necessary, to generate a complete description of a given illness occurrence. For this reason, they tend to form the pool from which presenting complaints are drawn. Finally, simple diagnostic categories make no reference to temporal sequence. Symptoms are either present or absent, and there is no necessary order to their successive appearances.

In contrast to these stand complex diagnostic categories. These superficially correspond to the "syndromes" of Western biomedicine, but include in their composition features of the illness drawn from domains other than the exclusively physiological ones.

A complex category may include reference to such features as the age and sex of the patient, the patient's activities immediately prior to the onset of the occurrence, the pathology of the illness, its prognosis, and the alternate forms its progress may take. Where simple diagnostic categories appear to be the terms in which illness is given shape, terms that can be applied by anyone, the classification of a given instance of illness into a complex category is often a matter of some speculation and requires an expert opinion. Similarly, complex categories are not generative, and cannot be used to create "new" descriptions of illness. Rather, an occurrence that does not display all the features of a given category may fall "between" categories, and be difficult to diagnose as a result.

The pattern established in Tabwa concepts of anatomy and bodily processes is thus continued here. Just as events unfolding within the body were identified with events occurring without, so do the very terms in which disease is conceptualized function to wed the physiological to the social circumstances and characteristics of the patient. Beyond even this, as well, is the problematic illness for which divination is sought, an occurrence such as the one affecting Kaputa's life.

A problematic illness is an occurrence of any kind that displays one or more of three characteristics: (1) it threatens the patient with permanent disability or death, (2) it is unintelligible (i.e., it falls "between" diagnostic categories), and (3) it is unresponsive to treatment. Any of these features is sufficient to prompt questioning as to the etiology of the occurrence, and, for BaTabwa, ultimate causes lie not in the patient's physiology but in that person's socio-historical circumstances. Divination is the only means by which etiology can be known, and it is regularly sought, as with Malaika's convulsions and fever, when an illness is life-threatening. Illnesses that are merely unintelligible and/or unresponsive to treatment, such as the swellings on the back of Malaika's head, do not require immediate investigation, although eventually some effort at deciphering them should be made.

When they have decided to divine, people have before them several alternatives of varying accuracy and expense. Regardless of which one they choose, the procedure by which the investigation is set in motion is the same: there is first an invocation (*kulandila*) of the "arrow" in which the cause of the illness is commanded to present itself to the diviner, which is then followed by a seance in which a diagnosis is presented. As we have observed in Kaputa's case, the diviner's hypothesis ties together the nature of the illness (both physiological and social), the history, circumstances, and kin of the patient and one of the four different etiological agents that are responsible for all problematic illness occurrences.

Of importance to this discussion is the profound communicative significance accorded to the unique event by the structure of the divinatory or oracular system. This significance has two domains: that of the problematic illness itself and that of the means by which it is deciphered or recognized.

First, the problematic illness, as described above, is an atypical or unique event, defined in the Tabwa medical system as the embodied and muffled communication of an etiologic agent such as an ancestor (*mzimu*), a spirit (*pepo*), an avenging ghost (*kibanda*), or sorcerer (*mlozi*). In this capacity, problematic illness has the privilege of precipitating what I have elsewhere called a "moment of concluding," a period in which the patient and the patient's kin meditate upon the combination of *circumstances* and *meanings* that together constitute an individual's personal identity, that is, what is known to be true to the person. In this developmental restructuring of the self, the process of divination and the discursive authority of the diviner (i.e., his right to define the patient's circumstances) both play important roles.

For BaTabwa, then, problematic illness is only superficially a punishment or an attack. At a more profound level it is, in its uniqueness, the indicator and potential revealer of significant truth. It is a message that is "unintelligible" (*haijulikani*) because it is said in the symptoms afflicting the body. When the message is made explicit in the diviner's words, the nonce communication unfolding in the body can cease and the patient can begin to show signs of improvement even without further modifications of his physiological therapy.

On the second level, that of divination itself, the unique event takes the form of the coincidence. Not only are the plausibility and elegance of the diviner's hypothesis determined by the extent to which he effectively correlates circumstances occurring in three different domains (the physiological, the social, and the spiritual), but the very hypothesis itself is often revealed and/or validated by the coincidence that is the voice of the oracle.

Whether it be the diviner's dreams—whose contents are governed by the instructions made during the preparation of the "arrow"—or the throwing of divinatory bones or objects, or the brewing of oracular beer, the converging epistemological implications of the process are both clear and deep. First, the communicative significance of the unique event proposes a relation between the hidden and the manifest which is such that knowledge of this relation can be obtained and validated without the intervention of mathesis (i.e., a mathematically based evaluative grid). Second, the definition of coincidence as an event of special discursive fullness gives particular epistemological emphasis to the witnessing eye. BaTabwa make the point more succinctly when they say that a diviner is like the laboratory technician at a clinic. Just as the technician examines one's blood, urine, and feces under the microscope and sees there parasites not visible to the naked eye, so does the diviner employ his special vision to see into one's affairs and discover there causes of illness to which a layperson would be blind.

The two optical images are important for our understanding. A microscope magnifies structures directly, rendering them accessible to vision and comprehension while maintaining their sanctity and uniqueness. So does the oracle in the divination cut directly to the heart of the problem, transcending the limits of normal insight and defining the particular illness occurrence without reference to an intervening network of crosscutting, statistically determined typical cases.

In addition, BaTabwa consider that the diviner's special power inheres in his vision (*mumacho yake*). Practitioners are said to "have eyes" (*kuwa na macho*) that enable them to see what others do not. Laypeople, in contrast, are "blind" (*kipofu*). They go about "like children" (*kama vile watoto*), with only the most superficial understanding of the nature of events. It is in his capacity as witness that the diviner is able to put into a meaningful whole circumstances and happenings that might remain unconnected, but for the capacity that lies at the center of his forehead and governs the way he sees.

What is being said here is that reality has a fluidity and an interactive quality that accords to the eye a status at once profound and powerful, for it is only under the gaze that an event assumes its truest nature. This nature derives from hidden "meaning," which for all its relative obscurity is nonetheless of the same order as the manifest events themselves, and takes as its shape such things as human motives and social rules.

RELIGIOUS AND MAGICAL PROCESSES

If the diviner's special vision enables him to witness the connection between the hidden and the manifest, his transformative powers enable him to manipulate it. For each of the four etiological agents that may cause problematic illness there is an appropriate nonbodily therapy—a therapy directed not toward the patient's physical person, but toward the social relations in which he exists. The restoration of order in social relations that have been disrupted and the realization (i.e., manifestation) in social life of the meanings that previously have been obscured within it are both processes essential to the patient's recovery. The four types of ceremony accomplish their aims in two complementary ways.

Ceremonies performed on behalf of ancestors (*mizimu*) and spirits (*pepo*) derive their particular shape from the nature of the beings with which they are concerned. Ancestors and spirits are those whose intent is the meaning hidden within a given situation. It is they whose will governs the ultimate outcome of the unfolding events, whether good or ill. A principal aim of ceremonies relating to them is the containment of their transformative power and its translation into words. Both of these are processes essential to the restoration of appropriate communications between these beings and humans.

With *mizimu* the containment is accomplished through the establishment of a small shrine. The process is initiated by the brewing of ordinary corn and millet beer (*kibuku*), which, in this instance, is transformed into a communicative device by means of an invocation (*kutambikia*). At the outset of the brewing, the ancestor is called on to express its will through the medium of the beer. A potent drink indicates that it is, indeed, the ancestor named who is responsible for this illness and that this being is wiling to enter into special relations with the patient. Beer that spoils constitutes a negative response and necessitates another divination.

Similarly, with *pepo*—possessing spirits whose arrival in Tabwaland dates from around the 1930s—the diviner's hypothesis must be confirmed by the spirit itself. At a ceremony called "arranging the spirit" (*kutengeneza pepo*), the afflicted individual (or his representative) is "mounted" by the *pepo*, which then speaks through him to state its name and to specify the benefits it has come to confer.

What occurs in both these cases is the use of material medium (the beer and the body) to realize an intention that is not otherwise directly or immediately accessible. Whether passively or actively, the will of the ancestor or of the spirit is given verbal articulation by means of this medium and is thus both made manifest in and contained by the wider social situation in which it was previously disruptive. If the communicative-transformative structure employed in these ceremonies is effective because it provides a vehicle by which the hidden can be made real, the structures employed to govern the two deadly types of etiological agents are effective because they obscure what is manifest.

As we saw in Kaputa's case, a potentially fatal connection to an avenging ghost can be severed by a ceremony called "throwing the person in the bush." In this, the patient and his family go to the bush at night and in silence. There they meet the diviner, who washes them with medicines that function to convince the ghost that it has already killed its intended victims and that the people leaving the site are "nothing" (*bure*) to it.

When an illness is caused by sorcery the connection between sorcerer and victim can sometimes be severed by the fabrication of an amulet (*erisi*). Called *mwanzambale*, the amulet is composed of plant and animal substances (*miti* and *vizimba*, respectively) and functions to protect the patient in several ways. It transforms the patient's appearance in the eyes of those who would attack him, making them see him kindly or with indifference. It also conceals the patient from those who came to harm him and prevents their magical medicines from crossing his path. Finally, it also reflects back to the sender whatever misfortune he may project toward the patient.

With avenging ghosts and sorcerers, then, the material medium (i.e., the medicinal infusion and the amulet) is a realization of the intentions of humans. Activated through invocations (*kusemelea*) spoken over them by the practitioner, such media both deploy human will in a social setting and give to that will proximate power over the wider situation. The power bestowed by amulets and infusions derives from changes they effect in the eye of the beholder. Threatening beings are held at bay by a process in which the manifest is made obscure.

Underlying and defining the effectiveness of these two types of nonbodily therapy (i.e., the religious and the magical) is the complex interconnection uniting words, objects, and events. It is by means of this that the relationship between the hidden and the manifest can be manipulated and the circumstances of the patient's life be gradually shaped to a given end.

In Tabwa thought, the power of words lies in their ability to make reality a process. In the single moment of their utterance, words unite past and future, tying them together with articulations of causality and of intention. In so doing, speech—like life, fire, and coitus—causes a thing to mature (*kukomesha*), to make manifest within itself the process by which it attains the fullness of its being. Speech is associated with continuity and with the east, the propitious direction from which the sun rises, and the dead return to be reborn. It is also associated with culture, with human consciousness, and with the transcendence of becoming over being. Like light, into which the voice (*sauti*) of a person is transformed at the person's death, speech makes things and people into what they really are.

Yet for all their ability to make simultaneously accessible past, present, and future, words are highly ephemeral. Their totality exists only in the moment of their saying; and to objects falls the task of synchronizing their temporality—in the case of religion, or of temporalizing their synchrony—in the case of magic.

Thus, through the medium of beer or of the body, objects make manifest the will of ancestors and spirits that might otherwise be known only by its unmediated, instantaneous effect on unfolding events. For ancestors and spirits, according to Tabwa thought, act directly. Their words *are* deeds.

Inversely, as magical infusions and amulets, objects function to preserve the worlds generated in the images of diviners' invocations. Such statements cause the amulets "to mature" (*kukomaa*), and become tiny microcosms (*kadunia*) of the world. Thus activated, they maintain the vitality of the client's intentions, while his thought returns, as it inevitably must, to the more pressing and pragmatic circumstances of ordinary life. In this way do amulets form things like holes in time, through which can be seen the clear intent of practitioner and client, however long ago it may have been expressed, and however obscured it may have been made by the force of intervening events.

Events, for their part, are diachrony itself. Composed as they are of the interweaving of meaning and circumstance, of intention and chance, they are the embodiment of history. In them are hidden processes first obscurely indicated, and then clearly revealed. In them as well can one decipher the ultimate will of the ancestors, and determine the extent to which one's own proximate will shall prevail.

The three entities of this transformative complex—words, objects, and events—can thus be said to be variations of one another. What can be expressed or created in one can be brought into being in another, yet each has an entirely different constitution with respect to time, materiality, and space. In the nonbodily therapies that are crucial to the Tabwa medical system, transformations of events are attempted by aligning in the desired way words and objects. If one does this, BaTabwa say, and God is willing, the circumstances themselves will also conform to the pattern.

CONCLUSION

This discussion of the Tabwa medical system was begun with the description of a particular case. In it, recourse was made to both European and traditional medicines, and to the process of divination. Subsequent consideration was devoted to the exposition of principles that were present, although tacit, in the case as given, and which are deeply rooted in Tabwa concepts, not only of illness and health but also of anatomy, bodily processes, and nonbodily transformations. Kaputa's decisions about his daughter were thus placed against a background of widening circles of comprehension. In this conclusion there will be a discussion of some of the widest domains of conceptualization, and then a return to the center, to the case, to accurately locate Western medicine within a total epistemological context.

In our consideration of the principles which underlie the theory and practice of medicine for BaTabwa, we have been led to concepts of the transposibility of symptoms, events, and words, to ideas about transformation, and to thoughts about the relationship between the material and the meaningful in the unfolding of events. Beyond all of these are Tabwa ideas about time and about change as these relate to the body and to health and illness.

Despite the presence and extensive use of clocks, calendars, and radios, there is an important respect in which time is not measured by BaTabwa in terms of minutes, hours, and days ticking off at a fixed and relentless rate. In an environment where mechanization has not made overwhelming inroads into the conceptualization of life, time may be defined as a sequence of coincident processes, all of which give way to one another in a regular and regularly moving order. Thus it is that the smoke of the dry season's bush fires rises to the sky where, people say, it forms the clouds which bring the rains of October. So, too, does the moon grow fatter and fuller as it moves from west to east, only to wane there, before returning, slender and rejuvenated, to the west. Human beings participate, as well, in this process. One is born, matures, and dies only to be reborn to a kinsman, or to be "rejuvenated" in the memory of oneself that is an infant namesake.

Within this broader unfolding also occurs the enacted or embodied time of which individual experience is composed. Its progress can be measured by the gradual clearing of a substantial field, by births of one's children, and by major events such as the deaths of one's close kin. In such a setting one is perhaps less *in* time than time is in oneself; identified with change, time comes into being in large measure by means of one's own activities and efforts, even when these are coordinated within an agricultural cycle. Such is the case at least when one is healthy and one's determination is one's action.

In illness, this relationship between experience and time is disrupted—indeed, is reversed. The passage of time is "felt" by one whose illness divides one's will from one's ability, and leaves one "without self-mastery" (*hajiwezi*), as people emphasize when speaking of serious illness. Time is doubled, as household members sit up all night (*kesha*) watching by the side of a sick kinsman, and determining the hour by the position of the Milky Way (*kipinda busiku* or "that which turns the night"). People will often say that someone was ill for three days, and then correct themselves to indicate that it was really six, because it was three days and three nights.

Further, illness brings to bear upon the family of the patient the pressure of time speeded up. Instead of basing their choices on their own necessities and convenience, people must move to the pace set by the progress of the disease. Procrastination can result in an illness that has become so serious that no practitioner would be willing to treat it, and it was with the danger of their daughter's fever in mind that Kaputa and Kalwa moved rapidly to seek divination.

In a situation such as this, then, time *is* change, and the body—or the material substance of a thing—is but the artifact of the processes that are time unfolding, blossom-like, from within it. In health, these go all unnoticed, but in illness, process becomes identified with deterioration and time becomes the product of the "Other" that governs the progress of the disease.

Modification can be effected from without, as when nonbodily therapy changes the context in which a patient lives as well as from within by means of traditional and European medicines; and it is here, in the relatively restricted domain of physiological therapies, that BaTabwa distinguish between *dawa ya kizungu* (European medicines) and *ya kinchi* (medicines of the land).

Each of the two has a distinctive form. Pills, injections, and liquid medicines characterize the first, while the latter is characterized by the use of plant and animal substances derived from the bush. Although its principal loci are the dispensary and the hospital, European medicine may also be obtained from itinerant merchants and fellow-villagers, as was the niridazole that Kaputa purchased. The Tabwa medical system includes a body of lay knowledge governing the use of European medicines, and this is known to virtually every adult in much the same way as every adult knows at least some of the traditional medicines that are readily available in the area.

While each type of medicine has its strengths and its weaknesses, what is more to the point of this discussion is the fact that both are *subordinate* in the same way to the broader epistemological concerns that give the Tabwa medical system as a whole its meaning and vitality. Thus it is that Kaputa and his wife and family could freely alternate between traditional and European medicines and never feel that the utilization of the latter necessitated the entry into an epistemological system whose underlying principles were fundamentally different from their own. Instead, their approach to Malaika's illness combined a pragmatism that would permit the use of any physiological medicine that would work with a meditative concern that sought to structure the divination in such a way as to obtain the most veracious insights possible.

In his essay on the form and meaning of magical acts, Tambiah suggests that "it is fundamentally mistaken to say that African religion and ritual are concerned with the same intellectual tasks that science in Western society is concerned with" (Tambiah 1973). While successful treatment is measured in both Europe and Africa by the effectiveness with which symptoms are made to remit, our discussion of the principles underlying the Tabwa medical system would indicate that success in it means something entirely different from success in a Western hospital. The Tabwa system, for all its use of European medicines, is essentially directed toward the alleviation of suffering as a fact of human experience. If it accomplishes this task by causing the remission of symptoms it is doubly successful; but the totality of its concerns is such that the persistence of symptoms is no measure of its failure.

Any medical system must fail to heal each of its constituents at least once in his life; hence, as important as the restoration of physical wholeness is the elaboration of a system of meaning, partly personal and partly cultural, that can expand to encompass the vicissitudes we experience and thus make sense of them. Although remission of symptoms remains the ultimate confirmation of a diagnosis, for BaTabwa "to recognize the illness" (*kutambuwa ujonguwa*) is to understand and speak about more than physiologic circumstances.

In the Tabwa medical system, the body holds the position of a defile or conduit through which flow and are united the mass of events that are the raw material of a patient's history and the several etiological agents which serve as anchoring points, giving structure to the flow of circumstance and transforming it into meaningful narrative. This is the task to which the Tabwa medical system rises and toward the fulfillment of which it directs even the use of European medicines.

NOTES

1. Reprinted from *Social Science and Medicine*, 15B (1981) (3): 309–316, with the permission of Pergamon Journals Ltd.

2. The material presented in this chapter derives from four years of field research (1974–1977) undertaken among the Lakeside Tabwa of Shaba, Zaire. Funds for the study were derived from a U.S. Public Health Service Training Grant, a Wenner-Gren Grant-in-Aid, and a Social Science Research Council Foreign Area Fellowship. Opinions expressed in this chapter are those of the author.

3. Words enclosed in quotes are English glosses of Swahili terms. In the village of Mpala, as well as in a substantial area surrounding it, Swahili has become the primary language, having been introduced nearly a century ago by Kingwana traders and European explorers. Although it is understood by the majority of the adult population, KiTabwa is not spoken by any but the most elderly or those born in the interior. Children born since independence speak and understand only Swahili. The culture described here appears to be a modification of the traditional system, changed and individualized by a coherent process of transformation into one better suited to the demands of present-day life.

4. The shore around Mpala is both rocky and steep. This effectively prevents the growth of the grasses eaten by the snails, which are the intermediate hosts of the blood flukes that cause bilharziasis. As a result, the only cases of the disease found in the area are those contracted elsewhere.

SIXTEEN

The Importance of Knowing about Not Knowing:[1] Observations from Hausaland

Murray Last

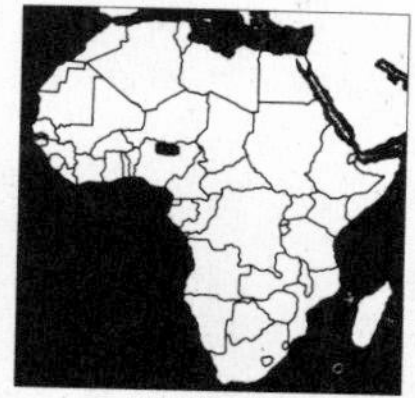

INTRODUCTION

I wish to raise the question of how much people know, and care to know, about their own medical culture and how much a practitioner needs to know in order to practice medicine. If the answer to both questions is "very little," then the concept of "medical system" will need to be reexamined, as will the notion of pluralism. In this essay I suggest that under certain conditions not-knowing or not-caring-to-know can become institutionalized as part of a medical culture and that it is inadequate, then, simply to claim there is still at work an unconscious system embedded, for example, in the language.

The reluctance in ethnography to record what people do not know is understandable; it is hard enough to record what they do know. On a superficial level every investigator has received the answer "don't know" and has been unsure whether the answer was the truth or simply a snub. Many anthropologists have relied on one "best" informant if for no other reason than that this person "knew" and could express this knowledge. Without such an informant models are apt to be constructed like a jigsaw from information collected piecemeal from the less knowledgeable; the process is embellished sometimes by the label "cross-checking." In an earlier paper (Last 1976, 116–119), I have argued that medical information in particular is liable to be layered, and as an outsider one may seep through into the inner layers of knowledge; yet the deeper one goes, the less certain is that knowledge. Furthermore, the researcher is always open to having a "leg pulled," particularly as the process of inquiry is often either richly comic or deeply aggravating to others. None of this should surprise us, accustomed as we are in our societies to the uneven, often bizarre distribution of knowledge, although I am astonished at our subsequent claims to know something as recondite as another medical culture. To discuss, then, the extent of not-knowing is presumptuous in the extreme; nonetheless to ignore the existence of not-knowing in medicine only negates our very claim to know another medical culture.

My other concern in this essay is the problem of alternative systems. Instead of treating them as isolates or even as competing equals, I rank them in a hierarchy of organization and access to government funds. For it is clear that the different methods of treatment vary widely in the extent to which they are systematized and recognized as a system by practitioners and patients. In short, the problem I suggest is one of inequality and the effect this has had on traditional medicine and its relationship to other methods of medicine.

The connection between not-knowing and/or not-caring-to-know and a hierarchy of medical systems lies in my argument that the medical system at the bottom of the hierarchy can become desystematized and that one striking symptom of this is a widespread attitude, to be found among patients and to a lesser extent among practitioners, of "don't know," "don't want to know." In our own societies lay disinterest in the intricacies of medicine is commonplace, but the public recognizes that there *is* a system. What I am suggesting here is that under certain conditions traditional medicine is not recognized even as a system, yet it can still be practiced widely and be patronized by the public.

To convince the skeptical reader I have to show first that there is a hierarchy of medical systems; second, that there is such a thing as a "nonsystem"; third (and hardest of all), that not-knowing and not-caring-to-know are genuine attitudes of mind and that they are very important to the medical culture. Negative evidence, which might reveal a nonsystem and extensive not-knowing, is not commonly recorded in ethnographies; their purpose was, naturally enough, to explain a *system* of medicine and to unravel the complexities of *knowledge*—and in the past, no doubt, systems were really systems. I am using the term "medical culture" for all things medical that go on within a particular geographical area. It is consequently a term wider than "medical system," as will become clear from the example that follows.

THE MEDICAL CULTURE OF THE MALUMFASHI AREA

Malumfashi (Kaduna State, Nigeria) is by Hausa standards a medium-sized district headquarters that in the 1963 census had a population of 17,000; the district's population was 177,000. A strongly Muslim Hausa town, it nonetheless had a Christian immigrant population from more southerly states of Nigeria and a scattered "pagan" Hausa or "Maguzawa" population in the surrounding countryside. I came to Malumfashi in 1969, after some six years of historical research elsewhere in Hausaland, in order specifically to study Hausa medicine. My three years of research were completed before large-scale studies by the Medical Research Council and the World Bank-financed Funtua Agricultural Development Project got under way. Most of my research was conducted from a Maguzawa house fifteen miles from Malumfashi, but only after an intensive survey of a Muslim village and a hamlet had been carried out. My data are best, therefore, for the most traditional end of the spectrum that makes up Malumfashi's medical culture.

At one end of the spectrum of medical practice is the set of treatments deriving from "Western" or hospital medicine. A branch of Ahmadu Bello University's teaching hospital is located on the outskirts of Malumfashi town; so too, are or were Protestant and Catholic mission dispensaries. Government dispensaries and leprosy clinics also operate in the area, as do—at a much more informal level—peddlers of pills, liniments, and even injections. Although conventionally one describes hospital medicine as a coherent system and the hospital as a single homogeneous unit, in reality, the hospital is staffed by people of widely different cultural and linguistic backgrounds and of varied technical competence; yet all these, in their private capacity, represent hospital medicine and may give advice or procure treatment after their own manner.[2]

At the other end of the spectrum is the enormous variety of treatments that is included under the label "traditional." The variety reflects not only the diversity within the culture of the dominant Hausa group, but also the large immigrant population, some of whom even import folk culture (for example, Rosicrucian ideas) from abroad. Between these two ends of the spectrum is Islamic medicine, relatively strongly systematized but that overlaps in its herbal specifics with "Western" medicine and in its concern for spirits or *jinn* with traditional cures. The core of its treatments is based on the use of Arabic texts, and its practitioners are expected to be Islamic scholars or students and to work within an Islamically orthodox framework. Government and universities, although providing education in Islamic studies, do not specifically include Islamic medicine, but much of what is taught is relevant to it; furthermore, the texts of Islamic medicine in Arabic are widely available.

The historical antecedents of this medical culture are broadly as follow. During the nineteenth century the area became depopulated by almost annual warfare; hence, Malumfashi town was only resettled less than 100 years ago. A large proportion of the present population migrated in from adjacent areas between 1890 and 1930 and still retain something of a frontier atmosphere there. Although the early-nineteenth-century Islamic reform movement was the source of the local political and ideological framework that governed the new frontier community, the community's territorial expansion was possible only under colonial rule. The early period (ca. 1903–1940) of colonial government also witnessed the burgeoning of a more strict Islamic culture throughout Hausaland, in part as a response to colonialism; by contrast the impact of Western culture, and Western medicine in particular, was slight. Only in the later colonial period (ca. 1945–1960) and during the decade since independence, has modern medicine become part of the area's medical culture; along with dispensaries there also came schools and all that better roads bring. The degree to which "Western" medicine was associated with colonialism (as, for example, in the manner described by Frantz Fanon in *A Dying Colonialism* [1967]) is not clear; certainly an unflattering folklore exists. Much more important historically, however, has been the role of Islam in "colonizing" the medical culture of the area. By according non-Muslims an inferior status politically and culturally, Islam has undermined the authority of traditional medicine. Maguzawa, although diverse and often Muslim in origin, now form part of a rural lower class and are treated almost as a pariah group for whom the peddling of traditional pagan ritual services is seen as an appropriate part-time occupation. Since other aspects of non-Muslim Hausa culture have been of less interest to the rest of the community, many of the traditional social ceremonies such as initiation and even weddings have been shorn of particular elements or gradually altered their significance. However, the formal continuation of non-Muslim culture has been necessary in order to validate some of the rituals of traditional medicine for the rest of the community, and if for no other reason, the specifically non-Muslim aspect of this segment of society still persists. Meanwhile Islamic medicine, faced with the recent extension of hospital medicine to the area, has become predominantly the medicine for social ills, preventing or curing unpopularity, warding off financial disaster. It still offers a wide range of specifics, especially for ailments that hospitals do not cure, but it faces considerable competition in this from patent remedies of a modernizing kind.

In short, the sequence of dominant medical systems within this medical culture is: (1) a putative traditional Hausa medicine[3] now maintained, probably in a much altered form, mainly by Maguzawa, (2) an Islamic medicine that was particularly strong during the early colonial period, and (3) hospital medicine, important in the late colonial period but now freed from its association with colonialism and financed by government.

HOW FAR IS TRADITIONAL MEDICINE IN MALUMFASHI STILL A "SYSTEM"?

The criteria I wish to use in assessing how far a method of medical practice is systematized or is seen by either its practitioners or its patients as a system are as follow. The top end of the scale would be occupied by a system in which:

1. There exists a group of practitioners, all of whom clearly adhere to a common, consistent body of theory and base their practice on a logic deriving from that theory.
2. Patients recognize the existence of such a group of practitioners and such a consistent body of theory and, while they may not be able to give an account of the theory, they accept its logic as valid.
3. The theory is held to explain and treat most illnesses that people experience.

Applying these criteria to traditional medicine in the Malumfashi area, we find: first, traditional healers form a category in M. G. Smith's terms, rather than a corporate group (Smith 1974, 100). They have no association, no examinations, no standard treatment. Indeed they compete with one another, using different curative techniques. There is in consequence no "local doctor" accepted by all the community, and as choice of practitioner is also governed as much by kinship links as by medical reputation or convenience, a more distant healer is often consulted before the neighborhood expert.

The various Hausa terms used, *boka*, *mai magani*, *mai Danko* (or *mai Ba-Gwari*, etc.), *Sarkin Mayyu*, do not denote either a hierarchy of skill or an area of medical specialization, although they might provide a clue to the healer's sex or ethnic background.[4] The distinction between, say, herbal remedies (from a *boka*) and spirit possession rituals (from a *mai Danko*) is spurious, since both a *boka* and a *mai Danko* will use both kinds of treatment.

The technicians of traditional medicine—the barber-surgeon (*wanzami*), the bone-setter (*madori*), the midwife (*ungozoma*)—form a separate group; they are treated more as professionals and tend, in any case, to be Muslims. Only the first, the barber-surgeon, is formally recognized as a craftsman with the local expert appointed as Master-Barber (*Sarkin Aska* or *Magajin Aska*) and is thus in effect licensed (e.g., to perform circumcisions). The other two professionals render strictly limited services but nonetheless vary widely in the details of their techniques. They are not required to diagnose illnesses since they are called in only to perform their specialized duties.

By contrast, the traditional healer not only has to diagnose but also may be called upon to render a range of services such as fortune-telling, supplying poison, and guarding or otherwise coping with wandering lunatics. In practical medicine, the practitioner's main rivals are the individuals, to be found in almost every house, who have inherited some specific nostrum (for example, against the pain of scorpion bites) or amateur practitioners of spirit possession. But major problems, like mental illness, are not amenable to do-it-yourself home remedies, and these, along with residual cases of medical catastrophes, are apt to end in the care of the *boka*.

Nevertheless, a proportion of all traditional healers has to take to the road and peddle their skills often among "foreign" communities such as the Yoruba; similarly healers from the Niger Republic tour the Malumfashi area. The value of their remedies lies in their very strangeness, in their *not* being part of a known system of medicine.

In short, the range of traditional healers that serve the Malumfashi area cannot be said to adhere to a single consistent theory of logic, except insofar as they are defined negatively, as *not* offering hospital or Islamic medicine. Nor, since traditional medicine is too diffuse to be monopolized, do healers form an exclusive group.

Second, patients and their kin do not expect their traditional doctors to have a consistent theory or form a cohesive group. Instead they accept that the different systems and methods of medicine have only a limited validity, although people do treat traditional medicine also as a residual category when other methods seem too dangerous or simply inadequate. This is best illustrated by a folk theory of ethnoecology which, given the social component in illness, has considerable sociological insight. According to this theory, each ethnic community carries within itself not only its own specific illnesses but also its own cures. Thus European medicine was necessary originally only for Europeans, then later for those who have to operate in European society; now, finally, as "modern medicine" it has the best cures for modern illnesses caught in modern society. Similarly, Muslim medicine, although much less sinister (and less powerful), is nonetheless essential for those who have to visit or work in a Muslim community, while non-Muslim medicine can cure, for all members of the community, not just the ailments caught deep in the bush but also aberrant "throw-backs" such as lunacy or a sinister malformation. Fulani pastoralists (who share the deep bush with Maguzawa) also have their own ailments and cures, but both groups tend to treat each other's patients for some illnesses, thus transferring to the other group not only the patient but also some of the blame for the existence of the illness.

In this ethnoecological theory, then, medicine is being seen not so much as a medical system but as part of the necessary cultural camouflage, like clothing and food, that enables one to survive, preferably unnoticed, in a diverse society. There are no "alternative" treatments, only appropriate ones—appropriate, that is, to the place where one happens to be.

However, the theory is more complicated in practice and has been modified over time. For example, hospitals are now recognized as at least temporarily effective against traditional illnesses since hospitals, so carefully fenced off and manned with guards, are "no-go areas" for spirits; relapses may occur, though, as soon as one leaves the gates. In contrast, and particularly in the past, one needed one's own medicine as well in order to survive a stay in a hospital, since hospitals are places of extreme danger (being one of the sources whence Europeans derived their magical power and domination over the local community), and one must be protected from the doctors, too. Implicit here is the recognition that the medical and geographic sphere in which traditional medicine is relevant is liable to shrink and indeed has shrunk in recent times. Certain classes of spirits, for example, have died out, while other spirit-linked illnesses are now confined to women. In short, one of the fundamental premises of traditional medicine—that spirits control illness—seems to be giving way, and if the present trend continues, only the herbal aspect of traditional medicine will survive while spirits become for some mere figures of the theatre.

Third, from what has already been said, for traditional medicine to have a single comprehensive theory to account for all illness is out of the question. But it seems that even a coherent set of ideas, embedded in the language or implicit in people's actions, has now disappeared. Fragments of a theory, with associated medical "facts," seem to survive, but it also seems impossible to make a proper historical reconstruction for any particular period, place or people; in the theory's breakup, the fragments and the "facts" have themselves been altered beyond the recall of people's memories. The most striking evidence for the difficulty in prizing a coherent theory out of the language is the lack of an agreed medical vocabulary not only among patients but also among practitioners. In trying to construct a Hausa medical dictionary I found what several others before me have found—as a comparison of all our vocabularies shows—that a large proportion of medical words (but especially terms for illnesses) have no standard meaning. The Ministry of Health issued a list of terms that are gradually gaining acceptance, but so far they remain "officialese," and patients in the know have learned to use the appropriate vocabulary in hospitals.[5] Hausa-speakers recognize the problem and also recognize how words change their meaning not only over time but also in differing places and subcultures. Such changes in the meaning of words can result in a new medical treatment which seems to contradict even the minimal logic behind the original, similarly named treatment. The best example of this is the elaboration of *gishiri*, an illness I have described elsewhere (Last 1979, 306–317). In medical discussions I have also heard people "incorrectly" applying to things Arabic-based labels new to them but standard in the towns. In this linguistic and dialectical diversity it is not surprising that certain stereotyped illnesses tend to be used not so much to describe a complaint as to preempt further discussion or diagnosis.

It is likely, although hard to prove, that the terminological confusion has grown rather than diminished over the years. Certainly, one effect of the lack of a widely agreed-upon medical terminology has been to prevent people now from recognizing any unified theory of Hausa medicine. My own efforts with informants at constructing such a theory tend to be met with polite interest rather than agreement! Despite this, I believe there is a "commonsense" knowledge for which the analyst can draw some general rules, although these rules may be more honored in the breach than observed. Indeed, the rules, like proverbs, may be contradictory and used by people only to judge whether a particular explanation "sounds possible."

From this brief account of the traditional segment of Malumfashi's medical culture, it should be clear that traditional medicine, if not perhaps a "nonsystem," is now extremely unsystematized in practice. Only a small part of traditional medical practice, the technical specialists, might be considered to constitute a system, and, perhaps in consequence, it is they who are being drawn gradually into the government's orbit.

SECRECY AND SKEPTICISM—CHARACTERISTICS OF A MEDICAL NONSYSTEM?

Although in suggesting that traditional medicine is no longer a system I have been describing it in rather negative terms, yet the resultant medical subculture is thriving *as* a nonsystem. It certainly has not withered away; rather, it has accentuated certain characteristics, some of which are familiar from other ethnographies (such as the Azande as described by Evans-Pritchard 1937) and are certainly not unique to Malumfashi. For people have, it seems, adapted to the lack of systematization in their traditional medicine and have over time adjusted their ideas and practices. In particular, the extent to which people now "don't know" or do not wish to know is remarkable, and old men complain about this (as, I admit, is the habit of old men!).

The most notable characteristic is the extreme, institutionalized secrecy surrounding medical matters. Practitioners are not expected to describe their methods. They are trade secrets. Nor is it appropriate for patients to discuss their ailments except among their closest kin. Generalities or even disinformation is given to, and expected by, solicitous or inquisitive neighbors. To reveal a knowledge of, say, anatomy or physiology, is dangerous since that implies witchcraft—a cause of illness seemingly on the increase because another consequence of the importance now given to secrecy is that individuals are not only a more obvious source of attack but also a more vulnerable target. Indeed, to show any interest at all in anyone ill is a social gaffe; witches are notoriously concerned for their victims and mourn them the most. With the gradual breakdown of lineages and wider kin groupings, individuals have to rely increasingly on their own medical defenses. The devolution of authority has also brought about the devolution of clan "secrets." Although the head of a house still retains his house's "secrets," increasingly individuals have their own personal "secrets," with the result, I think, that there is now a third layer to many people's idea of themselves. At the risk of systematizing the unsystematic, I suggest that whereas in the past there were two layers to one's self—the natural, physical inner layer sustained by food and cured by herbs; the social, psychological outer layer sustained through kinship and cured supernaturally—now there is a third, one's individual self, undefined, unknowable, largely indefensible except through "secrecy." Islamic culture supports this idea but does not dispel the disquiet. With the cures of traditional medicine now no longer wholly valid (because there is a new layer of oneself at risk now), illnesses are redefined as an endless, shifting state of being, to be alleviated but never cured, not even ultimately diagnosed. In short people really do *not* know, truly "don't know" through a combination of secrecy, uncertainty, and skepticism.

Skepticism, then, is the second salient characteristic. Skepticism about the motives and self-image (although not the naked power) of external authority has long been entrenched in the culture; the joking and mockery have become traditional, for example, in spirit possession. But fun is also made of local healing rituals and exposes the deceit involved. Admittedly, to do so is considered risqué, but people are amused, not shocked. A very tenuous veil of fiction is maintained over spirit possession. The skepticism is different from the familiar levity in ritual that so shocks the solemn or from jokes of the committed believer (such as only Catholics or Jews can make in our own societies). Similarly, the value of actually taking the medicines prescribed by the healers consulted is de facto questioned since little of the medicine is usually consumed; on occasions I have known the herbs to not even be collected. Such skepticism is not confined to traditional medicine—hospital medicines are often treated as cavalierly—and a high price does not guarantee a medicine will be taken. Furthermore, failure to take medicines may actually be a wise precaution. I have heard it argued that babies die because they cannot resist the medicine they are given, as can adults.

One consequence of the general skepticism is that any potential placebo effect is placed in jeopardy. Without that placebo effect the failure rate would be very high, indeed. In practice doubt is directed instead as much against the diagnosis as against the treatment. Treatments then may remain valid despite the lack of success. Paradoxically, perhaps, this seems to encourage rather than prevent a proliferation of practitioners offering new cures, especially panaceas. A few such panaceas succeed briefly in attracting patients with widely differing ailments from several hundred miles away. In other cases it is the treatment, not the practitioner, that becomes fashionable. Their eventual decline brings out wry comments from ex-patients about the profits made. The general acceptance of novelty, either as a patient or as a would-be practitioner, makes it possible for various individuals in the community to set themselves up in practice without any apprenticeship. They can buy or invent "traditional" prescriptions, some of which may run counter to traditional "commonsense" partly because secrecy protects them but also partly because skepticism has eroded both the old paradigm and the limits of naïveté.

Characteristically the rest of the medical culture is affected, too. Islamic and hospital methods of treatment are not immune to inventive entrepreneurial flair; the intellectual "bending" of the system meets a ready response from the community. Despite government's intentions, the varieties of treatments that patients lump together under the label "hospital medicine"—prescribed as often as not far away from a proper hospital—are a travesty of government-regulated medicine. Gross examples are injections into the eye or amateur (and often fatal) excision of goiter. As a result a further characteristic of this medical culture is for government to intervene, in pursuit of systematization as well as the safety of patients, and license the distribution of drugs, the right to give injections or to perform surgery, or the practice of midwifery. Elsewhere in Nigeria associations of healers have been encouraged or a hospital provided for bone-setters. In short the very lack of system brings about the enforced systematization of medical culture.

Finally, one characteristic is in fact absent, although it might have been predicted had there been a state of Durkheimian anomie in the culture. The incidence of ill health reportedly has not increased in the segment of the culture most affected by the desystematization of traditional medicine. If anything, compared with the rest of the community they are better off and are able to provide both shelter and cures for those "dropping out" of the town-centered culture. The rural rate of infant and maternal mortality remains high, but as hospital medicine is popularly thought to have introduced new illnesses into the community (and, indeed, the regular epidemics of cerebrospinal meningitis and cholera affect the towns more than the countryside), on balance people still see the countryside as enjoying "rude health."

In short, I am suggesting here that the origin of "not-knowing" lies in the breakup of traditional medicine as a system; and from this not-knowing there has developed first, a secrecy that tries to conceal the lack of knowledge and certainty; and second, a skepticism in which people suspect that no one really "knows," that there is no system. But the social conventions of politeness—as well as people's real need to find a cure for their ills—keep the veils of secrecy and skepticism sufficiently in place, for themselves and for others. Thus, visitors, on the lookout for systems, are easily misled.

CONCLUSIONS

It is easy for the visitor to take implicitly the doctor's point of view, describe the latter's method of treatment as a system, and so, by repeating the process, end up with a set of alternative systems to analyze. But what may seem to the outsider a Babel of different medical ideas is to the insider an adequately homogeneous means of coping with illness in all its forms. What I have tried to show here is that patients do not see the doctors' different systems as "alternatives"; furthermore, some of the doctors do not act as part of a system. Instead, there is a whole medical culture within which the various systems or nonsystems have affected each other over time, to the extent that a segment of the medical culture can flourish in seeming anarchy. The clue to why this can be so lies in part in people not knowing and not wishing to know, and therefore I suggest that people's disinterest in medicine is an important medical phenomenon. Not merely are the "don't-knows" significant, but also, behind many a pat, right answer, I suspect lies a "don't-care."

In the analysis of "alternative systems" then, I am suggesting that people in practice do not so much "switch codes" as simply switch off. An analogy may make this clearer. A passenger on a Malumfashi lorry knows where he wants to go, but does not know (nor want to know) anything about engines, highway, codes, or maps . And when he walks the final stretch home or uses a donkey to carry his loads, he is not "switching codes." Indeed (to his father's disgust), he may be as ignorant about donkeys as he is about lorries. People do not, in my experience, face intellectual problems in embarking on the appropriate method of treatment (or travel)—there are many more pressing, practical problems with which to cope.

If my suggestion is correct, at least two further implications arise from it. First, how common is the phenomenon I have described for the Malumfashi area? Would some other ethnographies, if reconsidered in a different light, reveal a similarly extensive "not-knowing" or a similar breakdown of one (yet still flourishing) system within a whole medical culture? Second, have the planners of health services been misled into thinking solely of differing systems, and how can new ideas be matched with old ones? Do the differences between "systems" really matter to patients and their kin—or does something else (like effectiveness, or kindness and concern) matter more?

Finally, I would stress that I do not see the situation as anything more than transitory. Although I do not know for how long there has been relative anarchy in traditional medicine (it may well have been longer than the sixty years of colonial rule and people's memories), the present situation as I have described it seems inherently unstable with only a part of the population affected. It is probable that out of the wider medical culture one dominant system will eventually emerge, through government impetus and representing a compromise, while the knowledge associated with it will be spread in primary and secondary schools. The "don't knows" will then have their ready answers again.[6]

POSTSCRIPT

Ten years later, events and further research have brought into sharper focus some of the issues raised in this essay. First, the proposals to organize, if not professionalize, healers have raised the question of what exactly are the boundaries and the logic of the expertise to be licensed and taught. The debate has moved from a general advocacy of traditional medicine on to particulars and cases; a critical element in that debate involves the notion of system (Last and Chavunduka, 1986).

Second, policy-makers have had to predict people's responses on the basis of analyses that take for granted the systematic nature of traditional medicine. Yet such systematic analyses, based necessarily largely on hindsight, omit such key contextual variables as emotions, expectations, and experience—indeed, the superficial data that hindsight cannot see, yet which contribute to the way people think and decide.

Third, charisma and entrepreneurship, important as they are in all kinds of medicine, are particularly so in the successful invention or elaboration of new "traditional" therapies—not the least when treating, for example, the new illnesses associated with AIDS. It is these qualities, not the logic or the consistency of discourse, that seems effective—indeed, is not the talent to break the rules outrageously and successfully a sure sign of real charisma?

Finally, it has become clearer how much cultures (and subcultures) vary at different periods in history in the emphasis they place on illness, and in the extent to which the idioms of medicine are used to express wider social malaise. The same point has recently been made again for some European countries and the United States, with Americans scoring high in their preoccupation with health generally (Payer 1988). It is more than expanding definitions of health (as in "holism"), and more, too, than merely a matter of metaphors—although the changing weight of meaning given to different metaphors and clichés needs to be measured critically. For many metaphors, used unthinkingly by people in daily life, are nonetheless being treated by analysts as if they were significant components of a medical system—much as a word's etymology is sometimes assumed to be a significant guide to its current meaning.

The suggestion, then, that it is useful to draw up a scale of systematization on which to differentiate between distinct bodies of medical practice is still, it seems, a practical one. To this might be added another scale, measuring the relative importance of medical discourse in a culture—in contrast to the idioms concerned with power or wealth.

Furthermore, the suggestion that people not only may not know, but also may have doubts about what they do know, is borne out by studies, for example, of noncompliance. Less easily quantifiable guides to skepticism are the jokes and gossip that help to mold attitudes to healers. Academic conferences are not immune; an old chestnut I have heard repeated at many seminars describes how a minister's car was seen at night outside a healer's door. But the problem remains as to how to assess the impact of such material. A recent northern Nigerian example would be the response to a widely discussed series of accidents in 1987/88 when three of four leaders of the main healers' organization then operative in northern Nigeria died in circumstances that questioned the real strength of their "powers." Two died in automobile crashes (such "accidents" being classic cover for magical attacks); the other collapsed with a heart attack on meeting the (conventional) Minister of Health. One of the three, so the standard, somewhat rather gleeful rumor had it, had just before his death been conned out of several hundred naira—again proof that his medicine was inadequate.

In a society like northern Nigeria's, damaging humor is a crucial weapon of the otherwise weak, and subverts almost any system the authorities seek to install. Analysts of other societies and their medical systems may miss such matters or disregard them as trivial; indeed, it may be that such subversive humor is missing from the society in question. I would argue, however, that for Nigeria, at least, it is still an essential ingredient.

Finally, it should be clarified that the primary field data for this essay came from living for two years in a single farmstead (population 120) in an area of similar dispersed farmsteads. The aim of the field work was to try to understand people's experience from the time they began to feel ill; hence it was necessary to stay permanently in one place, watching and listening. The essay was written later, while I had another two years in northern Nigeria, during which time I frequently visited the farmstead. Living initially with a farming family for that length of time and being dependent on them for all ordinary conversation and companionship (and concern when I was unwell) meant that I very rarely "questioned" people formally. In return for their hospitality I ran a kind of clinic, hand-fed an orphan, and ferried a few to hospital if they agreed; obviously in these particular circumstances medical matters were discussed at length, but mainly in reference to specific cases, past and present. In my second year there I was told substantially different things from what I learned in year one, not least about their doubts; indeed, the picture people presented to me became in some ways substantially less sharply drawn. It is precisely these nuances that I have tried to reflect here and which I think have wider value.

NOTES

1. An earlier version of this chapter appeared in *Social Science and Medicine*, 15B (1981) (3): 387–392. Revised by the author and published with the permission of Pergamon Journals Ltd.

2. Doctors staffing the hospital at different times included Nigerians trained in a number of countries as well as Britons, Finns, and a Dutchman; their command of Hausa was often limited or nil. The nursing and ancillary staff were drawn from different parts of Nigeria (and some from abroad), and so rarely shared the culture or religion of their patients even when they spoke a common language. As a consequence, the same illness could be understood and treated in different ways. Patients, knowing this, sought to work the system to their satisfaction—and in the process

subverted that "system" still further, although the senior medical staff were not always aware of it.

3. "Putative" because what we assume to have been a Hausa medical system may itself have been more a medical culture composed of competing systems derived from distinct cultural groups. Throughout the nineteenth century, despite attempts at reform, traditional medicine remained dominant at the popular level and distinct from Islamic medicine.

4. These terms denote general practitioners in contrast to the technical specialists discussed in the next paragraph: *boka*—"healer"; *mai magani*—"master of medicine"; *mai Danko, mai BaGwari*—"master of Danko" (a particularly fearsome spirit), "master of the *Gwari* (spirit)"—*Gwari* being non-Muslims south of Hausaland; and *Sarkin Mayyu*—"king of witches."

5. Although Hausa medical terminology may become systematized by being reduced to writing again (for it occurs in Arabic script earlier), it may not necessarily catch on. Folk medical vocabularies can survive unsystematized in literate cultures, too; conversely, highly systematized vocabularies exist in some nonliterate societies. A good example of the latter is put forward by D. M. Warren (1974, chap. 6) for the Techiman-Bono in Ghana. But there are major difficulties in creating accurate terminologies for parts of the body and for symptoms that are not readily visible; and there is a tendency to reflect the language of specialists rather than of the general public—not least because specialists are more systematic and consistent. For a generalized summary of Hausa terms, see Lewis Wall's *Hausa Medicine* (1988). Although based on primary fieldwork near Malumfashi, his data are embedded in a wider literature; the reader will find his approach different from the one presented here.

6. I am grateful to Social Science Research (United Kingdom) for supporting the research on which this essay is based, to the Nigerian authorities (particularly in Kankara and Malumfashi districts) for enabling the work to be done, and to the people of Gidan Jatau who helped me and still extend hospitality to me.

Postcolonial Medicine

SEVENTEEN

The Social Production of Health in Kenya

F. M. Mburu

INTRODUCTION

When colonization in Kenya started about the end of the nineteenth century, indigenous ethnic groups and their systems of government were subjugated under a new, imposed Western system. Africans were specifically excluded from the arena that determined their existence. Decisions were made by the white settlers on behalf of Africans. The denial of political rights to the African was the basis for other areas of expropriation, because having lost rights to political power, the indigenous populations had lost their right to make decisions (Kaggia 1975).

Following closely behind political conquest was the loss of economic rights. That conquest changed the existing modes of production and distribution of benefits and reversed the rationale for economic activity. Under colonial rule, however, the rationale of production, and the associated economic activities and result were for the benefit of the citizens of the United Kingdom. The African populations were used as a cheap means of profit-making for Europeans and the Asian entrepreneurs (Kenya Association of Manufacturers 1988). The laborers were not citizens, comparable to the European immigrants. On the contrary, they were relegated to the lowest rank in a two-tiered or three-tiered sociopolitical system. Cultural conquest destroyed, or attempted to destroy, the African ways of living and belief systems, religious and social-assimilation patterns, and customs. For example, the pulpit was used not always to spread words of Christian love and justice, but often to condemn some fundamental African customs. Notable among these areas of antagonism was the Agikuyu female circumcision and related ceremonial activities. Kenyatta's famous defense of female circumcision in the early 1920s became a rallying point in the struggle for independence (Kenyatta 1937).

MEDICAL CONQUEST

Related to colonial domination was the introduction of a new medical care system largely intended to create an environment for effective exploitation of the natives. It was realized early that the white settler needed an effective medical care for himself and for his servants.

When the modern medical system was established, it was believed that a minimum standard of health of the "natives" was a necessary condition for the African to be able to provide minimum work performance in whatever assignments were given to him (Kenya Medical Department, *Annual Report* 1927). Furthermore, the health of the European settlers was indeed partly dependent on the health status of the natives. The danger from communicable disease to which the European had built no immunity was always a monstrous threat to the white settler. The European employers were therefore advised by the colonial health department to invest in the health of their native laborers, for in them lay the very survival and success of the employer in order to reduce that risk to the minimum and to enhance economic environment which the white community dominated (Kenya Medical Department, *Annual Report* 1949, 1953).

The then government, however, allocated a relatively small budget toward health services for Africans in comparison to what was allocated to European health care services. Public medical services were limited to the urban centers and to those areas considered to have adequately accepted colonial rule, and urban areas were among them (Leys 1975). The relationship between the provision of medical services and the administration was not quite incidental. In most cases medical and educational services were common rewards for subservience. In this regard the administration differed markedly from the missionary: the latter used medical and educational services to gain access to the native souls.

For the government, however, medicine and politics were seen as the legendary "carrot and stick." A pioneering colonial doctor, for example, once said that it was necessary to give "the native tangible evidence that government is something more than mere tax collection" (Beck 1970) in justifying his recommendations for increased budget for the health department. The major causes of death, plague, malaria, sleeping sickness, influenza, and environmental sanitation hazards remained largely untouched. In addition, the introduction of the new medical technology was not accompanied by concomitant changes in the living styles. Consequently, the new technology was used to treat diseases without any significant attempt to get at causes of the illness. No medical system can be successful if it works in that kind of a vacuum where the society, which gives rise to the health problems intended to be controlled, is ignored.

Whatever the form of economic activity, it required a population with a minimum standard of health. Where necessary, however, the minimum standard was set aside, presumably to increase the profit margin and also because health was not thought to have a direct contribution to profit-making. Until the late 1940s medical services—as a rule, private commercial enterprises—limited their health services to the employees of the company, excluding their relatives. The quantity and quality of the services offered progressively declined from the Europeans through the Asians to the Africans. Interestingly, today private companies and other institutions subsidize health services of all their employees and their spouses and children.

Although missionaries opened up outposts in remote areas and larger "health centers" in their more important areas, the impact of missionary health services in the reserves remained low in a few places and nil in most communities.

The second half of the 1920s saw the expansion of both administrative and missionary medical work in response to the earlier disappointment. By and large, however, the religious medical services went exclusively to the African and Asian communities. In spite of dubious motives, initially missionary medical activities were the single most important attempt to affect Africans, in their own environment, outside the prevailing colonial structure. The missionaries may not have provided quality care but provided a significant portion of the services, although not adequate in quality and extent of coverage. For example, in 1914–1916 Africans were subjected to medical examinations to determine eligibility for military service, and at least 34 percent were judged unfit for any work in the army (Beck 1981).

Such was the condition of the formative years of the Kenya Colony. As would be expected, Nairobi was a major part of the colony, a position it is not likely to relinquish in independent Kenya.

GROWTH OF NAIROBI: PHYSICAL SEGREGATION

The structure and character of Nairobi has emerged as a result of the interaction of a number of significant factors. The physical background of the site had its own limitations. The racial composition of the original town about the turn of the century dragged behind it the colonial demands for white supremacy in a situation where whites were a numerical minority. Most important, the political-administrative rationale of both the city and the colony ignored extant priorities, especially in the provision of public services for a rapidly growing population.

Large tracts of land outside the boundary had been alienated to private individuals of European extraction with little thought to the future development of the budding town. To date, speculation has been the dominant factor and catalyst in urban services development, as was the case at the turn of the century.

Lack of control on land use and excessively generous respect for the rights of European land owners contributed to that problem. The 1947 Master Plan comments, "there was evidenced an erroneous respect for the sanctity of private rights of property, including the right to do wrong." Outside the central area, then, development was far-flung, haphazard, and uneconomical as far as services were concerned. There were a few "autonomous" European residential estates, including Muthaiga, which was a township in its own right with its own Town Clerk! This was, and still remains the residential area for the wealthy power elite. The developments of the turn of the century set the guidelines for the considerably disproportionate concentration of economic enterprises serving the needs of an incipient urban population, mostly people of European and Asian stock.

A further characteristic feature of the colonial settler was lack of control once he left England. A policy of laissez-faire existed in Nairobi and other parts of the country for many years. That tendency has persisted throughout the growth of the city, especially among the elite groups. Perhaps the rationale is, if the city could have thrived under the influence of unfettered European settlers and the Asian merchants and junior technocrats, why should the emerging African elite be denied similar latitude of freedom?

The ethics of laissez-faire "development" is a key-stone to capitalist modes of production—and Nairobi has not been an exception in the application of this rule. For instance, even at present there is no statutory urban or rural planning control. Planning by-laws control the use of buildings, but not of land, a serious hindrance to effective planning and development controls. As in the early days, in the 1980s large tracts of land were leased or sold to wealthy individuals or groups with little or no consideration for the future of the expanding city populations. As the various sociopolitical and economic groups run the administration of the city, their values have always dominated the pattern of growth of the city. By 1960, only three years before independence, Nairobi's development was judged not by the availability of public service and the potential for higher heights, but by the look of the business area. The development of Nairobi had attracted from rural areas a large labor pool. Poor education and lack of the necessary industrial skills led to concomitantly poor salaries and family poverty. The health status of lumpenproletariat was extremely low. The health outcome was perhaps the ineluctable result of the laissez-faire policy since the beginning of the city, which allowed the European and Asian entrepreneurs to exercise their liberty to do as they pleased.

In terms of administration and the creation of a national character, alien practices and values characteristic of radically different social climate and cultural background were imposed on the Kenyan environment. A confusion of standards of housing, living conditions, and public hygiene, among others, was presented to the indigenous population who, although numerically

TABLE 17.1. Growth of Five Urban Centers in Kenya, 1948–1979

	Urban population (×1,000)				*Average annual growth rates (%)*		
	1948	1962	1969	1979	1948–1962	1962–1969	1969–1979
Nairobi	119	267	509	828	5.9	9.7	5.1
Mombasa	85	180	247	341	5.5	4.7	3.3
Kisumu	11	24	32	153	5.7	4.7	16.8
Nakuru	18	38	47	93	5.7	3.1	7.0
Machakos	2	4	6	84	5.7	5.3	29.6

Population censuses rounded to 1,000.

strong, were an insignificant minority in policy formulation and urban development. With the exception of colonial ideology residential patterns determined the distribution and size of the population, health needs, and demands.

The Africans tended to settle in what is known as "Eastlands." The newer and better-quality housing is found further to the east in such estates as "Jericho," "Jerusalem," and the newly developed major housing schemes, Kariobangi and Buru Buru. On the whole, Eastlands is not as attractive a region as parts of the formerly Asian and European areas where boulevards and valleys provide scenic variety. Expectedly, in Eastlands income and rents are relatively low, and the population density is vastly higher than in other parts of Nairobi. Predictably, there is a disproportionate number of single men who have left wives and families behind in the rural areas of origin while the men work in the city (table 17.1). This skewed sex ratio is reflective of poor earning capacity and, therefore, an equally low living standard for the male in the city *and* almost inevitably the family left behind in the rural fringes. The city life has concomitant unstable influence on the family for the majority of the African working class.

But there have been significant changes in the populations that immigrate to Nairobi and other cities as more women immigrate to the cities and thus reduce the proportionate male dominance. Not only do wives now tend to follow husbands; young girls also tend to go to the city in the hope of finding jobs or educated and employed husbands. As female access to education increases, urban female employment opportunities attract an increasing number of women (see table 17.1)

THE URBAN SOCIAL PERIPHERY

In Kenya since Nairobi and other towns were established there has been massive migration of the African population from rural areas to the urban

TABLE 17.2. Housing and Environmental Sanitation in Selected Poor Areas of Nairobi, 1980

	Central city		*Intermediate zone*				*Permanent zone*			
	Shauri Moyo	Pumwani	Mathare	Mathare	Mathare	Mathare	Thayu	Ngei	Huruma	Kariobangi
Household size (*N*)	5.6	4.7	3.8	4.2	4.1	4.2	3.8	4.3	4.4	4.8
Occupants per room (*N*)	4.9	3	2.9	3.2	3.2	3.6	2.9	3.7	3.7	4.2
House with only one room (%)	88	78	91	90	87	94	78	84	86	90
Toilets										
Own	5	32	0	0	3	3	1	1	2	3
Sharing	95	68	100	99	79	77	60	81	70	94
Without	0	0	0	1	19	20	40	17	30	4
Kitchens										
Without	0	69	98	97	98	99	98	93	99	99
Materials										
Permanent	100	58	0	0	1	13	0	46	30	13

SOURCE: *The Situation of Women and Children in Kenya*, CBS/UNICEF, 1984.

areas. That is now an established feature of Kenya's spatial population dynamics. On the whole, the population structure underlines the dominance of the male population, especially in the major urban concentrations of Nairobi, Mombasa, Kisumu, Nakuru, Eldoret, and Thika. (Nairobi's growth rate from 1969 to 1979 was 5.1 percent, with an intercensal change of over 60 percent; see table 17.2.)

Accelerated urban growth stimulated by the rural and urban influx of African population is a source of many significant urban problems. Employment is an increasingly strong pulling factor toward social peripherization. Table 17.1 shows that youthful unemployment is a growing phenomenon and is related to increasing peripheralization. It is estimated that in Nairobi about 35 percent of the population live in slums, compared to Addis Ababa, 79 percent; Kinshasa, 60 percent; and Dakar, 30 percent. The acute shortage of housing, reflected in the mushrooming shanty dwellings and in the inflationary housing rents, is among the serious problems facing local authorities (Temple 1973). Social services, including education, health, and other amenities, are similarly overstretched. Food and water scarcity among urban-dwellers are chronic problems. Rapid urbanization has always been a source of many development problems that continue to tax the meager socioeconomic infrastructure available to the urban centers (Ominde 1981). For example, in 1974, while the population of Nairobi grew by 9.0 percent, approved housing increased by 1.5 percent. Thus peripheralization and its consequences were inevitable.

Lack of basic amenities is an indicator of a growing social periphery that may be defined by a variety of factors, including poor housing, sanitation, clean, potable water, and even employment, all of which indicate the presence of poverty. Of the 35 percent of Nairobi's population estimated to live in slums, a vast majority live in absolute poverty. They lack proper sanitation and clean water. Houses are mainly made of recycled materials such as cardboard, plastics, mud, and wooden remnants. Large families have to share toilet facilities that are often poorly maintained. The flammable housing materials make fires as big a threat as rain, both of which compete with the City Council Security Officers in demolishing the "illegal" constructions. Recent surveys of housing and environmental sanitation showed that poor Nairobi-dwellers have inadequate housing, living in overcrowded environments that are a public health hazard (see table 17.3).

URBAN POLITICS AND ADMINISTRATION

Development of health services in Nairobi has to be within some defined national and intracity policies. The national policy states the general principles and priorities to be pursued by the various segments of the country. Government ministers are responsible for determining the national policies.

TABLE 17.3. Employment Status of Young Adult Urban Population by Sex, 1978

	Employed and at work (%)	Employed but not at work (%)	Unemployed (%)	Housework (%)	School or outside labor force (%)
			Male		
15–19	12.6	3.1	8.2	6.1	70.0
20–24	53.5	7.6	19.2	3.6	16.1
25–29	81.0	11.7	0.3	0.7	6.3
Total	68.0	10.2	5.7	1.8	14.3
			Female		
15–19	9.7	8.1	5.2	48.0	29.0
20–24	23.8	9.1	4.7	54.0	8.1
25–29	31.4	11.5	0.9	49.1	7.1
Total	25.4	10.9	2.5	49.4	11.8

SOURCE: *Economic Survey 1977/78*, Government of Kenya, 1981.

Under the Minister of Health are the Permanent Secretary and the Director of Medical Services. The latter is the technical adviser to the city Medical Officer of Health. But the relationship between the city and the national policy makers is direct only in theory. City Council administrative officers are responsible to their own political-administrative officers who are elected and thus hold political posts within the Council.

Central Government Control

As a whole, the City Council is under the Ministry of Local Government which has a relatively elastic influence on the programs of the Council. Various other ministries have corresponding control of the relevant departments of the Council, as is indicated by the role of the Ministry of Health. In the formulation and implementation of policy there are three factors to be considered: (1) the ministries of the central government; (2) the elected councilors, who may or may not hold administrative positions; and (3) the administrative and technical officers in the various departments of the Council on whom the councilors depend for advice.

At any given time, these three have their own vested sociopolitical, administrative, and even purely economic interests, which may facilitate or hinder the pursuit of any defined public goals. The pursuit of sometimes conflicting goals creates coalitions rather than team work within the City Council. The coalitions are due to the fact that councilors are elected on some political platform—on the basis of some promises to deliver to the electors defined benefits, material or otherwise.

In a rapidly urbanizing polity represented by the councilors, material demands are often significant demands on the councilors. Demands include houses, jobs, business plots, contracts, plots to conduct what would otherwise be illegal or unhygienic businesses, and protection against harassment by the electorate. Once elected, a councilor has to fulfill some portion of the promises or will lose popularity. At the same time actually all urban leaders (like all leaders) have to pursue their own personal goals, especially to enhance their own economic positions on which a future election may depend. Invariably, the councilors are often in collision course with the administrative officers of the Council (Temple 1973).

Councilors versus Educated Bureaucrats

In most cases officers of the Council are highly specialized bureaucrats who have come up "learning the ropes" or have been hired purely on the basis of professional qualification. Once in position, the officers have to make the city function and, in so doing, protect their own acquired or established powers. As is common in bureaucracies, the most powerful are those who command the highest amount and quality of *information* (Michels 1962). The city officers have a vast advantage over the councilors. The latter may know the available options, but the officers control the operating administrative machinery and can therefore limit the options open to the councilors. In most cases officers pursue compromises that are consonant with the options favorable to them, and many senior officers such as the town clerks, treasurers, directors, and other heads of departments have been dismissed by the Council for failure to implement resolutions adequately. Policy deliberations are held in full council sessions or in committees both of which are "advised" by the employed officers. Predictably, the officers' disproportionate mastery of the technical expertise needed in the evaluation of policy options invariably transforms the offices into roles of leadership in the Council. The councilors depend on the advice of the officers.

Most councilors are not half as well educated as the officers and invariably suffer immense disadvantage in technical matters as they cannot make prior preparation for deliberations and are probably unable to weigh the consequences of the various options. It is therefore inevitable that policy options are narrowed down largely to those that appeal to those who understand and execute policies.

Above all, councilors are often more interested in allocational decisions, especially those which have potential benefits to themselves or to their supporters. The city may have some clearly definable development needs. What may ultimately determine urban development policy are the demands from interest groups. Development aspects such as health cannot be dished out as gifts to any interest group. Admittedly, urban health improvement often calls for an increase or restructuring of health services delivery points. But beyond the benefits accruing to those who win contracts to construct and provide equipment and supplies (and these are limited in number and diversity), it is not possible to own a service. Houses, jobs, contracts, business plots, and so forth are easily used as incentives for support. The 1979 election showed that material rewards and other similar favors could be used for purposes of manipulating the electorate. In some sections of Nairobi plots of land and newly constructed houses were promised or given to the supporters of those in control of City Hall. During the general election the then mayor of Nairobi was accused of giving away city plots and houses preferentially to his political supporters. As it turned out, only a certain amount of votes can be bought. There was massive support for the opposition.

Political Gamesmanship

The fact that health services are not tangible also significantly lessens their political visibility. Equally they are less likely to be viewed as priorities vis-à-vis other development areas. In most instances, neither the officers nor, even more so, the councilors understand the relationship between the health needs of a community and the development of a new health facility. Health care is just a necessary service that lacks the quality urban "fathers" scramble for in comparison to other urban development needs. In addition, the type, structure, and size of proposed health facilities are generally seen to be in the purview of the medical professionals. Even for them, beyond the basic (clinical) health needs necessary for a community, virtually little else is deemed necessary. In any case, following the established norms in health development in the city effectively avoids the complicated intricacies of urban politics common when seeking support from the councilors. Once health centers are established, it has become impossible to restructure or expand the health facilities clinics or health centers in Nairobi, even in the face of much larger population.

The similarity between the facilities is as remarkable as the diversity of the populations the services are supposed to serve. The facilities bear little or no semblance to the size, structure, and needs of their catchment populations; the potential volume of demands appears to be an irrelevant determining factor. For example, the health centers in Dagoretti and Kangemi were established over twenty years ago. They have not been expanded to cope with the much increased populations in those periurban areas of Nairobi. Councilors would not readily notice this discrepancy. Although a significant portion of the city budget goes to health, this is routine and the allocations are consumed by supplies and personnel.

If the many cases of reported corruption are anything to go by, there is no reason to believe that the stupendous health expenditures go to serve the people they are supposed to serve. For instance, the (national) Auditor-General revealed that from 1979 to the end of 1980, the City Council had illegally diverted U.S. $12 million from intended use. Such illegal uses included purchase of expensive vehicles for the control of communicable diseases such as cholera, and even some deals involving acquisition of drugs that could neither be traced nor even be accounted for. Mere rapid growth of the population did not sufficiently explain such a vast disbursement.

THE CITY HEALTH SECTOR

The city medical services may be grouped into two main categories: those services provided by the City Health Services Department and those services provided by private individuals or groups out to make profit.

The largest of the City Council hospitals is Pumwani Maternity in Eastlands, with a bed capacity of only about seventy. The hospital runs a daily maternal and child health clinic. Only those mothers who have consistently attended the Nairobi Council of Health clinic and booked for delivery at Pumwani are allowed to deliver at the hospital. Any other women who might turn up for an emergency delivery are turned away, however critical they may be.

Such women have to either deliver unattended by qualified health personnel, go to private hospitals or go to Kenyatta National Hospital (KNH). Maternity services are far inadequate for the city's women of child-bearing age, the majority of whom cannot meet the high fees charged by the private hospitals.

The Nairobi City Council has relatively efficient neighborhood clinics (NCs) (health centers and dispensaries) in most locations. The NCs provide comprehensive curative services of preventive and promotive care.

Most of the services are intended for mothers and children under five years. The NCs cater to out-patients only. Patients requiring admittance are referred to KNH or to the private hospitals. A limited number of pregnant women attending prenatal clinics may be referred to Pumwani. But congestion at the latter makes referrals a difficult proposition except in extreme cases.

The growth of the city population is predictably faster than the development of resources, including health services. There is always a gap between a new settlement (in thousands of households) and the time the community gets a new NC. Large areas in Eastlands (planned and unplanned) have no NCs of their own. In some cases none is planned, as the settlement itself is illegal according to the city's regulations. According to these regulations, perhaps nearly 40 percent of the city's estimated 1.6 million inhabitants are unplanned for, their housing is illegal, and the services are not provided. Eventually, however, the city accepts the settlements with a few changes to allow the city to bring in water, a sewage-drainage system, and electricity. Kangemi and Kawangware are prime examples of unplanned settlements that were institutionalized (see table 17.3 for other examples).

The City Council has provided neither acceptable housing nor concomitant services in Mathare Valley, an area with over one million people lacking in all basic services found in other areas. The quantity, type, and structure of services to be provided and the time frame for such accomplishment will depend on availability of resources, political will, foresight, and diligence of the city fathers, the urban political machinery and the administrative capacity of the City Hall officers. The latter have to provide the rationale and guidance while the politicians provide the necessary legitimacy and the money. Without these, nothing is achievable. The national health system is far too constrained by the more immediate rural health services needs to worry about improving urban health care. That is specifically the dilemma nationwide.

THE PRIVATE HEALTH SECTOR

The development outlined above has, indeed, carried equally even into the private sector. This private sector consists of two levels:

1. Large-scale and complex metropolitan hospital services operated on rules of the marketplace. The genesis of these hospitals is related to the historical racial segregation system propagated by the colonial government. Accordingly, the hospitals had been set up to serve the European, Asian, or other communities (Mburu 1979, 1981). The system flourished after independence because of the growing market among the African elite. These hospitals were, and still are, to be found in the major cities. Nairobi has the largest of them, inherited from the colonial period.
2. A host of private clinics of varying size and capability, usually held by one or more doctors, most of whom are general practitioners. The thrust of the practice is curative medicine, mostly in the city center, where the market is large. Indeed, relatively few people can afford the services of private doctors, especially the specialized cadre.

The private health care system provides a total of twenty institutions, with a combined bed capacity of about 1,300. As under the economic and sociopolitical structure of colonial times, the private sector tends to operate on a business pattern. Characteristically, specialization is a growing tendency, and is considered to be a necessary achievement in most hospitals. The physicians' specialization requires specialized diagnostic and curative equipment. Consequently, the molding of exceptional centers of excellence is already a reality and the norm. Surprisingly, the government health manpower development system, in which specialists are produced at the expense of the public, inadvertently serves the goals of the private sector. The quest for equitable distribution of the quantity and quality of care cannot be met in this manner as private health centers are business propositions, pure and simple.

The hospitals have to "maintain themselves," a euphemistic expression referring to the profit component. And that condition reduces accessibility to these institutions by the indigent sections of the society. The charges are so high that most of the users must have some insurance cover. For all practical purposes people do not like buying preventive health care. For that reason, the private hospitals provide curative services.

Predictably, the clinics are to be found in the city center sharing offices with other business concerns. Private clinics are very rarely situated in the locations where people live, in the city periphery. Business brings money. That business is in the city center; the peripheries are often inhabited by people who could not afford the services.

There are small but very well organized clinics run by industrial concerns such as the East African Industries, East African Power and Lighting, breweries, the armed forces, prison, and many others. The services offered are available only to the families of the employees.

By their very nature, size, location, and service fees, the private health facilities contribute little accessibility of health services among those who are in greatest need. However, the sector reduces congestion in hospital by the middle class and others who can afford the service fees. The planning and organization of private services are predicated on demand rather than need. It is well known that those who demand services do not necessarily need them, but all those who need care do not often have access to the available services. The discordance between need and demand of health care is an inextricable paradox in developing societies.

TRADITIONAL HEALTH CARE

One other health system warrants mention because it is widespread in the city, it is used across socioeconomic classes and tends to cost relatively less vis-à-vis modern health care (Thomas 1970). Traditional health care systems vary from one ethnic group to another. Scope does not allow close examination of the practices in this system. In one city location where extensive research has been conducted, the practitioner: population ratio was found to be 1:800. This compares favorably with the ratio in the modern system, which is about 1:1,000. The traditional system is largely loathed and often curbed from many angles—social, religious and even politically. Only traditional midwives are tolerated, although they are not allowed to work alongside the nurses and midwives trained in the formal sector. Even for a traditional care system there is immense disparity from one city region to another disproportionately favoring the poorer sections of the city. Exploitation is rife, and competition is an accepted part of the system (Mburu 1977).

THE PUBLIC HEALTH SYSTEM IN NAIROBI

In Nairobi, the central government provides Kenyatta National Hospital (KNH), the largest in the country, with a bed capacity of over 2,000 beds. The hospital accounts for more than 50 percent of doctors in the public service. There are plans to construct a large hospital to serve as the Nairobi "provincial-district" hospital. The services at KNH, and the proposed hospital, are provided to all citizens indiscriminately free of charge to the user in line with all the public health services since 1964. Almost invariably the public health care system is for the poor. There is congestion and perceived poor or inadequate service. Kenyatta National Hospital is near the city center. Suffice it to say that the construction of one more high-cost hospital would not dramatically improve the health status of the residents of the city. People living around the socioeconomic fringes of the city like Mathare Valley, Kangemi, Kibera, Kawangware, and the growing shanties in the eastern part of the city will continue to suffer relative deprivation vis-à-vis the well-to-do middle and upper socioeconomic classes.

Problems of relative deprivation may be illustrated by a 1984 strike by the doctors in public service on which the majority of the city population depends. On one hand, the doctors view their own level of remuneration as too low compared to their contemporaries with much less strenuous training and working conditions. Indeed, this is true. On the other hand, the government maintains that health care is an essential service, although, paradoxically, those who provide it cannot be paid as highly as the duty calls for, leave alone as they would like. By 1980 lawyers and the armed forces, however, were better remunerated than were the doctors. The younger doctors went on strike; their senior colleagues—consultants or specialists—refused to join them. National hospitals were deserted except by the seriously ill. As the strike continued, even the in-patients were hustled out. Those able to move to private hospitals did so; the poor either stayed home or sought care in the neighboring district hospitals. One major consequence of the doctors' strike was lowering of death in the hospital!

The government's attempt to combat the worsening situation fell on deaf ears. The political-administrative machinery had to be used to get the doctors back to work. The Kenya African National Union (KANU) declared the strike illegal and said the doctors were at once "self-serving individualists" and also "mercenaries" out to kill the poor!

The doctors were threatened with deregistration and criminal prosecution. Public sentiments against the doctors were created through newspapers, radio, television, and political rallies. Eventually, the doctors returned to work, but at a progressively slow work pace, which affected the performance of KNH and other large public hospitals. Like the poor, the doctors in public service are at the mercy of the government.

Class struggle cannot be ruled out. The existing elite control the channels of status improvement for the emerging lower-status groups. The doctors would like to command as much salary as the market could bear in their attempt to climb the class ladder. The urban lumpenproletariat want service only freely available in the public health service system. The medical professionals' demand for higher pay is viewed as a contradiction, first in the maintenance of the status quo for the lower classes and the provision of inexpensive health services to the poor.

CONCLUSIONS

Nairobi's planning problems must be regarded in the context of the country as a whole, since it is out of Kenya's problems that those of Nairobi arise. For very many years, the wealth of the country has been concentrated in the hands of a minority, and only recently has a *selective* redistribution process begun but ownership of a piece of land by everyone is an ideal that cannot be fulfilled (Mburu 1981).

The country, however, is unable to provide employment for the landless. Nairobi occupies such a strategic position, in terms of logistics, wealth, and power that its influence and attraction throughout the whole of Kenya are far greater than those of African cities of comparable size. It is the magnet to which the landless and the unemployed are drawn in hopes of work and shelter. Yet there are limitations on what the city can offer. Nor would it be appropriate or practical for it to attempt to solve a countrywide problem. Thus its future structure is intimately related to any central government policy that attempts to reduce the drift to urban areas. Nairobi's overriding planning problems derive from this situation (Rodney 1974).

For the last ten or twenty years the two leading cities in Kenya, Nairobi and Mombasa, have had an increasing doctor–patient—and paramedic–patient—population ratio, far in excess of what prevails in the rest of the country. In 1970, the ratio was 1:1,500 but had improved to 1:1,000 by 1981. There are 190 beds per 100,000 population in Nairobi, or about 1 bed for 500 people.

Such statistics are often deceptive for two major reasons. First, they do not shed light on the proportionate allocation among the various population groups, areas, population target groups, and, most importantly, problem areas. Second, the per capita figures do not show the differences among the various socioeconomic groups. The ranges of health and poverty are irreconcilably immense. The poorer segments of the community receive fewer doctors, fewer hospital beds, and less attention by the doctors and paramedical staff who serve in those institutions. Most of the hospitals and the facilities therein are private. They are run on a fee-for-service basis, a system not within easy reach of the poorer communities. However, no drastic policy measures have been taken toward *structural change* of the health care system since independence. Understandably, structural changes in large organizations and bureaucracies are difficult and rare. In addition, structural changes are economically expensive. More often than not, bureaucracies do their best to avoid having to make structural changes. But in a poor developing country, such changes are necessary if social justice is to be equitably distributed.

The major hindrances to the formulation of more effective health systems would appear to be the value systems of the elite groups and agencies and the structure these produce. Attempts to solve priority problems among the largest proportion of the population leave much to be desired. Although much has been achieved in Kenya, existing health structures and strategies fly in the face of available evidence on effective systems and strategies (Mburu 1979). In the conflict between political necessity and economic reality, many problems have been shelved rather than solved. The challenge in modern health care practice is to design systems that are not only fair and just to all but efficient and effective. It is not a small challenge. The performance of Kenya's political-administrative institutions should thus be assessed in that context.

The expansion of the health services has been effective in providing preventive and basic curative care, which is a major contribution toward socioeconomic democratization. In a fundamental manner, democracy must also include equitable accessibility to basic needs of life, of which health is one. The question in this chapter is directed toward how far the existing system and its institutions could produce an equitable expansion of health services necessary to bring health to the whole urban population.

EIGHTEEN

Health Care and the Concept of Legitimacy in Sierra Leone[1]

Carol P. MacCormack

INTRODUCTION

A disconcerting gap yawns between sensitive studies of indigenous systems of health and illness on one hand and national health planning on the other. Planners in the ministry of health or a planning ministry construct a hierarchy of health-workers with highly trained physicians at the apex, descending to poorly trained and poorly paid health workers in villages, where most productive labor in developing countries actually takes place.[2] Planners are concerned with training manuals for literate school-leavers and diagnostic flowcharts that can be used with rapidity and impersonality. Ideally, this hierarchy, especially at the lowest level, will function with rapid computer-like logic and efficiency. This kind of planning has a perspective, a point of view. Services, training, supervision, drugs, building materials, vehicles, and petrol are allocated down the system, from central government to provinces, districts, and villages. In the ideal plan, downward flows are somewhat complemented by statistics for evaluation and replanning flowing upward in the system.

Health services conceived and planned in this way have a rational-legal legitimacy in the Weberian sense. Plans and administrative procedures arise from expediency, rational values, or both. In national health planning they arise from expediencies caused by limited health funds and from rational values of Western science and medicine. For Weber, the purest exercise of rational-legal authority is through bureaucratic administration. Staff is ranked by status. The staff's competence is enhanced by a systematic division of labor with all workers knowing their respective roles thoroughly, the whole integrated bureaucracy functioning with impersonal efficiency.

Bureaucratic administration and medicine share an orientation based on the methods of technology. It is an orientation in which the systematic application of organized knowledge to practical tasks is achieved by forcing the division and subdivision of any task into its component parts. In administration this expertise resides especially in the "technostructure" (Galbraith 1967); in medicine it resides especially with specialist clinicians, supported by laboratory scientists. It is a method of proven success, and the discovery of effective drugs has perhaps led some to view health care as curing, without reference to whole social persons. In planning and administration one consequence of efficient technological divisions and specializations is alienation, or not "caring."

Weber is very clear in his view that in the interest of efficiency, spontaneous "community action" is always inferior to "societal action," which is methodically ordered. Bureaucracy is the means for converting community action into rational function (Weber 1946, 228–229). Although Weber was constructing an ideal type based on a kind of rational legitimacy never found in pure form, his construction has become a tenet of faith for Western-trained planners, secure in their claim for rational and legal legitimacy for their work. However, there are other kinds of legitimacy as we shall see.

Health services in Africa often fall short of the WHO-UNICEF goal of primary health care for all (WHO 1978*a*), especially for the rural sector, for many reasons. National wealth is finite, and there may be few funds in an absolute sense. Or, the ministry of health may be in a weak bargaining position against the ministry of finance. Navarro (1974, 5) has argued that Third World countries do not have a shortage of capital in an absolute sense, but large quantities of wealth are diverted to ends that are neither productive nor designed to meet basic needs throughout the country.

When a country genuinely seeks to extend primary health care, the assumptions of a market economy often shape the advice that international bodies give and the solutions that national physicians and planners adopt. For example, drug imports put a heavy strain on the national balance of payments (Gish and Feller 1979). As a solution, indigenous medicines are seen as raw materials from which chemicals might be extracted for national use (WHO 1978*a*). Chemicals will be extracted with technological apparatus, separated from all therapeutic ritual to practitioners and patients alike. They become a product. Once medicine becomes "pills," local people no longer command the meaning of those medicines and are made more dependent, a trend some have wished to reverse through community action in health care (Werner 1977*b*).

Some of the literature on drugs in developing countries suggests self-help (Barker 1975), but most is concerned with the "problem" of poor countries not having a petrochemical industry, byproducts of which can be used for synthesizing drugs with precise quality control. At the root of these discussions is often an assumption about professional expertise and village ignorance. However, with many common diseases such as diarrhea and malaria, people are able to monitor the states of their own bodies and adjust dosages more accurately than a doctor in a district hospital or a village health worker could do for them. But no one in the planning process comes forward to advocate the growing of cinchona trees in every kitchen garden or village common. Where cinchona trees do grow, people remove the bark and treat themselves for malaria (Kilama 1980). This rendering of plants into remedies by village people is socially as well as medically functional in that it fosters confidence and self-reliance, where a top–downward health system based on rational-legal bureaucracy is disfunctional at the bottom because it fosters dependence and lack of initiative in preventive and curative health care.

Perhaps the most profound fault in the current literature on drugs in developing countries arises from a Westernized assumption that people can purchase health passively (Titmuss 1964). People in rural African communities are wise, with rich, full concepts of well-being. They know well-being to be embedded within networks of intellectual meaning and social interdependence, networks that must constantly be reexamined for meaning and expressed in rituals of healing and social reconciliation.

On one hand, top–downward health planning is shaped by Westernized assumptions of effcient individualistic mechanistic function, and on the other hand is constrained by financial and political exigencies. For example, governments cannot ignore the demands of their own urban sector. It is a near-at-hand aggregate of influential people with a strong political voice. The urban elite demand good curative hospital services, and so a single teaching hospital may consume more than half the total health budget. Because of an urban bias in planning throughout the Third World (Lipton 1977), only a small fraction of national wealth is allocated for primary health care at the periphery.

Although bureaucracy as an ideal may be efficient, in practical application in Africa the district medical officer often feels abandoned and demoralized at the periphery. A solution is to desolve more planning and management responsibility downward to the district level. However, the political reality is that many African governments do not have a very firm grip on their periphery and in political terms cannot afford to devolve much authority. In some instances politicians at the center need to bind political clients through the deployment of funds, such as health funds. Thus some governments are constructed largely as a network of patron–client relationships, the center binding the periphery to itself through asymmetrical reciprocities (Clapham 1978; Gellner and Waterbury 1977; Williams and Turner 1978). Allocation of health care resources is part of this highly personalized system, far removed from the Weberian ideal of rational-legal legitimacy expressed in bureaucracy. Only hierarchy is preserved.

Hierarchy may even "float" without functional ties to poor rural communities in cases where the communities do not wish to participate in primary health care programs. Villagers may be profoundly wary of anything proposed by government officials (Bailey 1967). Or some communities may be destructively factionalized by party politics played out at the village level, with "health" being a political resource in the game (Feachem et al. 1978).

On an equally pragmatic level of analysis, Westernized urban planners either genuinely do not know, or seek to confirm, their elite status by professing not to know, what traditional practitioners are doing at the periphery.[3] In a field guide for articulating traditional midwives with national health services, WHO provided sample questionnaires that might be administered to traditional midwives (WHO 1979*b*). The faith that a questionnaire can plumb the depths of midwives' wisdom and local status is touching. However, that kind of evaluative effort seems a rather anachronistic solution, more appropriate to some colonial past. Why not just invite traditional midwives and other practitioners to be part of the planning process from the beginning? If pure top–downward planning persists, it will continue to be often culturally inappropriate at the local level, will not work as intended, and will be largely a waste of the limited resources for health that the country has.

LEGITIMACY AND THE CONCEPT OF APPROPRIATE HEALTH CARE

People invest legitimacy in the healers to whom they turn, whether they are scientifically trained physicians in state or private bureaucracies or traditional practitioners. In seeking legitimacy in healers, people reassure themselves that the system of healing has meaning and they can undertake the quest for health with conviction. Practitioners have legitimacy to command patients' "uncoerced obedience" to the system they represent (Weber 1947, 324–345).

Rational-legal legitimacy arises from the ideal of a society maintained through impersonal, efficient procedures. But rationality is not exclusive to the Western scientific tradition. Ethnographic literature often contains descriptions of empirical observation and hypothesis testing in small-scale rural societies (Ellen and Reason 1979), and a case can be made for pervasive rationality in all societies once we clarify our terms (Horton and Finnegan 1973; Wilson 1974). However, "rural rationality" is not necessarily expressed in bureaucracy.

For Weber, there are three types of legitimacy: (1) rational-legal, (2) traditional, and (3) charismatic. Any discussion of traditional practitioners might benefit from consideration of the latter two types.

Traditional legitimacy develops through time as qualities of merit, valor, and holiness become associated with a corporate group, such as a lineage or sodality. In the African context, traditional legitimacy is often associated with the wisdom of ancestral time. "Uncoerced obedience" arises from personal loyalty to those recognized as the heirs and bearers of legitimacy.

The third type of legitimacy, charismatic legitimacy, is analogous to the idea that God and His manifestations cannot be anything other than pure legitimacy. People of exceptional heroism and sanctity present a vision of hope and health. Believers follow in obedience to attain those goals. They have personal trust in the extraordinary qualities of healers and their revelations.

Paradoxically, a medical system based on traditional legitimacy may have more flexibility in responding to changing conditions than one based on rational-legal bureaucracy. In the latter, people are loyal to the rules. But with traditional legitimacy, the obligation of obedience is based on personal loyalty, free from cumbersome rules. In the case of traditional healers, as long as their action follows what Weber called principles of substantive ethical common sense, they are quite free to innovate. Their patients follow the regimen out of personal loyalty. Change does not come from legislation. Rather, it is claimed to have always been in force but only recently to have become known through the wisdom of the healer.

Charismatic authority is potentially most flexible, even revolutionary. But it has the drawback of being unorganized and not amenable to replication or to systematic administration over wide geographical areas or through time. When charismatic authority becomes organized the system has transformed into one of the other types of legitimacy.

Most indigenous healers in Africa enjoy traditional legitimacy. For example, midwives in Sierra Leone are officials in Sande, a women's sodality commanding wisdom obtained in ancestral time. During initiation ceremonies, when girls become women eligible to procreate, the ancestors become manifest as masked figures (MacCormack 1979, 1981). Some healers and carers are charismatic figures. But the point to be stressed is that traditional and charismatic healers have no less legitimacy to practice than those trained in Western biomedicine. How effectively they practice will depend to some extent on national and international politics.

I have referred to "traditional" practitioners and the "traditional" medical system because I wish to link them with Weber's concept of traditional legitimacy. However, I do not intend "traditional" to mean archaic, unchanging sociocultural relics from the past. Herbalists often add a wide range of commercial pharmaceuticals to their healing repertoire, and midwives who have been through a training program may use new therapies, techniques, and perhaps even new equipment from a UNICEF kit. Those who have been to school may have new conceptual models of disease transmission and prevention as well.

THE ARTICULATION OF WESTERNIZED AND TRADITIONAL SYSTEMS

Having established legitimacy for the "uncoerced obedience" of people following an indigenous medical system, let us return to the question of national health planning. Aspects of Western medicine are clearly superior. Far fewer babies will die of neonatal tetanus if the umbilical cord is not dressed with earth or dung. Herbalists who buy antibiotics and other drugs from pharmacists or traders will clearly benefit from more knowledge about the therapeutic powers and harmful side effects of the drugs they prescribe (Ebin 1982).

Seldom is an African traditional practitioner's office automatically inherited. The practitioner's status is largely achieved, not ascribed. Practitioners therefore have a vested interest in learning selectively from Western medicine, to improve their effectiveness and therefore their following. The allegations that indigenous practitioners are closed-minded and conservative is seldom true.

Traditional practitioners, voluntarily seeking to augment their knowledge with Western medical skills, therefore constitute a natural link in a comprehensive health system. A training program of sharing on-the-job skills between district-level health workers and traditional health workers might promote this linkage, an idea that will be developed in the next section. The district is the appropriate administrative level for linkage because it is the lowest level likely to have a hospital staffed by a doctor and a range of other skilled professionals who could be teachers. Also, at this administrative level ethnic, linguistic, and class "distance" between hospital staff and village people may be less of a barrier to constructive interaction. Ideally, hospitals or health center staff would go to rural villages for at least some training sessions. By going outside the hospital or clinic, the staff will begin to see a different range of illness and may come to appreciate the need for preventive services.

In actual practice, district health workers are quite overworked, treating the large numbers of people who come for curative services. The same staff cannot treat all who come and also work in villages with their traditional-sector counterparts. Either the numbers of workers at the district level will have to be increased, or some curative services, which people very much want, will have to be curtailed. Realistically, government commitment to primary health care will require additional expenditure on health.

Genuine collaboration will require some accommodation on the part of district-level personnel. For example, if the local traditional bone-setter is demonstrably more effective, the district health workers may wish to refer their cases to him, or they may wish to serve an apprenticeship under him, paying requisite fees for learning such valuable secret knowledge. Where women's initiation societies exist, district midwives will be most effective if they are initiated members of the sodality, within the moral community of women, having a legitimacy for effective collaboration with their village counterpart (MacCormack 1982).

Certainly not all practitioners may wish to become recognized village health workers. Bone-setters or healers of skin diseases may have successful professional secrets that they do not wish to relinquish. Spirit mediums may feel they have little to learn from the kind of psychiatric medicine practiced in their country. Traditional midwives may feel denigrated by their trained counterpart, or the traditional midwife may be a substantial political figure at the local level who outranks and dominates young educated midwives. Traditional practitioners are rewarded not only with respect but also in money and kind. To be incorporated as the bottom rung in a government medical service, poorly paid and defined by the system as least professional, may be a singularly unattractive proposition. These local contingencies are a further reason why considerable discretion in planning and administration should be devolved to the district level. A centrally planned health care system can never be sensitive enough to local situations to promote the most constructive collaboration possible.

Any collaboration must be voluntary. Requiring traditional practitioners to be licensed is a way for the national bureaucracy to control them, to bring them within its sphere of rational-legal legitimacy, but would probably drive most underground. In such a climate charlatans might flourish, where traditional practitioners have been outlawed but no adequate primary health care system has been provided, the practitioners have either worked illegally or been driven away. In these cases the first step in linking the indigenous system and the national system is to undo the damage that has been done, building a relationship of legality, public approval and respect. A WHO document (WHO 1978*a*) suggests that traditional practitioners form their own associations to maintain standards. This approach may work well for Ayurvedic, Unani, homeopathic, and other professionalized groups in Asia, but the variety of practitioners and institutional contexts is rather different in Africa. Spirit mediums, for example, practice as a result of having themselves been ill, possessed, and taken within a healing cult (Jules-Rosette 1979; Lewis 1971). The legitimacy they enjoy is not achieved in schooling and examinations nor expressed in bureaucratic organization that maintains rules and standards. They are a congregation (Turner 1967).

Some kinds of healing specialists do meet with each other (Ngubane 1981, 361), and negatively sanction the less worthy, but this is probably the exception rather than the rule in Africa. Virtually every rural adult knows the healing qualities of a variety of plants and helps self and others. Those recognized as having particular healing expertise are usually part-time specialists. Some specialize in a very limited range of ills, and their services may be sought only one or two times a year. Especially in sparsely populated areas, no group of assessor peers could be present to monitor standards, even if a list of standards could be agreed upon. Practitioners *are* assessed though, perhaps in the best way possible, by the people themselves. A practitioner who does not relieve suffering, or who causes more suffering, soon can be found "sitting alone."

A MODEL FOR THE INTEGRATION OF WESTERNIZED AND TRADITIONAL SYSTEMS

On one hand, health planning must necessarily originate in the ministry of health; on the other hand, one also hopes that rural people's knowledge for effective self-help will grow from strength to strength. These two sets of expectations meet in the planning process when traditional practitioners become advisors at early stages of planning. In organization and implementation of health plans, the two systems join in integrated function at the district level (see fig. 18.1).

In a national system, each district usually has one or more doctors and a range of other trained health workers: nurses with broad curative and preventive training, midwives, dispensers, and perhaps others. They are community workers on the leading edge of the upper triangle. Ideally, they spend some of their work time outside the hospital, participating in training workshops with their village counterparts. This is teaching by working together

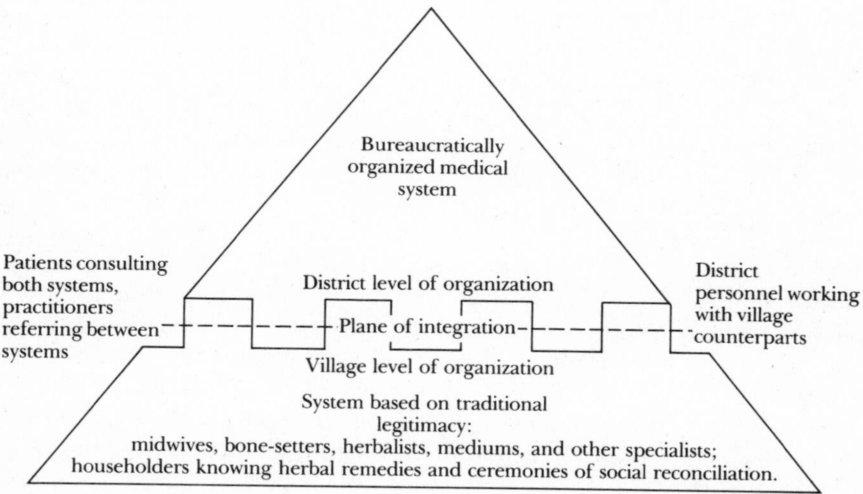

Figure 18.1. A model for integration of bureaucratically and traditionally organized medical systems.

and does not require literacy skills or a curriculum based on abstract principles. Potentially, it is appropriate, high-quality teaching if the participants are trained, are not overworked, are cooperative, and are willing to learn as well as teach. It is a very labor-intensive method, appropriate in countries that have not yet industrialized. In the example of midwives, all in the district could not enter into the collaborative scheme at once. Therefore, if possible, midwives in a local area might choose who will participate first and who will join the program later.

Enhancing the skills of a range of traditional practitioners (midwife, bonesetter, herbalist, etc.) may be a better strategy than training one village health worker, especially if that person will not be paid a full wage by the government. Some descriptions of village health workers' tasks stipulate a staggering range of curative and preventive services that they are to carry out after a few weeks' or months' training.[4] In rural villages they are all alone, without reliable backup from coworkers or laboratory services. They are on the vulnerable end of a limb compared with the doctor in the district hospital who may be seeing the same kinds of illnesses and emergencies, but with *far* more training and backup. In rural villages, referral of emergency cases seldom is possible where there are no roads, where transport is unpredictable, or where some people cannot afford the cost of transport to a hospital.

There is also the possibility that the village health workers will be poorly supplied, or irregularly supplied with drugs. Without these essential accoutrements, their legitimacy will diminish. Traditional practitioners, however, have years or generations of knowledge and self-assurance behind them. They have resources in the physical and social environment to call upon if drug supplies or in-service training are not reliably supplied to the periphery.

The alternative to augmenting the skills of traditional practitioners is to train young people with primary-school or secondary-school qualifications as village health workers. They can be taught less expensively, in large classes. Literacy allows more concentrated communication. Students are given books, and told to read them, in preparation for examinations. Evaluation by written examination is cheaper and easier to organize than on-the-job supervision. The risk, however, is that this kind of education will be based on abstract principles. When workers actually go to an isolated village, they may not know how to get on with the practical task of diagnosing and treating illness or initiating preventive activities. They may not remain in the village. In age-stratified societies they may lack prestige and authority for mobilizing community activities. In contrast, if older people with lesser literacy skills, or even illiterate traditional practitioners, are trained by doing, the method of education approximates that of clinical training. It is an expensive method in terms of labor-time of the trainers and may cause manpower bottlenecks in the short run, but this labor-intensive approach may be the most appropriate for the country in the long run.

Useful knowledge, the closely guarded secrets of Western medicine, must be shared out or the exercise will be a sham. Western medical knowledge comes down to villages, and knowledge about useful local medicines, other therapies, and local needs and preferences go up to the planners. Linkage is also achieved by referrals going both ways, as indeed today doctors refer to the traditional sector for some ills and traditional practitioners refer other kinds of cases to the district hospital. Patients also, on their own initiative, seek help where they perceive best results (Ademuwagun et al. 1978).

With traditional practitioners thus voluntarily linked with a national health care system there is potential for constructive planning from the bottom upward. Practitioners' therapies usually involve talking with patients at length and understanding their hopes and fears. Most, with the possible exception of "modern" herbalists (Ebin 1982), treat whole people embedded in human society. In planning maternal and child health services, for example, when traditional midwives are in the planning process at the beginning, plans—especially for preventive measures—have a better chance of being culturally appropriate, feasible to implement, and actually carried out at the local level. If the plans are *their* plans, traditional midwives are more likely to implement them. If they are excluded from the early planning stages they have tremendous influence for obstructing implementation. But to fully absorb the traditional sector into a national health system would destroy some of the best aspects of its caring services. Traditional midwives, for example, give such a wide range of services that they cannot be integrated into a health service that measures performance in terms of efficiency. Too many of the services they give are outside the job descriptions of medical services conceived in Western thought (MacCormack 1982).

The traditional sector can maintain its autonomy by practitioners continuing to work on a fee-for-service basis. They are people deeply embedded in local social networks and are not likely to exploit their patients. If they attempt to exploit, patients will simply turn to someone else, as they always have. Because traditional practitioners know so much about their patients as social persons, they are able to adjust fees without bureaucratic means-testing. Traditional practitioners may be offered an additional stipend for collecting statistics (or seeing that a literate member of their household keeps them), or for attending planning and training workshops, but they should not be given full salary as a device for controlling their activities.

Finally, the traditional sector must remain autonomous and only loosely integrated with the national health care system as an alternative, should the planned national bureaucracy become excessively inefficient or corrupt.

Now, after decades of ethnographic field studies, we know more than

Weber could have known about the practical implications of social systems based on traditional legitimacy. Because of his admiration for Bismarck's Germany, and the value he put on efficiency, he foresaw unequivocally the triumph of bureaucratic "societal action" over "community action." But the vitality for effective self-help resides in community action at the local level. Indeed, new Western medical knowledge is actively sought because of its observed efficacy. But any village that accepts it, bureaucratically imposed from the top downward, is in risk of losing its soul. Western medical knowledge can be liberating and revitalizing, engendering optimism and strength through self-help, or it can engender dependence and passivity (Werner 1977*a*).

This model has suggested a solution that maintains both traditional and Westernized medical systems in a symbiotic relationship where the two are loosely linked and neither controls the other. One continues its emphasis on technological methods for successful curing of certain complaints, and the other continues to follow traditional—but changing—wisdom in restoring a sense of well-being to whole people in social groups.

NOTES

1. Reprinted from *Social Science and Medicine*, 15B (1981) (3): 423–428, with the permission of Pergamon Journals Ltd.

2. Senior physicians, usually with a high level of technical training and specialization, are often the planners within a health ministry, or their views and behavior can effectively override the work of planners.

3. This is more likely to be the case for older professionals trained abroad. Many young doctors, trained in their own country or region, are much more comfortable with their cultural roots.

4. The WHO-UNICEF report, *Primary Health Care*, suggests that primary health care service "will include at least: promotion of proper nutrition and an adequate supply of safe water; basic sanitation; maternal and child care, including family planning; immunization against the major infectious diseases; prevention and control of locally endemic diseases; education concerning prevailing health problems and controlling them; and appropriate treatment for common diseases and injuries" (Jules-Rosette 1979).

BIBLIOGRAPHY

Aaby, P., J. Bukh, and A. Smits. 1983. "The Black Child's Grave: Measles, Overcrowding and Child Mortality in Africa." Paper presented to African Studies Association Meetings, Boston.

Aazevede, M. J. 1981. "The Human Price of Development: The Brazzaville Railroad and the Sara of Chad," *African Studies Review* 24 (1), 1–20.

Abu-Lughod, J. L. 1971. *Cairo: 1001 Years of the City Victorious*. Princeton: Princeton University Press.

Ackerknecht, E. H. 1971. *Medicine and Ethnology*. Baltimore: Johns Hopkins University Press.

———. 1965. *History and Geography of the Most Important Diseases*. New York: Hafner.

———. 1982. *A Short History of Medicine*. Baltimore and London: Johns Hopkins University Press.

Ademuwagun, Z. A., J. Ayoade, J. Harrison, and D. M. Warren, eds. 1978. *African Therapeutic Systems*. Waltham, Mass.: Crossroads Press.

Ajaegbu, H. I. 1977. "The Demographic Situations in Pre-Colonial and Early Colonial Periods in West Africa: An Assessment of the Usefulness of Non-Conventional Data Sources." In Edinburgh, *African Historical Demography*, pp. 169–194.

al-Bakri, Abu 'Ubaidallah ibn Adbul-'Aziz. 1960. *Al-Mughrib fi Dhikr Bilad 'Lfriqiya wal Maghrib*. Baghdad: Maktabat al-Muthanna.

al-Din, Rashid. 1911. *Al-Fakhri fi al-Adab*. Ed. T. Bochet. Vol. 1. Leiden.

al-Ghazali, Abu Hamid Muhammad ibn Muhammad al-Tusi. 1967. *Tahafut al-Falasifa*. Cairo: Editions Sulayman Dunya.

al-Hajj Sa'id, M. A., trans. 1966. "A Seventeenth Century Chronicle on the Origin and the Missionary Activities of the Wangarawa." *Kano Studies* 4: 7–42.

al-Idrīsī, Abū 'Abd Allāh Muhammad al-sharif. 1971. *Nuzhat al-Mushtag*. Cited in N. Levtzion, "The Early States of Western Sudan." In J. F. A. Ajayi and M. Crowder, eds., *History of West Africa*, 2 vols. London: Longman.

Allan, P., 1924. *Report of the Tuberculosis Survey of the Union of South Africa*. Cape Town.

———. *Report of the Native Laws Commission to the SAIMR*.

al-Majusi, Ali ibn Abbas. N.d. *Kamil al-Sina'a al-Tibbiya*. Cairo.

al-Maqarri, Ahmad b. Muhammad al-Tilimsani. n.d. *Nafh al-Tib fi ghusn al-Andalus al-ratib*. Ms. No. 562, Bibliothèque nationale, Rabat, p. 7.

al-Naqar, Umar. 1972. *The Pilgrimage Tradition in West Africa*. Khartoum: Khartoum University Press.

al-Tabari, Ali Ibn Abbas. 1885. *Firdaws al-Hikma*. Cairo: Bulaq.

al-Tabari, Muhammad ibn Jarir. 1879–1901. *Ta'rikh al-rusul wa-l-muluk*. Ed. M. J. de Goeje. (15 vols.). Leiden: Lugduni Batavorum.

Amerine, M. A., R. M. Pangbourn, and E. B. Roessler, 1965. *Principles of the Sensory Evaluation of Food*. New York: Academic Press.

Amin, S., ed. 1974. *Modern Migrations in Western Africa*. London: Oxford University Press.

Ampofo, O. 1977. "Plants that Heal." *World Health*, November.

Anderson, W. B. 1977. *The Church in East Africa 1840–1974*. Dodoma: Central Tanganyika Press.

Anderson-Morshead, A. E. M. 1955. *The History of the Universities' Mission to Central Africa*, vol. 1, *1859–1909*. London: Universities' Mission to Central Africa.

Andersson, N., and S. Marks. 1983. "Epidemics and Social Control in Twentieth Century South Africa." Paper presented to the African Studies Association, Boston.

Andrews, M. 1984. "The State, the Building Industry and the 1953 Group Areas Act in South Africa." Ph.D. dissertation, University of London.

Anker, R., M. Buvinic, and N. H. Youssef, eds. 1982. *Women's Roles and Population in the Third World*. London: Croom Helm.

Annett, H. E. 1902. *Report of the Malaria Expedition to Nigeria of the London School of Tropical Medicine and Medical Parasitology*. London: Liverpool School of Tropical Medicine, Memoir 3: 54–56.

Arabin, G. 1979. "First Tuberculosis Prevalence Survey in Kwazulu." *South African Medical Journal* 56: 434–438.

Armor, M. 1962. "Migrant Labour in the Kalabo District of Barotseland." *Bulletin Inter-African Laboratory Institute*. IX: 5.

Arom, S. 1985. *Polyphonies et polyrhythmies instrumentales d'Afrique centrale*. Paris: Société d'Etudes Linguistiques et Anthropologiques de France (2 vols).

Asl al-Wangarayyin al-Ladhina ma-a al-Shaykh. Seventeenth century [1968]. (trans. M. A. al-Hajj) "A Seventeenth Century Chronicle on the Origin and the Missionary Activities of the Wangarawa." *Kano Studies* 4: 7–42.

Augé, M. 1985. "Introduction." *Interpreting Illness* (special issue). *History and Anthropology* 2 (1): 1–15.

Austen, R. 1977. "Duala Versus Germans in Cameroon." *Revue française d'histoire d'outre-mer* 64: 477–497.

———, and R. Headrick. 1983. "Equatorial Africa under Colonial Rule." In Birmingham and Martin, eds., *History of Central Africa*, 2: 27–94.

Azevedo, M. J. 1976. "Sara Demographic Instability as a Consequence of French Colonial Policy in Chad, 1890–1940." Ph.D. dissertation, Duke University, Durham, N.C.

———. 1978. "Epidemic Disease Among the Sara of Southern Chad, 1890–1940." In Hartwig and Patterson, eds., *Disease in African History*, pp. 118–152.

Bailey, F. G. 1967. "The Peasant View of the Bad Life." School of African and Asian Studies and Institute of Development Studies Joint Report Series 7. Brighton: University of Sussex.

Baker, C. 1976. "The Government Medical Service in Malawi: An Administrative History, 1891–1974." *Medical History* 20: 296.

———. 1983. "A Long-Term Check." *Africa Now* (January): 59.

Ball, N. 1976. "Understanding the Causes of African Famine." *Journal of Modern African Studies* xiv: 517–523.

Banghawe, A.F., E. N. Mingola, and G. Maina. 1972. *The Use and Abuse of Drugs and Chemicals in Tropical Africa.* Nairobi: Kenya Literature Bureau.

Bannerman, R. B., and Ch'en Wen Chieh, eds. 1983. *Traditional Medicine and Health Care Coverage.* Geneva: World Health Organization (WHO).

Barber, T. X. 1984. "Changing 'Unchangeable' Bodily Processes by (Hypnotic) Suggestions: A New Look at Hypnosis, Cognitions, Imagining, and the Mind-Body Problem." *Advances* 1, 2. New York: Institute for the Advancement of Health.

Barker, C. 1975. "Pharmaceutical Production in a Less Developed Country." In M. Segall and C. Baker, eds., *Two Papers on Pharmaceuticals in Developing Countries.* Sussex: Institute of Development Studies, Communication No. 119.

———. 1981. "The Human Price of Development: The Brazzaville Railroad and the Sara of Chad." *African Studies Review* 24(1): 1–20.

Barotse Annual Reports, 1929. Nalolo. National Archives of Zambia.

Bastian, A. 1874. *Die deutsche Expedition an der Loango-Küste.* Jena: Costenoble.

Battel, A. 1814. "The Strange Adventures of Andrew Battel." In J. Pinkerton, ed., *A General Collection of the Best and Most Interesting Voyages.* London: Kimber & Conrad.

Bayliss-Smith, T. 1981. "Seasonality and Labour in the Rural Energy Balance." In Chambers et al., eds., *Seasonal Dimensions to Rural Poverty*, pp. 30–38.

Bayoumi, A. 1976. "The History and Traditional Treatment of Smallpox in the Sudan." *Journal of East African Research and Development* 6: 2.

———. 1979. *The History of Sudan Health Services.* Nairobi: Kenya Literature Bureau.

Beck, A. 1970. *A History of the British Medical Administration of East Africa.* Cambridge, Mass.: Harvard University Press.

———. 1977. "Medicine and Society in Tanganyika, 1890–1930." *Transactions of the American Philosophical Society* 67: 3.

———. 1981. *Medicine, Tradition and Development in Kenya and Tanzania, 1920–1970.* Waltham, Mass.: Crossroads Press.

Beckinsale R. P., and J. M. Houston, eds. 1968. *Urbanization and Its Problems: Essays in Honour of E. W. Gilbert.* Oxford: Blackwell.

Bedson, H. S., K. R. Dumbell, and W. R. Thomas. 1963. "Variola in Tanganyika." *Lancet* 2: 1085–1088.

Behm, H. 1980. "Socio-Economic Determinants of Mortality in Latin America." *Population Bulletin of the United Nations* 13: 1–15.

Beinart, W. 1979. "Joyini Nkomo: The Origins of Labour Migrancy in Pondoland." *Journal of Southern African Studies* 5 (2): 199–219.

———. 1983. *The Political Economy of Pondoland, 1860–1930.* Cambridge, New York: Cambridge University Press.

Bello, M. N.d. *Talkhis tibb an-Nabi.* Unpublished manuscript.

Belsey, M. A. 1976. "The Epidemiology of Infertility. A Review with Special Reference to Sub-Saharan Africa." *Bulletin of the World Health Organization* 54: 319–342.

Benenson, A. S., ed. 1975. *Control of Communicable Disease in Man*, 12th ed. Washington: American Public Health Assoc.

Benoît, D., B. Lacombe, P. Levi, P. Livenais, and F. Sodter. 1982. *Mariatang: enquête de sources complémentaires en pays Dagara (Haute-Volta)*. Paris: ORSTOM. (Document de travail, No. 16.)

Benyoussef, A., J. C. Cutler, A. Levine, P. Mansourian, T. Phan-Tan, R. Baylet, H. Collomb, S. Diop, B. Lacombe, J. Ravel, J. Vaugelade, and G. Diebold. 1974. "Health Effects of Rural-Urban Migration in Developing Countries—Senegal." *Social Science and Medicine* 8: 243–254.

Berque, J. 1958. "Médinas, villeneuves et bidonvilles." *Cahiers de Tunisie* 6: 5–42.

Betts, R. F. N.d. "The Establishment of the Medina in Dakar Senegal, 1914." *Africa* 41: 143–152.

Bhebe, N. 1978. "The Ndebele and Mwari Before 1893." In J. M. Schoffeleers, ed., *Guardians of the Land*. Gwelo: Mambo Press.

———. 1979. *Christianity and Traditional Religion in Western Zimbabwe*. London: Longman.

Bhila, H. H. K. 1982. *Trade and Politics in a Shona Kingdom*. Essex: Longman, Harlow.

Bibeau, G., E. Corin, Mulinda, Mabiala, Matumona, Mukuna, and Nsiala. 1980. *Traditional Medicine in Zaire*. Ottawa: International Development Research Centre.

———. 1981. "The Circular Semantic Network in Ngbandi Disease Nosology." *Social Science and Medicine* 15B (3): 295–308.

Birmingham, D., and P. Martin. 1983. *History of Central Africa* (2 vols.) London: Longman.

Bloch, M. 1973. "The Long Term and the Short Term: The Economic and Political Significance of the Morality of Kinship." In Goody, ed., *The Character of Kinship*, pp. 75–87.

Bochalli, R. 1954. *Robert Koch: Der Schöpfer der modernen Bacteriologie*. Stuttgart: Wissenschaftliche Verlagsgesellschaft.

Bohannan, P., and L. Bohanna. 1969. *Source Notebook on Tiv Religion*. New Haven, Conn.: Human Relations Area Files.

Bonner, P. 1982. "The Transvaal Native Congress, 1917–1920: The Radicalization of the Black Bourgeoisie on the Rand." In Marks and Rathbone, eds., *Industrialisation and Social Change in South Africa*, pp. 270–313.

Booth, N., ed. 1977. *African Religions: A Symposium*. New York, London, Lagos: Nok.

Borrell, J. 1981. "Zimbabwe Government Sees Witch Doctors as Valuable for Herbal Cures, Psychiatry." *Wall Street Journal* 24 (July): 25.

Botha, H. P. 1950*a*. "Karl Bremer." *Dictionary of National Biography*. 4: 104.

———. 1950*b*. "Better Health If You Live Long Enough." *Rand Daily Mail* 11:1.

———. 1961. *Nog Meer as 'n Dagtaak. Die Lewe van Karl Bremer*. Cape Town: Nasionale Raad vir Sosiale Navorsing.

Bourdieu, P. 1977. *Outline of a Theory of Practice*. Cambridge: Cambridge University Press.

Bourdillon, M. F. 1972. "The Manipulation of Myth in a Tavara Chiefdom." *Africa* 42: 112.

———. 1974. "Spirit Mediums in Shona Belief and Practice." *Native Affairs Department Annual*, p. 30.

Bourgeois-Pichat, J. 1952. "Essai sur la mortalité biologique de l'homme." *Population* 7 (3): 381–394.

Boyes, J. 1912. *A White King in East Africa.* New York: McBride, Nast and Co.

Bozzoli, B., ed. 1983. *Town and Countryside in the Transvaal.* Johannesburg: Ravan Press.

Breman, J. G., A. B. Alecaut, and J. M. Lane. 1977. "Smallpox in the Republic of Guinea, West Africa. I. History and Epidemiology." *American Journal of Tropical Medicine and Hygiene* 26: 756–764.

Brockelmann, C. 1898–1902. *Geschichte der Arabischen Litteratur* (2 vols.) Weimar: E. Felber.

———. 1937–1942. *Geschichte der Arabischen Litteratur,* Supplement, 3 vols. Leiden.

———. 1947. *History of the Islamic Peoples,* J. Carmichael and M. Perlmann, trans. New York: G. P. Putnam's Sons.

Brown, A. W. A., J. Haworth, and A. H. Zahar. 1976. "Review Article: Malaria Eradication and Control from a Global Standpoint." *Journal of Medical Entomology* 13 (1): 1–25.

Browne, G. E. 1921. *Arabian Medicine.* Cambridge: Cambridge University Press.

Browne, W. G. B. 1806. *Travels in Africa, Egypt, and Syria from the Year 1792 to 1798.* London: T. Cadwell.

Bruce-Chwatt, L. J. 1980. *Essential Malariology.* London: Heinemann Medical Books.

Bryceson, D. F. 1980. "Changes in Peasant Food Production and Food Supply in Relation to the Historical Development of Commodity Production in Pre-Colonial and Colonial Tanganyika." *Journal of Peasant Studies* vii.

Bucher, H. 1980. *Spirits and Power.* Cape Town: Oxford University Press.

Bundy, C. 1979. *The Rise and Fall of the South African Peasantry.* Berkeley, Los Angeles, London: University of California Press.

Burckhardt, J. L. 1819. *Travels in Nubia*: London: J. Murray.

Bürgel, J. C. 1976. "Secular and Religious Features of Medieval Arabic Medicine." In Leslie, ed., *Asian Medical Systems,* 44–62.

Burke, G., and P. Richardson. 1978. "The Profits of Death: A Comparative Study of Miner's Phthisis in Cornwall and the Transvaal." *Journal of Southern African Studies* 4 (2): 147–171.

Burnet, F. M., and D. O. White. 1974. *The Natural History of Infectious Disease,* 3d ed. Cambridge: Cambridge University Press.

Burney, P., and S. Shahyar, 1980. "Tuberculosis in the Transkei." In F. Wilson and G. Westcott, eds., *Economics of Health in South Africa,* Vol. 2, *Hunger, Work and Health.* Johnannesburg: Raven Press for the South Africa Labour and Development Unit, pp. 343–365.

Burnham, P. 1975. "*Regroupement* and Mobile Societies: Two Cameroon cases." *Journal of African History* 16 (4): 577–594.

———. 1980. "Raiders and Traders in Adamawa." In J. Watson, ed., *Asian and African Systems of Slavery.* Berkeley, Los Angeles, London: University of California Press, pp. 43–72.

Burrows, E. H. 1958. *A History of Medicine in South Africa Up to the End of the Nineteenth Century.* Cape Town and Amsterdam: A. A. Balkema.

Burton, L. E., H. H. Smith, and A. W. Nichols. 1980. *Public Health and Community Medicine,* 3d ed. Baltimore: Williams & Wilkins.

Burton, R. F. 1872. *Zanzibar: City, Island, and Coast.* London: Tinsley Bros.

Burton, W. F. P. 1961. *Luba Religion and Magic in Custom and Belief.* Tervuren: Museé Royal de l'Afrique Centrale.

Busvine, J. R. 1978. "Current Problems in the Control of Mosquitoes." *Nature* 273 (June 22): 604–607.

Cagnolo, C. 1933. *The Akikuyu: Their Customs, Traditions, and Folklore.* Nyeri: Mission Printing School.

Caldwell, J. C. 1975*a*. "Fertility Control." In Caldwell, Addo, et al., eds., *Population Growth and Socio-Economic Change in West Africa*, pp. 58–97.

———. 1975*b*. *The Sahelian Drought and Its Demographic Implications.* Washington, D.C.: American Council on Education, Overseas Liaison Committee, Paper No. 8.

———. 1977. "Major Questions in African Demographic History." In Edinburgh Center of African Studies, ed., *African Historical Demography*, pp. 7–22.

———. 1985. "The Social Repercussions of Colonial Rule—Demographic Aspects." In Adu Boahen, A., ed., *Africa Under Colonial Domination, 1880–1935*, vol. 7, *UNESCO General History of Africa*. Berkeley, Los Angeles, London: Heinemann and University of California Press.

———. 1986. "Routes to Low Mortality in Poor Countries." *Population and Development Review* 12 (2): 171–200.

———, ed., with N. O. Addo, S. K. Gaisie, A. Igun, and P. S. Olusanya. 1975. *Population Growth and Socio-Economic Change in West Africa.* New York and London: Columbia University Press.

———, and P. Caldwell. 1977. "The Role of Marital Sexual Abstinence in Determining Fertility: A Study of the Yoruba in Nigeria." *Population Studies* 31 (2): 193–213.

Caldwell, P., and J. C. Caldwell. 1981. "The Function of Child-Spacing in Traditional Societies and the Direction of Change." In Page and Lesthaeghe, eds., *Child-Spacing in Tropical Africa: Traditions and Change*, pp. 73–92.

Campbell, D. J., and D. D. Trechter, 1982. "Strategies for Coping with Food Consumption Shortage in the Mandara Mountains Region of North Cameroon." *Social Science and Medicine* xvi: 2117–2127.

Cansever, G. 1965. "The Psychological Effects of Circumcision." *British Journal of Medical Psychology* 38: 321.

Cantrelle, P. 1975. "Mortality: Levels, Patterns, and Trends." In Caldwell et al., *Population Growth and Socio-Economic Change in West Africa*, pp. 98–118.

———. 1979. "Inégalités face à la mort." In Union Internationale pour l'Étude Scientifique de la Population, ed., *La science de la population au service de l'homme.* Liège: UIESP, pp. 81–93.

Caplan, G. L. 1970. *The Elites of Barotseland, 1878–1969.* Berkeley, Los Angeles, London: University of California Press.

Carter, J. P. 1982. "The Physiology of Fasting, Famine, Starvation and Stress." In J. P. Carter, ed., *Famine in Africa: Proceedings of the Conference of a Working Group on Famine in Africa, Kinshasa, January 1980.* Oxford and New York: Pergamon Press, pp. 19–20.

Cartwright, A. P. 1971. *Doctors on the Mines. A History of the Mine Medical Officers' Association of South Africa.* Cape Town, Johannesburg, London, and New York.

Carver, R. 1983. "Integrating Traditional Healing." *Africa Now* (January): 57.

Castro, J. de. 1977. *The Geopolitics of Hunger.* New York: Monthly Review Press.

Cell, J. W. 1982. *The Highest Stage of White Supremacy: The Origins of Segregation in South*

Africa and the American South. Cambridge: Cambridge University Press.

Chambers, R., R. Longhurst, and A. Pacey, eds. 1981. *Seasonal Dimensions to Rural Poverty*. London: Frances Pinter.

Chavunduka, G. L. 1978. *Traditional Healers and the Shona Patient*. Gwelo: Mambo Press.

Chhabra, S. C. 1984. "Phytochemical Screening of Tanzanian Medicinal Plants. I." *Journal of Ethnopharmacology* 11: 157.

Chigunda, H. 1975. Interview. Rondo, Tanzania.

Christophers, S. R., and J. W. W. Stephens. 1900. "Destruction of Anopheles in Lagos." In *Reports of the Malaria Committee of the Royal Society*, 10 vols. London: Royal Society.

Christopherson, J. B. 1921. "The UMCA and Medical Work at Magila." *Central Africa* 39: 86, 91.

Clapham, C. 1978. "Liberia." In J. Dunn, ed. *West African States: Failure and Promise*. Cambridge: Cambridge University Press, pp. 117–131.

Cissoko, S. M. 1968. "Famines et épidemies à Tombouctou et dans la Boucle du Niger du XVI–XVII siècle." *Bulletin de L'IFAN* 30/3, Series B: 806–821.

Cliffe, L. 1974. "Capitalism or Feudalism? The Famine in Ethiopia." *Review of African Political Economy* i (1): 34–40.

Cluver, E. H. 1935. "Typhus and Tyhpus-like Disease in South Africa." Report to the Pan African Health Conference, Johannesburg.

Clyde, D. F. 1962. *History of the Medical Services in Tanganyika*. Dar es Salaam: The Government.

Coale, A. J., and F. Lorimer. 1968. "Summary of Estimates of Fertility and Mortality." In W. I. Brass, A. J. Coale, P. Demeny, D. Heisel, F. Lorimer, A. Romaniuk, and F. Van de Walle, eds. *The Demography of Tropical Africa*. Princeton: Princeton University Press, pp. 151–167.

Cobbing, J. 1977. "The Absent Priesthood: Another Look at the Rhodesian Risings of 1896–1897." *Journal of African History* 18: 61–84.

Coillard, F. 1887–1892. *Journal Intime*. Paris: Bibliothèque du DEFAP.

Collins, T. F. B. 1982. "The History of Southern Africa's First Tuberculosis Epidemic." *South African Medical Journal* 62: 780–789.

Colson, E. 1971. *The Social Consequences of Resettlement*. Manchester: Manchester University Press.

Comaroff, J. 1981. "Healing and Cultural Transformation: The Tswana of Southern Africa," *Social Science and Medicine*. 15B: 367–378.

———. 1985. *Body of Power, Spirit of Resistance*. Chicago: University of Chicago Press.

Comhaire, J. L. L. 1953. *Aspects of Urban Administration in Tropical and Southern Africa*. Cape Town: University of Cape Town.

Comstock, G. W. 1975. "Frost Revisited: The Modern Epidemiology of Tuberculosis." *American Journal of Epidemiology* 101: 363–382.

Conacher, D. 1957. "Smallpox in Tanganyika 1918–54." *East African Medical Journal* 34: 157–181.

Condamy. 1906. "Habitations coloniales." *Revue des troupes coloniales* 6: 21–28.

Conti, A. 1979. "Capitalist Organization of Production through Non-Capitalist Relations: Women's Role in a Pilot Resettlement Project in Upper Volta." *Review of African Political Economy* 15–16: 75–92.

Cooper, F . 1981. "Peasants, Capitalists and Historians." *Journal of Southern African Studies* 7: 2.

Coquery-Vidrovitch, C. 1972. *Le Congo au temps des grandes compagnies concessionnaires, 1898–1930.* Paris: Mouton.

———. 1976. "L'Afrique coloniale française et la crise de 1930: Crise structurelle et genèse du sous-développement." *Revue française d'histoire d'outre-mer* 63 (232–233): 386–424.

———. 1977. "Population et démographie en Afrique Équatoriale Française dans le premier tiers du XXe siècle." In Edinburgh, ed., *African Historical Demography*, 331–351.

———, and H. Moniot. 1974. *L'Afrique noire de 1800 à nos jours.* Paris: Presses Universitaires de France.

Cordell, D. D. 1983*a*. "Low Fertility in Africa: An Evaluation of the Bio-Medical Approach of Anne Retel-Laurentin." Quebec: paper presented at the annual meeting of the Canadian Association of African Studies.

———. 1983*b*. "The Savanna Belt of North Central Africa." In Birmingham and Martin, eds., *History of Central Africa*, I: 30–74.

———. 1985*a*. *Dar al-Kuti and the Last Years of the Trans-Saharan Slave Trade.* Madison: University of Wisconsin Press.

———. 1985b. "La sous-fécondité et l'histoire en Centrafrique." Paper presented to the département de démographie, Université de Montréal.

———. 1987*a*. "Extracting People from Precapitalist Production: French Equatorial Africa from the 1890s to the 1930s." In D. D. Cordell and J. W. Gregory, eds., *African Population and Capitalism: Historical Perspectives.* Boulders, Colo.: Westview Press, pp. 137–152.

———. 1987*b*. *Où sont tous les enfants: la démographie historique de la sous-fécondité en Centrafrique.* Memoire, Departement de démographie. Université de Montréal, 182 pp.

———, and J. W. Gregory. 1982. "Labor Reservoirs and Population: French Colonial Strategies in Ouagadougou, Upper Volta, 1914 to 1939." *Journal of African History* 23 (2): 205–224.

———. J. W. Gregory, and V. Piché. 1987. "African Historical Demography: The Search for a Theoretical Framework." In D. D. Cordell and J. W. Gregory, eds., *African Population and Capitalism: Historical Perspectives.* Boulder, Colo.: Westview Press, pp. 14–32.

Corin, E. 1979. "A Possession Psychotherapy in an Urban Setting: Zebola in Kinshasa." *Social Science and Medicine* 13B: 327.

———, and G. Bibeau. 1975. "De la forme culturelle au vécu des troubles psychiques en Afrique." *Africa* 45: 280.

Coulibaly, S., J. Gregory, and V. Piché, 1980. *Les migrations voltaique.* Tome l: *Importance et ambivalence de la migration voltaique.* Ottawa: CRDI pour la République de la Haute-Volta.

Crapanzano, V. 1973. *The Hamadsha: A Study in Moroccan Ethnopsychiatry.* Berkeley, Los Angeles, London: University of California Press.

Crawford. 1906. "Some Kikuyu Customs and Superstitions." *Mercy and Truth* 10: 87–88.

Crosby, A. 1972. *The Columbian Exchange.* Westport, Conn.: Greenwood.

Cruise O'Brien, R. 1972. *White Society in Black Africa: The French in Senegal*. London: Faber and Faber.

Crush, J. 1983. "The Struggle for Swazi Labour." Ph.D. dissertation, Queens University, Canada.

Curtin, P. D. 1984. *Cross-Cultural Trade in World History*, New York: Cambridge University Press.

Cutler, P. 1982. "Some Current Arguments on the Causes of Famine." Paper presented by the Nutrition Policy Unit, London School of Hygiene and Tropical Medicine, to the UNICEF/FAO/NPU/ICAR Workshop on Nutrition in Agriculture. Hassar, India (April 1982).

Dampierre, E. de. 1967. *Un ancien royaume Bandia du Haute-Oubangui*. Paris: Plon.

Daneel, M. L. 1970. *The God of the Matopo Hills*. The Hague: Mouton.

———. 1971. *Old and New in Southern Shona Independent Churches*, Vol. I. The Hague: Mouton.

Dapper, 0. 1668. *Naukeurige Beschryuinge der Afrikaensche Gewesten*. Amsterdam: Jacob von Meurs. [German edition: 1670. *Beschreibung von Afrika*. Amsterdam.]

Dawson, M. H. 1978. "Disease in Nineteenth-Century Kenya." Historical Association of Kenya Annual Conference.

———. 1979. "Smallpox in Kenya, 1880–1920." *Social Science and Medicine* 13B (4): 245–250.

———. 1981. "Disease and Population Decline of the Kikuyu of Kenya, 1890–1925." In Edinburgh, ed., *African Historical Demography*, II: 121–138.

———. 1983. "Social and Epidemiological Change in Kenya: 1880–1925." Ph.D. dissertation, University of Wisconsin.

———. 1987. "Health, Nutrition, and Population in Central Kenya, 1890–1945." In D. D. Cordell and J. W. Gregory, eds., *African Population and Capitalism: Historical Perspectives*. Boulder, Colo.: Westview Press, pp. 201–217.

De Craemer, W., J. Vansina, and R. Fox. 1976. "Religious Movements in Central Africa: A Theoretical Study." *Comparative Studies in Society and History* 18: 458–475.

De Heusch, L. 1972. *Le roi ivre, ou l'origine de l'état*. Paris: Gallimard.

Demers, L. 1981. *Morbidité et mortalité en Haute-Volta*: 1960–1976. Ouagadougou: Institut National de la Statistique et de la Démographie. (Dossier technique No. 4, PO1, Projet "Population et Développement." Nations-Unies et Haute-Volta.)

Dermenghem, E. 1954. *Le Culte des Saints dans l'Islam Maghrébin*. Paris: Gallimard.

Dewhurst, K. 1966. *Dr. Thomas Sydenham (1624–1689): His Life and Original Writings*. Berkeley and Los Angeles: University of California Press.

Dias, J. R. 1981. "Famine and Disease in the History of Angola *c*. 1830–1930." *Journal of African History* 22 (3): 349–378 .

Disler, P., and C. Oliver. 1984. "Some Diseases Associated with Poverty." Paper presented to Second Carnegie Inquiry into Poverty and Development, Southern Africa, Cape Town.

Dixon, C. W. 1962. *Smallpox*. Essex: Churchill.

Dobyns, H. F. 1963. "An Outline of Andean Epidemic History to 1720." *Bulletin for the History of Medicine* 37: 493–515.

Dormer, B. A. 1943. "A South African Team Looks at Tuberculosis." *Proceedings of the Transvaal Mine Medical Officers Association* 23: 86–90.

———. 1948. "Tuberculosis in South Africa." *British Journal of Tuberculosis* 50 (1): 53.

Doutté, E. 1908. *Magie et Religion dans l'Afrique du Nord.* Algiers: Jourdan.

Dresch, J. 1948. "Villes congolaises: Etude de géographie urbaine et sociale." *Revue de géographie humaine et de l'ethnographie* 1: 3–14.

———. 1950. "Villes d'Afrique occidentale." *Cahiers d'outre-mer* 3:200–230.

Dubos, R. 1953. *The White Plague.* Boston, London: Little, Brown.

———. 1959. "The Host in Tuberculosis." *ACTA Tuberculosea Scandinavica* 37: 43–62.

Duffy, J. 1979. *The Healers: A History of Medicine in America.* New York: McGraw-Hill.

Dumbell, K. R., and F. Huq. 1975. "Epidemiological Implications of the Typing of Variola Isolates." *Transactions of the Royal Society of Tropical Medicine and Hygiene* 69: 303–306.

Dumett, R. G. 1968. "The Campaign Against Malaria and the Extension of Scientific Medical Services in British West Africa." *African Historical Studies* 1: 153–197.

Dupré, G. 1982. *Un ordre et sa destruction: Économie, politique et histoire chez les Nzabi de la République populaire du Congo.* Paris: ORSTOM.

Durban Joint Council. 1931. "Report of Committee Appointed to Investigate and Report on Health of Durban Natives," pp. 3–4.

Du Toit, B., and I. H. Abdalla, eds. 1985. *African Healing Strategies.* Owerri, New York, London: Trado-Medic Books.

Dutta, H. M., and A. K. Dutt. 1978. "Malaria Ecology: A Global Perspective." *Social Science and Medicine* 12: 69–84.

Dwyer, D. H. 1978. *Images and Self-Image: Male and Female in Morocco.* New York: Columbia University Press.

Dybowski, J. 1893. *La Route du Tchad du Loango au Chari.* Paris: Librairie de Paris, Firmin-Didot et Cie.

East, R., trans. 1939. *Akiga's Story: The Tiv Tribe as Seen by One of its Members.* London: Oxford University Press.

Ebin, V. 1982. "Interpretations of Infertility; the Aowin People of South-West Ghana." In MacCormack, ed., *The Ethnography of Fertility and Birth*, pp. 141–160.

Edinburgh, University of, Centre of African Studies. 1977. *African Historical Demography.* Proceedings of a Seminar held April 29, 30.

———. 1981. *African Historical Demography*, Vol. II. Proceedings of a Seminar held in the Centre of African Studies, University of Edinburgh, April 24, 25.

———.1986. *African Medicine in the Modern World.* Centre of African Studies, University of Edinburgh. Seminar Proceedings 27.

Ehret, C., and M. Posnansky. 1982. *The Archaeological and Linguistic Reconstruction of African History.* Berkeley, Los Angeles, London: University of California Press.

Eickleman, D. C. 1976. *Moroccan Islam: Tradition and Society in a Pilgrimage Center.* Austin: University of Texas Press.

Elgood, C. 1962. "Tibb ul-nabbi or Medicine of the Prophet, by Al-Suyuti. Translation with commentary." *Osiris* XIV: 33–192.

Ellen, R. F., and O. Reason, eds. 1979. *Classifications and Their Social Context.* London: Academic Press.

Elling, R. 1981. "Political Economy, Cultural Hegemony, and Mixes of Traditional and Modern Medicine." *Social Science and Medicine* 15A: 89.

El-Nadoury, R. 1981. "The legacy of Pharaonic Egypt." In *General History of Africa II: Ancient Civilizations of Africa.* G. Mokhtar, ed., Paris and Berkeley (Calif.): UNESCO and Heinemann, pp. 155–177.

EMIS (Enquête de mortalité infantile au Sahel)-Burkina Faso. 1988. *Enquête sur la mortalité infantile dans le Sahel. Vol. III: Rapport d'analyse.* Ouagadougou: Institut national de la statistique et de la démographie; Bamako: Institut du Sahel, Unité socio-economique et de démographie.

Evans-Pritchard, E. E. 1937. *Witchcraft, Oracles and Magic among the Azande.* Oxford: Clarendon Press.

———. 1956. *Nuer Religion.* Oxford: Clarendon Press.

Fagan Commission. 1948. *Report of the Native Laws Commission, 1946–8.* South Africa.

Fanon, F. 1967. *A Dying Colonialism.* New York: Grove Press.

Feachem, R., E. Burns, S. Cairncross, R. Cronin, P. Cross, D. Curtis, M. Khalid Khan, and H. Southall, eds. 1978. *Water, Health and Development: An Interdisciplinary Evaluation.* London: Tri-Med Books.

Feierman, S. 1974. *The Shambaa Kingdom.* Madison: University of Wisconsin Press.

———. 1979. *Health and Society in Africa: A Working Bibliography.* Waltham, Mass. Crossroads Press.

———. 1981. "Therapy as a System-in-Action in Northeastern Tanzania." *Social Science and Medicine* 15B (3): 353–360.

———. 1985. "Struggles for Control: The Social Roots of Health and Healing in Modern Africa." *African Studies Review* 28 (2–3): 73–145.

Ferguson, A., and N. Folbre. 1981. "The Unhappy Marriage of Patriarchy and Capitalism." In L. Sargent, ed., *Women and Revolution.* Montreal: Black Rose Books, pp. 314–338.

Fofana, B., P. Imperato, and J. Nedvideck. 1971. "The Transmission Pattern of Smallpox in Eastern Mali." *Acta Tropica* 28: 175–179.

Ford, J. 1971. *The Role of the Trypanosomiases in African Ecology: A Study of the Tsetse-fly Problem.* Oxford: Clarendon.

———, and R. de Z. Hall. 1947. "The History of Karagwe (Bukoba District)." *Tanganyika Notes and Records* 24: 21.

Forde, D. 1965. *African Worlds.* London: Oxford University Press.

Fortune, G. 1973. "Who Was Mwari?" *Rhodesian History* 4: 1.

Foster, G. M. 1976. "Disease Etiologies in Non-Western Medical Systems." *American Anthropologist* 78 (4): 773–782.

———. 1978. "Hippocrates' Latin American Legacy: 'Hot' and 'Cold' in Contemporary Folk Medicine." In R. C. Wetherington, ed., *Colloquia in Anthropology*, Vol. II. Dallas, pp. 3–19.

———. 1979. "Methodological Problems in the Study of Intracultural Variation: The Hot/Cold Dichotomy in Tzintzuntzan." *Human Organization* 38: 2

Foster, S. O., A. Gadir, H. El Sid, and A. Deria. 1978. "Spread of Smallpox Among a Somali Nomadic Group." *Lancet* 2 (October): 831–833.

Fourie, L. 1934. Report of the Assistant Medical Offcer of Health. South Africa Government (GES), Pretoria.

Fourie, P. B., G. S. Townshend, and H. Kleeburg. 1980. "Follow-up Tuberculosis Prevalence Survey in the Transkei." *Tubercle* 61: 71–79.

———. 1986. "The Importance of Tuberculosis." *Proceedings of the First TBRI Symposium*, August 8–9, 1985, reported in *South African Journal of Science* 82: 386.

Fox, F. W., and D. Back. 1938. *A Preliminary Survey of the Agricultural and Nutritional Problems of the Ciskei and Transkeian Territories with Special Reference to Their Bearing on the Recruiting of Labourers for the Mining Industry*. Johannesburg: University of the Witwatersrand Archives.

Frack, I. 1943. *A South African Doctor Looks Backwards—and Forward*. Johannesburg: Central News Agency.

Frankenberg, R., and J. Leeson. 1974. "Sociology of Health Dilemmas in the Post-Colonial World: Intermediate Technology and Medical Care in Zambia, Zaire, and China." In E. DeKadt and E. Williams, eds., *Sociology and Development*. London: Tavistock, pp. 255–278.

———. 1977*a*. "Disease, Illness and Sickness: Social Aspects of the Choice of Healer in a Lusaka Suburb." In Loudon, ed. *Social Anthropology and Medicine*, pp. 223–258.

———. 1977b. "The Patients of Traditional Doctors in Lusaka." *African Social Research* 23: 217.

Frishman, A. 1977. "The Population Growth in Kano, Nigeria." In Edinburgh, ed., *African Historical Demography*, pp. 212–250.

Fukiau. A. 1969. *Le mukongo et le monde qui l'entourait*. Kinshasa: Office nationale de la recherche et de développement.

Galbraith, J. K. 1967. *The New Industrial State*. Boston: Houghton Mifflin.

———. 1970. "The Aftermath." In H. Gluckman, ed., *Abiding Values: Speeches and Addresses*. Johannesburg: Caxton, pp. 495–517.

Galdston, I., ed. 1963. *Man's Image in Medicine and Anthropology*. New York: International Universities Press.

Gale, G. 1938. *A Suggested Approach to the Health Needs of the Native Rural Areas of South Africa*. Benoni: privately published.

Gale, T. S. 1980. "Segregation in British West Office." *Cahiers d'études africaines* 20: 495–508.

Ganon, M. F. 1975. "The Nomads of Niger." In Caldwell, et al., eds. *Population Growth and Socio-Economic Change in West Africa*, pp. 694–700.

Gaud, F. 1911. *Les Mandia (Congo Français)*. Brussels: de Wit.

Gauvreau, D., J. W. Gregory, M. Kempeneers, and V. Piché, eds. 1985. *Stratégies de survie: populations et sociétés dans le Tiers-Monde*. Montréal: Nouvelle optique.

Gear, H. S. 1938. "South African Public Health Services," In F. Brümmer and B. J. Versfeld, eds, *Report of the National Conference on Social Work*. Johannesburg, March 9–10, 1936. Pretoria.

Geertz, C. 1968. *Islam Observed*. Chicago: University of Chicago Press.

Gelfand, M. 1953. *Tropical Victory: An Account of the Influence of Medicine on the History of Southern Rhodesia, 1890–1923*. Johannesburg: Juta.

———. 1961. *Northern Rhodesia in the Days of the Charter: A Medical and Social Study*, 1878–1924. Oxford: Basil Blackwell & Mott.

Gellner, E. 1969. *Saints of the Atlas*. London: Weidenfeld and Nicolson.

———. 1974. *Legitimation of Belief*. Cambridge: Cambridge University Press.

———. 1976. *A Service to the Sick*. Gwelo: Mambo Press.

———, and J. Waterbury, eds. 1977. *Patrons and Clients in Mediterranean Societies*. London: Duckworth.

Getz, H. R. 1951. "A Study of the Relationship of Nutrition to the Development of Tuberculosis: Influence of Ascorbic Acid and Vitamin C." *American Review of Tuberculosis* 64: 681.

Ghose, A. K. 1982. "Food Supply and Starvation: A Study of Famines with Reference to the Indian Subcontinent." *Oxford Economic Papers* xxxiv.

Gibb, H. A. R. 1965. *Shorter Encyclopedia of Islam.* Ithaca, N. Y.: Cornell University Press.

Gilges, V. 1955. "Notes on Luvale Therapy." *Some African Poison Plants and Medicines of Northern Rhodesia.* Livingstone: Rhodes-Livingstone Institute.

Gillies, E. 1976. "Causal Criteria in African Classifications of Disease." In Loudon, ed. *Social Anthropology and Medicine*, pp. 358–395.

Gilliland, D. S. 1971. "African Traditional Religion in Transition: The Influence of Islam on African Traditional Religion in Northern Nigeria." Ph.D. dissertation, The Hartford Seminary Foundation, Hartford, Conn.

Gish, O., and L. L. Feller 1979. *Planning Pharmaceuticals for Primary Health Care: Supply and Utilization of Drugs in the Third World.* Washington: American Public Health Association.

Glick, L. B. 1967. "Medicine as an Ethnographic Category: The Gimi of the New Guinea Highlands." *Ethnology* 6: 31–56.

Gluckman, H. 1939. Motion to South African House of Assembly. *Hansard.* May 12.

Gluckman, M. 1968. *Analysis of a Social Situation in Modern Zululand.* Manchester: Manchester University Press.

Glucksberg, H., and J. Singer. 1982. "The Multinational Drug Companies in Zaire: Their Adverse Effect on Cost and Availability of Essential Drugs." *International Journal of Health Services* 12: 381.

Good, B. J. 1977. "The Heart of What's the Matter. The Semantics of Illness in Iran." *Culture, Medicine and Psychiatry* 1: 25–58.

Good, C. M. 1978. "Man, Milieu, and the Disease Factor: Tick-Borne Relapsing Fever in East Africa." In Hartwig and Patterson, eds., *Disease in African History*, pp. 46–87.

———. 1987. *Ethnomedical Systems in Africa.* New York, London: The Guilford Press.

Goody, J. 1968. *Literacy in Traditional Societies.* Cambridge: Cambridge University Press.

———, ed. 1973. *The Character of Kinship.* Cambridge: Cambridge University Press.

Gorgas, W. C. 1914. *Recommendations as to Sanitation Concerning Employees on the Mines of the Rand.* Johannesburg: Argus Printing and Publishing Co.

Goutalier, R. 1979. "Au debut du 20e siécle: un problème vital pour les pays et protectorats du Tchad: L'établissement de la route de revitaillement." In *Recherches sahariennes.* Paris: CNRS.

Gran, P. 1979. "Medical Pluralism in Arab and Egyptian History." *Social Science and Medicine* 13B (4): 339–348.

Greenberg, J. 1955. *Studies in African Linguistic Classification.* New Haven, Conn.: Yale University Press.

Greenwood, B. P. 1984. "Cultural Factors in the Perception and Treatment of Illness in Morocco." Ph.D. dissertation, Cambridge University.

Gregory, J. W. 1974. "Development and In-Migration in Upper-Volta." In Amin, ed., *Modern Migrations in Western Africa;* 305–330.

———. 1976. "Levels, Rates, and Patterns of Urbanization in Upper Volta." *Pan African Journal* 9 (2): 125–134.

———. 1982. "African Population: Reproduction for Whom?" *Daedalus* 111 (2): 179–209.

———. 1984. "Migration, Labour and Wages: West and East." *Canadian Journal of African Studies* 18 (2): 455–447.

———. 1985. "Modes de production et régime démographique." *Canadian Journal of African Studies* 19: 1.

———. 1986*a*. "Démographie, impérialisme et sous-développement: Le cas africain." In D. Gauvreau, J. W. Gregory, M. Kempeneers, and V. Piché, eds. *Démographie et sous-développement dans le Tiers-Monde*. Montreal: Centre for Developing Area Studies, McGill University, pp. 10–16. (This is a French version of *The Demographic Process in Peripheral Capitalism Illustrated with African Examples*. Working Paper Series 29, 1981.)

———. 1986b. "Population, santé et développement: Cadre conceptuel, variables clés et possibilités méthodologiques." In Centre de recherches pour le développement international, ed., *Les actes du seminaire méthodologique sur les interrelations population, santé et développement*. Ottawa: CRDI; Bamako: USED, pp. 33–78 (IDRC-MR141f; Études et travaux de l'USED, No. 6).

Gregory, J. W., and E. Mandala. 1987. "Dimensions of Conflict: Emigrant Labor from Colonial Malawi and Zambia, 1900–1945." In D. D. Cordell, and J. W. Gregory, eds., *African Population and Capitalism*, Boulder, Colo.: Westview Press, pp. 221–240.

———, and Piché, V. 1981. *The Demographic Process of Peripheral Capitalism Illustrated with African Examples*. Montréal: Centre for Developing Area Studies, McGill University. (Working Paper No. 29.)

Gregory, J. W., G. Neill, V. Piché, and J. Poirier. 1988. *Division du travail et structures des ménages en Guadeloupe: Rapport de recherche*. Montréal: Département de démographie, 199 pp.

Guibbert, J. 1949. *Le coton en Oubangui-Chari*. Paris: Mémoire du Centre des hautes études sur l'Afrique et l'Asie modernes.

Guillemin, R. 1956. "L'évolution de l'agriculture autochtone dans les savanes de l'Oubangui." *L'agronomie tropicale* 11 (1): 39–61.

Gusmer, C. W. 1974. *The Ministry of Healing in the Church of England: An Ecumenical Liturgical Study*. Great Wakering (U.K): Mayhew-McCrimmon.

Guthrie, M. 1967–1971. *Comparative Bantu*, 3 vols. Hampshire: Gregg Press.

Guttentag, M., and P. F. Secord. 1983. *Too Many Women? The Sex Ratio Question*. Beverley Hills, Calif.: Sage.

Gwatkin, D. 1980. "Indication of Change in Developing Country Mortality Trends: The End of an Era." *Population and Development Review* 6 (4): 615–644.

Hahn, R. A. 1982. "'Treat the Patient, Not the Lab': Internal Medicine and the Concept of 'Person.'" *Culture, Medicine and Psychiatry* 6 (3): 219–236.

Hamarneh, S. 1962. "Development of Hospitals in Islam." *Journal of the History of Medicine* 17: 366–384.

———. 1965. "The First Known Independent Treatise on Cosmetology in Spain." *Bulletin of the History of Medicine* 38: 390–335 .

———. 1968. "The Climax of Medieval Arabic Professional Pharmacy." *Bulletin of the History of Medicine* 42: 450–461.

———. 1970*a*. "Medical Education and Practice in Medieval Islam." In C. D. O'Malley, ed., *The History of Medical Education*. Berkeley, Los Angeles, London:

University of California Press.

———. 1970*b*. "Sources and Development of Arabic Medical Therapy and Pharmacology." *Sudhoffs Archiv* 54: 30–48.

———. 1971. "The Physician and the Health Profession in Medieval Islam." *Bulletin of the New York Academy of Medicine* 47: 1008–1110.

———. 1974. "Ecology and Therapeutics in Medieval Arabic Medicine." *Sudhoffs Archiv* 58: 165–185.

———. 1977. "Surgical Developments in Medieval Arabic Medicine." *Viewpoints* 5 (4): 13–18.

Hannah, M. 1959. *Standard Shona Dictionary*, London: Macmillan.

Harjula, R. 1980. *Mirau and His Practice: A Study of the Ethnomedicinal Repertoire of a Tanzanian Herbalist*. London: Tri-Med.

Harlan, J. R., J. M. J. Wet, and A. Stemler, eds. 1976. *Origins of African Plant Domestication*. The Hague, Paris: Mouton.

Harlow, V., and E. M. Chilver, eds. 1965. *History of East Africa* vol. 2. Oxford: Clarendon Press.

Harms, R. 1975. "The End of Red Rubber: A Reassessment." *Journal of African History* 16 (1): 73–88.

———. 1981. *River of Wealth, River of Sorrow*. New Haven and London: Yale University Press.

———. 1983. "Sustaining the System: Trading Towns along the Middle Zaire." In Robertson and Klein, eds., *Women and Slavery in Africa*, pp. 95–110.

Harries, L. P. 1945. *"The Christian Life in Central Africa," Central Africa* 63: 122.

Harrington, J. 1977. "Infant and Early Childhood Survivorship in Upper Volta." In D. Ian and S. Kulibali, eds., *Demographic Transitions and Cultural Continuity in the Sahel*. Ithaca, N.Y.: International Population Program, Cornell University, pp. 172–277.

———. 1979. "Demographic Considerations in East Africa during the Nineteenth Century." *International Journal of African Historical Studies* 12: 664–666.

———. 1981. "Smallpox in the Sudan." *International Journal of African Historical Studies* 14: 5–33 .

Hartwig, G. W., and K. D. Patterson. 1978. *Disease in African History: An Introductory Survey and Case Studies*. Durham N. C.: Duke University Press.

Haswell, M. 1953. *Economics of Agriculture in a Savannah Village: Report on Three Years' Study of Genieri Village and Its Lands, The Gambia*. London: Colonial Offiice.

———. 1963. *The Changing Pattern of Economic Activity in a Gambia Village*. Department of Technical Cooperation, Overseas Research Publication No. 2. London: HMSO.

———. 1975. *The Nature of Poverty*. London: Macmillan.

———. 1981. "Food Consumption in Relation to Labour Output." In Chambers, Longhurst, and Pacey, eds., *Seasonal Dimensions to Rural Poverty*, 38–41.

Haute-Volta, Ministère de l'économie nationale. 1962. *Recensement de la ville de Ouagadougou: Résultats Provisoires*. Ouagadougou.

———, Service de la statistique. 1970. *Enquête démographique par sondage en RHV, 1960–1961*. Paris: INSEE and Secrétariat d'état aux affaires étrangères.

———, Institut national de la statistique et de la démographie. 1979. *Recensement général de la population, 1975*. Ouagadougou.

Headrick, R. 1981. "Sleeping Sickness at Nola (Central African Republic)." Bloomington, Ind.: paper presented at the annual meeting of the African Studies Association.

Hedberg, I. et al. 1982. "Inventory of Plants Used in Traditional Medicine in Tanzania: I. Plants of the Families Acanthaceae-Cucubitaceae." *Journal of Ethnopharmacology* 6: 29–60.

———. 1983. "Inventory of Plants Used in Traditional Medicine in Tanzania. II. Plants of Dilleniaceae-Opiliaceae." *Journal of Ethnopharmacology* 9: 105–128.

Helman, C. 1978. "'Feed a Cold and Starve a Fever'—Folk Models of Infection in an English Suburban Community." *Culture, Medicine and Psychiatry*, 2: 107–137.

Henderson, D. 1976. "The Eradication of Smallpox." *Scientific American* 235: 25–33.

Henderson, R. H., and M. Yekpe. 1969. "Smallpox Transmission in Southern Dahomey: A Study of a Village Outbreak." *American Journal of Epidemiology* 90: 423–428.

Henderson, W. O. 1965. "German East Africa, 1884–1918." In Harlow and Chilver, eds, *History of East Africa*, vol. 2: 123–162.

Henige, D. P. 1974*a*. *The Chronology of Oral Tradition: Quest for a Chimera*. Oxford: Oxford University Press.

———. 1974*b*. "Kingship in Elmina Before 1869: A Study of 'Feedback' and the Traditional Idealization of the Past." *Cahiers d'Études Africaines* 55: 499–520.

Hesse, M. 1978. "Theory and Value in the Social Science." In C. Hookway and P. Pettit, eds., *Action and Interpretation: Studies in the Philosophy of the Social Sciences*. Cambridge: Cambridge University Press, pp. 1–16.

Hill, P. 1977. *Population, Prosperity and Poverty: Rural Kano 1900 and 1970*. Cambridge: Cambridge University Press.

Hitti, P. 1951. *History of the Arabs from the Earliest Times to the Present*. New York: Macmillan.

Hine, J. 1924. *Days Gone By*. London: J. Murray.

Hodgson, M. G. S. 1974. *The Venture of Islam: Conscience and History in a World Civilization*, 3 vols. Chicago: University of Chicago Press.

Hoover, J. 1978. "The Seduction of Ruwej: Reconstructing Ruund History (The Nuclear Lunda; Zaire, Angola, Zambia)." Ph.D. dissertation, Yale University.

Hopkins, D., J. M. Lane, E. C. Cummings, and J. D. Miller. 1971. "Smallpox in Sierra Leone: I. Epidemiology." *American Journal of Tropical Medicine and Hygiene* 20: 689–704.

Horton, R. 1967. "African Traditional Thought and Western Science." *Africa* 37: 50–72, 155–187.

———, and R. Finnegan, eds. 1973. *Modes of Thought: Essays on Thinking in Western and Non-Western Societies*. London: Faber & Faber.

Howard, R. 1913/14. "Medical Missionary Work in Zanzibar Diocese." *Central Africa* 31: 136; 32: 44.

Hughes, C. C. 1963. "Public Health in Non-Literate Societies," In Galdston, ed. *Man's Image in Medicine and Anthropology*, pp. 157–233.

———, and J. M. Hunter. 1970. "Disease and 'Development' in Africa." *Social Science and Medicine* 3: 443–493.

Hunwick, J. 1974. *Literacy and Scholarship in Muslim West Africa in the Pre-Colonial Period*. Lagos: University of Nigeria Press.

Huot. 1921. "L'epidémie d'influenza de 1918–1919 dans les colonies françaises." *Annales de médecine et de pharmacie coloniale* 443–462.

Hyman, L. M., and J. Voorhoeve, eds. 1980. *L'Expansion Bantoue.* (3 vols.) Paris: Société d'Études Linguistique et Anthropologique de France et CNRS.

Ibn Abi Dinar. 1967. *al-Mu'nis fi Akhbar Ifriqiya wa Tunis.* Tunis: Al-Matba'a al-Haditha.

Ibn Abi 'Usaybi'a, Ahmad b. al-Qasim. 1883. *'Uyun al-'Anba' fi Tabaqat al-'Atibba'*, 2 vols. Cairo: al-Matba 'a al-Wahbiya (1st ed.).

Ibn al-'Arabi, Abu Bakr Muhammad b. Ali Muhyi al-Din. 1809. "*al-Futuhat al-Makkiya.*" Cairo: Bulaq. (Rabat: Ms. No. D1240, Bibliotheque Nationale.)

Ibn Khaldun, Abdul Rahman b. Muhammad. 1867. *Kitab al-'Aibar wa Diwan al-Mubtada wal Khabar*, 7 vols. Cairo: Bulaq Press.

———. 1900. *al-Muqaddima*, Beirut: al-Matba'a al-Adabiyya.

Ibn Khalikan, Ahmad b. Muhammad. 1948 [1885]. *Wafiyyat al-'Ayan wa 'anba' 'abna' al-zaman*, vol. 2. Ed. Muhammad Abdul Hamid. Cairo: Bulaq Press.

Iles, M. 1924. "Medical Work." *Universities Mission to Central Africa Annual Report for 1924*, p. 125.

Iliffe, J. 1989. "The Origins of African Population Growth." *Journal of African History* 30 (1): 165–169.

Illich, I. 1977. *Limits to Medicine.* Middlesex: Harmondsworth.

Imperato, P. J. 1972. "La Variole en République du Mali." *Afrique Médicale* 11: 983–994.

———, S. Ousmane, and B. Fofana. 1973. "The Persistence of Smallpox in a Remote Unvaccinated Village During Eradication Program Activities." *Acta Tropica* 30: 261–268.

Inikori, J. E. 1981. "Under-Population in 19th Century West Africa: The Role of the Export Slave Trade." In Edinburgh, ed., *African Historical Demography*, pp. 283–314.

Irvine, L. G., A. Mavrogodato, and H. Pirow. 1930. *A Review of the History of Silicosis on the Witwatersrand Goldfields.* International Silicosis Conference, Johannesburg.

Isaacman, A. 1972. *Mozambique: The Africanization of a European Institution.* Madison: University of Wisconsin Press.

Jackson, K. A. 1976. "The Family Entity and Famine among the Nineteenth Century Akamba of Kenya: Social Responses to Environmental Stress." *Journal of Family History* 1: 193–216.

Jacottet, E. 1896, 1899, 1901. *Etudes sur les langues du haut Zambèze I–III.* Paris: Ernest Leroux.

Jalla, A. N.d. *Notes privées.*

———. 1931. *Tableau Synchronique.*

Janzen, J. M. 1971. "Kongo Religious Renewal." *Canadian Journal of African Studies* V: 135–143.

———. 1975. "The Dynamics of Therapy in Lower Zaire." In T. R. Williams, ed., *Psychological Anthropology.* The Hague: Mouton, pp. 441–463.

———. 1976/77. "Traditional Medicine Now Seen as National Resource in Zaire and other African Countries." *Ethnomedizin* IV (1/2): 167–70.

———. 1977. "The Tradition of Renewal in Kongo Religion." In Booth, ed., *African Religions: A Symposium*, pp. 69–116.

———. 1978*a*. "Pluralistic Legitimation of Therapy Systems in Contemporary Zaire." In Ademuwagun et al., eds., *African Therapeutic Systems*, 208–216.

———. 1978*b*. *The Quest for Therapy in Lower Zaire*. Berkeley, Los Angeles, London: University of California Press.

———. 1978*c*. "The Comparative Study of Medical Systems as Changing Social Systems." *Social Science and Medicine* 12: 121–129.

———. 1979. "Ideologies and Institutions in the Pre-Colonial History of Equatorial African Therapeutic Systems." *Social Science and Medicine* 13B: 317–326.

———. 1981. "The Need for a Taxonomy of Health in the Study of African Therapeutics." *Social Science and Medicine* 15B (3): 185–94.

———. 1982. *Lemba 1650–1930: A Drum of Affliction in Africa and the New World*. New York: Garland.

———. 1987. "Therapy Management: Concept, Reality, Process," *Medical Anthropology Quarterly* I (1): 68–84.

———. 1989. "Health, Religion, and Medicine in Central and Southern African Traditions." In L. Sullivan, ed., *Caring and Curing*. New York: Macmillan.

———, and W. MacGaffey. 1974. *An Anthology of Kongo Religion: Primary Texts from Lower Zaire*. Publications in Anthropology No. 5. Lawrence: University of Kansas.

———, and S. Feierman. 1979. *The Social History of Disease and Medicine in Africa*. (Special Issue of *Social Science and Medicine* 13B [4]:239–356.)

———, and G. Prins. 1981. *Causality and Classification in African Medicine and Health*. (Special Issue of *Social Science and Medicine* 15B [3]: 169–437.)

Jelliffe, D. B., and P. Jelliffe. 1971. "The Effects of Starvation on the Function of the Family and of Society." In G. Blix, Y. Hofvander, and B. Valquist, eds., *Famine: A Symposium Dealing with Nutrition and Relief Operations in Times of Disaster*. Stockholm: Swedish Nutrition Foundation.

Jelly, D., and P. O'Keefe. In press. "Focusing on Mothers and Children: Primary Health Care in Mozambique." *Canadian Journal of African Studies*.

Joki, W. 1943. "A Labour and Manpower Survey of the Transkeian Territories." Johannesburg: University of Witwatersrand Archives, MS Institute of Race Relations File.

Jules-Rosette, B., ed. 1979. *The New Religions of Africa*. Norwood, Mass.: Ablex.

Junod, H. 1962. *The Life of a South African Tribe*, Vol. I. New York: University Books.

Kaggia, B. 1975. *Roots of Freedom 1921–1963* (autobiography). Nairobi: East African Publishing House.

Kalck, P. 1970. "Histoire de la République centrafricaine des origines à nos jours." Paris: Doctorat d'état, Université de Paris (Sorbonne), 4 vols.

———. 1974. *Histoire de la République centrafriaine des origines préhistoriques à nos jours*. Paris: Berqer-Levrault.

———. 1980. *Historical Dictionary of the Central African Republic*. Thomas O'Toole (trans.). Metuchen: Scarecrow Press.

Kano Chronicle. N.d. [1908]. *Journal of the Royal Anthropological Society* 38: 58–98; also published in *Sudanese Memoirs*, 1967. London: Cass and Co.

Kark, S. L., and G. W. Steuart. 1962. *A Practice of Social Medicine: A South African Team's Experiences in Different African Communities*. Edinburgh and London: Livingstone.

Katz, E. 1980. "Silicosis on the South African Gold Mines." In Westcott and Wilson, eds., *Hunger, Work and Health: Economics of Health in South Africa*, 2: 187–244.

Keharo, J. 1972. "La pharmacopée africaine traditionelle et récherche scientifique." *Présence Africaine* 475–499.

Kenya Association of Manufacturers. 1988. "Opportunities and Constraints in Providing Basic Infrastructure." Report.

Kenya Central Bureau of Statistics. *1979 Census*.

Kenya Medical Department. 1927, 1949, 1953. *Annual Report*. Nairobi: Kenya Government Printer.

Kenyatta, J. 1937. *Facing Mt. Kenya: The Tribal Life of the GiKuyu*. New York: Vintage. Also published 1938, London: Secker & Warburg.

Kershaw, G. 1972. "The Land and People: A Study of Kikuyu Social Organization in Historical Perspective." Ph.D. dissertation, University of Chicago.

Keys, A., J. Brozek, A. Henschel, O. Mickelsen, and H. L. Longstreet Taylor. 1950. *The Biology of Human Starvation*, 2 vols. (Vol. ii, *The Edema Problem*.) Minneapolis: University of Minnesota Press.

Khan, A. K., S. Akhtar, and H. Mahtab. 1980. "Treatment of diabetes mellitus with Coccinia indica." *British Medical Journal* 280: 1044.

Kilama, W. I. N. 1980. Director, Tanzania Medical Research Institute. Personal communications, Dar es Salaam.

Kimble, D. 1963. *A Political History of Ghana*, 1850–1928. Oxford: Clarendon Press.

Kimble, J. 1982. "Labour Migration in Basutoland, 1870–1885." In Marks and Rathbone, eds., *Industrialisation and Social Change in South Africa*, pp. 119–141.

King, A. D. 1976. *Colonial Urban Development: Culture, Social Power, and Environment*. London, Boston: Routledge and Kegan Paul.

Kjekshus, H. 1977. *Ecology Control and Economic Development in East African History*. Berkeley, Los Angeles, London: University of California Press.

Kleeberg, H. H. 1982. "The Dynamics of Tuberculosis in South Africa and the Impact of the Control Program." *South African Medical Journal*, Special Issue (November) 17: 22–23.

Kleinman, A. M. 1973. "Medicine's Symbolic Reality. On a Central Problem in the Philosophy of Medicine." *Inquiry* 16: 206.

Knapp, W. 1977. *North West Africa: A Political and Economic Survey*, 3d ed. London: Oxford University Press.

Koch, E. 1983. "'Without Visible Means of Subsistence': Slumyard Culture in Johannesburg 1918–1940." In Bozzoli, ed., *Town and Countryside in the Transvaal*, pp. 151–175.

Koch, E. 1900. "Professor Koch's Investigations on Malaria." *British Medical Journal* 1: 324–327, 1183–1185, 1597–1598.

Koestler, A. 1959. *The Sleepwalkers*, 1st ed. London: Macmillan.

Kokwaro, J. O. 1976. *Medicinal Plants of East Africa*. Kampala, Nairobi, Dar es Salaam: East African Literature Bureau.

Kuhn, T. S. 1970. *The Structure of Scientific Revolutions*, 2d ed. Chicago: University of Chicago Press.

Kuper, H. 1963. *The Swazi*. New York: Holt Rinehart & Winston.

LaFontaine, C. J. 1970. *City Politics: A Study of Leopoldville, 1962–63*. Cambridge: Cambridge University Press.

Laidler, P. W. 1938. "The Unholy Triad: Tuberculosis, Venereal Disease and Malnutrition." *South African Medical Journal* 659.

Laird. 1842. Memorandum to West Africa Committee, *British Parliamentary Papers* xi (551): 350–351.

Lamburn, R. 1970. *The Yao of Tunduru. An Essay in Missionary Anthropology*. Unpublished manuscript.

Langer, W. L. 1976. "Immunization Against Smallpox before Jenner." *Scientific American* 234: 112–117.

Langworthy, H. W. 1969. "A History of Undi's Kingdom to 1890." Ph.D. dissertation, Boston University.

———. 1971. "Conflict Among Rulers in the History of Undi's Chewa Kingdom." *Transafrican Journal of History* 1: 1.

Larson, L. E. 1976. "Problems in the Study of Witchcraft Eradication Movements in Southern Tanzania." *Ufahamu* 6: 88.

Lasker, J. 1977. "The Role of Health Services in Colonial Rule: The Case of the Ivory Coast." *Culture, Medicine and Psychiatry* 1 (3): 277–297.

Last, M. 1976. "The Presentation of Sickness in a Community of non-Muslim Hausa." In Loudon, ed., *Social Anthropology and Medicine*, pp. 104–149.

———. 1979. "Strategies against Time." *Sociology of Health and Illness* 1: 306–317.

———. 1981. "The Importance of Knowing about Not Knowing." *Social Science and Medicine* 15B (3): 387–392.

———, and G. L. Chavunduka, eds. 1986. *The Professionalisation of African Medicine*. Manchester: Manchester University Press.

Laurence, J. ed., 1977. *The Great White Hoax: South Africa's International Propaganda Machine*. London: Africa Bureau.

Leach, E. 1965. *Political Systems of Highland Burma*. Boston: Beacon Press.

Leakey, L. S. B. 1978. *The Southern Kikuyu before 1903*, Vol. II. New York: Academic Press.

Leboeuf, P. N. A., G. Martin, and E. Roubaud. 1909. *Rapport de la mission d'études de la maladie du sommeil au Congo-Français (1906–1908)*. Paris: Masson.

Leclerc, L. 1876. *Histoire de la médecine arabe*, 2 vols. Algiers.

Lee, A. A. 1976. "Ngoja and Six Theories of Witchcraft Eradication." *Ufahamu* 6: 101.

Lee, N. 1969. *The Search for an Abortionist*. Chicago: University of Chicago Press.

Lehuard, R. 1977. *Les pfemba du Mayombe*. Paris: Arts d'Afrique Noire.

Lerner. D. 1958. The *Passing of Traditional Society. Modernizing the Middle East*. New York: Free Press.

Le Roy Ladurie, E. L. 1979. "Amenorrhea in Time of Famine, Seventeenth to Twentieth Century." In Ladurie, ed. *The Territory of the Historian*. (trans. B. Reynolds and S. Reynolds). Chicago: University of Chicago Press.

Leslie, C., ed. 1976. *Asian Medical Systems*. Berkeley, Los Angeles, London: University of California Press.

Lévi-Strauss, C. 1949. *Les structures élémentaires de la Parenté*. Paris: Presses universitaires de France.

———. 1963. *Structural Anthropology*. London: Allen Lane.

Lewis, I. M. 1971. *Ecstatic Religions*. Harmondsworth: Penguin.

Leys, C. 1975. *Underdevelopment in Kenya: The Political Economy of Neo-Colonialism*. London: Heinemann.

Lipton, M. 1977. *Why Poor People Stay Poor: Urban Bias in World Development*. Cambridge: Harvard University Press.

Livingstone, D. 1858. *Missionary Travels and Researches in South Africa.* New York: Harper.

———. 1960 *Private Journals*, I. Schapera, ed. London: Chatto & Windus.

Livingstone. F. B. 1967. "The Origin of the Sickle-Cell Gene." In C. Gabel and N. R. Bennett, eds., *Reconstructing African Culture History.* Boston: Boston University Press, pp. 139–166.

Lodge, T. 1983. *Black Politics in South Africa since 1945.* London and New York: Longman.

Lofchie, M. F. 1975. "Political and Economic Origins of African Hunger." *Journal of Modern Africa Studies* xiii: 551–567.

Loram, C. T. 1930. "The Training of Natives in Medicine and Public Health." *Journal of the Medical Association of South Africa* (BMA) 13 (September): 515.

Loudon, J. B., ed. 1976. *Social Anthropology and Medicine.* London and New York: Academic Press.

Lovejoy, P. E., ed. 1986. *Africans in Bondage: Essays Presented to Philip D. Curtin on the Occasion of the 25th Anniversary of the African Studies Program.* Madison, Wisc.: African Studies Program, The University of Wisconsin.

Lucas, V. 1914. "That We May Never Forget." *Central Africa* 32: 238.

———. 1919. "Report." *Central Africa* 37: 170.

Lux, A. 1976. "Le problème de la stérilité en Afrique et ses implications de politique démographique: À propos deux ouvrages récents." *Canadian Journal of African Studies* 10: 143–155.

McCall, D. F. 1969. *Africa in Time-Perspective.* New York: Oxford University Press.

MacCormack, C . P . 1979 . "Sande: The Public Face of a Secret Society." In Jules-Rosette, ed., *The New Religions of Africa*, 27–37.

———. 1981. "Proto-Social to Adult: A Sherbro Transformation." In C. MacCormack and M. Strathern, eds., *Nature, Culture and Gender.* Cambridge: Cambridge University, pp. 95–118.

———. 1982. "Health, Fertility and Birth in Moyamba District, Sierra Leone." In C. MacCormack, ed., *The Ethnography of Fertility and Birth.* London: Academic Press.

———. 1988. Personal communications.

MacGaffey, W. 1970. "The Religious Commissions of the Bakongo." *Man* 5: 27–38 .

———. 1976. "Corporation Theory and Political Change: The Case of Zaire." In S. Newman, ed., *Small States and Segmented Societies.* New York: Praeger.

———. 1977 . "Fetishism Revisited: Kongo Nkisi in Sociological Perspective." *Africa* 47: 147–152.

———. 1986. *Religion and Society in Central Africa.* Chicago: University of Chicago Press.

McMaster, D. N. 1968. "The Colonial District Town in Uganda." In Beckinsale and Houston, eds. *Urbanization and Its Problems: Essays in Honour of E. W. Gilbert*, pp. 341–342.

McVicar, N. 1908. "Tuberculosis among South African Natives." *South African Medical Record* 6: 198–205.

Maher, V. 1974. *Women and property in Morocco.* Cambridge: Cambridge University Press.

Maine, H. 1960. *Ancient Law*, London: Dent.

Malonga, J. 1958. "La sorcellerie et l'ordre du 'Lemba' chez les Lari ." *Liaison* 62: 45–49, 51–61.

Manning, P. 1981. "The Enslavement of Africans: A Demographic Model." *Canadian Journal of African Studies* 15 (3): 499–526.

Maran, R. 1938. *Batouala*. Paris: Editions Albin-Michel.

Maret, P., de. 1980. "Bribes, Debris et Bricolage." In L. M. Hyman and J. Voorhoeve, eds. *L'Expansion Bantou*, Vol. III. Paris: SELAF, pp. 715–730.

Marks, S., and R. Rathbone, eds. 1982. *Industrialisation and Social Change in South Africa*. New York: Longman.

Martel. 1912. "Considérations sur les progrès hygiéniques réalisés dans la ville de Tamatave." *Annales d'hygiène et de médecine coloniale* 15: 528–529.

Martin, P. 1972. *The External Trade of the Loango Coast* 1576–1870. Oxford: Clarendon Press.

Marty, M. 1982. "Tradition and the Traditions in Health/Medicine and Religion." In M. Marty and K. Vaux, eds., *Health/Medicine and the Faith Traditions*. Philadelphia: Fortress Press, pp. 3–26.

Marwick, M. 1950. "Another Modern Anti-Witchcraft Movement." *Africa* 20: 100.

Mason, P. 1958. *The Birth of a Dilemma: The Conquest and Settlement of Rhodesia*. London: Oxford University Press.

Mataa, J. 1935. *Likalafo za sintu*. (Unpublished manuscript.)

Matthews. 1879. "Report on the Sanitary Condition of Kimberley." *Diamond News* (March 29).

Mbacke, C., and E. van de Walle. 1990. "Les facteurs socio-économiques et l'influence de la fréquentation des services de santé." In G. Pison, E. van de Walle, and M. Sala-Diakanda, eds., *Mortalité et société en Afrique au sud du Sahara*. Paris: Presses universitaires de France (INED, Travaux et Documents, pp. 124).

M'Bokolo, E. 1982. "Peste et société urbaine à Dakar: L'épidémie de 1914." *Cahiers d'études africaines* 22: 13–46.

Mburu, F. M. 1977. "The Duality of Traditional and Western Medicine in Africa: Mystics, Myths and Reality." In P. Singer, ed., *Traditional Healing: New Science or New Colonialism?* New York, Owerri, London: Conch Magazine Ltd., pp. 158–185.

———. 1979. "Rhetoric-Implementation Gap in Health Policy and Health Services Delivery for a Rural Population in a Developing Country." *Social Science and Medicine* 13A (3): 577–583.

———. 1981. "Socio-Political Imperatives in the History of Health Development in Kenya." *Social Science and Medicine* 15A: 521–527.

Medical Officer, Cape Colony. 1906. *Public Health Report*, 1905, reported in *South African Medical Record* 4 (9): 2.

———. 1907. *Public Health Report*, 1906, reported in *South African Medical Record*, 5 (10) (1907): 311.

Meillassoux, C. 1975. *Femmes, greniers et capitaux*. Paris: Maspero.

Mernissi, F. 1975. *Beyond the Veil. Male-Female Dynamics in a Modern Muslim Society*. New York: Schenkman.

Merriman, J. X. 1960–1969, in 4 vols. *Selections from the Correspondence of John X. Merriman, 1870–1890*. Cape Town: Van Riebeeck Society.

Merritt, E. H. 1975. "A History of the Taita of Kenya to 1900." Ph.D. dissertation. Indiana University.

Meyerhof, M. 1926. "New Light on Hunayn Ibn Ishaq and His Period." *Isis* 8: 685–724.

———, ed. 1928. *The Book of the Ten Treatises on the Eye Ascribed to Hunain b. Ishaq.* Cairo.

———. 1929. "Climate and Health in Old Cairo According to Ali Ibn Ridwan." In *Comptes rendues du congrès international de médecine tropicale et d'hygiène.* Cairo.

———. 1931. "Science and Medicine." In T. Arnold and A. Guillaume, eds. *The Legacy of Islam.* Oxford: Clarendon Press.

———. 1935. "Thirty-three Clinical Observation by Rhazes ca. 900." *Isis* 23: 321–355.

Michels, R. *Political Parties.* 1962. New York: Free Press.

Millar, J. G. 1908. "On the Spread and Prevention of Tuberculosis Disease in Pondoland, South Africa." *The British Medical Journal* 24 (September): 380.

Miller, J. C. 1982. "The Significance of Drought, Disease and Famine in the Agriculturally Marginal Zones of West-Central Africa." *Journal of African History* 23 (1): 17–61.

Minick, A. 1973. "Sociological Illness, *Mdulo* among the Chewa." University of Zambia research seminar paper.

Monsted, M., and P. Walji. 1978. *A Demographic Analysis of East Africa: A Sociological Interpretation.* Uppsala: Scandinavian Institute of African Studies.

Mosley, W. H. 1983. "Will Primary Health Care Reduce Infant and Child Mortality? A Critique of Some Current Strategies with Special Reference to Africa and Asia." Paris: paper prepared for the International Union for the Scientific Study of Population, Seminar on Social Policy, Health Policy, and Mortality Prospects, February 28–March 4.

Msigala, K, N.d. *Reminiscences Started in July 1955.* Unpublished manuscript trans. from Swahili by C. Blood.

Msonthi, J. D. 1983. "Traditional Medicine Research in Malawi." *Journal of Social Science* (University of Malawi) 120–131.

Munro, J. F. 1975. *Colonial Rule and the Kamba: Social Changes in the Kenya Highlands 1889–1939.* Oxford: Oxford University Press.

Murdock, G. P. 1959. *Africa. Its Peoples and Their Culture History.* New York: McGraw-Hill.

Muriuki, G. 1974. *A History of the Kikuyu 1500–1900.* Oxford: Oxford University Press.

Murray, C. 1981. *Families Divided: The Impact of Migrant Labour in Lesotho.* Cambridge: Cambridge University Press.

Mwaniki, H. S. 1974. *Embu Historical Texts.* Nairobi: East African Literature Bureau.

Navarro, V. 1974. "The Underdevelopment of Health or the Health of Underdevelopment: An Analysis of the Distribution of Human Health Organizations in Latin America." *International Journal of Health Services* 4: 5.

Nayenga, P. 1979. "Busoga in the Era of Catastrophes." In Ogot, ed., *Ecology and History in East Africa*, pp. 153–178.

Neill, G. 1988. "Démographie, femmes et développement: Une mise en perspective critique," Examen de synthèse, Département de démographie, Université de Montréal.

Newman, S., ed. 1976. *Small States and Segmented Societies.* New York: Praeger.

Newitt, M. D. D. 1973. *Portuguese Settlement on the Zambesi.* London: Longman.

Ngubane, H. 1976. "Some Aspects of Treatment among the Zulu," in Loudon, ed., *Social Anthropology and Medicine*, pp. 318–357.

———. 1977. *Body and Mind in Zulu Medicine*. London and New York: Academic Press.

———. 1981. "Aspects of Clinical Practice and Traditional Organization of Indigenous Healers in South Africa." *Social Science and Medicine* 15B: 361–366.

Nicholson, R. A. 1964. *Studies in Islamic Mysticism*. Cambridge: Cambridge University Press.

Nsemi, I. 1974. "Sacred Medicine (Minkisi)." In J. Janzen and W. MacGaffey, *Anthology of Kongo Religion*. Lawrence: University of Kansas Publications in Anthropology, p. 5.

Nyasaland Government. 1932. *Report of the Census of 1931*. Zomba.

———. 1940. *Annual Report of the Labour Department for 1939*. Zomba.

———. 1950. *Annual Report of the Labour Department for 1949*. Zomba.

O'Brien, J. 1987. "Differential High Fertility and Demography Transitions: Peripheral Capitalism in the Sudan." In D. D. Cordell and J. W. Gregory, eds., *African Population and Capitalism: Historical Perspectives*. Boulder, Colo.: Westview Press, pp. 173–186.

Ogot, B. A. 1963. "British Administration in Central Nyanza District on Kenya, 1900–60," *Journal of African History* 1.

———, ed. 1979. *Ecology and History in East Africa*. Hadith 7, Nairobi: Kenya Literature Bureau.

O'Meara, D. 1983. *Volkskapitalisme: Class, Capital and Ideology in the Development of Afrikaner Nationalism, 1934–1948*. Cambridge: Cambridge University Press.

Omer-Cooper, J. D. 1969. *The Zulu Aftermath*. Evanston, Ill.: Northeastern University Press.

Ominde, S. 1981. "The Population Issue in Kenya." In A. R. Ngoju, P. M. Tukei, and J. M. Roberts, eds. *Proceedings of 1st Annual Medical Scientific Conference*. Nairobi: KEMRI.

Onchere, S. R., and R. Slooff, 1981. "Nutrition and Disease in Machakos District, Kenya." In Chambers et al., eds., *Seasonal Dimensions to Rural Poverty*, pp. 41–45.

Orde-Browne, Major G. Saint J. 1935. "Witchcraft and British Colonial Law." *Africa* 8: 481.

———. 1970 [1925]. *The Vanishing Tribes of Kenya*. Westport, Conn.: Negro Universities Press.

Orenstein, A. J. 1923. "Compound Sanitation." *South African Medical Record* 21: 131.

Orubuloye, I. O., and J. C. Caldwell. 1975. "The Impact of Public Health Services on Mortality: A Study of Mortality Differentials in a Rural Area in Nigeria." *Population Studies* 29 (2): 259–272.

O'Toole, T. 1984. "The 1928–1931 Gbaya Insurrection in Ubangui-Shari: Messianic Movement or Village Self-Defense?" *Canadian Journal of African Studies* 18 (2): 329–344.

Ouedraogo, M.-M. 1988. "Premiers prioritiés des politiques urbaines confrontées à une croissance rapide: Le cas du Burkina Faso." *African Population Conference, Dakar 1988*. Liège: IUSSP.

Oughton, E. 1980. "The Maharashtra Droughts of 1970–73: An Analysis of Scarcity." *Oxford Bulletin of Economics and Statistics* xliv.

Owen, W. E. 1925. "The Kavirondo Practice of Inoculation with Smallpox." *Kenya Medical Journal* 1: 333–335.

Packard, R. M. 1984. "Maize, Cattle and Mosquitoes: The Political Economy of Malaria Epidemics in Colonial Swaziland." *Journal of African History* 25: 189–212.

———. 1990. *White Plague, Black Labor: Tuberculosis and the Political Economy of Health and Disease in South Africa*. Berkeley, Los Angeles, Oxford: University of California Press; Capetown: David Philip.

———, B. Wisner, and T. Bossert, eds. "The Political Economy of Health and Disease in Africa and Latin America." *Social Science and Medicine*, Special Issue, 28: 5.

Page, H. J. and R. Lesthaeghe, eds. 1981. *Child-Spacing in Tropical Africa: Traditions and Change*. London: Academic Press.

Palmer, H. R. 1967. *Sudanese Memoirs, Being Mainly Translations of a Number of Arabic Manuscripts Relating to the Central and Western Sudan*. London: Frank Cass & Co.

Palmer, R., and N. Parsons. 1977. *The Roots of Rural Poverty in Central and Southern Africa*. Berkeley, Los Angeles, London: University of California Press.

Pankhurst, R. 1965. "The History and Traditional Treatment of Smallpox in Ethiopia." *Medical History* 9: 344–356.

———. 1966 . "The Great Ethiopian Famine of 1888–1892: A New Assessment." *Journal of the History of Medicine* xxi.

Patterson, K. D. 1977. "The Impact of Modern Medicine on Population Growth in Twentieth Century Ghana: A Tentative Assessment." In Edinburgh, ed., *African Historical Demography*, pp. 437–452.

———. 1979 . "Health in Urban Ghana: The Case of Accra," *Social Science and Medicine* 13B (4): 251–268.

———. 1981*a*. "The Demographic Impact of the 1918–19 Pandemic in Sub-Saharan Africa: a preliminary assessment." In Edinburgh, ed., *African Historical Demography*, II: 401–431.

———. 1981*b*. *Health in Colonial Ghana: Disease, Medicine, and Socio-Economic Change*. Waltham, Mass.: Crossroads Press.

———, and G. W. Hartwig. 1978. "The Disease Factor: An Introductory Overview." In Hartwig and Patterson, eds., *Disease in African History: An Introductory Survey and Case Studies*, pp. 3–24.

———, and G. F. Pyle. 1983. "The Diffusion of Influenza in Sub-Saharan Africa During the 1918–1919 Pandemic." *Social Science and Medicine* 17: 1299–1307.

Patterson, W. J. 1919. "Some Medical Aspects of the East Africa Campaign (1916–1918)." M. D. thesis, University of Edinburgh.

Paviot, J. J. 1967. "Prevalence of Tuberculosis in Africa." *Bulletin of the International Union of Tuberculosis* 38: 125–137.

Payer, L. 1988. *Medicine and Culture: Varieties of Treatment in the United States, England, West Germany and France*. New York: Henry Holt & Co.

Pechuel-Loesche, E. 1907. *Volkskunde von Loango*. Stuttgart: Strecker & Schröder.

Perrot, C.-H. 1981. "Traditions orales et démographie historique: À propos de la population du Ndenye au XVIIe et XIXe siècles." In Edinburgh, ed., *African Historical Demography*, II: 443–455.

Phillips, R. E. 1930. *The Bantu Are Coming*. London: The Student Movement Press.

———. 1938. "The Bantu in the City," Ph.D. dissertation, Yale University, New Haven, Conn.

Phillipson, D. W. 1977. *The Later Prehistory of Eastern and Southern Africa*. London: Heinemann.

Phimister, I. 1978. "African Labour Conditions and Health in the Southern Rhodesian Mining Industry, 1898–1953." In I. Phimister and C. Van Onselen, eds., *Studies in the History of African Mine Labour in Colonial Zimbabwe*. Gwelo: Mambo Press, pp. 102–150.

Pillsbury, B. 1982. "Policy Evaluation Perspectives on Traditional Health Practitioners in National Health Care Systems." *Social Science and Medicine* 16 (21): 1825–1834.

Pison, G., E. van de Walle, and M. Sala-Diakanda, eds. 1990. *Mortalité et société en Afrique au sud du Sahara*. Paris: Presses universitaires de France (INED, Travaux et Documents, 124).

Planning for Health in South Africa. Johannesburg, December 1941, January 1942.

Playfair, E. 1958. *History of Medicine*. New York: Oxford University Press.

Plowden, W. C. 1868. *Travels in Abyssinia*. London: Longmans, Green.

Poirier, J., H. Dagenais, and J. W. Gregory. 1985. "Démographie et approche féministe. Reflexion méthodologique a partir d'une récherche en cours." *Cahiers quebecois de démographie* XIV (2): 227–283.

———, V. Piché, and G. Neill. In Press. "Travail des femmes et de fécondité dans les pays en dévéloppement: Que nous a appris l'Enquête mondiale de la fécondité?" *Cahiers quebecois de démographie*.

Pool, I. D. 1977*a*. "A Framework for the Analysis of West African Historical Demography." In Edinburgh, ed., *African Historical Demography*, pp. 45–61.

———. 1977*b*. "The Growth of the City of Ouagadougou and Fertility Trends." In Pool and Coulibaly, eds., *Demographic Transition and Cultural Continuity in the Sahel*, pp. 127–148.

———, and S. P. Coulibaly, eds. 1977. *Demographic Transition and Cultural Continuity in the Sahel*. Ithaca, N. Y.: International Population Program, Cornell University.

Population Reference Bureau. 1984. *1984 World Population Data Sheet*. Washington, D.C.: Population Reference Bureau.

———. 1988. *1988 World Population Data Sheet*. Washington, D.C.: Population Reference Bureau.

Press, I. 1980. "Problems in the Definition and Classification of Medical Systems." *Social Science and Medicine* 14B: 45–57.

Price-Williams, D. R. 1962. "A Case Study of Ideas Concerning Disease among the Tiv." *Africa* 32: 122–131.

Prins, G. 1978. "Grist for the Mill: On Researching the History of Bulozi." *History in Africa* 5: 311.

———. 1979. "Disease at the Crossroads: Towards a History of Therapeutics in Bulozi Since 1876." In Janzen, and Feierman, eds., *The Social History of Disease and Medicine in Africa*, pp. 285–315.

———. 1980. *The Hidden Hippopotamus*. Cambridge: Cambridge University Press.

Prins, P. 1907. "L'Islam et les musulmans dans les sultanats du Haut Oubangui." *L'Afrique française: reseignements coloniaux* 17 (6): 136–142.

Prioul, C. 1981. *Entre Oubangui et Chari vers 1890*. Paris: Société d'ethnographie et Laboratoire d'ethnologie et de sociologie comparative, Université de Paris X (Nanterre). (Recherches oubanguiennes, No. 6.)

Prothero, R. M. 1968. *Migrants and Malaria in Africa*. Pittsburg, Pa.: University of Pittsburg Press.

Rangeley, W. H. J. 1952. "Two Nyasaland Rain Shrines—Makewana, the Mother of All People." *Nyasaland Journal* 5: 31.

Ranger, T. O. 1968. "Nationality and Nationalism: The Case of Barotseland." *Journal of the Historical Society of Nigeria* IV: 228.

———. 1971. "Christian Independency in Tanzania. In D. B. Barrett, ed., African Initiatives in Religion. Nairobi: East African Publishing House, pp. 122–145.

———. 1975. *Dance and Society in Eastern Africa, 1890–1970*. London: Heinemann.

———. 1978*a*. "Growing From the Roots: Reflections on Peasant Research in Central and Southern Africa." *Journal of Southern African Studies* 5: 99–133.

———. 1978*b*. "Healing and Society in Colonial Southern Africa." Social History of South Africa Seminar. School of Oriental and African Studies.

———. 1979. "The Mobilization of Labor and the Production of Knowledge: The Antiquarian Tradition in Rhodesia." *Journal of African History* 20: 507–524.

———, and I. Kimambo, eds. 1972. *The Historical Study of African Religion*. Berkeley, Los Angeles, London: University of California Press.

Rankin, F. H. 1836. *The White Man's Grave: A Visit to Sierra Leone in 1834*, 2 vols. London.

Rashid al-Din. 1911. *al-Fakhri fi al-'Adad*, vol. 1. Ed. T. Bochet. Leiden.

Rattray, R. S. 1953. *Hausa Folklore, Customs and Proverbs, etc.*, 2 vols. Oxford: Clarendon Press.

Reefe, T. Q. 1981. *The Rainbow and the Kings: A History of the Luba Empire to 1891*. Berkeley, Los Angeles, London: University of California Press.

Retel-Laurentin, A. 1974*a*. *Infécondité en Afrique Noire: Maladies et consèquences sociales*. Paris: Masson et Cie.

———. 1974*b*. *Sorcellerie et Ordalies*. Paris: Editions Anthropos.

———. 1979*a*. *Cause de l'infécondité dans la Volta Noire*. Institut national d'études démographiques avec le concours du CNRS Travaux et Documents, Cahier no. 87. Paris: Presses Universitaires de France.

———. 1979*b*. *Un pays à la dérive: Une société en régression démographique. Les Nzakara de l'est centrafricain*. Paris: Jean-Pierre Delarge.

———, and D. Benoit. 1976. "Infant Mortality and Birth Intervals." *Population Studies* 30 (2): 279–293.

Reyna, S. P. 1983. "Dual Class Formation and Agrarian Underdevelopment: An Analysis of the Articulation of Production Relations in Upper Volta." *Canadian Journal of African Studies* 17 (2): 211–233.

Reynaud, G. 1903. *Hygiène coloniale* 1: 165–171.

Richards, A. I. 1935. "A Modern Movement of Witch-Finders." *Africa* 8: 448–461.

———. 1939. *Land, Labour and Diet in Northern Rhodesia*. London: Oxford University Press.

Rita-Ferreira, A. 1966. *Os Cheuas da Macanga*. Lisbon: Instituto de Investigaçào Cientifica de Moçambique.

Robertson, C., and M. Klein, eds. 1983. *Women and Slavery in Africa*. Madison: The University of Wisconsin Press.

Rodney, W. 1974. *How Europe Underdeveloped Africa*. Washington, D.C.: Howard University Press.

Romaniuk, A. 1967. *La fécondité des populations congolaises*. Paris and the Hague: Mouton.

———. 1980. "Increase in Natural Fertility during the Early Stages of Modernization: Evidence from an African Case Study, Zaire." *Population Studies* 34: 293–310.

Rondet-Smith, M. 1911. *L'Afrique équatoriale française*, 2d ed. Paris: Plon.

Rosen, G. 1958. *A History of Public Health*. New York: MD Publications.

Rosenberg, C. E. 1977. "The Therapeutic Revolution: Medicine, Meaning, and Social Change in Nineteenth-Century America." *Perspectives in Biology and Medicine* 20: 485–506.

———. 1979. "Florence Nightingale on Contagion: The Hospital as Moral Universe." In C. E. Rosenberg, ed., *Healing and History: Essays for George Rosen*. New York: Science History Publications, pp. 116–136.

Ross, R. 1902. "The Campaign against Malaria and the Extension of Scientific Medical Services in British West Africa." *African Historical Studies* 1: 153–197.

———. 1910. *Prevention of Malaria*. Liverpool School of Tropical Medicine, Memoir 2, London, pp. 285–286; and *Malarial Fever*, pp. 45–46.

Rowland, M. G. M. 1981. "Seasonality and the Growth of Infants in a Gambian Village." In Chambers et al., eds., *Seasonal Dimensions to Rural Poverty*, pp. 164–175.

Rudin, H. 1938. *Germans in the Cameroons*. New Haven: Yale University Press.

Rüger, A. 1968. "Die Duala und die Kolonialmacht, 1884–1914: Eine Studie über die historischen Ursprünge des afrikanischen Antikolonialismus." In H. Stoecker, ed. *Kamerun unter deutscher Kolonialherrschaft*. Berlin: Akademie Verlag, pp. 220–254.

Russell, W. 1906. "An Analysis of the Consumptive Cases Admitted into Kimberley Hospital." In *South African Medical Record* 4 (14): 214.

Ruzika, L. T. 1983. "Mortality Transition in the Third World Countries: Issues for Research." *Bulletin de liaison* (Liège, IUSSP), No. 17 (January–April): 60–82.

Sabatier, R. 1988. *Blaming Others: Prejudice, Race, and Worldwide AIDS*. Washington and Philadelphia: The Panos Institute and New Society Publishers.

Sabben-Clare, E. E., ed. 1980. *Health in Tropical Africa during the Colonial Period*. London: Oxford University Press.

Saberwal, S. 1970. *The Traditional System of the Embu of Central Kenya*. Nairobi: East African Publishing House, Makerere Institute of Social Research, East African Studies 35.

Saint-Pierre, M.-H., J. W. Gregory, and A. B. Simmons. 1986. "Structure démographique des ménages et comportement migratoire en Haute-Volta." In Gauvreau, et al., eds., *Stratégies de survie: populations et sociétés dans le Tiers-Monde*, pp. 111–141.

Salanoue-Ipin. 1911. "Notes sur les causes d'insalubrité des casernements et établissements militaires de Tananarive." *Annales d'hygiène et de médecine coloniale* 14: 38.

Samarin, W. J. 1984*a*. "Bondjo Ethnicity and Colonial Imagination." *Canadian Journal of African Studies* 18 (2): 345–365.

———. 1984*b*. "La communication par les eaux et les mots oubanguiennes." *Recherches centrafricaines: problèmes et perspectives de la recherche historique*. Aix-en-Provence: Institut de l'histoire des pays d'outre-mer, Université de Provence. (Etudes et documents, No. 18.)

Samuelson, P. A. 1970. *Economics*, 8th ed. New York: McGraw-Hill.

Sanagoh, G. 1977. "Une décennie de planification voltaique." Paris: Doctoral dissertation, Université de Paris I.

Sanders, D. 1982. "Nutrition and the Use of Food as a Weapon in Zimbabwe and Southern Africa." *International Journal of Health Services* 12 (2): 201–213.

———, with R. Carver. 1985. *The Struggle for Health.* Basingstoke and London: Macmillan.

Sankara, T. 1983. Discours d'orientation politique prononcé à la radio-television nationale le 2 octobre 1983, cited in Jean Ziégler *Sankara: Un nouveau pouvoir africain.* Lausanne: Pierre Marcel Favre/ABC édition, pp. 121–151.

Santandrea, S. 1957. "Sanusi, Ruler of Dar Banda and Dar Kuti in the History of the Bahr el-Ghazal." *Sudan Notes and Records* 38: 151–155.

Sarton, G. 1927–1948. *Introduction to the History of Science*, 4 vols. Baltimore: Carnegie Institute of Washington Publication No. 376, William & Wilkins.

Sautter, G. 1966. *De l'Atlantique au fleuve Congo: Une géographie du sous-peuplement*, 2 vols. Paris: Mouton.

———. 1967 "Notes sur la construction du chemin de fer Congo-Océan (1921–1934)." *Cahiers d'études africaines* 7(26): 219–299.

Savage, D. C., and J. F. Munro. 1966. "Carrier Corps Recruitment in the British East Africa Protectorate 1914–18." *Journal of African History* 7: 322.

Schapera, I. 1947. *Migrant Labour and Tribal Life.* London: Oxford University Press.

Schapiro, K. 1987. "Doctors or Medical Aids—the Debate over the Training of Black Medical Personnel for the Rural Black Population in South Africa in the 1920s and 1930s." *Journal of Southern African Studies* 3: 2.

Schipperges, H., E. Seidler, and P. Unschuld, eds. 1978. *Krankheit, Heilkunst, Heilung.* Freiburg, Munich: Karl Alber.

Schoenmaeckers, R., I. H. Shah, R. Lesthaege, and O. Tambashe. 1981. "The Child-Spacing Tradition and the Post-Partum Taboo in Tropical Africa: Anthropological Evidence." In Page and Lesthaeghe, eds., *Child-Spacing in Tropical Africa: Traditions and Change*, pp. 25–71.

Schoffeleers, J. M. 1972. "The History and Political Role of the M'Bona Cult Among the Mang'anja." In Ranger and Kimambo, eds., *The Historical Study of African Religion*, pp. 71–94.

———. 1973. "Towards the Identification of a Proto-Chewa Culture." *Journal of Social Science* 2: 47.

———. 1978. "The Chisumphi and Mbona Cults in Malawi: A Comparative History," in J. M. Schoffeleers, ed., *Guardians of the Land: Essays on Central African Territorial Cults.* Gwelo: Mambo Press, pp. 147–186.

———, and R. Mwanza. 1978. "An Organizational Model of the Mwari Shrines." In Schoffeleers, ed., *Guardians of the Land: Essays on Central African Territorial Cults.* Gwelo: Mambo Press, pp. 297–315.

Scott, D. C., and A. Hetherwick, 1970. *Dictionary of the Nyanja Language.* Lusaka.

Scott, H. H. 1939. *A History of Tropical Medicine.* London: E. Arnold and Co.

Scrimshaw, N. S., C. E. Taylor, and J. E. Gordon, 1968. *Interactions of Nutrition and Infection.* Geneva: WHO. Monograph Series, No. 57.

Seaman, J., and J. Holt. 1980. "Markets and Famines in the Third World." *Disasters* iv.

Seck, A. 1970. *Dakar: Métropole ouest-africaine.* Dakar.

Sehoza; S. N.d. *A Year in Chains*. Westminster.

Sen, A. K. 1981. *Poverty and Famines: An Essay on Entitlement and Deprivation*. Oxford: Clarendon Press.

———. 1983*a*. "The Battle to Get Food." *New Society* (October 13).

———. 1983*b*. "Economics and the Family." Public lecture in the Distinguished Speaker Series of the Asian Development Bank, Manila, September 15.

Serre, J. 1960. "Histoire économique et sociale du district de Grimari (1907–1958)." University of Paris: Ph.D dissertation, 2 vols.

Shapiro, A. K. 1960. "A Contribution to the History of the Placebo Effect." *Behavioral Science* 5: 109.

Siddiqi, M. N.d. *Studies in Arabic and Persian Medical Literature*.

Sigerist, H. E. 1961. *A History of Medicine*, 2 vols. New York: Oxford University Press.

Simkins, C. 1981. "Agricultural Production in the African Reserves." *Journal of Southern African Studies* 7: 256–283.

Simpson, W. J. 1914. "Report on Sanitary Matters in the East African Protectorate, Uganda, and Zanzibar." Protectorate Archive CO 879/115; 879/114.

Sindzingre, N. 1985. "Healing is as Healing Does: Pragmatic Resolution of Misfortune among the Senufo (Ivory Coast)." *History and Anthropology* 2: 33–57.

Skorupski, J. 1976. *Symbol and Theory: A Philosophical Study of Theories of Religion in Social Anthropology*. Cambridge: Cambridge University Press.

Slater, H. 1980. "The Changing Pattern of Economic Relations in Rural Natal." In S. Marks and A. Atmore, eds., *Economy and Society in Pre-Industrial South Africa*. London and New York: Longman.

Smith, F., and A. Pearse. 1904. "Fevers in Sierra Leone (Mount Aureol), Being a Preliminary Account of an Inquiry into the Causes of the Continued Prevalence of Ill-Health in the Apparently Favourably Situated Hill Station." *Journal of the Royal Army Medical Corps* 2: 278–282.

Smith, H. F. C. (Abdullahi). 1975. "The Contemporary Significance of the Academic Ideals of the Sokoto Jihad." Paper read at the Sokoto History Seminar.

Smith, J. T. 1977. "Economy and Demography in a Mossi Village," Ph.D. dissertation, University of Michigan, Ann Arbor.

Smith, M. G. 1974. *Corporations and Society*. London: Duckworth.

Smythies, C. A. 1892. "Medical Missionaries." *Central Africa* 11: 51.

South Africa, Union of. 1914. *Report of the Tuberculosis Commission*. Cape Town.

———. 1932. *Report of the Native Economic Commission, 1930–32*.

———. 1944. *Report of the National Health Services Commission*. Pretoria.

South African Government. 1942. *Report of the Inter-Departmental Committee on the Social, Health and Economic Conditions of Urban Natives*. Pretoria, 1942.

———. 1977. *The Health of the People. A Review of Health Services in the Republic of South Africa in the Mid-seventies*. Johannesburg: Chris van Rensburg Publications.

South African Institute of Medical Research (SAIMR). 1932. *Tuberculosis in South African Natives with Special Reference to the Disease Amongst the Mine Labourers of the Witwatersrand*. Johannesburg.

———. N.d. *Tuberculosis in the South African Natives*.

Spanton, C. 1935. "Speech to the Anniversary." *Central Africa* 51: 148.

Spear, T. 1978. *The Kaya Complex: A History of the Mijikenda Peoples of the Kenya Coast to 1900*. Nairobi.

Spitz, P. 1980. *Drought and Self-Provisioning*. Geneva: Working Paper, United Nations Research Institute for Social Development.

Spitzer, L. 1968. "The Mosquito and Segregation in Sierra Leone." *Canadian Journal of African Studies* 2: 49–61.

Stepan, J. 1983. "Patterns of Legislation Concerning Traditional Medicine." In Bannerman and Chieh, eds., *Traditional Medicine and Health Care Coverage*, pp. 290–313.

Steuer, R. O., and J. B. de C. M. Saunders. 1959. *Ancient Egyptian and Cnidian Medicine: The Relationship of their Aetiological Concepts of Disease*. Berkeley and Los Angeles: University of California Press.

Stirling, L. 1940. "The Progress of Surgery." *Central Africa* 58.

———. 1945. "Speech at the Anniversary." *Central Africa* 63: 80.

———. 1947. *Bush Doctor*. Westminster: Parrett and Neves for the Universities Mission to Central Africa.

———. 1977. *Tanzanian Doctor*. London: C. Hurst.

Stone, B. 1975. Interview. Rondo, Tanzania.

Stradling, L. E. 1960. *A Bishop on Safari*. SPCK.

Strahan, H. 1901. *Paper on the Health Conditions of West Africa*. Liverpool.

Strobel, M. 1983. "Slavery and Reproductive Labor in Mombasa." In Robertson and Klein, eds., *Women and Slavery in Africa*, 111–129.

Stürzinger, U. 1983. "The Introduction of Cotton Cultivation: The Role of the Administration, 1920–1936." *African Economic History* 12: 213–225.

Sullivan, L., ed. 1988. *Caring and Curing: Health and Medicine in World Religious Traditions*. New York: Macmillan.

Sundkler, B. G. M. 1961. *Bantu Prophets in South Africa*. London, New York, Toronto: Oxford University Press, for the International African Institute.

Suret-Canale, J. 1964. *Afrique noire occidentale et centrale II: L'ère coloniale (1900–1945)*. Paris: Editions sociales.

Swanson, M. W. 1979. "The Sanitation Syndrome: Bubonic Plague and Urban Native Policy in the Cape Colony, 1900–1909." *Journal of African History* 18 (3): 387–410.

Swaziland Government. 1931. *Annual Medical and Sanitation Report*. Swaziland National Archives.

———. 1932. *Annual Medical and Sanitation Report*. Swaziland National Archives.

Swindell, K. 1981. "Domestic Production, Labour Mobility and Population Change in West Africa, 1900–1980." In Edinburgh, ed., *African Demographic History*, pp. 655–690.

Symons. 1956. "Notes on Nkoya Therapy." In O. Coates-Palgrave, ed., *The Trees of Central Africa*. Salisbury: National Publication Trust, Rhodesia & Nyasaland.

Tabutin, D. 1984. "La fécondité et la mortalité dans les recensements africains des 25 dernières années." *Population* 39 (2): 295–312.

Tambiah, S. J. 1973. "Form and Meaning in Magical Acts: A Point of View." In Horton and Finnegan, eds., *Modes of Thought: Essays on Thinking in Western and Non-Western Societies*, pp. 199–229.

Tate, H. R. 1904. "Notes on the Kikuyu and Kamba of British East Africa." *Journal of the Royal Anthropological Institute* 34: 135.

Taylor, C. F. 1929. "Medical Work in Africa: 11, Sindano." *African Tidings* 38: 13.

Taylor, E. 1976. "The Place of Indigenous Medical Practitioners in the Modernisation of the Health Services." In C. Leslie, ed., *Asian Medical Systems.* Berkeley, Los Angeles, London: University of California Press, pp. 285–299.

Tempkin, O., and C. L. Tempkin. 1967. *Ancient Medicine: Selected Papers of Ludwig Edelstein.* Baltimore: The Johns Hopkins University Press.

Temple, F. T. 1973. "Politics, Planning and Housing Policy in Nairobi." Ph.D. dissertation, Massachusetts Institute of Technology.

Thomas, A. E. 1970. *Adoption to Modern Medicine in Lowland Machakos, Kenya.* Ph.D. dissertation, Stanford University.

Thomas, G. C. 1981. "The Social Background of Childhood Nutrition in the Ciskei." *Social Science and Medicine* 15A: 551–555.

Thomas, J. M. 1963. *Les Ngbaka de la Lobaye: Le dépeuplement rural chez une population forestière de la République Centrafricaine.* Paris and The Hague: Mouton.

Thomson, D. R. 1974. "Tuberculosis as a World Problem: The Current Epidemiological Position." *Tropical Doctor* 4: 155.

Thornton, J. 1977. "Demography and History in the Kingdom of Kongo." *Journal of African History* 18 (4): 507–530.

———. 1980. "The Slave Trade in Eighteenth Century Angola: Effects on Demographic Structures." *Canadian Journal of African Studies* 14 (3): 417–427.

Thylefors, B., and A. M. Tonjum. 1980. "A Three-Year Follow-up of Ocular Onchocerciasis in an Area of Vector Control." *Bulletin of the World Health Organization* 58 (1): 107–119.

Titmuss, R. M. 1964. "Sociological Aspects of Therapeutics." In P. Talalay, ed., *Drugs in Our Society.* Baltimore: John Hopkins University Press.

Tomé, B. 1979. "Medicina Tradicional: Estudar as Plantas Que Curam." *Tempo* 460: 13.

Trapnell, G. G., and J. N. Clothier. 1937. *The Soils, Vegetation and Agricultural Systems of North Western Rhodesia.* Lusaka: Northern Rhodesia Government.

Trimingham, H. S. 1961. *A History of Islam in West Africa.* London: Oxford University Press.

Turner, V. W. 1967. *The Forest of Symbols.* Ithaca: Cornell University Press.

———. 1968. *The Drums of Affliction.* Oxford: Clarendon.

———. 1975. *Revelation and Divination in Ndembu Ritual.* Ithaca, N.Y.: Cornell University Press.

Turrell, R. 1982*a*. "Capital, Class and Monopoly: The Kimberley Diamond Fields, 1871–1889." Ph.D. dissertation, University of London.

———. 1982*b*. "Kimberley Labour and Compounds, 1871–1914." In Marks and Rathbone, eds., *Industrialisation and Social Change in South Africa,* 45–76.

———. 1984. "Kimberley's Model Compounds." *Journal of African History* 25 (1): 59–75.

Turshen, M. 1984. *The Political Ecology of Disease in Tanzania.* New Brunswick, N.J.: Rutgers University Press.

Twaddle, M. 1974*a*. "On Ganda historiography." *History of Africa* 1: 85.

———. 1974*b*. "Ganda Receptivity to Change." *Journal of African History* XV: 303.

Twumasi, P. A. 1975. *Medical Systems in Ghana: A Study in Medical Sociology.* Accra-Tema: Ghana Publishing Corp.

Tylor, E. B. 1873. *Primitive Culture,* 2d ed. London: John Murray.

Ullmann, M. 1978. *Islamic Medicine.* Edinburgh: Edinburgh University Press.

United Nations. 1986. *Rapport sur l'Evaluation du Programme par Pays du Burkina Faso.* New York: United Nations Fund for Population Activities (UNFPA).

United Nations, Secretariat. 1982. "Infant Mortality: World Estimates and Projections: 1950–2025." *Population Bulletin of the United Nations* 14: 31–53.

United States, Agency for International Development (USAID) and Centers for Disease Control. 1975. *Disease and Demographic Survey Project Status Report (January 1975).* Atlanta, Ga.: Centers for Disease Control (CDC).

Unterhalter, B. 1982. "Inequalities in Health and Disease: The Case of Mortality Rates for the City of Johannesburg, South Africa, 1910–1979." *International Journal of Health Services* 12 (4): 625–626.

Vail, L. 1977. "Ecology and History: The Example of Eastern Zambia." *Journal of Southern African Studies* 3, 2: 129–155.

———. 1983. "The political economy of East-Central Africa." In Birmingham, and Martin, eds., *History of Central Africa* 2: 200–250.

Vallin, J. 1976. "La mortalité infantile dans le monde. Évolution depuis 1950." *Population* 31 (4–5): 801–838.

Van Binsbergen, W. M. J. 1977. "Regional and non-Regional Cults of Affliction in Western Zambia." In Werbner, ed., *Regional Cults*, 141–175.

———. 1981. *Religious Change in Zambia: Exploratory Studies.* London and Boston: Kegan Paul International.

Van Dijk, M. P. 1986. *Burkina Faso: le secteur informel de Ouagadaougou.* Paris: L'Harmattan.

Van Noten, F. 1982. *The Archaeology of Central Africa.* Graz: Akademische Druck u. Verlagsanstalt.

Van Onselen, C. 1976. *Chibaro: African Mine Labour in Southern Rhodesia 1900–1933.* London: Urizen Books.

———. 1983. *New Babylon.* Johannesburg: Ravan Press.

Van Overbergh, C. 1911. "Introduction." In F. Gaud, ed., *Les Mandja (Congo Français).* Brussels: deWit, pp. i–xxiv.

Vansina, J. 1961. *De la tradition orale: Essai de methode historique.* Tervuren: Musée Royal d'Afrique Centrale.

———. 1966. *Kingdoms of the Savanna.* Madison, Wisc.: University of Wisconsin Press.

———. 1968. "The Use of Ethnographic Data as Sources for History." In T. Ranger, ed., *Emerging Themes of African History.* Nairobi: East African Publishing House, pp. 97–124.

———. 1973. *The Tio Kingdom of the Middle Congo 1880–1892.* London: Oxford University Press.

———. 1974. "The Power of Systematic Doubt in Historical Inquiry." *History of Africa* 1: 109.

———. 1978. *The Children of Woot: Essays in Kuba History.* Madison: University of Wisconsin Press.

———. 1984*a*. *Art History in Africa.* London: Longman.

———. 1984*b*. "Western Bantu Expansion." *Journal of African History* 25: 129–145.

———. 1985. *Oral Tradition as History.* Madison: University of Wisconsin Press.

Vaughan, M. 1987. *The Story of an African Famine.* Cambridge: Cambridge University Press.

Wade, M., ed. 1976. *Martindale's Extra Pharmacopoeia.* London: Pharmaceutical Press.

Wain, H. 1970. *A History of Preventive Medicine*. Springfield, Ill.: Thomas.

Waite, G. 1980. "Spirit Possession Dance in East-Central Africa." *Journal of the Association of Graduate Dance Ethnologists UCLA* 4(1980): 31–38.

———. 1981. "A History of Medicine and Health Care in Pre-Colonial East-Central Africa. Ph.D. dissertation, University of California at Los Angeles.

———. 1987. "Public Health in Precolonial East-Central Africa," *Social Science and Medicine* 24 (3): 197–208.

———, and C. Ehret. In press. "Linguistic Perspectives on the Early History of Southern Tanzania." *Tanzania Notes and Records*.

Waliggo, J. M. 1976. "The Catholic Church in the Buddu Province of Buganda, 1879–1925." Ph.D. dissertation, University of London.

Walker, I. L., and B. Weinbren. 1961. *2,000 Casualties—a History of Trade Unions and the Labour Movement in South Africa*. Johannesburg: South African Trade Union Council.

Walker, K. 1955. *The Story of Medicine*. New York: Oxford University Press.

Wall, L. L. 1988. *Hausa Medicine: Illness and Well-Being in a West African Culture*. Durham, N.C.: Duke University Press.

Walter, J., and K. Wrightson. 1976. "Death and the Social Order in Early Modern England." *Past and Present* 71: 22–42.

Waltisperger, D. 1988. "Tendances et causes de la mortalité." In T. Dominique, ed., *Population et sociétés en Afrique au sud du Sahara*. Paris: L'Harmattan, pp. 279–308.

Ware, H. 1978. *Population and Development in Africa South of the Sahara: A Review of the Literature, 1970–1978*. International Review Group of Social Science Research on Population and Development, Appendix 7A. Mexico City: IRG, El Colégio de México.

Warren, D. M. 1974. *Disease, Medicine and Religion among the Techiman-Bono of Ghana: A Study in Cultural Change*. Ph.D dissertation, University of Indiana, Bloomington.

Watt, J., and E. Breyer-Brandwijk. 1962. *Poisonous and Medicinal Plants of East Africa*. Edinburgh and London: Livingstone.

Watts, M. 1983. *Silent Violence: Food, Famine & Peasantry in Northern Nigeria*. Berkeley, Los Angeles, London: University of California Press.

Weber, M. 1946. *From Max Weber*. (Trans. ed. H. H. Gerth and C. W. Mills.) New York: Oxford University Press.

———. 1947. *The Theory of Social and Economic Organization*. (Ed., trans. T. Parsons). New York: Free Press.

Webster, D. 1981. "The Political Economy of Food Production and Nutrition in Southern Africa in Historical Perspective." *Critical Health* (November): 6–28.

Webster, M. 1972, 1973. "A Review of the Development of the Health Services of Rhodesia from 1923 to the Present Day." *Central African Journal of Medicine* 18: 244; 19: 7–48.

Weinstein, B. 1970. "Felix Eboué and the Chiefs: Perceptions of Power in Early Oubangui-Chari." *Journal of African History* 11 (1): 107–126.

Weisbrod, B. A., R. L. Andreano, R. E. Baldwin, E. H. Epstein, A. C. Kelly, and T. W. Helminiak. 1973. *Disease and Economic Development: The Impact of Parasitic Diseases in St. Lucia*. Madison: University of Wisconsin Press.

Welsh D. 1971. "The Growth of Towns." In Wilson and Thompson, eds., *The Oxford History of South Africa*, 2: 172–243.

Werbner, R. P., ed. 1977. *Regional Cults*. Anthropological Studies Association of the Commonwealth Monograph No. 16. London, New York, San Francisco: Academic Press.

Werner, D. 1977*a*. *The Village Health Worker: Lackey or Liberator?* Palo Alto, Calif.: Hesperian Foundation.

———. 1977*b*. *Where There is No Doctor*. Palo Alto, Calif.: Hesperian Foundation.

West, M. 1975. *Bishops and Prophets in a Black City: African Independent Churches in Soweto Johannesburg*. Cape Town: David Philip.

Westcott, G., and F. Wilson. 1979. *Economics of Health in South Africa*, vol. 1: *Perspectives on the Health System*. Johannesburg: Ravan Press for the South Africa Labour and Development Research Unit.

Westerdorf, W. 1978. "Altes Aegypten." In Schipperges et al., eds., *Krankheit, Heilkunst, Heilung*, pp. 115–141.

Westermarck, E. 1914. *Marriage Ceremonies in Morocco*. London: Curzon Press.

———. 1926. *Ritual and Belief in Morocco*, 2 vols. London: Macmillan.

White, G. F., D. J. Bradley, and A. U. White. 1972. *Drawers of Water: Domestic Water Use in East Africa*. Chicago and London: University of Chicago Press.

Wilks, I. 1964. "The Growth of Islamic Learning in Ghana." *Journal of the Historical Society of Nigeria* 3: 123–135.

———. 1975. *Asante in the Nineteenth Century: The Structure and Evolution of a Political Order*. London: Cambridge University Press.

Willet, F. 1971. *African Art: An Introduction*. New York: Praeger.

Williams, G., and T. Turner. 1978. "Nigeria." In J. Dunn, ed., *West African States: Failure and Promise*. Cambridge: Cambridge University Press.

Williams, Mrs. 1880. *Universities Mission to Central Africa Annual Report 1880–1881*.

Williams-Myers, A. 1978. "The Nsenga of Central Africa," Ph.D. dissertation, University of California, Los Angeles.

Wilson, B. R., ed. 1974. *Rationality*. Oxford: Blackwell.

Wilson, F. 1972. *Labour in the South African Gold Mines, 1911–1969*. Cambridge: Cambridge University Press.

———, and G. Wescott. 1980. *Economics of Health in South Africa*, vol. *2: Hunger, Work and Health*. Johannesburg: Ravan Press for the South African Labour and Development Research Unit.

Wilson, G. H. 1914. "Mponda's." *Central Africa* 32: 302

Wilson, M., and L. Thompson, eds. 1971. *The Oxford History of South Africa*, 2 vols. Oxford: Oxford University Press.

World Bank. 1980. *World Development Report*. Washington, D.C.

World Health Organization (WHO). 1978*a*. *The Promotion and Development of Traditional Medicine*. Technical Report Series 622. Geneva.

———. 1978*b*. "Biological Control of Insect Vectors of Disease." *Bulletin of the World Health Organization* 56 (3): 377–378.

———. 1979*a*. *Science and Technology for Health Promotion in Developing Countries*. Geneva.

———. 1979*b*. *Traditional Birth Attendants: A Field Guide to Their Training, Evaluation and Articulation with Health Services*. Geneva: World Health Organization, Offset Publication 44: 49–65.

———. 1983. *Apartheid and Health*. Geneva.

Worthington, E. B. 1977. *Arid Lands Irrigation: Environmental Problems and Effects*.

Oxford: Pergamon Press.

Wrigley, C. C. 1979. "Population in African History." *Journal of African History* 20 (1): 127–131.

Xuma, A. B. 1931. "Response to Thornton's Proposal." *Journal of the Medical Association of South Africa* 24 (1): 40–41.

Ylvisaker, M. H. 1979. *Lamu in the Nineteenth Century*. Boston: African Studies Center, Boston University.

Yoder, P. S., ed. 1982. *African Health and Healing Systems: Proceedings of a Symposium*. Los Angeles: Crossroads Press.

Young, A. 1976. "Some Implications of Medical Beliefs and Practices for Social Anthropology." *American Anthropologist*, 78 (1): 5–24.

Yudelman, D. 1983. *The Emergence of Modern South Africa: State, Capital, and the Incorporation of Organized Labor on the South African Gold Fields, 1902–1939*. Westport, Conn. and London: Greenwood Press.

Yudkin, J. S. 1980. "The Economics of Pharmaceutical Supply in Tanzania." *International Journal of Health Services* 10: 455.

Zoctizoum, Y. 1983. *Histoire de la Centrafrique (tome 1), 1879–1959: Violence du développement, domination et inégalités*. Paris: L'Harmattan.

INDEX

Designer: U.C. Press Staff
Compositor: Asco Trade Typesetting Ltd., Hong Kong
Text: 10/12 Baskerville
Display: Baskerville
Printer: Haddon Craftsmen Inc.
Binder: Haddon Craftsmen Inc.

5021

SEP 2 1993